THE REAGAN MOMENT

THE REAGAN MOMENT

AMERICA AND THE WORLD IN THE 1980s

Edited by Jonathan R. Hunt and Simon Miles

CORNELL UNIVERSITY PRESS
Ithaca and London

Cornell University Press and the editors gratefully acknowledge the financial support of the Duke University Program in American Grand Strategy, Sanford School of Public Policy at Duke University, and the University of Southampton.

Copyright © 2021 by Cornell University

All rights reserved. Except for brief quotations in a review, this book, or parts thereof, must not be reproduced in any form without permission in writing from the publisher. For information, address Cornell University Press, Sage House, 512 East State Street, Ithaca, New York 14850. Visit our website at cornellpress.cornell.edu.

First published 2021 by Cornell University Press

Library of Congress Cataloging-in-Publication Data

Names: Hunt, Jonathan R., 1983– editor. | Miles, Simon, 1988– editor.
Title: The Reagan moment : America and the world in the 1980s / edited by Jonathan R. Hunt and Simon Miles.
Description: Ithaca, [New York] : Cornell University Press, 2021. | Includes bibliographical references and index.
Identifiers: LCCN 2021004294 (print) | LCCN 2021004295 (ebook) | ISBN 9781501760686 (hardcover) | ISBN 9781501760693 (paperback) | ISBN 9781501760716 (ebook) | ISBN 9781501760709 (pdf)
Subjects: LCSH: Reagan, Ronald. | United States—Foreign relations—1981–1989.
Classification: LCC E876 .R3973 2021 (print) | LCC E876 (ebook) | DDC 973.927092—dc23
LC record available at https://lccn.loc.gov/2021004294
LC ebook record available at https://lccn.loc.gov/2021004295

Contents

Foreword: Reagan in the World
WILLIAM INBODEN   ix

Introduction: The Man, or the Moment?
JONATHAN R. HUNT   1

PART ONE: GLOBAL AND DOMESTIC ISSUES   23

1. Ronald Reagan and the Cold War
   MELVYN P. LEFFLER   25

2. Energy and the End of the Evil Empire
   DAVID S. PAINTER   43

3. Reagan and the Evolution of US
   Counterterrorism CHRISTOPHER J. FULLER   64

4. Global Reaganomics: Budget Deficits,
   Capital Flows, and the International
   Economy MICHAEL DE GROOT   84

PART TWO: WESTERN AND EASTERN EUROPE   103

5. Confronting the Soviet Threat:
   Reagan's Approach to Policymaking
   ELIZABETH C. CHARLES AND
   JAMES GRAHAM WILSON   105

6. Once More, with Feeling: Transatlantic
   Relations in the Reagan Years
   SUSAN COLBOURN AND MATHIAS HAEUSSLER   123

7. Ronald Reagan and the Nuclear
   Freeze Movement STEPHANIE FREEMAN   144

CONTENTS

PART THREE: HUMAN RIGHTS AND DOMESTIC POLITICS   163

8. Rhetoric and Restraint: Ronald Reagan and the Vietnam Syndrome
   MARK ATWOOD LAWRENCE   165

9. Compartmentalizing US Foreign Policy: Human Rights in the Reagan Years
   SARAH B. SNYDER   188

10. Between Values and Action: Religious Rhetoric, Human Rights, and Reagan's Foreign Policy
    LAUREN F. TUREK   212

PART FOUR: LATIN AMERICA   235

11. Reframing Human Rights: Reagan's "Project Democracy" and the US Intervention in Nicaragua
    WILLIAM MICHAEL SCHMIDLI   237

12. Reagan and Pinochet's Chile: The Diplomacy of Disillusion
    EVAN D. McCORMICK   260

13. Anticommunism, Trade, and Debt: The Reagan Administration and Brazil, 1981–1989 JAMES CAMERON   281

PART FIVE: THE MIDDLE EAST AND AFRICA   301

14. The Limits of Triumphalism in the Middle East: Israel, the Palestinian Question, and Lebanon in the Age of Reagan SETH ANZISKA   303

15. The Central Front of Reagan's Cold War: The United States and Afghanistan
    ROBERT B. RAKOVE   324

16. The Reagan Administration and the Cold War Endgame in the Periphery: The Case of Southern Africa
    FLAVIA GASBARRI   345

PART SIX: SOUTH AND EAST ASIA — 365

17. Reagan and the Crisis of Southwest Asia ELISABETH LEAKE — 367

18. Adam Smith's Arthritis: Japan and the Fears of American Decline JENNIFER M. MILLER — 387

19. One World, Two Chinas: Dreams of Capitalist Convergence in East Asia JONATHAN R. HUNT — 414

Conclusion: Reagan Reconsidered SIMON MILES — 437

List of Contributors 445

Index 449

FOREWORD

Reagan in the World

WILLIAM INBODEN

We appear to be at the outset of a very fruitful period of scholarship on the Ronald Reagan administration and international politics in the 1980s. This volume exemplifies this new era and establishes many of the parameters of future lines of inquiry into this most consequential of presidencies and most consequential of decades. It began as a three-day conference convened in January 2017 at the University of Texas at Austin by the Clements Center for National Security, with generous additional support provided by other University of Texas at Austin entities, including the Robert S. Strauss Center for International Security and Law, the Lyndon B. Johnson School of Public Affairs, and the Departments of History and Government, as well as Southern Methodist University's Center for Presidential History. The editors Jonathan Hunt and Simon Miles merit special commendation for their intellectual vision, indefatigable labor, grit, and good cheer in designing the conference and then refining its most trenchant findings into this book. Its chapters represent a broad array of fresh insights into and perspectives on the foreign and defense policies of the Reagan administration and their manifestations around the world.

Four reasons in particular illuminate why the present moment marks the beginnings of an ideal period for scholars to study the Reagan presidency, all of which are evidenced by the chapters in this book. First, recent years have brought an abundance of newly declassified archives documenting the deliberations, policy developments, and decisions made by the Reagan administration. While scholars in previous years had to rely disproportionately on journalistic accounts and memoirs, these new primary sources provide fresh new insights into the administration's policymaking. When combined with the openings of many additional archives overseas, these new collections provide a further global perspective on the policies of other nations and their perspective on the United States. Second, the Reagan presidency was recent enough that many of its main policymakers are still alive and available to be interviewed, offering their firsthand accounts of the policies and events of the time. Third, now that three decades have passed since Reagan left office, sufficient time has elapsed for us to engage in retrospective assessment. Simply put, we now know how many of the stories ended—or at least have the historical and global context to draw provisional conclusions about the consequences of Reagan administration policies toward the Soviet Union, nuclear weapons, Asia, Latin America, the Middle East, terrorism, international economics, and many other issues. Fourth, a new generation of scholars has come of age since the Reagan presidency ended and thus have been spared the partisan fevers that sometimes beset Reagan's apologists and detractors while he was in office. Even in hindsight such passions sometimes can cloud the objectivity of older historians who have firsthand memories of the Reagan years; younger scholars are generally immune to such intellectual afflictions. It is perhaps no coincidence that the preponderance of chapters in this book are penned by a new generation of historians.

While no single collection can provide a definitive account of any presidency, this volume covers a capacious array of themes and will be of value to all future scholars studying Reagan administration foreign policy. In particular this book highlights the interplay between US domestic politics, US foreign policy, and international history; explores the relationship between economic trends and grand strategy; suggests ways to think about human rights in relation to soft and hard power, including the Reagan doctrine; illuminates the importance of the Cold War relative to other consequential concurrent trends such as the limited reform and opening up of China or the broader transformations in international markets and the information revolution; and, most fundamentally, considers the extent to which Reagan did or did not change the material and symbolic bases of American power in the world.

As the twenty-first century unfolds, it becomes surpassingly clear that many of the global issues and policy challenges shaping the current era—such as terrorism, great power competitions in Europe and Asia, political ferment in Latin America, Africa, and the Middle East, shifts and strains in alliances, globalization and communications revolutions, energy competition, and economic growth and inequality—trace their roots to the 1980s. We cannot understand our contemporary moment without understanding the Reagan administration and its tumultuous decade. This book is indispensable for doing so.

THE REAGAN MOMENT

Introduction

The Man, or the Moment?

JONATHAN R. HUNT

The end of the 1970s was nothing if not eventful. In April 1979, revolutionary students in Teheran took fifty-two Americans hostage weeks after Grand Ayatollah Ruhollah Khomeini founded the Islamic Republic of Iran, triggering an international crisis that fatally wounded Jimmy Carter's presidency. In July, Sandinista rebels deposed Nicaraguan dictator Anastasio Somoza, installing a new, leftist government unbeloved in Washington, DC. Later that year in the fall, two families floated their way from communist East Germany to capitalist West Germany in a hot-air balloon. In December, Japanese Prime Minister Ōhira Masayoshi unveiled a new foreign aid program to the People's Republic of China (PRC), and NATO approved the deployment to Western Europe of nuclear-tipped missiles capable of incinerating Moscow within ten minutes. By Christmas, Soviet Red Army tanks had rolled into Afghanistan on a mission to stabilize the People's Democratic Party in Kabul.[1] From a global standpoint, democracy and capitalism looked in terminal decline as the new decade arrived—researchers would recognize only thirty-seven major countries as democracies in 1980 while the misery index (the sum of monetary inflation and unemployment) in the United States reached 20.76 in 1981—and every dollar earned on January 1, 1980, would be worth around eighty-eight cents on January 1, 1981, when over 7 percent of Americans who wanted a job could not find one.

How much can change in a decade? In 1990, seventy-four countries possessed governments whose citizens held them periodically accountable in competitive elections, and the American misery index had been cut in half.[2] From 1989 to 1991, the United States, Great Britain, France, and the Soviet Union signed off on German reunification in the Treaty on the Final Settlement with Respect to Germany, Khomeini died and was succeeded by Ayatollah Ali Khamenei on the same weekend that the People's Liberation Army crushed student protests in Beijing's Tiananmen Square, Nicaragua's general elections handed Violeta Chamooro's National Opposition Union a hard-fought victory over President Daniel Ortega's Sandinista National Liberation Front, and the superpowers committed by treaty to halve their nuclear arsenals over the next forty months.

Revolutions now transformed living rooms and home offices as often as concrete barriers and public squares. When Republican nominee Ronald Reagan walked away with the US presidential election on November 4, 1980, there were as many as one million personal computers in the United States, three years after Steve Jobs unveiled the Apple I. By the end of the decade, there were fifty-four million, and Microsoft Corporation, led by Harvard dropout Bill Gates, was set to release Windows 3.0 on October 20, 1991.[3]

The final month of that year was particularly busy. On December 10, official delegates from the European Communities assembled in Maastricht, The Netherlands, to further bind their markets and peoples together. The Treaty of Maastricht would inaugurate the European Union two months later, and, for most of its member states, a new currency—the euro. On Boxing Day 1991, the Supreme Soviet voted to dissolve the Union of Soviet Socialist Republics, whose rights as a nuclear-weapon state and permanent member of the United Nations Security Council fell to the Russian Federation on New Year's Eve. In the space of five weeks, a new European super-state had materialized just as a seventy-year-old multiethnic empire passed out of existence—save in history books like the one you're now reading.

Major continuities accompanied these tectonic changes, above all the industrial axis that bridged the Atlantic Ocean and increasingly the Pacific, speeding the globalization of Western consumer culture in all its frivolity, dynamism, inequality, and waste.[4] In the fourth quarter of 1979, the Atari VCS was the most popular gift in American stores, bringing arcade games such as Asteroids, Pac-Man, and Space Invaders into the dens and basements of families across the country. Ten years later, more kids found a Nintendo Game Boy in their stockings than any other Christmas present. Even these echoes carried discordant notes, however. Atari, Inc., was based in Sunnyvale, California; Nintendo in Kyoto, Japan.[5] For decades the leading player in high-end consumer electronics, US blue chips were increasingly on the defensive against their foreign rivals. During the Democratic primary in 1992, former Massachusetts senator Paul Tsongas would declare the Cold War "over" and insist that "Japan won."[6] Thirty years later, it seemed the People's Republic of China may have snuck into the lead, just under the wire.

The relationship between the United States and the world transformed itself over the course of the "long 1980s," and over these developments towered the figure of Ronald Reagan. A middling Hollywood actor, Screen Actors Guild president, General Electric spokesman, and two-term California governor, Reagan would lead a two-term presidential administration of squabbling neoconservatives, neoliberals, moral majoritarians, and party-line Republicans. From January 20, 1981, to January 20, 1989, they remodeled American power, purpose, and prosperity by tapping the prodigious energies of an increasingly integrated, interdependent world economy with West Coast technologists, Texas wildcatters, Sunbelt entrepreneurs, Hollywood producers, Wall Street bankers, and Rustbelt laborers at its beating heart.[7]

The United States bestrode the world anew by 1989, even though its shoulders slumped with fresh-stacked debt. Upon his appointment as Federal Reserve chairman in August 1987, Alan Greenspan beheld a poisoned chalice: "Huge government deficits under Reagan had caused the national debt to the public to almost triple, from just over $700 billion at the start of his presidency to more than $2 trillion at the end of fiscal year 1988."[8] By the time Reagan's vice president and chosen successor, George H. W. Bush, left office five years later, the federal debt had ballooned to $4 trillion—66 percent as a share of gross domestic product (GDP), up from just 33 percent twelve years before.[9] The public sector held no monopoly on liabilities—total credit to the nonfinancial private sector hit $7.52 trillion on December 31, 1991, up from $2.38 trillion twelve years earlier.[10]

The 1980s was after all the decade when investment banks such as Goldman Sachs, Bear Sterns, Morgan Stanley, and Merrill Lynch became corporate superstars. In exchange, American society, together with international allies, multinational corporations, and global civil society, left the malaise of the 1970s behind for the boom-and-bust of the next forty years, as the United States' transition from an industrial to a service-led, rentier-dominated economy bore ever onward and the international communist movement retreated to a handful of redoubts in the Lao People's Democratic Republic, the Socialist Republic of Vietnam, the Republic of Cuba, the Democratic People's Republic of North Korea, and the People's Republic of China (PRC).[11] The lesson was not lost on future powerbrokers. When President George W. Bush's treasury secretary, Paul O'Neill, warned about the economic effects of yawning deficits after 9/11, Vice President Dick Cheney deadpanned in response, "You know . . . Reagan proved deficits don't matter."[12]

Like Thomas Jefferson, Andrew Jackson, Abraham Lincoln, Theodore Roosevelt, and Franklin Roosevelt, Reagan lent his name to an age by forging a new electoral coalition, proclaiming a fresh governing creed, and transforming his country's role in the world—for better and for worse.[13] Like them as well, the country's ensuing good fortunes have driven many of his presidency's complexities, contradictions, and controversies into the historical background. As late as 1987, Reagan's admirers, who feared he had broken his promise to face down Moscow, and his detractors, who believed his dogmatic anticommunism had inflicted undue suffering abroad and injustice at home, would both have been shocked to hear him dubbed "the conquering hero of the Cold War."[14] They might have used other names, some less flattering than others: conservative, radical, appeaser, militarist, conciliator, interventionist, free-marketeer, protectionist, warmonger, abolitionist, human rights champion, law-breaker.

As Reagan and the 1980s retreat farther into our collective memory, the necessity for historical reappraisal mounts. To turn Reagan's life and times into an epic for recitation, whether tragic or triumphant, rather than a subject for reflection, deadens our sense of historical structure and agency, of cause and effect, of continuity and change, and, above all, of the swirl of human choice and unexpected contingency that periodically bend history's arc. Historians owe those who witnessed the decade as well as those who now carry its debts an honest accounting of the world that Reagan and his contemporaries made. After all, this volume's editors (and many of its contributors) were born in the 1980s. By the time this volume is published, our college-age students will have no living memory of a time before Reagan's body came to rest beneath the grounds of his presidential library in Simi Valley, California.

This volume therefore aims to make sense not just of Reagan, but also the world he believed it was within his power to remake. His reputation has risen largely in recognition of his feats abroad—a cascade of earth-shaking events—many of which his vice president and successor, George H. W. Bush, presided over from 1989 to 1993: the fall of the Berlin Wall and Germany's reunification; Operation Desert Storm; the Soviet Union's dissolution; free elections in Eastern Europe, East Asia, and Latin America; Beijing's rising wealth and power.[15] Most striking has been the general perception that Reagan served as his own chief strategist, especially vis-à-vis the Soviet Union and the nuclear arms race. After his second landslide victory, even some of his harshest critics felt moved to acknowledge that he had "cut a figure of world-historical importance."[16]

The political battles of the 1980s, turbocharged by culture wars over religion, history standards, sexual and gender identity, labor rights, and family planning, cast Reagan as a single-minded foe of Marxist-Leninism, with villainous or heroic coats applied according to one's party colors or ideological hue. Early appraisals were unsurprisingly split. Cold War triumphalists fixated on his presence beside the death beds of the Warsaw Pact and the Soviet Union, attributing Western victory to Reagan and his supporting band of neoconservatives (many on loan from the Democratic Party).[17] Others were less impressed, emphasizing cynical, bloody, at times illegal covert operations in Nicaragua, Iran, and Guatemala; cynical support for South Africa's apartheid regime; blowback from funding and arming Islamic fundamentalists in war-torn Afghanistan; failed nuclear nonproliferation efforts in South Asia; expanded military spending; and creeping military involvement throughout the Middle East.[18]

Although many of these fires still smolder, scholars are beginning to substitute the heat of contemporary passion for the light of thoughtful retrospection. More than thirty years since Reagan left office, he routinely ranks among the top ten presidents in surveys polling scholars of the office and, among the public, first among those who have served since 1945.[19] The claims of recent histories of US foreign relations and international history in the 1980s have grown more nuanced and broadly favorable, if not necessarily more modest.[20] His willingness to defy his own neoconservative backers and work with Soviet general secretary Mikhail Gorbachev has won general plaudits.[21] So, too, has his heartfelt embrace of dramatic reductions, even categorical eliminations, of nuclear-weapon systems—first in the 1987 Intermediate Range Forces Treaty, and then the Strategic Arms Reduction Treaty (START) that Bush and Gorbachev signed in 1991.[22] To nuclear freeze activists, European allies, and American hawks, who all, in one way or another, thought they were living through a "year of maximum danger" in 1983, when a Soviet Su-15 interceptor shot down Korean Air Lines 007, claiming the lives of all 269 passengers and crew aboard, and NATO military exercise Able Archer reportedly triggered warnings of nuclear war, Reagan's record as a nuclear arms controller and a vocal abolitionist would have been unimaginable.[23] To many, his nuclear idealism now looks more momentous than his anticommunism.[24]

The events that dominated headlines from 1985 to 1991—the reactor meltdown in Chernobyl, Ukraine, Gorbachev's repudiation of the Brezhnev doctrine, the collapse of communist regimes throughout Eastern Europe, and the Soviet Union's break-up into fifteen republics on December 26, 1991—have defined Reagan's legacy as a statesman. Yet the drama of the Cold War's twilight struggle and largely bloodless finale were, in many ways, the fruits of human agency and structural constraints that long predated him and whose impacts remain with us still, decades later. A third wave of literature has accordingly widened the scope of historical inquiry along two axes: analytically, to better integrate matters of culture, society, domestic politics, ideas, finance, technology, race, national identity, and ideology into studies of US foreign relations and global affairs; and geographically, to better reconnoiter regions at the core and on the periphery of the Cold War, as well as off that map altogether.[25]

The contours of US foreign relations and international history in the 1980s therefore merit sustained, focused scholarly treatment, and this volume endeavors to provide it. Key themes bind its nineteen chapters together, though their common subtext is the perennial tension between the elite history of "great leaders" such as Ronald Reagan, Margaret Thatcher, Helmut Kohl, Deng Xiaoping, Yasuhiro Nakasone, Mikhail Gorbachev, or George H. W. Bush, and the social, economic, cultural, technological, and political contexts that conditioned their actions, themselves the product of those whose names will never grace a book's cover. As Harry S. Truman once pledged, "the buck stops" in the White House Oval Office, but even US presidents do not make history entirely as they please; this is therefore as much a study of the world that shaped Reagan's presidency as a book about the world his presidency shaped.

The first set of themes centers on the US-Soviet struggle. It is vital to distinguish between the subject as a geo-ideological conflict and as a historical era that stretched back to the Second World War, the Russian Revolution, or the Paris Commune, depending on the storyteller.[26] Although the Cold War was history's fulcrum from 1947 to 1991, not every event drew its meaning from the global struggle between liberal capitalism and authoritarian communism, let alone that between the United States and the Soviet Union. Early appraisals divided between those who praised Reagan for firming up US containment of international communism and the Kremlin more narrowly, and those who believed a cult of deterrence had steered US foreign policy down treacherous lanes.[27] John Lewis Gaddis singled out Reagan for praise, ranking him as one of the grandest of grand strategists in the nation's hall of honor by virtue of "his ability to see beyond complexity to simplicity"—namely, his intuition that the Kremlin remained fundamentally adversarial even as collectivist solutions sapped communist societies of their full potential. Melvyn Leffler, by contrast, looked inward for Reagan's strengths, above all "his willingness to reach out to a leadership he abhorred, men whose values he detested; to appreciate the concerns of the adversary; and to learn from experience."[28]

Whether simple or complex, Reagan's handling of the Cold War resists easy answers. Leffler begins this volume by asking a deceptively simple question: Did Reagan aim to win, or to end, the Cold War? Reagan had a knack for personal diplomacy, even with adversaries. At four summits in Geneva, Reykjavik, Washington, DC, and Moscow, he persuaded Gorbachev that he "was seeking not to win the Cold War, but to end it." Thus reassured, the Soviet general secretary, ever the impatient reformer, launched *glasnost* (transparency) and *perestroika* (restructuring) in hopes of catching up with East Germany and Japan while holding off a reforming and opening PRC, and then renounced Moscow's right under the Brezhnev doctrine to preserve Eastern European communism at rifle point.[29] Reagan's penchant for quiet, firm diplomacy, in Leffler's telling, made him "Gorbachev's minor, yet indispensable partner."

Elizabeth C. Charles and James Graham Wilson ask more pointed questions about US-Soviet relations: To what extent did Reagan perceive a Soviet threat? How did he and his staff plan to meet it? And did they succeed on their own terms? Reagan's foreign policy gained serious momentum in July 1982, when he made George Shultz, an economist and director of the Bechtel Group, the largest construction company in the United States, his second secretary of state. When Richard Pipes—a hardline National Security Council staffer on loan from Harvard University's Department of History—prioritized the need for the US government to "contain and over time reverse Soviet expansionism" in National Security Decision Directive (NSDD) 75, Shultz was instrumental in addressing the next two bullet points: to "promote . . . the process of change in the Soviet Union toward a more pluralistic political and economic system" and to "engage the Soviet Union in negotiations" on arms control, bilateral issues, and regional conflicts consistent with "the principle of strict reciprocity and mutual interest."[30] With Shultz at the helm, Reagan's "quiet diplomacy" achieved remarkable breakthroughs, first with Pentecostals seeking asylum at the US embassy in Moscow, then with arms control talks, and finally in Afghanistan.

Reagan's Cold War tactics never lacked a sharper edge, which gave rise to problems with more risk-averse allies and less compromising activists. NSDD 75's first goal, which *Wall Street Journal* columnist Charles Krauthammer styled the "Reagan doctrine" in 1985, would make life difficult for West European members of the North Atlantic Treaty Organization (NATO), for whom Warsaw Pact countries, however troublesome, were nonetheless neighbors. Together, Susan Colbourn and Mathias Haeussler explain why Reagan's abandonment of détente "put the United States at odds with many of his counterparts" in Bonn, Rome, Paris, and London, who prized the headway they had made during the 1970s with Moscow and its comrades in the

Warsaw Pact on matters of trade, war, and peace, even as Moscow deployed mounting numbers of nuclear-tipped missiles close to their territories. However well anti-détente rhetoric played with conservative audiences back home in the United States, in the end Reagan found it impossible to abandon the "dual-track strategy" that Western European capitals had devised with Carter to simultaneously deploy and negotiate over the so-called Euromissiles. As Stephanie Freeman demonstrates in her own chapter on the nuclear freeze movement, which called to halt the development, acquisition, and deployment of atomic arsenals on both sides of the Iron Curtain, antinuclear campaigners in Western Europe and North America, including key members of the US Congress, developed a "discordant relationship" with the president, notwithstanding their "shared interest in nuclear disarmament." This salutary rivalry forced more hawkish members of the first Reagan administration to reconcile themselves to the game of disarmament, which resulted in a set of "sweeping nuclear arms reduction agreements" during his final, and George H. W. Bush's only, term in office.

The Cold War's character varied from region to region and place to place, and the general applause Reagan would win in Europe would have more tragic echoes in Latin America, Asia, Africa, and the Middle East. Eager to sign communism's death warrant in the "Third World," his swashbuckling administration backed resistance forces to the hilt against Soviet proxies and leftist regimes in southern Africa, Afghanistan, and Central America.[31] The human cost was staggering, at times even genocidal. The Guatemalan civil war claimed 200,000 lives—most of them poverty-stricken Mayan villagers. Funded, trained, and armed by the US government, the Guatemalan military was responsible for 93 percent of those deaths.[32] The collapse of the Portuguese empire in Africa, which Flavia Gasbarri recounts in her chapter on southern Africa, yielded a similarly fraught proxy battleground in the Southern Hemisphere, where Reagan's readiness to counter Cuban and Soviet interventions in the Angolan Civil War collided head-on with a tenacious anti-apartheid movement. Conducted by Assistant Secretary of State for African Affairs Chester Crocker, Reagan's policy of "constructive engagement" toward South Africa eventually bore fruit thanks to parallel progress in US-Soviet relations, but his preference for incremental reform rather than swift progress toward black majority rule helped keep South Africa's apartheid regime on life support for years.

Afghanistan's reputation as a "graveyard of empires" is as hyperbolic as it is superficial. Yet two decades before US troops entered the rugged, landlocked country, the Soviet Red Army made war to pacify its nations and peoples. Its efforts came to naught because of resistance fighters whose ranks swelled in response to Soviet brutality and an international jihad that Wahhabi clerics declared from Saudi Arabia. Robert Rakove suggests that in the 1980s Afghanistan supplanted central Europe as the Cold War's "central front." Over time Washington's drive to turn the country into Moscow's "Vietnam" became an end in itself, hindering diplomacy and leaving behind a failed state whose lurch toward political Islam would offer al Qaeda critical sanctuary in the decade before 9/11. The Reagan doctrine produced similar tensions in Central America, which Jeane Kirkpatrick, an influential Democratic neoconservative at Georgetown University whom Reagan would make his United Nations ambassador, deemed "the most important place in the world."[33] Michael Schmidli demonstrates how US policymakers came to conflate democracy promotion and human rights in their efforts to contain leftist foes abroad and post-Vietnam liberals at home.[34] Democracy promotion was a double-edged sword. On the one hand, Bush's government spent more per voter on Nicaragua's election in 1990 than his own presidential campaign had spent on US voters two years earlier. On the other hand, the militarization of democracy and human rights normalized "a distinctive form of interventionism" in elite discourse back home—an exceptionalism that would resound during Bill Clinton's presidency when Secretary of State Madeleine Albright christened the United States the world's "indispensable nation."[35]

The second set of themes flows from Reagan's romantic statecraft.[36] In the *National Interest* in 1989, Francis Fukuyama claimed that "something very fundamental [had] happened in world history," namely "the end point of mankind's ideological evolution and the universalization of Western liberal democracy as the final form of human government."[37] Reagan might have called this result providential, as his personal optimism always sat uneasily with the philosophical pessimism that neoconservative and neoliberal writings exuded. Fukuyama had borrowed Friedrich Nietzsche's idea of the "last man" to think through what would happen when capitalism, democracy, private property, the rule of law, and human rights found universal expression. This package of liberal nostrums would supply material plenty and political legitimacy, but he doubted they could ever bestow transcendental meaning. Broadly shared prosperity would instead democratize ennui, leading average workers to turn to thoughtless consumption in a glittering marketplace, or, worse yet, to demagogic strongmen peddling grievances against their social betters (among whom he included Donald Trump alongside fellow New York fraudsters Leona Helmsley, Ivan Boesky, and Michael Milken).[38]

Reagan would have found this future intolerable for the same reason his presidency proved so dynamic. Whether due to his ecumenical Presbyterianism, his actor's sense of theater, or his Disneyfied image of American history, his world abounded with heroes, whose dramas, both tragic and uplifting, were to him just as gripping when they unfolded on main streets, in office towers, or in living rooms as when they were staged in marbled parliaments, on dusty battlefields, or aboard NASA's new Space Shuttle.[39]

This romantic worldview may have unnerved scientists of nuclear deterrence or the corporate balance sheet, but it also helped Reagan persuade Gorbachev—whose own architectural visions of democratic socialism and a "common European home" also possessed a heroic sweep—that they could accomplish great things together.[40] It also helped Reagan to sell the federal interventions—lender-of-last resort central banking, inflation-quelling interest rates, military spending, the Strategic Defense Initiative (SDI), and the War on Drugs, among others—in the context of a political platform that otherwise denigrated the Washington bureaucracy.

Reagan's faith in individuals led him badly astray at times, such as when National Security Adviser Robert McFarlane tasked Oliver North, a brash US Army lieutenant colonel, with overthrowing the elected government of Nicaragua by trading arms for hostages with the Islamic Republic of Iran, in defiance of common sense and congressional statute. It also led him to push against doors which others thought locked, convincing him, for example, that Stinger-armed mujahideen could defeat the vaunted Red Army in Afghanistan. Elisabeth Leake surveys how this confrontational approach yielded instability and crisis throughout southwest Asia, as a decade-long Central Intelligence Agency operation sped centrifugal forces of ethnonational separatism and Islamic fundamentalism that threatened to tear the countries of Iran, Afghanistan, Pakistan, and India apart. US officials may have handed their Soviet counterparts a black eye in local and global opinion, but their focus on nation-states also generated failures—to grasp the ethno-nationalist patchwork of Southwest Asia's borderlands, to invest in civil society, or to resolve many-sided regional conflicts—leaving a cluster of failed or failing states in their wake.

The Israeli-Palestinian conflict and the gathering clouds of international terrorism also resisted Reagan's good-versus-evil worldview. Seth Anziska recounts how Reagan's fondness for Israel and his fixation on pressing the Soviets led him to confirm Tel Aviv as a strategic partner and the Palestinian Liberation Organization (PLO) as a Soviet proxy-cum-terrorist group. Washington and Tel Aviv's tacit alliance served to embolden Israeli Prime Minister Menachem Begin, the founder of the Likud Party, who ramped up settlement construction in the West Bank, authorized airstrikes against Iraq's Osirak nuclear reactor, turned a blind eye toward the PLO's moderation, and launched a bloody incursion into Lebanon. To quell a bloodbath in Lebanon, Reagan dispatched US marines to Beirut. There, they bore the brunt of the deadliest terrorist attack in American history to date, and the worst military death toll since the

Vietnam War.[41] Christopher Fuller narrates how the death or injury of more than 300 service members at the US Marine barracks touched off a turf war back in Washington that pit Shultz and CIA Director William Casey against Secretary of Defense Caspar Weinberger, who insisted that military operations enjoy a public hearing, clear war aims, and a lack of political handcuffs. With the Pentagon more worried about reprising Vietnam than in battling terrorism, Casey formed the CIA Counterterrorism Center to synchronize human and signals intelligence around the world and develop new, low-profile weapon systems, including the first military drone. The fallout from the Iran-Contra affair decimated its top ranks, however. In his post-presidential memoirs Reagan would concede that, for all their efforts, the Middle East remained "an adders' nest"—a loaded term if there ever was one.[42]

Reagan's greatest heroes were the United States' soldiers. In their honor, he broached the subject that had shattered the consensus around anticommunist containment a decade earlier—the Vietnam War. Mark Lawrence places Reagan's struggles against the "Vietnam syndrome" in the context of the conservative movement he led. In his contest with Carter, Reagan branded the war a "noble cause," casting his lot with US veterans, prisoners of war, those missing in action, and the "silent majority" who maintained faith with the nation's martial virtues. Here as well Reagan proved less inflammatory once in the Oval Office, from where he sidestepped the uproar over Maya Lin's elegiac Vietnam War memorial and restricted US military operations abroad to small peacekeeping operations. In fact, his most successful armed intervention involved the deployment of a small expeditionary force to the tiny Caribbean island nation of Grenada. Weinberger's doctrine ruled out most military operations short of all-out war, but Reagan's "ability to convince ordinary American to see the world his way" nevertheless shifted the terms of debate over US armed might, foreshadowing its unsheathing over the next thirty years, first with George H. W. Bush's ejection of Iraqi dictator Saddam Hussein from Kuwait in 1990, then with limited military actions in Somalia, Serbia, Bosnia, Libya, Syria, and Yemen, and finally with two major conflicts in Afghanistan and Iraq, the first of which has now surpassed Vietnam as the longest war in American history.[43]

A third set of themes relates to the global expansion of liberalism: the package of political constructs—self-determination, democracy, the rule of law, human rights, private property, market practices—whose adherents, however diverse in their philosophical outlooks or political orientations, generally seek to enumerate the rights and responsibilities of private actors and public authorities in the belief that individual self-expression ranks utmost and that, in the absence of clear discrimination or external threat, the total, voluntary actions of individuals will redound to the greatest good.

Anticommunism and pro-liberalism were never one and the same. Reagan had earned his anticommunist bona fides in his 1964 speech on behalf of Republican presidential candidate Barry Goldwater, which his later protests against the pursuit of détente with Moscow and Beijing by Richard Nixon, Gerald Ford, Henry Kissinger, and Jimmy Carter only strengthened in the Republican Party and among the general public. Periodic broadsides against the "evil empire" notwithstanding, President Reagan proved less dogmatic than this pre-election rhetoric would have suggested. This was in part temperamental—Reagan's abundant self-confidence inclined him to shoot the moon. On a deeper level, however, his concrete love of individual action, whether via high-level summitry or in private enterprise, led him to raise his liberal dreams above his fear of collectivism. As conservative *Washington Post* columnist George Will noted when President Reagan canceled the punitive grain embargo that Carter had imposed on the Soviet Union after the Afghan invasion, "The administration evidently loves commerce more than it loathes Communism."[44]

The reality was more complex. The Reagan administration handled external relations in the context of huge structural changes to the national and world economy, which had gathered pace since the Bretton Woods system of gold-backed dollar finance had collapsed under Nixon.[45] Economic affairs had undergone three major sea changes since the early 1970s. First, after fifty years in abeyance, international banking reemerged as a global force. Skyrocketing oil prices and a cascade of scraped capital controls—beginning with the United States in the mid-1960s and concluding with the European Community, Scandinavia, and Japan in the late 1980s—gave rise to a massive pool of footloose, offshore capital: $160 billion in 1973 became $1.5 trillion ten years later and more than $5 trillion ten years after that, with more than $1 trillion loaned out each year.[46] Second, the death of Bretton Woods' "embedded liberal" order of mixed economies financing welfare states through Keynesian macroeconomics and freer trade gave way before "the spread of market practices less encumbered by social welfare provisions," as extolled by Nobel Prize-winning, supply-side economists such as Milton Friedman and Robert Mundell.[47] The rising clout of financial institutions—both central and private—weakened industrial planners and unions throughout the developed world, ushering in a more interconnected and equitable global economy as industry decamped for cheaper labor markets and national inequality began its steady rise as asset prices marched upward and deindustrialization curtailed secure working-class employment against a secular backdrop of stagnating growth.[48] Globalization and financialization accelerated just as revolutionary gifts of a "special century" of life-changing inventions—electricity, modern sanitation, radio, automobiles, airplanes, telecommunications, modern credit, plastics, and the semiconductor—started to peter out. As the pace of meaningful innovation slowed, that of labor productivity and economic growth did as well.[49]

The third sea change sprang from the previous two: the mutation of the United States from the world's biggest lender to its greatest borrower. In his chapter Michael De Groot surveys international monetary and trade relations in the 1980s, when "the US economic relationship with the world underwent a fundamental transformation." The sky-high interest rates imposed by Federal Reserve Chairman Paul Volcker in 1980 to tighten the dollar supply so as to vanquish inflation hindered the White House's efforts to jumpstart the economy through tax cuts, deregulation, and spending cuts. Foreign investment in US Department of Treasury securities shot upward as investors jumped on ten-year Treasury yields that exceeded 15 percent at one point, easily funding federal deficits that peaked at 6 percent in 1983 before falling to just over 3 percent in 1989—an average of 4 percent of GDP per year across the decade.[50]

What German Chancellor Helmut Schmidt dubbed "the highest real interest rates since the birth of Christ" upended state finances and economic growth around the globe.[51] Most consequentially, it rendered many developing and socialist countries insolvent, as a tsunami of capital flowed into the United States and out of Eastern Europe and the developing world, which had taken out massive loans in the mid-1970s to finance industrial modernization and import substitution.[52] By 1983, thirty-four countries in the developing and socialist worlds were renegotiating their loans with international lenders. By decade's end, before they lent more money, Western financial institutions were requiring certification by the International Monetary Fund, whose leadership pressed on sovereign debtors structural readjustment programs, which prioritized deficit reduction over aggregate demand, secure retirement, or social safety nets.[53] This one-two punch of capital flight and government austerity would make the 1980s a "lost decade" for Latin America and an antechamber to revolution in Eastern Europe.[54]

Robert Mundell's prediction in 1982 that oil-rich Saudi Arabia would ultimately fund a fast-rising US debt proved clairvoyant. In 1984, plunging oil revenues led the Saudi finance minister to seek more liquid assets for the $90 billion he had under management.[55] According to David Painter's chapter, that was more or less the extent of US-Saudi collusion against the Soviet Union. Rumors have long swirled that US officials convinced Saudi King Fahd bin Abudulaziz Al Saud to slash oil prices by ramping production up halfway through the decade, with a view to reverse the windfall oil-and-gas profits that were subsidizing Moscow's creaky factories and overgrown military industry. While the Reagan administration was not above economic warfare—punishing European allies, for instance, for approving a new transcontinental pipeline pumping gas from Siberia after the Polish strikes of 1981—Riyadh was too worried about its own red ink to spare much thought for Moscow's, while Moscow was more worried about its communist dependencies in Eastern Europe, whose total foreign-owned debt mushroomed from $6 billion in 1970 to $90 billion in 1990.[56] This debt would play an outsized role in the sequence of events that ended in the fall of the Berlin Wall, as East European leaders hungry for West German loans looked the other way as thousands fled the German Democratic Republic, whose own leaders acquiesced to unification with the Federal Republic of Germany in 1991 lest they have to face their international lenders alone.[57]

Although the challenges the advanced economies faced proved more manageable, they would have prolonged afterlives. At its economic meridian in the 1980s, Japan became a huge investor in the US economy. The *Wall Street Journal* reported in 1985 that Nippon Life Insurance Co., a major Japanese financial firm, "with US partners, owns skyscrapers in New York, Houston, and Los Angeles. It is becoming a major holder of the US national debt. It buys so many foreign bonds, in fact, that it is planning to set up its own Tokyo trading room to handle them."[58] Jennifer Miller relates how Japan's rising sun sparked "fears of American decline." Wall Street's marbled money and the Midwest's rusting factories were used to communist competitors, not Japanese corporatism, which married export-driven national champions to industrial planning, collaborative unionism, and lifetime employment. Foreign-held assets in the United States doubled from 1982 to 1986, and even though German, French, and British firms held more in their portfolios, Japanese investors received the most flak.[59] One critic of Japan's "free-riding" on the US security umbrella was Donald Trump, who, perhaps frustrated that Japanese investors were outbidding him for tony Manhattan real estate, took out advertisements in major newspapers calling on Reagan to "end *our* vast deficits by making Japan, and others who can afford it, pay. . . . Let's not let our great country be laughed at any more."[60]

My own contribution shows how foreign investment, arms sales, and human rights formed a triangular web among Washington, Taipei, and Beijing in the 1980s, with the former two ultimately carrying the day. Reagan's campaign buoyed hopes that the latest military kit and formal recognition would be made available to Taiwan. Instead, Reagan and PRC vice chairman Zhao Ziyang set ceilings on US arms sales to the diplomatically isolated island in 1982. Growing American, Japanese, Hong Kong, and eventually Taiwanese investment in mainland China, where Communist Party chairman Deng Xiaoping had launched a campaign of "reform and opening up," pointed to a lucrative convergence of "greater China," a sales pitch that Anna Chennault, an uncrowned queen of Washington high society and Deng's US confidant, made to Reagan's cabinet. Foreign investment into "special economic zones"—Shantou, Shenzhen, and Zhuhai in Guangdong across from Hong Kong and Xiamen in Fujian across from Taiwan—jumpstarted growth in the People's Republic in the 1980s, whose GDP would eclipse Russia's by the end of the 1990s. It also cushioned US-PRC ties when democracy promotion prompted a violent crackdown in Tiananmen Square in 1989.[61] As James Lilley, Bush's ambassador in Beijing, put it, CCP leaders might "close the door to beat the dog" by ejecting foreigner observers from the mainland, but that door would not remain closed for long to nuclear reactors, antisubmarine torpedoes, or navigation computers for Boeing jets.[62]

Human rights had emerged as touchstones for US foreign policy after Carter issued a clarion call in 1977 for Washington to serve as their "undisputed champion."[63] Sarah Snyder judges Reagan's human rights policies as being "highly compartmentalized," with his administration's policies falling generally along lines of geography. While still at Georgetown, Kirkpatrick had roasted Carter for abandoning Somoza and Iranian Shah Reza Pahlavi in a naïve attempt to retain the moral high ground. While such concerns were rarely decisive in most of Latin America and the Middle East, Reagan's administration was more than happy to rake communist regimes over the coals in Warsaw, Moscow, or Havana. Over time, they weighed them more heavily in cases where injustice appeared especially acute, for instance, in South Africa, the Philippines, and Chile. Reagan's approach was also distinct because, as Lauren Turek explains in her chapter, the modern conservative movement primarily approached human rights from the standpoint of religious freedoms. Human rights became animating principles in US foreign policy after Vietnam, when liberal and conservatives alike moved to reclaim their nation's virtue in the face of their country's sins abroad.[64] This "moral crusade" resonated with the Republican Party's emerging base—evangelical Christians and by-the-Book Catholics—who were willing to absolve his administration from working with authoritarian dictators so long as it proclaimed and pursued a holy war against atheistic communists worldwide.

For all the criticism Reagan's crusades in Nicaragua and Guatemala bred during the Iran-Contra scandal, his administration showed greater ambivalence toward South American dictators. As James Cameron and Evan McCormick note in their chapters, the US bond market's gravitational pull deprived Brazil and Chile of the foreign investment with which they had aimed to modernize their economies. Cameron chronicles how the Reagan administration's focus in Brazil correspondingly shifted from ardent anticommunism to a "push to create a world economy that safeguarded US business interests and maximized their access to foreign markets," most of all the intellectual property and investment rights that Silicon Valley and Wall Street coveted. In Chile, meanwhile, Augusto Pinochet's neoliberal reforms emboldened US officials, who grew confident that to condemn the torture, rape, and disappearance of political dissidents in the country would strengthen rather than undermine civil society. McCormick recounts how in a stark reversal of his earlier indulgences of Pinochet's felonies, Reagan's watch-phrase in Chile became "a prompt transition to civilian democracy." Disillusionment arose on both sides: for Reagan and Bush, at Pinochet's irreformability; for Pinochet, at Reagan and Bush for ultimately sounding just like Carter.

If there was a North Star to Reagan's thinking, it sparkled within a larger constellation of neoliberal values: free markets, free enterprise, and free expression. These maxims informed a governing mindset in which political and economic rights ranked higher than social justice. Shultz and Reagan believed that, when combined with the sheer size of the American economy, the animal spirits unleashed by deregulation, tax cuts, easy money, and globalization would speed victory against the Soviet Union. When the Joint Chiefs of Staff presented Shultz with the bill for the potential elimination of ballistic missiles after the Reykjavik summit in October 1986, the secretary of state's response was as self-assured as it was grandiose: "Why are we not willing to pay a little more for [this]? The American economy is so big and dynamic it's awesome!"[65]

Not everyone shared their faith that deficit-financed economic growth would furnish a silver bullet with which to end the Cold War. In a letter to the editor of the *Wall Street Journal* in February 1988, Yale University historian Paul Kennedy reflected on a recent review of his surprise bestseller, *The Rise and Fall of Great Powers*: "I thought it ironic, on the same day . . . elsewhere in your paper it was reported that President Reagan's final budget contained yet another massive federal deficit, and that no one in Congress was willing to propose any serious action this year to close the gap between spending and revenue." He rifled through history for comparisons: "One wonders whether the public ethos and political culture of contemporary America really are so different from those that hobbled Olivare's Spain or Louis XVI's France," both of which had collapsed in their quenchless thirst for opulence and imperium.[66]

While this volume's center of gravity lies in the 1980s, the historical legacy of US foreign relations and international history in that decade remains tightly bound up in the record of the George H. W. Bush presidency from 1989 to

1993. His service as Reagan's vice president and their common home in the Republican Party notwithstanding, Bush's administration brought a new style to the White House. Robert Hutchings, a prominent National Security Council staffer, would reminisce how "an entirely new team came in, representing foreign policy approaches fundamentally at odds with those of the Reagan administration." "Before 1989 there was Reagan," he underlined for effect; "afterwards there was Bush."[67]

"We set out to change a nation," Reagan had rhapsodized at a White House tribute to his "political soulmate," UK prime minister Margaret Thatcher, in 1988; "instead, we changed the world."[68] Aided by White House Chief of Staff James Baker and National Security Adviser Brent Scowcroft, Bush's ambitions proved more modest. Before a joint session of the US Congress on September 11, 1990, he envisaged a "new world order" where "the rule of law supplants the rule of the jungle," "nations recognize the shared responsibility for freedom and justice," and "the strong respect the rights of the weak." Most of all, it would be a world in which "America will not be intimidated."[69] Weeks earlier, the world had watched the technological marvel of the US military forged by Reagan to defeat the Warsaw Pact blow the world's fourth largest army to smithereens in the dusty plains of Iraq.

Would a third Reagan administration have pursued a more ambitious vision of post–Cold War global reconstruction? Any plans for grants and loans in the spirit of the Marshall Plan would have run afoul of the Balanced Budget and Emergency Deficit Control Reaffirmation Act, which the US Congress had passed in 1987 to lessen the deficits that Reagan was piling up. In the event, his heroic globalism set the terms for Bush's "conservative revolution" over the next four years, which would itself sow disorder throughout the international system. Over the past thirty years, the achievement of Cold War victory on Western terms has lost some of its luster as the numbers of failed states, civil conflicts, migrants floods, financial crises, nuclear proliferation, growing inequality, resurgent populism, rampaging epidemics, and expeditionary wars have risen apace.

Nixon, Ford, and Carter had each curtailed state involvement in the economy while expanding the role that capital flows, financial products, and economic markets played in national and international society: a global regime of free-floating exchange rates in lieu of Bretton Woods' gold-backed pegs; the deregulation of commercial air travel, rail shipping, and motor carriage; the replacement of military conscription with an all-volunteer force; and the coordinated extension of lender-of-last resort provisions by the Federal Reserve and other central banks via the Swiss-based Bank of International Settlements.[70]

Reagan welcomed without reservations these Promethean forces, and also those of democratic protest, human rights, and religious revival, further revising the relationship between the private and the public spheres in the United States and around the globe. His willingness to treat nonstate actors and individual conscience as policy objects as momentous as international institutions or balances of military power lowered the drawbridge between the nation-state, the market, and the individual, fostering a global landscape in which the United States' market-military state wielded decisive advantages over one-party, fiscal-military states like that of the Soviet Union. His and Bush's failures to invest equally in international institutions stood in marked contrast. The result has been the continued ascent of American wealth and might, ever more unbound by multilateral groupings, competing ideologies, or rival power blocs. Former World Bank chief economist and Nobel-Prize winner Joseph Stiglitz described the perverse result as "global governance without global government."[71] International relations scholar Susan Strange warned of a state of global "ungovernance," ripe for exploitation by the rich and the powerful, or by one-party authoritarian powers like a rising People's Republic of China.[72]

The new world order has worked for some more than others. Ronald Reagan's legacy will turn on how long the conception of the American nation that his speeches, his policies, and his administration conjured into being survives and prospers, at home and across the world. Thirty years since Reagan vacated the Oval Office, we are still living through this moment. We will wrestle with its aftermath, its failures and successes, for decades more to come.

Notes

1. Christian Caryl and Timm Bryson, *Strange Rebels: 1979 and the Birth of the 21st Century* (New York: Basic Books, 2014).

2. Max Roser, "Democracy," *Our World in Data*, Oxford Martin Programme on Global Development, https://ourworldindata.org/democracy (accessed 1 October 2019).

3. Daniel Knight, "Personal Computer History: 1975–1984," 26 Apr. 2014, http://lowendmac.com/2014/personal-computer-history-the-first-25-years/; "Personal Computer History: 1985–1994," 5 Mar. 2018, http://lowendmac.com/2018/personal-computer-history-1985-1994/.

4. Thomas Piketty and Arthur Goldhammer, *Capital in the Twenty-First Century* (Cambridge, MA: The Belknap Press of Harvard University Press, 2014).

5. Mia Consalvo, *Atari to Zelda: Japan's Videogames in Global Contexts* (Cambridge: MIT Press, 2016); Andrew C. McKevitt, *Consuming Japan: Popular Culture and the Globalizing of 1980s America* (Chapel Hill: University of North Carolina Press, 2017);

Michael Z. Newman, *Atari Age: The Emergence of Video Games in America* (Cambridge: MIT Press, 2017).

6. Quoted in McKevitt, *Consuming Japan*, 21.

7. Thomas H. Oatley, *A Political Economy of American Hegemony: Buildups, Booms, and Busts* (New York: Cambridge University Press, 2015).

8. H. W. Brands, *Reagan: The Life* (New York: Anchor Books, 2016).

9. Jeffry A. Frieden, *Global Capitalism: Its Fall and Rise in the Twentieth Century* (New York: Norton, 2007), 462.

10. "United States Credit to Private Non-Financial Sector," CEIC Data, https://www.ceicdata.com/en/indicator/united-states/credit-to-private-nonfinancial-sector (accessed October 2019).

11. Greta R. Krippner, *Capitalizing on Crisis: The Political Origins of the Rise of Finance* (Cambridge, MA: Harvard University Press, 2012).

12. Adam Tooze, *Crashed: How a Decade of Financial Crises Changed the World* (New York: Penguin, 2019), 36.

13. Both admirers and detractors set Reagan's name atop the decade's marquee. For a sympathetic view, see Steven F. Hayward, *The Age of Reagan. The Conservative Counterrevolution, 1980–1989* (New York: Crown Forum, 2009). For a more critical interpretation, see Sean Wilentz, *The Age of Reagan: A History, 1974–2008* (New York: Harper, 2008).

14. Hayward, *The Age of Reagan*, 141.

15. The literature on these four pregnant years is impressive and growing. In addition to Jeffrey Engel's *When the World Seemed New: George H. W. Bush and the End of the Cold War* (New York: Houghton Mifflin Harcourt, 2017), Kristina Spohr maintains that a "conservative revolution" locked in Western gains without reforming international institutions for a post–Cold War world in *Post Wall, Post Square: How Bush, Gorbachev, Kohl, and Deng Shaped the World after 1989* (New Haven: Yale University Press, 2020). On German unification, the best monograph is Mary Elise Sarotte, *1989: The Struggle to Create Post–Cold War Europe* (Princeton: Princeton University Press, 2014).

16. "After the Fall," *The Nation*, 17 Nov. 1984, https://www.thenation.com/article/archive/after-fall/.

17. Martin Anderson, *Revolution: The Reagan Legacy* (Stanford, CA: Hoover Institution Press), 1990; Paul Kengor, *The Crusader: Ronald Reagan and the Fall of Communism* (New York: Regan Books, 2006); Thomas C. Reed, *At the Abyss: An Insider's History of the Cold War* (New York: Ballantine Books, 2004); Peter Schweizer, *Victory: The Reagan Administration's Secret Strategy That Hastened the Collapse of the Soviet Union* (New York: Atlantic Monthly Press, 1994).

18. Bob Woodward, *Veil: The Secret Wars of the CIA, 1981–1987* (New York: Simon and Schuster, 1987); Malcolm Byrne, *Iran-Contra: Reagan's Scandal and the Unchecked Abuse of Presidential Power* (Lawrence: University Press of Kansas, 2014); Morris H. Morley, ed., *Crisis and Confrontation: Ronald Reagan's Foreign Policy* (Totowa, NJ: Rowman & Littlefield, 1988); Walton L. Brown, "Presidential Leadership and US Nonproliferation Policy," *Presidential Studies Quarterly* 24, no. 3 (1994): 563–575; Frances FitzGerald, *Way out There in the Blue: Reagan, Star Wars, and the End of the Cold War* (New York: Simon and Schuster, 2000); Raymond L. Garthoff, *The Great Transition: American-Soviet Relations and the End of the Cold War* (Washington, DC: Brookings Institution, 1994);

Andrew J. Bacevich, *America's War for the Greater Middle East: A Military History* (New York: Random House, 2017).

19. "Presidential Historians Survey 2017," C-Span, https://www.c-span.org/presidentsurvey2017/; "Poll—Presidents since the Second World War," Quinnipiac University, 7 Mar. 2018, https://poll.qu.edu/images/polling/us/us03072018_uplm87.pdf.

20. Kenneth L. Adelman, *Reagan at Reykjavik: Forty-Eight Hours That Ended the Cold War* (New York: Broadside Books, 2014); Hal Brands, *Making the Unipolar Moment: US Foreign Policy and the Rise of the Post–Cold War Order* (Ithaca, NY: Cornell University Press, 2016).

21. Beth A. Fischer, *The Reagan Reversal: Foreign Policy and the End of the Cold War* (Columbia: University of Missouri Press, 1997); Jim Mann, *The Rebellion of Ronald Reagan: A History of the End of the Cold War* (New York: Viking, 2009); James Graham Wilson, *The Triumph of Improvisation: Gorbachev's Adaptability, Reagan's Engagement, and the End of the Cold War* (Ithaca, NY: Cornell University Press, 2014).

22. Melvyn P. Leffler, *For the Soul of Mankind: The United States, the Soviet Union, and the Cold War* (New York: Hill and Wang, 2007).

23. Simon Miles, "The War Scare That Wasn't: Able Archer 83 and the Myths of the Second Cold War," *Journal of Cold War Studies* 22, no. 3 (2020): 86–118.

24. Jack F. Matlock, *Reagan and Gorbachev: How the Cold War Ended* (New York: Random House, 2004); Don Oberdorfer, *The Turn: From the Cold War to a New Era: The United States and the Soviet Union, 1983–1990* (New York: Poseidon Press, 1991); Paul Vorbeck Lettow, *Ronald Reagan and His Quest to Abolish Nuclear Weapons* (New York: Random House, 2005); David E. Hoffman, *The Dead Hand: The Untold Story of the Cold War Arms Race and Its Dangerous Legacy* (New York: Doubleday, 2009).

25. Jeffrey L. Chidester and Paul Kengor, eds., *Reagan's Legacy in a World Transformed* (Cambridge, MA: Harvard University Press, 2015); Bradley Lynn Coleman and Kyle Longley, eds., *Reagan and the World: Leadership and National Security, 1981–1989* (Lexington: University Press of Kentucky, 2017).

26. In order of periodization: John Lewis Gaddis, *Strategies of Containment: A Critical Appraisal of American National Security Policy during the Cold War* (New York: Oxford University Press, 2005); Melvyn P. Leffler, *The Specter of Communism: The United States and the Origins of the Cold War, 1917–1953* (New York: Hill and Wang, 1994); Odd Arne Westad, *The Cold War: A World History* (New York: Basic Books, 2017).

27. Gaddis, *Strategies of Containment*, 349–353; Richard Ned Lebow and Janice Gross Stein, *We All Lost the Cold War* (Princeton, NJ: Princeton University Press, 1995).

28. John Lewis Gaddis, *The Cold War: A New History* (New York: Penguin, 2005), 217; Leffler, *For the Soul of Mankind*, 341.

29. David Reynolds and I reach a similar conclusion in "Geneva, Reykjavik, Washington, and Moscow, 1985–1988," in *Transcending the Cold War: Summits, Statecraft, and the Dissolution of Bipolarity in Europe, 1970–1990*, ed. Kristina Spohr and David Reynolds (New York: Oxford University Press, 2016), 151–179.

30. National Security Decision Directive 75, "US Relations with the USSR," 17 Jan. 1983, https://fas.org/irp/offdocs/nsdd/nsdd-75.pdf. For more on the drafting of NSDD-75 and US-Soviet relations from 1980 to 1985 more generally, see Simon Miles, *Engaging the Evil Empire: Washington, Moscow, and the Beginning of the End of the Cold War* (Ithaca, NY: Cornell University Press, 2020).

31. Odd Arne Westad, *The Global Cold War: Third World Interventions and the Making of Our Times* (New York: Cambridge University Press, 2005), 7.

32. "Guatemala," United States Institute for Peace, 1 Feb. 1997, https://www.usip.org/publications/1997/02/truth-commission-guatemala.

33. Quoted in Walter LaFeber, *Inevitable Revolutions: The United States and Central America*, 2nd ed. (New York: Norton, 1993), 271.

34. This argument offers a neat twist on Barbara Keys's distinction between conservative and liberal human rights in the 1970s in her *Reclaiming American Virtue: The Human Rights Revolution of the 1970s* (Cambridge, MA: Harvard University Press, 2014).

35. Stefan-Ludwig Hoffmann, "Human Rights and History," *Past & Present* 232, no. 1 (2016): 294.

36. Brian C. Rathbun, *Reasoning of State: Realists, Romantics and Rationality in International Relations* (New York: Cambridge University Press, 2019), 246–302.

37. Francis Fukuyama, "The End of History," *National Interest*, Summer 1989, http://www.wesjones.com/eoh.htm.

38. Francis Fukuyama, *The End of History and the Last Man* (New York: Free Press, 1992).

39. Ronald Reagan, Remarks at the Annual Convention of the National Association of Evangelicals in Orlando, Florida, 8 Mar. 1983, https://www.reaganlibrary.gov/research/speeches/30883b.

40. Sarotte, *1989*, 33; William Taubman, *Gorbachev: His Life and Times*. (New York: Norton, 2018).

41. Douglas Brinkley, ed., *The Reagan Diaries* (New York: HarperCollins, 2007), 95.

42. Ronald Reagan, *An American Life* (New York: Simon and Schuster, 1990), 407.

43. David Fitzgerald, David Ryan, and John M. Thompson, eds., *Not Even Past: How the United States Ends Wars* (New York: Berghahn Books, 2020), 259.

44. Quoted in Hayward, *Age of Reagan*, 132.

45. Daniel J. Sargent, *A Superpower Transformed: The Remaking of American Foreign Relations in the 1970s* (Oxford: Oxford University Press, 2015).

46. Frieden, *Global Capitalism*, 464.

47. G. John Ikenberry, ed., *Power, Order, and Change in World Politics* (New York: Cambridge University Press, 2014), 96.

48. Thomas Piketty and Arthur Goldhammer, *Capital in the Twenty-First Century* (Cambridge, MA: The Belknap Press of Harvard University Press, 2014).

49. Robert J. Gordon, *The Rise and Fall of American Growth: The US Standard of Living since the Civil War* (Princeton, NJ: Princeton University Press, 2016).

50. "Table 14.6—Total Government Surpluses or Deficits in Absolute Amounts and as Percentages of GDP: 1948–2019," Historical Tables, White House Office of Management and Budget, https://www.whitehouse.gov/omb/historical-tables/ (accessed 14 Mar. 2021).

51. Daniel Yergin and Joseph Stanislaw, *The Commanding Heights: The Battle between Government and the Marketplace That Is Remaking the Modern World* (New York: Simon & Schuster, 1999), 347.

52. Frieden, *Global Capitalism*, 456.

53. Joseph E. Stiglitz, *Globalization and Its Discontents* (New York: Norton, 2002).

54. Frieden, *Global Capitalism*, 457–458; Mark Blyth, *Austerity: The History of a Dangerous Idea* (New York: Oxford University Press, 2015).

55. Robert Mundell's remark was recorded in Robert L. Bartley, *The Seven Fat Years: And How to Do It Again* (New York: Free Press, 1995), 59; Michael R. Sesit, "Cash-Strapped Arab Governments Move to More-Liquid Investments," *Wall Street Journal*, 23 Mar. 1984; David Ignatius, "Royal Resources: Saudi Central Bank Is Secretive, Conservative and Enormously Rich," *Wall Street Journal*, 13 Mar. 1981.

56. Engel, *When the World Seemed New*, 258.

57. Mary Elise Sarotte, *The Collapse: The Accidental Opening of the Berlin Wall* (New York: Basic Books, 2015).

58. E. E. Browning, "Gnomes of Tokyo: Japanese Step Up Role of Investing Overseas in Bonds, Real Estate," *Wall Street Journal*, 15 Aug. 1985, ProQuest Historical Newspapers, 1.

59. Engel, *When the World Seemed New*, 74–75.

60. Donald Trump, "There's Nothing Wrong with America's Foreign Defense Policy that a Little Backbone Can't Cure," *New York Times*, 2 Sept. 1987; Ilan Ben-Meir, "That Time Trump Spent Nearly $100,000 on an Ad Criticizing US Foreign Policy in 1987," *Buzzfeed News*, 10 July 2015, https://www.buzzfeed.com/ilanbenmeir/that-time-trump-spent-nearly-100000-on-an-ad-criticizing-us.

61. Stiglitz, *Globalization and its Discontents*, 20.

62. Engel, *When the World Seemed New*, 235.

63. Jimmy Carter, "A Time for Peace: Rejecting Violence to Secure Human Rights," 22 May 1977, https://www.cartercenter.org/news/editorials_speeches/a-time-for-peace-06212016.html.

64. Keys, *Reclaiming American Virtue*.

65. "JCS Briefing on Response to NSDD 250," 26 Feb. 1987, Ronald Reagan Presidential Library, Executive Secretariat–NSC, National Security Decision Directives, box 91297.

66. Paul M. Kennedy, "Rise and Fall of Great Powers," *Wall Street Journal*, 25 Feb. 1988.

67. Quoted in Sarotte, *1989*.

68. Engel, *When the World Seemed New*, 26.

69. George H. W. Bush, Address before a Joint Session of Congress, 11 Sept. 1990, https://web.archive.org/web/20160602115313/http://millercenter.org/president/bush/speeches/speech-3425.

70. Francis J. Gavin, *Gold, Dollars, and Power: The Politics of International Monetary Relations, 1958–1971* (Chapel Hill: University of North Carolina Press, 2003); Daniel J. Sargent, *A Superpower Transformed: The Remaking of American Foreign Relations in the 1970s* (Oxford: Oxford University Press, 2015).

71. Stiglitz, *Globalization and Its Discontents*, 21.

72. Susan Strange, *The Retreat of the State: The Diffusion of Power in the World Economy* (New York: Cambridge University Press, 1996), 32.

Part One

Global and Domestic Issues

CHAPTER 1

Ronald Reagan and the Cold War

MELVYN P. LEFFLER

Scholars love debating the role of Ronald Reagan in the Cold War. Some say he aimed to win the Cold War; others claim he wanted to end the Cold War. Some say he wanted to abolish nuclear weapons and yearned for a more peaceful world; others say he built up American capabilities, prepared to wage nuclear war, and quested to destroy communism and the "evil empire" that embodied it. Noting these contradictions and Reagan's competing impulses, some writers claim that he wanted to do all these things.[1]

The real truth is that figuring out what Ronald Reagan wanted to do, or, more precisely, figuring out what things he wanted *most* to do, may be impossible. When you read the memoirs and the interviews what impresses, and what surprises, is that many of those who adored him, who worked for him, and who labored to impress his legacy on the American psyche regarded the great communicator as "impenetrable."

Yes, Ronald Reagan was genial, upbeat, courteous, respectful, self-confident, and humble, but he was also opaque, remote, distant, and inscrutable (about many things). Ronnie was a "loner," Nancy Reagan wrote in her memoir. "There's a wall around him. He lets me come closer than anyone else, but there are times when even I feel that barrier."[2] His advisors agreed. Charles Wick, his long-time friend and head of the United States Information Agency (USIA), acknowledged, "No matter how close anybody was to him, . . . there still is a very slight wall that you don't get past."³ "No one was close to Reagan," said Ken Adelman to an interviewer. "He laughed, he was a wonderful warm human being, but there was something impenetrable about him. Really, he wouldn't share—some views were out there, but otherwise he just went to a different drummer—a strange person."⁴

Of course, Reagan had a set of strong convictions that he preached for most of his long career as a spokesperson for General Electric, as governor of California, as an aspirant for the highest office in the land, and as president. "He wasn't a complicated person," Nancy explained: "he was a private man, but he was not a complicated one."⁵ Everyone thought they knew what Reagan believed in: he loved freedom and hated communism, he revered free enterprise and abhorred big government, he wanted to cut taxes and catalyze private entrepreneurship, he adored the city on the hill and detested the "evil empire."⁶

But things got complicated for his advisors when they learned that he also yearned for peace, detested nuclear weapons, thought MAD was mad, feared that nuclear war would lead to Armageddon, and embraced compromise. When tradeoffs were necessary, when priorities needed reconciling, when complicated options begged for resolution, Reagan was opaque. He "gave no orders, no commands; asked for no information; expressed no urgency," said David Stockman, his first budget director. Although Stockman would become a harsh critic, Reagan's admirers did not disagree. Martin Anderson, among his most important economic advisers and a long-time friend, wrote: "He made no demands, and gave almost no instructions." Frank Carlucci, who served as deputy secretary of defense in the early years of the first Reagan administration and then returned as national security advisor and secretary of defense toward the end of the second term, noted that the president often seemed in a daze; well, not exactly a daze, Carlucci said, but very preoccupied. At National Security Council (NSC) meetings, said Richard Pipes, a renowned Soviet expert, Reagan sometimes seemed "really lost, out of his depth, uncomfortable." William Webster, who headed the CIA at the end of Reagan's presidency, one day approached Colin Powell, then the national security advisor, and confided, "I'm pretty good at reading people, but I like to get a report card. I can't tell whether I'm really helping him or not because he listens and I don't get a sense that he disagrees with me or agrees with me or what." Powell replied, "Listen, I'm with him a dozen times a day and I'm in the same boat. So don't feel badly about that."⁷

Nonetheless, there has emerged an interpretive trend praising Reagan's strategy for winning the Cold War. There is abundant evidence for this, say its proponents, and they highlight National Security Decision Directives (NSDD) 32 and 75. Those directives, formulated in 1982 and early 1983, do outline a strategy: build strength, constrain and contract Soviet expansion, nurture change within the Soviet empire (to the extent possible), and negotiate.[8] The sophisticated analysts who rely on these NSDDs and who regard Reagan as a grand strategist do acknowledge the disarray in the administration, the feuding between the State Department, the Defense Department, and the National Security staff, and the internal bickering inside the White House between James Baker, Michael Deaver, Ed Meese, and Nancy Reagan (to some extent). Yet they claim—with a good deal of evidence—that when Judge William Clark, Reagan's close friend, took the role of national security advisor in 1982, he sorted this all out, imposed discipline, and orchestrated a polished and refined strategy that triumphed over the evil empire.[9] Judge Clark himself, in a lengthy interview at the Miller Center in 2003, took pride in forcing the Soviets to reshape their behavior through economic warfare, an ideological crusade, and military power.[10]

These interpretations in the hands of sophisticated scholars such as Hal Brands, Will Inboden, and John Gaddis appear persuasive.[11] But when the evidence is examined closely, there is room for skepticism. Coherence was often lacking even when the directives were drafted. At a key meeting of the NSC, for example, when NSDD-75 was being discussed and approved, Secretary of Defense Caspar Weinberger interjected impatiently, "Yes, we are clear about our policy, it does not matter what is in the paper." But then Reagan concluded the meeting by stating: "To summarize, our goal [regarding technology transfers] is not to facilitate a Soviet military buildup, but at the same time I don't want to compromise our chance of exercising quiet diplomacy."[12]

So, just what was the strategy? In November 1983, soon after Pipes left the NSC, General Alexander Haig left the State Department, and Clark left the White House, Jack Matlock, Pipes's successor, began organizing Saturday morning breakfasts for senior officials to clarify the administration's policy. George Shultz, the new secretary of state, attended, as did Bud McFarlane, the new national security advisor, as well as Secretary of Defense Weinberger and Vice President George H. W. Bush. There were sharp differences of opinion, Matlock subsequently wrote, "but nobody argued that the United States should try to bring the Soviet Union down. All recognized that the Soviet leaders faced mounting problems, but understood that US attempts to exploit them would strengthen Soviet resistance to change rather than diminish it. President Reagan was in favor of bringing pressure to bear on the Soviet Union, but his objective was to induce the Soviet leaders to negotiate reasonable agreements, not to break up the country."[13]

These senior officials outlined the key goals: reduce the use and threat of force in international disputes, lower high levels of armaments, and establish minimal amounts of trust with the hope of verifying past agreements and effectuating progress on human rights, confidence-building measures, and bilateral ties.[14] These top policymakers also agreed that they should not challenge the legitimacy of the Soviet system, seek military superiority, or force the collapse of the Soviet system ("as distinct from exerting pressure on Soviets to live up to agreements and abide by civilized standards of behavior").[15] They also agreed that they should pursue a policy of realism, strength, and negotiation. Realism meant "that our competition with the Soviet Union is basic and there is no quick fix." Strength was necessary to deal with the Kremlin effectively. Negotiations aimed to reduce tensions, not to conceal differences.[16]

So, what should we conclude? We have Judge Clark and NSDD-75 on the one hand, and we have Ambassador Matlock and the November 19 Saturday morning breakfast memo on the other. We also know that Secretary Shultz presented his own memorandum to the president on Soviet-American relations shortly after he replaced General Haig, and that that memorandum resembled the Saturday breakfast memo.[17] What should we make of this? Was there a strategy to win the Cold War? Was there a strategy to end the Cold War?

While pondering these questions, we should consider two of the most famous quotations and stories about Ronald Reagan and the Cold War. In 1977, in a private conversation with Richard Allen, the man who would become his first national security advisor, Reagan explained that his theory of the Cold War was simple: "We win, they lose." Allen was stunned by the simplicity and brilliance of this formulation. And others have cited it as the most cogent framework for illuminating the evolution of Reagan's strategy.[18]

Thomas Reed, a special assistant to President Reagan for national security and a former secretary of the air force in the Ford administration, narrates the other story. Reed reports that Stuart Spencer, Reagan's political consultant, accompanied the candidate in July 1980 on a flight from Los Angeles to the Republican nominating convention in Detroit. Spencer asked, "Why are you doing this, Ron?" With no hesitation, Reagan answered, "To end the Cold War." "I am not sure how," Reagan went on to say, "but there has to be a way." Reagan focused on the weakness of the Soviet system, his fear of nuclear war, and his frustration with détente. Reed then adds, "Reagan was not a hawk. He did not want to 'beat' the Soviets. He simply felt that it would be in the best interests of both countries, or at least of their general citizenry, 'to end this thing.'"[19]

Reed goes on to emphasize that Reagan believed that the way to end the Cold War was by winning it.[20] But a more careful reading might conclude that

Reagan was not talking about "beating" the Soviets, but rather seeking to end the Cold War.

We often conflate these ideas: "winning the Cold War" and "ending the Cold War." But we should ponder them carefully when thinking about the strategy and aims of the Reagan administration. Was there a strategy to win the Cold War, as many triumphalists claim, or was there a strategy to end the Cold War? What would it take to win the Cold War? What would it take to end the Cold War? What assumptions would shape the pursuit of one or the other? Where would they diverge—requiring different approaches, different goals, different tactics—and where would they overlap?

In the many Miller Center interviews of leading officials in the Reagan administration, they often were asked whether Reagan had a strategy. Clark said yes. Richard Allen implied so as well. Frank Carlucci was not at all certain what Reagan had in mind, but he enormously admired the president's intuition. Things worked out; indeed, the results were breathtaking.[21] But because things worked out does not mean there was a strategy. In fact, George Shultz said that Reagan did not have a strategy to spend the Soviets into the ground. He reiterated the points he and Matlock had outlined in 1983: realism, strength, negotiation. Weinberger concurred that Reagan did not have a strategy to bankrupt the Soviet Union. The president, said Weinberger, wanted to win the Cold War by building strength and convincing the Kremlin that it could not win a hot war. Reagan's strategy was simple: negotiate from strength. James Baker pretty much agreed with Weinberger, but stressed that the president was a pragmatic compromiser. Reagan's aim, said Baker, was "peace through strength," not the breakup of the Soviet empire, the dissolution of the Soviet Union, or the destruction of communism.[22]

Ken Adelman's interview is one of the most interesting. Adelman recalled his own disbelief that the Cold War would ever end. Nor did he believe that the United States could bankrupt the Kremlin. As for Reagan's mastery of strategic issues, according to Adelman, it was nonexistent. "He had no knowledge, no feel, and no interest in whether it was missiles, warheads, CEPs [circular error probability], throw-weights, none of that," Adelman emphasized. When the president and Mikhail Gorbachev broached an agreement on nuclear abolition at Reykjavik, Adelman thought "they were in fairyland." And when Reagan kept insisting on sharing Strategic Defense Initiative (SDI) technology with Soviet leaders, Adelman thought it was "crazy." Yet he was quick to acknowledge that the results were spectacular, awesome, incredible. Adelman's interview ended with a rapturous homage to Reagan: "I'm so startled by the changes he made, and how that changed our world." The president was "impenetrable"; you could never grasp "his inner core," Adelman commented. But, so what, Adelman concluded—it is what he accomplished that counts. Everyone can see what he "really, really did," and that is what matters.[23]

So, what did Reagan really do, and what precisely mattered? Adelman, Wick, Baker, Weinberger, Allen, like so many others, assign huge importance to SDI. This is Paul Wolfowitz's contention, for which he cites an anecdote about a young Russian who came to visit Dick Cheney when he was secretary of defense in 1992. The young man explained how Reagan had won the Cold War. We Russians, he said, thought we were invincible until Reagan plowed ahead with the stealth bomber (the B-2) and with SDI. Then, we knew we could not compete unless we changed.[24] In this telling, SDI won the Cold War. Critics of this viewpoint, and I am one of them, need to be honest: you can find numerous quotations from Soviet officials and military people attesting to its veracity.[25]

But once again, let's nurture some skepticism: just as I am casting doubt on Reagan's strategic genius, I am casting doubt on the decisive role of SDI (and indirectly the US military buildup) in bringing about the end of the Cold War. Those who occupied the summit of Soviet power shared such skepticism. "We were not afraid of SDI," Gorbachev reflected in 1999, "first of all, because our experts were convinced that this project was unrealizable, and, secondly, we would know how to neutralize it." In fact, in 1985, when he assumed power, Gorbachev believed that Reagan's military buildup was not likely to be sustained. His closest aide, Anatoly Chernyaev, scorned the argument that Gorbachev had acted as a result of external pressure: "I do not believe that the anti-Communist, anti-Soviet rhetoric and the increase in the armaments and military power of the United States played a serious role in our decision-making.... I think perhaps they played no role whatsoever." Anatoly Dobrynin, the long-term Soviet ambassador to the United States who returned to the Kremlin in 1986 to lead the international department of the Communist Party of the Soviet Union, agreed entirely with Chernyaev. "The Soviet response to Star Wars," he writes, "caused only an acceptable small rise in defense spending." Our fundamental problems, writes Dobrynin, stemmed from autarchy, low investment, and lack of innovation. Alexander Bessmertnykh, the deputy foreign minister, recalled that "very soon we realized that it [SDI] was impractical.... [It] was a fantasy." The department chief of the Main Intelligence Division of the General Staff later confided: "I was in contact with our senior military officers and the political leadership. They didn't care about SDI. Everything was driven by departmental and careerist concerns."[26]

Nor do many of the most renowned historians of Soviet leaders and Kremlin decision-making think that SDI and the military buildup were critical. Mark Kramer, Vladislav Zubok, and Archie Brown downplay the importance of SDI.[27] In his 2015 book on the end of the Cold War, Robert Service presents a nuanced discussion of SDI, in which he does not discount its salience, but he stresses that Gorbachev eventually decided to ignore it. William Taubman pretty much concurs with this assessment in his 2017 masterful biography of Gorbachev. And in his excellent account, *The Dead Hand*, David Hoffman concludes: "Gorbachev's great contribution was in deciding what not to do. He would not build a Soviet Star Wars. He averted another massive weapons competition." In short, SDI was not the decisive factor shaping Gorbachev's behavior, a point that Beth Fischer argues forcefully in her new book, *The Myth of Triumphalism*.[28]

So, what did Reagan do that made a real difference? Let us first acknowledge some critical facts. Many of the most important events that defined the end of the Cold War—the eradication of the Berlin Wall, free elections in Poland and Hungary, unification of Germany inside the North Atlantic Treaty Organization (NATO), the Strategic Arms Reduction Treaty, and the dissolution of the Soviet Union—all came after Reagan left office. They were the result of socioeconomic and political crosscurrents in Eastern Europe, structural problems beleaguering the Soviet economy, nationality conflicts inside the Soviet Union, Gorbachev's policies and predilections, internal politics in the Kremlin, and diplomatic interactions between Gorbachev and George H. W. Bush, Helmut Kohl, and Francois Mitterand, among others.[29] Ronald Reagan had little to do with these matters.[30]

So, back to the key question: What were Reagan's key contributions? Shultz says it was the combination of strength, realism, and negotiation.[31] But would not Dean Acheson, John Kennedy, Richard Nixon, Henry Kissinger, and Zbigniew Brzezinski—to name but a few—have said much the same about their own approaches: that they combined the pursuit of strength, realism, and negotiation? Ken Adelman says it was the unique combination of seeking arms cuts, building strength, championing SDI, and delegitimizing the Soviet Union.[32] Yet building arms and extolling SDI, as already noted, did not shape Soviet policies decisively. And although US covert actions and Reagan's ideological offensive certainly put Gorbachev on the defensive, the US arms buildup, the deployment of Pershing IIs and cruise missiles, the genocidal actions of the United States' authoritarian associates in Central America and South America, and Washington's reluctance to separate itself from the apartheid regime in South Africa garnered widespread opprobrium and tarnished the image of the United States. Although the new literature persuasively shows that Reagan and his advisers merit credit for their shift to promoting democracy and supporting human rights, one should not forget that at the time that Reagan left office, it was Gorbachev who drew wildly enthusiastic crowds wherever he went, not Reagan (whose Teflon reputation was badly tarnished from the Iran-Contra affair).[33]

In the end, the Soviet system lost its legitimacy, not because of the US ideological offensive, but because of its performance. We now know that even before Gorbachev took office, his comrades grasped that their system was faltering and required radical overhaul. Gorbachev infused conviction, energy, and chaos into efforts to remake and revive socialism. He knew the system was stagnating; indeed this was evident around the world, as China embarked on a new trajectory and as country after country evolved away from command systems and statist controls.[34]

Reagan merits credit for understanding these trends, and then extolling and even intensifying them. His advisers merit credit for exploiting developments in the international economy to the United States' advantage. In his 2014 book, Hal Brands brilliantly assesses the ability of Reagan administration officials to capitalize on globalization, technological change, the communications transformation, and the electronics revolution.[35] These initiatives did reconfigure the United States' position in the international arena as the Cold War drew to a close, but they did not cause the end of the Cold War. In his recent scholarly account of Gorbachev's economic policies, Chris Miller shows that Gorbachev and his advisers were far more influenced by what was going on economically in Japan and especially in China than what was happening in the United States.[36]

So, back again, to the basic query: What were Reagan's unique contributions? Ken Adelman gets at it when he stresses Reagan's desire for real cuts in armaments; Shultz get at it when he stresses negotiation; James Baker gets at it when he underscores Reagan's negotiating skills and dwells on his pragmatism.

But these laudatory comments understate Reagan's true gifts and unique contributions to the end of the Cold War. To say that Reagan wanted to negotiate is far too facile. He fiercely wanted to talk to Soviet leaders. He wanted to talk to them from his first days in office.[37] When Vice President Bush attended Chernenko's funeral in March 1985, he brought with him a set of talking points for his first meeting with Gorbachev. He was scripted to say the following: "I bring with me a message of peace. We know this is a time of difficulty; we would like it to be a time of opportunity. . . . We know that some of the things we do and say sound threatening and hostile to you. The same is true for us." Reagan wanted to transcend that distrust. "We are ready to embark on that path with you. It is the path of negotiation."[38]

Once again, to say that Reagan wanted to negotiate trivializes his approach. After Bush conversed with Gorbachev at Chernenko's funeral, Secretary of State Shultz turned to the new Soviet leader and said, "President Reagan told me to look you squarely in the eyes and tell you: 'Ronald Reagan believes that this is a very special moment in the history of mankind. You are starting your term as general secretary. Ronald Reagan is starting his second term as president.... President Reagan is ready to work with you.'"[39] That determination and anticipation shaped Reagan's first meeting with Gorbachev at Geneva in November 1985. Read the opening pages of his autobiography and you can sense the president's excitement: having looked forward to this encounter with a Soviet leader for more than five years, his "juices" were flowing. "Lord," he wrote in his diary, "I hope I'm ready."[40]

He was ready. He felt that his policies had built up US military might and strengthened his negotiating position. He thought that the Soviet Union was an economic basket case.[41] But neither US military strength nor Soviet economic weakness explains what ensued. They were part of the puzzle, important parts, but they had been around at other times during the Cold War, and it had neither ended nor been won.[42]

What was different now? It was not simply Reagan's desire to negotiate. It was his sensibility, empathy, conviction, skill, charm, and self-confidence. Informed of the intricacies of the Single Integrated Operational Plan (SIOP) and the mechanics of decision-making in times of nuclear crisis, Reagan was appalled by the thought that he would have only six minutes to determine whether "to unleash Armageddon!" "How could anyone apply reason" in those circumstances, he mused.[43] Perhaps his growing empathy for his adversary sprang from that realization, along with the tutoring he was receiving in Soviet history and culture.[44] "Three years had taught me something surprising about the Russians," he wrote in his diary. "Many people at the top of the Soviet hierarchy were genuinely afraid of America and Americans. Perhaps this shouldn't have surprised me, but it did."[45] In fact, he talked to foreign ambassadors about Soviet perceptions and recorded their views in his diary. Learning that the Soviets were insecure and genuinely frightened, he tried to insert this understanding in his handwritten letters to Chernenko before the Soviet leader died.[46] Reagan told his national security advisors, "We need talks which can eliminate suspicions. I'm willing to admit that the USSR is suspicious of us."[47]

This empathy subsequently infused his meetings with Gorbachev. Although Reagan wanted armaments to cast shadows and bolster his negotiating posture, he also grasped Soviet perceptions of SDI. "We do not want a first-strike capability," he told his advisors, "but the Soviets probably will not believe us." Intuiting that after the nuclear disaster at Chernobyl Gorbachev was facing growing internal challenges, Reagan prodded his subordinates to reach an agreement that did not "make [Gorbachev] look like he gave up everything."[48] Gorbachev, he stressed, mustn't be forced "to eat crow"; he mustn't be embarrassed. Let "there be no talk of winners and losers." The aim was to establish a process, a series of meetings, "to avoid war in settling our differences in the future."[49]

The deliberations of the NSC after 1985 do not reveal officials designing a strategy to win the Cold War; they reveal officials struggling to shape a negotiating strategy that would effectuate arms reductions. They reveal a president pushing hard for real arms cuts. They reveal a president who feared nuclear war, believed in SDI, and wanted to share it. They reveal a president who desired to abolish nuclear weapons.[50] His advisors felt that he was living in fantasyland, as Adelman said in his interview.[51] Occasionally, they politely interrupted him: "Mr. President," they would say, "there is a great risk in exchanging technical data"; "Mr. President, that would be the most massive technical transfer the western world has ever known." But Reagan was not dissuaded: "There has to be an answer to all these questions because some day people are going to ask why we didn't do something new about getting rid of nuclear weapons. You know," he went on, "I've been reading my Bible and the description of Armageddon talks about destruction, I believe, of many cities and we need absolutely to avoid that. We have to do something now."[52]

Of course, he was not very good at getting his advisors to do things that they bickered over or did not want to do. But Reagan was good, superb even, at dealing with people. He could set you "utterly at ease," wrote his critic, David Stockman. Devoid of facts and short on knowledge, said Richard Pipes, Reagan nonetheless "had irresistible charm." "Easy to like," said Shultz, Reagan "was a master of friendly diplomacy." Endowed with "boundless optimism and a sunny disposition," recalled James Baker, "he made people feel good."[53]

He worked hard at it, prepared for his talks, grasped the rhythm of negotiations, and understood the value of stubborn patience.[54] Gorbachev sometimes disparaged him at Politburo meetings. But in their new book, Svetlana Savranskaya and Thomas Blanton show how deeply affected he was at Reykjavik by Reagan's conviction to abolish nuclear weapons. At the emotional end of their last conversation, Reagan pled with Gorbachev to allow SDI testing: "Do it as a favor to me so that we can go to the people as peacemakers." Gorbachev said no, but was deeply affected nonetheless. "I believe it was then, at that very moment," wrote Chernyaev, that Gorbachev "became convinced that it would 'work out' between him and Reagan."[55]

Reagan engaged Gorbachev in a way no American leader had ever engaged a Soviet leader in the history of the Cold War. Of course, he was dealing with a special, new type of Soviet leader. But it was to Reagan's credit that he realized this. It took intuition and courage. Other than Shultz, hardly any of his advisors felt this way—not Weinberger, or Clark, or Casey, or Carlucci, or Baker, or Bush, or Gates. Not even outside critics such as Henry Kissinger, who presented himself as the high priest of US-Soviet détente. Nor is it clear that his Democratic foes would have seized the opportunity, and, even if they did, it is not likely that they could have orchestrated the same type of political support for engagement with the Soviet leader.

Reagan made it possible for Gorbachev to forge ahead. Gorbachev needed a partner to tamp down the arms race and end the Cold War so that he could revive socialism inside the Soviet Union. He wanted to cut military expenditures, accelerate the Soviet economy, and improve living conditions inside the Soviet Union.[56] Propelled by his own ideals and by his recognition of material realities, he gradually made all the key concessions.[57] Reagan's stubborn patience incentivized Gorbachev to sign the zero-zero Intermediate Nuclear Force Treaty and to withdraw from Afghanistan. Reagan's sincerity, affability, and goodwill encouraged Gorbachev to believe that the Soviet Union was endangered not by foreign adversaries but by superior economies.[58] Reagan embodied a capitalist system that Gorbachev disdained, but also democratic and humane values with which he did not disagree. By reconfiguring Soviet foreign policy, championing conventional as well as strategic arms cuts, and retrenching from regional conflicts, he hoped to find the time and space to integrate the Soviet Union into a new world order and a common European home in a way that would comport with Soviet economic needs and security imperatives.

Gorbachev sensed that Reagan was seeking not to win the Cold War, but to end it. He recognized that Reagan wanted arms cuts, believed in nuclear abolition, and sincerely championed human rights and religious freedom. He also understood that Reagan and his advisors wanted to exploit Soviet vulnerabilities and weaknesses to enhance the United States' position in international affairs. But Gorbachev did not think that these matters endangered Soviet power and security, and he believed that the president's own predilections coincided with his own. Gorbachev, explained Chernyaev, felt "that Reagan was someone who was concerned about very human things, about the human needs of his people. He felt that Reagan behaved as a very moral person."[59]

Gorbachev was right. Reagan's rhetoric, actions, and behavior during his last years in office reveal what he most wanted to do: negotiate arms cuts, reduce tensions, champion human rights, and promote stability and peace. He and his advisors were not discussing ways to win the Cold War or to break up the Soviet Union. At meetings, they occasionally expressed confidence that they had the Soviets on the run, but far more often they remonstrated about the constraints imposed by Congress and acknowledged that Soviet economic problems, as bad as they were, were not likely to cause a Soviet collapse or even a rebalancing of military power. Their discussions implied an understanding that, at best, they might reduce tensions, mitigate chances of nuclear conflict, manipulate the Soviets into restructuring their forces, and curtail Soviet meddling in Central America, southern Africa, and parts of Asia. Reagan hectored them to move forward and to prepare a strategic arms reduction treaty that he could sign. He still distrusted the Soviets; he still wanted to negotiate from strength; he still prodded Gorbachev to advance human rights and religious freedom. But he knew that it was counterproductive to talk of winners and losers.[60] Neither he nor his closest associates discussed victory in the Cold War. "Truth be told," wrote Robert Gates, the deputy director of the CIA, in January 1989, nobody in the US government was predicting free elections in Eastern Europe, or the unification of Germany inside NATO, let alone the dissolution of the Soviet Union.[61]

Although these conditions that have come to define victory in the Cold War were not expected when he left office, Reagan nonetheless took tremendous pride in what he had accomplished. By seeking peace through strength, by striving to avoid a nuclear confrontation, by aspiring to abolish nuclear weapons, by aiming to check Soviet expansion while engaging Soviet leaders, by showing empathy, displaying goodwill, and appreciating the changes Gorbachev was making, by hoping to end the Cold War rather than win it, Reagan reassured Gorbachev that Soviet security would not be endangered as the Soviet leader struggled to reshape Soviet political, economic, and social institutions.[62]

In 2001, long after he left power, Gorbachev attended a seminar in London and listened to academics blithely condemning Reagan as a lightweight. The professors had it all wrong, Gorbachev interjected. Reagan was a "man of real insight, sound political judgment, and courage." Three years later, in June 2004, he unexpectedly showed up at Reagan's funeral and went to the Capitol Rotunda where Reagan's coffin was draped in an American flag. Slowly, he approached the casket, extended his right hand, and gently rubbed it back and forth over the stars and stripes. "I gave him a pat," Gorbachev later commented, a pat that well symbolized the "personal chemistry" they had forged.[63]

When Gorbachev's initiatives after 1989 produced havoc within the Soviet Union and disintegration within the Soviet empire, Reagan heralded the United States' victory in the Cold War. But his own contribution was more modest and paradoxical. By seeking to engage the Kremlin and end the Cold War, he helped to win it. Negotiation was more important than intimidation. Reagan's emotional intelligence was more important than his military buildup; his political credibility at home was more important than his ideological offensive abroad; his empathy, affability, and learning were more important than his suspicions. By striving to end the nuclear arms race and avoid Armageddon, he inadvertently set in motion the dynamics that led to the dissolution of the Soviet Union. These ironies should not detract from Reagan's significance, but they should put it in proper perspective. He was Gorbachev's minor, yet indispensable partner, setting the framework for the dramatic changes that neither anticipated happening anytime soon.

Notes

This essay is a slightly revised version of my article, "Ronald Reagan and the Cold War: What Mattered Most," *Texas National Security Review* 1, no. 3 (2018): 77–89.

1. John Prados, *How the Cold War Ended: Debating and Doing History* (Washington, DC: Potomac Books, 2011); Artemy Kalinovsky and Craig Dagle, "Explanation for the End of the Cold War," in *The Routledge Handbook of the Cold War*, ed. Artemy Kalinovsky and Craig Daigle (London: Routledge, 2014). For Reagan's competing impulses, see, for example, James G. Wilson, *The Triumph of Improvisation: Gorbachev's Adaptability, Reagan's Engagement, and the End of the Cold War* (Ithaca, NY: Cornell University Press, 2014); Jacob Weisberg, *Ronald Reagan* (New York: Times Books, 2016); Beth Fischer, *The Myth of Triumphalism: Rethinking President Reagan's Cold War Legacy* (Lexington: University Press of Kentucky, 2020), 110–128.

2. Nancy Reagan, with William Novak, *My Turn: The Memoirs of Nancy Reagan* (New York: Random House, 1989), 106. See also Lou Cannon, *President Reagan: The Role of a Lifetime* (New York: Public Affairs, 1991), 172–195; Edmund Morris, *Dutch: A Memoir of Ronald Reagan* (New York: Random House, 1999), 61.

3. Charles Wick, Miller Center Interview, 24–25 Apr. 2003, 42.

4. Kenneth Adelman, Miller Center Interview, 30 Sept. 2003, 45

5. Nancy Reagan, *My Turn*, 104.

6. A wonderful compendium of Reagan's beliefs and views can be found in Kiron K. Skinner, Annelise Anderson, and Martin Anderson, eds., *Reagan in His Own Hand* (New York: Simon and Schuster, 2001).

7. David Stockman, *The Triumph of Politics: How the Reagan Revolution Failed* (New York: Harper and Row, 1986), 76; Martin Anderson, *Revolution: The Reagan Legacy* (Stanford, CA: Hoover Institution Press, 1990), 289–290; Richard Pipes, *Vixi: Memoirs of a Non-Belonger* (New Haven, CT: Yale University Press, 2003), 166; Frank Carlucci,

Miller Center Interview, 28 Aug. 2001, 28–30; William Webster, Miller Center Interview, 21 Aug. 2002, 27.

8. NSDD-32, "US National Security Strategy," 20 May 1982, https://fas.org/irp/offdocs/nsdd/nsdd-32.pdf; NSDD-75, "US Relations with the USSR," 17 Jan. 1983, https://fas.org/irp/offdocs/nsdd/nsdd-75.pdf.

9. Hal Brands, *What Good Is Grand Strategy?: Power and Purpose in American Statecraft from Harry S. Truman to George W. Bush* (Ithaca, NY: Cornell University Press, 2014), 102–119; John Lewis Gaddis, *Strategies of Containment: A Critical Appraisal of American National Security Policy During the Cold War*, rev. ed. (New York: Oxford University Press, 2005), 342–379; William Inboden, "Grand Strategy and Petty Squabbles: The Paradox and Lessons of the Reagan NSC," in *The Power of the Past: History and Statecraft*, ed. Hal Brands and Jeremi Suri (Washington, DC: Brookings Institution, 2016), 151–180.

10. William Clark, Miller Center Interview, 17 Aug. 2003, 34.

11. Brands, *What Good Is Grand Strategy?*; Gaddis, *Strategies of Containment*; Inboden, "Grand Strategy and Petty Squabbles."

12. Jason Saltoun-Ebin, *The Reagan Files: Inside the National Security Council*, 2nd ed. (Santa Barbara: Seabec Books, 2014), 215–217.

13. Jack F. Matlock Jr., *Reagan and Gorbachev: How the Cold War Ended* (New York: Random House, 2004), 75–77.

14. Matlock, *Reagan and Gorbachev*, 75–77.

15. Matlock, *Reagan and Gorbachev*, 75–77.

16. Matlock., *Reagan and Gorbachev*, 76.

17. Shultz to Reagan, "Next Steps in US-Soviet Relations," 16 Mar. 1983, http://thereaganfiles.com/19830316-shultz.pdf; George P. Shultz, *Turmoil and Triumph: My Years as Secretary of State* (New York: Scribner, 1993), 269–271.

18. Richard Allen, Miller Center Interview, 28 May 2002, 26–27; Hal Brands, "The Vision Thing," in *Peril: Facing National Security Challenges*, ed. Melvyn P. Leffler and William Hitchcock (Charlottesville, VA: Miller Center, 2016), http://firstyear2017.org/essay/the-vision-thing.

19. Thomas Reed, *At the Abyss: An Insider's History of the Cold War* (New York: Ballantine Books, 2004), 234–235.

20. Reed, *At the Abyss*, 236–237.

21. Clark, Interview, 14–16, 34; Allen, Interview 26–27, 74–75; Carlucci, Interview, 28–34, 40–42, 47–48.

22. George P. Shultz, Miller Center Interview, 18 Dec. 2002, 13, 18–19; Caspar Weinberger, Miller Center Interview, 19 Nov. 2002, 10–11, 28–31; James Baker, Miller Center Interview, 15–16 June 2004, 13, 44.

23. Adelman, Interview, 60, 57, 58, 39, 64–66; see also Ken Adelman, *Reagan at Reykjavik: Forty-Eight Hours That Ended the Cold War* (New York: Broadside Books, 2014), 64–66.

24. Paul Wolfowitz, "Shaping the Future: Planning at the Pentagon, 1989–1993," in *In Uncertain Times: American Foreign Policy after the Berlin Wall and 9/11*, ed. Melvyn P. Leffler and Jeffrey W. Legro (Ithaca, NY: Cornell University Press, 2011), 44.

25. See, for example, Hal Brands, *Making the Unipolar Moment: US Foreign Policy and the Rise of the Post–Cold War Order* (Ithaca, NY: Cornell University Press, 2016), 89–90;

Peter Schweizer, *Reagan's War: The Epic Story of His Forty-Year Struggle and Final Triumph over Communism* (New York: Anchor Books, 2002), 151–152; Paul Kengor, *The Crusader: Ronald Reagan and the Fall of Communism* (New York: Regan, 2006), 300–302.

26. For Gorbachev, see Andrei Grachev, *Gorbachev's Gamble: Soviet Foreign Policy and the End of the Cold War* (Cambridge, UK: Polity, 2008), 84; see also Yakovlev to Gorbachev, 12 Mar. 1985, in *The Last Superpower Summits: Gorbachev, Reagan, and Bush: Conversations that Ended the Cold War*, ed. Svetlana Savranskaya and Thomas Blanton (Budapest: Central European University Press, 2016), 26–27. For Chernyaev's comment, see Beth Fischer, "Reagan and the Soviets: Winning the Cold War?" in the *Reagan Presidency: Pragmatic Conservatism and Its Legacies* (Lawrence: University Press of Kansas, 2003), 126; Anatoly Dobrynin, *In Confidence: Moscow's Ambassador to America's Six Cold War Presidents* (New York: Random House, 1995), 610–611. For Bessmertnykh, see *Witnesses to the End of the Cold War*, ed. William C. Wohlforth (Baltimore: Johns Hopkins University Press, 1996), 14. Quotation by V. V. Shlykov, in *The Destruction of the Soviet Economic System: An Insiders' History*, ed. Michael Ellman and Vladimir Kontorovitch (Armonk: M. E. Sharpe, 1998), 57.

27. Private e-mail correspondence, December 2016. See also Archie Brown, *The Gorbachev Factor* (Oxford: Oxford University Press, 1997), 226, 232, 235; Archie Brown, *The Human Factor: Gorbachev, Reagan, and Thatcher, and the end of the Cold War* (New York: Oxford University Press, 2020), 292–294; Vladislav Zubok, *A Failed Empire: The Soviet Union in the Cold War from Stalin to Gorbachev* (Chapel Hill: University of North Carolina Press, 2007), 273, 276, 287, 292.

28. Robert Service, *The End of the Cold War, 1985–1991* (New York: Public Affairs, 2015), 192–195, 274–278, 296; William Taubman, *Gorbachev: His Life and Times* (New York: Norton, 2017), 294–305; David E. Hoffman, *The Dead Hand: The Untold Story of the Cold War Arms Race and Its Dangerous Legacy* (New York: Doubleday, 2009), 206–225, 243–244, 266; James Mann, *The Rebellion of Ronald Reagan: A History of the End of the Cold War* (New York: Viking, 2009), 345; Luigi Lazzari, "The Strategic Defense Initiative and the End of the Cold War," MA thesis, Naval Postgraduate School, 2008; Fischer, *Myth of Triumphalism*, 110–128.

29. For brief discussions of many of these matters, see the essays, among others, by Archie Brown, Alex Pravda, Helga Haftendorn, and Jacques Levesque, in Melvyn P. Leffler and Odd Arne Westad, eds., *Cambridge History of the Cold War*, vol. 3, *Endings* (Cambridge: Cambridge University Press, 2010).

30. Of course, Reagan was instrumental in shaping the INF Treaty and in urging Gorbachev to withdraw Soviet troops from Afghanistan.

31. Shultz, *Turmoil and Triumph*, 500, 1136.

32. Adelman, *Reagan at Reykjavik*, 64–66.

33. For new findings on Reagan and democracy promotion and human rights, see, for example, Sarah Snyder, "Principles Overwhelming Tanks: Human Rights and the End of the Cold War," in *The Human Rights Revolution: An International History*, ed. Akira Iriye, Petra Goedde, and William I. Hitchcock (New York: Oxford University Press, 2012), 265–283; Robert Pee, *Democracy Promotion, National Security and Strategy: Foreign Policy under the Reagan Administration* (London: Routledge, 2016); Evan D. McCormick, "Breaking with Statism? US Democracy Promotion Programs in Latin America, 1984–1988," *Diplomatic History* 42, no. 5 (2018): 745–771; Joe Renouard, *Human*

Rights in American Foreign Policy: From the 1960s to the Soviet Collapse (Philadelphia: University of Pennsylvania Press, 2015), 167–207. For Iran-Contra, see Malcolm Byrne, *Iran-Contra: Reagan's Scandal and the Unchecked Abuse of Presidential Power* (Lawrence: University Press of Kansas, 2014); Richard Reeves, *President Reagan: A Triumph of Imagination* (New York: Simon and Schuster, 2005), 364–365.

34. Stephen G. Brooks and William C. Wohlforth, "Power, Globalization, and the End of the Cold War: Reevaluating a Landmark Case for Ideas," *International Security* 25, no. 3 (2000): 5–53; Service, *End of the Cold War*; Chris Miller, *The Struggle to Save the Soviet Economy: Mikhail Gorbachev and the Collapse of the USSR* (Chapel Hill: University of North Carolina Press, 2016); Zubok, *A Failed Empire*, 265–335; Archie Brown, *The Rise and Fall of Communism* (London: Bodley Head, 2009); Chen Jian, "China and the Cold War after Mao," in *Cambridge History of the Cold War*, eds. Melvyn P. Leffler and Odd Arne Westad (Cambridge: Cambridge University Press, 2010), 3:181–200

35. Brands, *Making the Unipolar Moment*.

36. Miller, *Struggle to Save the Soviet Economy*.

37. Melvyn P. Leffler, *For the Soul of Mankind: The United States, the Soviet Union, and the Cold War* (New York: Hill and Wang, 2007), 347–365.

38. Leffler, *For the Soul of Mankind*, 364–365.

39. Shultz, *Turmoil and Triumph*, 531–532.

40. Ronald Reagan, *An American Life* (New York: Pocket Books, 1990), 11–14, 634–641.

41. Douglas Brinkley, ed., *The Reagan Diaries* (New York: Harper Collins, 2007), 368.

42. Leffler, *For the Soul of Mankind*.

43. Reagan, *An American Life*, 257.

44. Matlock, *Reagan and Gorbachev*, 132–134; Robert C. McFarlane and Zophia Smardz, *Special Trust* (New York: Cadell and Davies, 1994), 308–309; James Mann, *The Rebellion of Ronald Reagan: A History of the End of the Cold War* (New York: Viking, 2009), 82–110.

45. Brinkley, *Reagan Diaries*, 198–199, 247; Reagan, *American Life*, 588, 589, 595.

46. Leffler, *For the Soul of Mankind*, 357–361.

47. "Discussion of Geneva Format and SDI," 10 Dec. 1984, in Saltoun-Ebin, *Inside the National Security Council*, 344.

48. "US-Soviet Relations," 6 June 1986, in Saltoun-Ebin, *Inside the National Security Council*, 426.

49. Reagan, "Gorbachev," Nov. 1985, in Savranskaya and Blanton, *Superpower Summits*, 44.

50. For his fears, see, Brinkley, *Reagan Diaries*, 199; Reed, *At the Abyss*, 243–245; Beth A. Fischer, *The Reagan Reversal* (Columbia: University of Missouri Press, 1997), 102–143; Nate Jones, ed., *Able Archer 83: The Secret History of the NATO Exercise That Almost Triggered Nuclear War* (New York: The New Press, 2016), 45–47. For his nuclear abolitionism, see especially Paul Lettow, *Ronald Reagan and His Quest to Abolish Nuclear Weapons* (New York: Random House, 2005); Martin Anderson and Annelise Anderson, *Reagan's Secret War: The Untold Story of His Fight to Save the World from Nuclear Disaster* (New York: Crown Publishers, 2009); Fischer, *Myth of Triumphalism*, 61–65, 141–146.

51. Adelman, Interview, 58.

52. "Review of United States Arms Control Positions," 8 Sept. 1987, in Saltoun-Ebin, *Inside the National Security Council*, 541, 543; Savranskaya and Blanton, *Superpower Summits*, 454.

53. Stockman, *Triumph of Politics*, 74; Shultz, *Turmoil and Triumph*, 131; Pipes, *Vixi*, 167; Baker, 40–41. See also Dobrynin, *In Confidence*, 605–612; Eduard Shevardnadze, *The Future Belongs to Freedom* (New York: Free Press, 1991), 81–90; Helmut Schmidt, *Men and Powers: A Political Retrospective*, trans. Ruth Hein (New York: Random House, 1989), 241–246.

54. For comments on Reagan's negotiating skill, see, for example, Shultz, *Turmoil and Triumph*, 145; Anderson, *Revolution*, 285; Michael Deaver, *A Different Drummer: My Thirty Years with Ronald Reagan* (New York: HarperCollins, 2001), 71; Dobrynin, *In Confidence*, 605–612; Baker, Interview, 41–42. For Reagan's own thoughts on negotiations, see, for example, "US Options for Arms Control at the Moscow Summit," 9 Feb. 1988, in Saltoun-Ebin, *Inside the National Security Council*, 574.

55. Savranskaya and Blanton, *Last Superpower Summits*, 136–137.

56. For Gorbachev, see, for example, Mikhail Gorbachev, *Perestroika: New Thinking for Our Country and the World* (New York: Harper and Row, 1987); Mikhail Gorbachev, *Memoirs* (New York: Doubleday, 1995); and especially, Mikhail Gorbachev and Zdenek Mlynar, *Conversations with Gorbachev on Perestroika, the Prague Spring, and the Crossroads of Socialism* (New York: Columbia University Press, 2002). Some of the best accounts by scholars include Archie Brown, *The Gorbachev Factor* (Oxford: Oxford University Press, 1997) and *Seven Years that Changed the World: Perestroika in Perspective* (New York: Oxford University Press, 2007); Taubman, *Gorbachev*, 205–305; Odd Arne Westad, *The Cold War: A World History* (New York: Basic Books, 2017), 534–552. For a critical view, see Zubok, *Failed Empire*, 278–335.

57. For an excellent dialogue about the role of ideas and material realities, see the exchanges between William Wohlforth and Stephen Brooks on the one hand and Robert English on the other: Brooks and Wohlforth, "Power, Globalization, and the End of the Cold War"; Robert D. English, "Power, Ideas, and New Evidence on the Cold War's End: A Reply to Brooks and Wohlforth," *International Security* 26, no. 4 (2002): 70–92; Brooks and Wohlforth, "From Old Thinking to New Thinking in Qualitative Research," *International Security* 26, no. 4 (2002): 93–11. See also the analysis by Joshua R. Itzkowitz Shifrinson, *Rising Titans, Falling Giants: How Great Powers Exploit Power Shifts* (Ithaca, NY: Cornell University Press, 2018).

58. See my discussion in Leffler, *For the Soul of Mankind*, 455–461. See also Chernyaev's comments in Svetlana Savranskaya, Thomas Blanton, and Vladislav Zubok, eds., *Masterpieces of History: The Peaceful End of the Cold War in Europe* (Budapest: Central European University Press, 2010), 190, 200; and in the same volume, Savranskaya, "The Logic of 1989: The Soviet Peaceful Withdrawal from Eastern Europe," 1–47; Fischer, *Myth of Triumphalism*, 138–141.

59. For Chernyaev's comment, see William C. Wohlforth, *Witnesses to the End of the Cold War* (Baltimore: Johns Hopkins University Press, 1996), 109; also the comments by Bessmertnykh, in the same volume, 107–108; Gorbachev, *Memoirs*, 405–411; Savranskaya and Blanton, *Superpower Summits*, 132–137, 373–380; Brown, *Gorbachev Factor*, 233. Reagan "bolstered Gorbachev on his risky journey that took him from

reformer of the existing system to systemic transformer within the space of four years." Brown, *Human Factor*, 307.

60. Reagan, "Gorbachev," Nov. 1985, in Savranskaya and Blanton, *Superpower Summits*, 44.

61. These generalizations are based on my reading of the many NSC discussions in 1987 and 1988 in Saltoun-Ebin, *Inside the National Security Council*, 462–624, and on the summitry documents in Savranskaya and Blanton, *Superpower Summits*, 254–478. For the quotation, see Robert M. Gates, *From the Shadows: The Ultimate Story of Five Presidents and How They Won the Cold War* (New York: Touchstone, 1996), 449.

62. Some of Reagan's most sincere convictions, hopes, and aims seem to be expressed in his autobiography, Reagan, *An American Life*, 266–268. See also Reagan, "Gorbachev," Nov. 1985, in Savranskaya and Blanton, *Superpower Summits*, 42–44. The argument here comports with Beth Fischer's themes in Fischer, *Myth of Triumphalism*, 129–146.

63. The two stories are narrated in Adelman, *Reagan at Reykjavik*, 314, 340. For the "personal chemistry," see Grachev, *Gorbachev's Gamble*, 227. See also comments by Chernyaev and Shultz, in Wohlforth, *Witnesses*, 109, 116; Brinkley, *Reagan Diaries*, 613.

CHAPTER 2

Energy and the End of the Evil Empire

DAVID S. PAINTER

The collapse of the Soviet system was one of the most important events in the twentieth century. Although most studies have focused on such issues as the burden of military spending, the cost of foreign involvement, the failure of communism to deliver economic prosperity and political freedom, and the impact of Western, especially US policies on the Soviet Union, a growing number of scholars has begun to examine the role of energy in the Soviet collapse.[1]

Oil and natural gas exports, aided by sharp increases in oil prices during the 1970s and growing demand for natural gas in Western Europe, accounted for almost 80 percent of the Soviet Union's hard currency revenues by the early 1980s. These earnings enabled the Soviet Union to import grain, machinery, and technology from the West to shore up its stagnating economy and continue high levels of military spending. Oil prices fell by two-thirds in real terms between 1980 and 1986, however, and the drop in oil prices, which also drove down natural gas prices, devastated the Soviet Union's balance of payments and its internal budget deficit and played an important role in the collapse of the Soviet system.[2]

Although the main sources of Soviet energy problems, like most of the factors that led to the Soviet collapse, were internal, energy resources were also an important element in the power position of the Soviet Union.[3] US leaders were aware that Soviet energy performance and prospects had important implications for US and Western interests because of their overall impact on the Soviet economy and their implications for choices in allocating resources among the competing objectives of defense, investment, and consumption. During the 1980s, the United States took a number of steps to hinder Soviet natural gas exports to Western Europe and to drive down oil prices. Some writers claim that these efforts played an important role in the collapse of communism and the end of the Cold War. These claims are an integral part of a larger set of claims that the Reagan administration's foreign policies "won" the Cold War.[4] Analysis of the Reagan administration's anti-Soviet energy efforts, internal Soviet developments, and changes in the world oil economy should therefore illuminate important issues about the impact of US policies and actions.[5]

During the 1970s, the center of Soviet oil production shifted to the west Siberian Basin, and by mid-decade the Soviet Union had surpassed the United States as the world's leading oil producer.[6] The Soviets also found several gigantic natural gas fields in western Siberia and overtook the United States as the world's top natural gas producer in the mid-1980s. Soviet oil exports rose from 1.9 million barrels per day (bpd) in 1970 to 3.2 million bpd in 1980, and natural gas exports increased from 3.3 to 54.2 billion cubic meters (bcm).[7]

Oil and gas accounted for around two-thirds of Soviet energy consumption, and Eastern Europe received 42 percent of Soviet energy exports in 1970 and 47 percent in 1978. Energy exports to Eastern Europe, of which oil was the most important, were a key element in Soviet efforts to maintain a sphere in the region. Except for Romania, Eastern Europe lacked significant indigenous oil reserves and depended on the Soviet Union for almost all its oil needs. Soviet deliveries of oil and natural gas were a critical energy source for most countries in the region, as the share of coal in total energy consumption declined during the 1960s and 1970s in every country except Romania.[8]

The sharp increase in oil prices resulting from the oil crises of the 1970s boosted Soviet hard currency export earnings. Soviet oil exports to hard currency markets increased from 620,000 bpd in 1970 to 1.1 million bpd in 1978, and as world oil prices rose from $1.80 a barrel in current dollars in 1970 to $36.83 a barrel in 1980, Soviet hard currency earnings from oil exports rose from $479.8 million in 1970 to $1.21 billion in 1980. By 1978, oil exports were responsible for around half of the Soviet Union's hard currency earnings and total energy exports for over 60 percent. The second oil shock of 1979–1980 further boosted export revenues.[9]

In December 1977, with oil production struggling to keep up with growing demand, the Soviet leadership decided to focus oil investment in western

Siberia. To stave off or slow the projected decline in oil production, the Soviets needed vast amounts of Western equipment and technology, such as rotary drills to drill deeper wells through harder rocks (Soviet turbo drills were not well suited for such conditions), high-capacity submersible pumps, and chemicals to enhance recovery from existing wells. They also needed Western exploration technology and Western offshore production technology. Although the Soviets could get most of what they needed from other Western countries, the United States was the leading producer of most of the equipment and technology they needed.[10]

The Soviets also decided to increase natural gas production and exports from western Siberia and began work on a large-diameter pipeline to supply markets in Eastern and Western Europe. This massive project involved construction of a 5,000-km (around 3,100 miles) pipeline with a projected cost of around $14 billion. At the same time, the Soviets were also building an extensive network of long-distance gas pipelines to serve their internal market. Substituting natural gas for oil in domestic markets and in Eastern Europe would free up more oil for export to hard currency markets. Natural gas exports to Western Europe would also earn needed hard currency that could help cover the massive cost of building the pipelines and help finance Western equipment and technology needed for the oil industry. In addition, the Eastern European nations that the pipeline crossed would receive natural gas in lieu of a transit fee, thus reducing some of Moscow's burden in supporting their economies. To build the pipelines, the Soviets needed high-quality large diameter pipe from Western suppliers, pipe-laying equipment, and high-capacity turbines for compressors to push the gas over the long distances involved. They looked to Western European governments and banks, as well as to Japanese banks, to supply most of the financing for the project.[11]

Following the December 1979 Soviet intervention in Afghanistan, the Jimmy Carter administration imposed a series of sanctions on the Soviet Union, including tight restrictions on the sale of oil and gas technology, which made it very difficult for the Soviets to acquire oil and gas equipment and technology from US companies. Rather than joining the United States in cutting trade with the Soviet Union, however, the major European countries increased their exports of oil and gas equipment and technology to the Soviet Union, often replacing US firms, which were forced to give up their contracts.[12]

Ronald Reagan had long been skeptical about trade with the Soviet Union, believing that Western technology propped up its economic system and undermined Western security by enhancing Soviet military power. CIA Director William Casey and Secretary of Defense Caspar Weinberger believed that anything that helped the Soviet economy ultimately strengthened Soviet military power. Convinced that imports of Western equipment and technology were crucial to the Soviet economy, they argued that the United States should deny the Soviets access to Western oil and gas equipment, technology, and credit. They focused on blocking the Siberian gas pipeline project, which analysts identified as the best prospect the Soviets had for substantial hard currency earnings.[13]

Pipeline opponents argued that Western Europe's huge financial investment in the project by Western banks would make Western governments vulnerable to Soviet pressure and reinforce tendencies toward neutralism. They also claimed that other energy sources, such as liquefied natural gas (LNG) from Algeria and Nigeria, natural gas from Norway, and increased coal imports from the United States were less risky and less expensive.[14]

Although he shared these concerns about the pipeline, Secretary of State Alexander M. Haig believed that the pipeline was too far along to stop. In addition, Haig pointed out that the alternatives proposed by embargo advocates were unrealistic and impractical. Even if environmental and political problems could be overcome, US port facilities were inadequate for exporting increased volumes of coal. In addition, the Norwegians had not agreed to increase their natural gas production, which was more expensive than Soviet gas. Given the pipeline project's economic importance to Western Europe, Haig argued that trying to block it would do more harm than good. Although the United States was a world leader in most aspects of oil and gas technology, the Soviets could obtain the technology they needed from other countries. Joined by Secretary of Commerce Malcolm Baldridge, Secretary of the Treasury Donald Regan, US Trade Representative William Brock, and Office of Management and the Budget Director David Stockman, Haig argued that instead of trying to block sales of equipment, which US allies would oppose and could undermine, the United States should focus on tightening controls over the transfer of oil and gas technology to the Soviet Union.[15]

West European governments and companies argued that the pipeline's benefits would outweigh its costs. Gas consumption was growing in Western Europe, and increased natural gas imports from the Soviet Union would help make up for the expected decline in Dutch gas shipments and in Soviet oil exports. The Europeans viewed the Soviet Union as a more reliable source of supply than Middle East producers. Access to Middle East oil had been threatened in 1956, 1967, and 1973, and Iran, Libya, and Algeria had canceled natural gas contracts in the past. In contrast, the Soviets had continued to deliver oil to Western Europe during the 1967 and 1973–1974 Arab oil embargoes. The Europeans also argued that the project would not appreciably increase their overall dependency on the Soviets for energy supplies due to declining oil imports from the Soviet Union. They could protect themselves from supply interruptions by building up strategic reserves and fuel substitution capacity and by not becoming overly dependent on any single supplier.[16]

The Europeans expected major economic benefits from the project. Western Europe was suffering from widespread unemployment, and sales of large-diameter pipe, compressors, and related equipment would generate thousands of jobs and billions of dollars in revenues. The project involved a large number of European companies, and for many of these companies, there were no other markets of comparable size. Moreover, European firms had already signed a number of contracts, and the contracts contained cancellation penalties. In addition, they expected the Soviets to spend a large portion of their earnings from gas sales in Western Europe.[17]

Beyond these concerns, the Europeans wanted to preserve détente in Europe and to avoid exacerbating East-West tensions. Some Europeans suspected that the Reagan administration opposed the pipeline because it reduced US leverage over Western Europe by providing an East-West economic link that supported European détente. Most Western European governments believed that economic and other ties with the Soviet Union would moderate Soviet behavior by creating mutual interdependence. In their view, European détente had been successful, especially in opening Eastern Europe to Western influence, and they wanted to maintain this access.[18]

Concerned that unilateral sanctions would harm US business without limiting Soviet access to Western oil and gas technology and equipment, Reagan initially hesitated to take action.[19] Pipeline opponents continued their efforts, and in late October 1981 Casey sent Reagan a CIA study that emphasized Soviet dependence on Western equipment and technology. A month later he sent the president a Special National Intelligence Estimate on how trade with the West strengthened Soviet military power, which concluded that "short of comprehensive trade restrictions, a Western embargo on oil and gas equipment would have the greatest impact" on the Soviets.[20]

Events in Poland provided Reagan with an opportunity to act. On December 12, 1981, with political authority deteriorating, unrest spreading, and a Warsaw Pact intervention apparently imminent, Polish Prime Minister General Wojciech Jaruzelski, who was also defense minister and first secretary of the Communist Party, declared a state of siege and ordered the arrest of more than 5,000 opposition leaders, including the leaders of the independent trade union Solidarity.[21]

The United States and its North Atlantic Treaty Organization (NATO) allies had issued several warnings against Soviet military intervention in Poland.

Although the Soviets refrained from sending troops, the Reagan administration, ignoring years of NATO contingency planning and agreements on how to respond to Soviet actions in Poland, unilaterally imposed an array of economic sanctions on the Soviet Union, including suspension of sales of oil and gas technology and licenses for various high-technology exports.[22] Some US companies, especially Caterpillar, were hard hit, but officials at the Commerce Department interpreted the restrictions as applying to equipment produced by subsidiaries of US companies abroad and equipment produced abroad under licenses issued by US companies. The Europeans rejected the US interpretation, noting that the sanctions affected them much more than they affected the United States. US exports of manufactured industrial goods to the Soviet Union amounted to around $300 million per year, whereas US sanctions threatened $4 billion–worth of European contracts related to the pipeline. British Prime Minister Margaret Thatcher, who supported political measures against the Soviets, warned Reagan on January 29 that "the French, Germans, and Italians cannot and will not give up on the gas pipeline project."[23]

Unmoved by these objections and bolstered by the appointment of William P. Clark Jr., a hardline Cold Warrior with direct access to the president, as national security adviser, Weinberger argued that events in Poland provided an opportunity to rally the Europeans behind US policy and that it was "time to mount a major effort to dismantle the project." He favored extending sanctions to the subsidiaries of US firms in other countries. Drawing on CIA reports, Norman Bailey of the National Security Council (NSC) pointed out that the Soviets faced a shortage of hard currency and that the pipeline represented "the Soviet Union's only hope for a new substantial source of hard currency in the future." Casey wanted the United States to focus on convincing its allies to limit government and government-guaranteed and subsidized credits to the Soviets. Casey also argued that the United States and its allies should be working to increase the availability of oil and gas in their own countries in order to limit dependence on Soviet oil and gas.[24]

Admitting that he had not understood the impact of the sanctions on the Europeans, Reagan decided to defer decision on the question of applying US sanctions to foreign companies pending a State Department mission to Europe to discuss restrictions on credits. After hearing a briefing on the Soviet economy in March 1982, however, Reagan wrote in his diary: "They are in very bad shape and if we can cut off their credit they'll have to yell 'Uncle' or starve." Harvard professor Richard Pipes, who was the Soviet specialist at the NSC in 1981–1982, warned that there was "virtually no chance" that the Europeans would agree to effective credit controls and that relaxing or ending sanctions would have a "catastrophic" impact on US credibility.[25]

Meanwhile, Clark and other hardliners, such as Thomas C. Reed, former secretary of the Air Force, and Pipes had drafted National Security Decision Directive (NSDD) 32, which called for aggressive policies to roll back Soviet power, including economic warfare against the Soviet Union in order to force the Soviet Union "to bear the brunt of its economic shortcomings" in the hope of precipitating regime change either through radical reform or economic collapse.[26]

As negotiations with the Europeans dragged on, Reagan grew impatient. The Soviet Union was "on the ropes economically," he exclaimed at an NSC meeting on May 24. "This is the time to punish them." With Casey and others continuing to argue for tougher action against the Soviets to delay the pipeline, the State Department conceded that if talks with the Europeans on credit restrictions failed, the United States should make the sanctions applicable to US subsidiaries abroad and foreign companies using US licenses.[27]

When the talks with the allies revealed little enthusiasm for credit restrictions, pipeline opponents decided that it was time to switch from persuasion to coercion.[28] At an NSC meeting that Assistant for National Security William Clark scheduled to take advantage of Haig's absence—he was meeting with Soviet foreign minister Andrei Gromyko in New York—Reagan agreed to extend the sanctions against the Soviet Union to include equipment produced by subsidiaries of US companies abroad and equipment produced abroad under licenses issued by US companies. Angered that the situation in Poland had not improved and convinced that the Soviets were vulnerable, Reagan declared that the United States had to take a strong stand. A week later, Haig, whose position was already tenuous, resigned.[29]

The major Western European nations protested the US action as an illegal attempt to impose extraterritorial trade sanctions and rejected the US argument that the proposed pipeline could provide the Soviets with a means of applying economic pressure on Western Europe. The announcement on July 30, 1982, of a large new US grain deal with the Soviets further infuriated the Europeans. Not convinced by arguments that grain sales absorbed hard currency while selling the Soviets oil and gas equipment helped them earn hard currency, the British, German, French, and Italian governments instructed their firms to honor their contracts with the Soviets. British Prime Minister Margaret Thatcher was especially upset, publicly stating that the US action left her "deeply wounded by a friend."[30] Privately, she told Weinberger that she "desperately needed some face-saving solution."[31]

As shipments of pipeline equipment started on their way to the Soviet Union, the Reagan administration announced that companies violating the US sanctions would be denied access to all US goods, services, and technology and would be subject to fines up to $100,000. By October, the US government had cited twelve European firms for defying the embargo. In response, the Europeans threatened retaliatory trade measures.[32]

The State Department warned that the tensions created by the sanctions, especially the retroactive and extraterritorial aspects, were creating "a new and formidable barrier" to the achievement of important US objectives. George P. Shultz, who had replaced Haig as secretary of state at the end of June, was especially concerned about negotiations on the deployment of intermediate-range nuclear missiles in Europe. Arguing that continuation of the sanctions would damage US interests, the State Department proposed relaxing them in exchange for a broader consensus on trade with the Soviet Union, including strengthening controls on the export of advanced technology, and monitoring export credits to the Soviet Union. Clark's resignation as national security adviser in mid-October further undermined the influence of hardliners.[33]

Although Reagan remained determined to "punish" the Soviets, he too began looking for a face-saving solution. The CIA pointed out that the sanctions would not prevent the Soviets from completing the pipeline, raising concerns that if the sanctions were still in place when the pipeline was completed it would magnify the appearance of failure. Rather than trying to halt exports of oil and gas equipment, pipeline opponents decided to shift their focus to getting the Europeans to limit their purchases of Soviet gas and to tighten controls on credit and advanced technology exports.[34]

The change in focus allowed the State Department to negotiate an agreement with US allies to withdraw the extended trade sanctions in return for promises of increased vigilance in trade matters. The Europeans also agreed not to sign or approve any new gas contracts with the Soviets while they and the United States conducted a study on alternatives to Soviet gas, improved enforcement of controls over export of advanced technologies, especially in the oil and gas sector, and made changes in officially backed export credit practices to include "substantially higher rates" to the Soviet Union, higher down payments, and shortened maturities. Reagan announced the lifting of the sanctions on November 13, 1982.[35]

Supporters of sanctions tried to salvage something from the reversal by committing the Europeans to limit Soviet gas imports to no more than 30 percent of total European gas supplies. In addition, NSDD-75, approved in January 1983, retained the objective of preventing the transfer of any technology that would either directly or indirectly contribute to Soviet military power. Although the Europeans agreed to a May 1983 International Energy Agency communiqué that called on member states to avoid "undue dependence" on any single supplier, they refused to agree to any binding ceiling or to single out the Soviet Union. Reflecting a long-standing and independent commitment by European governments not to become dependent on any single supplier, the communiqué also called on member states to diversify sources of energy imports by developing indigenous natural gas resources in North America and the North Sea.[36]

Meanwhile, angered by US actions, the Soviet leadership made completion of the pipeline a top priority. Although the Soviets announced in January 1984 that the first shipment of gas from Siberia had arrived in France, the gas traveled through the already existing pipeline system, not the new line, which opened in late 1985. The US embargo caused some delays and increased costs, but it failed to prevent natural gas sales to Western Europe from increasing and becoming an important source of hard currency earning for Soviet Union. Western Europe bought less Soviet gas than originally projected because energy use had fallen due to slower economic growth. As a result, earnings, while significant, were less than originally projected.[37] Earnings were also smaller because the price of Soviet natural gas was linked to the price of oil, and world oil prices dropped dramatically between 1980 and 1986.

During the 1970s, world oil prices skyrocketed from $1.80 a barrel in 1970 to $36.83 in 1980. (In 2018 dollars, from $11.63 to $112.64.)[38] Over time, higher prices led to increases in supply and decreases in demand. In addition, the advanced industrial nations launched a coordinated campaign via the Organization for Economic Cooperation and Development (OECD) and the International Energy Agency (IEA) focused on reducing oil consumption through greater efficiency and conservation, replacing oil with other energy sources, particularly in electricity generation, and reducing oil imports from the members of the Organization of the Petroleum Exporting Countries (OPEC), and especially from the Middle East, by increasing oil production elsewhere.[39]

Although these efforts lagged due to a drop in real prices for oil between 1974 and 1978, the second oil shock of 1979–1980 revived them. Between 1979 and 1985, oil consumption in the noncommunist world fell from 51.6 to 46.3 million bpd. Over the same period, non-OPEC "free world" oil production, mainly from Alaska, the North Sea, and Mexico, increased from 17.7 to 22.6 million bpd. The result was a 10.2 million bpd drop in demand for OPEC oil. (These figures exclude Soviet and Chinese oil production, which combined increased by over a million bpd in the same period.) These changes in the world oil economy put enormous pressure on oil producers. After peaking in the fourth quarter of 1980 at $38.60 per barrel, the average spot price of a barrel of light crude oil fell to $34.17 in 1981, $31.76 in 1982, $28.67 in 1983, to a range around $27 in 1984–1985.[40]

The drop in prices hit Saudi Arabia especially hard. Saudi decisions on pricing and production levels were calculated to maximize and protect their income over the long run. The Saudis preferred prices that would discourage the development of alternative sources of oil and alternatives to oil and not harm Western economies, where they had significant investments. These interests aligned them more with the oil-importing countries than with the other major oil-exporting countries.[41] The Saudis initially attempted to stabilize prices around $29 a barrel by cutting back their production. Other producers, including other OPEC members, failed to reduce their production, however, and the Saudis lost markets and the price of oil continued to fall. Saudi production fell from an average of 10.27 million bpd in 1980 to around 2.2 million bpd in August 1985, and Saudi revenues fell from $113.2 billion in 1981 to $25.9 billion in 1985, forcing the kingdom to cut back many government programs and draw down its foreign-exchange reserves. Low oil production levels also meant less associated gas production, threatening the Saudi petrochemical industry, which used natural gas as its main feedstock. Natural gas was also essential to power Saudi Arabia's seawater desalination plants.[42]

Tired of cutting back production in a futile effort to maintain prices, the Saudis decided in September 1985 to regain their position as the leading OPEC producer, stem the drop in oil revenues, and ensure a long-term market for their oil by increasing production. An added bonus was that lower prices would also hurt Iran, which was engaged in a bloody war with Iraq and threatened Saudi Arabia and other Gulf producers, which were aiding Iraq. Rather than selling oil at a fixed price, the Saudis would be paid based on what refined products sold for in the marketplace minus a fixed profit for the refiner. The new "netback" system put a premium on volume rather than price and led to a collapse of world oil prices, which fell to around $17 a barrel in the first quarter of 1986 and $11 in the second quarter.[43]

The collapse in world oil prices decimated Soviet hard currency earnings. Initially the decline in the price of oil was, in part, offset by the rise in the value of the dollar against other major Western currencies, which enhanced the Soviet Union's foreign purchasing power because Soviet oil and gas exports were priced in dollars while most of their hard currency purchases were made in Western Europe and Japan in nondollar currencies. The depreciation of the dollar beginning in the mid-1980s, on the other hand, eroded the purchasing power of Soviet energy revenues.[44]

Oil production declined in 1985, and hard currency oil export earnings, which had reached approximately $15.6 billion in 1983, fell to around $6.96 billion in 1986. The Soviets restored oil production levels in 1986 by pouring huge additional amounts of money, workers, and equipment into western Siberia. Due to a slight increase in oil prices in 1987, hard currency export earnings rose from $6.96 billion in 1986 to almost $10.3 billion in 1987. Prices fell again in 1988, however, and earnings from hard currency exports dipped to around $9.77 billion in 1988, even though the volume of oil exported increased from 3.92 million bpd in 1987 to 4.09 million bpd in 1988. Low oil prices also took a toll on hard currency earnings from gas sales. Natural gas earnings fell from almost $4 billion in 1981 to a little over $2.6 billion in 1988 despite an increase in exports from 61.7 bcm in 1981 to an estimated 86 bcm in 1988.[45]

The drop in oil prices also hurt Soviet weapons exports, because many of their best customers were oil exporters. According to a CIA study, around 5 percent of Soviet hard currency earnings and 10 percent of Soviet oil exports were derived from re-exported Middle East oil, obtained mostly in exchange for Soviet arms. Soviet exports of arms and military goods to nonsocialist countries denominated in hard currencies fell from $9.18 billion in 1984 to $7.49 billion in 1985. Although sales recovered in 1987 to $10.4 billion and rose to $11.8 billion by 1989, actual Soviet gains were probably less, because significant portions of the sales were on credit. As a result, Third World debt to the Soviet Union grew from $34.8 billion in 1985 to $67.4 billion by the end of 1989. In 1990, the value of Soviet arms sales fell to $9.4 billion.[46]

The decline in earnings presented the new Soviet government of Mikhail Gorbachev, who took power in March 1985, with difficult choices. Gorbachev

Table 1 Oil prices and Soviet hard-currency oil and natural gas export earnings, 1980–1988 (current US $)

| | | EXPORT EARNINGS | |
YEAR	OIL PRICE PER BARREL	OIL	NATURAL GAS
1980	36.83	12,123,700,000	2,710,200,000
1981	35.93	11,886,900,000	3,967,900,000
1982	32.97	14,823,800,000	3,672,800,000
1983	29.55	15,569,200,000	3,193,500,000
1984	28.78	15,111,300,000	3,753,900,000
1985	27.56	11,471,000,000	3,813,200,000
1986	14.43	6,962,800,000	3,638,400,000
1987	18.44	10,274,300,000	2,768,600,000
1988	14.92	9,767,800,000	2,621,400,000

Source: CIA, *Soviet Energy Data Resource Handbook*, SOV 90-10021, May 1990, CIA Electronic Reading Room; *BP Statistical Review of World Energy 2019*, http://www.bp.com/statisticalreview.

initially planned to hold energy investment steady and use oil and gas earnings to finance modernization of Soviet industry and improve living standards. Instead he had to increase energy investment and import more Western equipment and technology to keep production from falling and to maintain exports. This policy meant cutting imports of machinery and equipment for his modernization program as well as imports of grain and consumer goods. Devoting additional domestic resources to oil production and to the manufacture of oil field equipment also reduced the availability of funds for plant construction and improved equipment in other industries. Theoretically, conservation and efficiency gains could cut domestic oil and gas consumption, thus freeing up more oil and gas for export, but prospects were dim. Both would require substantially higher energy prices to reflect increasing costs, radical changes in the economic system to ensure that higher prices led to energy conservation, and increased investment in more efficient machinery.[47]

Rather than providing the funds to help him overcome the problems facing the Soviet Union, as he had hoped, the energy sector had, by 1989, become a major barrier to Gorbachev's plans. There was no easy way out. If he continued to allow energy to soak up a growing share of investment resources, his modernization and consumer welfare goals would be out of reach. At the same time, energy shortages and declining hard currency earnings, which would result from failure to maintain production and exports, would be equally devastating to his reform plans. Cutting domestic consumption to increase exports risked starving the domestic economy of needed energy, while cutting exports to Eastern Europe and other clients carried the risk of exacerbating political unrest.[48]

Labor and political unrest, shortages of equipment, and general economic disruption due to the uneven impact of Gorbachev's economic reforms, combined with the natural depletion of fields, led to a decline in oil production to 12.254 million bpd in 1989, 11.523 million bpd in 1990, and 10.431 million bpd in 1991. In addition, mounting violence between Azerbaijan and Armenia contributed to shortages in oil equipment, most of which came from Azerbaijan.[49] Falling oil output undermined the domestic economy and the Soviet Union's ability to service its growing foreign debt, which rose from $14.9 billion in 1985 to $45.36 in 1990. As earnings from foreign trade fell, the Soviet state budget deficit rose from 1.7 billion rubles in 1985 to 10.3 billion rubles in 1990.[50]

By 1990, the Soviet Union's balance-of-payments problem had become acute, in part because of the sharp decline in revenues from oil and gas exports, and the central government's ability to pay its international debts had declined sharply.[51] The Soviet system collapsed in 1991, when the piecemeal economic reforms Gorbachev instituted led to economic chaos and to the defection of a large portion of the Soviet elite, whose continued privileges were threatened by political reforms.[52]

Analysis of US efforts to hinder Soviet natural gas exports to Western Europe and US policies to influence oil prices by pressing Saudi Arabia to increase production does not support claims that US policies and actions had an important impact.

Roger W. Robinson Jr., who was on the NSC staff from 1982 to 1985, argues that that US export controls limiting Soviet access to Western credits, technology, and equipment hindered Soviet gas exports and cost the Soviet Union billions of dollars in export earnings. Thomas C. Reed, who served as special assistant for national security affairs, 1982–1983, claims that software, secretly altered by the CIA and illegally obtained by the Soviets resulted in a massive explosion that destroyed a segment of the pipeline in October 1982, costing the Soviets massive amounts of money and delaying completion.[53] Many studies uncritically repeat Reed's account.

US efforts to block the construction of the Siberian gas pipeline caused some delays and imposed some costs, but natural gas production and exports nevertheless increased and became a major source of foreign exchange earnings for the Soviet Union. Claims that US actions were effective overstate the costs imposed by US policies by comparing actual volumes and revenues to earlier exaggerated projections about the pipeline and ignore changes in economic conditions and independent decisions by European governments. Moreover, US efforts to block the pipeline damaged US relations with its Western European allies and hindered efforts to craft effective controls on strategic exports.[54]

While the CIA may have had a program to corrupt software stolen by the Soviets, and while there was an explosion at a Soviet natural gas pipeline in Siberia in 1982, there is no independent evidence connecting the two. According to former CIA staff historian Nicholas Dujmovic, who researched the issue for the agency during the 1980s, Reed's account is a "persistent myth." Vladimir Zakhmatov, a scientist who worked on safety measures for Soviet oil and gas pipelines at the time, has pointed out that Soviet gas pipelines in the 1980s did not use computer controls. Reed also erroneously had the pipeline running through Kazakhstan.[55]

Conservative journalist Peter Schweizer claims that the Reagan administration orchestrated the oil price collapse of 1986 and that economic pressures caused by the drastic drop in oil prices were a key factor in Gorbachev's efforts to improve relations with the West and end the Cold War. Drawing largely on interviews, Schweizer recounts alleged conversations with high Saudi officials, including King Fahd, during which President Reagan, Secretary of Defense Weinberger, and CIA Director Casey, who often met with Saudi leaders to secure funding for anti-Soviet insurgents in Afghanistan and Nicaragua, urged the Saudis to cut oil prices. The Reagan administration also made extensive efforts to assure Saudi Arabia of US friendship through arms sales, personal diplomacy, and public declarations of support for the Saudi regime[56] Weinberger later claimed that "one of the reasons we were selling the Saudis all those arms was to get lower prices."[57] With the fate of the shah of Iran in mind, Reagan, Haig, Casey, and Weinberger made it clear that they would not permit the Saudi monarchy to be overthrown, a policy that conservative journalist William Safire labeled the "Reagan Corollary" to the Carter doctrine.[58]

The collapse in oil prices in the mid-1980s had a devastating impact on the Soviet economy, and Casey and others probably urged the Saudis to increase oil production, but there is no evidence that links the Saudi decision in September 1985 to increase oil production and thereby drive down prices to US lobbying. Most records of these meetings are still classified, and other accounts of US-Saudi relations in the 1980s make no mention of discussions about oil prices.[59] Maintaining Western access to Saudi oil had been a US policy priority since World War II, and the United States already had a long history of arms sales to Saudi Arabia, including during the Carter administration. Reagan administration officials had been pressing the Saudis to increase production since 1981, but the Saudis did not act until the fall of 1985, when it had become clear that their policy of cutting production to maintain higher oil prices had failed. Thus, even if US officials encouraged the Saudis to increase production, the Saudis had good reasons—apart from US pressure—to act.[60] While economic problems, including energy problems, were a factor in Gorbachev's calculations, there is little evidence that the Reagan administration's policies forced him to end the Cold War on US terms.[61]

Analysis of US efforts to undermine the Soviet energy sector reveals the limits of US influence and undermines claims that aggressive US policies caused the collapse of the Soviet system. The Reagan administration engaged in economic warfare against the Soviet energy sector, and energy problems played an important role in the collapse of the Soviet economy, but correlation is not causation. In the end, the problems that plagued the Soviet energy sector were not due to US policies and actions, but rather were the result of the inefficiencies and contradictions of their command economy and developments in the world oil economy over which they (and the United States) had little control. Indeed, the problems of the Soviet energy sector both reflected and often exacerbated the larger problems that led to the collapse of the Soviet system. In neither case were aggressive US policies and actions the decisive factor.

Notes

1. Yegor Gaidar, *Collapse of an Empire: Lessons for Modern Russia*, trans. Antonina W. Bouis (Washington, DC: Brookings Institution, 2007); Yegor Gaidar, "The Soviet Collapse: Grain and Oil," Apr. 2007, American Enterprise Institute, http://www/aei.org/wp-content/uploads/2011/10/2007040419_Gaidar.pdf; Stephen Kotkin, *Armageddon Averted: The Soviet Collapse, 1970–2000* (Oxford: Oxford University Press, 2001), 10–27; Olga Skorokhodova, "The Double Shock: The Soviet Energy Crisis and the Oil Price Collapse of 1986," in *Counter-Shock: The Oil Counter-Revolution of the 1980s*, ed. Duccio Basosi, Giuliano Garavini, and Massimiliano Trentin (London: I. B. Tauris, 2018), 180–198. Chris Miller, *The Struggle to Save the Soviet Economy: Mikhail Gorbachev and the Collapse of the USSR* (Chapel Hill: University of North Carolina Press, 2016), 62, 146, tends to minimize the importance of the oil price collapse, but still confirms it had a role.

2. Alan Smith, *Russia and the World Economy: Problems of Integration* (London: Routledge, 1993), 80–81; "Cheaper Oil: Many Winners, a Few Bad Losers," *The Economist*, 25 Oct. 2014, 16.

3. A key "take-away" from Vladislav Zubok, "The Collapse of the Soviet Union," in *Cambridge History of Communism*, vol. 3, *Endgame? Late Communism in Global Perspective, 1965 to the Present*, ed. Juliane Fürst, Silvio Pons, and Mark Selden (Cambridge: Cambridge University Press, 2017), 250–257, is the overwhelming role of internal factors and the relatively minor impact of US policies and actions.

4. David S. Painter and Thomas S. Blanton, "The End of the Cold War," in *A Companion to Post-1945*, ed. Jean-Christophe Agnew and Roy Rosenzweig (Malden, MA: Blackwell Publishing, 2002), 479–500.

5. This essay draws on my chapter "From Linkage to Economic Warfare: Energy, Soviet-American Relations, and the End of the Cold War," in *Cold War Energy: A Transnational History of Soviet Oil and Gas*, ed. Jeronim Perović, (Cham: Palgrave Macmillan, 2017), 283–318.

6. Jeronim Perović, "The Soviet Union's Rise as an International Energy Power: A Short History," in *Cold War Energy: A Transnational History of Soviet Oil and Gas*, ed. Jeronim Perović, (Cham: Palgrave Macmillan, 2017), 1–43, provides a concise overview of Soviet energy development.

7. *BP Statistical Review of World Energy 2019*, http://www.bp.com/statisticalreview; CIA, *Soviet Energy Data Resource Handbook: A Reference Aid*, SOV-90-10021, May 1990, CIA Electronic Reading Room (CIAERR), https://www.cia.gov/library/readingroom/home.

8. CIA, *Soviet Energy Policy toward Eastern Europe: A Research Paper*, June 1980, CIAERR; Marshall I. Goldman, *The Enigma of Soviet Petroleum: Half-Empty or Half-Full* (London: George Allen and Unwin, 1980), 49–54.

9. In 2018 dollars, oil prices rose from $11.63 in 1970 to $112.64 in 1980; *BP Statistical Review of World Energy 2019*; CIA, *Soviet Energy Policy toward Eastern Europe*, June 1980, CIAERR; CIA, *Soviet Energy Data Resource Handbook: A Reference Aid*; Goldman, *The Enigma of Soviet Petroleum*, 7. On the oil crises, see David S. Painter, "Oil and Geopolitics: The Oil Crises of the 1970s and the Cold War," *Historical Social Research* 39, no. 4 (2014), 186–208.

10. CIA, *The Impending Soviet Oil Crisis*, ER 77-10147 U, Mar. 1977, CIAERR; CIA, *Prospects for Soviet Oil Production*, ER 77-10425, Apr. 1977, CIAERR; CIA, *Prospects for Soviet Oil Production: A Supplemental Analysis*, ER-10270, July 1977, CIAERR; CIA, *The Value to the USSR of Economic Relations with the US and the West*, ER M 77-10525, Aug. 1977, CIAERR; US Department of State, *Foreign Relations of the United States, 1977–1980 (FRUS)*, vol. 6, *Soviet Union* (Washington, DC: US Government Printing Office, 2013), doc. 40.

11. Thane Gustafson, *Crisis amid Plenty: The Politics of Soviet Energy Under Brezhnev and Gorbachev* (Princeton: Princeton University Press, 1989), 29–35; US Congress, Senate Committee on Banking, Housing, and Urban Affairs, *Proposed Trans-Siberian Natural Gas Pipeline*, 97th Congress, 1st Session, 12 Nov. 1981, 165–167; CIA, *Outlook for the Siberia-to-Western Europe Natural Gas Pipeline*, SOV 82-10120, Aug. 1982, CIAERR; CIA, *USSR-Western Europe: Implications of the Siberia-to-Europe Gas Pipeline*, ER 81-10085, Mar. 1983, CIAERR; Bruce Jentleson, *Pipeline Politics: The Complex Political Economy of East-West Energy Trade* (Ithaca, NY: Cornell University Press, 1986), 163–169.

12. *FRUS 1977–1980*, vol. 6, docs. 250, 252, 257; Jentleson, *Pipeline Politics*, 161–163; Michael Mastanduno, *Economic Containment: CoCom and the Politics of East-West Trade* (Ithaca, NY: Cornell University Press, 1992), 220–229.

13. Tyler Esno, "Reagan's Economic War on the Soviet Union," *Diplomatic History* 42, no. 2 (2018): 281–304; *FRUS 1981–1988*, vol. 3, docs. 68 and 70; Weinberger to Allen, 8 July 1981, Margaret Thatcher Foundation (MTF), http://www.margaretthatcher.org/archive; Casey to Reagan, 9 July 1981, "CIA Memorandum on Siberian Pipeline," 8 July 1981, CIAERR; Jentleson, *Pipeline Politics*, 174–179; Mastanduno, *Economic Containment*, 233–240.

14. See the testimony of Assistant Secretary of Defense Richard Perle in US Congress, *Proposed Trans-Siberian Natural Gas Pipeline*, 113–118; US Department of State, *American Foreign Policy: Current Documents (AFP)* (Washington, DC: Government Printing Office, 1983), 443.

15. *FRUS 1981–1988*, vol. 3, docs. 68, 70; Alexander M. Haig Jr., *Caveat: Realism, Reagan, and Foreign Policy* (New York: Macmillan, 1984), 225–254; Bjørn Vidar Lerøen, *Troll: Gas for Generations* (Oslo: A/S Norske Shell and Statoil, 1996), 77–82; Jentleson, *Pipeline Politics*, 185–188; Mastanduno, *Economic Containment*, 240–243.

16. Stephan Kieninger, *The Diplomacy of Détente: Cooperative Security Policies from Helmut Schmidt to George Shultz* (New York: Routledge, 2018), 83–148, details the difference between American and European views. CIA, *USSR-Western Europe: Implications of the Siberia-to-Europe Gas Pipeline*, Mar. 1981, CIAERR; CIA, *Economics of the Siberia-to-Europe Gas Pipeline*, Sept. 1981, CIAERR; US Congress, *Proposed Trans-Siberian Natural Gas Pipeline*, 167–170; Per Högselius, *Red Gas: Russia and the Origins of European Energy Dependence* (New York: Palgrave Macmillan, 2013), 190–195.

17. *FRUS 1981–1988*, vol. 3, doc. 213; Jentleson, *Pipeline Politics*, 181–185; CIA, *Implications of the Siberia-to-Europe Gas Pipeline*, Mar. 1981, CIAERR; CIA *The Soviet Gas Pipeline in Perspective*, SNIE 3-11/2-82, 21 Sept. 1982, CIAERR.

18. *FRUS 1981–1988*, vol. 3, doc. 213; Jentleson, *Pipeline Politics*, 190–192; Kieninger, *Diplomacy of Détente*.

19. *FRUS 1981–1988*, vol. 3, docs. 68, 71, 94.

20. *FRUS 1981–1988*, vol. 3, docs. 98, 102, 105.

21. Raymond L. Garthoff, *The Great Transition: American-Soviet Relations and the End of the Cold War* (Washington, DC: Brookings Institution, 1994), 546–547.

22. Garthoff, *Great Transition*, 547–549; *AFP*, 636–637; Andrea Chiampan, "'Those European Chicken Littles': Reagan, NATO, and the Polish Crisis, 1981–1982," *International History Review* 37, no. 4 (2015): 682–689; Esno, "Reagan's Economic War," 290–291.

23. Haig to Reagan, 29 Jan. 1982, MTF; Thatcher to Reagan, 29 Jan. 1982, MTF; Margaret Thatcher, *The Downing Street Years* (New York: HarperCollins, 1993), 253–255; Ksenia Demidova, "The Deal of the Century: The Reagan Administration and the Soviet Pipeline," in *European Integration and the Atlantic Community*, ed. Klaus Kiran Patel and Kenneth Weisbrode (Cambridge: Cambridge University Press, 2013), 66–76; Kieninger, *Diplomacy of Détente*, 111–112; Jentleson, *Pipeline Politics*, 204–206; Haig, *Caveat*, 254–256.

24. Esno, "Reagan's Cold War," 191; *FRUS 1981–1988*, 3, docs. 139, 141, 145, 152; Bailey quoted in Kieninger, *Diplomacy of Détente*, 116; CIA, *The Soviet Economic Predicament and East-West Economic Relations*, SOV 82-10001X, Jan. 1982, CIAERR; CIA, *Soviet Economic Dependence on the West*, SOV 10012, Jan. 1982, CIAERR; Casey to Reagan, 25 Mar. 1982, CIAERR; CIA, *Western Alternatives to Soviet Natural Gas: Prospects and Implications*, 17 May 1982, CIAERR.

25. *FRUS 1981–1988*, vol. 3, docs. 145, 172; Douglas Brinkley, ed., *The Reagan Diaries* (New York: Harper Collins, 2007), 75.

26. *FRUS 1981–1988*, vol. 3, doc. 160; Esno, "Reagan's Economic War," 291–292; James Graham Wilson, *The Triumph of Improvisation: Gorbachev's Adaptability, Reagan's Engagement, and the End of the Cold War* (Ithaca, NY: Cornell University Press, 2014), 30–34.

27. *FRUS 1981–1988*, vol. 3, docs. 146, 152, 172, 174; CIA, *The Soviet Bloc Financial Problem as a Source of Western Influence*, NIC M 82-10004, Apr. 1982, CIAERR.

28. Kieninger, *Diplomacy of Détente*, 112–113; Henry R. Nau, *The Myth of America's Decline: Leading the World Economy into the 1990s* (New York: Oxford University Press, 1990), 309–312.

29. Minutes of NSC Meeting, 18 June 1982, The Reagan Files (RF), www.thereaganfiles.com; Brinkley, *Reagan Diaries*, 137–139; Haig, *Caveat*, 312–314. Reagan's decision was released as National Security Decision Directive 41 on 22 June 1982: http://www.reagan.utexas.edu/archives/reference/Scanned%20NSDDS/NSDD41.pdf; *AFP*, 436–441. Telegram, 13 July 1982, Ronald Reagan Presidential Library (RRPL), Jack F. Matlock Jr. Files, box 25, folder: "USSR–Economy (5/10)."

30. Kieninger, *Diplomacy of Détente*, Esno, "Reagan's Economic War, " 298–299; *FRUS 1981–1988*, vol. 3, doc. 190; Thatcher to Reagan, 25 June 1982, MTF; Thatcher, TV interview for BBC, 1 Sept. 1983, MTF; Thatcher, *Downing Street Years*, 256; Mastanduno, *Economic Containment*, 255–258; "Europe Protests Reagan Sanctions on

Pipeline Sales," *New York Times*, 13 Aug. 1982; "Europeans Protest US Pipeline Sanctions," *Washington Post*, 13 Aug. 1982.

31. Weinberger to Clark and Shultz, 9 Sept. 1982, MTF.

32. *FRUS 1981–1988*, vol. 3, doc. 208; Jentleson, *Pipeline Politics*, 195–196; Mastanduno, *Economic Containment*, 258–259; Kieninger, *Diplomacy of Détente*, 128, 130; Demidova, "Deal of the Century," 77–79.

33. Dan Morgan, "Position Is Contrary to Thinking in Administration," *Washington Post*, 24 July 1982; L. Paul Bremer III to David E. Pickford, 14 Sept. 1982, RRPL, Executive Secretariat–National Security Council, Meeting Files, folder: "NSC 0006/22 Sept. 82 (1/4)"; Minutes, Senior Interdepartmental Group, International Economic Policy, 16 Sept. 1982, RRPL, Executive Secretariat–National Security Council, Meeting Files, folder: "NSC 0006/22 Sept. 82 (2/4)"; *FRUS 1981–1988*, vol. 3, doc. 212; NSC Meeting, 21 Sept. 1982, RF; Memorandom to the Director of Central Intelligence, 15 Sept. 1982, CIAERR; George P. Schultz, *Turmoil and Triumph: My Years as Secretary of State* (New York: Scribner, 1993), 136–143; Kieninger, *Diplomacy of Détente*, 128–129; Esno, "Reagan's Economic War," 300–302.

34. *FRUS 1981–1988*, vol. 3, docs. 213, 214, 223; Brinkley, *Reagan Diaries*, 156, 163; CIA, *Outlook for the Siberian-to-Western Europe Natural Gas Pipeline*, Aug. 1982, CIAERR; CIA, *The Soviet Gas Pipeline in Perspective*, SNIE 3/11-2/82, 21 Sept. 1982, CIAERR; Casey to MacFarlane, 18 October 1982, CIAERR.

35. *FRUS 1981–1988*, vol. 3, docs. 231, 232, 246; AFP, 446–447; Mastanduno, *Economic Containment*, 260–262; Jentleson, *Pipeline Politics*, 197–198.

36. *FRUS 1981–1988*, vol. 3, docs. 223, 226; NSDD-75, "US Relations with the USSR," 17 Jan. 1983, https://www.reaganlibrary.gov/sites/default/files/archives/reference/scanned-nsdds/nsdd75.pdf; Roger W. Robinson Jr., "Reagan's Soviet Economic Take-Down Strategy: Financial and Energy Elements," in *The Grand Strategy That Won the Cold War: Architecture of Triumph*, ed. Douglas E. Streusand (Lanham, MD: Lexington Books, 2016), 167–169; Paul Lewis, "Economic Parley Will Seek to Settle Disputes," *New York Times*, 9 May 1983; Steven R. Weizman, "US Depicts Allies as Wary on Soviet," *New York Times*, 28 May 1983; Jentleson, *Pipeline Politics*, 198–203; Lerøen, *Troll*, 80–83; Kieninger, *Diplomacy of Détente*, 95.

37. Jentleson, *Pipeline Politics*, 199–203, 211–214; Gustafson, *Crisis amid Plenty*, 152, 156–157, 202–208; CIA, *The Role of Western Equipment in Soviet Oil and Gas Development*, SOV 84-10153X, Sept. 1984, CIAERR; CIA, *Soviet Energy Data Resource Handbook*.

38. *BP Statistical Review of World Energy 2019*.

39. Henning Turk, "Reducing Dependence on OPEC Oil: The IEA's Energy Strategy between 1976 and the Mid-1980s," in *Counter-Shock: The Oil Counter-Revolution of the 1980s*, ed. Duccio Basosi, Giuliano Garavini, and Massimiliano Trentin (London: I. B. Tauris, 2018), 241–258.

40. Edward T. Dowling and Francis G. Hilton, "Oil in the 1980s: An OECD Perspective," in *The Oil Market in the 1980s: A Decade of Decline*, ed. Siamack Shojai and Bernard S. Katz, (New York: Praeger, 1992), 74–75; *BP Statistical Review of World Energy 2019*; Francesco Petrini, "Countershocked? The Oil Majors and the Price Slump of the 1980s," in *Counter-Shock: The Oil Counter-Revolution of the 1980s*, ed. Duccio Basosi, Giuliano Garavini, and Massimiliano Trentin (London: I. B. Tauris, 2018), 76–96; R. Tyler Priest, "Shifting Sands: The 1973 Oil Shock and the Expansion of Non-OPEC Supply," in *Oil Shock:*

The 1973 Crisis and its Economic Legacy, ed. Elisabetta Bini, Giuliano Garavini, and Federico Romero (London: I. B. Tauris, 2016), 117–141; Giuliano Garavini, *The Rise and Fall of OPEC in the Twentieth Century* (New York: Oxford University Press, 2019), 301–346.

41. CIA, *Saudi Arabia: Perspectives on Oil Policy*, NIC M 81-10013, Nov. 1981, CIAERR.

42. Ian Skeet, *OPEC: Twenty-Five Years of Prices and Politics* (Cambridge: Cambridge University Press, 1988), 194–212, 241; Majid Al-Moneef, "Saudi Arabia and the Counter-Shock of 1986," in *Counter-Shock: The Oil Counter-Revolution of the 1980s*, ed. Duccio Basosi, Giuliano Garavini, and Massimiliano Trentin (London: I. B. Tauris, 2018), 99–105; Garavini, *Rise and Fall of OPEC*, 339, 345–346; CIA, "Threat Outlook: Lower Oil Prices: Impact on the Soviet Union," 13 Feb. 1985, CIAERR; CIA, *Saudi Arabia, Kuwait, UAE: Asset Management in Austere Times*, GI 85-10099, Apr. 1985, CIAERR; CIA, *OPEC: Narrowing Options in a Softening Oil Market*, GI 85-10165, June 1985, CIAERR; CIA, *The Saudi Oil Offensive*, GI M 86-20084, 31 Mar. 1986, CIAERR. The Energy Information Administration (EIA) of the US Department of Energy puts Saudi production in August 1985 at 2.34 million bpd: EIA, *Historical Monthly Energy, 1973–1992* (Washington, DC: Energy Information Administration, 1992), 309.

43. Daniel Yergin, *The Prize: The Epic Quest for Oil, Money, and Power* (New York: Simon & Schuster, 1991), 745–751; Skeet, *OPEC*, 215–221; Al-Moneef, "Saudi Arabia and the Counter-Shock of 1986," 111–116; CIA, *The Saudi Oil Offensive*, 31 Mar. 1986, CIAERR; CIA, *Saudi Arabia's Oil Policy: Implications for the United States*, GI M 86-20186, 8 Aug. 1986, CIAERR; Dowling and Hilton, "Oil in the 1980s," 74.

44. CIA, "Threat Outlook: Lower Oil Prices: Impact on the Soviet Union," 13 Feb. 1985, CIAERR; CIA, *Implications of the Decline in Soviet Hard Currency Earnings*, NIE 11-23-86, Sept. 1986, CIAERR; Smith, *Russia and the World Economy*, 139.

45. CIA, *USSR: Facing the Dilemma of Hard Currency Shortages*, SOV 86-10027X, May 1986, CIAERR; CIA, *Soviet Energy Data Resource Handbook*, May 1990, CIAERR; CIA, *USSR: Coping with the Decline in Hard Currency Revenues*, Apr. 1988, CIAERR. Smith, *Russia and the World Economy*, 81, 91, gives slightly different figures.

46. Smith, *Russia and the World Economy*, 91, 147–148. According to CIA figures, Soviet arms sales were $4.9 billion in 1985 and increased to an average of $7.3 billion in 1986–1987: CIA, *USSR: Coping with the Decline in Hard Currency Revenues*, SOV 88-10014X, April 1988, CIAERR.

47. CIA, *Implications of an Oil Price Decline*, SNIE 3-85, Aug. 1985, CIAERR; CIA, *USSR: Implications of Reduced Oil Exports*, 4 Sept. 1985, CIAERR; Hoffman to Meyer, "Soviet Oil: Gorbachev's Alternatives," 2 Oct. 1985, CIAERR; CIA, *Soviet Oil Production through 1990: Hard Choices Ahead*, SOV 86-10051, Nov. 1986, CIAERR; CIA, *Soviet Energy Data Resource Handbook*. Gustafson, *Crisis Amid Plenty*, 227–262, provides a detailed analysis of the poor prospects for conservation.

48. CIA, *USSR: Investment Trade-Offs Between Energy Production and Conservation, 1986–95*, SOV 87-10059, Oct. 1987, CIAERR; CIA, *The Soviet Energy Plight: Runaway Investment or Energy Shortfalls*, SOV 89-10002, Jan. 1989, CIAERR; Stephen Kotkin, "The Kiss of Debt: The East Bloc Goes Borrowing," in *The Shock of the Global: The 1970s in Perspective*, ed. Niall Ferguson, Charles S. Maier, Erez Manela, and Daniel J. Sargent (Cambridge, MA: Harvard University Press, 2010), 80–93. For a fuller analysis, see Painter, "From Linkage to Economic Warfare," 298–302.

49. Thane Gustafson, *Wheel of Fortune: The Battle for Oil and Power in Russia* (Cambridge, MA: Harvard University Press, 2012), 30–62; *BP Statistical Review of World Energy 2015*.

50. Smith, *Russia and the World Economy*, 159; Vladimir Mau and Irina Starodubrovskaya, *The Challenge of Revolution: Contemporary Russia in Historical Perspective* (New York: Oxford University Press, 2001), 247.

51. CIA, *Beyond Perestroika: The Soviet Economy in Crisis*, DDB 1900-164.91, June 1991, CIAERR; Gaidar, *Collapse of an Empire*, 220–249; Smith, *Russia and the World Economy*, 156–176; Marshall I. Goldman, "Soviet Economy Heads for a Crash," *Wall Street Journal*, 27 June 1990.

52. Mark Harrison, "Coercion, Compliance, and the Collapse of the Soviet Command Economy," *Economic History Review* 55, no. 3 (2002): 397–433; Anders Åslund, "The Demise of the Soviet Economic System," *International Politics* 48, no. 3 (2011), 552–558; David Kotz and Fred Weir, *Revolution from Above: The Demise of the Soviet System* (London: Routledge, 2002); Zubok, "Collapse of the Soviet Union."

53. Robinson, "Reagan's Soviet Economic Take-Down Strategy," 159–174; Thomas C. Reed, *At the Abyss: An Insider's History of the Cold War* (New York: Random House, 2004), 266–269; "Update: Agent Farewell and the Siberian Pipeline Explosion," National Security Archive, https://nsarchive.wordpress.com/2013/04/26/agent-farewell-and-the-siberian-pipeline-explosion.

54. CIA, "Role of Western Equipment in Soviet Oil and Gas Development," Sept. 1984, CIAERR; CIA, *The Soviet Energy Plight*, Jan. 1989, CIAERR; Jentleson, *Pipeline Politics*, 212–214. On US relations with its European allies, see the chapter by Colbourn and Haeussler in this volume.

55. Nicholas Dujmovic, "Review of David E. Hoffman, *Billion Dollar Spy*," *Studies in Intelligence* 60, no. 1 (2016), 59; Esno "Reagan's Economic Warfare," 293, also doubts Reed's account; V. D. Zakhmatov, V. V. Glushkova, and O. A. Kryazhich, "Explosion, Which . . . Was Not!" 25 June 2011, http://ogas.kiev.ua/perspective/vzryv-kotorogo-ne-bylo-581. For an alternative explanation of the explosion, see Anatoly Medetsky, "KGB Veteran Denies CIA Caused '82 Blast," *Moscow Times*, 18 Mar. 2004.

56. Peter Schweizer, *Victory: The Reagan Administration's Secret Strategy That Hastened the Collapse of the Soviet Union* (New York: Atlantic Monthly Press, 1994); Peter Schweizer, *Reagan's War: The Epic Story of His Forty-Year Struggle and Final Triumph Over Communism* (New York: Doubleday, 2002), 238–241.

57. Schweizer, *Victory*, 31

58. *AFP*, 659, 809, 812–813, 816, 818, 820, 823–824; Schweizer, *Victory*, 29–32; William Safire, "The Reagan Corollary," *New York Times*, 4 Oct. 1981.

59. Correspondence with former CIA staff historian; Rachel Bronson, *Thicker than Oil: America's Uneasy Partnership with Saudi Arabia* (New York: Oxford University Press, 2006), 168–190; Bob Woodward, *Veil: The Secret Wars of the CIA, 1981–1987* (New York: Simon and Schuster, 1987); Jonathan Marshall, "Saudi Arabia and the Reagan Doctrine," *Middle East Report* 155 (1988), http://www.merip.org/mer/mer155.

60. Author's correspondence with former State Department specialists on Saudi Arabia. Weinberger admitted to Schweizer that the Saudis probably acted for internal reasons: Schweizer, *Victory*, 242.

61. In addition to the studies cited in Painter and Blanton, "The End of the Cold War," see Vladislav M. Zubok, *Failed Empire: The Soviet Union in the Cold War from Stalin to Gorbachev* (Chapel Hill: University of North Carolina Press, 2007), 265–335; and Archie Brown, "The Gorbachev Revolution and the End of the Cold War," in *Cambridge History of the Cold War*, vol. 3, *Endings*, ed. Melvyn P. Leffler and Odd Arne Westad (Cambridge: Cambridge University Press, 2010), 244–260.

CHAPTER 3

Reagan and the Evolution of US Counterterrorism

CHRISTOPHER J. FULLER

On September 29, 2001, the White House released a picture of President George W. Bush sitting at a shadowy Camp David table with his chief of staff, Andrew Card, and national security advisor, Condoleezza Rice. Opposite sat the director of Central Intelligence (DCI), George Tenet, using a map of Afghanistan to brief the group on the United States' planned retaliation against al-Qaeda and their Taliban hosts following the September 11 attacks.[1] Considering the purpose of the meeting, Secretary of Defense Donald Rumsfeld was conspicuous in his absence, and shortly afterward sent a frustrated memo to the chairman of the Joint Chiefs bewailing that the Department of Defense (DoD) "can't do anything on the ground in Afghanistan until the CIA people go in first." "Given the nature of the world," Rumsfeld continued, his department was clearly "lacking a capability we need."[2] The roots of 9/11, why Afghanistan became the site of the United States' first major war of the twenty-first century, and how Langley rather than the Pentagon came to be at the forefront of America's retaliation can all be traced back to a series of policy decisions and conflicts within the Ronald Reagan administration. While much of the record of American statecraft through the 1980s discloses bold policies that subsequently contributed to the favorable flow of global events, the Reagan administration's approach to counterterrorism serves as a reminder that behind the narrative of strong vision and decisive action, Reagan's White House was plagued by division, dysfunction, and a lack of foresight, which ultimately planted the seeds of the most catastrophic terrorist incident in US history.[3]

While the Reagan administration's disorder played a significant role in creating the environment in which al-Qaeda and its ambitious terrorist plot was able to evolve, its actions also helped lay the political, legal, and structural foundations of what became the United States' War on Terror. This chapter thus demonstrates that counterterrorism under Reagan is best viewed as paradoxical, having fostered the ideological climate and terrorist infrastructure that enabled the radical Islamist cause to thrive, while simultaneously establishing the fundamentals of the hard-line pursuit of these terrorists. It makes evident the extent to which counterterrorism policy, while significant in Reagan's public rhetoric, was treated as a lower-tier issue compared with wider Cold War objectives such as the arms buildup and the Reagan doctrine, approaches that not only served to obscure the administration's efforts to reduce the terrorist threat, but actively undermined it, weakening those charged with tackling the violent phenomenon while uniting and emboldening those who would become its greatest practitioners.

Reagan came to office at a time when terrorist incidents around the world had increased dramatically, rising over 300 percent between 1970 and 1980.[4] In addition to the accelerating tempo of attacks, the perpetrators were becoming progressively more capable, as funding and training from rogue regimes such as Muammar Gaddafi's Libya and post-revolution Iran transformed amateur rebels into hardened militia, employed to wage what RAND's Brian Jenkins described at the time as "covert acts of surrogate warfare."[5] Hezbollah's devastating assault on American interests in Lebanon demonstrated this deadly evolution, with the bombing of the US embassy in Beirut on April 18, 1983, killing seventeen Americans, including seven members of the CIA who were the explicit targets of the attack. Six months later a suicide bomber dispatched by the same group drove an explosive-laden truck into a barracks containing US marines, who had been posted to the Lebanese capital as a part of a multinational peacekeeping force during the nation's civil war, killing 241 American service personnel and injuring sixty more. Four months later the efficacy of this tactic was revealed when Reagan authorized the withdrawal of the remaining US troops from the war-torn country, despite the peacekeepers not having achieved their original objective.[6]

Reagan's early capitulation to terrorist tactics was a long way from the fiery rhetoric he had employed in the 1980 election campaign, when the former governor chastised President Jimmy Carter for failing to lead the United States against what he described as this "scourge of civilization."[7] In the candidates' only debate Reagan had implied weakness and inaction on the part of his opponent by stating that under *his* leadership the "civilized countries of the world" would "make it plain that there is no room worldwide for terrorism."[8] He had also established the use of a war paradigm for discussing terrorist incidents by describing the fifty-two American diplomats held hostage by Iran's revolutionary authorities during Carter's presidency as "prisoners of war." Following his election Reagan continued to employ this hard-line rhetoric, vowing that his administration would maintain "an unrelentingly tough line against any such future acts of terrorism."[9] "Let terrorists be aware," the president warned within days of his inauguration, "that when the rules of international behavior are violated, our policy will be one of swift and effective retribution."[10] As the events in Beirut notably exposed, however, despite the president's tough talk, the early years of his tenure saw US officials struggle to find a policy solution that matched his assertive language.

While the relationship between a president's rhetoric and the agenda he pursues matters for all occupants of the White House, the way that Reagan spoke about a particular matter took on extra significance due to his unique approach to policymaking. The president typically set his political goals through speeches. His addresses focused on style, symbolism, and populist ideals of American exceptionalism, leaving the task of translating his rhetorical flourishes into actionable policies to his advisors.[11] More critical observers have attributed Reagan's disconnection from the formal responsibilities associated with policymaking to his notoriously short attention span and consequent disinterest in the finer details of the process.[12] Others have suggested a more nuanced assessment, arguing that Reagan was driven above all by his showman's desire to remain popular, bypassing the hard and at times divisive challenges of governance in favor of keeping his audience engaged with his broad agenda.[13] The art of remaining the "great communicator" was, as Gary Wills has suggested, "a matter of remaining understood, step by step, never breaking the sequence of easy exposition."[14] Thus, rather than being responsible for implementing any sort of specific policy himself, Reagan lived in what Francis Fitzgerald described as "a world of rhetoric, performance and perceptions," in which his job was to sell, rather than formulate, policies.[15]

Reagan's style of leadership meant that when noteworthy terrorist events occurred, in particular those involving American citizens, he responded with simple but lofty rhetoric, declaring that the superiority of the United States' values combined with the nation's will to confront evil would prevail and ensure that the perpetrators would be brought to some undefined form of justice. As recent history has demonstrated, however, terrorism is a form of violence that defies simplistic definitions, black and white notions of justice, and quick solutions. It is a threat that turns the very values of a free and open society Reagan cited as the United States' advantage into a source of vulnerability. Rather than being in a position to apply justice swiftly, the United States quickly found that when faced with unconventional enemies who employ asymmetric tactics to fight with secrecy and surprise, its military superiority was bypassed, and the vastness of its international presence transformed from a geopolitical advantage to indefensible frontiers. Given these circumstances there was no obvious translation of Reagan's rhetoric into a coherent counterterrorism policy. The complexity of the task and the simplicity of the leadership offered thus ensured US counterterrorism policy had a distinctly stuttering character during the 1980s.

The most hawkish voices on the matter of how to respond to terrorism were those of Secretary of State George Shultz and Central Intelligence Agency Director William Casey. As a former member of the Marine Corps himself, Shultz had witnessed soldiers with whom he had a strong sense of brotherhood bombed in their bunks, while his department's embassies—symbols of the United States' global presence—had become primary targets for terror attacks. As a consequence of one such attack, which specifically targeted a meeting of CIA officers at the Beirut embassy on April 18, 1983, Casey had endured the deadliest day in his agency's history. From the newly drawn front line of the emerging conflict, both men spoke out in an increasingly forceful manner. During a public address in October 1984, Shultz described state-sponsored terrorism as a "weapon of unconventional war" being employed against the democracies of the West. Six months later, Casey told an audience at Tufts University that the United States was "engaged in a new form of low intensity conflict" and that international terrorism had become "a perpetual war without borders."[16] Shortly afterward Reagan's DCI repeated the claim to lawmakers, telling a closed session of the Senate Intelligence Committee that "the United States is at war" with terrorism.[17] The only way to effectively deal with this rising threat, the pair argued, was to adopt the use of preventive or preemptive force against terrorist groups. The secretary of state acknowledged that such a policy would necessitate the development of a public consensus around the right to the use of force without "the kind of evidence that can stand up in an American court of law," but warned that a failure to adapt would leave the United States hamstrung by confusion and indecisiveness.[18]

Shultz and Casey's hard line found form with the introduction of National Security Decision Directive (NSDD) 138 in April 1984. Titled simply "Combating Terrorism," the document was written predominantly by Oliver North, the National Security Council (NSC) member responsible for low-intensity warfare, self-declared "de-facto counterterrorism coordinator," and a mentee of Casey.[19] The fact that combating terrorism was such a significant part of the president's public discourse, yet was overseen by a single junior member of the NSC reinforces the rhetoric-first manner in which the Reagan administration functioned, and the extent to which in actual policy terms it remained a low-tier issue. Drawn from a combination of the president's bold statements and the approach championed by Shultz and Casey, NSDD-138's proposals were later described by Tim Naftali as "a declaration of war against international terrorism," while Noel Koch, who had served as the Pentagon director of special planning with responsibility for antiterrorism and counterterrorism at the time, later reflected that the approach marked "a quantum leap in countering terrorism."[20] The directive acknowledged for the first time that terrorism posed a threat to the national security of the United States and ordered the development of capabilities to enable the "pre-emptive neutralization of anti-American terrorist groups" and of a clandestine capability for overseas reprisals.[21] Reagan's willingness to sign off on the aggressive measures revealed his acute awareness of the political damage terrorism could cause a president. He had witnessed Carter's authority bleed out as a result of the Iranian hostage crisis—a situation he and his campaign team exploited to present the beleaguered president as feckless and weak. The increasing tempo of terrorist incidents, including Reagan's own hostage crisis in Lebanon where Hezbollah was kidnapping, and in some cases killing, American and European citizens, forced the president into action. Unfortunately, as with so many policy initiatives introduced by the Reagan administration, the directive's origins in populist rhetoric rather than a coordinated administration-wide strategy ensured its measures failed to become embedded as the necessary follow-through and details were overlooked, and wider Cold War objectives that were directly contradictory to the counterterrorism agenda won priority.[22]

One consequence of basing policymaking upon presidential rhetoric was that officials often acted independently on what they believed to be the operant assumptions of "Reaganism." While Reagan invoked a war paradigm against terrorism in his speeches, and NSDD-138 framed counterterrorism in national security terms, the agenda the president had articulated for his secretary of defense was a long way from Delta Force raids on terrorist safe havens or military strikes against its state sponsors. During the 1980 election the Reagan campaign had formulated a narrative—with some veracity—that the US defense budget had declined more than 20 percent through the 1970s, causing the nation's military might to wither. The fear among Reagan's neoconservative advisors was that any sense of American weakness could encourage the Soviet Union to include military action in its foreign policy calculus. As a result, Reagan campaigned on, and his secretary of defense, Caspar Weinberger, delivered, the largest peacetime military buildup in American history.[23] The strategic purpose behind this investment was articulated in NSDD-75, commonly known as the Reagan doctrine, which stated, "Soviet calculations of possible war outcomes under any contingency must always result in outcomes so unfavorable to the USSR that there would be no incentive for Soviet leaders to initiate an attack."[24]

Key to achieving the military buildup was the maintenance of congressional support and the restoration of the public's faith in the US military. Post-Vietnam defeatism, combined with the hostility that had developed between the civilians who had protested the war and the veterans who had fought in it, required a realignment of the American psyche.[25] To help achieve this goal, the Pentagon reached out to screenwriters and production studios in Hollywood, Israel and Canada, as well as developing collaborations with authors, artists, and even toy manufacturers to create what has been dubbed the "military-entertainment complex."[26] The highly patriotic, action-orientated output of this alliance eschewed the complex morality behind the geopolitical conflicts that characterized the international tensions fueling the terrorism of the 1980s. Instead, Americans were sold a simplified fantasy world in which the United States represented the forces of good, fighting for freedom against the "evil empire" of the Soviet Union, the tyrannical desires of Middle Eastern dictators, and the mindless violence of bloodthirsty terrorists. In this alternative reality, the United States' victory was assured as the indomitable Chuck Norris freed American hostages from Beirut in *The Delta Force*, Louis Gosset Jr. aided a young pilot to free his father from an Arab dictator in *Iron Eagle*, and Tom Clancy's fictional CIA analyst Jack Ryan foiled IRA terror plots in the novel *Patriot Games*.

The jingoistic fantasies of the military-entertainment complex achieved their primary purpose, rehabilitating the military's image and generating the support necessary for Reagan's arms buildup. But the need to maintain the simplified view of the world they created paralyzed Pentagon counterterrorism efforts. Combating terrorism is, as the political analyst and former CIA operations officer Graham Fuller has observed, a "very rough game." As opposed to the black and white world projected by the pro-American propaganda, terrorism and efforts to prevent it tend to exist in what Fuller describes as a "gray area." "Sometimes to win," Fuller asserts, "you have to use very rough tactics."[27] Shultz had addressed the moral difficulties presented by active measures of counterterrorism during his 1984 address, admitting that "fighting terrorism will not be a clean or pleasant contest," before adding that as a primary target of such tactics, the United States had "no choice but to play it."[28] The disastrous consequences of Operation Eagle Claw four years earlier had exposed the high risk reality of counterterrorism operations. Desperate to free the American hostages from their Iranian captors, Carter had authorized the Pentagon's recently formed Delta Force counterterrorism unit to undertake an audacious rescue mission in April 1980. Bad luck, poor planning, and a lack of experience saw the mission end in the Iranian desert before the rescue team got near Tehran, with eight personnel losing their lives as the result of an aircraft collision.[29] Already politically weakened by the hostage crisis, the failure of the operation amplified the acute sense of incompetence surrounding Carter, prompting one of his advisors to lament that "the President's chances of re-election probably died on the desert of Iran with the eight brave soldiers who gave their lives trying to free the American hostages."[30]

The political risk associated with counterterrorism missions did not escape Weinberger's notice. He knew that a repeat scenario would jeopardize the support the DoD was rebuilding and subsequently put the military buildup at risk. Speaking at the National Press Club in November 1984, the secretary of defense challenged the hard-line position Shultz had proposed a month earlier, setting out new guidelines for the use of force that explicitly precluded the sort of small-scale operation Delta Force had been created to undertake. The Weinberger doctrine, as the guidelines became known, stated that any military deployment was to be fully briefed to Congress and the American public before commencement, removing the element of surprise necessary for preemptive operations. Furthermore force was only to be deployed "wholeheartedly," taking the option of small-scale raids and rescue missions off the table.[31] As a result, despite the continued rise in terrorist violence during Reagan's time in office, Delta Force was not deployed. "For many years, they were kind of a joke," reflected Colonel W. Patrick Lang, a former member of US Special Forces and Intelligence. "They were the 'Big, Bad, Weightlifting Guys,' you know, down at Fort Bragg, . . . but they never got to fight anybody."[32] While the military buildup and its subsequent glorification via the military-entertainment complex enabled the DoD to project a rehabilitated image of strength and confidence on the world stage, the Pentagon's refusal to play a counterterrorism role left the wider US government looking hesitant and inert.

The Weinberger doctrine created paralysis among the upper echelons of Reagan's administration. Shultz and Casey were confident that their hard-line agenda channeled the president's desire to respond forcefully to terrorism, while the secretary of defense was adamant that his prioritization of the military buildup was sanctioned by Reagan. The administration was saddled with what Hal Brands has dubbed "the worst-of-both-worlds policy," with tough talk and very little action.[33] By September 1985 the American public, for whom terrorism had been a matter of concern since the Iranian hostage crisis, were beginning to share Shultz's and Casey's frustration at the government's inability to mount a meaningful response. Officials working for Vice President George H. W. Bush reported that 78 percent of Americans favored a "major effort" to "take steps to combat terrorism," an increase of 24 percent from the previous year. Reflecting blowback from the exaggerated glory of the military-entertainment complex, the same officials noted: "The American people seem to be waiting for Dirty Harry, Rambo and John Wayne to 'stick it to 'em.'"[34] With the president's authority on the line, the national security advisor, Robert McFarlane, warned Reagan that he "did not have a team in national security affairs." "Your Secretaries of State and Defense agree on next to nothing." McFarlane implored the president to either sack one of the two men or to get more involved in the policy process by determining which of his conflicting visions should take priority. Reagan, however, remained aloof, unwilling to risk one of his central Cold War policies in the form of the arms buildup to address the growing terrorist threat, and instead instructed his disgruntled national security advisor to "just make it work."[35]

The deadlock over the use of military force against terrorists was temporarily broken following the bombing of West Berlin's La Belle discothèque in April 1986. The venue was deliberately targeted due to its popularity with US service personnel in an attack that killed two Americans and a Turkish woman and injured 229, including seventy-eight military staff. A communications intercept by the NSA directly linked the attack to the Libyan dictator Muamar Gaddafi, a terrorist sponsor whom Reagan had accused of perpetrating at least twenty-five terrorist incidents in the previous year.[36] The direct targeting of DoD personnel ensured that the reluctant secretary of defense would be forced to support a military response by a president finally stung into action. "I felt we must show Qaddafi that there was a price he would have to pay for that kind of behavior, that we wouldn't let him get away with it," Reagan later reflected.[37] Although the incident galvanized the divided administration into action, the retaliation revealed further problems with the US counterterrorism capability. After six years of sidelining the matter, the Pentagon had limited options. Cruise missile strikes were rejected over concerns that the wreckage of the cutting-edge technology could be passed on to the Soviet Union for reverse engineering, while Oliver North's aggressive plan to deploy Navy SEALs was vetoed by commanders as too risky.[38] In the end, the Pentagon opted for a sledgehammer over a scalpel, launching a large-scale bombing raid, code-named "Operation El Dorado Canyon," on April 15, 1986.

Numerous sites across the Libyan capital of Tripoli and the eastern city of Benghazi were targeted for their connection to terrorist infrastructure, including Gaddafi's own residence. Despite careful planning and the US aircraft utilizing the latest in precision guidance technology, the decision to drop tons of munitions onto targets located in crowded urban environments exposed the difficulty associated with undertaking forceful counterterrorism operations against opponents who conceal their forces among noncombatants. Thirty-seven civilians were reported killed, with hundreds more injured, putting the loss of innocent life from the United States' retaliation well beyond that caused by Gaddafi's initial act of terror.[39] Two American aviators were also killed when their F-111 was shot down by a Libyan surface-to-air missile. In the short term the attack reduced the tempo of violence, but intelligence reports later concluded that Gaddafi had not been deterred; the analysis was confirmed two years later by the regime's bombing of Pan Am Flight 103 over Lockerbie, Scotland, in which all 259 passengers lost their lives, as did a eleven victims on the ground.[40] Politically the operation was met with international condemnation. The United Nations General Assembly rejected the Reagan administration's justification that the raid was an act of self-defense under Article 51 of the UN Charter and instead adopted a resolution condemning the raid as a violation of international law.[41] Domestically, however, the raid was generally well received, with a *New York Times*/ABC poll revealing that 77 percent of American public approved.[42] Although Reagan's delivery on the threat he had been making since his first election campaign played well with voters, the high collateral damage, international backlash, and limited impact on Gaddafi's terror campaign ensured Operation El Dorado Canyon was the administration's only foray into military counterterrorism. Its consequences seemed to validate Weinberger's argument that American military force was the wrong tool for the job and ensured that the raid was a one-off, rather than the adoption of a war paradigm against terrorism.

Two months prior to Operation El Dorado Canyon, with debate still rife over the administration's counterterrorism agenda, Casey delivered a speech at Fordham University titled "Scouting the Future." The DCI used the address to share his belief that it was the responsibility of the intelligence community, in particular the CIA, to look "across the broad spectrum of international political, economic, military, sociological, and demographic developments . . . and to distill from them careful assessments of problems we will face now and past the year 2000."[43] In identifying the rising tide of terrorism as a legitimate national security threat and correctly predicting that the US lacked the necessary tools to successfully counter it, Casey had exercised this foresight. A month before the Fordham speech, under intense pressure from Reagan to show greater initiative in the fight against terrorism, Casey had set out to evolve the CIA into an agency that could fill the vacuum left by the DoD's disengagement.[44] NSDD-207 was introduced on January 20, 1986, and while it reiterated much of what had been proposed in NSDD-138 two years earlier, it bypassed the interdepartmental deadlock that had undermined the preceding directive by explicitly giving the CIA responsibility to "establish an all-source fusion center for international terrorism" and authorizing Langley to oversee the rapid establishment of a "clandestine service capability for preventing, pre-empting and/or disrupting international terrorist activity."[45] Two weeks later the CIA's Counterterrorism Center (CTC) was formed under the leadership of the respected but controversial operations officer Duane Clarridge.

The CTC was, in its founder's own words, "nothing short of a revolution within the CIA" and set a number of important precedents in the United States' approach to counterterrorism. It was unique in bringing together staff from across the directorates of intelligence, operations, and science and technology, which ensured that the agency's full capabilities could be brought to bear against international terror groups. The center was also the first CIA entity to transcend Langley's traditional regional structure. In recognizing the new waves of terrorism as worldwide in their inception and execution, Casey authorized Clarridge's request for a global remit to hunt terrorists. Lacking the DoD's support to act on this new authority, Clarridge sought a technological solution to enable him to wage a global war against terrorists. Drawing a lesson from Operation El Dorado Canyon, the CTC chief instructed his staff to develop "a better way to send a message" to terrorists than an "expansive military raid with heavy collateral damage." The cutting-edge solution was a small, pilotless drone. Dubbed the "Eagle Program," the CTC's five prototypes were fitted with small rockets and explosives to enable the precise targeting of individuals and low-noise wooden propellers, intercept equipment, and an infrared camera for close surveillance of targets.[46] While wider events, discussed below, prevented the CTC from developing this approach during Reagan's remaining time in office, its foundations eventually saw the center charged with tracking and neutralizing Osama bin Laden in the late 1990s, and spearheading the United States' war against his group and their Taliban hosts following the 9/11 attacks. The armed drone, through a staggered and spluttering development, eventually evolved into General Atomics' Predator, the platform that, along with its successor the Reaper, became the primary tool in the CTC's extensive post-9/11 targeted killing program, a campaign based upon the founding principles of the CTC.[47] While Reagan's failure to manage the deadlock between his officials left the DoD lacking the necessary capacity to combat terrorism, it sparked a wave of innovation within the CIA, which established the architecture that eventually become the backbone of the United States' global War on Terror.

For all that the Reagan-era reforms eventually helped empower the CIA in its aggressive pursuit of terrorists, the administration undermined these positive developments through the catastrophic impact of two policies spawned directly from the Reagan doctrine—an approach that conclusively illustrates the priority the Reagan administration gave to its Cold War confrontation with the Soviet Union over its counterterrorism policies. Established in January 1983, the doctrine's key strategic intention was to provide overt and covert aid to anticommunist guerrillas and resistance movements with the aim of rolling back what were perceived to be Soviet-backed governments in Africa, Asia, and Latin America. Hailed by Reagan's proponents as the bold approach that ultimately helped overwhelm the Soviet Union and bring the Cold War to an end, the willful short-termism involved in the doctrine's challenge to communist regimes at any cost made a mockery of Casey's advocacy for thoughtful foresight. The breaking of the Iran-Contra scandal in November 1986 exposed the administration's illegal funding of the Contra rebels against the Sandinista government in the tiny country of Nicaragua, and with it, the hypocrisy inherent in Reagan's doctrine. The brutal rebels were no better than the terrorist groups the president had railed against since assuming office, and their actions raised questions about the United States' own role as a state sponsor of terror. Furthermore, for all of Casey's talk of scouting the future, the decision to back the Contras was based upon an outdated perspective on Latin America, drawn from what Senator Frank Church described as the persistent myth of "Communism as a single, hydra-headed serpent," which Casey and his coconspirators believed it was the CIA's duty to "cut off each ugly head, wherever and however it may appear."[48] By failing to differentiate between the hapless Sandinistas and legitimate national security threats, Casey severely undermined his credibility and with it the counterterrorism agenda he had championed.

The Iran portion of the scandal, which saw the government breaching international sanctions to covertly sell arms to the revolutionary government, in part to raise the funds for the Contras and as a misbegotten plot to free the American hostages held by Iran's Lebanese proxy, Hezbollah, was even more damaging. The deal exposed the administration's collusion with the very sponsors of terrorism Reagan had been spouting fiery rhetoric against since the first hostage crisis under Carter. Although Reagan and his Republican successor, George H. W. Bush, survived Iran-Contra without a major upheaval, the same cannot be said for the administration's counterterrorism agenda.[49] Casey died of a brain tumor in May 1987 before he could testify to Congress for his role in the affair; North, heavily implicated in the deal, was dismissed by Reagan in November 1986; and Clarridge, closely linked to the Contras, was forced to retire on June 1, 1987. With two of the key architects of the hard-line counterterrorism agenda gone, and the man selected to lead their offensive forced out of the CIA, the appetite for risk taking at Langley evaporated. The CTC abandoned Clarridge's "war room" vision and instead adopted the traditional report-writing culture the hard-liners had sought to replace. "Casey had envisaged it as something different than what it eventually became," rued Vincent Cannistraro, an operations officer who had arrived at the CTC shortly after it was founded.[50] It would not be until nonstate terrorism had fully demonstrated its potential by toppling the twin towers of the World Trade Center that the CTC would once again function as the aggressive counterterrorism hub its founders had intended.

As the fallout from the Reagan doctrine's application in Latin America weakened the United States' counterterrorism capability, its execution in the Asian states of Afghanistan and Pakistan dramatically strengthened the nation's future terrorist enemies. The CIA's covert activity in the region predated the Reagan administration, with Carter, prompted by his national security advisor, Zbigniew Brzezinski, signing a finding on July 3, 1979, authorizing the covert provision of $500,000 of nonlethal aid to the self-styled Afghan mujahideen fighters, who had declared a religious struggle—or jihad—against the country's USSR-aligned government.[51] The Soviet Union's invasion of Afghanistan in December of the same year had been intended to crush the rebels and contain the spread of their Islam-inspired insurgency to other Muslim territories along the Soviet Union's central Asian frontier. Instead, the brutal tactics employed by the Red Army, coupled with the unwelcome presence of a foreign atheistic power, inflamed the religious dimension of the conflict and swelled the mujahideen's ranks. Seeking to capitalize on the growing anti-Soviet jihad, the Carter administration deepened American involvement and permitted the CIA to begin providing weapons to the mujahideen, which were covertly funneled over the border by Pakistan's influential Inter-Services Intelligence (ISI).[52]

The United States' close links to the Pakistani military dated back to the early years of the Cold War, when President Dwight D. Eisenhower had authorized the establishment of a military aid program to the young nation, designed to act as a counterbalance to neighboring India, which was judged by policymakers as being too close to the Soviet Union.[53] Billions of dollars were poured into Pakistan's armed forces to transform the state into a bulwark against South Asian socialism.⁵⁴ Two decades later, the military establishment had become so powerful that following a period of civil and political disorder, it staged a coup. The four-star general behind the uprising, Zia-ul-Haq, assumed the role of dictator and promptly initiated a set of reactionary Islamic reforms in which liberal elements of the Pakistani government were purged and a strict Salafist puritanism was enforced. Cautious of Zia's Islamist agenda, the Carter administration kept the covert aid program modest, investing enough to harass the Soviet occupation, but restricting the types of weapons and training the ISI could provide their mujahideen clients. The Reagan doctrine transformed this delicate balance, establishing the more ambitious goal of forcing the Soviets out of Afghanistan. Despite Zia's strict Islamist outlook, his regional goal to encompass Afghanistan in his "Islamic renaissance," and the fact that the United States was itself struggling with Islamic-tinged terrorism, the Reagan administration opted to further empower the Islamist cause by dramatically increasing the flow of arms.⁵⁵ Predictably, given Zia's ideological outlook, the ISI purposefully funneled the new resources to the most radical elements of the mujahideen, such as the warlord Gulbuddin Hekmatyar, whose group, Hezb-i-Islami, advocated the establishment of a political order rooted in archaic Islamic precepts.

In line with NSDD-75's stated objective to "keep maximum pressure on Moscow for withdrawal and to ensure that the Soviets' political, military, and other costs remain high while the occupation continues," the Reagan administration sought to draw more fighters to the anti-Soviet jihad.⁵⁶ In a deal struck with its ally Saudi Arabia, the kingdom agreed to match every American dollar invested into the mujahideen and to promote its jihadist cause.⁵⁷ Additional funds flowed into the hard-line groups from Islamic charities and mosque collections across the Sunni community, forming ideological and financial support networks that continued to funnel money and recruits into the extremist cause long after the Soviets had withdrawn.⁵⁸ In March 1985 Reagan further escalated American support by signing NSDD-166, which instructed the CIA to use "all available means" to support the mujahideen.⁵⁹ Within months the ISI was running a network of formal training camps. As with the Reagan administration's support for the Contras, these American-funded camps blurred the line between guerrilla warfare and terrorism, with fighters trained in sabotage techniques and the targeted killings of Soviet officers. Despite his hard-line support for aggressive counterterrorism techniques, Casey openly endorsed attacks in urban areas against Soviet supporters, describing the consistent low-intensity warfare taught in the camps as "death by a thousand cuts."⁶⁰ As many as 18,000 recruits passed through these camps each year, including an influx of Arab volunteers steered to the conflict by the Saudi state,

Wahhabi clerics, and recruitment centers established in the Pakistani border town of Peshawar.[61] Collectively these changes distorted the nature of Afghan jihad, radicalizing its agenda from one of local resistance to a global vision of Islamic revolution.

As American and Saudi funds enabled the insurgency to drag on, Afghanistan's refugee crisis worsened. Pakistan and Saudi Arabia took advantage of the chaos, pouring money into the creation of thousands of new madrassas along the Afghanistan-Pakistan border. Where in 1971 there were some 900 of these religious schools, by 1988 that number had increased to over 8,000.[62] While in principle these schools provided education, shelter, and safety for the vulnerable youth displaced by a decade of conflict, many of the new madrassas were places of extreme proselytization, where the Pakistani government allowed the leadership of the radical mujahideen groups free rein over the increasingly hard-line curriculum.[63] From 1986 to 1992, the United States Agency for International Development (USAID) directly supported this indoctrination, sponsoring a $50 million education program geared at promoting jihadist ideology. An example taken from a mathematics textbook provided through the US program clearly illustrates the nature of the propaganda: "Grade 4—The speed of a Kalashnikov bullet is 800 meters per second. If a Russian is at a distance of 3,200 meters from a mujahid, and that mujahid aims at the Russian's head, calculate how many seconds it will take for the bullet to strike the Russian in the forehead."[64]

Thus many of the conflict's young male orphans were raised in what Neamatollah Nojumi has described as "a socio-psychological environment that guided them to understand the world in black and white, which was out of context with reality."[65] Tens of thousands of refugees were indoctrinated in a radical version of Islam, etched with ideas of military training and the importance of undertaking a forceful interpretation of jihad.[66] Once these young men graduated, the networks of training camps ensured that they could develop the deadly skills necessary to advance their singular vision of a righteous Islamic society, governed under the strict medieval interpretation of Sharia that had formed their upbringing. Tragically the consequences of the Reagan doctrine were not unknown to the policymakers who advocated it. As the Soviet Union prepared to withdraw from Afghanistan, CIA analysts reported that the factions left in control of the devastated country would be "strongly fundamentalist" and "actively hostile, especially toward the United States."[67] Such warnings were overlooked in favor of the doctrine's core goal of demonstrating to the Soviet Union the costs of "unacceptable behavior" in the world, which as Robert Rakove argues in his chapter on Afghanistan in this volume, was seen as having such profound global significance to the Cold War that it overruled the lower-tier counterterrorism agenda, even among those such as Shultz and Casey who pushed for a hard-line approach.[68]

As predicted, the religious fervor stoked by the United States, Pakistan, and Saudi Arabia did not end when the Soviets withdrew. The mujahideen fractured into hundreds of lethal shards, including al-Qaeda, the Taliban, and the Haqqani Network. Having vanquished one superpower, these groups quickly turned their attention to the next impediment to their dreams of a global caliphate, their former patron. When the anti-American attacks began with Ramzi Yousef's bombing of the World Trade Center in 1993, the FBI's investigation labeled the movement he represented a "new generation of Sunni Islamic terrorism." Assessing the emergence of this new threat, the FBI's report highlighted the importance of the radical's "worldwide network of support for funding, training and safe haven," the "crucial" nature of the Afghan training camps, the access to "technical resources" and the environment that enabled the recruitment of "like-minded radicals."[69] The al-Qaeda leader Ayman al-Zawahiri later supported the FBI's analysis, writing shortly after 9/11 that the Afghan jihad "was a training course of the utmost importance to prepare Muslim mujahidin to wage their awaited battle against the superpower that now has sole dominance over the globe, namely, the United States."[70] The emergence of the jihadists from Afghanistan's training camps was, as the CIA analyst Paul Pillar explained, a "watershed in global terrorism—the debut of the new generation of unaffiliated, religious/political violence," and while the movement's roots can be traced back to well before the Reagan doctrine's application in Afghanistan, it was the infrastructure, training, financial connections, and jihadist narrative that the anti-Soviet jihad provided that truly transformed the jihadist cause into something capable of waging a sustained guerilla warfare campaign against the United States.[71]

Reagan entered the White House having campaigned in part on his determination to defeat terrorism. He had presented his predecessor as weak and incompetent, suggesting that if only he had the will to confront the growing menace, the United States could eradicate it. Once Reagan was in office, however, it became clear that there was a gulf between talking tough about terrorism and formulating a successful strategy to counter it. After seven bruising years in which his administration failed to score any decisive victories against either the perpetrators of terrorist attacks or those who funded them, Reagan acknowledged his administration's lack of progress in a meeting of the National Security Planning Group on February 24, 1987, when he lamented that "experience has taught us that there is no clear, easy solution to this problem."[72] Some scholars have agreed with Reagan's assessment, citing the fact that the administrations that succeeded Reagan struggled with many of the same fundamental issues.[73] Such a resignation however overlooks the extent to which much of the Reagan administration's failures in counterterrorism were of its own making, as well as the degree to which its own wider Cold War policies exacerbated the challenges faced by its successors.

The president's inability to manage the divisions between his senior staff over the best approach to combating terrorism exposed both his personal indecisiveness and the administration's lack of a coherent strategy. The failure to coordinate policies across the government—a signature of the Reagan administration and a responsibility that ultimately rests with the president himself—saw one initiative pulling against the other. And in a battle between Cold War objectives and a focused campaign against terrorism, it was the United States' superpower competition that consistently won out, thereby not just depriving the counterterrorism agenda of the focus it required, but frequently exacerbating the root causes and problems. The much vaunted military buildup, promoted as vital to the United States' national security, stymied aggressive counterterrorism measures, and the failure to secure the DoD's support for the agenda left the United States sorely ill equipped to deal with the hostage-taking tactics employed by groups such as Hezbollah. This lack of options led to desperation, and with it the administration's grievous sin of negotiating with the very terror sponsors Reagan had verbally committed his government to destroying. While the creation of the CTC, efforts to push for the aggressive neutralization of terrorists, and the adoption of an early unmanned drone as a tool for surveillance and precision strikes set important precedents, the fallout of the Iran-Contra scandal stunted these approaches precisely when they were needed. The Reagan administration's reforms made the CIA the lead agency in the United States' battle against international terrorism just before the fallout of its illegal use stripped Langley of the talent, the energy, and the will necessary to execute its new mission. In its evaluation of the CIA's failings in the run-up to the September 11 attacks, the 9/11 commission explicitly identified the agency's aversion to risk as key in their failure to neutralize Osama bin Laden and his terrorist network.[74] A number of factors were identified as contributing to this mindset, including budget cuts, miscommunication between policymakers and agents, and a lack of clear legal authorization from President Clinton. However, the evaluation overlooked the long-term impact of Iran-Contra, which had defanged the CTC in the very year that al-Qaeda was formed.

When evaluating counterterrorism policy, one must distinguish between approaches that fail to prevent terrorism and those that actively enable it. Unfortunately for the United States, the Reagan doctrine falls into the latter category. Premised on coopting geopolitically useful but otherwise distasteful allies against the Soviet Union, the strategy ensured that fundamentalist anti-Western groups were ascendant within the fragmented Afghan insurgency. The Afghan jihad catalyzed Islamist sentiment throughout the Sunni Muslim world, forging a vast cohort of individuals in the intoxicating ideological flames the Reagan administration stoked. While in the short-term its application may have been the bane of the Soviet Union, it was a boon for militant Islam, injecting an energy and dynamism that transformed the radical movement. For all its effort to establish an efficient way to kill terrorists, the Reagan administration's exploitation of Sunni Islamic radicalism fueled an ideological fervor that has proven much more dangerous and harder to eliminate than any individual terrorist.

Notes

1. President George W. Bush receives a briefing during a meeting with CIA Director George Tenet, National Security Advisor Condoleezza Rice, and Chief of Staff Andy Card at Camp David, Saturday, Sept. 29, 2001, White House photo by Eric Draper, White House News and Policies, September 2001, George W. Bush White House Archives, 29 Sept. 2001, https://georgewbush-whitehouse.archives.gov/news/releases/2001/09/images/20010929.html.

2. Rumsfeld to Myers, 17 Oct. 2001, http://nsarchive2.gwu.edu//NSAEBB/NSAEBB358a/doc19.pdf.

3. Hal Brands, *Making the Unipolar Moment: US Foreign Policy and the Rise of the Post–Cold War Order* (Ithaca, NY: Cornell University Press, 2016), 340–341.

4. "Global Terrorism Database," National Consortium of the Study of Terrorism and Responses to Terrorism, http://www.start.umd.edu/gtd/globe/index.html (accessed 12 Mar. 2021).

5. Brian Michael Jenkins, *New Modes of Conflict* (Santa Monica, CA: RAND Corporation, 1983), 3, http://www.rand.org/content/dam/rand/pubs/reports/2006/R3009.pdf.

6. Frank M. Benis, *US Marines in Lebanon, 1982–1984* (Washington, DC: US Marine Corps History and Museums Division, 1987), 133–134; Timothy J. Gerathy and Alfred M. Gray Jr., *Peacekeepers at War: Beirut 1983—The Marine Commander Tells His Story* (Washington, DC: Potomac Books, 2009), 91–123.

7. Reagan, "A Strategy for Peace in the '80s," 19 Oct. 1980, American Presidency Project (APP), https://www.presidency.ucsb.edu.

8. "President Jimmy Carter and Governor Ronald Reagan Presidential Debate," 28 Oct. 1980, APP.

9. George C. Wilson, "Pentagon Scrubbed a Second Iranian Rescue Plan as Too Dangerous," *Washington Post*, 25 Jan. 1981.

10. Reagan, "Remarks at the Welcoming Ceremony for the Freed American Hostages," 27 Jan. 1981, APP.

11. Sean Wilentz, *The Age of Reagan: A History, 1974–2008* (New York: HarperCollins, 2009), 151; Ronald Reagan, *An American Life* (New York: Pocket Books, 1990), 161.

12. Robert Timberg, *The Nightingale's Song* (New York: Touchstone, 1995), 448.

13. Haynes Johnson, *Sleepwalking through History: America in the Reagan Years* (New York: Norton, 2003), 142.

14. Garry Wills, *Reagan's America: Innocents at Home* (New York: Touchstone, 1995), 423–425.

15. Francis Fitzgerald, *Way out There in the Blue: Reagan, Star Wars and the End of the Cold War* (New York: Touchstone, 2000), 15.

16. William Casey, "The Practice of International Terrorism Has to Be Resisted by All Legal Means," Fletcher School of Law and Diplomacy, 17 Apr. 1985, in *Scouting the Future: The Public Speeches of William J. Casey*, ed. Herbert E. Meyer (Washington, DC: Regnery Gateway, 1989), 193–204.

17. Casey, "The Practice of International Terrorism," 193.

18. George P. Shultz, "Terrorism and the Modern World," address at Park Avenue Synagogue, 25 Oct. 1984, *Air Force Magazine*, 1 Dec. 2010, https://www.airforcemag.com/article/1210keeperfile/.

19. Neil Livingstone, *Cult of Counterterrorism* (Washington, DC: Lexington Books: 1990), 231–232; Oliver L. North and William Novak, *Under Fire: An American Story* (New York: HarperCollins, 1991), 179–182, 197; Joseph Persico, *Casey: The Lives and Secrets of William J. Casey from the OSS to the CIA* (New York: Penguin, 1990), 397.

20. "Secret Policy on Terrorism Given Airing," *Washington Post*, 18 Apr. 1984; Livingstone, *Cult of Counterterrorism*, 234

21. NSDD-138, "Combating Terrorism," 3 Apr. 1984, https://fas.org/irp/offdocs/nsdd/nsdd-138.pdf.

22. David Wills, *The First War on Terrorism: Counter-Terrorism Policy during the Reagan Administration* (Lanham, MD: Rowman and Littlefield, 2003), 84.

23. Jesús Velasco, *Neoconservatives in US Foreign Policy under Ronald Reagan and George W. Bush: Voices behind the Throne* (Baltimore: Johns Hopkins University Press, 2010), 111.

24. NSDD-75, "US Relations with the USSR," 17 Jan. 1983, https://fas.org/irp/offdocs/nsdd/nsdd-75.pdf.

25. Adrian R. Lewis, *The American Way of War: The History of US Military Force from World War II to Operation Iraqi Freedom* (New York: Routledge, 2007), 295.

26. Georg Löfflmann, "Hollywood, the Pentagon, and the Cinematic Production of National Security," *Critical Studies on Security* 1, no. 3 (2013): 280–294; David Sirota, "How the '80s Programmed Us for War," *Salon*, 15 Mar. 2011, http://www.salon.com/2011/03/15/sirota_excerpt_back_to_our_future/.

27. Richard Sale, *Clinton's Secret Wars: The Evolution of a Commander in Chief* (New York: Thomas Dunne Books, 2009), 290.

28. Shultz, "Terrorism and the Modern World."

29. Mark Bowden, *Guests of the Ayatollah: The First Battle in the West's War with Militant Islam* (London: Atlantic Books, 2007), 460–467; "Holloway Report into Operation Eagle Claw," 23 Aug. 1980, National Security Archive, https://nsarchive.gwu.edu/dc.html?doc=6536632-National-Security-Archive-Doc-10-Final-Report-of.

30. Theodore H. White, *America in Search of Itself: The Making of the President 1956–1980* (New York: Harper and Row, 1982), 21.

31. Caspar Weinberger, "The Uses of Military Power," 28 Nov. 1984, National Press Club, PBS.org, https://www.pbs.org/wgbh/pages/frontline/shows/military/force/weinberger.html.

32. Jeremy Scahill, *Dirty Wars: The World Is a Battlefield* (New York: Nation Books, 2013), 54.

33. Brands, *Making the Unipolar Moment*, 251.

34. Brands, *Making the Unipolar Moment*, 251–252.

35. Timberg, *The Nightingale's Song*, 359; Robert McFarlane and Zofia Smardz, *Special Trust* (New York: Cadell and Davies, 1994), 268.

36. Reagan, "Remarks at the Annual Convention of the American Bar Association," 8 July 1985, APP.

37. Reagan, *An American Life*, 518.

38. Ben Bradlee Jr., *Guts and Glory: The Rise and Fall of Oliver North* (New York: Donald I. Fine, 1988), 353–354.

39. Mark E. Kosnik, *An Analysis of the United States Use of Force against Terrorism*, 1999, Weatherhead Center for International Affairs, Harvard University, https://wcfia.harvard.edu/publications/analysis-united-states-use-military-force-against-terrorism; David C. Martin and John Walcott, *Best Laid Plans: The Inside Story of America's War on Terrorism* (New York: Simon and Schuster, 1989), 310; Brian L. Davis, *Qaddafi, Terrorism, and the Origins of the US Attack on Libya* (New York: Praeger, 1990), 169.

40. CIA, "Libya: Reviewing Terrorist Capabilities," Apr. 1989, CIA Electronic Reading Room (CIAERR), https://www.cia.gov/library/readingroom/home.

41. UN General Assembly Resolution 41/38, 20 Nov. 1986, https://undocs.org/en/A/RES/41/38.

42. Reagan, *An American Life*, 520; Seymour Hersh, "Target Qaddafi," *New York Times*, 22 Feb. 1987.

43. Casey, "Scouting the Future: Meeting the Challenges of a Rapidly Changing World," 25 Feb. 1986, in *Scouting the Future: The Public Speeches of William J. Casey*, ed. Herbert E. Meyer (Washington, DC: Regnery Gateway, 1989), 120–121.

44. Duane Clarridge with Digby Diehl, *A Spy for All Seasons: My Life in the CIA* (New York: Scribner, 1997), 320.

45. NSDD-207, "The National Program for Combatting Terrorism," 20 Jan. 1986, https://fas.org/irp/offdocs/nsdd/nsdd-207.

46. Clarridge, *A Spy for All Seasons*, 339; Steve Coll, *Ghost Wars: The Secret History of the CIA, Afghanistan and Bin Laden* (New York: Penguin, 2005), 143.

47. Christopher Fuller, *See It/Shoot It: The Secret History of the CIA's Lethal Drone Program* (New Haven, CT: Yale University Press, 2017), 116–121.

48. "CIA: Maker of Policy or Tool?," *New York Times*, 25 Apr. 1966.

49. Rhodri Jeffreys-Jones, *Cloak and Dollar: The History of American Secret Intelligence* (New Haven: Yale University Press, 2002), 244.

50. Coll, *Ghost Wars*, 162.

51. Robert Gates, *From the Shadows: The Ultimate Insider's Story of Five Presidents and How They Won the Cold War* (New York: Simon and Schuster, 2006), 143–146.

52. Steve Coll, "Anatomy of a Victory: CIA's Covert Afghan War," *Washington Post*, 19 July 1992; Coll, *Ghost Wars*, 55.

53. Eisenhower, "Statement by the President on Military Aid to Pakistan," 25 Feb. 1954, APP.

54. Sultan Afroz, "The Cold War and United States Military Aid to Pakistan 1947–1960: A Reassessment," *South Asia* 18, no. 1 (1994), 67–72.

55. Charles G. Cogan, "Shawl of Lead," *Conflict* 10, no. 3 (1990): 189–204.

56. NSDD-75.

57. Coll, *Ghost Wars*, 65, 121; George Crile, *My Enemy's Enemy* (New York: Grove Atlantic, 2003), 238.

58. Yahia Baiza, *Education in Afghanistan: Developments, Influences and Legacies since 1901* (London: Routledge, 2013), 139.

59. Kirsten Lundberg, "Politics of a Covert Action: The US, the *Mujahideen*, and the Stinger Missile," John F. Kennedy School of Government, Harvard University, 9 Nov. 1999, https://case.hks.harvard.edu/politics-of-a-covert-action-the-u-s-the-mujahideen-and-the-stinger-missile/.

60. Persico, *Casey*, 429.

61. Coll, *Ghost Wars*, 126–127; Persico, *Casey*, 428–429; Bruce Riedel, *The Search for Al-Qaeda: Its Leadership, Ideology, and Future* (Washington, DC: Brookings Institution Press, 2010), 42–43.

62. Neamatollah Nojumi, *The Rise of the Taliban in Afghanistan: Mass Mobilization, Civil War, and the Future of the Region* (New York: Palgrave Macmillan, 2002), 98.

63. Nafay Choudhury, "The Localized Madrasas of Afghanistan: Their Political and Governance Entanglements," *Religion, State & Society* 45, no. 2 (2017), 120–140.

64. Craig Davis, "'A' Is for Allah, 'J' is for Jihad," *World Policy Report* 19, no. 1 (2002), 90–94.

65. Nojumi, *Rise and Fall of the Taliban*, 98.

66. Nojumi, *Rise and Fall of the Taliban*, 97–98; Coll, *Ghost Wars*, 283–289.

67. CIA, "USSR: Withdrawal from Afghanistan," Mar. 1988, CIAERR.

68. NSDD-75.

69. FBI, "Ramzi Yousef: A New Generation of Sunni Islamic Terrorists," 1995, in Steve Coll, *Ghost Wars: The Secret History of the CIA, Afghanistan, and bin Laden from the Soviet Invasion to September 10, 2001* (London: Penguin, 2005), 278–279; Walter Pincus, "Mueller Outlines Origin, Funding of Sept. 11 Plot," *Washington Post*, 6 June 2002.

70. Ayman al-Zawahiri, *Knights Under the Prophet's Banner*, in Laura Mansfield, *His Own Words: A Translation of the Writings of Dr. Ayman al Zawahiri* (New York: TLG Publications, 2006).

71. State Department Office of the Coordinator for Counterterrorism, "1994/1995 Patterns of Global Terrorism," https://fas.org/irp/threat/terror.htm; Coll, *Ghost Wars*, 261.

72. National Security Planning Group meeting record, 24 Feb. 1987, Ronald Reagan Presidential Library, Executive Secretariat–NSC, NSPG Records, box 90138, folder "NSPG 0146."

73. Brands, *Making the Unipolar Moment*, 254.

74. "The 9/11 Commission Report," 22 July 2004, https://9-11commission.gov/report/.

Chapter 4

Global Reaganomics

Budget Deficits, Capital Flows, and the International Economy

Michael De Groot

During Ronald Reagan's first term as president, the US financial relationship with the world transformed. Rather than serving as a net exporter of capital, as it had during most of the postwar period, the United States became a net importer. "The huge inflow reverses the nation's traditional role," *New York Times* journalist James Sterngold observed in November 1984. "Particularly since World War II, the United States has economically nurtured many other countries, offering finance, aid and direction. Now the nation has to wrestle with its own sudden dependence."[1] Capital flows into the United States contributed to financing American budget deficits, inaugurating an era of dependence on foreign investors that prevails to the present day. Foreign capital helped ensure that Washington could continue running budget deficits rather than making a difficult political decision about whether to make significant cuts to spending in defense or social safety nets or to increase taxes.

The existing literature on Reagan's economic policies has focused on the extent to which they benefited the domestic economy, a debate still colored by partisanship. On the one hand, critics contend that "Reaganomics" contributed to economic inequality, diminished the power of organized labor, hurt manufacturing industries, and introduced budget deficits the likes of which the country had never seen. On the other hand, proponents argue that

Reagan's policies helped tame inflation and led to one of the most impressive economic expansions in US history.

Often overlooked in this literature is the impact that Reaganomics had on international affairs, particularly the unexpected utility of finance and monetary policy as foreign policy tools.[2] Given the centrality of the United States in the international economy, the effects of Reaganomics rippled across the globe. For some countries, particularly those in Western Europe and East Asia, the US economic expansion ultimately served as an engine for their own recovery. The demand for dollar-denominated assets placed upward pressure on the dollar, making imports relatively cheap for American consumers. Americans' appetite for foreign products stimulated the Western European and East Asian economies, helping to lift them out of recession. Other countries were not so fortunate. Attracted by the American market, investors turned away from Eastern Europe and the developing world, magnifying the growing sovereign debt crisis in those regions.

These developments also played an important role in the collapse of the Soviet bloc. As Melvyn P. Leffler argues in this volume, Reagan did not have a grand strategy to bring the Soviet Union to its knees, but the president deserves credit for his willingness to engage his Soviet counterpart, Mikhail Gorbachev, in an effort to end the Cold War. This chapter suggests that Reagan's economic policies inadvertently made an additional contribution. The recovery of the capitalist economies enhanced the West's ideological authority to wage the Cold War at a time when the Soviet bloc sunk deeper into crisis. Additionally, high interest rates, the exchange rate of the dollar, and the US domination of capital markets had unintended second-order effects across the Iron Curtain. They caused a "credit crunch" in the socialist countries, which aggravated the interlinked economic and political crises already in motion across Eastern Europe.

When Reagan entered the White House in January 1981, he charted an ambitious agenda to revitalize American economic power. He inherited an economy struggling to recover from the travails of stagflation in the 1970s and still stumbling from high unemployment, rampant inflation, and low economic growth. Supported by policymakers such as secretary of the treasury Donald Regan and head of the Office of Management and Budget (OMB) David Stockman, Reagan embraced supply-side economics, which posits that reducing taxes and eliminating regulations on the market provides the best path to growth. Proponents of supply-side economics contend that taxes and onerous regulations stunt economic activity by reducing incentives; if the government instead lowered tax rates and deregulated markets, they argue, state revenue would actually increase thanks to higher rates of growth.

Reagan railed against what he saw as excessive government spending. The president preached the mantra of small government, telling the nation in February 1981, "We cannot delay in implementing an economic program aimed at both reducing tax rates to stimulate productivity and reducing the growth in government spending to reduce unemployment and inflation." Government spending, burdensome regulations, and high taxes had run out of control, he warned. Previous administrations had kicked the can down the road, refusing to live within their means, but now "we no longer have that luxury. We're out of time."[3]

Reagan accelerated the push for deregulation that had begun under the Carter administration, muscling the Economic Recovery and Tax Act (ERTA) through Congress in July 1981 and slashing income tax rates across the board. The ERTA called for a $749 billion tax cut to be phased over five years. The Reagan administration forecast a balanced budget by 1983, or 1984 at the latest.[4]

Despite Reagan's rhetoric about the importance of balanced budgets, a combination of factors dragged the government's finances deeper into the red than at any time in American history to that point. First, the Reagan administration expected that accelerating economic growth would help pay for the tax cuts, but officials grossly miscalculated. The promises of supply-side economics proved groundless in this case: tax cuts slashed government receipts, and the OMB had little idea how to compensate. "None of us really understands what's going on with all these numbers," Stockman admitted to journalist William Greider in the December 1981 issue of *Atlantic Monthly*. "People are getting from A to B and it's not clear how they are getting there." Stockman had to face reality, Greider wrote: "The economic theory behind the President's program wasn't working."[5] The article offered the first glimpse to the average American of what the Reagan revolution looked like behind the curtain, and it was not pretty. It almost led to Stockman's dismissal. Between 1980 and 1983, government spending rose by 2.2 percent and the budget deficit increased by 3.5 percent.[6] Furthermore, the Federal Reserve's successful battle against inflation brought "tax bracket creep" to an end as well. The tax system was not indexed for inflation, and in a high inflation economy, taxpayers' gross income increased and pushed them into higher tax brackets. As inflation decreased, the Treasury's inflation windfall fell too. "The Laffer curve couldn't pay for both" inflationary bracket creep and tax cuts, Stockman reflected. "Not even close."[7] About 40 percent of the reduction in government receipts stemmed from the fact that the OMB had not accounted for the decline of inflation in its calculations.[8]

Second, the OMB planned to pay for the tax cuts in part by slashing spending on social programs. "The success of the Reagan Revolution," Stockman wrote in his memoirs, "depended upon the willingness of the politicians to turn against their own handiwork—the bloated budget of the American welfare state."[9] A formidable bipartisan coalition of members of Congress, however, who worried that their senior constituents would abandon them if they gutted New Deal— and Great Society–era programs, bitterly opposed the plan. Social Security, in particular, was a "near-untouchable 'third rail' of American politics," insuring 140 million Americans and providing support to 36 million retirees, disabled workers, and their families.[10] Representative Claude Pepper (D-FL) blasted the cuts, saying that the "impunity with which this administration goes about slashing promised benefits is both astounding and frightening." Representative Olympia Snowe (R-ME) wondered "if the White House switchboard has been ringing like the phone in my district office."[11] Opponents charged that cutting benefits for the needy was immoral in the face of the large tax cuts, which disproportionately benefited the wealthy. Reagan was disappointed. The Democratic "leadership has refused to tackle the problem in an effort to find a bi-partisan solution," Reagan lamented. "They are staking it out as an '82 campaign issue in which we'll be portrayed as trying to pinch the Sr. Citizens."[12] Some programs had to tighten their belts: housing subsidies for low-income families, for example, fell from $84.7 billion in 1979 to $26 billion in 1984.[13] Nevertheless, most programs survived. "The American welfare state emerged from the ordeal largely intact," to Stockman's regret.[14]

Finally, spending on the military increased the budget deficit. While the administration aggressively pushed for cuts in many domestic programs, Reagan wanted to increase defense spending. Arguing that the Soviets had seized the initiative in the arms race and in the developing world, Reagan accelerated an arms buildup that Carter had started. He frequently charged that proponents of détente had allowed the Soviet Union to achieve military superiority. "You often hear that the United States and the Soviet Union are in an arms race," he said in an address to the nation in November 1982. "The truth is that while the Soviet Union has raced, we have not. . . . Today, in virtually every measure of military power, the Soviet Union enjoys a decided advantage."[15]

This narrative did not align with the findings of the Central Intelligence Agency, which disputed that Moscow had a decisive edge. Reagan, however, subscribed to the so-called "Team B" perspective, which held that the Soviets were much stronger than the CIA claimed. The president appointed hawks who shared his view, such as Secretary of Defense Caspar Weinberger, to important posts in his administration. The White House launched a massive military buildup with expenditures that totaled $1.5 trillion over five years, spending enormous sums on new missiles, bombers, fighter jets, and submarines.[16] Committed to overcoming the logic of "mutually assured destruction," Reagan introduced the Strategic Defense Initiative in March 1983, envisioning a missile defense system that would use space-based lasers to destroy incoming Soviet missiles. The president realized that military spending would weigh on the government's resources, but he believed that the Soviet challenge demanded a forceful response. "I wanted a balanced budget," Reagan wrote in his memoirs. "But I also wanted peace through strength."[17]

Reaganomics created unprecedented budget deficits. Stockman wrote that by 1982, "The fiscal situation was an utter, mind-numbing catastrophe."[18] The national debt increased at an alarming rate, from $914 billion in 1980 to $2.7 trillion in 1989. Reagan added more to the national debt in six years than all presidents combined in the previous 190 years.[19] Given his views about the dangers of big government, Reagan grasped the irony. "We who were going to balance the budget face the biggest budget deficits ever," Reagan wrote in his diary in December 1981.[20]

The key to financing these budget deficits came from an unexpected source: the Federal Reserve. Its chairman, Paul Volcker, had launched an aggressive program in October 1979 to reduce inflation and regain control over the money supply. He prioritized discipline over expansion and employment, seeking to create the necessary conditions for sustainable noninflationary economic growth. Interest rates skyrocketed to an astounding 18.5 percent by April 1980, and, after a brief recovery, the economy descended into a painful recession. Volcker's commitment to a tight monetary policy created enemies both inside the government and out. "That the country's, not to mention the Western world's economic (and therefore social and political) future should be subject to the personal whim of Volcker and his colleagues is simply unacceptable," National Security Council (NSC) staffer Norman Bailey complained.[21] "You have all but shut down the auto and housing industries, you are driving many businesses out of existence, and are the cause of the horrible unemployment problem," a woman from Florida wrote Volcker angrily.[22] Despite unemployment that rose a postwar high of 11 percent, Volcker refused to lower interest rates. He believed that they were the key to fighting inflation.[23] The standoff between Volcker's tight monetary policy and Reagan's fiscal spending "resembled cold war brinksmanship," economist William Silber writes.[24] Each man blamed the other for pursuing a policy that handicapped America's ability to achieve sustainable noninflationary growth.

Despite the domestic pressure to replace Volcker, Reagan stuck with him, even as Republicans suffered at the polls during the 1982 midterm elections. Although the medicine was painful, the president recognized that it was necessary. "We are attacking the core problems," Reagan assured British prime minister Margaret Thatcher in September 1983.[25] Nevertheless, despite modest fiscal cuts and increased income taxes, Reagan refused to change his approach in a way that would meaningfully close the budget deficit. The constellation of economic forces was set. "As long as the United States has very large budget deficits," the chairman of the Council of Economic Advisers, Martin Feldstein, wrote in January 1983, "we are likely to have high real interest rates, a very strong dollar, and sizeable trade deficits."[26]

The primary rationale for keeping interest rates high was to tackle inflation, but Volcker and his colleagues at the Federal Reserve recognized that the high interest rates could serve another purpose: the policy could help fund the budget deficits by attracting foreign capital. Investors with deep pockets in Japan, West Germany, and elsewhere flocked to the United States, attracted by the opportunity to capitalize on US debt. The real rate of interest on twenty-year Treasury bonds had averaged only 0.6 percent during 1979 but rose to 5.4 percent during the height of the 1981–1982 recession. In early 1983, the real rate on US debt rose to 6.6 percent and would climb even higher to 8.4 percent by the end of the year. Corporate bonds' interest rates averaged 8.2 percent in 1983–1984. Using interest rates as a means to attract foreign investors became a matter of policy. Vice chairman of the Federal Reserve Preston Martin explained, "We have to have rates high enough to bring in the capital. All of us have to consider the government financing very seriously. . . . Keeping the rates high enough to attract foreign investors is the argument that's made and it's an awareness we all had."[27] Foreign investors understood that higher interest rates in the United States would yield greater profits than elsewhere, particularly as the dollar continued to appreciate.

The capital that poured into the United States greased the wheels of the country's recovery. Eighty-three billion dollars flowed into the United States in 1983, $103 billion in 1984, $129 billion in 1985, and $221 billion in 1986.[28] The ability of the United States to attract foreign capital turned the outflow of $46.8 billion from the "Group of Seven" countries–seven of the richest industrial democracies–in the 1970s into an inflow of $347.4 billion in the 1980s.[29] Relying on this inflow, the United States abdicated its traditional role as the "world banker." Rather than recycle the capital and reinvest abroad, an increasing share of the money stayed at home. In 1981, 110 percent of the capital inflows left the United States again, but by 1984, that figure dropped to 13 percent.[30]

The flow of capital financed as much as one-half of the budget deficit in 1985 and kept interest rates at least 5 percent lower than they would have been otherwise.[31] This represented a path of least political resistance. By relying on capital flows, the Reagan administration could postpone difficult decisions about government spending. It did not have to make tough choices about whether to cut spending on defense or social safety nets or to increase taxes significantly to close the deficit.

The general turn toward liberalizing international financial markets in the early 1980s facilitated the large flows of capital into the United States. The Treasury launched a campaign to deregulate financial markets and abolish capital controls at home and abroad, and it issued a new bond specifically for foreign buyers. The yen-dollar agreement of 1984, for example, promoted inflows and outflows of Japanese capital, making Japanese savings available for the American market.[32]

A biproduct of the push to invest in dollar-denominated assets was the rapid appreciation of the dollar, a trend that Volcker's strict control of the money supply reinforced. Between July 1980 and March 1985, the dollar rose 18.1 percent against the Japanese yen, 94.5 percent against the West German Deutsche Mark, and 122.6 percent against the British pound.[33] The notion that large budget deficits would lead to a strong currency did not make sense in most contexts. In the United States, however, Volcker's disciplinary medicine meant that Reagan's budget deficits did not cause an increase in inflation. Investors realized that in the case of the United States, financial flows and the opportunities to capitalize on their investments mattered more than traditional indicators such as trade balances.

US officials did not believe that the dollar's appreciation posed a significant problem. Even if they had, they doubted whether they had the capacity to influence its course. Hundreds of billions of dollars changed hands every day in markets across the globe, and central banks would need to spend enormous sums of money to influence the markets. Intervention, Reagan officials believed, could not offset the shifts that were caused by such "fundamental factors as changes in inflation, budget deficits, and the price of oil."[34] Focusing on intervening in the foreign exchange markets, an NSC staffer argued, would only reduce pressure on governments to change the monetary and fiscal policies that had caused the currency to become over- or undervalued in the first place.[35]

Exchange rates reflected perceptions of real issues, and Washington placed the emphasis on convergence of economic policies. "We can't have one country going one way and others in the other direction," Regan said.[36] Except in the extreme case of "disorderly markets," such as in the aftermath of the attempted assassination of Reagan in March 1981, the Reagan administration took a stance of "benign neglect" toward the dollar, a policy that previous administrations had generally followed as well. Furthermore, an attempt to bring down the dollar would have undermined the Treasury's efforts to sell bonds to foreign investors, hurting the country's ability to attract capital.

The strength of the dollar made foreign products cheaper in the United States, and foreign products flooded the American market. The trade deficit increased. Conditions in the international system also contributed—the sovereign debt crises in Latin America, for example, limited demand for US goods—but the dramatic increase in the trade deficit owed much to the rise of the dollar. Its rise of 63 percent between 1980 and 1985 was equivalent to taxing US exports by the same amount, and it also provided imports with an equal subsidy.[37] Agricultural producers in the United States were greatly disadvantaged. Grain farmers lost more than a third of their share of the global market between 1981 and 1983 as the export price of their wheat and corn doubled. The auto industry was badly hit, losing ground to foreign manufacturers, particularly Japanese, who capitalized on the dollar's rise to seize a greater share of the US market. "Even after we're all done fixing quality and productivity, and fuel efficiency and performance," a Chrysler official complained, "the Japanese still have a $2,000 per car advantage in US showrooms. . . .] With the yen undervalued against the dollar, by at least twenty percent and probably more, their cars and other products are much cheaper than they would be if the yen reflected its true purchasing power in the open market."[38] The administration may have portrayed the strong dollar as a symbol of renewed American strength, but it contributed to the elimination of hundreds of thousands of jobs, particularly unionized jobs in manufacturing. Faced with increased competition, calls for Washington to protect American industries became louder. "This administration is going to be under a great deal of political pressure this year to raise the barriers of Fortress America," Regan predicted in 1984.[39] In 1980, the trade deficit totaled only $15 billion, which represented 0.5 percent of the gross domestic product (GDP). Seven years later, the trade deficit jumped almost ten times to $143 billion, which totaled more than 3 percent of GDP.[40]

Using foreign capital to fuel America's economic recovery served several interests in the short term. It allowed the Reagan administration to have its cake and eat it too, and the strong dollar whetted the country's appetite for products from beyond its borders. Nevertheless, contemporaries worried that the reliance on the rest of the world to help drive US economic growth was unsustainable in the long run and would simply prolong the day when the country would need to enact painful adjustments. Speaking to the Senate Committee on Banking, Housing and Urban Affairs in February 1984, Volcker stressed that "we simply can't afford to become addicted to drawing on increasing amounts of foreign savings to help finance our internal economy. Part of our domestic industry—that part dependent on exports or competing with imports—would be sacrificed." At some point, "other countries will increasingly need their savings. While we don't know when, at some point the process would break down."[41] The fiscal stimulus of the White House and the discipline of the Federal Reserve reflected the contested nature of economic policy during the first Reagan administration as both sides attempted to unlock the secret to noninflationary growth. The resulting dependence on finance from beyond US shores bought the country time, but, as Volcker warned, it also placed the United States at the mercy of foreign capital.

The US dominance of financial markets and the strong dollar had consequences that reverberated around the world, altering capital flows and opportunities for economic growth. In her chapter in this volume, Jennifer Miller covers the ways in which Japanese exporters benefited from the American recovery. The Western Europeans understood that their future was tied in large part to developments across the Atlantic and that the United States would have to serve as the locomotive for the resurgence of capitalism. The Western Europeans had far fewer tools available to them than US policymakers, given the size of the US economy and centrality of the dollar in international trade and finance. "The prospects for world economic recovery," a British Treasury report concluded in the midst of the 1981–1982 recession, "continue to depend to a large extent on the course of US economic policy."[42]

Western European critics believed that US policies slowed economic growth on their side of the Atlantic. "Because of the world role of the dollar there is a limit to what . . . we can do to get our own interest rates down," British chancellor of the exchequer Geoffrey Howe wrote Thatcher in June 1982.[43] High interest rates in Britain helped lower inflation to 4.6 percent in 1983, but between 1979 and 1983, GDP fell by 4.2 percent, industrial production dropped 10.2 percent, manufacturing was down 17.3 percent, and unemployment totaled three million Britons.[44] The recession in the United States contributed to similar conditions in Western Europe, particularly for those countries that relied on export industries. Growth in West Germany and Italy, for example, fell to zero or negative between 1981 and 1983 and collapsed even further in Britain and the Netherlands.[45]

Anxiety also centered on the dollar. Schmidt told Reagan in early 1982 that "often these countries could only finance their capital imports at interest rates above those of the US. The dollar's superior position on the international financial markets makes it easier for the US to finance its capital imports, and the same circumstance makes it more difficult for partners."[46] Western European calls for Washington to bring down the dollar in the early 1980s contrasted with their concerns just several years prior. In the late 1970s, American allies denounced the Carter administration for refusing to support the depreciating dollar. In the early 1980s, the opposite was true: they complained that the Reagan administration did nothing to prevent the dollar from climbing too high. The rise of the dollar put pressure on the new European Monetary System, a regional project that had come into existence only in January 1979. They also balked at the perceived disconnect between Reagan's demand that Western Europe behave as US allies in the context of the escalating so-called "second Cold War" but accept American policies that hindered economic recovery across the Atlantic. French official Jacques Attali, Mitterrand's longtime collaborator and personal representative for the 1982 G7 summit in Versailles, told US policymakers that "you cannot expect consensus on security issues and at the same time create recession in Europe."[47] Tempers ran high at the G7 summits in the early 1980s, as the Western Europeans challenged Reagan and accused Washington of making them pay for the large US budget deficits with its high interest rate policy.[48]

The United States commanded the attention of global financial markets and limited opportunities for Western Europe to receive capital. Their economies needed investment too, West German chancellor Helmut Schmidt grumbled to French president François Mitterrand, but lenders could receive rates of 15 to 17 percent in New York, in comparison to 10 percent in Frankfurt and 14 or 15 percent in Paris.[49] Western European officials pleaded with their American counterparts to lower US interest rates. "As long as interest rates are too high and exchange rates are erratic, money is not moving into Europe for investment," European Community president Gaston Thorn said to Reagan.[50] "High interest rates suck into New York City all the liquidity in the world," Schmidt added, and "pessimism reigns" in many Western European countries. "Please remember that what you do has consequences," he implored Reagan. "There can be political destabilization as a result."[51]

Recession portended social discontent. "There is a risk that the world recession could lead to world depression," Schmidt worried. "Economic insecurity threatens social unrest and the strategic danger of political destabilization."[52] With unemployment averaging 10 percent in Western Europe in 1982, Secretary of State Alexander Haig wrote Reagan, "the state of the world economy has become a powerful force in the domestic politics of many of our European friends."[53]

The criticism from across the Atlantic softened by the mid-1980s. A conservative revival across Western Europe brought more leaders to power who sympathized with Reagan's economic ideology, and the economic situation began to improve. Painful structural adjustments and the decline of oil prices in the early 1980s helped reduce stagflation, and the US economic recovery provided a stimulus for exports. American consumers, armed with valuable dollars in their pockets, purchased Western European goods ranging from West German machinery to French wine and spent dollars as they traveled abroad in growing numbers. A chief economist at the Organization for Economic Cooperation and Development calculated that the strong dollar and recovery underway in the United States accounted for approximately one-third of Western European economic growth in 1984.[54] After a 9 percent gain in 1983, the value of Western European exports to the United States increased by a quarter in 1984, totaling $60 billion. In 1984, West German and French exports to the United States each rose by 30 percent to $16.5 billion and $7.9 billion, respectively, and Italian exports increased by 37 percent to $7.5 billion. In sum, Western Europe achieved a $5 billion trade surplus with the United States in 1984, compared with a $30 billion deficit in 1980.[55] The economic recovery in Western Europe during the second half of the 1980s contributed to political and social stability across the region, ensuring that Western Europe could serve as a model of social democracy for reformers across the faltering Soviet bloc.

While the US recovery ultimately served as an engine for the industrial democracies' economic resurgence, not all regions of the world benefited. The American dominance of the capital markets, for example, worsened the emerging sovereign debt crisis in Eastern Europe, crowding out the socialist states that had come to rely on loans from capitalist banks to finance their standard of living. Struggling to make the transition from extensive to intensive growth in the late 1960s, many Eastern European countries took advantage of decreased East-West tensions and reengaged the industrial democracies economically, planning to use Western credits to import technology and goods with which they would create robust export industries of their own. These plans failed to bear fruit, and the Eastern Europeans became increasingly dependent on Western capital to compensate for their shortcomings. In the mid-1970s, capitalist banks—flush with cash as international liquidity exploded—accommodated the socialists. Believing in Eastern Europe's political stability and assuming that the Soviet Union would step in to rescue its allies in the event of an financial crisis, the banks extended credits to meet demand.

As the US Federal Reserve tightened the money supply in its fight against inflation, global liquidity decreased. The "flood" of credits to the Soviet bloc in the 1970s transitioned into the "drought" of the 1980s.[56] The president of the East German Außenhandelsbank, Werner Polze, reported that on the Euromarket, the volume of credits during the first half of 1980 decreased by 15 percent in comparison to the same period the previous year. "The share of socialist countries in Eurocredits fell the most," he worried. In the first half of 1980, the socialist countries managed to raise $950 million from capitalist banks. "That is less than a fifth of the volume of the first half of 1979."[57] The escalating crisis in Poland in 1980 and 1981 also alarmed the capitalist banks about the stability of Eastern European socialist regimes, causing them to scramble in the early 1980s to minimize their exposure to the region.

Confidence in Eastern Europe as a prudent investment deteriorated in the aftermath of the Polish crisis, and high interest rates in the West acted as a magnet that attracted capital flows away from the socialists. Characterizing US domination of capital markets as an expression of imperialism, Horst Kaminsky, the president of the East German Staatsbank, wrote in April 1982 that high interest rates in the United States had "weakened US competitors in the other capitalist centers and caused an increased inflow of capital to finance US budget deficits in connection with the military buildup. This is a new and extremely serious situation. The socialist countries must adapt to it."[58]

When the socialists did receive loans, they struggled to pay the higher interest rates, compounding the "credit crunch" across the region.[59] Even Bulgaria, the most isolated of the Eastern European socialist countries, felt the squeeze. The Bulgarian general secretary Todor Zhivkov explained to a Soviet counterpart that Sofia managed to reduce its debt to capitalist banks in the late 1970s and early 1980s, but "the problem still remains. Why? Because we pay annually about $400 million in interest. For a country of our scale, with our capabilities, this is a lot. . . . We have to reduce those debts that have high interest rates."[60] As interest payments claimed a significant share of the socialist states' dwindling reserves of convertible currency, high interest rates also threatened Eastern Europe's capacity to receive further loans. With limited ways to earn hard currency through exports, the Eastern Europeans depended on loans to purchase necessary goods from the nonsocialist world. "If the capitalist banks no longer grant credits," the East German State Planning Commission feared, "the GDR within just a few months would no longer be solvent and could no longer receive imports."[61]

In the event that the socialists no longer had the capacity to purchase goods from the capitalists, they would be forced to limit consumption in their countries.

Socialist policymakers understood that such austerity measures posed an enormous threat to their regimes: recent crises such as those in Poland in 1970, 1976, and 1980–1981 over the rising cost of food demonstrated that the people would take to the streets in response. Rather than having access to relatively cheap credit in the 1970s, the US dominance of financial markets contributed to a tougher environment for the Eastern Europeans, who struggled in the early 1980s to find creditors. When they did, they had trouble paying interest rates that ranged from 14 to 16 percent.[62] For the moment at least, "the door of the Euromarket had closed on Comecon," an article in *Euromoney* explained in September 1982, "quietly, politely, but firmly."[63]

Isolated from capital markets, the Eastern Europeans launched an "export offensive" between 1980 and 1984 in a desperate effort to remain solvent. While they managed to increase exports by 25 percent, the strategy exhausted what little remained of Eastern European reserves.[64] The situation stabilized somewhat in the mid-1980s, when capital once again began to flow, but debt rose quickly thereafter as the Eastern Europeans struggled to find buyers for their products. The depreciation of the US dollar after 1985 (which increased the value of debt expressed in other currencies) and the oil countershock of 1985–1986 also contributed. According to the state bank of the Soviet Union (Gosbank), collective Council for Mutual Economic Assistance (CMEA) debt jumped from $87.5 billion in 1984 to $121.1 billion in 1986 and climbed to $143.8 billion by 1988.[65] When the Eastern European revolutions of 1989 erupted, most teetered on the brink of insolvency.[66]

The diversion of capital flows to the United States certainly did not cause the revolutions, but they eliminated a bandage that had been previously available to socialist policymakers to mask their inability to transition to intensive economic growth.[67] The accumulation of Eastern European debt also made it more costly for the Soviet Union, which plunged into its own economic crisis by the late 1980s, to countenance interventioning to suppress the revolutions or extending economic aid. Moscow did not have the resources to take on a collapsing ally "as a dependent," as Anatoly Chernyaev wrote in his diary in the summer of 1981.[68] The Soviet capacity to do so only diminished as the decade wore on.

While Eastern Europe struggled to adapt to the changes in capital flows, developing countries in the global South, particularly in Latin America and sub-Saharan Africa, suffered from a similar predicament. Countries in East Asia such as Singapore, Taiwan, and South Korea enjoyed export-led growth in the 1980s, both stimulated by and in imitation of Japan's impressive performance. They took advantage of the heightened US demand for imports and experienced a boom in manufacturing, trade, and investment. For many least developed countries (LDCs) in the global South, however, the outlook was far from rosy. As in Eastern Europe, many LDCs took out loans during the 1970s as a means of financing their oil imports and other domestic projects. These loans allowed LDCs to maintain growth levels, but they accumulated debt that they lacked the capacity to repay. Buoyed by inflation in the commodities markets in the 1970s, members of the developing world suffered from decreased demand in the industrialized world, which was stumbling from the recession of the early 1980s. Investment began to taper off. As French Minister of Finance Jacques Delors observed in May 1983, "High interest rates in the United States are . . . making it virtually impossible for many Third World countries to borrow."[69] The reorientation of capital markets toward the United States did not cause the sovereign debt crisis that enveloped many LDCs in the 1980s, but it did contribute to their hardships. Capital flows to the United States crowded out LDCs, pushing them toward default.

In Latin America, the collective debt ballooned from $59 billion in 1975 to $331 billion in 1982.[70] Mexico provided the cautionary tale. After the Volcker shock dried up the credit markets and oil prices dropped, Mexico suffered from an acute debt crisis. A battle raged in Mexico City about the proper course of action. On the one hand, technocrats such as Finance Minister Jesús Silva-Herzog wanted to appeal to the international financial community for assistance. On the other hand, economic nationalists such as President José López Portillo wanted to turn their backs on the global economy, deciding instead to nationalize the banks. The issue was decided when a new Mexican government under Miguel de la Madrid turned to the International Monetary Fund (IMF) for assistance in the fall of 1982. In return for a loan of $3.7 billion, Madrid agreed to a reform program that decreased the budget deficit, increased taxes, and devalued the peso. The crisis started a chain reaction. Within a few weeks, similar crises erupted in Argentina and Brazil.[71] As fear grew that poorer countries would not have the capacity to repay their debts, lenders ceased to extend credits. Desperate developing countries had to stop payments on their credits, which only reinforced bankers' unwillingness to invest in those countries. By 1983, Latin American collectively spent half its export earnings to pay interest and principal on foreign debt. The only avenue available was the IMF, which demanded structural adjustments in return for aid, reversing Latin America's reliance on import-substitution industrialization that had been in place since the Great Depression.[72]

Many sub-Saharan African countries had not accumulated the same levels of debt that Latin American countries held. Out of the $1 trillion that developing countries owed to creditors, sub-Saharan African countries had to pay a total of $91 billion, spread among 43 different countries. Their debts, however, were large in proportion to the size of their economies, and they lacked the capability to increase exports. Many sub-Saharan African countries were hit hard by the 1973 oil crisis and borrowed heavily to weather the storm. The reorientation of capital markets toward the United States in the early 1980s meant that investment to the African countries slowed considerably, even though the inflows necessary to support development programs were relatively small. Net investment in the region fell steadily after 1982, dropping from an inflow of $1.52 billion to an outflow of $290 million by 1984.[73] The ratio of external debt to GNP rose from 25 percent in 1980 to more than 80 percent in 1994.[74] As in Latin America, the debt crisis forced many sub-Saharan African countries into the arms of the IMF. The IMF demanded strict conditionality in return for loans, as the institution believed that the chief problem rested with the statist development model rather than exogenous shocks.

The US economic recovery under Reagan drew strength from the privileged position of the dollar as well as the size and attractiveness of the domestic market. No other country in the world had the capacity to follow a similar path. The former Council of Economic Advisers chairman Herbert Stein wrote in October 1986, "Could France count on a similar result? If it cut taxes and raised the budget deficit by x billion francs, could it expect a capital inflow of approximately the same amount? The answer to that is almost certainly negative."[75] The United States stumbled into this arrangement, created by an unusual constellation of monetary policy, budget deficits, and the availability of global capital searching for a profitable home.

The consequences of Reagan's economic policies were far-reaching. In the short-term, the ability of the United States to attract foreign investors created the opportunity for the country to live beyond its means, delaying the difficult decisions about how to decrease budget deficits and national debt. After a period of heightened tension with the Western Europeans, the US recovery also served as the engine for the economic recovery in the Western world, allowing the industrial democracies to adapt to the challenges of economic globalization, a fact that became quite clear in the Cold War against a stagnating and buckling socialist bloc. By redirecting capital flows, the United States inadvertently undermined the stability of the socialist regimes in Eastern Europe, forcing them to make the difficult decisions about how to handle their debts.[76]

The long-term ramifications are still unfolding. Financing US budget deficits has depended on the willingness of foreigners to purchase US debt. The attraction of US debt has permitted the United States to spend liberally on national security and social programs without having to raise taxes, but the day of reckoning will arrive when investors no longer wish to play their part. As

Volcker warned the Senate Committee on Banking, Housing and Urban Affairs in February 1984, there is no such thing as a free lunch.[77]

Notes

1. James Sterngold, "A Nation Hooked on Foreign Funds," *New York Times*, 18 Nov. 1984.

2. This approach aligns with Daniel Sargent's *A Superpower Transformed: The Remaking of American Foreign Relations in the 1970s* (New York: Oxford University Press, 2015), which analyzes how American policymakers in the 1970s attempted to navigate a changing global environment. In contrast to a growing literature on international economic affairs during the 1970s, scholarship on these issues during the 1980s based on archival research has yet to develop. An important exception is Hal Brands, *Making the Unipolar Moment: US Foreign Policy and the Rise of the Post–Cold War Order* (Ithaca, NY: Cornell University Press, 2015), 172–223.

3. Ronald Reagan, "Address to the Nation on the Economy," 5 Feb. 1981, http://www.presidency.ucsb.edu/ws/?pid=43132.

4. Harold James, *International Monetary Cooperation since Bretton Woods* (New York: Oxford University Press, 1996), 416.

5. William Greider, "The Education of David Stockman," *Atlantic Monthly*, Dec. 1981, https://www.theatlantic.com/magazine/archive/1981/12/the-education-of-david-stockman/305760/.

6. James M. Poterba, "Federal Budget Policy in the 1980s," in *American Economic Policy in the 1980s*, ed. Martin Feldman (Chicago: University of Chicago Press, 1994), 238.

7. David Stockman, *The Triumph of Politics: How the Reagan Revolution Failed* (New York: Harper and Row, 1986), 10–11.

8. Michael J. Boskin, *Reagan and the Economy: The Successes, Failures, and Unfinished Agenda* (San Francisco: Institute for Contemporary Studies Press, 1987), 176.

9. Stockman, *The Triumph of Politics*, 135.

10. James T. Patterson, *Restless Giant: The United States from Watergate to Bush v. Gore* (New York: Oxford University Press, 2005), 163.

11. Spencer Rich, "Cuts in Social Security 'Negotiable,' Hill Assured," *Washington Post*, 22 May 1981.

12. Douglas Brinkley, ed., *The Reagan Diaries* (New York: Harper, 2007), 39.

13. Judith Stein, *How the United States Traded Factories for Finance in the Seventies* (New Haven, CT: Yale University Press, 2010), 268.

14. Stockman, *The Triumph of Politics*, 204.

15. Ronald Reagan, "Address to the Nation on Strategic Arms Reduction and Nuclear Deterrence," 22 Nov. 1982, https://www.reaganlibrary.gov/research/speeches/112282d.

16. James Graham Wilson, *The Triumph of Improvisation: Gorbachev's Adaptability, Reagan's Engagement, and the End of the Cold War* (Ithaca, NY: Cornell University Press, 2014), 16–23.

17. Ronald Reagan, *An American Life* (New York: Simon and Schuster, 1990), 235.

18. Stockman, *The Triumph of Politics*, 356.
19. Diane B. Kunz, *Butter and Guns: America's Cold War Economic Diplomacy* (New York: Free Press, 1997), 286.
20. Brinkley, *The Reagan Diaries*, 53.
21. Bailey to Clark, "The Course of the US Economy," 24 Aug. 1982, Ronald Reagan Presidential Library (RRPL), Roger W. Robinson Files, box 3, folder "International Financial: 04/20/1982–11/16/1982."
22. Letter, 22 Feb. 1982, Seely G. Mudd Library, Paul A. Volcker Papers, box 9, folder "General January–August 1982."
23. Kunz, *Butter and Guns*, 285.
24. William L. Silber, *Volcker: The Triumph of Persistence* (New York: Bloomsbury Press, 2010), 210.
25. "Memorandum of Conversation," 29 Sept. 1983, RRPL, Executive Secretariat–NSC (ESNSC), Subject Files (SF), box 51, folder "Memorandums of Conversation—President Reagan (09/28/1983–09/30/1983)."
26. Real interest rates refer to interest rates after adjusting for inflation. Feldstein to Reagan, "Japanese Trade and the Yen," 17 Jan. 1983, RRPL, Martin Feldstein Files (MFF), Chronological File (CF), box 5, folder "Memos and Correspondence, January 1983."
27. Quoted in William Greider, *Secrets of the Temple: How the Federal Reserve Runs the Country* (New York: Simon & Schuster, 1989), 561–63.
28. Greta Krippner, *Capitalizing on Crisis: The Political Origins of the Rise of Finance* (Cambridge, MA: Harvard University Press, 2012), 189.
29. Giovanni Arrighi, "The World Economy and the Cold War, 1970–1990," in *The Cambridge History of the Cold War*, vol.3, *Endings*, ed. Melvyn P. Leffler and Odd Arne Westad (New York: Cambridge University Press, 2010), 35.
30. Robert Triffin, "W. M. S.: The World Monetary System or Scandal?," in *International Banking and World Economic Growth: The Outlook for the Late 1980s*, S. K. Kaushik (New York: Praeger, 1987), 41.
31. Eric Helleiner, *States and the Reemergence of Global Finance: From Bretton Woods to the 1990s* (Ithaca, NY: Cornell University Press, 1994), 148.
32. I. M. Destler and C. Randall Henning, *Dollar Politics: Exchange Rate Policymaking in the United States* (Washington, DC: Institute for International Economics, 1989), 28–29.
33. James, *International Monetary Cooperation*, 419.
34. Feldstein to Reagan, "European Concerns at Williamsburg," 4 May 1983, RRPL, MFF, CF, box 5, folder "Memos [Including to the President] and Correspondence, May 1983."
35. Nau to Poindexter, "US Support for Mark and Franc," 15 Nov. 1982, RRPL, Roger W. Robinson Files, box 3, folder "International Financial: 11/17/1982–12/31/1982."
36. "Memorandum of Conversation," April 21, 1983, RRPL, ESNSC, SF, box 51, folder "Memorandums of Conversation—President Reagan (May 1983)."
37. Stein, *Pivotal Decade*, 269.
38. Quoted in Greider, *Secrets of the Temple*, 593.
39. Quoted in Brands, *Making the Unipolar Moment*, 186.
40. Martin Feldstein, "American Economic Policy in the 1980s: A Personal View," in *American Economic Policy in the 1980s*, ed. Martin Feldman (Chicago: University of Chicago Press, 1994),63.

41. US Congress, *The Federal Reserve's First Monetary Policy Report for 1984: Hearings before the Senate Committee on Banking, Housing and Urban Affairs*, 98th Congress, 2nd Session, 8 Feb. 1984, 20–21.

42. S. H. Broadbent, "World Economic Prospects: Autumn 1982 Forecast," 19 Oct. 1982, National Archives of the United Kingdom (TNA), FCO 59/1921.

43. Howe to Thatcher, "President Reagan and the US Budget Debate," 3 June1982, TNA, PREM 19/943.

44. William I. Hitchcock, *The Struggle for Europe: The Turbulent History of a Divided Continent, 1945–2002* (New York: Doubleday, 2003), 325.

45. Duccio Basosi, "The European Community and International Reaganomics, 1981–1985," in *European Integration and the Atlantic Community in the 1980s*, ed. Kiran Klaus Patel and Kenneth Weisbrode (New York: Cambridge University Press, 2013), 140–141.

46. "Gespräch des Bundeskanzlers Schmidt mit Präsident Reagan in Washington," 2 Jan. 1982, in *Akten zur Auswärtigen Politik der Bundesrepublik Deutschland, 1982 (AAPD)* (Munich: Oldenbourg Verlag, 2013), doc. 3.

47. Nau to Clark, "Report on Summit Preparatory Meeting," 2 Mar. 1982, RRPL, Douglas N. McMinn Files (DNMF), box 12, folder "France—Chron (02/25/1982–03/08/1982)."

48. Basosi, "The European Community and International Reaganomics, 1981–1985," 144–145.

49. "Gespräch des Bundeskanzlers Schmidt mit Staatspräsident Mitterrand in Paris," 25 Feb. 1982, in *AAPD, 1982*, doc. 65.

50. "Memorandum of Conversation," 21 Apr. 1983, RRPL, ESNSC, SF, box 51, folder "Memorandums of Conversation—President Reagan (May 1983)."

51. "Memorandum of Conversation," 21 May 1981, RRPL, ESNSC, Country File, box 14, folder "FRG Vol. I (1/20/81–6/30/81) (4)"

52. "Gespräch des Bundeskanzlers Schmidt mit Präsident Reagan in Washington," 2 Jan. 1982, in *AAPD, 1982*, doc. 3.

53. Haig to Reagan, "US-European Economic Relations," 22 Feb. 1982, RRPL, DNMF, box 12.

54. Paul Lewis, "Ambivalence on the Dollar: Europeans' Wary View," *New York Times*, 13 Jan. 1984.

55. CIA Directorate of Intelligence, "Western Europe: Coping with the Dollar," June 1985, CIA Electronic Reading Room (CIAERR).

56. Arrighi, "The World Economy and the Cold War, 1970–1990," 34.

57. Werner Polze, "Information über die Lage auf den kapitalistischen Geld- und Kreditmärkten," 13 Aug. 1980, Bundesarchiv-Berlin (BAB), DN 10/616.

58. Kaminsky to Stoph, 8 Apr. 1982, Stiftung Archiv der Parteien und Massenorganisationen der DDR (SAPMO), DY 30/25765.

59. Directorate of Intelligence, "Eastern Europe's Credit Crunch," March 1982, CIAERR.

60. "Sreshta na Politbyuro na TsK na BKP s drugarya Nikolai Tikhonov—chlen na Politbyuro na TsK na KPSS i predsedatel na Ministerskiya savet na Savetskiya sayuz," 5 July 1981, Tsentralen Darzhaven Arhiv Balgariya (TsDA), f. 1B, op. 60, a.e. 281.

61. "Konzeption zum Abbau der Höhe der Verbindlichkeiten der DDR gegenüber dem nichtsozialistsichen Wirtschaftsgebiet vom 27.6.1980," 5 May 1989, BAB, DE 1/58746, Bd. 1.

62. Iván T. Berend, *Central and Eastern Europe, 1944–1993: Detour from the Periphery to the Periphery* (Cambridge: Cambridge University Press, 1996), 231.

63. Padraic Fallon and David Shirreff, "The Betrayal of East Europe," *Euromoney* (1982): 22.

64. Berend, *Central and Eastern Europe*, 231.

65. Valyutno-ekonomicheskoe upravlenie Gosbanka SSSR, "O valyutno-finansovom polozhenii sotsialisticheskikh stran," 24 Feb. 1988, Rossiiskii Gosudarstvennyi Arkhiv Ekonomiki, f. 2324, op. 33, d. 696.

66. The exception was Romania, which embarked on a draconian austerity policy that eliminated the debt but came at the cost of alienating the Romanian people.

67. See André Steiner, "The Decline of Soviet-Type Economies," in *The Cambridge History of Communism*, vol. 3, *Endgames? Late Communism in Global Perspective, 1968 to the Present*, ed. Juliane Fürst, Silvio Pons, and Mark Selden (Cambridge: Cambridge University Press, 2017), 203–223.

68. Anatoly Chernyaev, *Sovmestyi iskhod: Dnevnik dvykh epoch 1972–1991 gody* (Moscow: Rosspen, 2008), 459.

69. "Botschafter Herbst, Paris, an das Auswärtige Amt," May 18, 1983, *AAPD, 1983* (Munich: Oldenbourg Verlag, 2014), doc. 148.

70. Brands, *Making the Unipolar Moment*, 199.

71. James, *International Monetary Cooperation*, 371, 374.

72. Jeffry A. Frieden, *Global Capitalism: Its Fall and Rise in the Twentieth Century* (New York: Norton, 2006), 374–376.

73. Scott Thomas, "The African Debt Problem, Occasional Paper No. 9," January 1988, RRPL, Stephen Danzansky Files, SF, box 1, folder: "Debt (1 of 3)."

74. Ngaire Woods, *The Globalizers: The IMF, the World Bank, and Their Borrowers* (Ithaca, NY: Cornell University Press, 2006), 143.

75. Quoted in Boskin, *Reagan and the Economy*, 244.

76. See, for example, Fritz Bartel, "The Power of Omission: The IMF and the Democratic Transitions in Poland and Hungary," in *New Perspectives on the End of the Cold War: Unexpected Transformations?*, ed. Bernhard Blumenau, Jussi M. Hanhimäki, and Barbara Zanchetta (London: Routledge, 2018), 200–221.

77. US Congress, *The Federal Reserve's First Monetary Policy Report for 1984*, 20–21.

Part Two

Western and Eastern Europe

CHAPTER 5

Confronting the Soviet Threat
Reagan's Approach to Policymaking

ELIZABETH C. CHARLES AND JAMES GRAHAM WILSON

"It has to be admitted that we all not only underestimated Reagan fairly frequently but also greatly oversimplified him," read the lead article in *Pravda* on January 20, 1989. "His outward simplicity was taken for simple-mindedness, his rhetoric for substance, and his ostentatious toughness for an inability to be flexible." Who was he really? "The Reagan of the years 1980–1981, who promised to 'leave communism on the ash heap of history'?" Or, the "Reagan of 1987–1988, whose signature is on the Soviet-US Treaty on Intermediate-Range and Shorter-Range Missiles, the first agreement in history on the physical elimination of two classes of nuclear weapons?" Gennadiy Vasilyev, the author of this profile, deferred to a recent edition of *Fortune Magazine*: "It is hard to evaluate Reagan's presidency because it abounds with paradoxes." Indeed, in Vasilyev's words, "One of the main paradoxes is . . . [the Reagan administration's] achievements in the area where it had no plans and where no one expected anything of it. . . . I mean the sphere of Soviet-US relations." How and why did this happen? "The answer is simple," Vasilyev argued, "the world has changed, people's sentiments have changed, in the United States itself, in Western Europe, and everywhere."[1]

Ronald Reagan would surely have smiled at the suggestion that he had entered office with no plans and low expectations when it came to the Soviet Union. As Melvyn P. Leffler writes in his contribution to this volume, Reagan had once confided in Richard Allen—who would become his first national security advisor—that his objective when it came to the Soviet Union and the Cold War was clear: "We win; they lose."[2] The former governor had explained to another political associate his sense of purpose: "To end the Cold War. . . . there has got to be a way."[3]

By the time he left office, however, Reagan regarded the Cold War as neither won nor over. Yet he and Soviet leader Mikhail Gorbachev had made great strides in lessening global tensions. "My view is that President Gorbachev is different from previous Soviet leaders," Reagan stated in his farewell Oval Office address to the American people on January 11, 1989. "I think he knows some of the things wrong with his society and is trying to fix them. We wish him well. And we'll continue to work to make sure that the Soviet Union that eventually emerges from this process is a less threatening one."[4]

This chapter focuses on Reagan's perception of the Soviet threat over the course of his presidency and how his administration managed the overall US relationship with the Soviet Union. It seeks to answer three questions: (1) How did Reagan perceive the Soviet threat in the early stages of his presidency? (2) How did his administration craft policies to mitigate that threat? and, (3) Did the Reagan administration successfully execute these policies?

In each instance, Reagan's optimism was the common variable in his thinking about and actions toward the Soviet Union. The president believed in the goodness of the United States and considered its democratic system as the enduring model for organizing societies. He also believed in his ability to negotiate with Soviet leaders and even bring them around to his way of thinking. Reagan's optimism motivated the president from January 1981 onward and fostered his cordial relationship with Gorbachev; it did not originate with the advent of a new type of Soviet leader. That quality—which critics and supporters often misinterpreted as mere rhetoric—proved to be political substance.

Reagan's singular personality trait sustained his approach to the Soviets throughout his eight years in office. Translating optimism into policies required key partners—most notably George Shultz, who came on board as secretary of state in the summer of 1982, and Mikhail Gorbachev, who became general secretary in the spring of 1985. During the first half of 1983, Shultz developed a four-part agenda to deal with the Soviet Union, which was focused on nuclear weapons reductions, human rights, bilateral relations, and regional issues—all issues that Reagan believed could be negotiated with Soviet leaders. The implementation of this four-part agenda, along with Reagan's continued optimism that relations could be improved, led to a lessening of tensions, and therefore, in Reagan's view, a lessening of threats posed to the United States by the Soviet Union.

Winning the Cold War was not necessarily the same thing as ending the Cold War, as Leffler correctly points out. The grand optimism that Reagan exuded drew no such distinctions. Grand optimism—as opposed to grand strategy—propounded the abolition of nuclear weapons and the eradication of communism. In the case of the Strategic Defense Initiative (SDI), it included a decades-long transition from mutual assured destruction to mutual assured survivability, a proposal that Reagan would lay out in a letter to Gorbachev a few months before their October 1986 encounter at Reykjavik.[5] It included a shift from arms control to arms reductions, meaning zero Soviet SS-20 missiles and a reduction in Soviet SS-18 missiles on the order of one-third to one-half. As Reagan and Gorbachev were preparing to sign the Intermediate-Range Nuclear Forces (INF) Treaty, in Washington on December 8, 1987, negotiating teams led by Paul Nitze and Sergei Akhromeyev were successfully hammering out the formula for the Strategic Arms Reduction Treaty (START), which remained in place until the eventual signing of that agreement in the summer of 1991.

Nothing about Reagan's grand optimism ought to detract from the role of Gorbachev, who made the hardest decisions; or that of Shultz, who attempted to rein in the president's competing impulses and impose discipline on the interagency process. Getting from the lousy state of affairs between the United States and the Soviet Union in January 1981 to the much-improved one in January 1989 required all of these things.

"The country is in the grip of a national sickness," *Pravda* reporter Vasilyev quoted "Peanut Farmer Jimmy Carter" as saying during the 1980 campaign. "'No,' Ronald Reagan [responded]. . . . 'America is walking tall once again and looking to the eighties with courage, confidence, and hope.'"[6] Nevertheless, Reagan also believed that the Soviets were on the march, as the December 1979 invasion of Afghanistan made clear to him. In January 1981, he entered office convinced that his predecessors had squandered the US strategic advantage that forced the Soviets to back down during the October 1962 Cuban Missile Crisis. In the aftermath of that near-cataclysmic encounter, Soviet leaders—who, Reagan sensed, acknowledged the logic of strength far better than their US counterparts—caught up and surpassed the United States when it came to nuclear capabilities.[7] Meanwhile, US involvement in Vietnam turned into a tragedy, because these same US policymakers—such as Secretary of Defense Robert McNamara, whom Reagan ridiculed as "that efficient disaster"—denied American GIs the opportunity to win. Similarly, détente failed either to check Soviet expansion or to halt the nuclear arms race, because American leaders were negotiating from a position of weakness, as Lyndon Johnson's domestic policies, which were largely upheld by Richard Nixon, had depleted the coffers of the federal government while (allegedly) thwarting the creative potential of the American people. Reagan aspired to roll back the "Great Society" and restore US military strength. He believed that a program of new conservatism would rejuvenate the American people and repel Soviet efforts to exploit Western malaise to further the longstanding communist objective of world domination.

Reagan assembled a national security team that included Secretary of State Alexander Haig, Secretary of Defense Caspar Weinberger, and Director of Central Intelligence William Casey, who did not agree on everything yet *did* agree that Soviet leaders were undermining noncommunist governments in Central America, seeking to paralyze the North Atlantic Treaty Organization (NATO) via information warfare, shoring up a foundering communist regime in Poland, and building on their advantage in strategic nuclear arms. Reagan and his top advisers were intent on distinguishing their policies toward the Soviet Union from those of Carter during the latter administration's early months in office.[8] "I don't have to think of an answer as to what I think their intentions are; they have repeated it," Reagan declared in his first press conference, on January 29, 1981: "I know of no leader of the Soviet Union since the revolution, and including the present leadership, that has not more than once repeated in the various Communist congresses they hold their determination that their goal must be the promotion of world revolution and a one-world Socialist or Communist state, whichever word you want to use."[9]

That objective threatened not only US allies abroad but also nations within its own hemisphere. "High spot a [National] Security Council meeting," Reagan, away from the cameras, wrote in his diary on February 11, 1981. "We have absolute proof of Soviet & Cuban activity in delivering arms to rebels in El Salvador—Also their worldwide propaganda campaign which has succeeded in raising riots & demonstrations in Europe & the US."[10] Temporary derailment in George Washington University Hospital, following an assassination attempt on March 30, did not distract the president from this focus. "Information available to me indicates a growing possibility that the Soviet Union is preparing to intervene militarily in Poland," Reagan wrote Soviet General Secretary Leonid Brezhnev in a message over the direct communication link (a.k.a., "the hotline") on April 3; "I wish to make clear to you the seriousness with which the United States would view such an action, to which we would be compelled to respond. I take this step not to threaten the Soviet Union, but to ensure that there is no possibility of your misunderstanding our position or our intentions."[11]

On April 24, after the threat of Soviet invasion of Poland had temporarily subsided, Reagan wrote a follow-up letter to Brezhnev in which he attributed the collapse of the détente to two Soviet actions: "First, the USSR's unremitting and comprehensive military buildup over the past 15 years, a buildup which in our view far exceeds purely defensive requirements and carries disturbing implications of a search for military superiority.... Second, the Soviet Union's pursuit of unilateral advantage in various parts of the globe and its repeated resort to the direct and indirect use of force."[12]

These letters to Brezhnev in April 1981 were candid expressions of Reagan's perception of the Soviet threat. He believed that the continued deterioration of the strategic nuclear balance between the United States and Soviet Union empowered communist ideologues in the Kremlin. The Warsaw Pact, by definition, included Poland, yet a potential Soviet invasion of that country would broadcast to the world that Moscow could violate the sovereignty of foreign countries with impunity. Moreover, the governments of NATO allies, which had shrugged at the Soviet invasion of Afghanistan in December 1979, were under pressure from domestic constituents who apportioned equal blame to East and West for the commencement of a "Second Cold War." In Reagan's mind, it was time to turn things around; that meant deployment of Pershing IIs (PIIs) in West Germany and ground-launched cruise missiles (GLCMs) in other NATO countries to offset Soviet SS-20 intermediate-range ballistic missiles. It also meant research, development, and deployment of the MX Peacekeeper intercontinental ballistic missile (ICBM), the Trident II submarine-launched ballistic missile (SLBM), air-launched cruise missiles (ALCMs) on B-52s, the B-1B bomber, and the B-2 "Stealth" Bomber. With the exception of the B-1, President Carter had signed off on all these systems; Reagan ramped up outlays for the next decade.

"Peace through strength" was one of Reagan's favorite slogans, and the sentiment behind it distinguished him from Carter, who embraced complexity and enmeshed himself in the details of US strategic systems. Slogans were not necessarily policy prescriptions, however; nor did they resolve internal debates about how to mitigate threats, real and perceived. The president's top advisers differed over whether to attempt to delay or derail Soviet construction of a trans-Siberian pipeline to transport natural gas to Western Europe, a complicated topic that pitted the United States against its NATO allies and came down to whether one believed that Moscow's potential economic gains automatically enhanced its military might. Secretary of Defense Weinberger was quite certain that they did. "Almost everything aids their military and helps their economy," he asserted on July 6, 1981. "We know that they will only be satisfied by world domination, and we cannot satisfy them by appeasing them."[13]

Reagan often expressed a similar outlook—yet he also had tremendous respect and affection for Prime Minister Margaret Thatcher, who disapproved of punishing British subsidiaries and licensees of US industrial conglomerates. And he was also reluctant to intervene in debates between high-octane personalities on his own team. "I must take the blame for having been careless," as he put it at an NSC meeting on February 26, 1982. "At the time that I announced the [first round of] sanctions, I believed that the United States was the dominant factor in what went into the production of the pipeline. Now, Maggie Thatcher has made me realize that I have been wrong"—that in fact the "important factors" were "subsidiaries and licensees of US corporations."[14] Nevertheless, following a June 18, 1982, NSC meeting while Haig was in New York for a special session of the United Nations, Reagan extended sanctions on oil and gas equipment exports to the Soviet Union.[15] A week later, Reagan accepted Haig's resignation.[16]

One of the first initiatives of the new secretary of state, George Shultz, was to convene a group of top-level officials in previous administrations to discuss strategies toward the Soviet Union. In it, Secretary of Defense Donald Rumsfeld and former Secretary of Commerce Pete Peterson stressed the importance of policies "sustainable for the long haul," which would "avoid the polar extremes of the past ten years in which we ask the American people to support either a soft-headed detente or an unyielding hard-line confrontation (with the broad swings in defense expenditures which accompany these poles.)"[17] A set of consistent and sustainable policies toward the Soviet Union would purchase time for the United States to recover. While Shultz did not regard himself as a grand strategist in the mold of Henry Kissinger, he also did not regard his brief as managing US decline. Rather, it was to embrace an optimistic future in which US core values and institutions would flourish.

An examination of a key period in the Reagan administration from January to June 1983 demonstrates three points: first, the decisive role that Secretary of State George Shultz played in understanding and furthering Reagan's vision and policies with respect to the Soviet Union; second, the dysfunction of the NSC and the interagency process; and third, how Reagan's reluctance to assert his will over his staff contributed to a lack of policy cohesion. Levels of coordination and efficiency during the deliberation and decision-making processes varied depending on the issues and the officials involved. Reagan's decision-making style depended on his personal interest and attachment to the issue at hand. When Reagan had strong beliefs about a subject—as with SDI, for instance, and the plight of the Pentecostalist families in the Moscow embassy—his involvement in meetings and the overall decision-making process was crucial. The Soviet Union and the nuclear arms race captured Reagan's attention throughout his administration; as a result, he played a more decisive role in decisions related to these subjects. Reagan's belief in his ability to negotiate with Soviet leadership and his continued optimism that the US system was superior and would eventually prevail over communism commanded his attention to these issues.

With the signing of National Security Decision Directive (NSDD) 75 in January 1983, the Reagan administration established a four-part agenda toward the Soviet Union focused on human rights, bilateral relations, regional issues, and arms control. Shultz endorsed consistent, fair dialogue with the Soviets framed through the four-part agenda. Weinberger held to a tougher line, believing that it would be impossible to reach arms control agreements with the Soviet Union that preserved the military systems vital to US national security. This left Reagan's national security advisers to weigh the options, mediate between these camps, and try to explain to the president the arguments of each side so that he could reach an informed decision. This process rarely worked smoothly.

Shultz took a pragmatic approach toward dealing with the Soviet Union. He was willing to have tough conversations about human rights and arms control and to continue dialogue with Soviet Foreign Minister Andrei Gromyko even after a Soviet interceptor shot down Korean Airlines Flight 007 on September 1, 1983. Shultz's willingness to negotiate even at difficult moments put the administration in a position to have productive summits once Gorbachev arrived on the scene. Shultz could not have done this alone. When longtime foreign service officer Jack Matlock became senior director for European and Soviet affairs on the NSC in the summer of 1983, Shultz gained an ally at the White House—one who saw eye to eye on Soviet issues and wanted to help the president better understand the Soviet Union and how its leaders thought. What Weinberger and others failed to recognize or chose to ignore was that Reagan wanted arms reductions. Reagan wanted to meet Soviet leaders because he was optimistic that conversations with them could improve US-Soviet relations.

Shultz recognized Reagan's aspirations during a private conversation in February 1983. When a blizzard prevented the Reagans from spending the weekend at Camp David, Shultz and his wife were invited for dinner at the White House. Shultz had just returned from a trip to Asia and later recalled: "President Reagan was fascinated by China and expressed openly his ideas about the Soviet Union. He recognized how difficult it was for him to move forward in dealing with either of these countries. . . . [and realized] that he was in a sense blocked by his own White House staff, by the Defense Department, by Bill

Casey in the CIA, and by his own past rhetoric." Shultz understood that Reagan's public rhetoric and harsh stance on communism did not mean that the president was unwilling to open a dialogue with Moscow or Beijing. Shultz believed Reagan would "relish" the opportunity to speak directly with communist leadership.[18]

Shultz was scheduled to meet Soviet Ambassador Anatoly Dobrynin the next day, February 15, and he told Reagan that he could secretly usher the Soviet ambassador into the White House. Over the objections of National Security Adviser William Clark and others, Shultz did just that. "Almost forgot—Geo. Shultz sneaked Ambassador Dobrynin (Soviet) into the W.H. We talked for 2 hours," Reagan wrote in his diary, "Sometimes we got pretty nose to nose. I told him I wanted George to be a channel for direct contact with Andropov—no bureaucracy involved. Geo. tells me that after they left, the ambas. said 'this could be an historic moment.'"[19]

After his discussion with Dobrynin, the president gave Shultz a mandate to conduct "quiet diplomacy" with the Soviets. Shultz and the State Department staff wrote a series of memoranda from January to May 1983, in preparation for a small White House meeting on June 15 to discuss US-Soviet relations.[20] Once there, Shultz outlined his ideas for promoting the four-part agenda and advancing dialogue with the communist rival. The memoranda laid out issues such as the opening of consulates in Kiev and New York; a long-term grain agreement; and restarting cultural exchanges. "While these proposals have merit," Clark responded to one such proposal, "taken together they may give the appearance of expanding ties and increasing cooperation, allowing the contention that we are tilting toward détente."[21] Shultz disagreed; he believed that some members of the NSC staff shared Weinberger's skepticism for arms control and cooperation with the Soviets and were obstructing the president's views on Soviet issues.

Clark's position was slightly more nuanced than Shultz recognized at the time. In a February 4 memorandum from Clark to Reagan titled "The Prospects for Progress in US-Soviet Relations," the national security adviser discussed how to deal with Yuri Andropov, the new Soviet leader, in a way that afforded the president options for how to formulate realistic policy toward the Soviets and their bilateral arms control talks. In the memo, Clark argued that INF seemed the most likely track for progress, as "it gives us substantial leverage and imputes a sense of urgency in Moscow."[22] He then discussed the benefits of traditional diplomatic dialogue versus a back channel, private approach, ultimately arguing for a private channel since "it has become virtually impossible for us to keep the substance of our negotiations private once they are circulated within the government."

"We have a separate but related problem," Clark wrote in the memorandum. "This concerns the very deeply-felt ideological bias which exists within your administration against arms control. This small group of professionals—centered in the Defense Department—believes that arms control generically is bad."[23] Because of the risk of leaks, "a private channel may offer the only means to proceed." Clark clearly understood the bureaucratic hurdles in moving forward on arms control. He argued that taking steps toward dialogue would "be worthwhile because it would make clear that you are not ideologically against solving problems with the Soviet Union; it would show that you are at least willing to try." He closed the memorandum explaining that he hoped it would "stimulate a discussion" that would help them "lay out a strategy," noting that he had "discussed this with no one."

Clark's memorandum is interesting for a few reasons. First, it followed NSDD 75, which clearly laid out a comprehensive, long-term strategy for dealing with the Soviet Union. In some ways he was reiterating the points of the NSDD, but with the discussion of the back channel, he was promoting a different means toward those chosen ends. Second, the ideas Clark endorsed were not too far off from Shultz's, the main difference being a private channel versus normal diplomatic communications. At least in this one memorandum, Clark seemed to promote improved strategic dialogue with the Soviets and progress on arms control—ideas similar to Shultz's. However, given that Clark did not discuss the memorandum with anyone on the NSC staff, or push the staff to promote these ideas, he did not succeed in his objectives.

Clearly there was a breakdown in communication between Shultz and Clark and possibly between Clark and his staff. Shultz's frustration mounted, focused, ironically, in on the like-minded national security advisor: "I could not let the White House staff interpret me to him [Reagan]. That was especially true when it came to Clark, because his views and instincts were different from mine, and he could not translate me accurately."[24] On March 10, Shultz attended a White House meeting on US-Soviet relations. When he entered the Oval Office, Reagan pulled him aside and told the secretary he did not want anyone to know about his earlier meeting with Dobrynin. Shultz wrote that "his remark reinforced my growing sense that the president was a prisoner of his own staff."[25]

Shultz continued his meetings with Dobrynin, in which he promoted the president's stated positions. "An hour meeting with Geo. S. just the 2 of us to talk about our quiet diplomacy efforts with Dobrynin," Reagan wrote in a diary entry of March 25. "We may get those Pentacostalists [sic] out of the embassy in Moscow yet."[26] Matters came to a head when Shultz and Reagan met late in the afternoon on April 6. In his diary entry, Reagan wrote: "Learned in office George S. is upset—thinks N.S.C. is undercutting him on plans he & I discussed for 'quiet diplomacy' approach to the Soviets."[27] The Soviets had released one of the Pentecostalists, Lydia Vashchenko, and she had arrived in Vienna that day. For Reagan and Shultz, this provided a concrete result of their quiet diplomacy in action.

Reagan's diary entries, as well as his comments to Shultz about keeping his private meeting with Dobrynin in February under wraps, illuminated the dysfunction in the NSC process with respect to Reagan's policies toward the Soviet Union. Reagan clearly was on the same page as Shultz, as he continued in his diary: "We had a meeting later in the day with George & cleared things up I think. Some of the N.S.C. staff are too hard line & dont [sic] think any approach should be made to the Soviets. I think I'm hard line and will never appease but I do want to try & let them see there is a better world if they'll show by deed they want to get along with the free world."[28]

This exemplified one of Reagan's greatest paradoxes: while "not appeasing" and remaining tough with the Soviets, he simultaneously reached out to Soviet leaders. And this again demonstrates Reagan's optimism that he could negotiate and improve relations with the Soviets.

Shultz pressed ahead with his quiet outreach to Dobrynin. Many of their discussions focused on the Pentecostalists who had been living in the basement of the US embassy in Moscow since 1978. The plight of the Pentecostals was a prime example of an issue that Reagan took a deep, vested personal interest in seeing resolved. He felt for these families, whom he believed had been unjustly persecuted merely for practicing their religion. Shultz promised Dobrynin that if they could secure the release of these families, the president would not publicly promote it as a US win over the Soviets. Reagan made the decision to push for their release because he was emotionally invested, as he wrote on April 12: "Today the Pentecostals left the Am. Embassy basement in Moscow where they've lived for 4 yrs. They left at our request. We think—well more than that we're sure we have a deal that they will be allowed to emigrate."[29] By July 1983, the families had been provided exit visas and allowed to emigrate to Israel. On July 20, Reagan wrote: "Incidentally the other Pentecostal family—15 people—has been allowed to leave the Soviet U. Quiet diplomacy is working."[30] Shultz recognized this as a major step forward in relations, explaining that "this 'special issue' was the first successful negotiation with the Soviets in the Reagan administration. The president's own role in it had been crucial. I always felt it was significant that Ronald Reagan's first diplomatic achievement with the Soviets—largely unknown to the public all these years—was on an issue of human rights. Was this episode also a test by the Soviet leaders of their ability to deal with Ronald Reagan? I thought so."[31]

Shultz went on to say that since the president did not "crow" publicly about the Pentecostalists "release," he demonstrated to the Soviets that a constructive relationship with him was possible.

Progress throughout the winter and spring 1983 on US-Soviet relations was slow, but nonetheless there was progress. That fall was tumultuous. Over the objections of Weinberger and others, Reagan authorized Shultz to maintain his scheduled meeting with Gromyko in Madrid a few short days after the KAL 007 disaster.[32] Even when difficult, dialogue did not cease. Then in November, NATO deployed Pershing II and ground-launched cruise missiles, after which the Soviets walked out of arms control negotiations in Geneva. The willingness of the Reagan administration to continue planned INF deployments in late November demonstrated a willingness to negotiate, not capitulate. Righting the balance on INF weapons and countering the Soviet threat in this arena allowed the Reagan administration to reassure NATO allies of US steadfastness.

While the Soviet walkout of INF and subsequently START negotiations in Geneva stalled any progress on arms negotiations in 1984, Reagan and Shultz prepared to move forward. During a series of meetings between Shultz and Gromyko in Geneva in January 1985, the two sides agreed to begin a new series of arms negotiations, the Nuclear and Space Talks (NST), to include three tracks: INF, START, and Defense and Space.[33] The first round of NST was set to begin on March 12. Then, Soviet General Secretary Konstantin Chernenko died on March 10 and the new Soviet leader, Mikhail Gorbachev, ascended to the post of general secretary the following day.

Even with the revolving door of national security advisers and resistance to arms control in some parts of the administration, Reagan and Shultz forged ahead with the four-part agenda. While initial assessments and reactions to Gorbachev in the Reagan administration were mixed, Gorbachev eventually proved to be an incomparable partner for Reagan in reducing the numbers of nuclear weapons in the US and Soviet arsenals. Reagan's willingness to negotiate with the new Soviet leader and his continued optimism that quiet diplomacy could improve relations with the Soviet Union (and, by extension, enhance US national security interests), coupled with Shultz's understanding of Reagan's vision, opened the door to a productive dialogue with Gorbachev and his new foreign minister, Eduard Shevardnadze.

"The Soviet Union remains the principal menace to our security and that of our allies," stated NSDD-165, which Reagan signed on March 8, 1985. As with NSDD-75, which the president had approved in January 1983, NSDD-165 called for agreements that would protect US interests and forward its objectives, chief among them the completion of its strategic modernization program. The deployment of Pershing II and ground-launched cruise missiles in Western Europe in the fall of 1983 notwithstanding, Reagan administration officials' perception of Soviet nuclear advantage persisted as the second term got underway. Moscow was about roll out SS-24s (MIRVed missiles in silos and on rail) and SS-25s (then-single warhead missiles on road-mobile launchers) for which there was no US equivalent deployed at the time.

In his early reform initiatives, Gorbachev did not halt these deployments; the US intelligence community expressed pessimism that he could. "While Soviet economic problems are severe, we see no signs that the Soviets feel compelled to forego important strategic programs or that they will make substantial concessions in arms control in order to relieve economic pressures," according to an April 1985 National Intelligence Estimate (NIE), titled "Soviet Capabilities for Strategic Nuclear Conflict through the Mid-1990s," which Reagan initialed. "Soviet force decisions and arms control decisions are likely to continue to be driven by calculations of political-strategic benefits and the dynamism of weapons technology," it went on to say.[34]

Contrary to these expectations, Gorbachev came to discount the political-strategic benefits and dynamism of weapons technology. Incredibly, both Soviet and American leaders in the mid-1980s agreed that military superiority conferred no advantage, while also rejecting mutual assured destruction. Here and elsewhere, decision directives and national intelligence estimates tell only part of the story. Execution of policies, as categorized in the four-part framework, came through interactions among individuals in Washington and Moscow. The Department of Defense's annual *Soviet Military Power*—a publication whose first issue included an overlay of a Soviet tank factory superimposed on the National Mall—did not misstate Soviet strategic capabilities; yet it offered scant evidence about how capabilities shaped Soviet intentions.[35] That was for leaders to decide.

When it came to US capabilities and intentions, Reagan did not fundamentally reevaluate his perception of threat from nuclear weapons or communism after the tense fall of 1983 and his smashing reelection victory one year later. While he may well have perceived and framed Soviet capabilities and intentions as inseparable, during his first few months as president, Reagan also espoused a fundamental optimism about human nature that superseded the grim logic of nuclear theorists. In the fall of 1981, Assistant Secretary of Defense Richard Perle and Secretary of Defense Caspar Weinberger probably regarded the zero option as a clever ploy to prevent the Soviets from derailing INF deployment with an interim agreement; Reagan, however, thought that it was a fine idea. Similarly, when his top advisers scoffed at Gorbachev's proposal, in January 1986, to eliminate all nuclear weapons by 2000, Reagan insisted that the proposal was consistent with what had been calling for all along. In support of the president's ambitions to achieve a blockbuster deal during his second administration, Shultz brought into his inner circle Paul Nitze, who had crafted NSC-68 ("United States Objectives and Programs for National Security") during the Truman administration and participated in every big debate about nuclear weapons ever since.[36]

Shortly after Reagan's second inauguration, Nitze delivered a speech to the World Affairs Council of Philadelphia in which he laid out a "strategic concept" for the next ten years that called for "radical reductions" in nuclear weapons toward the ultimate goal of zero.[37] Wary of Nitze's attacks on the unratified SALT II Treaty during the Carter administration, many arms control advocates doubted his sincerity on reducing nuclear arsenals; a number of arms control skeptics within the administration figured that Nitze intended to trade away SDI to secure his own ambitions to broker a deal.[38] As with the zero option four years earlier, the president seized on the positive vision that Nitze sketched out—a transition from strategic offenses to strategic defenses—and made it his own.

"The United States does not possess the numbers of weapons needed to carry out an effective first strike; nor do we have intention of acquiring such a capability," Reagan wrote Gorbachev in a July 25, 1986, letter that fleshed out Nitze's strategic concept. The president proposed three phases by which the United States and Soviet Union could research and deploy strategic defenses while providing assurance against a first-strike capability. During the first five years both sides would limit themselves to research, development, and testing of the strategic defense concept, under the terms of the 1972 Anti-Ballistic (ABM) Treaty, to establish a proof of concept. Reagan was prepared to sign a treaty stipulating that the party that decided to proceed beyond research, development, and testing, in 1991, agreed to "share the benefits of such a system with the other providing there is mutual agreement to eliminate the offensive ballistic missiles of both sides." Should the two sides fail to reach a sharing arrangement within the span of two years after 1991, either side would be free to deploy ABM systems after giving six months' notice. "I believe you would agree that significant commitments of this type with respect to strategic defenses would make sense only if made in conjunction with the implementation of immediate actions on both sides to begin moving toward our common goal of the total elimination of nuclear weapons," Reagan reiterated. "Toward this goal, I believe we also share the view that the process must begin with radical and stabilizing reductions in the offensive nuclear arsenals of both the United States and Soviet Union."[39]

Reagan hoped to employ the Strategic Defense Initiative (SDI) to transcend his perception of the ultimate threat in the nuclear age, by providing the "means of rendering these nuclear weapons impotent and obsolete." Following his interactions with Gorbachev—most dramatically, at Reykjavik in October 1986—the president was confident that Washington could share SDI with Moscow in the hope of someday eliminating these weapons. While NSDD-75 had called for encouraging liberalization of the Soviet system, the pursuit of that objective came not by proclamation but rather through Reagan and Shultz's pressing the case for dissidents and refuseniks in meetings with Gorbachev and Shevardnadze. In other words, the NSDDs alone did not explain the policies, which were fluid and reversible in the hands of US policymakers who faced internecine strife and external shocks. An example of fluidity was Shultz's defiance of hard-liners and Congress in his trip to Moscow in March 1987 following the Soviet penetration of the US embassy.[40]

In reading NSDD-75, moreover, there is no evidence of Reagan's ambitions to achieve radical nuclear arms reductions, starting with his execution of the policy of zero-zero on INF, which led to the first effectively verifiable nuclear arms reduction treaty in December 1987. Nowhere in NSDD-75 did it say anything about sharing a defensive missile shield with the Soviet Union to help facilitate the elimination of nuclear weapons. Yet that is what Reagan aspired to do. NSDD-75 *did* list as a key objective helping facilitate change within the Soviet system, which Reagan attributed to his championing of freedom, the enduring vitality of democratic capitalism, and above all to Gorbachev. The president saw his own role in facilitating change in the Soviet Union as exercising quiet diplomacy in private, as with the Pentecostalists, dissidents Anatoly Shcharansky and Andrei Sakharov; and, speaking truth in public, as he did in front of a giant statue of Lenin at Moscow State University in 1988. Elsewhere on that same trip, he famously stated that his phrase "evil empire" referred to "another time, another era."[41]

Reagan's anticommunism was clearly a core attribute of his extraordinary political career—yet that proclamation, in Red Square, was as consequential to the revolutions of 1989 as his previous exhortation: "Mr. Gorbachev: Tear down this wall!" In one of his last conversations with Soviet Foreign Minister Eduard Shevardnadze, on September 23, 1988, Reagan "recalled that in June 1987, he had gone to Berlin and made a speech in front of the Berlin Wall, a speech which called upon the Soviet Union to work with the West to improve the situation in that city. It had perhaps been unrealistic to have suggested then that the Berlin Wall be torn down in its entirety." Indeed, the president "realized that the division of Germany and of Berlin was a product of World War II, and the feeling on the part of the Soviet Union and many others that

Germany should never again be allowed to be the strongest and most dominant power in central Europe. But since we had talked earlier about the elimination of mistrust between us, one clear way of eliminating mistrust in Europe would be to allow the two parts of Berlin to work together, and the two parts of Germany to work together. This would be good for Europe and the world."[42]

Needless to say, the fall of the Berlin Wall came a lot faster than Reagan anticipated as he was preparing to leave office. That does not mean that Reagan and his national security team failed to execute their policies toward the Soviet Union by the end of December 1988—even though Reagan had once aspired to "win the Cold War" or, at least, "end the Cold War." Rather it shows how remote the termination of that conflict seemed at the start of the 1980s. Reagan's unceasing optimism set him apart from other US elected officials. It is no denigration to his legacy to state that Gorbachev—who signed the INF Treaty, agreed to the counting formula for START, released Sakharov and Shcharansky, committed to withdraw from Afghanistan, abandoned international class conflict, and gave up on attempting to split Western Europe from the United States—remains the figure most indispensable to the end of the Cold War.

"Because of strength and philosophy, the US-Soviet relationship will always be unique and always difficult to manage," Shultz wrote Reagan on November 18, 1987, "but it is increasingly clear that the Soviet Union is going to be seen by history as Ronald Reagan's 'China.'" Shultz went on to cite progress in the four areas of the Reagan agenda: arms control, human rights, bilateral issues, and regional affairs. "The Soviet Union is now changing also because of fear—fear of China's reforms, fear of Eastern European restlessness—but most of all because of fear of falling permanently behind the US." It was in the US interest to "keep the Russians well behind us but not so far behind that they become desperate and dangerous." "We have entered one of those rare historical periods when significant planned change is possible in relations between states," Shultz wrote in the closing paragraph. "We are at a crossroads where East and West could transform the nature of their postwar relationship with a more constructive form of competition. It is American ideas, strengths, and policies that have drawn the Soviets in this direction. It will be up to us to carefully manage its continued progress through a balance of toughness and inducement."[43]

Indeed, careful management was required after the breakthroughs of the Reagan-Gorbachev era led to new challenges. For example, the INF Treaty, which eliminated an entire class of nuclear weapons and initiated a regime of onsite inspections, raised the specter of a nuclear battlefield limited to

Germany, which ushered in the need for ambitious reductions in conventional forces—which, in turn, raised the prospect of a European continent without nuclear weapons or a US military presence. Moreover, Reagan's optimism about Gorbachev's prospects did not necessarily accord with the intelligence community's assessments—either when it came to the Soviet leader, the future of the Soviet system, or Soviet strategic capabilities. In a follow-up NIE issued at the tail end of Reagan's presidency, Soviet watchers within the US intelligence community predicted that "the large sunk costs in production for new strategic weapons and the fact that such production facilities cannot readily be converted to civilian uses mean that Gorbachev's industrial modernization goals almost certainly will not have major effects on strategic weapons deployments through the mid-1990s."[44]

While Gorbachev's devotion to new thinking led him to announce reductions in conventional forces, and later to accept the opening of the Berlin Wall and the broadly peaceful collapse of Soviet power in Eastern Europe, it had not overcome the inertia of the Soviet strategic build-up. Achieving that objective took the signing of START in 1991, the technical complexities of which outweighed Reagan and Shultz's enthusiasm to sign by January 20, 1989. What lay in store for Reagan's successor in the White House was the necessity for more imaginative thinking and ever-skillful diplomacy. The perception of Soviet threat, during 1989–1991, was the potential for mass violence amidst the collapse of a multinational empire with thousands of nuclear weapons—a fundamentally different set of perceived threats than what the Reagan administration had encountered.[45]

Notes

The views expressed here do not necessarily reflect those of the Department of State or the US government. This chapter is based on declassified and publicly available sources. The authors compiled the *Foreign Relations* volumes covering the Soviet Union and nuclear arms control that are among the fifty-two volumes in the Reagan subseries that are either available or will be available at https://history.state.gov/historicaldocuments/reagan.

1. Profile of Reagan, *Pravda*, 20 Jan. 1989, https://web.archive.org/web/20120510213231/http://www.foia.cia.gov/Reagan/19890120.pdf.

2. Richard Allen, Miller Center Interview, 28 May 2002. See also Hal Brands, *Making the Unipolar Moment: US Foreign Policy and the Rise of the Post–Cold War Order* (Ithaca, NY: Cornell University Press, 2016).

3. Stuart Spencer, quoted in Thomas C. Reed, *At the Abyss: An Insider's History of the Cold War* (New York: Ballantine Books, 2004), 234.

4. Reagan, Farewell Address to the Nation, 11 Jan. 1989, https://www.reaganfoundation.org/ronald-reagan/reagan-quotes-speeches/farewell-address-to-the-nation-2.

5. Reagan to Gorbachev, 25 July 1986, https://www.thereaganfiles.com/19860725.pdf.

6. Profile of Reagan, *Pravda*, 20 Jan. 1989.

7. In a series of radio addresses in October 1978, then–former governor Reagan read portions of a recent speech by Eugene Rostow arguing that the loss of American strategic superiority after the Cuban Missile Crisis had encouraged Soviet aggression around the world. Rostow, who had been the undersecretary of state for political affairs during the Johnson administration, would go on to head the Arms Control and Disarmament Agency from 1981 to 1982. See Kiron K. Skinner, Annelise Anderson, and Martin Anderson, eds., *Reagan, in His Own Hand: The Writings of Ronald Reagan That Reveal His Revolutionary Vision for America* (New York: Free Press, 2001), 92–96.

8. Distinguishing it from the last year of the Carter administration was complicated by the fact that Carter had already boosted defense spending following the Soviet invasion of Afghanistan in December 1979. See Brian J. Auten, *Carter's Conversion: The Hardening of American Defense Policy* (Columbia: University of Missouri Press, 2008). See also Edward Keefer, *Harold Brown: Offsetting the Soviet Military Challenge, 1977–1981* (Washington, DC: Historical Office, Office of the Secretary of Defense, 2017).

9. Reagan News Conference, 21 Jan. 1981, http://www.presidency.ucsb.edu/ws/?pid=44101.

10. Douglas Brinkley, ed., *The Reagan Diaries* (New York: Harper, 2009), 1:19. The minutes of the NSC meeting are available at http://www.thereaganfiles.com/19810211-nsc-2.pdf.

11. *Foreign Relations of the United States, 1981–1988*, vol. 3, *Soviet Union, January 1981–January 1983* (Washington: US Government Printing Office, 2016), doc. 39.

12. *FRUS, 1981–1988*, vol. 3, doc. 47.

13. *FRUS, 1981–1988*, vol. 3, doc. 68.

14. *FRUS, 1981–1988*, vol. 3, doc. 145.

15. *FRUS, 1981–1988*, vol. 3, doc. 189.

16. *FRUS, 1981–1988*, vol. 3, doc. 191.

17. *FRUS, 1981–1988*, vol. 3, doc. 205.

18. George Shultz, *Turmoil and Triumph: My Years as Secretary of State* (New York: Scribner's, 1993), 167.

19. Brinkley, *The Reagan Diaries*, 1:198. *FRUS, 1981–1988*, vol. 4, *Soviet Union, January 1983–March 1985*, docs. 9, 10, 11.

20. *FRUS, 1981–1988*, vol. 4, docs. 1, 19, 61, 62.

21. *FRUS, 1981–1988*, vol. 4, doc. 36.

22. *FRUS, 1981–1988*, vol. 4, doc. 7.

23. According to Tom Simons, who headed the Office of Soviet Union Affairs, the State Department also had its "watchdogs," such as Paul Wolfowitz in Policy Planning: "So it was not just the Pentagon. It was not just Secretary Weinberger and Richard Perle. Douglas [Feith] . . . was there. Frank Gaffney was there. So the little team was there, and their role was to block things and prevent things from happening." Tom Simons, Association for Diplomatic Studies and Training Interview, 22 July 2004, http://adst.org/wp-content/uploads/2012/09/Simons-Thomas-W1.pdf.

24. Shultz, *Turmoil and Triumph*, 167; *FRUS, 1981–1988*, vol. 4, doc. 16.
25. *FRUS, 1981–1988*, vol. 4, doc. 17; Shultz, *Turmoil and Triumph*, 267.
26. Brinkley, *The Reagan Diaries*, 1:210.
27. Brinkley, *The Reagan Diaries*, 1:212. For documents on the Pentecostalists, see *FRUS, 1981–1988*, vol. 4, docs. 12, 20, 34, 42, 74.
28. Brinkley, *The Reagan Diaries*, 1:212.
29. Brinkley, *The Reagan Diaries*, 1:215.
30. Brinkley, *The Reagan Diaries*, 1:249.
31. Shultz, *Turmoil and Triumph*, 171.
32. *FRUS, 1981–1988*, vol. 4, docs. 104, 105.
33. *FRUS, 1981–1988*, vol. 4, docs. 355–363.
34. National Intelligence Estimate, 11-3/8-84/85, "Soviet Capabilities for Strategic Nuclear Conflict Through the Mid-1990s," 25 Apr. 1985, https://web.archive.org/web/20120505204855/http://www.foia.cia.gov/Reagan/19850425.pdf.
35. Perhaps the most authoritative sources of Soviet strategic capabilities are the texts of INF and START. Also, see the interviews with former Soviet generals and officials sponsored by the Office of Net Assessment, which William Burr and Svetlana Savranskaya have curated and made available at http://nsarchive.gwu.edu/nukevault/ebb285.
36. On Nitze's role in the Cold War, see Strobe Talbott, *The Master of the Game: Paul Nitze and the Nuclear Peace* (New York: Knopf, 1988).
37. Nitze, Address Before the World Affairs Council of Philadelphia, 20 Feb. 1985, in Department of State, *Bulletin*, Apr. 1985, 27–28.
38. These fault lines are laid out in Talbott, *The Master of the Game*.
39. Reagan to Gorbachev, 25 July 1986, http://www.thereaganfiles.com/19860725.pdf.
40. For the National Security Planning Group minutes on the topic of Soviet penetration in advance of Shultz's trip, see *FRUS, 1981–1988*, vol. 6, *Soviet Union, October 1986–January 1989* (Washington: US Government Printing Office, 2016), doc. 31.
41. See *FRUS, 1981–1988*, vol. 6, doc. 155.
42. *FRUS, 1981–1988*, vol. 6, doc. 177.
43. *FRUS, 1981–1988*, vol. 6, doc. 94.
44. National Intelligence Estimate 11-3/8-88, Dec. 1988, https://www.cia.gov/library/center-for-the-study-of-intelligence/csi-publications/books-and-monographs/at-cold-wars-end-us-intelligence-on-the-soviet-union-and-eastern-europe-1989-1991/16526pdffiles/NIE11-3-8-88.pdf.
45. On the transition from Reagan to Bush as well as the latter's policies toward the Soviet Union, see Philip Zelikow and Condoleeza Rice, *To Build a Better World: Choices to End the Cold War and Create a Global Commonwealth* (New York: Twelve Books, 2019); Jeffrey Engel, *When the World Seemed New: George H. W. Bush and the End of the Cold War* (Boston: Houghton Mifflin Harcourt, 2017); and Svetlana Savranskaya and Thomas Blanton, *The Last Superpower Summits: Gorbachev, Reagan, and Bush Conversations that Ended the Cold War* (New York: Central European University Press, 2016).

CHAPTER 6

Once More, with Feeling

Transatlantic Relations in the Reagan Years

SUSAN COLBOURN AND MATHIAS HAEUSSLER

Ronald Reagan's first term as president was marked by sharp and often heated disputes over transatlantic relations. Contemporaries often viewed these difficulties as the product of Reagan's bombastic, anti-Soviet rhetoric and abrasive foreign policy style, which seemed to mark a clear break from the détente of the 1970s. The Reagan administration's outlook exacerbated tensions with key allies across Western Europe, many of whom sought to preserve and strengthen East-West contacts and connections despite the deterioration of superpower relations. The repercussions of such tensions stretched far beyond high politics, as widespread public opposition toward US policies throughout the Atlantic alliance threatened the very foundations of the transatlantic relationship, with Reagan serving as a galvanizing force against which antinuclear and peace activists unified.[1]

Yet, Reagan's diplomatic tone was far from the root cause of these transatlantic difficulties. Many of the problems that plagued transatlantic relations during Reagan's first term in office in fact emerged out of larger questions that had plagued the West's approach to the Cold War since the signing of the North Atlantic Treaty in 1949. Rather than marking a sharp break from the past, Reagan's new approach merely revealed the existing contradictions and tensions between superpower and inner-European détente that had already been simmering within the transatlantic alliance.[2] And, just as in previous episodes, those on both sides of the Atlantic tried to reconcile their interests by working toward common positions in line with NATO's longer-term dual strategy: the simultaneous pursuit of deterrence and dialogue. As the Reagan administration made strides in improving relations with the Soviet Union during the second term, a different set of familiar problems resurfaced: fears that the United States might sell out its allies as part of a deal with the Soviet Union. Tracing how these familiar dynamics played out in the 1980s, this chapter highlights just how much of the transatlantic relationship was shaped by structural forces and constraints. This is not to suggest that individuals did not influence policy or transatlantic relations in critical ways. Reagan's own outlook—his frustration with détente, his nuclear abolitionism, or his commitment to working with Mikhail Gorbachev—all played a decisive role and brought about many of the most critical issues in transatlantic relations during the president's two terms in office.

Since its founding in the late 1940s, NATO had experienced cyclical patterns of harmony and despair. The asymmetrical distribution of power among the Western allies made these tensions more or less inevitable, as did their various allies' very different geographic positions relative to the Soviet Union. In the late 1960s, for example, fears of an emerging nuclear parity between the superpowers made many Western Europeans worry about the continuing credibility of the US security guarantee and fear a potential superpower condominium taking place over their heads; in turn, the more autonomous stance of European leaders, notably the French president Charles de Gaulle, made US decision-makers apprehensive about a potential agreement with the Soviet Union that could lead to the neutralization or "Finlandization" of Europe.[3] In the early 1970s, too, the European Community's growing political and economic power fueled anxieties in Washington about its future leadership of NATO, resulting not least in Henry Kissinger's ill-fated demand for a so-called Year of Europe.[4] Though tensions calmed somewhat during Gerald Ford's brief stint in office, they quickly resurfaced under Jimmy Carter.

Carter's disagreements and testy exchanges with West German Chancellor Helmut Schmidt, as well as with other Western European leaders such as the French president Valéry Giscard d'Estaing, boiled down to competing philosophies in how to manage the Cold War. By the late 1970s, détente's achievements seemed increasingly uncertain. Vast investments into the Soviet Union's military capabilities appeared to underwrite a new sense of confidence in Moscow, which now behaved as a truly global superpower. Détente, critics charged, had done little to contain Soviet growth, a frustration compounded by a more general sense of pessimism about US power in the wake of Vietnam and Watergate.[5] Carter advocated a more realistic version of détente, adopting a tougher line on the Soviet Union's human rights record. But he believed this could be done without jeopardizing other elements of US-Soviet détente, particularly the Strategic Arms Limitation Talks (SALT). Carter's approach alarmed many in Western Europe. Not only were they much closer to the Soviet Union geographically and, accordingly, felt Moscow's military threat more acutely, but they were often also tied in longer-term trade relationships and economic interdependencies with the Eastern bloc.[6] Indeed, already during his very first meeting with Carter, the British prime minister James Callaghan was at pains to stress how most Western Europeans "felt themselves too close to the Soviet Union for comfort," given that they "had to continue to live with the Soviet Union" and were therefore "nervous about anything which might upset the existing balance."[7]

By the time Carter took office in January 1977, the rapid growth of Soviet military capabilities fueled such anxieties further, particularly the deployment of two new medium-range systems, the Backfire bomber and the SS-20 intermediate-range ballistic missile. With the deployment of these new, more advanced nuclear forces targeting Western Europe, some worried about the superpowers' continuing embrace of strategic parity, enshrined in SALT, and a growing insecurity in Europe as a result. NATO lacked comparable systems to counter the SS-20s, and the new Soviet weapons remained outside the scope of existing arms control negotiations, falling in a so-called "gray area" between SALT and the Mutual and Balanced Force Reduction (MBFR) talks. Wary of an irrevocable shift in the balance of power that might leave Western Europe exposed to Soviet pressure, the Schmidt government in particular lobbied the Carter administration to take the threat to Europe seriously and to restore parity either by increasing NATO's own tactical-nuclear capabilities or "negotiating away" the Soviet deployments.[8] After much wrangling, the transatlantic alliance eventually adopted a paired path forward in December 1979: in what became known as NATO's dual-track decision, the allies planned to deploy 572 medium-range missiles to Western Europe—a combination of Pershing II ballistic missiles and Gryphon ground-launched cruise missiles—and, simultaneously, to pursue negotiations with the Soviet Union to limit these same theater nuclear forces (TNFs).[9]

The Soviet invasion of Afghanistan later that month exacerbated intra-alliance tensions, bringing the various competing definitions of détente to the fore. Carter and his advisers, outraged by the invasion, moved quickly to introduce steep political and economic sanctions on the Soviet Union and asked their transatlantic partners to follow suit. But the administration's efforts to gain widespread support foundered, as the Western Europeans were reluctant to take measures that would hurt their own economies and compromise inner-European détente. In March 1980, Zbigniew Brzezinski, Carter's national security adviser, bemoaned the Western Europeans' seeming refusal to act, complaining to the president that they had effectively "done nothing in their bilateral relations with the Soviets to show their displeasure and concern over the invasion of Afghanistan."[10] Although Brzezinski's frustration conveniently overlooked the support that some Western European governments did give the administration's sanctions, such as Schmidt's reluctant backing of the Olympic boycott despite his own domestic political difficulties, the national security adviser's scathing assessments belied a larger fissure at the heart of the alliance.

By 1980, détente had become heavily contested, both at home in the United States and across the alliance. It was against this backdrop that Ronald Reagan ascended to the presidency, having positioned himself early as one of détente's fiercest critics. During his 1976 run for the Republican nomination, he had attacked Ford heavily for signing the Helsinki Final Act and quipped that détente had given the United States little more than the right to sell Pepsi in Siberia.[11] He had also lamented what he saw as the more general erosion of US power and influence across the globe, a deterioration that he viewed, at least in part, as the product of détente. "All I can see," he told an audience in March 1976, "is what other nations the world over see: collapse of the American will and the retreat of American power. There is little doubt in my mind that the Soviet Union will not stop taking advantage of détente until it sees that the American people have elected a new President and appointed a new Secretary of State."[12] In 1980, he doubled down on such rhetoric by heavily attacking Carter's foreign policy, even accusing the incumbent president for having brought the United States' position in the world to "an all-time low."[13] Once elected president, Reagan prepared to make good on his campaign promises.

Despite Reagan's aggressive rhetoric on the campaign trail, many of the Western allies greeted his election as a welcome change. Frustrated by the vacillations and uncertainties under Carter, key partners hoped that the new administration would bring greater consistency back to the policymaking process in Washington. Helmut Schmidt, in a conversation with the British prime minister Margaret Thatcher, lamented that the United States had been operating without a grand strategy since the Nixon years and added that the two things needed now were "leadership from the United States and much more consultation."[14] Reagan's foreign policy team, for one, was keen to exercise what it regarded as some much-needed leadership as well.[15]

If the new administration provided leadership, it hardly went in the direction that Washington's partners had hoped it would. The most acute problems centered unsurprisingly on the new president's outspoken anti-Soviet rhetoric: in his very first press conference, Reagan again dismissed détente as a "one-way street" that had enabled the Soviet Union to get ahead in the superpower competition while curtailing the United States' progress.[16] Remarks like these heightened already existing anxieties about the deterioration of East-West relations across Western Europe. By the spring of 1981, Secretary of State Alexander Haig concluded that there were "deep—though I believe mistaken—apprehensions in Europe that we are on a collision course with an increasingly desperate Soviet Union."[17]

Such fears crystalized around NATO's dual-track decision. Reagan's own inflammatory rhetoric, as well as the more general hostility to arms control found among some members of his administration, left many convinced that the president would abandon the decision's negotiating track entirely. As a result, Western European governments moved quickly to shape and moderate the administration's approach, and in so doing often proceeded in tandem. Before Margaret Thatcher visited Washington in February 1981, for instance, Helmut Schmidt urged her to convey in the strongest possible terms that the United States needed to retain its commitment to the negotiating track. "I would stick to that decision and make it stick," he remarked, obliquely referencing concerns that his government might back away from the December 1979 decision, "but please in order to make it stick I have to be sure that the United States . . . would stick to the words of that decision." Schmidt went on, emphasizing the critical importance of negotiations and of a mutual balance, something the chancellor had championed for decades. The Federal Republic would adhere to both "the deployment of such weapons in Europe" and to the Western efforts "to negotiate mutual balance—ceilings—or whatever you call them. Both are necessary and the Americans must not give the impression to the European public . . . that the second half of the decision does not really matter and what matters is just the first half."[18] Already, governments across Western Europe faced significant domestic pressure from a rapidly growing number of antinuclear campaigns, which feared the seeming return to the Cold War of recent years and explicitly opposed the planned deployment of the Pershing IIs and ground-launched cruise missiles. Thatcher dutifully carried Schmidt's message throughout the year. As Haig reported to Reagan in the spring of 1981, the British prime minister seemed "deeply concerned that we take into account the situation in the FRG. Mrs. Thatcher almost pleaded with me in London that we take care not to isolate Chancellor

Schmidt." Few of Haig's colleagues cared as much as the secretary of state. Next to Haig's note, Reagan's first national security adviser, Richard Allen, scribbled: "Who cares? State does, but why? ... Not our job to keep Schmidt in power—or any of the others." Allen worried that Haig and his compatriots at the State Department were more focused on "saving European governments" and all too willing to let that "become overriding concern in setting US policy."[19]

Allen's griping aside, the Reagan administration appreciated the degree to which the dual-track decision's fate depended on the support of governments across Europe. Though most members of the administration agreed that arms control negotiations were unlikely to yield results in the short term, the intensity of public opposition meant that Washington simply could not preserve support for deployment without demonstrating a genuine commitment to arms control.[20] Only earnest negotiations with Moscow—or, at least, the appearance thereof—could prevent a rift with Bonn, address mounting public concerns at home and abroad, and avoid a larger split within the alliance over East-West relations.[21] The initial US negotiating position reflected those considerations. In a speech at the National Press Club on November 18, 1981, Reagan laid out the administration's opening position for the arms control negotiations, now known as the intermediate-range nuclear force (INF) talks, scheduled to begin later that month. He proposed to stop the planned Pershing II and cruise missile deployments if the Soviet Union removed its existing medium-range systems—the so-called zero option. While Reagan's personal support for the proposal may have stemmed, at least in part, from its simplicity and sweeping reductions, which appealed to the president's sense of nuclear abolitionism, others within the administration saw it as a mechanism to keep the deployments on track.[22] Not only would the zero option demonstrate that the United States was willing to negotiate, people such as Secretary of Defense Caspar Weinberger or Richard Perle, the assistant secretary of defense for global strategic affairs, mused, but it would also strengthen the deployment track over the long term. When the Soviet Union invariably rejected the proposal, or so the thinking went, the Western Europeans would have no choice but to accept the deployments.[23]

The dual-track decision was far from the only issue plaguing transatlantic relations as 1981 came to close. After the introduction of martial law in Poland in December, the Reagan administration responded with a series of sanctions targeting both the Polish government and that of the Soviet Union. What ensued bore striking similarity to earlier allied disagreements following the invasion of Afghanistan. Once more, the Western Europeans tried to avoid any actions likely to further compromise East-West relations or jeopardize their existing trade relations with the East. For many governments in Western Europe, not only were there philosophical and strategic questions at stake, but the issue also impacted vital economic interests: by 1982, Western Europe's trade with the Soviet Union amounted to a total of $41 billion, compared to the United States' $2.5 billon.[24] Schmidt, for one, opposed the Reagan administration's calls for sanctions outright, even going so far as to claim that martial law was an internal Polish affair under the Helsinki Final Act.[25] The British, too, though somewhat bewildered by Germany's legalistic line, largely shared Schmidt's concerns.[26] The fact that the sanctions seemed to inordinately impact the Western Europeans only aggravated the situation. The Reagan administration's decision not reintroduce a grain embargo, for instance, seemed a clear example of US hypocrisy as halting grain sales would have impacted the lion's share of US-Soviet trade. In July 1982, the announcement of a US-Soviet grain deal further added to the sense that the administration's measures were punitive and lopsided.

What aggravated the Western Europeans most were the Reagan administration's thinly veiled attempts to use the sanctions to stop the construction of the Urengoy-Pomary-Uzhgorod pipeline. Once constructed, the extensive 5,000-kilometer pipeline would connect Soviet natural gas in Siberia to markets in Western Europe. The United States had long opposed to the project, believing that it would serve only to inject much-needed hard currency into the ailing Soviet economy, as well as hand over a critical lever to blackmail the governments of Western Europe over energy supply.[27] For the Western European governments, by contrast, the pipeline represented a much-needed economic link across the Iron Curtain, as well as a chance to diversify their energy sources after the shocks and shortages of the 1970s. It was also seen as an opportunity to create political and economic interdependencies that might diffuse, transform, and perhaps eventually even dismantle the divisions of the Cold War. These radically divergent positions unsurprisingly put the United States at odds with its Western European allies invested in the project. As British Foreign Secretary Lord Carrington put it to Washington in uncharacteristically sharp language, it seemed "questionable for the Americans to block unilaterally a project of vital importance to the Europeans in the guise of an Alliance reaction to Poland."[28]

Faced by almost complete opposition from its NATO partners, the Reagan administration eventually backtracked. George Shultz, who replaced Haig as secretary of state in the summer of 1982, understood the diplomatic damage done by the disputes over the Siberian pipeline. A veteran of the Nixon administration, with strong connections across Western Europe from his previous service, Shultz believed that the sanctions would only hurt US interests over the long term given the considerable anti-American sentiment found in Western Europe.[29] On November 13, Reagan announced that the sanctions would be lifted, thanks to a series of new allied initiatives to study alternative sources for Western energy, streamline strategic controls, and harmonize Western credit policies. The issue's resolution could hardly be seen as a victory for NATO, but Oliver Wright, the new British ambassador in Washington, concluded that it was "an almost total defeat for the Americans." Worse yet, the entire situation could easily happen again. The underlying questions about how best to manage East-West relations had not been resolved.[30]

The "year of the missile"—1983—would test the alliance to its very core; surviving that test would be critical to the future of the entire transatlantic partnership. Support for the dual-track decision's deployment track remained fragile. In the Federal Republic, Helmut Schmidt's government coalition had collapsed in October 1982, partly because of significant opposition against missile deployments within Schmidt's Social-Democratic Party, and Schmidt was replaced by the Christian Democrat Helmut Kohl.[31] Any uncertainty in Bonn's position alarmed other allied leaders as the Federal Republic was linchpin of the dual-track decision. On January 20, 1983, French President François Mitterrand used his remarks at the Bundestag marking the twentieth anniversary of the Élysée Treaty to express his strong support for the INF deployments in an attempt to sway German public opinion.[32]

Antinuclear demonstrations continued apace on both sides of Atlantic. In October 1983, as part of "Action Week," protestors gathered across Europe to express their ongoing opposition to the impending deployments of the Pershing IIs and ground-launched cruise missiles. A crowd of 400,000 gathered in the West German capital, where former chancellor Willy Brandt addressed the crowd, as did Petra Kelly, the prominent founder of the Green Party.[33] But the three critical governments stood firm. The British, Italian, and West German parliaments all voted to accept missiles deployments; the Soviets responded to the final decision in Bonn by walking out of the negotiations in Geneva. East-West relations seemed headed from bad to worse, and a string of other crises added to this sense of anxiety. On September 1, the Soviet Union shot down a passenger aircraft, Korean Airlines flight 007, killing all 269 passengers on board. The next month, as protestors rallied in Action Week demonstrations, two truck bombs struck US forces in Lebanon, and the United States invaded Grenada. Canadian Prime Minister Pierre Trudeau launched a self-proclaimed "peace mission" that same week, pointing to these recent crises as prime evidence of the need for meaningful dialogue between East and West lest the world become even more dangerous.[34]

What of another seeming brush with danger that autumn—NATO's now-infamous command-and-control exercise, Able Archer 83? Part of a larger simulation, Able Archer rehearsed the transition from conventional to nuclear weapons. According to one school of thought, based largely off of information provided by a Soviet defector, Oleg Gordievskii, Able Archer nearly led to nuclear war. The Soviet Union, this telling goes, believed the exercise to be a cover for a nuclear first strike and even contemplated launching one of their own.[35] Material from archives across the Warsaw Pact suggests that Gordievskii's claims were wildly exaggerated. Far from seeing it as a potential first strike scenario, Soviet observers understood the exercise's basic purpose and saw few reasons to be alarmed.[36] For contemporaries, however, Gordievskii's warnings underscored the severe tensions in East-West relations and offered yet more reasons to pursue a more comprehensive and overt dialogue with the Soviet Union. "I feel the Soviets are so defense minded," Reagan confided in his diary on November 18, "so paranoid about being attacked that without being in any way soft on them we ought to tell them no one here has any intention of doing anything like that. What the h—l have they got that anyone would want."[37]

Much of the Reagan administration's first term was marked by transatlantic disagreements about how to manage relations with the Soviet Union and Eastern Europe, with Washington's allies frequently making the case for greater dialogue. By early 1983, the Reagan administration set out a four-part approach to manage relations with the Soviet Union in a comprehensive strategy paper, National Security Decision Directive 75. It identified arms control, bilateral issues, regional questions, and human rights as the four main topics that should guide relations, and in so doing set the tone for much of the administration's later engagement with the Soviet Union, including the historic breakthroughs and summits of Reagan's second term.[38]

George Shultz again played a major part in developing and communicating the administration's strategy. In June 1983, he laid out the four-part approach in a clear, concise testimony before the Senate Foreign Relations Committee. The British ambassador to the United States, Oliver Wright, viewed the testimony as the sign of a new era, claiming that Shultz's approach seemed to mark the beginning of a "comprehensive, coherent and conciliatory" Soviet policy.[39] Over the following months, the Reagan administration sent a steady stream of signals that it hoped to do business with the Soviet Union. "The United States," the president affirmed in November, "will never walk away from the negotiating table. Peace is too important. Common sense demands that we persevere, and we will persevere."[40] On January 16, 1984, in a major foreign policy address, Regan again underscored his desire for dialogue with the Soviet Union, famously musing about a chance encounter between four ordinary citizens of both nations, Ivan, Anya, Jim, and Sally.[41] As he confided to his diary afterward, it was an address that "held the door open to the Soviets if they mean what they say about loving peace to walk in."[42] Others derided it as cynical electioneering, designed to secure the president's reelection in November.[43]

Even as the Reagan administration shifted tone, progress remained slow. During Konstantin Chernenko's brief tenure as general secretary, he agreed to reopen arms control negotiations with a new package of umbrella talks, the Nuclear and Space Talks (NST). As part of these negotiations, the United States and the Soviet Union agreed to hold simultaneous discussions on strategic forces, intermediate-range weapons, and what the Soviets referred to as "the militarization of space." The last of these topics centered on Reagan's Strategic Defense Initiative (SDI), first unveiled in March 1983 and quickly dubbed "Star Wars." "What if," the president had asked, "free people could live secure in the knowledge that their security did not rest upon the threat of instant US retaliation to deter a Soviet attack, that we could intercept and destroy strategic ballistic missiles before they reached our own soil or that of our allies?"[44] The idea was as simple as it was ambitious: a missile defense system based not on US soil, but rather in space, which might eventually render nuclear weapons obsolete. Yet, few within the alliance shared Reagan's affection for SDI. Officials across the alliance dismissed Reagan's vision of a space-based defensive system as fanciful, if not downright insane, and charged that the president hoped to turn space into the next battlefield. Reagan's desire to shift away from mutual deterrence, some in Western Europe worried, could undermine the security of Washington's partners by loosening the US commitment to Europe and accelerating the administration's existing isolationist tendencies. The Kohl government, for instance, wondered if SDI would damage arms control and decouple Europe's security from that of the United States.[45]

Reagan's October 1986 meeting with Chernenko's successor, Mikhail Gorbachev, presented a new and rather unexpected twist on SDI. At the Reykjavik summit, the two leaders flirted with sweeping proposals to rid the world of nuclear weapons altogether; the only thing that stopped them was a disagreement over SDI. Reagan refused to sacrifice the program, while Gorbachev refused to remove SDI from the overall package. Relieved by the summit's failure, policymakers across the alliance rushed to make sure that the president appreciated the implications about what had nearly transpired in Iceland.

Within the United States, the Joint Chiefs of Staff tried to secure guarantees from the president that he understood the implication of the Soviet Union's conventional force advantages.[46] SDI's role as the spoiler of Reykjavik also made the proposal far more popular with the Western Europeans, who had been alarmed by Reagan's willingness to consider such sweeping arms control proposals—a far cry from their earlier concerns that the president was hostile to any and all arms control. Margaret Thatcher in particular had little patience for the president's abolitionist thought, believing that one simply could not reverse time to put the proverbial nuclear genie back in the bottle. Helmut Kohl, too, underscored the importance of arms control agreements that ensured the West's continued security in the face of Soviet Union's conventional, chemical, and short-range nuclear capabilities during a visit to Washington a few weeks after the summit.[47]

Kohl's and Thatcher's views spoke to an increasingly unified Western European position, which was wary of the president's position at Reykjavik and its potential to damage NATO's defenses.[48] Seen from Western Europe, Reagan's willingness to entertain a nuclear-free world threatened to undercut their own security and unravel the Atlantic alliance, a prospect that revived old nightmares about a superpower condominium where Moscow and Washington might do a deal over their heads. Horst Teltschik, one of Kohl's chief advisers, bemoaned the latest round of requests that the West Germans not "overburden the president's attention span" in the weeks after the summit. "This was the same president who had negotiated for eleven hours with Gorbachev."[49] Ivo Daalder succinctly summed up the Western European dilemma: "Europe loves arms control, but not too much of it," he wrote in November 1986, mere weeks after the superpowers' summit at Reykjavik. "It does not like star wars, but finds it useful in blocking arms control deals that go too far. It likes nuclear weapons, but must deal with a sizable public minority that clamors for their removal. It likes superpower summits, but only ones on which it is consulted."[50]

Reykjavik eventually paved the way for an arms control agreement that limited both sides' intermediate-range forces. In February 1987, Gorbachev indicated he was willing to break INF out of the arms control package.[51] Over the course of the year, the United States and the Soviet Union ironed out an agreement, based on Reagan's initial zero option proposal from 1981. The final result, the INF Treaty signed at the Washington summit that December, eliminated all intermediate-range missiles between 500 and 5,000 kilometers, including the SS-20s, Pershing IIs, and ground-launched cruise missiles. Despite allied support for the zero option, many within NATO circles expressed severe reservations about a deal that did away with all intermediate-range systems, not least because they had previously accepted the zero option on the assumption that it would never form the basis of an actual agreement. The Western allies thus refocused their attention on the proposal's shortcomings and on the original logic behind the dual-track decision.[52] Supreme Allied Commander General Bernard Rogers was only one of many voices warning of the dangers inherent in the further denuclearization of Europe. "Let's not sacrifice the long-term security of Western Europe on the altar of political expediency," he implored.[53] Within Western Europe, too, old anxieties returned as to what, exactly, the superpowers might be willing to accept. In Bonn, for example, it was feared that the INF Treaty's elimination of intermediate-range weapons would place greater emphasis on conventional, chemical, and short-range nuclear forces (SNFs)—precisely the systems that would be used on German soil if a conflict were to break out. No matter the dramatic breakthroughs in East-West relations, the transatlantic alliance still stared down difficult problems about how to defend the West at the end of Reagan's tenure.[54]

Though structural constraints and perennial problems loomed large in transatlantic relations—the realities of geography and the asymmetry of power regularly led to discord and disagreement between the Western allies—so too did individual leaders, their relationships, and their personal chemistry. At Reagan's funeral in 2004, two of the president's closest transatlantic partners, Margaret Thatcher and Brian Mulroney, the former Canadian prime minister, delivered heartfelt eulogies. Already during Reagan's presidency, both relationships had been celebrated prominently. Reagan and Mulroney's March 1985 summit—the so-called Shamrock summit—embodied that close feeling, as the two men comfortably swapped stories and told jokes. What grabbed headlines, at least in Canada, was a rendition of "When Irish Eyes Are Smiling" including the presidents and their wives; some Canadian critics derided it as embarrassing and a sign of an almost pathetic willingness to pander to the Americans.[55] Margaret Thatcher's close relationship with Ronald Reagan has been held up even more prominently as a prime example of the allegedly "special" Anglo-American relationship, at times evoking comparisons to the partnership between Winston Churchill and Franklin Delano Roosevelt. Indeed, Reagan later described their relationship as "soul mates when it came to reducing government and expanding economic freedom," and Thatcher proclaimed at Reagan's funeral to "have lost a dear friend."[56]

Strong leadership and personal connections could have important effects on policy and process, as in the case of Canada. After George Shultz became secretary of state, he spearheaded efforts to get his counterparts in Washington to take Canada seriously, appreciating that it was the United States' largest trading partner by far. "I was frustrated that so few people in Washington appreciated Canada's significance to us," he later wrote. Trying to strengthen the bilateral relationship, Shultz initiated regular meetings with his Canadian counterpart Allan MacEachen, whom he had known for decades going back to their time at the Economics Department at MIT.[57] These informal quarterly meetings, which continued throughout the Reagan administration and held with both Liberal and Conservative governments in Ottawa, facilitated close consultations on a wide range of issues and irritants from acid rain to apartheid, even if they did not always result in agreement.

Among the most contentious and consequential of these issues was free trade. In 1982, Pierre Trudeau had appointed the Royal Commission on the Economic Union and Development Prospects for Canada, better known as the Macdonald Commission after its chair, former finance minister Donald Macdonald, to study the country's economic policies. When the commission's findings were released in the autumn of 1985, they injected new momentum into the idea of free trade. Mulroney, now prime minister, seized on the report to initiate free trade talks with the United States; these negotiations began in April 1986. Congress fast-tracked the talks: if an agreement was reached before midnight on October 3, 1987, then it could be put to an up-down vote. The negotiations went down to the wire on October 3, as the two sides argued about a dispute settlement mechanism, a must-have item for Ottawa. Mere hours before the deadline, the Canadian negotiators in Washington called the prime minister to tell him that there would be no deal. Secretary of the Treasury James Baker finally broke the stalemate when he burst in on the Canadian negotiators and offered up the settlement mechanism they had wanted.[58] After a rocky and heated election campaign in Canada, which centered on the question of free trade and Canada's relationship with the United States, the agreement went into effect on January 1, 1989.[59] These bilateral negotiations paved the way for a trilateral deal with Mexico—what became the North American Free Trade Agreement (NAFTA). Looking back, Mulroney credited his close personal relationship with the president—and the network of contacts cultivated by the longtime Canadian ambassador in Washington, Allan Gotlieb—for making free trade possible.[60]

Yet, when thinking of Reagan's closest partners, it is Margaret Thatcher who most frequently comes to mind. The two leaders, however, disagreed frequently, and at times heavily, over actual policy decisions.[61] Thatcher, as seen earlier, largely shared the concern of other Western European leaders about Reagan's vision of a nuclear-free world, and later described it as one of the few instances where Reagan's "aspirations" had allegedly "left the reality of human nature."[62] Economic policy also proved surprisingly contentious, even with Reagan's and Thatcher's ideological affinity. True to her monetarist convictions, however, the British prime minister shared the concerns of London's continental partners about skyrocketing US interest rates, and she frequently voiced them in Washington.[63] In June 1982, Thatcher sided with Schmidt to confront Reagan directly about his deficit spending at the G-7 summit in Versailles, and afterward boasted to the chancellor how "she had tackled President Reagan about the US deficit."[64] In so doing, Thatcher expressed grievances shared by both Schmidt and François Mitterrand, who repeatedly indicated his frustration with the president's economic policies.[65] The most infamous clash between Thatcher and Reagan, however, came over the US invasion of Grenada in October 1983, which took place without any advance notice to Thatcher in spite of her well-known reservations. "She's upset & doesn't think we should do it," Reagan confided in his diary after one telephone conversation. "I couldn't tell her it had started."[66] That lack of consultation left Thatcher embarrassed and in a political bind. "At best, the British government had been made to look impotent," she later wrote. "At worst we looked deceitful."[67]

Reagan's relationships with his counterparts in Bonn and Paris reveal similar patterns. Again, these similarities point to some broader structural dynamics underlying transatlantic tensions under Reagan. Helmut Schmidt, for example, initially appeared fond of Reagan's plain-spokenness—and enjoyed the simple fact that he was not Carter—but soon became disillusioned by what he regarded as Reagan's lack of sensitivity to Western European interests in critical geostrategic and macroeconomic questions.[68] After Schmidt's fall from office, his successor Kohl worked hard to develop a strong relationship with Reagan, partly to defuse some of the anti-American sentiment gaining ground in the Federal Republic during the early 1980s.[69] Their relationship—and the heavy weight of the past that still defined that relationship—was perhaps best illustrated by the Bitburg affair. In November 1984, during a visit to Washington, Kohl invited Reagan to the Federal Republic the following spring. The president's visit, Kohl hoped, would demonstrate the strength of the German-American relationship and underscore the two nations' reconciliation since the Second World War, not unlike the chancellor's highly publicized stop at Verdun, where he and François Mitterrand clasped hands on the historic battlefield. After it came to light that the planned site—the cemetery at Bitburg—included graves of soldiers who had served in Heinrich Himmler's Waffen-SS, the press had "a field day."[70] Elie Wiesel, the famed writer and Holocaust survivor who served as chair of the US Holocaust Memorial Council, implored the president not to go. "That place," he remarked, "is not your place. Your place is with the victims of the SS."[71] But Kohl warned that if the president revised his plans, it would undercut the chancellor's political position. Thomas Niles, who served as Deputy Assistant Secretary in the European Bureau, later explained Reagan's decision to stick with the stop as the product of friendship. The president was "a person who valued friendship and put high store on loyalty to friends." So when Kohl made it clear that the appearance mattered to him, Reagan stayed the course.[72]

A French socialist, François Mitterrand was not a fellow conservative like Mulroney, Thatcher, or Kohl.[73] Certainly, no shortage of issues plagued the relationship. The French, to give but one example, came out swinging against the Reagan administration's sanctions threatening the Siberian pipeline project. Claude Cheysson, the French foreign minister, insisted that the United States and Western Europe were headed toward a "progressive divorce." Those in Washington, as he bemoaned in one televised interview, seemed "totally indifferent to our problems."[74] But Mitterrand proved a critical ally when it mattered most: over the dual-track decision. Despite France's detached attitude toward the alliance since the country's withdrawal from the integrated command structure in 1966, Mitterrand came out in favor of the dual-track decision (including in his January 1983 Bundestag remarks) in appeals designed to bolster the pro-deployment forces within the Federal Republic. Their shared sense of anticommunism brought the two together, leaving Reagan to remark on one occasion that the French president's comments about the Soviet Union "sounded like me."[75]

Transatlantic relations in the 1980s often covered familiar ground. At the dawn of the decade, Washington's allies worried about the hardline bombast popular among Americans and urged a more conciliatory approach to the Soviet Union with far greater dialogue. As that dialogue picked up steam, they then worried about what kind of bargains the superpowers might strike. Neither was all that surprising given the asymmetrical nature of the relationship; these oscillations were, to borrow a phrase from Geir Lundestad, "dependency swings."[76] Anxieties like these infused the Western allies' debates throughout the decade, be they economic, strategic, or nuclear debates. For all the familiar dynamics at play in the 1980s, the Atlantic alliance stared down critical challenges that threatened to undermine and unravel the transatlantic relationship entirely. The implementation of the dual-track decision called into question assumptions at the heart of the alliance, not least NATO's reliance on nuclear deterrence to defend its various members on both sides of the Atlantic. Even after the deployment of the Pershing IIs and ground-launched cruise missiles began in the autumn of 1983, many observers worried that the transatlantic security consensus had broken down and could no longer sustain the alliance's existing nuclear policies. We now know that the alliance did not fall apart; instead, the Berlin Wall did, followed by the Warsaw Pact and, then, the Soviet Union itself. But, to contemporaries, the acrimonious debates over the Pershing IIs and ground-launched cruise missiles suggested a broader erosion of the alliance's foundations. During Reagan's two terms, then, transatlantic relations bore striking familiarity to decades past and, simultaneously, navigated the single most significant challenge of the Atlantic alliance's history during the Cold War.[77]

This paradox was far from the only one to shape these eight years. Reagan's seemingly incongruous attitudes inflected and inspired many of the problems in transatlantic relations. Over his two terms, the president railed against détente with the Soviet Union, tried to stymie NATO allies' efforts to build economic ties with Moscow, and signed a sweeping arms control agreement eliminating a whole set of missiles. Protestors took to the streets across the alliance in the largest demonstrations since 1945, armed with placards condemning the president as a warmonger who flirted with nuclear strikes. Yet, it was that same man who dreamed of a world without nuclear weapons and almost did away with them at Reykjavik in the autumn of 1986. As with so many aspects of the Reagan administration's eight years in power, these seeming contradictions shaped much about the transatlantic relationship and the issues the Western allies confronted, reminding many of the chronic tensions found within the alliance.

Notes

1. For earlier historical studies of the transatlantic relationship during the Reagan years, see N. Piers Ludlow, "The Unnoticed Apogee of Atlanticism? US-Western European Relations during the Early Reagan Era," in *European Integration and the Atlantic Community*, ed. Klaus Kiran Patel and Kenneth Weisbrode (Cambridge: Cambridge University Press, 2013), 17–38; Timothy Andrews Sayle, *Enduring Alliance: A History of NATO and the Postwar Global Order* (Ithaca, NY: Cornell University Press, 2019), 205–215. For Reagan as a unifying factor within the peace movements of Western Europe, see Holger Nehring and Benjamin Ziemann, "Do All Paths Lead to Moscow? The NATO Dual-Track Decision and the Peace Movement—A Critique," *Cold War History* 12, no. 1 (2012): esp. 9–10.

2. Historians have since identified a far more gradual change in US Cold War strategy, beginning at least in the Carter years. For a recent overview, see Olav Njølstad, "The Collapse of Superpower Détente, 1975–1980," in *The Cambridge History of the Cold War*, vol. 3, *Endings*, ed. Melvyn P. Leffler and Odd Arne Westad (Cambridge: Cambridge University Press, 2010), 135–155.

3. Frédéric Bozo, *Two Strategies for Europe: De Gaulle, the United States, and the Atlantic Alliance* (Lanham, MD: Rowman and Littlefield, 2001); Thomas A. Schwartz, *Lyndon Johnson and Europe: In the Shadow of Vietnam* (Cambridge, MA: Harvard University Press, 2003), 92–140.

4. Luke Nichter, *Richard Nixon and Europe: The Reshaping of the Postwar Atlantic World* (Cambridge: Cambridge University Press, 2015); Daniel Möckli, *European Foreign Policy during the Cold War: Brandt, Pompidou and the Dream of Political Unity* (London: Bloomsbury, 2009).

5. Julian Zelizer, "Détente and Domestic Politics," *Diplomatic History* 33, no. 4 (2009): 653–670.

6. For the more general differences between superpower and inner-European détente, see Daniel Sargent, *A Superpower Transformed: The Remaking of American Foreign Relations in the 1970s* (Oxford: Oxford University Press, 2015), 59–67; Stephan Kieninger, *Dynamic Détente: The United States and Europe, 1964–1975* (Lanham, MD: Rowman and Littlefield, 2016).

7. Callaghan-Carter record of discussion, 10 Mar. 1977, National Archives of the United Kingdom (TNA), PREM 16/1485.

8. Kristina Spohr, "Conflict and Cooperation in Intra-Alliance Nuclear Politics: Western Europe, the United States, and the Genesis of NATO's Dual-Track Decision, 1977–9," *Journal of Cold War Studies* 13, no. 2 (2011), 39–89; Kristina Spohr, *The Global Chancellor: Helmut Schmidt and the Reshaping of the International Order* (Oxford: Oxford University Press, 2016).

9. For an overview of the origins of the Dual-Track Decision, see Leopoldo Nuti, "The Origins of the 1979 Dual Track Decision—A Survey," in *The Crisis of Détente in Europe: From Helsinki to Gorbachev, 1975–1985*, ed. Leopoldo Nuti (Abingdon: Routledge, 2009), 59–71.

10. Brzezinski to Carter, 18 Mar. 1980, Jimmy Carter Presidential Library (JCPL), Remote Access Capture (RAC), NLC-17-131-4-2-2.

11. "The President's News Conference," 13 Feb. 1976, *Public Papers of the Presidents of the United States: Gerald Ford 1976–1977* (Washington, DC: US Government Printing Office, 1979), 1:267–268.

12. Jon Nordheimer, "Reagan, in Direct Attack, Assails Ford on Defense," *New York Times*, 5 Mar. 1976.

13. "Televised Address by Governor Ronald Reagan: 'A Strategy for Peace in the '80s'," 19 Oct. 1980, https://www.reaganlibrary.archives.gov/archives/Reference/10.19.80.html.

14. Thatcher-Schmidt note of conversation over dinner, 17 Nov. 1980, TNA, PREM 19/471; "Gespräche BK mit PM Thatcher und AM Carrington," 17 Nov. 1980, Bundesarchiv (BA), B 136/17115.

15. Ra'anan to Iklé, "Toward the Evolution of a 'Reagan Doctrine' on Global Strategy: Some Considerations," 26 May 1980, Hoover Institution Archives (HIA), Fred Iklé Papers, box 14, folder "Soviet Union."

16. "The President's News Conference," 29 Jan. 1981, *Public Papers of the Presidents of the United States: Ronald Reagan (PPP: RR) 1981* (Washington: US Government Printing Office, 1982), 57.

17. Haig to Reagan, 29 Apr. 1981, Ronald Reagan Presidential Library (RRPL), Executive Secretariat NSC (ESNSC), Meeting Files (MF), folder "NSC0008."

18. Thatcher-Schmidt record of telephone conversation, 24 Feb. 24, 1981, TNA, PREM 19/762. On Helmut Schmidt's earlier thinking about balance, see Spohr, *Global Chancellor*, 33–60.

19. Haig to Reagan, 29 Apr. 1981, RRPL, ESNSC, MF, folder "NSC0008."

20. Rostow to Casey, "Reflections on My Trip to Brussels, SHAPE, Bonn, and London, September 24, to October 13, 1981," 26 Oct. 1981, CIA Electronic Reading Room.

21. Ermarth, "TNF and Arms Control," July 1981, RRPL, Sven Kraemer Files, box 90556, folder "NATO-TNF-Arms Control–State Conference (1)."

22. See Stephanie Freeman's chapter in this volume. See also Paul Lettow, *Ronald Reagan and His Quest to Abolish Nuclear Weapons* (New York: Random House, 2005). For a rebuttal of this view, see Doug Rossinow, "The Legend of Reagan the Peacemaker," *Raritan* 32, no. 3 (2013): 56–76.

23. NSC record of meeting, 13 Oct. 1981, http://reaganfiles.com/19811013-nsc-22.pdf.

24. US-Soviet trade was smaller, in part because the Jackson-Vanik Amendment had severely reduced the scope of superpower trade relations by curtailing the president's ability to grant most favored nation status (MFN) to the Soviet Union. See Michael Cotey Morgan and Daniel Sargent, "Helsinki 1975," in *Transcending the Cold War: Summits, Statecraft, and the Dissolution of Bipolarity in Europe, 1970–1990*, ed. Kristina Spohr and David Reynolds (Oxford: Oxford University Press, 2016), 104; Angela Romano, "The Main Task of European Political Cooperation: Fostering Détente in Europe," in *Perforating the Iron Curtain: European Détente, Transatlantic Relations, and the Cold War, 1965–1985*, ed. Poul Villaume and Odd Arne Westad (Copenhagen: Museum Tusculanum Press, 2010), 137. On the significance of economics and trade in European conceptions of détente more generally, see Werner D. Lippert, *The Economic Diplomacy of Ostpolitik: Origins of NATO's Energy Dilemma* (New York: Berghahn Books, 2011).

25. Gregory F. Domber, "Transatlantic Relations, Human Rights, and Power Politics," in *Perforating the Iron Curtain: European Détente, Transatlantic Relations, and the Cold War, 1965–1985*, ed. Poul Villaume and Odd Arne Westad (Copenhagen: Museum Tusculanum Press, 2010), 197.

26. Thatcher-Carrington memorandum of telephone conversation, 27 Dec. 1981, TNA, PREM 19/871.

27. NSC record of meeting, 9 July 1981, RRPL, ESNSC, MF, folder "NSC00017." David Painter's contribution to this volume offers a detailed overview of the various arguments, both within the administration and between the Western allies over the pipeline. See also Bruce W. Jentleson, *Pipeline Politics: The Complex Political Economy of East-West Energy Trade* (Ithaca, NY: Cornell University Press, 1986); Ksenia Demidova, "The Deal of the Century: The Reagan Administration and the Soviet Pipeline," in *European Integration and the Atlantic Community in the 1980s*, ed. Klaus Kiran Patel and Kenneth Weisbrode (Cambridge: Cambridge University Press, 2013), 59–82; Andrea Chiampan, "'Those European Chicken Littles': Reagan, NATO, and the Polish Crisis, 1981-2," *International History Review* 37, no. 4 (2015): 682–699.

28. Carrington, "Poland, the USA, and the Alliance," 26 Jan. 1982, TNA, PREM 19/873.

29. Susan Colbourn, "An Interpreter or Two: Defusing NATO's Siberian Pipeline Dispute, 1981–1982," *Journal of Transatlantic Studies* 18, no. 2 (2020): 131–151.

30. "Summary of Washington Despatch of 10 December, The Siberian Pipeline: Lessons for the Future," 13 Dec. 1982, TNA, FCO 33/5362.

31. For the role of the Social Democrats, see Jan Hansen, *Abschied vom Kalten Krieg? Die Sozialdemokraten und der Nachrüstungsstreit, 1977–1987* (Berlin: De Gruyter Oldenbourg, 2016).

32. Frédéric Bozo, "France, the Euromissiles, and the End of the Cold War," in *The Euromissile Crisis and the End of the Cold War*, ed. Leopoldo Nuti, Frédéric Bozo, Marie-Pierre Rey, and Bernd Rother (Washington, DC: Woodrow Wilson Center Press, 2015), 199–202.

33. William Drozdiak, "More Than a Million Protest Missiles in Western Europe," *New York Times*, 23 Oct. 1983.

34. Pierre Elliott Trudeau, "A Peace Initiative from Canada," *Bulletin of the Atomic Scientists* 40, no. 1 (1984): 15. On the peace mission and its links to transatlantic relations, see Susan Colbourn, "'Cruising toward Nuclear Danger': Canadian Anti-Nuclear Activism, Pierre Trudeau's Peace Mission, and the Transatlantic Partnership," *Cold War History* 18, no. 1 (2018): 19–36.

35. Christopher Andrew and Oleg Gordievsky, *KGB: The Inside Story of Its Foreign Operations from Lenin to Gorbachev* (London: Hodder and Stoughton, 1990), 502–503; Nate Jones, *Able Archer 83: The Secret History of the NATO Exercise That Almost Triggered a Nuclear War* (New York: New Press, 2016).

36. Beatrice Heuser, "The Soviet Response to the Euromissiles Crisis," in *The Crisis of Détente in Europe: From Helsinki to Gorbachev, 1975–1985*, ed. Leopoldo Nuti (Abingdon: Routledge, 2009), 137–49; Mark Kramer, "Die Nicht-Krise um Able Archer 83: Fürchtete die sowjetische Führung tatsächlich einen atomaren Großangriff im Herbst 1983," in *Wege zur Wiedervereinigung: Die beiden deutschen Staaten in ihren Bündnissen, 1970 bis 1990*, ed. Oliver Bange and Bernd Lemke (Munich: Oldenbourg, 2013), 129–149; Dmitry Adamsky, "'Not Crying Wolf': Soviet Intelligence and the 1983 War Scare," in *The Euromissile Crisis and the End of the Cold War*, ed. Leopoldo Nuti, Frédéric Bozo, Marie-Pierre Rey, and Bernd Rother (Washington, DC, and Stanford, CA: Woodrow Wilson Center Press and Stanford University Press, 2015), 49–65; Gordon Barrass, "Able Archer 83: What Were the Soviets Thinking?," *Survival* 58, no. 6 (2016): 7–30; Simon Miles, "The War Scare that Wasn't: Able Archer 83 and the Myths of the Second Cold War," *Journal of Cold War Studies* 22, no. 3 (2020): 86–118.

37. Douglas Brinkley, ed., *The Reagan Diaries* (New York: Harper, 2009), 1:290.

38. Elizabeth Charles and James Graham Wilson's chapter in this volume offers a detailed overview of the four-part agenda and its implementation, including the administration's internal debates. For an overview that situates the administration's 1983 conversations in the broader context of US-Soviet relations, see Simon Miles, *Engaging the Evil Empire: Washington, Moscow, and the Beginning of the End of the Cold War* (Ithaca, NY: Cornell University Press, 2020), 57–83.

39. Wright, "US Policy towards the Soviet Union," 20 June 1983, TNA, PREM 19/1033.

40. "Address before the Japanese Diet in Tokyo," 11 Nov. 1983, *PPP: RR 1983*, 2:1576.

41. "Address to the Nation and Other Countries on United States-Soviet Relations," 16 Jan. 1984, *PPP: RR 1984*, 1:40–44.

42. Brinkley, *Reagan Diaries*, 1:308.

43. Mary McGrory, "Despite His Handlers' Hype, Reagan Didn't Sound Converted," *Washington Post*, 19 Jan. 1984. For an overview of Reagan's seeming shift and

the role of domestic politics, see Simon Miles, "The Domestic Politics of Superpower Rapprochement: Foreign Policy and the 1984 Election," in *The Cold War at Home and Abroad*, ed. Andrew L. Johns and Mitchell B. Lerner (Lexington: University Press of Kentucky, 2018), 267–288.

44. "Address to the Nation on Defense and National Security," 23 Mar. 1983, *PPP: RR 1983*, 1:442.

45. On European reactions and attitudes toward SDI, see Sean N. Kalic, "Reagan's SDI Announcement and the European Reaction: Diplomacy in the Last Decade of the Cold War," in *The Crisis of Détente in Europe: From Helsinki to Gorbachev, 1975–1985*, ed. Leopoldo Nuti (Abingdon: Routledge, 2009), 99–110; Edoardo Andreoni, "Ronald Reagan's Strategic Defense Initiative and Transatlantic Relations, 1983–86," PhD diss., University of Cambridge, 2017.

46. Brinkley, *Reagan Diaries*, 2:652.

47. Margaret Thatcher, *The Downing Street Years* (New York: HarperCollins, 1993), 462; Helmut Kohl, *Erinnerungen, 1982–1990* (Munich: Droemer, 2005), 584.

48. Brussels (NATO) to External Affairs, "SCG: 02Feb," 28 Jan. 1987, Library and Archives Canada (LAC), Record Group (RG) 25, vol. 28853, file 27-4-NATO-1-INF, pt. 12.

49. Bonn to Foreign and Commonwealth Office, "Reykjavik Summit: German Views," 15 Oct. 1986, TNA, PREM 19/1759.

50. Ivo H. Daalder, "Europe's Post-Reykjavik Ambivalence," *Christian Science Monitor*, 3 Nov. 1986.

51. Elizabeth C. Charles, "Gorbachev and the Decision to Decouple the Arms Control Package: How the Breakdown of the Reykjavik Summit Led to the Elimination of the Euromissiles," in *The Euromissile Crisis and the End of the Cold War*, ed. Leopoldo Nuti, Frédéric Bozo, Marie-Pierre Rey, and Bernd Rother (Washington, DC: Woodrow Wilson Center Press, 2015), 66–84.

52. Marilena Gala, "The Euromissile Crisis and the Centrality of the 'Zero Option'," in *The Euromissile Crisis and the End of the Cold War*, ed. Leopoldo Nuti, Frédéric Bozo, Marie-Pierre Rey, and Bernd Rother (Washington, DC: Woodrow Wilson Center Press, 2015), 168–169.

53. Paul Lewis, "General Sees Missile Plans as a Mistake," *New York Times*, 24 June 1984.

54. Sayle, *Enduring Alliance*, 213–215.

55. Tasha Kheiriddin, "Brian Mulroney Remembers His Friend Ronald Reagan," *National Post*, 4 Feb. 2011.

56. Ronald Reagan, *An American Life* (New York: Simon and Schuster, 1990), 204; "Eulogy for President Reagan," 11 June 2004, https://www.margaretthatcher.org/document/110360.

57. George P. Shultz, *Turmoil and Triumph: Diplomacy, Power, and the Victory of the American Ideal* (New York: Charles Scribner's Sons, 1993), 129.

58. Derek Burney, *Getting It Done: A Memoir* (Montreal: McGill-Queen's University Press, 2005), 119–120; Brian Mulroney, *Memoirs: 1939–1993* (Toronto: McClelland & Stewart, 2007), 572–573.

59. "Border," 1988, https://www.youtube.com/watch?v=jKQPw9vmG04. On the free trade election, see Robert Bothwell, *The Penguin History of Canada* (Toronto: Penguin, 2006), 480–482.

60. Elaine Smith, "Personal Relationships Key to Successful Diplomacy: Mulroney," *U of T News*, 13 Oct. 2011, https://www.utoronto.ca/news/personal-relationships-key-successful-diplomacy-mulroney.

61. Richard Aldous, *Reagan and Thatcher: The Difficult Relationship* (London: Norton, 2012).

62. "Margaret Thatcher interviewed about Ronald Reagan," 8 Jan. 1990, https://www.margaretthatcher.org/document/109324.

63. Duccio Basosi, "The European Community and International Reaganomics," in *European Integration and the Atlantic Community in the 1980s*, ed. Klaus Kiran Patel and Kenneth Weisbrode (Cambridge: Cambridge University Press, 2013), 133–153.

64. "Record of Meeting Held between PM and Chancellor Schmidt at Versailles," 5 June 1982, TNA, PREM 19/724. For more detail, see Mathias Haeussler, *Helmut Schmidt and British-German Relations: A European Misunderstanding* (Cambridge: Cambridge University Press, 2019), 196–199.

65. Frank J. Prial, "Bonn and Paris Agree to Oppose US Rate Policy," 14 July 1981, *New York Times*.

66. Brinkley, *Reagan Diaries*, 1:279. See also Coles to Fall, "Grenada," 26 Oct. 1983, TNA, PREM 19/1048.

67. Thatcher, *Downing Street Years*, 331.

68. Haeussler, *Schmidt*, 182–188, 196–205.

69. Alice Siegert, "120,000 Germans at rally: 'Yankee don't go home,'" *Chicago Tribune*, 6 June 1982.

70. Brinkley, *Reagan Diaries*, 1:444.

71. Bernard Weinraub, "Wiesel Confronts Reagan on Trip," *New York Times*, 20 Apr. 1985.

72. Thomas M. T. Niles, Association for Diplomatic Studies and Training Interview, 5 June 1998, 105.

73. For a discussion of their ideological differences and similarities, see William I. Hitchcock, "The Sense of History: Ronald Reagan and François Mitterrand," in *Reagan and the World: Leadership and National Security, 1981–1989*, ed. Bradley Lynn Coleman and Kyle Longley (Lexington: University of Kentucky Press, 2017), 147–150, 153–155.

74. Flora Lewis, "France Defies Ban by US on Supplies for Soviet Pipeline," *New York Times*, 23 July 1982.

75. Hedrick Smith, "Reagan, Reflecting on Ottawa Parley, Praises Mitterrand," *New York Times*, 23 July 1981.

76. Geir Lundestad, *The United States and Western Europe since 1945: From "Empire by Invitation" to Transatlantic Drift* (Oxford: Oxford University Press, 2005), 228.

77. For a more detailed version of this argument, see Susan Colbourn, *Euromissiles: A Transatlantic History* (Ithaca, NY: Cornell University Press, 2022).

Chapter 7

Ronald Reagan and the Nuclear Freeze Movement

Stephanie Freeman

On December 6, 1982, Ronald Reagan met with Helen Caldicott in the White House library to discuss the nuclear arms race. Caldicott was one of the most prominent antinuclear activists in the world—an Australian pediatrician who had revived Physicians for Social Responsibility and created Women's Action for Nuclear Disarmament. Reagan agreed to this meeting as a favor to his daughter, Patti Davis, who was a frequent spokesperson for antinuclear organizations in California. Davis hoped that a conversation with Caldicott would lead her father to abandon his nuclear modernization plans, which she feared might precipitate a nuclear war.[1]

The meeting quickly turned contentious, leaving both Reagan and Caldicott upset. Reflecting on the encounter in his diary, the president wrote that Caldicott was "all steamed up & knows an awful lot of things that aren't true. I tried but couldn't get through her fixation."[2] Caldicott characterized the meeting as "the most disconcerting hour and a quarter of my life."[3] Caldicott and Reagan each advocated a disarmament strategy that the other considered dangerous. Caldicott argued that the United States and the Soviet Union should adopt a nuclear freeze as a first step toward nuclear disarmament. She worried that a nuclear build-up would bring about a nuclear war, as the superpowers would be more likely to use new counterforce weapons in a crisis rather than chance losing them to an enemy first strike.[4] Reagan thought that the United States needed to modernize its nuclear forces in order to incentivize the Soviet Union, which he believed was winning the arms race, to reduce its nuclear weapons. He called this the "peace through strength" strategy. Reagan cautioned that a freeze would simply cement Soviet advantages in the arms race.[5]

This meeting illuminates the discordant relationship between Reagan and grassroots nuclear freeze activists. Although they shared the goal of nuclear disarmament, Reagan and the activists promoted conflicting strategies for achieving their common aim, which led them to dislike and mistrust one another. Drawing on recently declassified US government documents, as well as underutilized sources from grassroots antinuclear organizations, this chapter considers the ways in which Reagan and US nuclear freeze activists' shared interest in nuclear disarmament reshaped US strategic arms control policy during Reagan's first term.[6]

The prevailing interpretations of the Reagan administration's nuclear policy tend to be one-sided, privileging either the grassroots antinuclear movement or Reagan's nuclear abolitionism as the single driving force behind US arms control policy in the early 1980s. One school of thought holds that the Reagan administration was unserious about nuclear arms control during its first term and pursued negotiations with the Soviets only due to pressure from antinuclear activists.[7] A second school contends that Reagan became a nuclear abolitionist in the late 1940s and that his antinuclearism was the most important factor shaping US policy.[8] This chapter demonstrates that both Reagan and nuclear freeze activists were crucial in shifting the US strategic arms control paradigm from arms limitation to arms reduction during Reagan's first term.

In initiating the pursuit of strategic arms reduction, this unlikely coalition brought about the first step toward reversing the US-Soviet nuclear arms race. A few weeks after entering the White House, Reagan's nuclear abolitionism led him to announce that his administration would seek nuclear arms reduction instead of arms limitation. Pressure from nuclear freeze activists, however, accelerated the Reagan administration's timetable for beginning strategic arms reduction (START) negotiations with the Soviets, emboldened its initial START proposal, and later prompted it to alter US proposals in a bid to make them more acceptable to the Soviets. US antinuclear activism was particularly important in leading Reagan's advisers, who were not nuclear abolitionists, to support the opening of START talks.

Freeze activists pressured the Reagan administration by winning support among the American electorate for a nuclear freeze. They also lobbied Congress to pass a nuclear freeze resolution and reject funding for the Reagan administration's strategic modernization program. Reagan was troubled by the increasing popularity of the nuclear freeze proposal, which he believed would endanger US national security if implemented. The president became eager to demonstrate that his "peace through strength" disarmament strategy would yield significant results. He accelerated his START negotiating timetable, set forth a dramatic opening START proposal, and then modified US proposals in an effort to address Soviet concerns. Reagan hoped that these actions would spur nuclear disarmament, but his advisers endorsed them merely in a cynical effort to curb grassroots antinuclear activism. Activists threatened public and congressional support for the US strategic modernization program, which Reagan's aides thought was essential to ensure the stability and security of the US nuclear deterrent.

Grassroots antinuclear activism was increasing as the 1980s got underway. The breakdown of détente and the intensification of the nuclear arms race bred concern among millions of ordinary individuals that a nuclear war was becoming more likely. Across the globe, citizens mobilized in support of nuclear disarmament.[9] Growing opposition in the US Senate to the second Strategic Arms Limitation Treaty (SALT II) led a group of American activists to begin promoting a nuclear freeze.[10] Randall Forsberg, a graduate student in international studies at the Massachusetts Institute of Technology, made the case for a bilateral nuclear freeze in *The Call to Halt the Nuclear Arms Race*, which was first published in April 1980. In this pamphlet, Forsberg urged the United States and the Soviet Union to "adopt a mutual freeze on the testing, production and deployment of nuclear weapons and of missiles and new aircraft designed primarily to deliver nuclear weapons." She envisioned the freeze as an "essential, verifiable first step" toward preventing a nuclear war, sharply reducing or eliminating nuclear weapons, and ending nuclear proliferation.[11]

Grassroots support for the nuclear freeze proposal grew in response to the failure of SALT II, which President Jimmy Carter withdrew from Senate consideration after the Soviet invasion of Afghanistan. The continued escalation of the nuclear arms race also galvanized support for a freeze. From March 20 to 22, 1981, 275 antinuclear activists from more than thirty states assembled in Washington, DC, for the first national nuclear freeze conference.[12] They endorsed a strategy for a national nuclear freeze campaign during their meeting.[13] The freeze movement would concentrate on "developing widespread public support for the freeze in the US and then making the freeze a national policy objective."[14] Activists believed that only an outpouring of public support for a freeze would convince US officials to halt the nuclear arms race.

While the freeze movement had been taking shape in 1980, Reagan was running for president. During his campaign, Reagan touted the "peace through strength" strategy, which called for modernizing US nuclear forces and then negotiating nuclear arms reduction with the Soviets.[15] Although Reagan overstated the disparity in the superpowers' nuclear arsenals, he truly wanted to reach an arms reduction agreement with the Soviet Union.[16] As governor of California from 1967 to 1975, Reagan had repeatedly told aides that the strategy of mutual assured destruction was immoral and dangerous. Martin Anderson and Michael Deaver, who advised Reagan during his presidential campaigns, claimed that Reagan's desire to end the threat of nuclear war motivated his political career.[17] On the 1980 campaign trail, Reagan vowed, "My goal is to begin arms reductions. My energies will be directed at reducing destructive nuclear weaponry in the world—and doing it in such a way as to protect fully the critical security requirements of our nation."[18]

During his first month as president, Reagan announced that his administration would seek to reduce strategic nuclear weapons instead of simply limiting their increase. Reagan declared at his first press conference, "We should start negotiating on the basis of trying to effect an actual reduction in the numbers of nuclear weapons. That would then be real strategic arms limitation." Yet Reagan's "peace through strength" strategy called for modernizing the US nuclear deterrent before beginning arms reduction talks. Reagan also endorsed the concept of linkage at this press conference, meaning that arms control negotiations would be dependent on Soviet good behavior across the globe.[19] Since the Soviets were waging war in Afghanistan and eyeing a possible intervention in Poland, it appeared unlikely that strategic arms reduction talks would begin in the near future.[20]

Reagan's statements about Soviet officials at his first press conference further undermined the prospects for strategic arms reduction negotiations. He famously asserted that Soviet leaders "have openly and publicly declared that the only morality they recognize is what will further their cause, meaning they reserve unto themselves the right to commit any crime, to lie, to cheat."[21] The Soviet press agency TASS condemned these comments as "unseemly" and "deliberate distortions," while also criticizing the US policy of linkage.[22] Despite Reagan's stated interest in pursuing strategic arms reduction negotiations with the Soviets, talks did not appear to be on the horizon.

Concern over the growing nuclear freeze movement, however, prompted the Reagan administration to decide to begin strategic arms reduction negotiations sooner than originally planned. In an August 17, 1981, National Security Council (NSC) meeting, US Arms Control and Disarmament Agency (ACDA) director Eugene Rostow, a nuclear hard-liner, stated that a modernized US nuclear deterrent would incentivize the Soviets to negotiate seriously. But Rostow also recognized the power of the growing grassroots antinuclear movement. He noted, "I am not suggesting that we wait to negotiate until we are rearmed. That is a rational position. . . . But we can't go so far, and the President has decided otherwise. As we have been forced to realize, the mystic faith in arms control agreements as guaranties of peace is simply too strong among our people and the people of Europe to be ignored." Reagan had resolved not to defer strategic arms reduction talks until after he had modernized US strategic forces. Rising antinuclear sentiment among Americans and West Europeans prompted even hard-liners like Rostow to agree with the president's decision. Rostow now sought only "firm commitments to rearm" before opening negotiations with the Soviets.[23]

The US nuclear freeze movement was on the march in late 1981. Concerned that US nuclear modernization was making a nuclear war more likely, Americans engaged in antinuclear activism to induce US officials to retreat from the nuclear abyss. In August 1981, Reagan decided to produce the neutron bomb, which was designed to kill people without destroying the surrounding infrastructure. Antinuclear activists feared that this indicated that Reagan was seriously contemplating a nuclear war.[24] Two months later, Reagan unveiled his plans for a strategic modernization program that would enhance all three legs of the US strategic triad—land-based intercontinental ballistic missiles (ICBMs), submarine-launched ballistic missiles, and strategic bombers.[25] In a conversation with newspaper editors on October 16, Reagan even suggested that it would theoretically be possible for the superpowers to fight a limited nuclear war in Europe.[26] The Reagan administration was also moving forward with plans to deploy US intermediate-range nuclear forces (INF) in Western Europe in 1983 in accordance with the 1979 NATO dual-track decision. This consisted of a proposed modernization of the alliance's long-range theater nuclear forces and a simultaneous offer of US-Soviet arms control negotiations on these forces.[27] These looming deployments galvanized massive antinuclear movements across Western Europe, which called on their governments to refuse to host US INF missiles and to eliminate nuclear weapons from Europe.[28] Although the US nuclear freeze movement did not prioritize the INF issue, the planned deployments were another example of the Reagan administration's commitment to nuclear modernization, which activists worried might precipitate a nuclear war.[29] In the wake of these developments, approximately 100,000 people attended "teach-ins" on the danger of nuclear war and the importance of nuclear arms reduction during the Union of Concerned Scientists' (UCS) convocation on Veterans Day. Events took place at 151 colleges and universities in thirty-seven states.[30] By June 1982, hundreds of town meetings, 144 city councils, thirty-one county councils, and eight state legislatures had approved freeze resolutions.[31]

The Reagan administration took note as the US antinuclear movement expanded. In a November 18, 1981, speech to the National Press Club, Reagan promised to begin talks on strategic nuclear weapons "as soon as possible next year." To reflect the shift from his predecessors' pursuit of strategic arms limitation, he announced that the negotiations would be called Strategic Arms Reduction Talks (START) instead of SALT. In this speech, Reagan also unveiled the zero option as his proposal for the INF negotiations. Under the zero option, the United States would cancel its planned INF deployments if the Soviet Union would dismantle its existing INF missiles.[32]

By the spring of 1982, members of Congress were joining ordinary Americans in endorsing the freeze proposal. On March 10, 1982, Edward Kennedy (D-MA) and Mark Hatfield (R-OR) introduced a bipartisan freeze resolution in the US Senate, while Edward Markey (D-MA), Jonathan Bingham (D-NY), and Silvio Conte (R-MA) did the same in the US House of Representatives. National Nuclear Weapons Freeze Campaign (NWFC) leaders had devised a plan to discuss the freeze with House members in December 1981.[33] Peter Franchot, an aide to Markey, read *The Call* and urged Markey, who had a long-standing concern about nuclear power and nuclear proliferation, to introduce a freeze resolution.[34] Kennedy, who was weighing another presidential bid in 1984, thought that it would be politically beneficial to back a proposal that was gaining popularity across the country. Markey and Kennedy found Republican colleagues who shared their concern about the nuclear arms race and convinced them to cosponsor the freeze resolution in order to broaden its appeal. Members of Congress began supporting the freeze resolution to express their disapproval of Reagan's nuclear modernization program and their desire for START negotiations.[35]

From April 18 to 25, 1982, the antinuclear organization Ground Zero sponsored activities across the country to teach Americans about the threat of nuclear war. "Ground Zero Week" featured rallies, discussions, and lectures in more than 600 communities and 350 college campuses. These events attracted significant media coverage, which expanded the reach of Ground Zero's warnings about the risk of nuclear war.[36]

In response to Ground Zero Week, National Security Adviser William P. Clark encouraged the Reagan administration to set forth dramatic arms reduction proposals in an accelerated time frame. Writing to Edwin Meese, James Baker, and Michael Deaver on April 22, Clark repeatedly noted that Reagan and grassroots antinuclear activists shared the aim of preventing a nuclear war, although they maintained different strategies for accomplishing this goal. He wrote, "Our effort should be directed toward convincing Americans whose anxieties are heightened by this movement that *our* policy solutions best meet their desire that the United States do something to lessen the prospect of a nuclear holocaust." Clark contended that the administration should advance its strategy not only by conducting a public relations campaign, but also by offering bold arms reduction proposals. "We must also focus on concrete policy and new initiatives," he wrote, "otherwise, our 'peace offensive' will be met with cynicism, both at home and abroad." For example, Reagan should unveil a new START proposal in May in an announcement "designed to capture the initiative by its boldness."[37]

A dramatic START proposal was in keeping with Reagan's nuclear abolitionism. During an April 21, 1982, NSC meeting, he noted, "It's too bad we cannot do in START what we did in INF, or what Ike [Eisenhower] proposed on all nuclear weapons. First, we need to restore the balance."[38] Reagan wished that his opening START position could call for the eradication of strategic nuclear weapons, as the zero option proposed the elimination of INF missiles. In a letter to a concerned citizen that was also dated April 21, Reagan wrote about his aim of abolishing nuclear weapons.[39] Yet Reagan thought that it would be unwise to propose the elimination of strategic nuclear weapons given Soviet conventional superiority. Nevertheless, the president wanted to set forth a bold proposal in the upcoming START talks.

Pressure from freeze activists prompted Reagan's advisers to seek a bold opening gambit in the START talks, which they hoped would curb support for the freeze movement. During the April 21 NSC meeting, both Rostow and Secretary of State Alexander Haig voiced concerns about the rise in grassroots antinuclear activism. Haig even told Reagan, "We need a dramatic proposal to reverse the momentum over the peace movement and put you on the side of the Angels."[40] Reagan's advisers hoped to quell the antinuclear movement with a bold START proposal, largely because they feared that antinuclear activists were undermining congressional support for the administration's strategic modernization program. Haig explained that it was important to craft a START proposal that would win public approval, "not only to reinforce our START negotiating position, but also to ensure Congressional approval of our defense budget, and maintain support for the firm foreign policy line we have taken with the Soviet Union across the board."[41]

For his part, Reagan wanted a START proposal that was not only bold, but also plausible to the Soviets. Although critics later argued that the initial US START position was unserious because it required the Soviet Union to engage in steeper reductions in ICBM warheads and strategic missile launchers than the United States, Reagan chose the most credible proposal presented by his aides. Alternative Defense Department and ACDA options called on negotiators to seek immediate reductions of throw-weight (a metric of the number and size of warheads a missile could carry) below the US level. These proposals would have mandated a 65 percent reduction in Soviet throw-weight without subjecting the Americans to any real cuts. Haig correctly noted that the Soviets would never agree to these terms.[42] Worried about the plausibility of the US START position, Reagan endorsed an initiative that the State Department, the Joint Chiefs of Staff, and Deputy National Security Adviser Robert "Bud" McFarlane promoted. It postponed direct reductions in throw-weight until a later stage of the talks.[43]

The opening US START position called for two phases of negotiations. During the first, US negotiators would propose that the superpowers reduce their strategic ballistic missile warheads to 5,000 apiece, with no more than 2,500 of those warheads deployed on ICBMs. Each side would also reduce its deployed strategic ballistic missiles to 850, of which only 210 could be heavy and medium ICBMs. Each superpower could deploy only 110 heavy missiles. During the second phase, US officials would call for reductions in ballistic missile throw-weight to an equal level below the current US figure. The Americans and the Soviets would also reduce their bombers to 250 each.[44] On May 9, 1982, Reagan outlined this START proposal in a commencement address at his alma mater, Eureka College.[45]

Antinuclear activists were critical of Reagan's START position. The Friends Committee on National Legislation (FCNL) pointed out that the Soviets would have to engage in sharper reductions of ICBM warheads, strategic ballistic missiles, and eventually throw-weight than the Americans because large ICBM warheads comprised the bulk of Soviet strategic nuclear forces. FCNL also lamented that Reagan's proposal did not mandate a freeze on weapons production and deployment during the START negotiations. "This proposal is so partial and one-sided that by the time the Soviets respond with their own initial positions, and by the time negotiators, after long sessions, finally hopefully reach agreement years hence, the proposals are likely to be overtaken by events and new weapons production," wrote an FCNL activist. Both FCNL and NWFC argued that the United States and the Soviet Union could halt the arms race only if they implemented a freeze on new nuclear weapons while they negotiated deep reductions in existing systems.[46]

Many Americans seemed to agree. In one of the largest political demonstrations in US history, 750,000 people rallied for a freeze and disarmament on June 12, 1982, in New York City. A coalition of antinuclear, environmental, union, religious, and minority groups had organized the protest, which took place during the United Nations' Second Special Session on Disarmament. The rally's aim was to pressure government officials to pursue "'a freeze and reduction of all nuclear weapons and a transfer of military budgets according to human needs.'" It drew a diverse group of participants that included pacifists, veterans, artists, scientists, students, and politicians. Demonstrators carried signs with slogans such as "Choose Life"; "A Feminist World Is a Nuclear-Free Zone"; "Build Houses Not Bomb Shelters"; and "Don't Blow It—Good Planets Are Hard to Find."[47] The size and composition of this protest revealed the extent of public discontent with US nuclear policy.

Despite the criticism from antinuclear activists, Reagan eagerly touted his START initiative, believing that it was a superior alternative to the freeze proposal for reducing US and Soviet nuclear weapons and preventing a nuclear war. He contended that a nuclear freeze would cement Soviet advantages in the arms race and eliminate the Soviets' incentive to negotiate arms reduction by halting US nuclear modernization.[48] Misconstruing the nuclear freeze as the end goal of the antinuclear movement rather than a first step toward nuclear disarmament, Reagan boasted that his START proposal provided for significant reductions in the superpowers' nuclear arsenals instead of just a halt in place.[49]

Yet antinuclear activists continued to win support for the freeze proposal from the American electorate, which was largely unmoved by Reagan's criticisms of the freeze. In the 1982 midterm elections, freeze resolutions passed in eight of the nine states with such a measure on the ballot. Voters in California, Massachusetts, Michigan, Montana, New Jersey, North Dakota, Oregon, and Rhode Island approved a freeze, while only Arizonans rejected it. The freeze had already won in Wisconsin in September. The residents of Chicago, Denver, Philadelphia, and Washington, DC, also adopted freeze measures. The *New York Times* reported that "the voting on the resolution, which is purely advisory, constituted the largest referendum on a single issue in the nation's history," as the states and cities that passed a freeze resolution "include about one-fourth of the country's population."[50] According to freeze activists, there were also fifteen House races in which an incumbent opposed to the freeze lost.[51]

One month later, freeze activists' congressional lobbying efforts paid off when the House voted to eliminate production funding for the MX missile from the fiscal year 1983 defense appropriations bill. The MX ICBM was a central element in Reagan's strategic modernization program. Rising public support for the freeze proposal and the cogency of antinuclear activists' arguments against the MX fueled congressional opposition to the missile. For the first time since the Second World War, a chamber of Congress refused to fund production of a major weapon system that a president had explicitly requested.[52]

Joining forces with environmental and religious groups, antinuclear activists had mounted a massive anti-MX campaign.[53] They wrote letters to members of Congress condemning the MX as a destabilizing and expensive missile that would hinder nuclear arms control negotiations with the Soviets.[54] Activists also denounced the proposed basing mode for the MX, which was called "dense pack." Under the "dense pack" plan, MX missiles would sit so close to one another in such a small area that incoming Soviet warheads would theoretically destroy one another without obliterating the majority of the MX missiles. The UCS, for example, sent information to senators on the problems associated with "dense pack."[55] They had an impact. During the House debate on the MX, representatives articulated many of the same arguments that antinuclear activists had been expressing against the MX. House members also cited public support for the freeze as a reason to oppose MX production funding.[56] On December 7, 1982, the House voted 245 to 176 to delete MX production funds from the fiscal year 1983 defense appropriations bill.[57]

Reagan regarded the House vote to eliminate MX production funding as a serious challenge to his disarmament strategy. He was unable to recognize the contradiction between building MX missiles and pursuing START negotiations. Rather, the president believed that the MX vote would impede progress in the ongoing START talks by removing a major incentive for the Soviets to reduce their strategic nuclear weapons. Characterizing the December 7 vote as "'a grave mistake,'" Reagan cautioned that "'unless reversed in coming days, it will seriously set back our efforts to protect the nation's security and could handcuff our negotiators at the arms table.'"[58] His private remarks attested to a fear of disastrous consequences if the START talks stalled in the wake of the MX vote. Reagan warned McFarlane, "'It's coming, Bud. This inexorable building of nuclear weapons on our side and the Russians' side can only lead to Armageddon. We've got to get off that track.'"[59]

Yet Congress dismissed Reagan's warnings, listening instead to antinuclear activists' concerns about the MX missile and the "dense pack" basing mode. Antinuclear activists scored a major victory when a House-Senate conference committee rejected MX production funding on December 19, 1982. While the conference committee did provide $2.5 billion for MX research and development, most of these funds could not be spent until Congress approved a basing mode for the MX.[60]

Freeze activists' increasing influence in Congress led the Reagan administration to alter its START proposal throughout 1983 in an effort to address Soviet concerns. Reagan hoped that these changes would yield a quick START agreement that would vindicate his disarmament strategy and undercut support for the grassroots freeze movement. Reagan's aides, on the other hand, endorsed these modifications in order to win congressional backing of the MX.

After the House voted to delete MX production funds, the Reagan administration created a commission of outside experts to examine the MX basing mode, the overall strategic modernization program, and US arms control policies. Brent Scowcroft, who had served as Gerald Ford's national security adviser, chaired this bipartisan panel. In its April 1983 report, the Scowcroft Commission urged Reagan to use arms control to help transition from large ICBMs with multiple warheads to small, single-warhead ICBMs, which were deemed more survivable and stable. Arms reduction proposals should be framed "not in terms of launchers, but in terms of equal levels of warheads of roughly equivalent yield." If launchers or missiles were the unit of account in arms reduction proposals, there would be "an incentive to build launchers and missiles as large as possible and to put as many warheads as possible into each missile."[61]

As the antinuclear movement pushed Congress to defund the MX permanently, several influential representatives and senators declared that their support for the MX was tied to the Reagan administration altering its START position. These members of Congress wanted Reagan to bring his START proposal into line with the Scowcroft Commission's recommendations and pursue new arms reduction initiatives.[62] Senators Charles Percy (R-IL), Sam Nunn (D-GA), and William Cohen (R-ME) suggested that the president create a bipartisan arms control advisory commission and pitch the idea of a "build-down" to the Soviets. Under the "build-down" proposal, the United States and the Soviet Union would eliminate two nuclear warheads for every new nuclear warhead deployed.[63]

While Congress debated the future of the MX, freeze activists won another important victory when the House passed a nuclear freeze resolution by a vote of 278 to 149 on May 4, 1983. Although this resolution included thirty-three amendments, it nevertheless maintained the basic idea that the United States and the Soviet Union should implement a freeze before negotiating arms reduction agreements.[64] By presenting an alternative arms control approach, the freeze resolution expressed displeasure with the Reagan administration's pursuit of arms control. Some House members backed it for this very reason.[65]

As the freeze movement fueled congressional dissatisfaction with Reagan's arms control policies, the administration reevaluated its START proposal. In letters sent to members of Congress on May 11 and 12, Reagan promised to alter the US START position in accordance with the Scowcroft Commission's report and congressional recommendations. The House Appropriations Subcommittee on defense and the Senate Appropriations Committee released MX research and development funds in response.[66] This horse-trading between the Reagan administration and Congress continued throughout 1983, leading to multiple adjustments to the US START proposal in exchange for congressional appropriation of MX production funds in November.[67]

While the president's advisers hoped that a revised START proposal would win congressional support for the MX, Reagan and Clark believed that it might actually yield some type of strategic arms reduction agreement. Reagan was eager for the START talks in Geneva to produce results. In a July 11, 1983, letter to Soviet leader Yuri Andropov, Reagan pledged that his administration was "dedicated to, 'the course of peace' and 'the elimination of the nuclear threat.'" He asked Andropov, "Could we not begin to approach these goals in the meetings now going on in Geneva?"[68] Clark thought that the modifications to the US START position might make possible "either a Vladivostok type agreement on the way to a full START Treaty and/or the implementation of some build-down provisions in the context of such an agreement."[69] On October 4, Reagan unveiled a round of changes to the US START proposal and proclaimed, "The door to an agreement is open. All the world is waiting for the Soviet Union to walk through."[70]

Reagan's hopes for a quick START agreement were dashed when the Soviets responded to US INF deployments in November by refusing to resume START negotiations after the fifth round concluded on December 8, 1983. Although START talks would remain dormant until the Nuclear and Space Talks opened on March 12, 1985, Reagan and the freeze activists had shifted the US strategic arms control paradigm from arms limitation to arms reduction during the president's first term. In his first presidential press conference, Reagan announced that his administration would pursue nuclear arms reduction instead of arms limitation. Pressure from freeze activists, however, accelerated the Reagan administration's timetable for initiating START negotiations and meaningfully shaped its START proposals. Antinuclear activism was key in motivating Reagan's advisers, who were not nuclear abolitionists, to support the opening of START talks.

This shift in the US nuclear arms control paradigm was the first step toward reversing the US-Soviet nuclear arms race. On the day before the Nuclear and Space Talks opened on March 12, 1985, Mikhail Gorbachev became Soviet general secretary. Reagan finally had a partner in the Kremlin with whom he could work for nuclear disarmament. Meanwhile, the US nuclear freeze movement was unable to overcome a series of setbacks between late 1983 and early 1985. These setbacks included congressional appropriation of MX production funding in November 1983; Reagan's reelection in November 1984; and the opening of the Nuclear and Space Talks without the implementation of a freeze in March 1985. By early 1985, freeze activists no longer influenced

US arms control policy. After his landslide victory in the 1984 presidential election, Reagan felt that he had an electoral mandate to pursue his strategy of negotiating arms reduction from a position of strength. Reagan focused on his personal diplomacy with Gorbachev, which he believed could pave the way for global nuclear abolition.[71]

But Reagan and Gorbachev's disagreements over the US Strategic Defense Initiative (SDI) frustrated their efforts to reach arms reduction agreements at their first two summits in Geneva in November 1985 and Reykjavik in October 1986. SDI was a missile defense program that Reagan had unveiled on March 23, 1983. Reagan believed that SDI would aid the transition to a nuclear-free world by making nuclear weapons obsolete and therefore easier to eliminate.[72] In Reagan's view, SDI would also protect against the revival of nuclear weapons after they had been abolished.[73] Gorbachev, however, feared that SDI was an effort to give the United States a first-strike capability. Protected by SDI, the United States could launch a nuclear attack against the Soviet Union without fear of retaliation.[74] Gorbachev therefore linked the reduction and elimination of nuclear weapons with restrictions on strategic defenses. Most notably, this was Gorbachev's position at the Reykjavik summit, during which he and Reagan came tantalizingly close to reaching an agreement to abolish their nuclear weapons in ten years. Yet the Reykjavik summit ended without an agreement because Reagan rejected Gorbachev's demand that a treaty eliminating nuclear weapons also restrict SDI to the laboratory for ten years.[75]

In February 1987, Gorbachev decided to pursue an INF treaty separately from agreements on START and strategic defenses. Gorbachev hoped that this decision would not only facilitate the conclusion of an INF treaty in the near future, but also jumpstart the START and defense and space negotiations, which were progressing more slowly than the INF talks. Gorbachev's decision removed the major obstacle blocking the conclusion of an INF agreement. On December 8, 1987, Reagan and Gorbachev signed the landmark INF Treaty, which eliminated US and Soviet land-based intermediate-range and shorter-range missiles. This was the first agreement to abolish an entire class of nuclear weapons.[76]

Although the Reagan administration was unable to conclude a START agreement before leaving office, its ideas of engaging in deep cuts in both strategic missiles and strategic warheads framed the rest of the START debate. The START Treaty, which Gorbachev and President George H. W. Bush signed on July 31, 1991, incorporated significant reductions in both strategic missiles and strategic warheads. These INF and START agreements marked the reversal of the US-Soviet nuclear arms race and were milestones in the Cold War's endgame.[77]

Although he is still revered as a conservative icon more than three decades after his presidency ended, Reagan's nuclear abolitionism made him an outlier among Republicans. Even within his own administration, no one shared his desire to eliminate nuclear weapons. In fact, it took a large and broad-based US nuclear freeze movement to persuade Reagan's advisers to endorse the opening of negotiations aimed at reducing US and Soviet strategic nuclear weapons. Freeze activists also convinced Reagan and his team to begin these talks sooner than the president had originally intended. Reagan contributed to the Cold War's endgame when he deviated from conservative orthodoxy, engaged Soviet officials, and sought sweeping nuclear arms reduction agreements.[78]

Notes

1. Helen Broinowski Caldicott, *A Desperate Passion: An Autobiography* (New York: Norton, 1996), 259–261; Ronald Reagan, *An American Life: The Autobiography* (New York: Simon and Schuster, 1990), 566.

2. Reagan diary, 6 Dec. 1982, https://www.reaganfoundation.org/ronald-reagan/white-house-diaries/diary-entry-12061982/.

3. Caldicott, *A Desperate Passion*, 265.

4. Counterforce weapons were generally intended to attack an adversary's nuclear forces in a first strike instead of providing a second-strike deterrence capability.

5. Caldicott, *A Desperate Passion*, 260–266; Reagan, *An American Life*, 566, 562.

6. Since this chapter considers the policy impact of Reagan and US nuclear freeze activists' common desire for nuclear disarmament, it focuses on US strategic arms control policy. This chapter does not detail the Reagan administration's efforts to reduce intermediate-range nuclear forces (INF). US nuclear freeze activists were less active in opposing US and Soviet INF deployments than European antinuclear activists, who formed their own distinct movements separate from the US nuclear freeze movement. On the reluctance of the freeze movement's leaders to engage the INF issue, see, for example, Pam Solo, *From Protest to Policy: Beyond the Freeze to Common Security* (Cambridge, MA: Ballinger, 1988), 120–121.

7. See, for example, Angela Santese, "Ronald Reagan, the Nuclear Weapons Freeze Campaign and the Nuclear Scare of the 1980s," *International History Review* 39, no. 3 (2017): 496–520; Lawrence S. Wittner, *The Struggle against the Bomb*, vol. 3, *Toward Nuclear Abolition: A History of the World Nuclear Disarmament Movement, 1971 to the Present* (Stanford, CA: Stanford University Press, 2003); Jeffrey W. Knopf, *Domestic Society and International Cooperation: The Impact of Protest on US Arms Control Policy* (Cambridge: Cambridge University Press, 1998); David S. Meyer, *A Winter of Discontent: The Nuclear Freeze and American Politics* (New York: Praeger, 1990); David Cortright, *Peace Works: The Citizen's Role in Ending the Cold War* (Boulder, CO: Westview Press, 1993); Robert Kleidman, *Organizing for Peace: Neutrality, the Test Ban, and the Freeze* (Syracuse, NY: Syracuse University Press, 1993); Douglas C. Waller, *Congress and the Nuclear Freeze: An Inside Look at the Politics of a Mass Movement* (Amherst: University of

Massachusetts Press, 1987); Bradford Martin, *The Other Eighties: A Secret History of America in the Age of Reagan* (New York: Hill and Wang, 2011).

8. See, for example, Paul Lettow, *Ronald Reagan and His Quest to Abolish Nuclear Weapons* (New York: Random House, 2005); Martin Anderson and Annelise Anderson, *Reagan's Secret War: The Untold Story of His Fight to Save the World From Nuclear Disaster* (New York: Crown Publishers, 2009).

9. On the rise of grassroots antinuclear activism during the 1980s, see Wittner, *Toward Nuclear Abolition*.

10. Randall Forsberg interview, 9 Nov. 1987, https://openvault.wgbh.org/catalog/V_F6CC542AF94B434FBC7E1DBE45F07024.

11. *The Call to Halt the Nuclear Arms Race*, reprinted in *Security Dialogue* 12, no. 4 (1981): 417–421.

12. "Coming Up . . . Freeze Strategy Conference," *Freeze Newsletter* 1, no. 1 (1981): 2.

13. "First Annual Freeze Conference, March 20–22, 1981," Swarthmore College Peace Collection (SCPC), SANE, Inc. Collection (SANE), series G, box 50, folder "Freeze, 1980–1981."

14. "Strategy for Stopping the Nuclear Arms Race," Mar. 1981, LSE Library (LSEL), END/19/17.

15. See, for example, Reagan, "A Strategy for Peace in the 80s," 19 Oct. 1980, https://www.reaganlibrary.gov/10-19-80.

16. In early 1982, the Reagan administration would acknowledge that the United States and the Soviet Union had a rough parity in strategic ballistic missile warheads. See NSC minutes, 21 Apr. 1982, Ronald Reagan Presidential Library (RRPL), Executive Secretariat–NSC (ESNSC), Meeting Files (MF), box 5, folder "NSC 00046 21 Apr 82 (2/5)"; Reagan, "The President's News Conference," 13 May 1982, The American Presidency Project (APP), https://www.presidency.ucsb.edu/.

17. Lettow, *Ronald Reagan and His Quest to Abolish Nuclear Weapons*, 23, 30–31.

18. See Reagan, "A Strategy for Peace in the 80s."

19. Reagan, "The President's News Conference," 29 Jan. 1981, APP.

20. For the argument that Afghanistan actually became the "central front" of the Cold War during this period, see Robert Rakove's chapter in this volume.

21. Reagan, "The President's News Conference," 29 Jan. 1981.

22. "Russia Answers Reagan Blast," *Los Angeles Times*, 30 Jan. 1981.

23. "Remarks of EVR at National Security Council Meeting at Los Angeles, August 17, 1981, on Strategic Weapons Systems, (somewhat edited)," RRPL, ESNSC, MF, box 2, folder "NSC 00020 17 Aug 1981 [East-West Trade, Central America, Strategic Forces]."

24. SANE to Reagan, 12 Aug. 1981, SCPC, SANE, series G, box 30, folder "Testimony, letters to Congress and President, 1980–1987."

25. Reagan, "Remarks and a Question-and-Answer Session with Reporters on the Announcement of the United States Strategic Weapons Program," 2 Oct. 1981, APP.

26. Reagan, "Remarks and a Question-and-Answer Session at a Working Lunch with Out-of-Town Editors," 16 Oct. 1981, APP.

27. NATO, "Special Meeting of Foreign and Defense Ministers (The 'Double-Track' Decision on Theatre Nuclear Forces)," 12 Dec. 1979, https://www.nato.int/cps/en/natolive/official_texts_27040.htm. In 1981, the Reagan administration began

referring to theater nuclear forces as INF. INF have a range capability between 1000 and 5500 kilometers.

28. For a more detailed examination of the NATO dual-track decision and West European demonstrations against the planned US INF deployments, see Susan Colbourn and Mathias Haeussler's chapter in this volume.

29. On US nuclear freeze movement leaders' unwillingness to prioritize the INF issue, see Solo, *From Protest to Policy*, 120–121.

30. Ben A. Franklin, "Thousands at Colleges Join Drive against Atomic Arms," *New York Times*, 12 Nov. 1981; Meyer, *A Winter of Discontent*, 126.

31. Meyer, *A Winter of Discontent*, 183.

32. Reagan, "Remarks to Members of the National Press Club on Arms Reduction and Nuclear Weapons," 18 Nov. 1981, APP.

33. "Minutes of the December 21, 1981, Meeting of the US Government Contacts Task Force of the National Nuclear Weapons Freeze Campaign, 1:00 to 3:00 p.m.," State Historical Society of Missouri at St. Louis (SHSM), National Nuclear Weapons Freeze Campaign Records (NNWFC), box 8, folder "US Government Relations Task Force, May 1981–Mar. 1982."

34. Waller, *Congress and the Nuclear Freeze*, 45–48.

35. Knopf, *Domestic Society and International Cooperation*, 214–215; Waller, *Congress and the Nuclear Freeze*, 65–66, 60.

36. Judith Miller, "Arms Control Drive to Open," *New York Times*, 18 Apr. 1982; Robert G. Kaiser, "Ground Zero Week, Despite Fizzles, Calls Attention to A-War Risk," *Washington Post*, 25 Apr. 1982.

37. Clark to Meese, Baker, and Deaver, 22 Apr. 1982, RRPL, David Gergen Files, box OA9422, folder "Nuclear [Freeze] (1 of 8)."

38. NSC minutes, 21 Apr. 1982.

39. Reagan to Adams, 21 Apr. 1982, in *Reagan: A Life in Letters*, ed. Kiron K. Skinner, Annelise Anderson, and Martin Anderson (New York: Free Press, 2003), 401–402.

40. NSC minutes, 21 Apr. 1982.

41. Haig to Reagan, 1 May 1982, RRPL, ESNSC, MF, box 6, folder: "NSC 00049 03 May 82 (1/2)."

42. "NSC, 5/3/82, START," RRPL, ESNSC, MF, box 6, folder "NSC 00049 03 May 82 (1/2)."

43. Strobe Talbott, *Deadly Gambits: The Reagan Administration and the Stalemate in Nuclear Arms Control* (New York: Knopf, 1984), 263–268.

44. NSDD-33, "US Approach to START Negotiations," 14 May 1982, https://www.reaganlibrary.gov/sites/default/files/archives/reference/scanned-nsdds/nsdd33.pdf; NSDD-44, "US Approach to START Negotiations—III," 10 July 1982, https://www.reaganlibrary.gov/sites/default/files/archives/reference/scanned-nsdds/nsdd44.pdf.

45. Reagan, "Address at Commencement Exercises at Eureka College in Illinois," 9 May 1982, APP.

46. Snyder, "A Commentary on President Reagan's 'START' Proposal," 11 May 1982, SHSM, NNWFC, box 6, folder "Reagan, 1980–1984"; "US and USSR Urged to Suspend Nuclear Arms during START Talks," SHSM, NNWFC, box 8, folder "US Govt. Relations Task Force, Apr.–July 1982."

47. Paul L. Montgomery, "Throngs Fill Manhattan to Protest Nuclear Weapons," *New York Times*, 13 June 1982; Robin Herman, "Protesters Old and New Forge Alliance for Antinuclear Rally," *New York Times*, 4 June 1982; Robert D. McFadden, "A Spectrum of Humanity Represented at the Rally," *New York Times*, 13 June 1982.

48. See, for example, Reagan, "Remarks in Columbus to Members of Ohio Veterans Organizations," 4 Oct. 1982, APP.

49. See, for example, Reagan, "Remarks at the Centennial Meeting of the Supreme Council of the Knights of Columbus in Hartford, Connecticut," 3 Aug. 1982, APP.

50. John Herbers, "Widespread Vote Urges Nuclear Freeze," *New York Times*, 4 Nov. 1982.

51. "Incumbents Opposed to Nuclear Weapons Freeze Who Lost on November 2, 1982 and Their Successful Opponents," SHSM, NNWFC, box 8, folder "US Govt. Relations Task Force, Aug.–Dec. 1982."

52. Richard Halloran, "House, 245–176, Votes Down $988 Million for MX Missile; Setback for Reagan Policy," *New York Times*, 8 Dec. 1982.

53. On the composition of the anti-MX coalition and its strategy for stopping the MX, see Cortright, *Peace Works*, 141–146; John D. Isaacs and Katherine Magraw, "The Lobbyist and the MX," *Bulletin of the Atomic Scientists* 39, no. 2 (1983): 56–57.

54. See, for example, Kendall to Addabbo, 26 Aug. 1982, SCPC, SANE, series K, box 21, folder "Defense appropriation, FY 83, 1982–1983." This letter was sent to each member of the House Appropriations Committee.

55. See, for example, Monfort to Biden, 15 Oct. 1982, SCPC, SANE, series K, box 21, folder "Defense appropriation, FY 83, 1982–1983"; Union of Concerned Scientists, "Dense Pack—How Much Will It Cost?," SCPC, SANE, series K, box 21, folder "Defense appropriation, FY 83, 1982–1983"; Union of Concerned Scientists, "Questions About Dense Pack," SCPC, SANE, series K, box 21, folder "Defense appropriation, FY 83, 1982–1983."

56. Representative Les AuCoin, 97th Congress, 2nd Session, 7 Dec. 1982, *Congressional Record* 128, H 29070–29071; Representative Edward Markey, 97th Congress, 2nd Session, 7 Dec. 1982, *Congressional Record* 128, H 29052–29053; Representative Patricia Schroeder, 97th Congress, 2nd Session, 7 Dec. 1982, *Congressional Record* 128, H 29073; Representative Harold Ford, 97th Congress, 2nd Session, 7 Dec. 1982, *Congressional Record* 128, H 29090–29091.

57. Halloran, "House, 245–176, Votes Down $988 Million for MX Missile; Setback for Reagan Policy."

58. Halloran, "House, 245–176."

59. Quoted in James Graham Wilson, *The Triumph of Improvisation: Gorbachev's Adaptability, Reagan's Engagement, and the End of the Cold War* (Ithaca, NY: Cornell University Press, 2014), 67.

60. Helen Dewar and Bill Peterson, "Conferees Drop Jobs Plan, Defy Reagan on MX," *Washington Post*, 20 Dec. 1982.

61. *Report of the President's Commission on Strategic Forces* (Washington, DC: The Commission, 1983), 22–24.

62. Clark to Reagan, 7 May 1983, RRPL, ESNSC, MF, box 8, folder "NSC 00079 10 May 83 [START] [1/2]." The members of Congress who expressed this sentiment to the White House included Senators William Cohen, Charles Percy, and Sam Nunn and Representatives Norman Dicks and Al Gore.

63. "Senator Nunn's Proposal for a Bipartisan Presidential Commission on Arms Control," RRPL, ESNSC, MF, box 8, folder "NSC 00079 10 May 83 [START] [2/2]"; "Cohen-Nunn Two for One Build Down Approach," RRPL, ESNSC, MF, box 8, folder "NSC 00079 10 May 83 [START] [2/2]."

64. H. J. Res. 13, 98th Congress (1983). NWFC congressional liaison Reuben McCornack proudly noted after the House vote that "'the nut of the freeze was preserved'" (quoted in Knopf, *Domestic Society and International Cooperation*, 220).

65. Meyer, *A Winter of Discontent*, 231.

66. Lou Cannon and George C. Wilson, "Reagan Reassures Congress, Is Rewarded with MX Vote," *Washington Post*, 12 May 1983; Lou Cannon and George C. Wilson, "President Backs Arms Build-Down," *Washington Post*, 13 May 1983.

67. Hedrick Smith, *The Power Game: How Washington Works* (New York: Random House, 1988), 545–549.

68. George P. Shultz, *Turmoil and Triumph: My Years as Secretary of State* (New York: Scribner, 1993), 359.

69. Clark to Reagan, 29 Sept. 1983, RRPL, ESNSC, National Security Planning Group Files, box 2, folder "NSPG 0071 29 Sep 1983 [START]." This supports Elizabeth C. Charles and James Graham Wilson's argument in their chapter in this volume that Clark seemingly sought progress on nuclear arms control at times during 1983.

70. Reagan, "Remarks to Reporters Announcing New United States Initiatives in the Strategic Arms Reduction Talks," 4 Oct. 1983, APP.

71. On Reagan and US nuclear freeze activists in 1985, see Stephanie Lynn Freeman, "Looking over the Horizon: Nuclear Abolitionism and the End of the Cold War, 1979–1989," PhD diss., University of Virginia, 2017, 150–210.

72. Reagan, "Address to the Nation on Defense and National Security," 23 Mar. 1983, APP.

73. See, for example, "Memorandum of Conversation, Second Private Meeting, November 19, 1985, 3:40–4:45 p.m.," https://nsarchive2.gwu.edu/NSAEBB/NSAEBB172/Doc19.pdf.

74. See, for example, "Memorandum of Conversation, Second Plenary Meeting, November 19, 1985, 2:30–3:40 p.m.," https://nsarchive2.gwu.edu/NSAEBB/NSAEBB172/Doc17.pdf.

75. "Memorandum of Conversation, Final Meeting, October 12, 1986, 3:25–4:30 and 5:30–6:50 p.m.," http://nsarchive.gwu.edu/NSAEBB/NSAEBB203/Document15.pdf.

76. On Reagan and Gorbachev's success in concluding the INF Treaty, see Freeman, "Looking over the Horizon," 271–318.

77. On Reagan and Gorbachev's inability to reach a START agreement after Reykjavik, see Freeman, "Looking over the Horizon," 271–318.

78. For a more detailed assessment of Reagan's role in ending the Cold War that also emphasizes the importance of his engagement with Gorbachev and his desire for nuclear abolition, see Melvyn P. Leffler's chapter in this volume.

Part Three

*Human Rights
and Domestic Politics*

CHAPTER 8

Rhetoric and Restraint
Ronald Reagan and the Vietnam Syndrome

Mark Atwood Lawrence

"For too long, we have lived with the 'Vietnam Syndrome.'" Thus declared Ronald Reagan, the Republican nominee for president, in a speech before the national convention of the Veterans of Foreign Wars on August 18, 1980. Reagan was not the first person to use the term as shorthand for the sense of caution and doubt about the use of American power that seemed to pervade the United States in the 1970s because of its military failure in Southeast Asia. Never before, however, had such a high-profile figure assailed the "syndrome" and urged Americans to regain the confidence that had allegedly perished in the jungles and paddies of Vietnam. Reagan's political advisers feared that his comments would alienate the broader American public even if the speech played well with the veterans in his audience.[1] But candidate Reagan held nothing back in urging the nation to rethink the lessons of the lost war in Vietnam. "It is time we recognized that ours was, in truth, a noble cause," he asserted. During the war, the United States had selflessly defended the independence of South Vietnam, "a small country newly free from colonial rule," from communist aggression. The US defeat, insisted Reagan, flowed not from a failure of motives or capabilities but from insufficient will. Henceforth, the nation must have "the means and the determination to prevail" when it used its power overseas. He drew his audience to its feet with his best-known line: "Let us tell those who fought in that war that we will never again ask young men to fight and possibly die in a war our government is afraid to let them win."[2]

Reagan, who had served as governor of California during the peak years of wartime turmoil, had struck these themes before and had even used some of the same words during his 1976 presidential campaign.[3] Perhaps for that reason, neither the *New York Times* nor the *Washington Post* paid much attention to his remarks in August 1980. Nor did President Jimmy Carter's spokesman, Jody Powell, offer much of a response, telling reporters only that he would leave Reagan's comments "to the judgment of the American people."[4] Yet the speech stands out in retrospect as a landmark moment when Reagan cast himself forcefully in the role of straight-talking iconoclast and tapped into the resurgent nationalism that would help carry him to victory in November. Reagan's refashioning of the war's meaning was central to his larger aspiration to reenergize American foreign policy, pump resources into the military, and rekindle the nation's willingness to use force around the world in pursuit of a reenergized Cold War. A few observers saw as much at the time. Scorning those who would inevitably criticize Reagan as a "wild man," the *Wall Street Journal* editorial page praised him for having "the nerve to open old wounds" at a time when the nation required vigorous new leadership to confront growing communist challenges. Reagan was proposing, in the *Journal*'s judgment, nothing less than "a new philosophical basis" for foreign policy necessary to "summon the sort of commitment he thinks America will need for the confrontations ahead."[5] Later historians and commentators have vigorously debated Reagan's take on history, but few have failed to highlight the "noble cause" speech as a seminal moment in the 1980 campaign and in his larger effort to turn back to the clock to the simpler days of unquestioned American power and exceptionalism.[6]

Acknowledging the rhetorical and political significance of Reagan's words does not, however, mean that Reagan succeeded in vanquishing the Vietnam syndrome. Reagan's skillful invocation of nationalist themes, popular and congressional endorsement of the major defense build-up that he urged, and widespread adoration of Reagan as a heroic cowboy who rescued the nation from an era of decline suggest real success in removing a major impediment to an emboldened foreign policy as the 1970s gave way to the 1980s. Yet the record of the Reagan years points to more mixed results. Although Reagan and his aides showed steady concern with the Vietnam syndrome and worked hard to overcome it, they achieved only limited success and, in fact, quietly respected the constraints imposed on them by persistent anxiety about becoming embroiled in new "Vietnams." Retrospect enables us, in short, to see a striking divergence between the boldness of Reagan's rhetoric and his private acceptance that his administration could do only so much to change the debate over the war's implications, much less settle it on his own terms. In the end, Reagan's contribution was more to stir new debate over the lessons of the Vietnam War—a debate that would grow increasingly vocal and intense because of the energy he injected into it—than to assure the triumph of the lessons he embraced. Reagan thus played a central role in the drama of Americans' attempts to come to terms with their lost war in Vietnam—just not the role that he aspired to.

Debate about the implications of the Vietnam War for American foreign policy was, of course, just one dimension of a much broader American reckoning with war's meaning in the late 1970s and early 1980s. Indeed, Reagan's decisions about the use of force overseas can be best understood within the context of the administration's attitudes toward an array of politically charged issues related to the war. Outside the realm of foreign affairs, three issues that commanded sustained attention within Reagan's White House demonstrate both the administration's eagerness to seize opportunities to recast Vietnam for its purposes and its attentiveness to limits on how far it could reasonably go in challenging widely held attitudes. On one of these matters—surging attention to the status of servicemen categorized as missing in action—the administration took a bold position designed to capitalize on changing public attitudes and shift policy in new directions. However, on two other subjects—the erection of a national monument to Vietnam veterans and planning for commemoration of the tenth anniversary of the fall of Saigon—the administration showed caution.

Reagan had good timing with respect to the status of Vietnam veterans in American society: the issue was ripe for political exploitation in 1980. Following the end of the US war in Vietnam in 1973, the federal government, like much of the American public, mostly ignored veterans, while Hollywood established the trope of the drug-addled, violence-prone misfit in films such as *Taxi Driver* (1976), *Coming Home* (1978), and *The Deer Hunter* (1978). For various reasons, however, predominant attitudes about Vietnam veterans were evolving rapidly by the end of the decade. The simple passage of time enabled Americans to overcome the initial shock of defeat and to appreciate the war, including the men who fought it, with greater nuance. At the same time, the Soviet invasion of Afghanistan, the Sandinista revolution in Nicaragua, and especially the Iran hostage crisis fueled a sense of national humiliation that stirred renewed respect for the military.

Reagan's political advisers correctly detected that many Americans yearned for a return to the era of confidence and ambition that predated the catastrophe in Southeast Asia. "The common wisdom holds that any mention of the word 'Vietnam' would be a political liability in a campaign year," asserted one 1980 campaign aide, Larry De Meo, a few weeks before the election. But De Meo suggested that attitudes were "now changing" and that large majorities of Americans believed that Vietnam veterans had been treated unfairly and deserved increased benefits. "In the perceptions of the American voter," he advised, "there is a very real, distinct difference in the meaning of the words 'Vietnam war' and 'Vietnam veteran.'" A golden opportunity had arisen, he asserted, to capitalize on broad sympathy for the plight of the men who fought in Vietnam while skirting controversies about the war itself.[7] At a minimum, concluded Reagan's team, the campaign had a chance to forge bonds with a veteran community increasingly inclined to reject prevailing attitudes and take pride in military service. "Veterans groups may offer one of the best sources of Republican Party support, if properly approached," asserted one campaign memo, noting that veterans were both well organized and "perhaps the most frustrated interest group" in all of American society with the Carter administration.[8]

Accordingly, candidate Reagan promised to pump new resources into veterans' services and sharply criticized Carter for ignoring veterans' affairs generally and Vietnam veterans in particular. As president, he also sought to tap into veteran support by pledging his dedication to the recovery of US servicemen categorized as missing in action in Vietnam—a subject Reagan ignored as a candidate but highlighted enthusiastically during his first term in the White House. The POW/MIA issue was tailor-made for Reagan since it could be a vehicle for demonstrating not only nationalist sensibilities and support for the military but also scorn for a treacherous and inept federal government. This blend was well represented in popular culture at the time, above all in a form that Reagan could easily appreciate: cinema. By the end of Reagan's first term, the first of the *Rambo* series and Chuck Norris's *Missing in Action*—movies depicting heroic rescues of POWs who had been shamefully abandoned in Vietnam—had become box office hits.[9] But Reagan needed no instruction from Hollywood to highlight the issue. The president declared that accounting for all of the approximately 2,500 US servicemen missing in Indochina was "of the highest national priority," and an interagency working group within the administration worked closely with the National League of Families of American Prisoners and Missing in Southeast Asia—a citizens' group established in 1970 to press for a full accounting of all Americans MIAs—to develop a public relations campaign to heighten awareness.[10] In June 1981, Reagan signed legislation designating July 17 "National P.O.W.-M.I.A. Recognition Day."[11]

Moreover, the administration launched a series of policy initiatives in 1982 and 1983 that went beyond mere public posturing. These endeavors led to intensified contacts with the Vietnamese and Laotian governments, including dispatch of a mission headed by Deputy Assistant Secretary of Defense Richard L. Armitage to address the issue with Vietnamese Foreign Minister Nguyen Co Thach in Hanoi in February 1982, despite the fact that the two nations had no formal diplomatic relations. The administration also promised new efforts by US intelligence services to investigate reports of "live sightings" of American servicemen in Indochina. By early 1982, US agencies had received 403 such reports since the collapse of South Vietnam in 1975. Although Reagan administration officials conceded that they had no proof that any Americans remained in Southeast Asia against their will, they also noted that the Vietnamese and Laotian governments had not been as forthcoming with information as they could be.[12] All in all, Reagan promised that the "full resources of our Government" would be focused on achieving "the return of all POW's, the fullest possible accounting of those still missing, and the repatriation of remains of those who died serving our Nation."[13] From 1984 to 1989, the Defense Department issued a POW-MIA fact book that stated, "it would be irresponsible to rule out the possibility that live Americans are being held."[14]

The administration's activism on the POW/MIA issue contrasted markedly with its caution in connection with controversies that swirled around the creation of the Vietnam Veterans Memorial. This divergence demonstrates Reagan's selective attention to Vietnam-related themes and sense of caution when the issue did not seem certain to work in favor of his broad policy goals. Congress voted in July 1980 to approve construction of a memorial on the National Mall, intending that the monument would "make no political statement about the war," as decorated Vietnam veteran Jan Scruggs, the founder and principal fundraiser for the initiative, put it. "Our nation," Scruggs added, "must separate the issue of the war itself from the issue of how veterans served the country."[15] When the memorial's design was selected in May 1981, however, many Americans quickly condemned the project for failing to strike the promised tone. The winning design—the famous black marble "V" designed by twenty-one-year-old Yale University architecture student Maya Lin—was "a black gash of shame and sorrow, hacked into the national visage that is the Mall," Army veteran Tom Carhart wrote in the *Wall Street Journal*.[16] Marine veteran and author James H. Webb, later a senator from Virginia, agreed, asking rhetorically, "At what point does a piece of architecture cease being a memorial to service and instead become a mockery of that service, a wailing wall for future anti-draft and anti-nuclear demonstrators?"[17] To blunt the criticism, which quickly drew support from dozens of members of Congress, the

Vietnam Veterans Memorial Fund and various organizations responsible for reviewing public statuary in Washington quickly offered a compromise that called for adding two additional elements—a flagpole and a "heroic sculpture" depicting three GI's in battle.[18]

Through all this controversy, the administration was remarkably quiet despite obvious opportunities to weigh in against what could surely have been decried as a grim insult to American servicemen and women. Behind the scenes, White House staffers paid careful attention to the issue and weighed three options as the controversy intensified in early 1982. The executive branch could, advised presidential aide Danny Boggs, kill the proposed design by withholding approval by the National Park Service. But Boggs warned that taking such a step would risk delaying construction of any Vietnam memorial "for many years or forever" while also stirring "political furor" that would draw the president "into expressing, directly or indirectly, some opinion on the design"—clearly not a happy prospect for the White House. Equally unappealing was the option of allowing the proposed design to proceed without amendment. Boggs cautioned that this path would also generate "considerable political discontent," including lawsuits, efforts within Congress to block construction, and even "direct action" by outraged veterans. The most appealing solution was the compromise formula that seemed to be gathering momentum in early 1982. Modifying the "trappings" surrounding the monument, wrote Boggs, seemed likely to defuse the crisis.[19]

The White House quietly promoted that outcome, making no pronouncement on the issue and allowing Interior Secretary James Watt, in his role as overseer of the National Park Service, to handle the controversy. Watt decided in February 1982 to withhold final approval of the memorial pending review of the compromise proposal—Lin's "wall" plus the flagpole and the statue of the three servicemen—by the US Commission of Fine Arts and the National Capital Planning Commission.[20] Watt did not insist on completion of a Gallup poll to test Americans' attitudes toward the proposed memorial, an idea advanced by billionaire businessman H. Ross Perot, a fierce opponent of Lin's design and self-appointed defender of veterans' interests. White House aide Morton Blackwell recommended that Watt accede to Perot's idea, noting that the poll could get the administration off the hook for a decision one way or another. ("If the combat veterans support the design, all effective opposition will collapse," wrote Blackwell. "If they oppose the design, it will be very difficult to criticize the Administration for adhering to their preference.") But Watt took no public position on Perot's idea, instead leaving the matter in the hands of the two relatively predictable review boards. Their approval stirred relief within the administration, and Watt signed off on the compromise on

March 11, 1982, allowing time to complete construction before a public unveiling on Veterans Day later that year. Watt's insistence, in his congratulatory letter to Scruggs, that the addition of the sculpture and the flag would "transform the design into one which honors both those who served the country and those who made the ultimate sacrifice" smacked of exaggeration since neither of the additional elements substantially changed the impression created by the massive marble monument.[21] What counted most, though, was to end the controversy without further attention.

Reagan similarly kept a low profile on the Vietnam War when questions arose in early 1985 about how the White House should mark the tenth anniversary of the fall of Saigon. To be sure, Reagan's aides were deeply divided over how the administration should handle a moment that seemed likely to attract significant attention. "A debate was raging within the administration, unnoticed by the media," Secretary of State George Shultz wrote in his memoir.[22] For his part, Shultz was eager to exploit the opportunity to challenge old thinking about the war, and, on April 25, 1985, he delivered a strongly worded speech in the State Department's vast diplomatic lobby insisting that the United States had pursued "noble ideals" in Vietnam and had subjected the peoples of South Vietnam, Laos, and Cambodia to "brutal tyranny" by failing to see its commitment through to the end.[23] Most striking of all, Shultz drew parallels to the ongoing crisis in Central America, warning that congressional constraints on the administration's ability to support pro-US forces in Nicaragua and El Salvador amounted to a similar failure of will that risked inviting dangerous communist advances. "Can we afford to be naïve again," asked Shultz, "about the consequences when we pull back, about the special ruthlessness of Communist rule?"[24] Presidential speech writer Pat Buchanan hoped that Reagan might invoke such themes in a "surprise" address that he proposed to entitle "The Lessons of Vietnam."[25] But National Security Adviser Robert C. "Bud" McFarlane and other aides wanted no part of such provocations, agreeing at a White House staff meeting that the best course in connection with the anniversary was "not to play it up."[26]

Such cautious advisers proposed that the White House's goal should be merely "to ensure that the anniversary does not open old wounds but contributes to healing them" and to "look forward rather than back as much as possible," as one internal memorandum put it. To that end, aides suggested, among other notably bland ideas, efforts to show the president's eagerness "to meet the concerns of the Vietnam veterans and the families of the POW/MIAs" and to demonstrate that the nation had "recovered from the trauma of our involvement in Vietnam."[27] On more controversial matters, there was strikingly little interest in the president taking any strong position. Above all, wrote Richard T. Childress, the NSC aide responsible for Vietnamese affairs, the White House must avoid commentary that would encourage comparisons to ongoing US initiatives in El Salvador or Nicaragua. "We should not place ourselves in the position of defending the war in Vietnam and especially in linking it in any specific way to Central America," he insisted, advocating an approach to the anniversary that "doesn't spark debates with us over lessons learned and current events in Central America and elsewhere."[28] Shultz recalled in his memoir that Childress objected vociferously to his insistence on giving a speech, calling the secretary "in a rage" in the days leading up to the anniversary to warn of the damage that might be done to US efforts to negotiate with Hanoi on POW/MIA issues.[29]

Reagan followed the lead of Childress and other cautious aides, making no speech and generating no significant headlines in connection with the anniversary. Unquestionably, Reagan demonstrated his continued interest in the issue—and likely his suppressed eagerness to speak out on the subject—during a news conference on April 18, when offered a lengthy response to a reporter's question about the lessons that the United States had learned from the war.[30] Yet Reagan stuck close to old themes and even phrases he had used so often in the past. He praised the "unselfish heroism" of the servicemen and women who had fought in Vietnam and criticized US leaders who had fed them into "this meat-grinder" even though "no one had any intention of allowing victory." Even so, Reagan asserted somewhat paradoxically, US forces did achieve victory and Washington signed a workable peace agreement in 1973, only to see Congress betray those achievements by refusing to help South Vietnam withstand renewed communist aggression. "We broke our pledge as a government," Reagan insisted.[31] He did not, however, connect these events to contemporary foreign policy challenges or otherwise draw lessons from the lost war, and the moment passed with little attention in the US media.

The administration's mixed and contradictory behavior carried over to Reagan's decision-making about foreign policy. After entering the White House, the president occasionally invoked the war as he pressed for a more assertive US role in the world and sounded nationalist themes that had served him well during the campaign. Aversion to international activism was, Reagan declared in a 1981 commencement speech at West Point, "a temporary aberration" that his administration was committed to ending. "Let friend and foe alike," he continued, "be made aware of the spirit that is once more sweeping across our land, because it means we will meet our responsibility to the free world." His conclusion was the headline-grabber: "The era of self-doubt is over," he told the graduating cadets. "We've stopped looking at our warts and rediscovered how much there is to love in this blessed land."[32]

Out of public view, however, the administration was divided over the meaning of the Vietnam War for US foreign relations. On one side, Reagan's secretary of state, Army General Alexander Haig, urged bold action consistent with Reagan's assertive rhetoric. For Haig, the key lesson of Vietnam was the need to act decisively against the enemy's main sources of strength. "The Vietnam War," Haig wrote later, "was prosecuted on the basis of a fallacious strategic theory—incrementalism—that gave the advantage to a weaker enemy by imposing irrational limits on the use of our own power." This approach sprang from the "arrogant sophistication" of defense intellectuals who believed they could apply military force in carefully measured doses to achieve precise political effects, Haig added. But in the end, the US approach amounted to "moral weakness and military folly."[33] In Central America and the Caribbean, the key regions of concern for the new administration, this outlook led Haig to advocate bold use of American power, even at the risk of war with Cuba or the Soviet Union, to block Cuba's ability to support leftist insurgencies throughout the region.[34]

On the other side, Defense Secretary Caspar Weinberger invoked Vietnam in support of a cautious approach to the Cold War at odds with Reagan's tough talk. Whereas Haig argued that Reagan's sweeping electoral victory gave the president space to defy American skepticism about a bold foreign policy, Weinberger called attention to the dangers of policy departures that lacked public support. "It is not really possible, no matter what the skill, nor the size, nor the effectiveness of the American forces, to fight a war that does not have the understanding of the American people," Weinberger asserted during his Senate confirmation hearing just before Reagan took office.[35] He later expanded on the point: "You can't fight Congress and public opinion and the enemy at the same time. That's why Vietnam was the crime of the century."[36] In the administration's early days, this outlook led the new defense secretary to oppose Haig's aggressive proposal for the Western Hemisphere. Instead, Weinberger recommended relatively modest measures aimed not at Cuba but at defeating insurgencies in Central America, especially in El Salvador.

Weinberger won the debate. Reagan's closest White House aides—Chief of Staff James Baker III along with subordinates Edwin Meese and Michael Deaver—concluded that the political risks were too grave to risk aggressive action.[37] These advisers wanted to focus on the president's domestic agenda and worked to deemphasize foreign policy challenges in the administration's opening months. Accordingly, when the administration announced its decision on March 2, 1981, to send $25 million in military aid to the government of El Salvador and increase the number of US military personnel in that country to fifty-four, it did so with notable understatement. The announcement came in a press briefing by State Department spokesman William J. Dyess, who stressed that the decision merely expanded aid programs begun by the Carter administration and that US troops "will not accompany Salvadoran armed forces outside their garrison areas or participate in any combat operations."[38] Reagan's team was also careful to describe American personnel as "trainers" rather than "advisers," a term the administration feared would conjure memories of Vietnam.[39] Officials had good reason to proceed in this way. In March 1981, a Gallup poll showed that two-thirds of "informed Americans" believed the situation in El Salvador could develop into "another Vietnam." Only 2 percent backed the idea of sending US combat troops. Meanwhile, Congress showed little enthusiasm for strong steps in Central America and jealously guarded its prerogatives to constrain the executive branch's activist impulses, attitudes that led Congress to bar covert US aid to the Contras in Nicaragua from 1982 to 1985.[40]

The administration affirmed its cautious approach in late 1981 and early 1982, when the National Security Council, with Reagan in the chair, devoted unprecedented attention to problems in Central America, which had seemed to grow only more urgent. "It is clear that the threat to the Caribbean is unprecedented in severity, and proximity and complexity," asserted National Security Adviser William P. Clark, who judged the crisis as more serious than the dangers posed to Latin American by the Nazis in the 1930s and 1940s and by Fidel Castro's Cuba in the 1960s.[41] UN Ambassador Jeane Kirkpatrick pointed to a different historical reference point—the Vietnam War—but suggested that problems in Central America were much graver than they had been in Southeast Asia. "The Vietnam War did not involve direct national security interests," she asserted on November 10, 1981. "The loss of Central America does."[42] Under these circumstances, Reagan's aides agreed that the United States needed to act more determinedly throughout the region, and their comments reverberated with tough talk.

Predictably, Haig spoke most aggressively—though only in generalities—about the need to "act" regardless of the public mood, insisting that the United States must deliver the message that "we mean business." Haig invoked the Vietnam War as evidence of the dangers of half measures and insufficient will. "We cannot start another Vietnam in our hemisphere," he declared in urging bold action to deal with the problem decisively. Mostly, though, officials emphasized that the administration could not risk steps that ran afoul of American opinion. Defense Secretary Caspar Weinberger ruled out "unilateral force."

Instead, he asserted, the United States must "go step by step" and work in tandem with "a coalition of Latin American countries" to craft solutions that enjoyed multilateral support.[43] National Security Adviser Clark also rejected Haig's proposal of relatively quick and decisive action and instead proposed a wide-ranging Caribbean basin initiative to focus US resources on the region over the long term. "There will be no quick fix," he lamented. "And it won't be cheap."[44] Most important of all, aides suggested, was to broaden support for US activism by working to reshape public attitudes. The secret seemed to lie in emphasizing the dire threat emerging within the hemisphere and the need to jettison old anxieties rooted in memories of Vietnam. The administration could not, in the worlds of NSC aide Robert C. McFarlane, "create a consensus overnight." Rather, generating support would be a "process that is going to take time," added McFarlane, who agreed with other officials on the need for a major presidential speech focused on this task.[45]

Most revealing of all were Reagan's own musings about the shadow that Vietnam cast over his administration. At the NSC meeting in November 1981, the president conceded the persistent power of the Vietnam syndrome by suggesting that one solution was to rely on "covert actions" that could be "truly disabling" to Latin American leftists while skirting public notice in the United States.[46] Thus did Reagan verbalize the logic that underpinned the secret dimensions of what political commentator Charles Krauthammer would, in 1985, dub the "Reagan doctrine," the administration's practice of backing anticommunist resistance forces around the world. Reagan had long advocated US backing for such groups, and during his presidency he made no secret of his desire to do so in countries ranging from Nicaragua and Suriname to Afghanistan and Angola.[47] In practice, however, US initiatives to support groups such as the Nicaraguan Contras and the Afghan mujahideen were often covert. One reason for secrecy was undoubtedly fear that overt meddling in communist-leaning nations might provoke dangerous clashes with Moscow, but it stands to reason that public aversion to bold foreign policy forays stemming from the Vietnam War also encouraged the administration to keep its activities as quiet as possible. Indeed, the administration's concerns about antagonizing public and congressional opinion in 1981 coincided with a series of decisions to support antigovernment guerrillas in Nicaragua almost entirely through covert channels, decisions that put the administration on a collision course with Congress and ultimately resulted in the Iran-Contra scandal.[48]

Although drawn to covert operations, Reagan also agreed with his advisers that the best way to regain the ability to carry out an assertive foreign policy was to mount a persuasion campaign to convince Americans to embrace renewed international activism. The president expressed confidence that an effective public-relations initiative could achieve his goals, noting that a key problem in Vietnam was that the war was "never explained" to the American people. A major question for the administration was, the president suggested, "How do we frame a speech that keeps the protesters out [in] the snow?" Yet Reagan also recognized that he could not go too far in sounding the alarm and implied the need to strike a balance between boldness and conciliation. "Can we do a speech without making it sound like war?" he wondered, suggesting that the most effective message to send to Central Americans might be decidedly dovish. "We should go to the Caribbean and say we are all neighbors," Reagan speculated in an almost stream-of-consciousness ramble that revealed the contradictions in his thinking. Addressing imaginary Central American interlocutors, he proposed, "Let's hear your ideas and together bring about the things you are interested in." The president reminded his aides that he had been a "hawk" on the Vietnam War "because I believe if you ask people to die you should give them a chance to win." But he immediately tacked to a more compromising tone, noting, "The best way to prevent war is to get to the problem early." All in all, he hoped to find a way to blunt communist advances in the region without the military action that would only affirm his reputation for belligerence. "Can I do something without adding to the perception of me as a hawk?" he asked rhetorically.[49]

Conflicting pressures intensified in the fall of 1983, when two nearly simultaneous crises—one in Lebanon and another in the tiny Caribbean island nation of Grenada—stirred new discussion of the Vietnam syndrome and its meaning for US policymaking. Above all, the two episodes affirmed that, even as the downing of Korean Airlines flight 007 and the staging of provocative NATO exercises in Western Europe intensified the Cold War to levels unseen since the early 1960s, Americans remained skeptical of intervention abroad. The Reagan administration, attuned to public opinion trends, appreciated that its options remained limited in the international arena.

The terrorist bombing of the US Marine barracks in Lebanon—a devastating explosion that killed 241 Americans taking part in a multinational peacekeeping operation—inflamed the Vietnam syndrome by reinforcing the perceived dangers of sending American forces into confusing, war-torn settings abroad. In fact, the legacies of Vietnam had haunted US decision-making toward Lebanon for many months before the bombing as the Reagan administration struggled to quell sectarian fighting that threatened American interests across the Middle East. When the administration first dispatched US Marines to Lebanon in August 1982, the force had a narrow remit to facilitate the withdrawal of Palestinian Liberation Organization guerrillas from Lebanon within thirty days and then pull out themselves. That plan represented a victory for Weinberger, as usual the most skittish of Reagan's senior advisers about the use of US military power, over Secretary of State George Shultz and others who believed that the US contingent should do more to promote an overall political settlement in Lebanon. At first, the operation appeared to be successful. After escorting the PLO fighters out of Lebanon, the Marines withdrew from the country in mid-September. Before long, however, Weinberger was on the defensive when pressures mounted to reintroduce US forces to take part in a reconstituted multinational force. That abrupt shift resulted from a drastic change in the context of US decision-making on September 17 and 18, 1982, when Christian militiamen, with the tacit support of the Israeli army, massacred more than 700 Palestinians in the Sabra and Shatila refugee camps in the southern part of the country.[50]

The sheer brutality of the attacks, probably accompanied by a sense of guilt over withdrawing the first US contingent too quickly, shifted the balance of power toward administration officials who advocated not only the reintroduction of US troops but also a relatively expansive mission aimed at strengthening the Lebanese government's authority. Weinberger, backed by Joint Chiefs of Staff Chairman John W. Vessey Jr., opposed the whole idea, worried about the ambition and imprecision of American goals. But he lost the debate, not least because the president took a strong position on the matter.[51] Shortly after the Marines arrived back in Lebanon, an unnamed aide made Reagan's logic explicit in comments to *Time* magazine: "The president believes the 'Viet Nam syndrome' has put ridiculous restraints on peace keeping, even when it is in American interests," the aide stated. "He is disturbed at the reluctance to use American military force when it can be a useful adjunct to our foreign policy."[52] Perhaps most remarkably, opinion polls gave officials no strong reason to fear an ambitious policy. Whereas polls about US policy toward Central America in early 1981 had revealed widespread anxiety about a new Vietnam-like quagmire, they now showed no such qualms in connection with Lebanon. As historian Gail Yoshitani observes, several factors help account for this momentary easing of the Vietnam syndrome: broad sympathy for Israel, revulsion at gruesome images of civilian casualties in Lebanon, and frustration about the US inability thus far to create stability.[53]

The return of US forces in September 1982 set the stage for disaster—and a powerful resurgence of the Vietnam syndrome—the following fall. The Reagan administration described the US contingent as a disinterested peacekeeping force, but as the Lebanese civil war escalated over the following months, the Americans became entangled in local political rivalries. Attacks on US troops accelerated during the first ten months of 1983, culminating in the bombing of the US barracks on October 23. International critics of the United States immediately invoked Vietnam to beat up on the Reagan administration. The Lebanon-based Hezbollah movement, for example, praised the bombers for inflicting on the United States an "utter defeat, not experienced since Vietnam."[54] In Moscow, *Pravda* suggested that "it looked like Vietnam was getting started again" in Lebanon.[55] Perhaps aware that foreign enemies were explicitly deploying the Vietnam analogy, Reagan's critics within the United States generally avoided explicit comparisons. Yet it required little imagination to hear echoes of Indochina in commentary by Democrats concerned that the administration had failed to articulate a clear rationale for the US mission in Lebanon and had carelessly exposed American servicemen to danger. "It hasn't been clear what our purpose, our mission, our strategy, is," complained Democratic Senator Christopher Dodd of Connecticut. Suggesting that the deployment was motivated mostly by the administration's desire to project an activist image, Dodd asserted, "I don't want to call . . . some Connecticut constituents and tell them that their son is no longer alive for pride and perception and images."[56]

Out of public view, Reagan's aides engaged with the Vietnam analogy and brainstormed arguments that the president, Weinberger, and Shultz would make over the following months to shield the administration from Vietnam-tinged criticism. Above all, officials sought to bolster the idea that the United States must preserve the ability to respond to international threats with measured uses of force that fell short of full-scale war and played an important role in reinforcing diplomatic initiatives. "In some regions of the world (e.g., the Middle East)," asserted one memo,

> the most relevant currency supporting diplomacy is military power and the demonstrated willingness to use it in support of limited objectives. If the US is to deal effectively in the Middle East and influence the perceptions of US adversaries and their willingness to agree to political accommodation, the US must be ready to apply measured force to protect important interests and objectives. This does not mean "war" in the traditional sense; rather, it is the use of military power to complement diplomacy.

The memo acknowledged that Americans had learned some "wise lessons" from the Vietnam War, including the point that "gradualism is a mistake." But it also insisted, "This does not mean . . . that limited uses of force for limited political objectives are no longer possible." Indeed, the paper contended that authoritarian nations such as North Vietnam would always have an "inherent advantage" over a democracy such as the United States because of their ability to use all-out force without the restraint of public opinion. The United States must exercise "voluntary self-discipline" to assure that it could defend its interests even while accepting the problems of waging limited war. "This is difficult to achieve," the memo concluded. "But if the Vietnamese example turns out to be a pattern for the future, then Western interests throughout the world will be in danger."[57]

The administration embraced this logic in ordering the invasion of Grenada on October 25, 1983, to overthrow the nation's Marxist regime. Reagan and his aides feared that the island was moving dangerously into the communist camp and, once it completed work on a new jet runway, would become capable of supporting Soviet and Cuban military activities. In a nationally televised address on October 27, Reagan heralded the success of Operation Urgent Fury and made the case for a vigorous and proactive foreign policy. Events in Lebanon and Grenada, he said, "though oceans apart," were "closely related" because they both stemmed from the machinations of the Soviet Union—a formidable adversary in every part of the world. At one time, the president continued, the United States could defend its interests with just a "standing army," "shore batteries," and "a navy to keep the sea lanes open for the shipping of things necessary to our well-being." Now, he added, "The world has changed. Today, our national security can be threatened in far-away places," and, he concluded, "It's up to all of us to be aware of the strategic importance of such places and to be able to identify them."[58] Only years later did Reagan take his analysis a step further by explicitly invoking the ghosts of Vietnam in explaining his decisions about Grenada. "I understood what Vietnam had meant for the country," he explained in his 1990 memoir, "but I believed the United States couldn't remain spooked forever by this experience."[59]

The administration was no doubt pleased with the initial public reaction to the invasion and Reagan's speech. Predictably, conservative voices sang the administration's praises. Success in Grenada showed that "when necessary and appropriate, the US can and should rely on its military power to achieve its political goals," declared a *Wall Street Journal* editorial that excoriated "Washington's self-reinforcing culture of opinion" for its unthinking aversion to such behavior since the Vietnam War.[60] Less predictably, calls to the White House, which reached unprecedented levels in the Reagan presidency during the hours after the address, showed strong support. Of 16,009 calls, more than 13,000 were positive, while only 998 were negative.[61] Opinion polls over the following days ran in the same direction. According to *USA Today*, for example, support for the decision to send the Marines to Lebanon climbed from 39 percent before the speech to 53 percent afterward, while support for keeping the

Marines in Lebanon increased from 48 to 59 percent. Regarding Grenada, support for Reagan's decision to invade leapt from 48 percent before the speech to 68 percent afterward.[62] An ABC News poll found even stronger backing for the administration after the speech. Support for US policy in Lebanon spiked from 50 to 80 percent and in Grenada from 64 to 84 percent.[63]

Yet the administration also confronted abundant evidence of persistent aversion to use of American power abroad. The Vietnam syndrome persisted despite the rally-around-the-flag effect produced by the disaster in Lebanon, the invasion of Grenada, and Reagan's speech. Even some of Reagan's allies drew a distinction between US policies in the Middle East and the Caribbean, expressing concern about the former even as they praised the latter. "The president is wrong on Lebanon," asserted GOP Senator Slade Gorton of Washington, who declared himself "100%" with the president on Grenada.[64] For their part, Democrats were predictably much more forthright in criticizing Reagan and sometimes invoked Vietnam. One line of attack emphasized that Reagan was overly aggressive in the international arena and hinted at his burning desire to overcome the Vietnam syndrome. "I think there was a desire to use force and show our strength," asserted Democratic Senator Alan Cranston of California, who described the president as "trigger happy and somewhat reckless." Colorado Senator Gary Hart quipped, "I don't know what this country's foreign policy will be when we run out of Marines."[65] The *New York Times* editorial page struck some of the same themes, berating Reagan for a "seductive and immature reaction" to a complex political situation in Grenada and speculating about where the United States would lash out next. "Watch out, Nicaragua. Beware, Syria. Keep out, Russia," the *Times* mockingly asserted.[66]

Meanwhile, opinion polls made clear that most Americans, even if they supported Reagan in Lebanon and Grenada, remained wary of embroilment overseas and skeptical of the administration's broad pattern of behavior. A poll conducted by the *New York Times* and CBS after Reagan's October 27 speech showed that pluralities harbored doubts. Some 49 percent of Americans agreed that Reagan "uses [the] military far too quickly" (compared to 38 percent who felt he used "diplomacy enough"). Meanwhile, 49 percent indicated that they were "uneasy with Reagan's approach to international crises (as opposed to 44 percent saying he handled crises "wisely"). Forty percent believed that Reagan had sent troops into Grenada merely "to show American military strength after the bombing of Lebanon," whereas only 39 percent considered the invasion "necessary."[67] Possibly even more troubling for the administration, Reagan's approval ratings for his handling of foreign policy had steadily deteriorated in the year leading up to the fall of 1983, with fully 50 percent expressing disapproval in September of that year. The bump in public approval at the time of Reagan's speech, then, came against a gloomy backdrop, with impressive numbers of Americans supporting the nuclear freeze, expressing wariness about the military buildup, and opposing other aspects of Reagan's policies.[68]

Did all this make a difference in Reagan's decision-making? The evidence is mostly circumstantial, but it appears that the administration was indeed constrained in various ways by public and congressional skepticism. For one thing, Reagan's Defense Department went to extraordinary lengths to control information about the Grenada invasion. Officially, administration officials claimed that they declined to brief Congress about the operation and excluded reporters from Grenada for the first four days of US military operation in order to preserve the element of surprise. Yet there is little doubt that the decision, which sparked fierce controversy, flowed from determination to shape public attitudes without concern about critical reporting.[69] Reagan admitted as much in his 1990 memoir, asserting, "I suspected that, if we told the leaders of Congress about the operation, even under the strictest confidentiality, there would be some who would leak it to the press together with the predictions that Grenada would become 'another Vietnam.'"[70]

Still more striking was the Reagan administration's decision not to retaliate in Lebanon against the terrorists responsible for the barracks bombing. At an urgent meeting with senior advisers shortly after the attack, Reagan declared, "The first thing I want to do is to find out who did it and go after them with everything we've got.[71] When US intelligence placed the blame on a splinter Shiite group known as the Husaini Suicide Force, CIA Director William Casey and Secretary of State Shultz backed a US air attack. As usual, though, Weinberger cautioned against quick action, warning especially that a US attack would inevitably kill innocent civilians and thereby damage the US image throughout the Middle East. Although the idea of a retaliatory strike lingered within senior decision-making circles, Reagan remained ambivalent, and the proposal went nowhere. Meanwhile, fearing congressional efforts to force an end to the mission in Lebanon, the administration began planning in December 1983 to pull out US forces. On February 7, Reagan ordered the Marines to withdraw to warships in the Mediterranean.[72]

Publicly, the Reagan administration continued after the dramatic events of fall 1983 to tout its determination to put the Vietnam syndrome to rest and restore vigor to US foreign relations. In an April 1984 speech, Schultz hit a typical note, asserting that Americans must accept that "there will always be risks" in foreign policy and that America's adversaries would surely "play rough" by putting the United States in difficult situations that defied easy solutions. The realities that would face the United States "in the 1980s, 1990s, or beyond" demanded flexibility and determination, Shultz insisted.[73] More remarkably, officials sometimes claimed that they had succeeded in bringing about the shift they so desired. When the administration confronted a surging communist danger in Grenada, asserted Vice President George H. W. Bush during the 1984 reelection campaign, Reagan had "acted before the crisis became humiliation." Such behavior, asserted Bush, stood in sharp contrast to the "paralysis, stagnation, and drift" that had characterized US policymaking four years earlier. On the campaign trail, Reagan himself asserted that the era of "paralyzing self-doubt" had ended under his watch and that the nation was once again comfortable with "just and legitimate uses of American power." He added: "Some nations thought they could threaten or harm the United States with impunity. We've changed this."[74]

Yet, as throughout Reagan's first term, the administration's statements were contradicted by its performance. Since entering the White House, Reagan and his advisers had demonstrated keen awareness of constraints imposed by public opinion, Congress, and cautious military commanders. Moreover, some of the administration's boldest actions brought disaster rather than triumph. The Lebanon intervention was widely derided as ill-planned and poorly executed, while secret US support of the Nicaraguan Contras set Reagan on a course to a major political crisis when evidence surfaced in 1986 about the administration's sales of arms to Iran in order to fund activities in Central America that were forbidden by Congress. Only the Grenada episode could be counted as a clear-cut success in pushing against the constraints imposed by the Vietnam syndrome, though a good deal of commentary highlighted that a US success in a tiny Caribbean spice island hardly counted as a major geopolitical accomplishment.

Perhaps the most revealing evidence of the administration's inability to reconcile words with behavior, though, was a significant rhetorical shift that occurred on November 28, 1984, just after the election. In a high-profile speech before the National Press Club in Washington, Defense Secretary Weinberger went further than any previous administration official in spelling out limits that he believed presidents must accept in wielding US military power in the future. He insisted that American forces should be deployed only when core interests of the United States or its allies were in play, when congressional and public support could be assured, when goals were clearly defined and achievable, and when all other options had been exhausted.[75] As usual, though, the administration hardly spoke with one voice. Secretary of State Shultz belittled Weinberger's caution, calling the speech "the Vietnam syndrome in spades, carried to an absurd level" and "a complete abdication of the duties of leadership."[76] All in all, later commentary has probably exaggerated the significance of the speech, which gained stature partly because General Colin Powell, Reagan's national security adviser during his last fifteen months in office, liked it so well that talk of a "Weinberger doctrine" morphed into the "Powell doctrine." In fact, as Shultz acknowledged in his 1993 memoir, Vietnam, combined with Watergate, had the United States "tied in knots." Trying to make policy under these circumstances was, he added, "like walking through a swamp."[77] Among the problems in discerning a clear US policy was a lack of direction from the top. Reagan took no clear position on Weinberger's speech during his second term, when the combination of declining Cold War tensions and the Iran-Contra scandal made US interventions less appealing for the Reagan administration. (Confrontations with Libya during Reagan's second term shed little light since those episodes did not appear to entail any significant possibility of a major US troop deployment.)

It is tempting, then, to castigate Reagan for hypocritical posturing in connection with the legacies of the Vietnam War. He claimed to defy the Vietnam Syndrome when doing so served his political purposes but otherwise quietly respected post-Vietnam political realities. Yet to take this position is to discount the importance of political rhetoric in evaluating the larger significance of the Reagan presidency. Whatever his performance in practice, Reagan lent credibility to the argument that the principal lesson of Vietnam was that the United States must use power more boldly in the future and give the military everything it needed to get the job done. This vision of the Vietnam War gained popularity during the 1980s and ultimately prevailed with a substantial part of the American population in the post–Cold War era, when the new unipolar world order made intervention more tempting than ever for US officials. This was no small achievement by Reagan and depended on his greatest asset in his formidable array of political tools: his ability to convince ordinary Americans to see the world his way. As Henry Kissinger later contended, Reagan's speeches were far more important than his policy decisions, for they helped remake the political landscape in ways that would endure far beyond his presidency and inspire a generation of conservatives far more attached to Reagan's core principles than concerned with his deviations.[78]

Assessing this contribution to the debate over the lessons of the Vietnam War is, of course, largely a matter of interpretation and political outlook. Some commentary suggests that Reagan merits enormous credit for restoring the nation's self-confidence and laying the groundwork for the end of the Cold War and the assertion of American power that followed. Others take Reagan to task for scrapping lessons that could have reoriented the nation in a more constructive, thoughtful, and moral direction, both in its domestic political culture and its behavior internationally. In this telling, Reagan encouraged the rewriting of history that explained away the American defeat in Vietnam and set the stage for the United States to make the same errors in the future. But there is also a third possibility. It may be that Reagan deserves credit for recognizing an opportunity to reorient public debate—to apply a "symbolic balm for America's wounded pride," as political commentator Peter Beinart puts it—in a way that actually assured him, whether deliberately or inadvertently, the ability to behave in a cautious, more realist manner.[79] In the disparity between rhetoric and behavior may lie a key to understanding Reagan's performance in the foreign policy arena. Reagan understood how to create and nurture a political movement rooted in patriotic themes even as he understood the limitations on the use of American power.

Notes

1. H. W. Brands, *Reagan: The Life* (New York: Anchor, 2015), 228.
2. Reagan, "Restoring the Margin of Safety," 18 Aug. 1980, https://reaganlibrary.archives.gov/archives/reference/8.18.80.html.
3. Lou Cannon, *President Reagan: The Role of a Lifetime* (New York: Public Affairs, 1991), 290.
4. "Powell: Reagan Is 'Trying to Have It Both Ways,'" *Washington Post*, 19 Aug. 1980.
5. "Vietnam Syndrome," *Wall Street Journal*, 20 Aug. 1980.
6. On Reagan's place within the longer history of the Vietnam syndrome, see David L. Anderson, "One Vietnam War Should Be Enough and Other Reflections on Diplomatic History and the Making of Foreign Policy," *Diplomatic History* 30, no. 1 (2006): 1–21; Robert J. McMahon, "Contested Memory: The Vietnam War and American Society, 1975–2001," *Diplomatic History* 26, no. 2 (2002): 159–184.
7. De Meo to Kelly, "Vietnam Veterans Issues and Their Effects on the Popular Vote," 22 Sept. 1980, Ronald Reagan Presidential Library (RRPL), 1980 Campaign Papers (CP), Citizens' Operations (CO), box 352.
8. "Veterans Affairs: Brief Sheet," RRPL, CP, CO, box 352.
9. Fred Turner, *Echoes of Combat: The Vietnam War in American Memory* (New York: Anchor Books, 1994), 90–95.
10. Reagan speech to National League of Families of American Prisoners and Missing in Southeast Asia, 28 Jan. 1983, RRPL, Morton C. Blackwell Papers (MCBP), box 45; Childress to Christiansen, "POW/MIA Issue," 19 Jan. 1982, RRPL, MCBP, box 45; Griffiths to Interagency Group on POW/MIAs, 3 Mar. 1982, RRPL, MCBP, box 45.
11. Reagan, "Proclamation 4848—National P.O.W.-M.I.A. Recognition Day, 1981," 12 June 1981, http://www.presidency.ucsb.edu/ws/?pid=43942.
12. Christiansen to Blackwell, "Interagency Group on POW/MIA Affairs," 8 Mar. 1982, RRPL, MCBP, box 45.

13. Reagan speech to National League of Families of American Prisoners and Missing in Southeast Asia, 28 Jan. 1983.

14. H. Bruce Franklin, *M.I.A., or Mythmaking in America* (New York: Lawrence Hill Books, 1992), 4–5.

15. "Yale Architecture Student Wins Vietnam Veterans Memorial Design Competition," 6 May 1981, RRPL, MCBP, box 53.

16. Tom Carhart, "Insulting Vietnam Vets," *Wall Street Journal*, 24 Oct. 1981.

17. James H. Webb Jr., "Reassessing the Vietnam Veterans Memorial," *Wall Street Journal*, 18 Dec. 1981.

18. Watt to Scruggs, 29 Sept. 1982, RRPL, MCBP, box 53. For details of these controversies, see James Reston Jr., *A Rift in the Earth: Art, Memory, and the Fight for a Vietnam Memorial* (New York: Arcade, 2017).

19. Boggs to Anderson, 18 Jan. 1982, RRPL, Elizabeth Dole Papers (EDP), box 58.

20. Benjamin Forgey, "Memorial Delayed: Vietnam Monument to be Reviewed," *Washington Post*, 27 Feb. 1982.

21. Watt to Scruggs, 29 Sept. 1982, RRPL, MCBP, box 53.

22. George P. Shultz, *Turmoil and Triumph: My Years as Secretary of State* (New York: Scribner, 1993), 552.

23. Shultz, *Turmoil and Triumph*, 553.

24. Bernard Gwertzman, "Shultz Likens Latin Left to Indochina Communists," *New York Times*, 26 Apr. 1985.

25. Buchanan to Regan, McFarlane, Elliott, and Poindexter, 5 Apr. 1985, RRPL, Richard T. Childress Papers (RTCP), box 4.

26. Childress to Poindexter, 3 Apr. 1985, RRPL, RTCP, box 4.

27. "Meeting on the Tenth Anniversary of the End of the Vietnam War," 27 Feb. 1985, RRPL, RTCP, box 4.

28. Childress to McFarlane, 10 Apr. 1985, RRPL, RTCP, box 4; Childress to Poindexter, 3 Apr. 1985, ibid.

29. Shultz, *Turmoil and Triumph*, 552.

30. Shultz remembered that Reagan energetically endorsed his speech on April 25; Shultz, *Turmoil and Triumph*, 553.

31. "Remarks and a Question-and-Answer Session with Regional Editors and Broadcasters," 18 Apr. 1985, http://www.presidency.ucsb.edu/ws/index.php?pid=38498.

32. "Address at Commencement Exercises at the United States Military Academy," 27 May 1981, http://www.presidency.ucsb.edu/ws/?pid=43865.

33. Alexander M. Haig Jr., *Inner Circles: How America Changed the World* (New York: Warner Books, 1992), 127.

34. Gail E.S. Yoshitani, *Reagan on War: A Reappraisal of the Weinberger Doctrine, 1980–1984* (College Station: Texas A&M University Press, 2012), 50–51.

35. Quoted in Yoshitani, *Reagan on War*, 54.

36. Quoted in Jeffrey Record, *Making War, Thinking History: Munich, Vietnam, and Presidential Uses of Force from Korea to Kosovo* (Annapolis, MD: Naval Institute Press, 2002), 89.

37. Record, *Making War, Thinking History*, 53.

38. Juan de Onis, "US Expands Military Aid," *New York Times*, 3 Mar. 1981.

39. Yoshitani, *Reagan On War*, 43–45, 170–171.

40. Cynthia Arnson, *Crossroads: Congress, the President, and Central America, 1976–1993* (Philadelphia: Penn State University Press, 1993), 65–67.

41. NSC meeting, 10 Feb. 1982, RRPL, National Security Planning Group (NSPG), box 1.
42. NSC meeting, 10 Nov. 1981, RRPL, NSPG, box 1.
43. NSC meeting, 10 Nov. 1981.
44. NSC meeting, 10 Feb. 1982.
45. NSC meeting, 10 Feb. 1982.
46. NSC meeting, 10 Nov. 1981.
47. Chester Pach, "The Reagan Doctrine: Principle, Pragmatism, and Policy," *Presidential Studies Quarterly* 36, no. 1 (2006): 75–88.
48. Record, *Making War, Thinking History*, 93, and Yoshitani, *Reagan on War*, 56.
49. NSC meeting, 10 Feb. 1982.
50. These events are well recounted in Robert Fisk, *Pity the Nation: Lebanon at War* (New York: Oxford University Press, 1990).
51. Cannon, *President Reagan*, 356–357; Marvin Kalb and Deborah Kalb, *Haunting Legacy: Vietnam and the American Presidency from Ford to Obama* (Washington, DC: Brookings Institution Press, 2011), 99–100; Yoshitani, *Reagan on War*, 85–90.
52. William E. Smith, "Looking to Washington," *Time*, 1 Nov. 1982.
53. Yoshitani, *Reagan on War*, 72–76.
54. Magnus Ranstorp, *Hizb'allah in Lebanon: The Politics of the Western Hostage Crisis* (New York: St. Martin's Press, 1997), 38.
55. Press briefing transcript, 24 Oct. 1983, RRPL, White House Office of Speechwriting–Research, box 119.
56. Transcript of NBC interview, 28 Oct. 1983, RRPL, Michael E. Baroody Papers (MEBP), box 18.
57. Teicher, "Lebanon Packet for Congress," 24 Jan. 1984, Donald R. Fortier Papers, box 4.
58. Reagan, "Address to the Nation on Events in Lebanon and Grenada," 27 Oct. 1983, https://reaganlibrary.archives.gov/archives/speeches/1983/102783b.htm.
59. Ronald Reagan, *An American Life* (New York: Simon and Schuster, 1990), 451.
60. "The Lessons of Grenada," *Wall Street Journal*, 28 Oct. 1983.
61. Roussel to Speakes, "Summary Regarding Speech Reaction," 11 Oct. 1983, RRPL, MEBP, box 10.
62. Roussel to Speakes, "Summary Regarding Speech Reaction."
63. "ABC Nightline Poll of Reaction to Speech on Lebanon and Grenada," 28 Oct. 1983, RRPL, MEBP, box 10.
64. Summary of responses to Reagan speech, 28 Oct. 1983, RRPL, MEBP, box 10.
65. "The Democratic Candidates on Grenada," Nov. 1983, RRPL, MEBP, box 10.
66. "Goliath in Grenada," *New York Times*, 30 Oct. 1983.
67. David Shribman, "Poll Shows Support for Presence of US Troops in Lebanon and Grenada," *New York Times*, 29 Oct. 1983; "CBS News/New York Times Poll," RRPL, MEBP, box 10.
68. "ABC News/Washington Post—September Poll," RRPL, MEBP, box 10.
69. See Yoshitani, *Reagan on War*, 122.
70. Reagan, *An American Life*, 451.
71. Quoted in Kalb and Kalb, *Haunting Legacy*, 104.

72. On these events, see Christian G. Appy, *American Reckoning: The Vietnam War and Our National Identity* (New York: Penguin, 2015), 287–290; Kalb and Kalb, *Haunting Legacy*, 107–111; Yoshitani, *Reagan on War*, 127.

73. Quoted in Yoshitani, *Reagan on War*, 126.

74. Francis X. Clines, "Reagan Turns 73 at Home in Illinois, Saying Nation's 'Self-Doubt' Is Over," *New York Times*, 7 Feb. 1984.

75. Weinberger speech, 28 Nov. 1984, National Press Club Archives.

76. Shultz, *Turmoil and Triumph*, 650.

77. Shultz, *Turmoil and Triumph*, 294, 286.

78. Jacob Weisberg, *Ronald Reagan* (New York: Times Books, 2016), 116.

79. Peter Beinart, *The Icarus Syndrome: A History of American Hubris* (New York: Harper, 2010), 386.

CHAPTER 9

Compartmentalizing US Foreign Policy
Human Rights in the Reagan Years
SARAH B. SNYDER

Fully understanding Ronald Reagan's personal beliefs and how they shaped his administration's policies challenged many contemporary observers and scholars writing in subsequent years. Apparent contradictions in his approach to US foreign policy have proved particularly confounding. These difficulties may explain why so many observers examining his approach to human rights have written geographically focused studies.[1] Such an approach makes sense given the highly compartmentalized process Reagan and his aides brought to considerations of human rights in US foreign policy.

In his published memoirs and private diaries, Reagan said relatively little about human rights.[2] Yet, in the assessment of political scientist Kathryn Sikkink, "No human rights policy in US history was more hotly contested in its time, or is more controversial today, than the practices and legacy of the Reagan administration."[3] This chapter explores the content of Reagan's human rights policy and the reasons for its enduring controversy. It also fits into a broader effort to examine conservative efforts to shape human rights institutions and utilize human rights as a tool in their approaches to domestic and foreign policy.[4]

To those committed to human rights, Ronald Reagan's election on November 4, 1980, caused considerable concern. Their basic worry was that Reagan would abandon Jimmy Carter's human rights policies. Joshua Rubenstein of

Amnesty International spoke for many human rights activists when he said, "We are concerned that the Reagan administration will not have a positive emphasis on human rights and in some parts of the world his election has been taken as a green light, an encouragement for repressive forces."[5] In some areas of the world, notably in Latin America, such concerns were borne out by the Reagan administration's justification of devastating human rights violations in the name of preventing the spread of communism.[6] In other spheres, particularly the Soviet Union and Poland, Reagan spoke forthrightly and repeatedly in defense of human rights activists and against repression in the Soviet bloc. Finally, in a number of cases such as South Africa, the Philippines, and Chile, the Reagan administration's stance evolved. The degree of credit that should be given to the US government for changes in those countries is often refracted through a political lens.[7] Overall, however, Reagan's record is difficult to characterize neatly, which is one of the reasons his policy remains so contested today.

Over the course of his administration, Reagan increasingly used the term "human rights" in his public statements, and the trends in his rhetoric echo what we see in other manifestations of his policy. Based on analysis of the American Presidency Project, we can see that Reagan's utterances increased most significantly from 1981, when he used the term nineteen times publicly, to 1982, with forty-nine mentions. Overall, his usage grew to ninety instances per annum by the last year of his administration. In his public statements, Reagan talked about human rights most frequently in connection with annual celebrations such as Human Rights Day, abuses suffered in the Soviet bloc, and the Conference on Security and Cooperation in Europe (CSCE) process.[8] He also devoted particular attention to the plight of Poles living under martial law, Jews seeking to emigrate from the Soviet Union, and prominent activists such as Andrei Sakharov.[9] In addition, he used the term in connection with African Americans, apartheid in South Africa, and Central America.[10] Throughout his presidency, however, Reagan adhered to a narrow definition of human rights that ignored social and economic rights as well as women's rights.[11]

Reagan, and many within his administration, had criticized elements of Carter's human rights policy before entering the White House, charging that it had not improved human rights meaningfully and had neglected the US national interests.[12] A number of early signals suggested that the new administration would implement changes informed by those criticisms. For example, Reagan appointed Jeane Kirkpatrick, who had reproached Carter for prioritizing human rights and neglecting the Cold War, to serve as US ambassador to the United Nations (UN).[13] Furthermore, the administration announced it would shift its focus to combating international terrorism. In his first press conference as secretary of state, Alexander Haig said, "International terrorism will take the place of human rights in our concern because it is the ultimate of abuse of human rights. And it's time that it be addressed with better clarity and greater effectiveness by Western nations and the United States as well."[14] Critics of Reagan also note that he invited the military dictators of South Korea and Argentina to visit the White House shortly after he took office.[15] Finally, Reagan's nomination of Ernest W. Lefever, a vocal critic of Carter's human rights policy, to head the State Department's Bureau of Human Rights and Humanitarian Affairs raised serious questions about the administration's dedication to human rights and strengthened early concerns about Reagan's commitment.[16]

Reagan's nomination of Lefever, announced in early February 1981, provoked considerable controversy at the time and continues to loom over scholarship on Reagan's human rights policy.[17] The most significant obstacle was a concern that Lefever would not be an effective champion of human rights, as he had a record of questioning the issue's relevance to US policy. Shortly after Carter's inauguration, Lefever had written in the *New York Times* that "a consistent and single-minded invocation of the 'human rights' standard in making United States foreign policy decisions would serve neither our interests nor the cause of freedom."[18] Such possibilities led the Senate Foreign Relations Committee chair, Senator Charles Percy (R-IL), to express skepticism about Lefever's positions, saying, "You seem in doubt about whether your job should exist."[19]

Some administration supporters argued that criticism of Lefever reflected opposition to Reagan's human rights approach, which in columnist William Safire's words "has just won an election."[20] Testifying before the Senate Committee, Representative Charles Wilson (R-TX) said, "I would point out to my friends with a differing viewpoint from mine, that Mr. Lefever is not the only man in the United States that believes that human rights can best be achieved by using less pyrotechnics and more diplomacy. The President can certainly find others to represent his policy, but I can assure you he is not going to appoint Pat [sic] Derian as Assistant Secretary for Human Rights, no matter what my friends say."[21] Indeed, some members of the committee suggested that no Reagan nominee would meet with their approval.[22]

After a June 4 executive session to enable Lefever to respond to the objections that had been raised against him, the committee voted thirteen to four against him.[23] Senate historians at the time said that it was the first instance since 1959 that a president's nominee had been rejected by a Senate committee.[24] In explaining his vote, Percy expressed apprehension about Lefever's commitment to human rights and personal integrity: "Concern for human rights is not just a policy of the United States. It is an underlying principle of our political system and a fundamental factor in the appeal of democracy to people throughout the world."[25] Percy also questioned Lefever's knowledge of policy issues, saying Lefever had "very little familiarity with the [human rights] provisions themselves" and characterized his testimony as "a series of broad generalizations without a willingness to discuss specific issues."[26]

In the wake of Lefever's withdrawal, the administration did not move quickly to propose a second nominee. Instead, the Reagan administration contemplated disbanding the bureau and eliminating the assistant secretary for human rights and humanitarian affairs position, which led to consternation among human rights groups and members of Congress, given that congressional legislation mandated the assistant secretary position.[27]

The concern and complaints from human rights advocates were not lost on the administration. Under Secretary of State Richard Kennedy wrote to Haig, "Congressional belief that we have no consistent human rights policy threatens to disrupt important foreign-policy initiatives. . . . Human rights has become one of the main avenues for domestic attack on the administration's foreign policy."[28] Kennedy, working alongside State Department officials Charles Fairbanks Jr. and Paul Wolfowitz, sought to shift the administration's approach.[29] To address persistent concerns and signal a new style, Haig gave a speech saying that human rights was "the major focus" of Reagan's foreign policy.[30]

The administration also leaked parts of a State Department memorandum that stated, "Human rights is at the core of our foreign policy because it is central to what America is and stands for. 'Human rights' is not something we tack on to our foreign policy, but is its very purpose."[31] The memorandum was greeted warmly when disclosed to the *New York Times* and when a similar version was disseminated to human rights organizations.[32] In advance of the planned announcement of a new nominee to head the Human Rights Bureau, the State Department asserted that the bureau was to be "strengthened and reinvigorated" as opposed to the reduction in influence many had feared.[33] The Reagan administration further proclaimed what it argued was a consistent approach to human rights abusers, writing in the 1981 *Country Reports on Human Rights Practices*, "US human rights policy will not pursue a policy of selective indignation."[34]

Most significantly, the White House announced its nomination of Elliott Abrams to head the State Department's Human Rights Bureau on October 30, 1981. Abrams had bipartisan support in Congress, having previously worked for Senators Daniel Patrick Moynihan (D-NY) and Henry Jackson (D-WA).[35] Abrams faced few difficult questions in his confirmation hearings, and

Republicans and Democrats alike expressed pleasure at his nomination. The Senate Foreign Relations Committee unanimously approved Abrams's nomination on November 17, 1981. The Senate unanimously confirmed him several days later. Skeptics, however, expressed less than overwhelming enthusiasm for Abrams's appointment, with one saying, "Everyone's saying Elliott Abrams is so great just because he's not Darth Vader."[36]

After Abrams's confirmation, Haig distributed a memorandum directing all regional bureaus to work with the Human Rights Bureau to ensure that "the promotion of political freedom . . . not be considered only as an afterthought."[37] Furthermore, Abrams articulated an intention to pursue an active approach: "There has been and will be less public criticism of friendly country governments . . . [but] you cannot make a clear distinction between East and West on the basis of freedom if the United States is supporting dictators around the world."[38] Such steps suggested that the administration hoped to signal a shift in its approach to human rights. In terms of personnel, George Shultz's replacement of Haig as secretary of state in July 1982 also affected the administration's human rights policy significantly in that Schultz devoted considerable attention to the question of protection of human rights in the Soviet Union and Eastern Europe, thereby heightening the administration's commitment to the issue.[39]

Within the literature on Reagan and human rights, nascent as it is, observers point to a "turnaround" in his approach to human rights. Tamar Jacoby has suggested the Reagan administration's attitude toward human rights underwent a fundamental reversal.[40] Sikkink also identifies a "turnaround" in Reagan's policy and argues that its "symbolic dimension . . . should not be underestimated."[41] In Sikkink's view, the mystery of the Reagan administration is "how one of the most ideologically conservative administrations in recent history had come to cautiously implement the very policies it had once so fervently challenged."[42] Elliott Abrams, however, has said that during the first year and a half of the Reagan administration, "There was no human rights policy. There was a critique of Carter policy, combined with an instinctive distrust of the phrase, crowd, and community associated with it."[43] Abrams's comments, however, neglect the extent to which the administration articulated a policy that represented more than a blind rejection of what had preceded it and the fact that it acted on it.

More importantly, despite any "turnaround," concern for human rights was highly compartmentalized as well as dependent on geopolitics and strategic interests. The Reagan administration was less willing than Carter to criticize states and leaders it considered allies of the United States. In addition, the administration overlooked human rights abuses in Argentina, Chile, the

Philippines, South Korea, and Turkey for many years and sought to reverse congressional legislation related to human rights.[44]

The root of harsh criticisms of Reagan's record on human rights is US policy toward Central America during his presidency. In 1983, Reagan argued that Central America was integral to the security of the United States, and Reagan's statement to Congress echoed Jeane Kirkpatrick's declaration two years before that "Central America is the most important place in the world for the United States today."[45] US policy toward Nicaragua, Guatemala, and El Salvador was driven by Cold War concerns that communists were gaining influence in the strategic region and needed to be thwarted at all costs.

Beginning with Nicaragua, the Reagan administration was funneling money and other forms of support to the Contras, who in their fight against the left-leaning Nicaraguan government, engaged in "kidnappings, torture, and murder of unarmed civilians," according to the human rights organization Americas Watch.[46] During the course of the fighting in Nicaragua, approximately 30,000 died. William LeoGrande points out that, in terms of a proportion of the population, that number represented more than the proportion of Americans lost in the Civil War, both World Wars, the Korean War, and the Vietnam War.[47] In historian Joseph Renouard's words, the Reagan administration had "to perform acrobatic leaps of obfuscation" to characterize the Contras as "democratic."[48] Yet, its opposition to the Sandinista government distorted the administration's evaluations of the human rights violations of each side and the strategic costs associated with each party's potential triumph. In the subsequent chapter, William Michael Schmidli explores the reasons why US policymakers saw Nicaragua as so significant strategically and identifies a range of geopolitical, strategic, and ideological factors.[49]

The Guatemalan government brutally murdered more than 100,000 Guatemalans in 1982 and 1983, yet, according to Sikkink, the Reagan administration manipulated Guatemala's human rights record to ensure that military assistance could continue to flow to that government. Describing the praise for the Guatemalan government as the "low point" for US policy in Central America, Sikkink argues that Reagan's rhetorical support for Ríos Montt, the Guatemalan president, signaled to the Guatemalan military that the United States would not be concerned by human rights violations: "At the height of the only genocide in recent Latin American history, the Reagan administration gave rhetorical and moral support to a murderous regime through both its public and private diplomacy."[50] Again, fears of a guerilla insurgency motivated the Reagan administration as it ignored its ally's human rights violations.[51]

With regard to El Salvador, the Reagan administration sent conflicting messages about its concern about abuses by right-wing groups.[52] Around 50,000 El Salvadorans were killed by the military and its right-wing allies between 1979 and 1985, yet, in order to keep aid flowing to El Salvador, the administration certified every six months that the government there was making progress on respecting human rights.[53] The Reagan administration was motivated by a desire to defend the government in El Salvador from the Farabundo Marti National Liberation Front (FMLN). In his memoirs, Reagan wrote, "Yes, it is true there were extreme right-wing outlaw elements in that country, including members of the government security forces, who were guilty of flagrant and grave human-rights abuses, sometimes against innocent Salvadorans. But the brutal pro-Marxist rebels . . . were infinitely more barbaric."[54] While the administration's reports underplayed the seriousness of the human rights situations in El Salvador, human rights organizations such as Amnesty International disagreed with the administration's characterizations. Accounts of a massacre in El Mozote, in which nearly 1,000 people were killed, further undermined the Reagan administration's certifications.[55]

Recognizing that such abuses threatened US backing, Reagan administration officials undertook efforts to convince San Salvador to curb its repression. During his December 1983 visit, Vice President George Bush signaled to the El Salvadoran government that the United States' continued support was conditioned on a reduction in abuses by right-wing paramilitary squads.[56] Urging the government to shift course, he said, "These cowardly death squad terrorists are just as repugnant to me, to President Reagan, to the US Congress, and to the American people as the terrorists of the left."[57] Shultz echoed Bush's message during a January 1984 visit. Shultz admonished the government there that "death squads and terror have no place in a democracy."[58]

Although Reagan administration officials belatedly exerted pressure on the El Salvadoran government to rein in the right-wing death squads, overall, the administration callously overlooked the massive loss of life in Central America for the goal of eradicating communism there. As one critic put it, "The United States has been a beacon of freedom for the oppressed and a leader of humanitarian causes for too long a time to have this asset sacrificed for transitory and perhaps illusory victories over revolutionary movements rooted in circumstances beyond US control."[59]

One of the spheres in which we can see the greatest Reagan administration activism on human rights was East-West relations. Shultz spurred much of this thrust by making human rights one of the four points on the agenda he formulated for discussions with the Soviets, but in many respects, Reagan's agreement to such an emphasis should not have been surprising.[60] Specifically, in National Security Decision Directive 75, the Reagan administration outlined an effort to move "the Soviet Union toward a more pluralistic political and economic system." To achieve such a goal, US officials needed to develop a policy with "an ideological thrust which clearly affirms the superiority of US and Western values of individual dignity and freedom."[61] For US leaders, championing human rights in the Soviet Union and Eastern Europe was a means to achieving internal liberalization and a weakening of ties among the Soviet bloc states.[62]

There was a strong connection between Reagan's anticommunism and support for human rights. Reagan sympathized with victims of communist repression, and, there were a number of individual cases with which the president became personally involved, the most prominent of which was the Pentecostal families living in the United States embassy in Moscow.[63] According to Foreign Service Officer Jack Matlock, Reagan's interest was driven by his concern for "identifiable human beings" and was linked to earlier work as a lifeguard and his desire to save people who needed help.[64] Reagan pressed Soviet leader Leonid Brezhnev for exit visas for the Pentecostal families.[65] Later, in a February 1983 meeting with the Soviet ambassador to the United States, Anatoly Dobrynin, Reagan asked that the two families be allowed to emigrate as a signal of goodwill to the United States.[66] In his public rhetoric regarding Soviet human rights abuses, Reagan supported congressional efforts to support human rights activists in the Soviet Union, such as members of the Ukrainian Helsinki Monitoring Group and spoke about Soviet dissidents such as Andrei Sakharov and Anatoly Shcharansky specifically and repeatedly.[67]

Reagan's first-term support for human rights in Eastern Europe was manifested primarily within the Conference on Security and Cooperation in Europe (CSCE) meeting in Madrid. The US ambassador to the meeting, Max M. Kampelman, pursued vocal and active diplomacy. Kampelman proposed to Shultz that as a prerequisite to a concluding document at Madrid, the United States require the release and possible emigration of a number of human rights activists and Jewish refuseniks. When Kampelman and Shultz discussed the proposal with the president, Reagan asked the ambassador to press for the emigration of the Pentecostals as part of a package agreement and pushed him to negotiate with the Soviets at Madrid to help Jewish refuseniks, saying, "Max, see what you can do to help these people," as he handed him a list.[68] The United States named 119 individuals of concern during the talks.[69]

After Mikhail Gorbachev became Soviet general secretary in March 1985, Reagan repeatedly affirmed the United States' commitment to human rights.[70] In a subsequent letter, Reagan cited continued Soviet human rights abuses in violation of CSCE agreements: "We believe strongly that strict observance of the Universal Declaration of Human Rights and of the Helsinki Final Act is an important element of our bilateral relationship."[71] Reagan's repeated efforts helped convince Gorbachev of the United States' commitment to human rights: Gorbachev later wrote that Americans had "an almost missionary passion for preaching about human rights and liberties."[72] Facing American and other entreaties on the issue, Gorbachev suggested that he was willing to discuss human rights broadly with the West, but not individual cases.[73]

For the first Soviet-American summit in six years, Reagan's briefing paper advised him to express concern at low Jewish emigration, Sakharov's exile, political prisoners, and divided spouses, among other issues.[74] Reagan wrote notes to himself in advance of the 1985 Geneva meeting; of the four and a half double-spaced pages he drafted, one full page was devoted to his thoughts on human rights: "We are somewhat publicly on the record about human rights. Front page stories that we are banging away on them on their human rights abuses will get us some cheers from the bleachers, but it won't help those who are being abused."[75] In their two days of meetings, Reagan told Gorbachev about American concern for families divided by the Iron Curtain, and he suggested that movement on human rights would facilitate other types of cooperation, such as trade.[76] Reagan assured Gorbachev he would not claim responsibility if the Soviets moved forward on some cases, and Gorbachev eventually agreed to examine the situations.[77]

After Geneva, Reagan wrote to Gorbachev to outline his concerns about Soviet human rights, emphasizing progress was critical to improving the broader US-Soviet relationship. He noted with pleasure Soviet efforts to reunite divided spouses in the aftermath of the summit but also outlined a number of other areas that he hoped Gorbachev would address, including dual citizens and family reunification requests.[78] After the summit, Reagan told his cabinet that he would no longer pressure the Soviet Union on human rights publicly.[79] He hoped to convince Gorbachev that respecting human rights was in the best interests of the Soviet Union, and he recognized that Gorbachev would be much more likely to implement changes if it did not appear as if he was reacting to Western demands.[80]

After Geneva, Reagan continued to stress human rights in his personal correspondence with Gorbachev, including by sending a letter to Gorbachev enumerating seventeen divided spouses, twenty-three cases involving dual citizenship, and 129 family reunification cases the United States hoped could be resolved.[81] The Soviet leader took a number of steps on human rights issues in the subsequent months, including granting exit visas for eight divided spouses and releasing several dissidents such as Shcharansky and Yuri Orlov in prisoner exchanges.[82] When he welcomed Orlov to the White House, Reagan said Orlov had "done more to inform the world of current Soviet human rights violations than any man on Earth." He went on to describe the dissident as "a hero for our time."[83]

At the October 1986 Reykjavik summit, Reagan intended to press Gorbachev on human rights issues, announcing he would link them to other areas of the US-Soviet relationship: "I will make it amply clear to Mr. Gorbachev that unless there is real Soviet movement on human rights, we will not have the kind of political atmosphere necessary to make lasting progress on other issues."[84] In their talks, Reagan told Gorbachev that he wished the Soviets could go further on human rights to facilitate more cooperation, and he gave him a list of 1,200 Soviet Jews who were waiting to emigrate.[85]

Matlock argues that after Reykjavik, Gorbachev realized he could achieve normalized relations with the United States only if he was willing to deal with "the full agenda of issues," which included human rights.[86] Shultz in particular was committed to pressing the issue, as Reagan noted in his diary after a meeting with Shultz: "He presented some material on his coming trip to Moscow having to do with Human Rights. He really wants to go after observance by the Soviets of the Helsinki Pact."[87] The following month, Shultz invited Jewish refuseniks to a seder at Spaso House over Passover in April 1987 to demonstrate to Soviet authorities that Jewish emigration was a priority for him.[88] Shultz's emphasis slowly produced results, and he began to see genuine change in the Soviet position when Shevardnadze told him in September 1987, "Give me your lists and we will be glad to look at them."[89] By October 1987, the Soviets had granted exit visas to 6,000 people, more than six times the number in 1986, although 7,500 cases remained.

As he had during the December 1987 Washington summit, Reagan pressed his human rights concerns in a number of ways in connection with the Moscow summit from May 29 to June 2, 1988.[90] According to Reagan, Gorbachev was more receptive to his concerns about religious freedom and human rights during the Moscow meeting than ever before.[91] During the summit, Reagan visited the Danilov Monastery to underline his commitment to religious freedom.[92] The monastery visit was one of a number of symbolic stops made by Reagan that were designed to demonstrate his commitment to human rights. Reagan's repetition began to gain traction in Moscow, and in their first one-on-one meeting, Gorbachev said Soviet leaders were ready to work with the Reagan administration and the US Congress to resolve outstanding humanitarian issues.[93]

Reagan's personal involvement culminated with his remarks to more than one hundred dissidents at Spaso House, the US ambassador's residence in

Moscow. Reagan praised Soviet progress on human rights, but in a common theme of the trip, emphasized that more work was needed to fulfill the obligations of the Helsinki Final Act and the Universal Declaration on Human Rights.[94] He expressed a strong commitment to advocating for the freedoms of religion, speech, and travel in his negotiations with the Soviets. The president also thanked the dissidents for their courage as they worked "with your very lives, day in, day out, year after year, risking your jobs, your homes, your all."[95] By the end of 1988, 600 political prisoners had been released, and emigration had swelled to 80,000.

The Reagan administration was also attentive to human rights violations elsewhere in the Soviet bloc, focusing considerable attention on the 1981 Polish decision to impose martial law in response the growing influence of Solidarity, the trade union movement there. Several days later Reagan asked Americans to follow his example and light a candle in their windows to demonstrate their solidary with Poles suffering under martial law.[96]

In the wake of the imposition of martial law, Reagan imposed sanctions on the Soviet Union and Poland. The US president targeted the Soviet airline Aeroflot, the export of technology to the Soviet Union, as well as maritime, exchange, and grain agreements. He and officials in his administration repeatedly pressed for the end of martial law, freeing political prisoners, and talks between the Communist Party, the Catholic Church, and the opposition. Reagan's political and economic sanctions against the Polish government affected fishing rights, access for the Polish airline to US airports, export of technology, agricultural assistance, and credits for Polish loans.[97] In a letter to the Polish general Wojciech Jaruzelski, Reagan framed his opposition to martial law in human rights terms: "The United States government cannot sit by and ignore the widespread violations of human rights occurring in Poland. To do so would make us party to the repression of the rights of the Polish people."[98] In the face of limited progress, the Reagan administration remained critical of the Polish record. US officials negotiated incremental lifting of US sanctions, including landing rights for the Polish airline and access to fishing grounds in US waters in order to achieve the release of Solidarity members imprisoned in Poland.[99]

South Africa was one of a few noncommunist countries toward which Reagan administration policy slowly evolved, becoming more engaged with human rights concerns over the course of his eight years in office.[100] The administration, however, shifted course largely due to congressional and nongovernmental pressure, raising questions about how much Reagan's stance truly developed over his presidency. Although as historian James H. Meriwether has emphasized, Reagan condemned apartheid repeatedly, the Reagan administration's policy toward South Africa was formulated within a Cold War context, which led officials to overemphasize the threat of communism to the country and the region.[101]

Shortly before being appointed assistant secretary of state for African affairs, Chester A. Crocker articulated what would become the Reagan administration's policy of "constructive engagement" in a *Foreign Affairs* article.[102] Crocker wrote, "Clearly, the fundamental goal is the emergence in South Africa of a society with which the United States can pursue its varied interests in a full and friendly relationship, without constraint, embarrassment or political damage. The nature of the South African political system prevents us from having such a relationship now."[103] Crocker went on to write, "As a multiracial democracy, the United States cannot endorse a system that is racist in purpose or effect."[104] Yet, by arguing that "Americans have no mandate to judge how much reform is enough," Crocker undercut one of the principal tenets of human rights activism—that human rights abuses such as racial discrimination do warrant international condemnation because human rights are universal and not bestowed by a national government.[105] Crocker's articulation of "constructive engagement" revealed early on a tendency to defer to South African officials about the best pace and course for "reform." Crocker later acknowledged that South African leaders saw Reagan's election "as the beginning of an embrace."[106]

In his attempt to avoid a showdown with an increasingly anti-apartheid Congress in 1986, Reagan issued an executive order intended to signal American displeasure with apartheid but without including some more far-reaching elements in the proposed congressional legislation. Announcing his executive order, Reagan said, "America's view of apartheid is simple and straightforward: We believe it's wrong. We condemn it, and we're united in hoping for the day when apartheid will be no more."[107] Reagan targeted bank loans to the South African government, the export of technology to South Africa, and purchases of South-African-made military, as well as engaged the Treasury and State Departments in planning for further steps against the South African government.[108] Critics at the time charged that he shifted away from "constructive engagement" only to prevent the passage of more far-reaching sanctions.[109] Reflecting criticism at the time, reporters pressed Reagan on if he had selected just "the weakest measures in the congressional package."[110]

Administration critics argued that Reagan's policy of "constructive engagement" toward South Africa had "failed" and that US policy had "actually exacerbated the situation inside South Africa by encouraging and indulging the white regime's divide-and-rule tactics."[111] When Reagan's executive order did not prevent more far-reaching congressional legislation, the president vetoed the Comprehensive Anti-Apartheid Act of 1986, arguing that it would "seriously impede the prospects for a peaceful end to apartheid and the establishment of a free and open society for all in South Africa."[112] According to historian Thomas Borstelmann, Reagan's veto put him out of step with other Americans.[113] Congress then overrode his veto. Later, in the administration's first annual, congressionally mandated report on South Africa's attempts to dismantle apartheid, officials wrote that the situation of Black South Africans was "bleak" given that they faced "increased repression, harassment, and . . . imprisonment."[114] The administration's report frankly addressed the problems in South Africa, reporting that the country was "not any closer in late 1987 to respecting free speech and free political participation by all its citizens than it was one year ago. No timetable has been set for the elimination of the remaining apartheid laws."[115] Rather than having any improvements to report, administration officials noted that political imprisonment had increased significantly and that civil and political rights were not respected.

Regarding the Philippines, US officials eventually supported the ouster of a repressive dictator but only very late in the game and, to use a second cliché, only when the writing was on the wall for Filipino President Ferdinand Marcos.[116] Marcos had declared martial law in 1972 ostensibly in the face of communist insurgents; it remained in place until early 1981. Rather than express concerns about the abrogation of democracy or abuses of human rights under martial law, Reagan focused on the Philippines' economic growth and stability.[117] The assassination of opposition leader Ninoy Aquino in 1983 precipitated a new crisis, but Reagan articulated his continued support for Marcos, saying that the United States would not "cut away from a person who, imperfect though he may be on human rights, has worked with us."[118] Despite Reagan's vocal support, others within the administration signaled that the United States should reconsider its position. Given such concerns, Reagan agreed to pressure Marcos to reform but would not withdraw his personal support.[119] The violence and fraud that marred Marcos's 1986 election against Aquino's widow, Corazon, ultimately forced even Reagan to bend. He called upon Marcos to allow a "peaceful transition to a new government."[120]

Finally, in the case of Chile, Reagan resisted efforts to distance the United States from Augusto Pinochet's dictatorship for several years. Reagan and his advisors had wanted to warm relations with Chile after the strain they had experienced at the end of the Ford administration and during the Carter years. Yet, in the 1980s, challenges to Augusto Pinochet's rule in Chile grew in the form of public protests and an economic crisis in 1982. Despite the efforts of

US diplomats and military officials to press Pinochet to moderate his response, they were unable to reduce his repression.[121] In addition, obstacles to investigating and adjudicating the Washington assassination of former Chilean foreign minister Orlando Letelier complicated administration efforts to resume support for Pinochet, although historian Alan McPherson argues that the stumbling block was the Chilean violation of US national sovereignty rather than its violation of human rights.[122] Faced with Pinochet's intransigence, State Department officials, including Shultz, expressed increasing frustration with the Chilean dictator's methods and raised questions about future Chilean-American relations.[123] Pinochet rationalized his harsh measures as necessary to prevent communists from coming to power, but American officials were increasingly worried that his methods risked precipitating such an outcome as a backlash.[124] Shultz and Elliott Abrams worked together to shift US policy away from support for Pinochet.[125]

In order to express its frustration with Pinochet, the United States abstained from voting on a 1985 World Bank loan for Chile.[126] Morris Morley and Chris McGillon argue that the new American position signaled to Pinochet that his broader economic interests, including loans from the International Monetary Fund and Bank Advisory Group, might be at risk. Shortly thereafter, he reduced the number of political prisoners and internal exiles, lifted the state of siege that was in place, and broadened freedom of the press.[127] Pinochet's steps eased administration concerns, but members of Congress remained opposed particularly in light of reports that arrests, torture, and other human rights abuses persisted.[128]

By July 1986, State Department officials were increasingly concerned that Pinochet sought to remain in power beyond the end of Reagan's presidency and intended to eliminate any moderate opposition that might succeed him.[129] As Reagan and Shultz debated how to influence Pinochet, the president suggested inviting the dictator for a state visit. Shultz refused, saying, "No way. This man has blood all over his hands. He has done monstrous things."[130] The United States sought to exert more pressure on Pinochet, with officials debating submitting a resolution to the United Nations General Assembly that criticized Chile's record on human rights.[131]

In the end, the United States signaled its dwindling support for Pinochet through a resolution at the UN General Assembly and a second abstention on the World Bank loan.[132] At the UN Human Rights Commission in Geneva in 1986, the United States introduced a resolution that criticized the use of torture in Chile and called on Pinochet to end it.[133] Whereas Shultz had hoped to vote against a November 1986 $250 million loan from the World Bank, he was authorized only to abstain.[134] The United States also devoted several million dollars, through the National Endowment for Democracy and Agency for International Development, to supporting the democratic process in Chile.[135] One observer described the US efforts as an "open collaboration" with opposition politicians to oust Pinochet.[136] After the success of the "no" campaign against Pinochet in 1988, the United States remained engaged in facilitating the country's transition to democracy.[137]

With the cases of South Africa, the Philippines, and Chile, Reagan personally moved to shift US policy only in the face of considerable pressure from members of Congress, his own State Department, and White House aides. And significantly, such pressure could succeed only because the specter of communism was fainter in these three countries than in Central America. In Human Rights Watch Executive Director Aryeh Neier's assessment, "Picking on Pinochet had high rewards and low costs."[138] Furthermore, in the final years of Reagan's presidency, the president met annually with Gorbachev. As the tensions of the Cold War diminished, supporting repressive dictators as bulwarks against communism seemed less necessary. Therefore improvements in Soviet-American relations may have enabled greater progress on human rights internationally.

By the end of the Reagan's presidency, Neier argues that his administration had "accepted that promoting human rights was a major goal and that the United States should be evenhanded in condemning abuses."[139] State Department official George Lister agreed, observing that over the course of the Reagan administration, "Human rights policy had become institutionalized."[140] Schmidli makes the same argument in his chapter in this volume, while noting that the definition of rights embraced was quite narrow.[141] Drawing a contrast with the early days of Haig's secretaryship, Neier argues that in the early days of George H. W. Bush's presidency, it was "unthinkable that Secretary of State James Baker would propose replacing a concern for human rights with a concern for any other cause."[142]

Progress was made on human rights in the Reagan years. To the extent to which a positive evaluation can be formulated, George Shultz's influence should be noted. His entry into the administration represented a turning point toward greater attention to human rights, and he pressed these issues throughout his secretaryship. But, the positive elements of Reagan's record were determined by geopolitics and not the human rights at stake. Setting aside the Soviet bloc, the administration's attention to human rights was at best belated and episodic. In Central America, US inattention was immoral, and its active involvement made the administration complicit in massive violations of human rights.

Reagan's compartmentalized approach to human rights was not unique among Cold War or post–Cold War US presidents. Carter has been similarly criticized over charges of inconsistency in his approach to human rights. A number of scholars have demonstrated that the Carter administration largely ignored human rights concerns when they did not coincide with its larger strategic goals.[143] Thus in many ways there was a good degree of consistency between Carter's and Reagan's policies regarding human rights.[144] What may have distinguished Reagan's policy was a different approach to thinking about where and when reform might be possible.

Notes

The author wishes to express her appreciation for research assistance to Jaclyn Fox.

1. See, for example, Kathryn Sikkink, *Mixed Signals: US Human Rights Policy and Latin America* (Ithaca, NY: Cornell University Press, 2004); Sarah B. Snyder, *Human Rights and the End of the Cold War* (New York: Cambridge University Press, 2011); Morris Morley and Chris McGillon, *Reagan and Pinochet: The Struggle over US Policy toward Chile* (New York: Cambridge University Press, 2015); Roger Peace, *A Call to Conscience: The Anti-Contra War Campaign* (Boston: University of Massachusetts Press, 2012). One exception is Joe Renouard, *Human Rights in American Foreign Policy: From the 1960s to the Soviet Collapse* (Philadelphia: University of Pennsylvania Press, 2016).

2. In his diaries, Reagan primarily noted his signing of annual human rights proclamations (the relevant index entries are Human Rights Commission, Human Rights Conference, Human Rights Day, Human Rights Week, and Human Rights Year) and delved into substance only on South Africa and a Soviet proposal to hold a human rights conference in Moscow. See Ronald Reagan, *An American Life* (New York: Pocket Books, 1990), 299, 305; Douglas Brinkley, ed., *The Reagan Diaries* (New York: HarperCollins, 2007), 286, 650, 728.

3. Sikkink, *Mixed Signals*, 179.

4. For other recent efforts, see Marco Duranti, *The Conservative Human Rights Revolution: European Identity, Transnational Politics, and the Origins of the European Convention* (New York: Oxford University Press, 2017); Carl J. Bon Tempo, "From the Center-Right: Freedom House and Human Rights in the 1970s and 1980s," in *The Human Rights Revolution: An International History*, ed. Akira Iriye, Petra Goedde, and William I. Hitchcock (New York: Oxford University Press, 2012), 223–244.

5. "Soviet Dissident Calls Reagan Human Rights Policy Dangerous," 10 Feb. 1981, Open Society Archives, Radio Free Europe / Radio Liberty Research Institute Records, Soviet Red Archives, Old Code Subject Files 1953–1994, box 691 folder "Human Rights, 1982–1983."

6. Sikkink has argued that instances of human rights abuses increased in the first year of the Reagan administration as leaders in repressive countries took Reagan's election and his early policies as a signal that such practices were now permissible. Sikkink, *Mixed Signals*, 154.

7. See for example Human Rights Watch Executive Director Aryeh Neier's criticism of the Reagan administration's record in difficult cases: "When the rewards were fewer and the costs were higher than those that followed from opposing Pinochet, the Reagan administration's practices . . . were generally not to serve as an advocate of human rights. Worse, it frequently defended the practices of such governments and, thereby, acted as an apologist for abuses." Aryeh Neier, "Human Rights in the Reagan Era: Acceptance in Principle," *Annals of the American Academy of Political and Social Science* 506 (1989): 34.

8. See for example, Reagan, "Address to Members of the British Parliament," 8 June 1982, The American Presidency Project (APP), https://www.presidency.ucsb.edu.

9. See for example, Reagan, "Address to the Nation about Christmas and the Situation in Poland," 23 Dec. 1981, APP; Reagan, "Remarks at a White House Meeting with Jewish Leaders," 2 Feb. 1983, APP; Reagan, "Message on the 60th Birthday of Andrei Sakharov," 2 May 1981, APP.

10. Reagan, "Radio Address to the Nation on the Anniversary of the Birth of Martin Luther King, Jr.," 15 Jan. 1983, APP; Reagan, "Remarks and a Question-and-Answer Session with Reporters on Signing the Executive Order Prohibiting Trade and Certain Other Transactions Involving South Africa," 9 Sept. 1985, APP; Reagan, "Radio Address to the Nation on the Situation in Central America," 13 Aug. 1983, APP.

11. See William Michael Schmidli's chapter in this volume for a broader discussion. For more on conservative approaches to social and economic rights, see Duranti, *The Conservative Human Rights Revolution*, 327–331. On Reagan's neglect of women's rights and human rights in the Islamic world more broadly, see Kelly J. Shannon, *US Foreign Policy and Muslim Women's Human Rights* (Philadelphia: University of Pennsylvania Press, 2018), 39.

12. David Carleton and Michael Stohl, "The Foreign Policy of Human Rights: Rhetoric and Reality from Jimmy Carter to Ronald Reagan," *Human Rights Quarterly* 7, no. 2 (1985): 208–209; David P. Forsythe, "Human Rights in US Foreign Policy: Retrospect and Prospect," *Political Science Quarterly* 105, no. 3 (1990): 444–445.

13. Tamar Jacoby, "The Reagan Turnaround on Human Rights," *Foreign Affairs* 64, no. 5 (1986): 1068–1069. Historian Greg Grandin charges that Jeane Kirkpatrick "provided the Republican administration with the argument it needed to justify continued support for brutal dictatorships." Greg Grandin, *Empire's Workshop: Latin America, the United States, and the Rise of the New Imperialism* (New York: Holt, 2007), 75.

14. "Excerpts from Haig's Remarks at First News Conference as Secretary of," *New York Times*, 29 Jan. 1981. Richard Schifter, who served as assistant secretary of state for human rights and humanitarian affairs in Reagan's second term, suggests the extent to which the Reagan administration intended to replace concern for human rights with attention to international terrorism was misinterpreted due to a verbal fumble by Haig. Richard Schifter, "Building Firm Foundations: The Institutionalization of United States Human Rights Policy in the Reagan Years," *Harvard Human Rights Journal* 2, no. 3–24 (1989): 4.

15. David F. Schmitz, *The United States and Right-Wing Dictators* (New York: Cambridge University Press, 2006), 201; William Michael Schmidli, *The Fate of Freedom Elsewhere: Human Rights and US Cold War Policy toward Argentina* (Ithaca, NY: Cornell University Press, 2013), 183. Yet, Joseph Renouard, a more sympathetic observer,

argues that each invitation was less an affront to human rights concerns than it seemed at the time. According to Renouard, Reagan administration officials invited General Roberto Viola of Argentina because they regarded him as "a pro-US moderate who favored a return to civilian rule." In addition, Renouard shows that Reagan's invitation to General Chun Doo-hwan was conditioned by a promise not to execute opposition politician Kim Dae Jung (Renouard, *Human Rights in American Foreign Policy*, 191, 195–196). Charles Maechling Jr., "Human Rights Dehumanized," *Foreign Policy* 52 (Autumn 1983): 128.

16. Forsythe, "Human Rights in US Foreign Policy," 442; John Dumbrell, *American Foreign Policy: Carter to Clinton* (New York: St. Martin's Press, 1997), 57; Hauke Hartmann, "US Human Rights Policy under Carter and Reagan, 1977–1981," *Human Rights Quarterly* 23, no. 2 (2001): 403, 424; Carleton and Stohl, "The Foreign Policy of Human Rights," 208–209; Charles Mohr, "Haig Aide Insists US Rights Policy Is Evenhanded," *New York Times*, 15 July 1981; Sandy Vogelgesang, "Diplomacy of Human Rights," *International Studies Quarterly* 23, no. 2 (1979): 230–231.

17. For further discussion of Lefever's nomination, see Sarah B. Snyder, "The Defeat of Ernest Lefever's Nomination: Keeping Human Rights on the United States Foreign Policy Agenda," in *Challenging US Foreign Policy: America and the World in the Long Twentieth Century*, ed. Bevan Sewell and Scott Lucas (New York: Palgrave Macmillan, 2011), 136–161. See also chapters by Lauren Turek and William Michael Schmidli in this volume.

18. Vogelgesang, "Diplomacy of Human Rights," 230–231

19. Anthony Lewis, "Advice at Home; Advise and Consent," *New York Times*, 21 May 1981.

20. William Safire, "The New Haynsworth," *New York Times*, 28 May1981.

21. "Nomination of Ernest W. Lefever," Hearings before the Committee on Foreign Relations, United States Senate, 97th Congress, 1st Session, 18–19 May and 4–5 June 1981.

22. "Nomination of Ernest W. Lefever."

23. The five Republicans who voted against Lefever were Charles Mathias, Nancy Kassebaum, Rudolph Boschwitz, Larry Pressler, and Charles Percy. All of the committee's Democrats opposed his nomination: Claiborne Pell, Joseph Biden, John Glenn, Paul Sarbanes, Edward Zorinsky, Paul Tsongas, Alan Cranston, and Christopher Dodd. His sole supporters were Howard Baker, Jesse Helms, Richard Lugar, and Samuel Hayakawa.

24. "Exit Lefever, with a Nudge," *New York Times*, 7 June 1981.

25. "Nomination of Ernest W. Lefever"; Extension of Remarks, *Congressional Record*, 9 June 1981, 11934–11936.

26. "Nomination of Ernest W. Lefever"; Extension of Remarks.

27. Congress established the position with an amendment (Section 624 (f)) to the Foreign Assistance Act of 1961.

28. Kennedy to Haig, 26 Oct. 1981, released to the author under the Freedom of Information Act. See also Jacoby, "The Reagan Turnaround on Human Rights," 1069–1070.

29. Jefferson Morley, "Rights and Reagan: Does the Appointment of Elliott Abrams Signal a Reversal in Human Rights Policy?" *Foreign Service Journal* (Mar. 1982): 20; "Elliott Abrams: A Neoconservative for Human Rights," *National Journal*, 1 May 1982.

30. Edwin S. Maynard, "The Bureaucracy and Implementation of US Human Rights Policy," *Human Rights Quarterly* 11, no. 2 (1989): 182–183.

31. Kennedy to Haig, 26 Oct. 1981, released to the author under the Freedom of Information Act. See also Maynard, "The Bureaucracy and Implementation of US Human Rights Policy," 182–183; Hartmann, "US Human Rights Policy under Carter and Reagan, 1977–1981," 425–426.

32. See, for example William Safire, "Human Rights Victory,'" *New York Times*, 5 Nov. 1981; Pell to Haig, 12 Nov. 1981, University of Rhode Island Archives, Claiborne Pell Papers, box 54, folder "Alexander Haig."

33. Barbara Crossette, "US to Name Human Rights Aide," *New York Times*, 30 Oct. 1981.

34. A. Glenn Mower, *Human Rights and American Foreign Policy: The Carter and Reagan Experiences* (New York: Greenwood Press, 1987), 46–47.

35. Judith Miller, "Man in the News: A Neoconservative for Human Rights Post," *New York Times*, 31 Oct. 1981; George Lardner Jr., "Human Rights Spokesman Reported Chosen," *Washington Post*, 30 Oct. 1981.

36. Morley, "Rights and Reagan," 25.

37. Schifter, "Building Firm Foundations," 19.

38. "Abrams, State's Human Rights Chief, Tries to Tailor a Policy to Suit Reagan," *National Journal*, 1 May 1982.

39. Shultz thought Haig's past experience working with Henry Kissinger may have led him to place insufficient emphasis on human rights. George Shultz Interview, Princeton University Archives (PUA), Don Oberdorfer Papers (DOP), box 3, folder 3.

40. Jacoby, "The Reagan Turnaround on Human Rights," 1066–1086.

41. Sikkink, *Mixed Signals*, 150.

42. Sikkink, *Mixed Signals*, 149.

43. Sikkink, *Mixed Signals*, 148.

44. Jacoby, "The Reagan Turnaround on Human Rights," 1068, 1078; Jerome J. Shestack, "An Unsteady Focus: The Vulnerabilities of the Reagan Administration's Human Rights Policy," *Harvard Human Rights Journal* 2 (1989): 33–34, 37–38; Sikkink, *Mixed Signals*, 150.

45. Walter LaFeber, *Inevitable Revolutions: The United States in Central America*, 2nd ed. (New York: Norton, 1993), 5, 271.

46. LaFeber, *Inevitable Revolutions*, 307. See also Schmidli's chapter in this volume.

47. William M. LeoGrande, *Our Own Backyard: The United States in Central America, 1977–1992* (Chapel Hill: University of North Carolina Press, 1998), 582.

48. Renouard, *Human Rights in American Foreign Policy*, 184.

49. See Schmidli's chapter in this volume.

50. Sikkink, *Mixed Signals*, 166–167, 169, 180. See also Jason M. Colby, "Reagan and Central America," in *A Companion to Ronald Reagan*, ed. Andrew L. Johns (Malden, MA: Wiley Blackwell, 2015), 445.

51. See Lauren F. Turek's chapter in this volume, where she points out that Montt's Pentecostal beliefs led conservative Christians in the United States to support sending more aid to Guatemala.."

52. Sikkink, *Mixed Signals*, 172.

53. LaFeber, *Inevitable Revolutions*, 10, 312, 315; LeoGrande, *Our Own Backyard*, 152–153.

54. Reagan, *An American Life*, 478.
55. LeoGrande, *Our Own Backyard*, 153–155, 171.
56. LeoGrande, *Our Own Backyard*, 235. See also Reagan, *An American Life*, 478.
57. Quoted in Renouard, *Human Rights in American Foreign Policy*, 189.
58. George P. Shultz, *Turmoil and Triumph: Diplomacy, Power, and the Victory of the American Ideal* (New York: Charles Scribner's Sons, 1993), 404.
59. Maechling, "Human Rights Dehumanized," 134.
60. Shultz, *Turmoil and Triumph*, 266n.
61. National Security Decision Directive 75, 17 Jan. 1983, https://fas.org/irp/offdocs/nsdd/nsdd-75.pdf.
62. NSDD 75.
63. The Vashchenko and Chmykhalov families forced their way into the United States embassy in June 1978 in an effort to secure emigration from the Soviet Union. Matlock regards Reagan's interest in Soviet human rights as genuine. Jack Matlock Jr. *Reagan and Gorbachev: How the Cold War Ended* (New York: Random House, 2004), 55–56; Arthur Hartman Interview, PUA, DOP, box 2, folder 16. See also Nicholas Daniloff, *Of Spies and Spokesmen: My Life as a Cold War Correspondent* (Columbia: University of Missouri Press, 2008), 377. Further evidence of Reagan's concern can be found in his personal letters to author Suzanne Massie, *Manchester Union Leader* publisher Nackey Loeb, and businessman Armand Hammer in which he discusses successful American efforts to secure the release of Soviet dissident Yuri Orlov and his wife and Soviet dissidents David and Cecilia Goldfarb. Kiron K. Skinner, Annelise Anderson, and Martin Anderson, eds., *Reagan: A Life In Letters* (New York: Free Press, 2003), 382–383. In Turek's view, Reagan's concern for the Pentecostalists connected with his broader policy goal of reforming the Soviet political system; Turek, in this volume.
64. Jack Matlock Interview with author, 3 Apr. 2006.
65. Shultz to Moscow, 15 Jan. 1982, Ronald Reagan Presidential Library (RRPL), Executive Secretariat–NSC (ESNSC), Head of State File (HSF), box 38, folder "USSR: General Secretary Brezhnev."
66. According to Soviet official Andrei Aleksandrov-Agentov, Dobrynin cabled Moscow after his meeting with Reagan, urging resolution of the problem. Gromyko agreed and facilitated their emigration. Matlock, *Reagan and Gorbachev*, 54; George Shultz Interview, PUA, DOP, box 3, folder 2; Andrei Aleksandrov-Agentov Interview, PUA, DOP, box 1, folder 2; Arthur Hartman Interview, PUA, DOP, box 2, folder 16.
67. Reagan, "Proclamation 4973," 21 Sept. 1982, APP; Reagan, "Remarks at a White House Meeting with Jewish Leaders," 2 Feb. 1983, APP; Reagan, "Proclamation 5063," 18 May 1983, APP; Reagan, "Remarks on Presenting Congressional Gold Medals to Natan and Avital Shcharansky and an Informal Exchange with Reporters," 11 Jan. 1989, APP.
68. Max M. Kampelman, "Rescue With a Presidential Push," *Washington Post*, 11 June 2004; Max Kampelman Interview with author, 13 Mar. 2007; Matlock, *Reagan and Gorbachev*, 57–58; George F. Will, "Helsinki Charade," *Washington Post*, 21 Aug. 1983.
69. Statement of Max M. Kampelman, 15 July 1983, in *Three Years at the East-West Divide*, ed. Leonard R. Sussman (New York: Freedom House, 1983), 115; "The Madrid CSCE Review Meeting," Nov. 1983, Organization for Security and Cooperation in Europe Archives; Millicent Fenwick, *Speaking Up* (New York: Harper and Row, 1982), 165–166.

70. Reagan to Gorbachev, 11 Mar. 1985, RRPL, ESNSC, HSF, box 39, folder "USSR-GSG 8590272–8590419."

71. Reagan to Gorbachev, 30 Apr. 1985, RRPL, ESNSC, HSF, box 39, folder "USSR GSG 8590475–8590495."

72. Mikhail Gorbachev, *Perestroika: New Thinking for Our Country and the World* (New York: Harper and Row, 1987), 215.

73. Gorbachev, *Perestroika*, 205.

74. "Human Rights in the Soviet Union," RRPL, Tyrus W. Cobb Files, box 21097, folder "Soviet Union (Binder)."

75. Matlock, *Reagan and Gorbachev*, 152.

76. Lou Cannon, *President Reagan: The Role of a Lifetime*, rev. ed. (New York: PublicAffairs, 2000), 675; Bernard Weinraub, "President Links Rights in Soviet to Summit Success," *New York Times*, 8 Oct. 1986.

77. Matlock, *Reagan and Gorbachev*, 161; Memorandum of Conversation, 20 Nov. 1985, RRPL, Jack F. Matlock Files, box 92137, folder "Geneva: Memcons (Reagan-Gorbachev Memcons Geneva Meeting 11/19–21/1985) 2 of 3."

78. Shultz to Reagan, 4 Dec. 1985, RRPL, ESNSC, HSF, box 40, folder "USSR GSG 8591241–8591245"; Reagan to Gorbachev, 7 Dec. 1985, RRPL, ESNSC, HSF, box 40, folder "USSR GSG 8591241–8591245"; Reagan, *An American Life*, 645.

79. Jacoby, "The Reagan Turnaround on Human Rights," 1082–1083. See also Sarah B. Snyder, "'No Crowing': Reagan, Trust, and Human Rights," in *"Trust, but Verify": The Politics of Uncertainty and the Transformation of the Cold War Order, 1969–1991*, ed. Reinhild Kreis, Martin Klimke, and Christian Ostermann (Palo Alto, CA: Stanford University Press, 2016), 42–62.

80. Jack Matlock Interview, 3 Apr. 2006; Shultz to Reagan, 14 Jan. 1986, RRPL, ESNSC, HSF, box 40, folder "USSR GSG 8690024–8690124."

81. Reagan to Gorbachev, 7 Dec. 1985, RRPL, ESNSC, HSF, box 40, folder "USSR General Secretary Gorbachev 8591241–8591245."

82. The Reagan administration's approach to human rights was shaped by human rights organizations such as Helsinki Watch, which advised US officials on which dissidents needed release most urgently. Sarah B. Snyder, "Bringing the Transnational In: Writing Human Rights into the International History of the Cold War," *Diplomacy and Statecraft* 24, no. 1 (2013): 108–109.

83. Ronald Reagan, "Remarks at a White House Meeting with Human Rights Advocates," 7 Oct. 1986, APP.

84. Weinraub, "President Links Rights in Soviet to Summit Success"; Briefing Book, RRPL, Fritz Ermath Files, box 92085, folder "President Reagan's Trip to Reykjavik, Iceland October 10–12, 1986: Overall Briefing Book."

85. Shultz proposed a working group to discuss human rights and regional issues. Matlock, *Reagan and Gorbachev*, 226; Cannon, *President Reagan*, 687.

86. Jack Matlock Jr., *Autopsy of an Empire: The American Ambassador's Account of the Collapse of the Soviet Union* (New York: Random House, 1995), 97. Other scholars such as Robert English have maintained the nuclear accident at Chernobyl in April 1986, not Reykjavik, spurred Gorbachev to focus more on respect for human rights issues, as it demonstrated the dangers of Soviet secrecy and the need to open the Soviet system. Robert D. English, *Russia and the Idea of the West: Gorbachev,*

Intellectuals and the End of the Cold War (New York: Columbia University Press, 2000), 220.

87. Brinkley, *The Reagan Diaries*, 484.

88. Max Kampelman Interview, 24 June 2003, http://memory.loc.gov/ammem/collections/diplomacy/; Charles Hill, written communication with the author, 29 Mar. 2010; Gal Beckerman, *When They Come for Us, We'll Be Gone* (New York: Houghton Mifflin Harcourt, 2010), 511–513.

89. Shultz, *Turmoil and Triumph*, 986. According to Ridgway, Shultz's repeated entreaties convinced Soviet leaders that changing their human rights practices was in the best interests of their reform efforts. Rozanne Ridgway Interview, PUA, DOP, box 2, folder 30.

90. National Security Decision Directive 305, 26 Apr. 1988, RRPL, National Security Decision Directives, box 2, folder 6.

91. Reagan, *An American Life*, 709. Joseph Renouard emphasizes the growing significance of religious freedom to Reagan over the course of his second term; Renouard, *Human Rights in American Foreign Policy*, 171. Reagan focused his rhetorical attention on those seeking religious freedom and the right to emigrate earlier in his presidency as well. See for example, Reagan, "Statement on Signing a Bill Concerning Human Rights in the Soviet Union," 22 Mar. 1982, APP.

92. Brinkley, *The Reagan Diaries*, 613; Remarks by the President, 30 May 1988, RRPL, Katherine Chumachenko Files (KCF), box OA19268, folder "Human Rights Day 1988 (5)."

93. Memorandum of Conversation, 31 May 1988, http://nsarchive.gwu.edu/NSAEBB/NSAEBB251/.

94. Don Oberdorfer, *From the Cold War to a New Era: The United States and the Soviet Union, 1983–1991* (Baltimore, MD: Johns Hopkins University Press, 1998), 297; Robert Kennedy Eichhorn, "The Helsinki Accords and Their Effect on the Cold War," MA thesis, California State University, Fullerton, 1995, 273; Cannon, *President Reagan*, 705–706; Press Briefing, 30 May 1988, RRPL, KCF, box OA18291, folder "Moscow Summit 1988 (7)"; Brinkley, *The Reagan Diaries*, 613–614.

95. Reagan, "Remarks to Soviet Dissidents at Spaso House in Moscow," 30 May 1988, APP. Lauren Turek's chapter in this volume shows how Reagan framed human rights violations in religious terms.

96. Reagan, "Address to the Nation about Christmas and the Situation in Poland," 23 Dec. 1981, APP.

97. Historian Gregory Domber sees little impact from Reagan's sanctions on Polish policy; Gregory F. Domber, *Empowering Revolution: America, Poland, and the End of the Cold War* (Chapel Hill: University of North Carolina Press, 2014), 254, 256. Reagan *An American Life*, 305.

98. Frustrated by the Reagan administration's response, Jaruzelski noted the contrast in Reagan's reaction to human rights violations in Poland, Romania, and Chile. Domber, *Empowering Revolution*, 33, 45.

99. Domber, *Empowering Revolution*, 130.

100. Joseph Renouard points to administration criticism of South Africa, South Korea, and El Salvador as evidence that its approach underwent "a profound change." Renouard, *Human Rights in American Foreign Policy*, 217.

101. James H. Meriwether, "Reagan and Africa," in *A Companion to Ronald Reagan*, , ed. Andrew L. Johns (Malden, MA: Wiley Blackwell, 2015), 380, 382.

102. Chester A. Crocker, "South Africa: Strategy for Change," *Foreign Affairs* 59, no. 2 (1980): 323–351.

103. Crocker, "South Africa," 324.

104. Crocker, "South Africa," 324.

105. Crocker, "South Africa," 348.

106. Chester A. Crocker, "Southern Africa: Eight Years Later," *Foreign Affairs* 68, no. 4 (1989): 159.

107. Reagan, "Remarks and a Question-and-Answer Session with Reporters on Signing the Executive Order Prohibiting Trade and Certain Other Transactions Involving South Africa," 9 Sept. 1985, APP. See also Schmitz, *The United States and Right-Wing Dictators*, 217–223.

108. Reagan, "Message to the Congress Reporting on the National Emergency with Respect to South Africa," 17 Mar. 1986, APP.

109. David L. Hostetter, *Movement Matters: American Antiapartheid Activism and the Rise of Multicultural Politics* (New York: Routledge, 2006), 130–132.

110. Reagan, "Remarks and a Question-and-Answer Session with Reporters on Signing the Executive Order Prohibiting Trade and Certain Other Transactions Involving South Africa," 9 Sept. 1985, APP.

111. Sanford P. Ungar and Peter Vale, "South Africa: Why Constructive Engagement Failed," *Foreign Affairs* 64, no. 2 (1985): 234–235; Helen Kitchen, "Africa: Year of Ironies," *Foreign Affairs* 64, no. 3 (1986), 572. For a more positive appraisal, see Renouard, *Human Rights in American Foreign Policy*, 230.

112. Reagan, "Message to the House of Representatives Returning without Approval a Bill Concerning Apartheid in South Africa," 26 Sept. 1986, APP.

113. Thomas Borstelmann, *The Cold War and the Color Line: American Race Relations in the Global Arena* (Cambridge, MA: Harvard University Press, 2001), 259.

114. Reagan "Transmitting a Report on Apartheid in South Africa," 1 Oct. 1987, APP.

115. Reagan "Transmitting a Report on Apartheid."

116. Renouard notes that Reagan's record toward the Philippines did not show him to be "a democratic visionary." Renouard, *Human Rights in American Foreign Policy*, 224.

117. Schmitz, *The United States and Right-Wing Dictators*, 231–232. See also William J. Burns, "The Reagan Administration and the Philippines," *World Today* 38, no. 3 (1982): 97–104.

118. See Schmitz, *The United States and Right-Wing Dictators*, 233.

119. Schmitz, *The United States and Right-Wing Dictators*, 234–237.

120. Schmitz, *The United States and Right-Wing Dictators*, 237–239.

121. Morley and McGillon, *Reagan and Pinochet*, 49–61.

122. Morley and McGillon, *Reagan and Pinochet*, 70, 233; Alan McPherson, *Ghosts of Sheridan Circle: How a Washington Assassination Brought Pinochet's Terror State to Justice* (Chapel Hill: University of North Carolina Press, 2019), 220–221.

123. Morley and McGillon, *Reagan and Pinochet*, 86–87; McPherson, *Ghosts of Sheridan Circle*, 221.

124. Morley and McGillon, *Reagan and Pinochet*, 85–7, 96, 108.

125. Reagan is largely absent from their account. Morley and McGillon, *Reagan and Pinochet*, 108, 123.

126. Morley and McGillon, *Reagan and Pinochet*, 119.

127. Morley and McGillon, *Reagan and Pinochet*, 126.

128. Morley and McGillon, *Reagan and Pinochet*, 127–8.

129. Morley and McGillon, *Reagan and Pinochet*, 164.

130. Morley and McGillon, *Reagan and Pinochet*, 191.

131. US policy toward Pinochet was constructed in the shadow of the final days of Marcos' rule in the Philippines. Morley and McGillon, *Reagan and Pinochet*, 194–5, 222.

132. Morley and McGillon, *Reagan and Pinochet*, 240–50.

133. Shultz, *Turmoil and Triumph*, 972.

134. Shultz, *Turmoil and Triumph*, 974.

135. Morley and McGillon, *Reagan and Pinochet*, 255; Shultz, *Turmoil and Triumph*, 974. For more on the Reagan administration's efforts at democracy promotion, see Schmidli's chapter in this volume.

136. Morley and McGillon, *Reagan and Pinochet*, 265, 322.

137. Morley and McGillon, *Reagan and Pinochet*, 276–278, 292.

138. Neier, "Human Rights in the Reagan Era," 33.

139. Neier, "Human Rights in the Reagan Era," 30.

140. Schmidli, *The Fate of Freedom Elsewhere*, 187.

141. See Schmidli's chapter in this volume.

142. Neier, "Human Rights in the Reagan Era," 31.

143. Luca Trenta, "The Champion of Human Rights Meets the King of Kings: Jimmy Carter, the Shah, and Iranian Illusions and Rage," *Diplomacy and Statecraft* 24, no. 3 (2013): 476–498; Kenton Clymer, "Jimmy Carter, Human Rights, and Cambodia," *Diplomatic History* 27, no. 2 (2003): 245–277; Bradley R. Simpson, "Denying the 'First Right': The United States, Indonesia, and the Ranking of Human Rights by the Carter Administration, 1976–1980," *International History Review* 31, no. 4 (December 2009): 798–826; Simon Stevens, "'From the Viewpoint of a Southern Governor': The Carter Administration and Apartheid, 1977–81," *Diplomatic History* 36, no. 5 (2012): 843–880; Rosemary Foot, *Rights beyond Borders: The Global Community and the Struggle over Human Rights in China* (New York: Oxford University Press, 2000), 89–90.

144. For similar arguments, see Carleton and Stohl, "The Foreign Policy of Human Rights," 218; Sikkink, *Mixed Signals*, 180.

CHAPTER 10

Between Values and Action
Religious Rhetoric, Human Rights, and Reagan's Foreign Policy

LAUREN F. TUREK

On March 5, 1986, President Ronald Reagan sat down in the White House library to film a five-minute video message about a civil war raging in Nicaragua. With Congress locked in a fierce battle over his request for $100 million in assistance for the US-backed Contras, the counterrevolutionary forces fighting to oust the Frente Sandinista de Liberación Nacional (FSLN) from power, the administration was anxious to sway public and congressional opinion about the conflict. Reagan and his supporters feared that a Sandinista victory would expand Soviet and Cuban influence in Central America, worsen a growing revolutionary insurgency in El Salvador, and hasten the spread of communism throughout the region.[1] Yet congressional opponents of the administration's policies had already passed several measures aimed at restricting appropriations for military funding to the Contras, citing concern about US involvement in efforts to overthrow the Nicaraguan government.[2] Mounting evidence of Contra human rights violations fueled further congressional resistance to the president's request.[3] In response, the Reagan administration launched a multifaceted public relations campaign aimed at seizing the moral high ground in the debate. The video message, which Reagan recorded specifically for Christian media providers to broadcast on their television and radio programs, constituted a crucial part of this effort to win public and congressional support for the Contras.

In the video, Reagan blended an overview of the national security threat that he believed the Sandinistas posed to the United States with references to core American values, religious language, and details about religious persecution in Nicaragua. He described FSLN human rights abuses, including the closure of the Catholic radio station, as assaults on the freedoms of the press and religion, and condemned the forcible relocation and mass killing of the (predominantly Protestant) Miskito Indian population as a genocide.[4] Reagan then argued that in a time when freedom and democracy had "flashed out like a great astonishing light" elsewhere in the world, it was "nothing less than a sin to see Central America fall to darkness."[5] Here, in addition to using the language of sin to describe the spread of communism, the speech made a subtle reference to Matthew 4:16 ("The people who sat in darkness have seen a great light"), with democracy as the force of national salvation.[6] Reiterating this theme, Reagan told his Christian audience that "if we work together . . . we can save Central America."[7] He ended the video message by requesting that viewers contact their senators and representatives and urge them to vote for Contra funding.

The messaging of the video encapsulated how as president Reagan used religious values, language, and imagery to frame human rights issues and his foreign policy objectives. From religious repression in the Soviet bloc to brutal state violence in Southern Africa, Central America, and other regions throughout the global South, human rights concerns lay at the heart of international politics in the 1980s. During the 1980 presidential campaign, Reagan had mounted an attack on Jimmy Carter's human rights policies, arguing that Carter alienated US allies by targeting violations in authoritarian regimes while turning a blind eye to abuses in the Soviet Union and other totalitarian states.[8] Reagan pledged to upend this approach, highlighting religious persecution and other human rights abuses in the communist world as matters of special concern.[9] Recently, scholars such as Sarah Snyder, Kathryn Sikkink, and Joe Renouard have begun to examine how the Reagan administration reoriented and redefined US human rights policies, delving into the key rhetorical shifts, bureaucratic changes, and legislative strategies the White House pursued.[10] Zeroing in on the religious content of the administration's rhetoric reveals much about how Reagan conceptualized human rights, how his interpretation reflected a conservative Christian perspective on human rights, and how his administration operationalized this perspective to achieve broader foreign policy objectives.[11]

In his public statements as president, Reagan merged his core religious beliefs, including a concept of universal human dignity rooted in scripture, with eternal American values such as the freedom of conscience in his calls to reappraise how human rights issues informed US policymaking. Although his administration's understanding and treatment of global human rights issues changed over the course of his presidency, Reagan made extensive use of religious rhetoric to explain his foreign policy agenda—and the role of human rights within it—throughout his time in office. This effort was both a conscious, expedient political strategy and a reflection of sincerely held beliefs.

Reagan also developed and drew on relationships with religious leaders and interest groups, especially politically conservative Christian and Catholic organizations, to build public support for his foreign policy decisions, as the intended audience for his video message on Contra funding attested.[12] Evangelical Christians became particularly reliable and influential allies of the administration, providing moral and philosophical backing for Reagan's policies in congressional hearings and debates. Evangelical organizations as well as the Christian media also publicized important foreign policy issues through television, radio, newsletters, and direct mail campaigns. Their effectiveness in advocating for Reagan administration policies reflected the considerable political power that the religious right had gained by the early 1980s.[13]

Religious rhetoric helped Reagan categorize human rights abuses in totalitarian as well as authoritarian regimes, develop and explain policy responses that reflected his broader national security aims, and rally religious interest groups to advocate for those objectives. How religion suffused the language, values, and actions the administration employed to address public concerns about human rights in the Soviet bloc, Central America, and Southern Africa was particularly revelatory. Transnational nongovernmental organizations played a significant role in pushing the United States to take up international human rights issues during the Carter and Reagan years.[14] Religious groups on both the political left and the political right made vital contributions to this moral crusade.[15] Yet the growing public interest in human rights threatened some of Reagan's foreign policy objectives, particularly his plans for confronting communism in Central America. In response, the Reagan administration used Christian nationalist rhetoric to reframe the goals of US human rights policies, harnessing the support of politically conservative religious groups to form a moral bulwark against public and congressional critics and reorienting the moral compass of American foreign policy in return.

The signals Reagan had sent on the campaign trail about his intentions to recalibrate US foreign and human rights policies alarmed religious critics, who confronted the new administration shortly after inauguration. The Ad Hoc Committee of the Human Rights Community, an umbrella organization of more than sixty groups that included the National Council of Churches and the Union of American Hebrew Congregations, assailed Secretary of State Alexander Haig for asserting at his first press conference that "international terrorism will take the place of human rights" as the administration's foreign policy priority.[16] Politically liberal and moderate Mainline Protestant, Catholic, and Jewish critics also decried Reagan's nomination of Ernest Lefever for assistant secretary of state for Human Rights and Humanitarian Affairs.[17] As Sarah Snyder makes clear in her contribution to this volume, the selection of Lefever—and the vociferous opposition that arose in Congress in response—was a signal moment in Reagan's first term, one that pushed the administration to adjust its public rhetoric on human rights, though not its core policy orientation. The religious beliefs and faith-based language that religious supporters and opponents alike employed in the Lefever hearing provide additional insight into the administration's rhetorical reorientation.

Lefever, the founder of a conservative public policy think tank, shared with Reagan, Haig, and other members of the new administration a stated commitment to target human rights abuses in totalitarian regimes while "improving relations with authoritarian regimes friendly to the United States."[18] Public, religious, and congressional human rights advocates feared that cozying up to authoritarians rather than holding them accountable for human rights abuses would embolden autocratic rulers by tacitly condoning repression in Central America and other regions of concern. The editor of the liberal Protestant journal *Christianity and Crisis* summed up critics' sentiments: "Lefever has in fact become an instant symbol of the Reagan-Haig shift away from giving official attention to human rights abuses and toward denunciation of Soviet-inspired 'international terrorism.' To human rights groups, the stress on terrorism and on Soviet sins heralds an undiscriminating attack on people's movements all over the world."[19] Rev. Martin Deppe, a Methodist minister and member of the interfaith peace organization Clergy and Laity Concerned, emphasized that such a change in the nation's foreign policy orientation would represent a step away from the core values of the United States and the Christian faith. He referenced Pope John Paul II's impassioned defense of "human dignity and human rights" and noted that, like the Catholic Church, the United Methodist Church affirmed the concept of universal human dignity, as described in the Book of Genesis, as a centerpiece of human rights.[20] Although the Reagan administration offered a robust defense of Lefever, bringing in the director of the National Association of Evangelicals and others to testify at the congressional hearings that Lefever's human rights views had a strong basis in scripture and upheld the concept of human dignity, the Senate Foreign Relations Committee rejected his nomination.[21]

Stung by this rebuff, the Reagan administration left the position unfilled for several months as it devised a strategy to advance its foreign policy objectives while neutralizing congressional critiques that its policies hindered the advancement and protection of human rights. Reagan and his advisors in the State Department and elsewhere recognized that "human rights has been one of the main directions of domestic attack on this Administration's foreign policy."[22] Yet the Reagan administration remained committed to intensifying pressure on the Soviet Union and other communist states while relying on quiet diplomacy in its relations with friendly anticommunist nations. As such, it did not intend to issue public rebukes of repressive authoritarian regimes as the Carter administration had, though the State Department acknowledged that Reagan could not totally ignore violations in allied nations.[23] For this reason, the administration began to discuss human rights in different terms.[24] Reagan's advisors believed that if they and the president could cast tyranny in the Soviet bloc as the most pressing human rights issue of the day and sell the efficacy of quiet diplomacy in dealings with autocrats, they might redefine the terms of the debate and win support for Reagan's approach to foreign affairs.

Conflating human rights with American political and religious values provided the Reagan administration with the rhetorical means to do so. Less than two months after he raised the hackles of human rights activists with his suggestions that the administration planned to dismantle Carter's policies, Haig assured the public that "we are a community of peoples devoted to human rights, democracy and the rule of law."[25] Liberal members of Congress remained skeptical, as Haig's statements suggested only a modest stylistic shift. When Haig's aide, Under Secretary of State for Political Affairs Walter J. Stoessel Jr., testified at a House subcommittee on Human Rights and International Organizations hearing in July 1981, he spoke more directly to congressional concerns and received a much warmer reception in return.[26] He pledged that "the protection and enhancement of human rights is a principal goal of our foreign policy" and asserted that "this administration opposes the violation of human rights whether by ally or adversary, friend or foe."[27] Stoessel argued that Reagan supported pragmatic human rights policies that took the political and cultural realities of each country the United States interacted with into account. As result, he suggested, Reagan would prove more effective at reducing human rights violations throughout the world than his predecessor.

Stoessel also emphasized the significance of religious liberty and religious principles to the new administration's human rights priorities. At the hearing, he insisted that Reagan believed that the United States would best foster global human rights if it shone "as a city upon a hill" and led the world by example, in a reference to John Winthrop's "A Model of Christian Charity" that the president employed often in his speeches.[28] Winthrop served to personify the pursuit of religious liberty and its status as a foundational American value, a principle Reagan viewed as the polestar of his fight against totalitarianism. When Stoessel highlighted the administration's "public human rights diplomacy" at the Conference on Security and Cooperation in Europe (CSCE) and the meeting of the United Nations Human Rights Commission in 1981, he spoke with pride about how these gatherings exposed and condemned religious persecution in the Soviet bloc.[29] He also celebrated "the [UN] Commission's adoption of the Declaration on the Elimination of all Forms of Intolerance and Discrimination Based on Religion or Belief."[30] This emphasis suggested that for the Reagan administration, religious liberty (and the freedom of conscience more broadly) formed the foundation for its conception of human rights.

Although the members of the subcommittee pressed Stoessel on how "evenhanded" Reagan's policy actually was with regard to abuses in authoritarian versus totalitarian regimes, they found his explanation of the administration's policies far more acceptable than those from past spokespersons.[31] Such senior officials as Paul Wolfowitz and Lawrence Eagleburger praised his testimony, arguing in a State Department memo that it "established a new direction for US human rights policy" that would bolster the administration's credibility on the issue.[32] They advocated for an elaboration of Reagan's human rights policy along the lines Stoessel had articulated in his public and congressional statements.

To promote its refashioned commitment to human rights to the American people, the administration leaked portions of a memorandum describing this "new" policy direction to the *New York Times*.[33] Elliott Abrams, Reagan's new appointee for the assistant secretary of state for Human Rights and Humanitarian Affairs position, excelled at couching the new policies in the more palatable language of American values and religious dignity.[34] So did George Shultz, whom Reagan named secretary of state in July 1982 after Haig's departure and who embraced the language of human rights and religious freedom in the realm of Soviet policy. One journalist recounted that while Haig had argued that the administration should not elevate human rights above other bilateral issues such as arms control, "in describing the US-Soviet agenda for negotiation and dialogue, the first item on Shultz's list was 'improvements in Soviet performance on human rights.'"[35] By 1983 the Reagan administration spoke consistently—in public forums and in private diplomatic exchanges—about religious persecution in the Soviet bloc as a major sticking point in US-Soviet relations.

Reagan and Shultz saw tremendous value in using human rights issues to exert pressure on the Soviet Union, both in bilateral relations and as part of a larger strategy for developing a Western consensus on Washington's dealings with the USSR. National Security Decision Directive 75 (NSDD-75), which Reagan signed in January 1983, noted that in order to achieve US security goals vis-à-vis the Soviet Union, "US policy must have an ideological thrust which clearly affirms the superiority of US and Western values of individual dignity and freedom."[36] These values, rooted in *imago dei*—the Christian belief that God created humans in his image and therefore granted all individuals dignity, equality, and freedom—formed the religious basis for Reagan's understanding of human rights. They also illustrated the moral gulf that Reagan perceived between the United States and the Soviet Union, which he viewed as atheistic and therefore fundamentally incapable of protecting human dignity and freedom of conscience. Calling attention to Soviet repression was an effective means of publicizing the American commitment to these values around the world. The administration believed that doing so would create an opening to "loosen Moscow's hold" on Eastern Europe, gradually reshape internal politics in the Soviet Union itself, and win Western European support.[37]

Evidence of escalating human rights abuses in the Soviet Union afforded grounds for more confrontational dialogue with Soviet leaders. In line with NSDD-75, human rights issues and cases of religious persecution figured prominently in discussions between Reagan and Soviet ambassador Anatoly Dobrynin, as well as in his later meetings with General Secretary Mikhail Gorbachev. In their early conversations with Dobrynin, Reagan and Shultz focused considerable energy on the plight of the Siberian Seven, two Pentecostal families who had taken refuge in the US embassy in Moscow in 1978 after the state repeatedly denied their requests to emigrate.[38] Reagan informed Dobrynin that public concern for the Siberian Seven, including attention from Congress and international advocacy campaigns from US religious organizations, made it politically difficult for the administration to negotiate with the Soviet Union on other important matters, such as arms control or trade.[39] The president also issued public statements on the Siberian Seven, most notably an open letter in which he praised the families for embarking on their "courageous course, a struggle that is an inspiration to all who value religious freedom and individual human rights."[40] Although quiet diplomacy would in the end prove most crucial to securing their release, the breakthrough revealed the power that human rights appeals could have in US-Soviet diplomacy.[41] Reagan henceforth incorporated pleas for specific victims of religious persecution and a more general emphasis on religious liberty into his discussions with Soviet leaders.[42] Domestic US and international public support for these goals provided Reagan with leverage to push for greater religious freedom in the Soviet Union as well as for concessions on a range of other significant issues, such as arms control and improved economic relations.

The administration worked to cultivate consensus among Western European leaders on how to best combat human rights violations in the Soviet Union and Eastern Europe. Reagan and his State Department agreed that the mission afforded an opportunity for the administration "to enlist the help of our Allies in devising a common human rights policy."[43] Allied support for intensified foreign policy pressure on the Soviet Union was an unspoken but obvious adjunct to this desired outcome. In July 1983, Reagan sent Walter Stoessel and Elliot Abrams on a special presidential mission to eight European countries and the Vatican for consultations on "Soviet anti-Semitism and repression of human rights" ahead of the final session of the Madrid CSCE meetings.[44] In official letters for European leaders and Pope John Paul II, the president asserted that the "situation concerns me because of the importance I attach to the Helsinki Final Act commitments, because of the terrible costs that are being paid by individual human beings, and because our overall relationship with the Soviets is seriously affected by human rights violations."[45] He highlighted Soviet attacks and restrictions on Jews and other religious minorities as particularly grievous.

Stoessel found that Western European leaders and the pope shared Reagan's concerns about Soviet abuses, which contributed to the adjustments to the Helsinki process that the Madrid CSCE made.[46] When he announced the Madrid CSCE document, Reagan highlighted its "provisions dealing with human rights," including more robust attention to "religious liberties," the "unification of families," and the "free flow of information" in the Soviet Union.[47] These commitments aligned well with the tougher line the administration wanted to take in reshaping Soviet internal affairs. They also reflected Reagan's concerns about the onerous restrictions the Soviet Union imposed on Jews, Pentecostals, and other religious minorities, including limitations or prohibitions on their ability to practice their faiths freely, to emigrate, and to access religious materials.

To publicize his administration's role in reinvigorating the Helsinki process—and showcase his personal dedication to human rights causes in the Soviet bloc—Reagan proclaimed August 1 "Helsinki Human Rights Day." The Helsinki accord had figured prominently in Reagan's Soviet views for a long time. When the Polish crisis escalated early in his first term, the president framed the political crackdown and declaration of martial law—which he attributed to the Soviets—as violations of human rights under Helsinki.[48] As his first term proceeded, Reagan emphasized the religious protections of the Helsinki Final Act with increasing force. The Helsinki Human Rights Day would both commemorate the anniversary of the signing of the Helsinki Final Act and bring vital attention to religious persecution in the communist world, which he condemned as an affront to the "principles of Helsinki."[49] In his proclamation, Reagan described the accord as "a powerful diplomatic instrument to advance the cause of human dignity and liberty," largely because it was an emblem of domestic and international condemnations of Soviet repression and expansionism.[50] This focus on religious values, and his characterization of human rights as an acceptance of fundamental human dignity (derived from Biblical teachings) with corresponding protections for individual liberties, resonated with the international community, the American public, and religious interest groups.

Such rhetoric also inspired the Reagan administration's efforts to enlist the support of friendly religious leaders and organizations and to mobilize them as public advocates for the president's policies. Part of this outreach campaign, which the Office of Public Liaison spearheaded, entailed inviting religious opinion leaders to the White House or the State Department for briefings on human rights issues, US foreign policy, and relevant pending legislation.[51] These colloquies ensured that conservative religious interest groups and other potential administration allies received tailored information from policymakers to share with their followers, inform their activism on key issues, and refer to when lobbying their congressional representatives.[52]

The State Department and members of the National Security Council took the lead in proposing one of these events in 1984—an International Conference on Religious Liberty. Proposed and co-sponsored by the Institute on Religion and Democracy, a conservative Christian think tank, the event demonstrated the administration's commitment to global human rights with an emphasis on religious freedoms.[53] Planning documents suggested that speakers from diverse political and religious perspectives would deliberate "on the status of freedom of religion in the world, identify its major abusers, and examine ways to help victims of religious repression."[54] The State Department requested that Reagan give an opening speech, and Shultz and National Security Adviser Robert McFarlane participate along with over two hundred religious leaders from across the globe. The speakers whom the Institute on Religion and Democracy invited ultimately proved less diverse than anticipated—most espoused conservative political views on domestic social issues as well as foreign policy and embraced the conservative Christian perspective that religious liberty provided the foundation for all human rights.[55] Although this stoked some controversy with politically moderate and liberal religious leaders, as well as with the press, it fostered a sense of shared purpose and a common language for discussing human rights issues among the administration and members of the religious right, as the speakers' interpretations of human rights and religious persecution tended to align closely with those of Reagan and his chief lieutenants.[56]

Reagan spoke at length about the relationship he saw between Christian values, human rights principles, and his foreign policy in his conference remarks. His speech clearly articulated his sense that democracy, civil liberties, and religious freedom were inalterably entwined and formed the basis for human rights. Reagan began by citing the Gospel of St. Matthew and asserting that all religions distinguished between the "temporal world and the spiritual world."[57] He stated that what the biblical injunction to maintain a separation between these worlds "teaches us is that the individual cannot be entirely subordinate to the state, that there exists a whole other realm, an almost mysterious realm of individual thought and action which is sacred and which is totally beyond and outside of state control."[58] Reagan maintained that this teaching provided the root of modern conceptions of human rights. Such a concept could only survive in a free, democratic society because only in those states that permitted religious liberty "could the idea of individual human rights take root, grow, and eventually flourish."[59] American democratic principles and practices had forged for him a nation "whose avowed purpose was and is the protection of . . . God-given rights."[60]

The speech also typified the essential distinctions about human rights violations that Reagan and his advisors drew when considering US relations with totalitarian versus authoritarian states. Here, too, Reagan elaborated to his audience about how notions of faith and religious freedom provided a foundation for his thinking about human rights: "Atheism is not an incidental element of communism, not just part of the package; it is the package. In countries which have fallen under Communist rule, it is often the church which forms the most powerful barrier against a completely totalitarian system. And so, totalitarian regimes always seek either to destroy the church or, when that is impossible, to subvert it."[61] Reagan insisted that "the most essential element of our defense of freedom is our insistence on speaking out for the cause of religious liberty."[62] Defending religious liberty abroad offered his government a chance to support a fundamental human right while also containing the expansion of communism. This involved more than just fighting for religious liberty in Eastern Europe and the Soviet bloc. He identified examples of

Soviet or Soviet-influenced religious persecution in Iran, Afghanistan, and Nicaragua and argued that the United States ought to rededicate itself to fighting human rights abuses throughout the world. The administration thus effectively claimed the mantle of human rights activism, offering a politically conservative yet morally grounded alternative to the human rights perspective liberal activists had claimed as their own.

Reagan's belief that human rights could not exist in countries that lacked religious freedom and democratic values also informed the rhetoric he used to explain his support for repressive autocratic regimes in Central America, Southern Africa, and elsewhere in the world. Throughout his time in office, the United States loaned material aid and encouragement to countries that actively resisted communist subversion, such as El Salvador, Guatemala, and South Africa. Even if these countries committed human rights abuses in order to oppose revolutionary groups, Reagan believed that if they succeeded in their fight against totalitarian forces, they would eventually transition to democracy and, therefore, abide by human rights norms.[63] For this reason, he praised even the most modest evidence of movement toward democracy, highlighting the flourishing of civic and religious groups and the promises of free elections in countries such as El Salvador.[64] In his view, totalitarian regimes, by contrast, lacked the capacity for any such transition to democracy and human rights compliance, a conviction that harkened back to the earliest days of his administration and that he reiterated even at the end of his presidency.[65]

Religious values and the support of conservative religious groups reinforced the connection Reagan saw between democratization and human rights and bolstered his advocacy for aid to autocratic yet anticommunist governments. His embrace of General José Efraín Ríos Montt, the Guatemalan dictator who seized power through a 1982 military coup, as a key ally in the fight against Cuban and Soviet subversion in Central America drew moral sustenance from his Christian human rights. Despite extensive evidence from international human rights groups that Ríos Montt's campaign against communist insurgents entailed the mass killing of innocent indigenous peoples in the Guatemalan highlands, Reagan pledged US military aid to the regime. Indeed, after a meeting with Ríos Montt in which the general described the political reforms he had enacted in Guatemala as part of a larger effort to oppose communism and lead the country to God, Reagan told reporters that "President Ríos Montt is a man of great personal integrity and commitment. His country is confronting a brutal challenge from guerrillas armed and supported by others outside Guatemala. I have assured the President that the United States is committed to support his efforts to restore democracy and to address the root causes of this violent insurgency. I know he wants to improve the quality of life for all Guatemalans and to promote social justice."[66]

Reagan's support seemed to rest on Ríos Montt's Christian faith and affirmation of religious values.[67] Conservative Christians in the United States, particularly evangelicals and those who shared Ríos Montt's Pentecostal beliefs, rallied to the cause of securing military aid for the Guatemalan regime, which Reagan began pushing for in earnest in early 1983.[68] Much like Reagan, these advocates argued that Ríos Montt's Christianity ensured that he would foster human rights and democracy; they saw religious and democratic values as inextricably linked. Intensive bureaucratic wrangling, coupled with mass-media and letter-writing campaigns from US evangelicals, helped secure some additional aid for Ríos Montt from a mix of religious, corporate, and government sources.

Concern about communist advances in Angola, Namibia, and Mozambique likewise led Reagan to emphasize the threat that totalitarianism posed to religious freedom and democracy when discussing US policy toward southern Africa. His administration feared that unrest stemming from racial segregation and repressive white minority rule in South Africa might encourage further Soviet involvement, compromising US interests in the region.[69] Indeed, the CIA expressed considerable anxiety about Soviet support for the African National Congress in its militant resistance to apartheid.[70] The White House also opposed the efforts of anti-apartheid activists and their congressional allies to impose sanctions on South Africa on the grounds that sanctions might threaten Pretoria's willingness to aid the United States in rolling back communism in neighboring countries.[71] Yet the moral righteousness of the anti-apartheid crusade, coupled with the significance of faith-based anti-apartheid activism, posed a challenge to Reagan's framing of US–South African relations in religious language.

Bishop Desmond Tutu, the Anglican secretary-general of the South African Council of Churches, and Dr. Allan Boesak, a clergyman in the Dutch Reformed Church in South Africa, gained international renown for their anti-apartheid activism—activism that they viewed as rooted in their faith. Tutu, who won the Nobel Peace Prize in 1984, stressed that the South African freedom struggle was "'thoroughly based on the Gospel . . . on a God who takes the side of nonentities.'"[72] Tutu and Boesak both emphasized Christian principles when speaking out against the Pretorian government and the brutal system of apartheid, which, as Boesak noted, "trampl[ed] on our humanity and our God-given dignity."[73] Pope John Paul II employed similar religious language in his condemnation of apartheid. A Vatican statement affirmed the Catholic belief that "man's *creation by God* 'in his own image' (*Gen.* 1, 27) confers upon every human person an eminent dignity; it also postulates *the fundamental equality of all human beings*," and thus it denounced the South African government for violating "the rights of the human person."[74] Religious anti-apartheid activists in the United States embraced these shared spiritual principles in protests, letter-writing campaigns, and testimony urging Congress and the Reagan administration to sanction the South African government.

Under pressure and determined to seize the moral high ground, the Reagan administration recruited conservative Christian leaders and their followers to call on their congressional representatives to oppose the sanctions movement and began explaining its policies toward South Africa using the language of faith-based human rights. In a 1986 speech, Reagan countered critiques from anti-apartheid activists that his opposition to sanctions indicated that he supported South Africa's racist edifice. He argued that he opposed apartheid but could not ignore the threat totalitarianism posed to the region, claiming that "in southern Africa, our national ideals and strategic interests come together. South Africa matters because we believe that all men are created equal and are endowed by their Creator with unalienable rights."[75] He seemed to believe that, unlike in Soviet-supported states nearby and despite the intractability, brutality, and inherent tyranny of apartheid, South Africa could and should reform apartheid to make its system democratic and thus compliant with human rights norms. He accordingly compared the autocratic apartheid regime favorably to totalitarian states, noting that while South Africa granted its citizens "a broad measure of freedom of speech, of the press, and of religion. . . . it's hard to think of a single country in the Soviet Bloc, or many in the United Nations, where political critics have the same freedom to be heard as did outspoken critics of the South African Government."[76] Given the appalling violence of apartheid, this explanation failed to sway most members of Congress, of course, but it did reflect Reagan's tendency to view communist human rights violations as more serious than authoritarian abuses, in part because it elevated religious liberty and democratic values above other categories of rights.[77]

Anticommunism was also behind the administration's financial and moral support for violent counterrevolutionary movements, such as the Contras in Nicaragua. As in the South African case, Reagan and his advisors viewed the emergence of the FSLN, with its ties to Cuba and the Soviet Union, as a threat to American interests in the surrounding region. And as in his statements on Soviet human rights abuses, Reagan reiterated that religious believers in Nicaragua experienced rampant persecution under the Sandinistas.[78] Framing the Contra war as a battle for religious liberty and democracy in Central America thus helped his administration mobilize conservative religious interest groups and mount a more effective challenge to liberal human rights activists who opposed Reagan's pro-Contra policies. The message he filmed for the Christian media, along with the other aspects of his public relations campaign, helped Reagan wring some funding from Congress for the Contra war despite broad public and congressional opposition.

Positing religious liberty as the core human right also influenced how Reagan addressed relations with noncommunist adversaries. In 1983, the president condemned Iran and the Ayatollah Khomeini for human rights abuses against religious minorities, specifically members of the Bahá'í faith. Calling for an end to the summary execution of Bahá'ís, Reagan noted, "These individuals are not guilty of any political offense or crime. . . . They only wish to live according to the dictates of their own consciences."[79] Khomeini rejected the president's critique, accusing him of hypocrisy for protesting abuses against the Bahá'ís while ignoring the violations of Iraqi and Iranian human rights that Iraq, then an ally of the United States, was perpetrating in its war with Iran.[80] Reagan continued to denounce Iran for restricting religious freedom, citing the country alongside the Soviet bloc countries for engaging in "rampant religious persecution," in his Human Rights Day and Week proclamations in 1983, 1984, and 1985 as well as in the remarks he made at the 1985 Conference on Religious Liberty.[81] Furthermore, in the 1985 Human Rights Day and Week proclamation, the president drew explicit connections between human rights, democracy promotion, and the goal of international peace: "Respect for human rights is essential to true peace on Earth. Governments that must answer to their peoples do not launch wars of aggression. That's why the American people cannot close their eyes to abuses of human rights and injustice, whether they occur among friend or adversary or even on our own shores."[82] Citing countries for religious persecution provided a means for the administration to act as a defender of human rights without compromising its strategic priorities.

Reagan entered office with a reputation as an opponent of human rights in a time when many in Congress and the American public championed the ideals of the international human rights movement. His attempt to reorient US human rights policies to better align with his conservative foreign policy objectives faced an uphill battle. Although Reagan did not sway committed liberal human rights activists to his perspective, as many of his policies aided repressive regimes, he did fashion a rhetorical framework for a conservative conception of human rights. This framework went beyond simply conflating human rights with democracy promotion. Though democratic principles provided a key aspect of Reagan's integration of human rights language into his foreign policy agenda, religious values, beliefs, and interest groups were indispensable. Emphasizing the scriptural basis for human rights—and thus prioritizing religious liberty in foreign policy as a means for protecting those rights—brought coherence to Reagan's human rights policies. It also gave him the moral and interest-group backing he needed to pursue his foreign policy goals despite organized congressional resistance.

Notes

1. David S. Painter, *The Cold War: An International History* (New York: Routledge, 1999), 99; "National Security Decision Directive on Cuba and Central America," 4 Jan. 1982, https://catalog.archives.gov/id/6879618

2. "Amendment Offered by Mr. Boland," *Congressional Record*, 97th Congress, 2nd Session, 8 Dec. 1982, vol. 12, pt. 21, H29468–H29469; "Amendment Offered by Mr. Boland," *Congressional Record*, 98th Congress, 1st Session, 20 Oct. 1983, vol. 129, pt. 20, H28560, H28572; *Continuing Appropriations for the Fiscal Year 1985*, PL 98-473, Stat. 1935–1937, sec. 8066.

3. Barbara Mikulski, "Opposing Aid to the Contras," Extension of Remarks, *Congressional Record*, 99th Congress, 2nd Session, 18 Mar. 1986, vol. 132, pt. 35, E919; Barney Frank, "Nicaragua," *Congressional Record*, 99th Congress, 2nd Session, 10 Apr. 1986, vol. 132, pt. 43, H1765.

4. Reagan, "Taping: Message on Contra Aid for Religious Programs," 5 Mar. 1986, Ronald Reagan Presidential Library (RRPL), Carl Anderson Files, box 10, folder "OA 17967: RR/Nicaragua Videotape for Christian Media 03/05/1986." Speechwriter Peggy Noonan authored the text for the video.

5. Reagan, "Taping: Message on Contra Aid for Religious Programs."

6. Mt. 4:16 (New Revised Standard Version). See also Jn 8:12, "Jesus the Light of the world."

7. Reagan, "Taping: Message on Contra Aid for Religious Programs."

8. Reagan, "1980 Ronald Reagan/Jimmy Carter Presidential Debate," 28 Oct. 1980, https://www.reaganlibrary.gov/archives/speech/1980-ronald-reagan-and-jimmy-carter-presidential-debate.

9. Reagan, "Republican National Convention Acceptance Speech," 17 July 1980, https://www.reaganlibrary.gov/archives/speech/republican-national-convention-acceptance-speech-1980; H. W. Brands, *Reagan: The Life* (New York: Doubleday, 2015), chap. 31.

10. See Sarah B. Snyder, *Human Rights Activism and the End of the Cold War: A Transnational History of the Helsinki Network* (New York: Cambridge University Press, 2011); Kathryn Sikkink, *Mixed Signals: US Human Rights Policy and Latin America* (Ithaca, NY: Cornell University Press, 2007); Joe Renouard, *Human Rights in American Foreign Policy: From the 1960s to the Soviet Collapse* (Philadelphia: University of Pennsylvania Press, 2015).

11. Much of the recent scholarly literature that assesses the religious underpinnings of human rights ideas and activism focuses on politically and theologically

liberal religious groups, such as mainline Protestants. See, for example, Samuel Moyn, *Christian Human Rights* (Philadelphia: University of Pennsylvania Press, 2015); David Hollinger, *Protestants Abroad: How Missionaries Tried to Change the World but Changed America* (Princeton, NJ: Princeton University Press, 2017). My work explores politically and theologically conservative religious groups, specifically evangelical Christians, who saw freedom of conscience (and thus openness to evangelism and salvation) as the foundational human right, and formulated their human rights agenda and activism on the basis of this precept.

12. Theresa Keeley has explored the role of conservative Catholics in providing such support for Reagan administration policies in Central America. See Theresa Keeley, *Reagan's Gun-Toting Nuns: The Catholic Conflict Over Cold War Human Rights Policy in Central America* (Ithaca, NY: Cornell University Press, 2020).

13. The religious right, which included politically conservative Catholics, evangelicals, fundamentalists, and other right-leaning faith groups, mobilized during the 1970s in response to the social and cultural changes of the era. They were initially galvanized by the threats that they perceived to their values through Supreme Court rulings that prevented segregated private schools from receiving tax-exempt status, affirmed women's rights to access birth control and abortion, and threatened compulsory prayer in schools, and began organizing politically in response. By the end of the 1970s, conservative religious lobbying groups, including the Christian Coalition and the Moral Majority, enjoyed considerable influence in Congress, and the religious right had emerged as an important voting bloc for the Republican Party. Ronald Reagan courted this constituency explicitly in both the 1980 and 1984 elections. In an August 1980 speech on religious liberty, Reagan famously appealed to the religious right when he asserted that he "endorsed" them and their agenda; in March 1983, he gave a well-known speech to the National Association of Evangelicals, where he framed the Soviet Union as an "evil empire" that infringed on the rights of religious believers and posed a threat to democracy and freedom worldwide. The religious right proved to be a key piece of the Reagan coalition, helping Reagan win election and lending him considerable support throughout his two terms in office. The scholarly literature on the rise of the religious right is extensive. Key works include William C. Martin, *With God on Our Side: The Rise of the Religious Right in America* (New York: Broadway Books, 1996); Lisa McGirr, *Suburban Warriors: The Origins of the New American Right* (Princeton, NJ: Princeton University Press, 2001); Daniel K. Williams, *God's Own Party: The Making of the Christian Right* (Oxford: Oxford University Press, 2010); Darren Dochuk, *From Bible Belt to Sunbelt: Plain-Folk Religion, Grassroots Politics, and the Rise of Evangelical Conservatism* (New York: W. W. Norton, 2011). As I argue in my book, the religious right did not limit their political lobbying to hot-button domestic social issues; by the late 1970s, evangelical Christians in particular had developed a cogent foreign policy agenda rooted in their evangelistic aims and had built a strong and effective lobby to advocate for those objectives in Congress. See Lauren Frances Turek, *To Bring the Good News to All Nations: Evangelical Influence on Human Rights and US Foreign Relations* (Ithaca, NY: Cornell University Press, 2020).

14. For recent work that addresses the role of NGOs in US human rights activism as well as the international human rights movement in the 1970s and 1980s, see Snyder, *Human Rights Activism*; Barbara Keys, "Anti-Torture Politics: Amnesty International, the Greek Junta, and the Origins of the US Human Rights Boom," in *Human

Rights in the Twentieth Century: An International History, ed. Akira Iriye, Petra Goedde, and William Hitchcock (New York: Oxford University Press, 2012), 201–221; Renouard, *Human Rights*; Barbara Thomas Davies, *NGOs: A New History of Transnational Civil Society* (Oxford: Oxford University Press, 2014).

15. The religious right tended to focus more narrowly on human rights violations in the communist world (particularly abuses against fellow believers) than the religious left, which had a broader focus. See Turek, *To Bring the Good News to All Nations*.

16. Don Oberdorfer, "Haig Calls Terrorism Top Priority," *Washington Post* 29 Jan. 1981; "Excerpts from Haig's Remarks at First News Conference as Secretary of State," *New York Times*, 29 Jan. 1981;

17. Charles Mohr, "Coalition Assails Reagan's Choice for State Dept. Human Rights Job," *New York Times*, 25 Feb. 1981; Hon. Richard L. Ottinger, "Wrong Signals on Human Rights," Extension of Remarks, *Congressional Record*, 97th Congress, 1st Session, 17 Feb. 1981, vol. 127, pt. 2, 2306.

18. John M. Goshko, "Ultraconservative May Get Human Rights Post at State," *Washington Post*, 5 Feb. 1981. In congressional hearings, Lefever called for the repeal of certain human rights policies and downplayed the severity of human rights abuses in authoritarian states. He, along with Reagan and Haig, embraced the ideas that Jeane J. Kirkpatrick advanced in her well-known article, "Dictatorships and Double Standards," *Commentary* (1979): 34–45. See also Ernest Lefever, "Statement of Ernest W. Lefever, Director of the Ethics and Public Policy Center, Georgetown University: The Trivialization of Human Rights," in House Committee on Foreign Affairs, *Human Rights and US Foreign Policy: Hearings before the Subcommittee on International Organizations of the Committee on Foreign Affairs, House of Representatives, 96th Congress, 1st Session, May 2; June 21; July 12; and August 2, 1979* (Washington, DC: US Government Printing Office, 1979), 239; Senate Committee on Foreign Relations, *Nomination of Ernest W. Lefever: Hearings before the Committee on Foreign Relations, United States Senate, 97th Congress, 1st Session, on the Nomination of Ernest W. Lefever to be Assistant Secretary of State for Human Rights and Humanitarian Affairs, May 18, 19, June 4, and 5, 1981* (Washington, DC: US Government Printing Office, 1981), 3–5, 83–84.

19. Leon Howell, "Ernest Lefever at the Edge of Power: A Profile in Consistency," *Christianity and Crisis*, 2 Mar. 1981, 37–38.

20. Gn 1:26–27 (New Revised Standard Version) describes humankind as made in God's image, and many Christians connected this concept of the *imago dei* with the sense that God had imbued them with universal dignity and core freedoms (such as spiritual freedom through eternal salvation in Jesus Christ) and thus human rights. Rev. Martin L. Deppe, "Prepared Statement of Rev. Martin L. Deppe," in Senate Foreign Relations Committee, *Nomination of Ernest W. Lefever*, 329.

21. Robert P. Dugan Jr., "Prepared Statement of Robert P. Dugan, Jr.," in *Nomination of Ernest W. Lefever*, 307. See also Carl F. H. Henry to the Senate Committee on Foreign Relations, 10 Mar. 1981, in *Nomination of Ernest W. Lefever*, 30. For more on the Lefever nomination and its significance to US human rights policies during the Reagan era, see Sarah Snyder, "The Defeat of Ernest Lefever's Nomination: Keeping Human Rights on the United States Foreign Policy Agenda," in *Challenging US Foreign Policy: America and the World in the Long Twentieth Century*, ed. Bevan Sewell and Scott Lucas (New York: Palgrave Macmillan, 2011), 131–161; Sikkink, *Mixed Signals*, 22, 155–156.

22. Wolfowitz and Eagleburger to Haig, "Human Rights Policy," 2 Oct. 1981, Chile Declassification Project.

23. Richard T. Kennedy to Alexander Haig, "Reinvigoration of Human Rights Policy," 26 Oct. 1981, https://history.state.gov/historicaldocuments/frus1981-88v41/d54.

24. In their respective chapters, Sarah Snyder and William Michael Schmidli also explore the Reagan administration's efforts to reframe human rights and interpret them narrowly enough to support its preexisting foreign policy objectives. This chapter homes in on the key role that religious language and conceptions of religious liberty played in the administration's rhetorical shift on human rights, including its embrace of the language of democracy promotion.

25. "Text of Haig's Speech on American Foreign Policy," *New York Times*, 25 Apr. 1981.

26. Charles Mohr, "Haig Aide Insists US Rights Policy Is Evenhanded," *New York Times*, 15 July 1981.

27. Walter J. Stoessel, Jr., "Statement," *Implementation of Congressionally Mandated Human Rights Provisions*, vol. 1, *Hearings before the Subcommittee on Human Rights and International Organizations of the Committee on Foreign Affairs, House of Representatives, Ninety-Seventh Congress, First Session, July 14, 30; September 17, 1981* (Washington, DC: US Government Printing Office, 1982), 6.

28. Stoessel, "Statement," 6–7.

29. Stoessel, "Statement," 8.

30. Stoessel, "Statement," 8.

31. Jonathan Brewster Bingham, *Implementation of Congressionally Mandated Human Rights Provisions*, vol. 1, *Hearings before the Subcommittee on Human Rights and International Organizations of the Committee on Foreign Affairs, House of Representatives, Ninety-Seventh Congress, First Session, July 14, 30; September 17, 1981* (Washington, DC: US Government Printing Office, 1982), 15–16.

32. Wolfowitz and Eagleburger to Haig, "Human Rights Policy."

33. Kennedy to Haig, "Reinvigoration of Human Rights Policy."

34. Senate Committee on Foreign Relations, *Nomination of Elliot Abrams: Hearing before the Committee on Foreign Relations, United States Senate, Ninety-Seventh Congress, First Session, on the Nomination of Elliot Abrams, of the District of Columbia, to be Assistant Secretary of State for Human Rights and Humanitarian Affairs, November 17, 1981* (Washington, DC: US Government Printing Office, 1981).

35. Don Oberdorfer, "Shultz Outlines Policy of Opposing Soviets," *Washington Post*, 16 June 1983.

36. National Security Decision Directive 75, "US Relations with the USSR," 17 Jan. 1983, https://fas.org/irp/offdocs/nsdd/nsdd-75.pdf. See the Charles and Wilson chapter in this volume, which contextualizes the human rights objectives of NSDD-75 within the Reagan administrations larger agenda for US-Soviet relations and explains the factors that encouraged the administration to emphasize quiet diplomacy on human rights (and other) policies.

37. NSDD-75, 4.

38. Reagan, Shultz, and Dobrynin, "Memorandum of Conversation," 15 Feb. 1983, Ronald Reagan Presidential Library (RRPL), William P. Clark Files (WPCF), box 8, folder "US-Soviet Relations Papers Working File (2)"; Shultz to Reagan, "Next Steps

in US-Soviet Relations," 16 Mar. 1983, RRPL, WPCF, box 8, folder "US-Soviet Relations Papers Working File (2)."

39. Shultz to Reagan, "USG-Soviet Relations—Where Do We Want to Be and How Do We Get There?," 3 Mar. 1983, RRPL, WPCF, box 8, folder "US-Soviet Relations Working File (3)."

40. Reagan, "Message to Lidiya and Augustina Vashchenko, Hunger Strikers in the United States Embassy in Moscow," 29 Jan. 1982, https://www.reaganlibrary.gov/archives/speech/message-lidiya-and-augustina-vashchenko-hunger-strikers-united-states-embassy.

41. Jack Matlock, *Reagan and Gorbachev: How the Cold War Ended* (New York: Random House, 2005), 57–59.

42. See, for example, Shultz to Reagan, "Progress in the US-Soviet Bilateral Relationship," 5 Nov. 1986, RRPL, European and Soviet Affairs Directorate (ESAD), box 14, folder "US-USSR Bilateral"; "1986 Reagan-Gorbachev Summit: Public Diplomacy Strategy," RRPL, Jack F. Matlock Files, box 44, folder "USIA Conference on Public Diplomacy London March 3–4"; "The President's First One-on-One Meeting with General Secretary Gorbachev," 29 May 1988, in Declassified Documents Reference System (DDRS) (Farmington Hills, MI: Gale, 2013), doc. CK3100550863.

43. Clark to Reagan, "Ambassador Stoessel's Mission to Europe for Consultations on Soviet Human Rights Performance," 13 June 1983, RRPL, ESAD, box 4, folder "USSR-Human Rights/Stoessel Mission (5 of 5)."

44. Clark to Reagan, "Ambassador Stoessel's Mission to Europe."

45. Reagan to Pope John Paul II, 2 July 1983, RRPL, ESAD, box 4, folder "USSR-Human Rights/Stoessel Mission (5 of 5)." The Helsinki Final Act included agreements stipulating that signatory nations would "respect human rights and fundamental freedoms, including the freedom of thought, conscience, religion or belief," as well as the rights of individuals to move more freely throughout the world. Conference on Security and Co-Operation in Europe Final Act (Helsinki, 1975), 6, 38. Available from https://www.osce.org/helsinki-final-act.

46. "Memorandum of the President's Meeting with Ambassador Stoessel: Report on Presidential Mission to Europe on Soviet Human Rights Performance," 18 July 1983, RRPL, ESAD, box 4, folder "USSR-Human Rights/Stoessel Mission (3 of 5)."

47. Bernard Gwertzman, "US Accepts Terms for Human Rights at Madrid Meeting," *New York Times*, 16 July 1983,

48. "The President's News Conference," 17 Dec. 1981,https://www.reaganlibrary.gov/archives/speech/presidents-new-conference-december-17-1981 ; Reagan, "Statement on US Measures Taken against the Soviet Union Concerning Its Involvement in Poland," 29 Dec. 1981,https://www.reaganlibrary.gov/archives/speech/statement-us-measures-taken-against-soviet-union-concerning-its-involvement-poland.

49. "Aug. 1 to Be Helsinki Rights Day," *New York Times*, 26 July 1983.

50. Reagan, "Proclamation 5075—Helsinki Human Rights Day," 25 July 1983, https://www.reaganlibrary.gov/archives/speech/proclamation-5075-helsinki-human-rights-day.

51. For an example of how explicitly the Office of Public Liaison discussed this strategy of outreach to religious groups, see "The Central American Outreach Effort," 1984, RRPL, Faith Ryan Whittlesey Records, Subject File, box 34, folder "Central America: Materials (1 of 7)."

52. For a longer treatment of the human rights activism and policy lobbying activity of conservative Christian groups during the Reagan administration, see Turek, *To Bring the Good News to All Nations*.

53. Marjorie Hyer, "State Department Backing of Religious Conference Stirs Debate," *Washington Post*, 20 Apr. 1985.

54. Kimmitt to Ryan, "Dinner and Speech to Conference on Religious Liberty," 31 July 1984, RRPL, Executive Secretariat–NSC (ESNSC), Subject File (SF), box 12, folder: "Human Rights (07/23/1984) Box 40."

55. Hyer, "State Department."

56. Hyer, "State Department."

57. Reagan, "Remarks at a Conference on Religious Liberty," 16 Apr. 1985, https://www.reaganlibrary.gov/archives/speech/remarks-conference-religious-liberty; "Render therefore unto Caesar the things which are Caesar's; and unto God the things that are God's" (Mt. 22:21; King James Version).

58. Reagan, "Remarks at a Conference on Religious Liberty."

59. Reagan, "Remarks at a Conference on Religious Liberty."

60. Reagan, "Remarks at a Conference on Religious Liberty." Reagan did not limit his use of faith-based explanations of human rights and US policies to meetings with religious leaders. For an example of similar rhetoric at an ostensibly secular human rights event, see Ronald Reagan, *Rededication to the Cause of Human Rights: December 10, 1984* (Washington, DC: US Department of State, Bureau of Public Affairs, 1984).

61. Reagan, "Remarks at a Conference on Religious Liberty."

62. Reagan, "Remarks at a Conference on Religious Liberty."

63. For an example regarding El Salvador and its efforts to transition to democracy and decrease its rampant human rights abuses, see Reagan, "Address Before a Joint Session of the Congress on Central America," 27 Apr. 1983, https://www.reaganlibrary.gov/archives/speech/address-joint-session-congress-central-america. For a more global example, see Reagan, "Message to the Congress on Freedom, Regional Security, and Global Peace," 14 Mar. 1986, https://www.reaganlibrary.gov/archives/speech/message-congress-freedom-regional-security-and-global-peace.

64. Reagan, "Radio Address to the Nation on Central America," 14 Apr. 1984, https://www.reaganlibrary.gov/archives/speech/radio-address-nation-central-america-0.

65. Reagan stated this explicitly in a speech he made near the end of his presidency proclaiming a Human Rights Day. See Reagan, "Remarks on Signing the Human Rights Day, Bill of Rights Day, and Human Rights Week Proclamation," 8 Dec. 1988, https://www.reaganlibrary.gov/archives/speech/remarks-signing-human-rights-day-bill-rights-day-and-human-rights-week-0. The sentiment reflects the ideas Jeane Kirkpatrick developed in her 1979 article "Dictatorships and Double Standards," William Michael Schmidli elaborates on the Reagan administration's linkage of human rights and democracy promotion in his contribution to this volume.

66. Reagan, "Remarks in San Pedro Sula, Honduras, Following a Meeting with President Jose Efrain Rios Montt of Guatemala," 4 Dec. 1982, https://www.reaganlibrary.gov/archives/speech/remarks-san-pedro-sula-honduras-following-meeting-president-jose-efrain-rios-montt. For details on the information that Reagan and Ríos Montt exchanged at their meeting, see General José Efraín Ríos Montt, "Mensaje del presidente Ríos Montt, durante su primer ano del gobierno," Dec. 1982, Centro de

Investigaciones Regionales de Mesoamérica, Archivo de Inforpress Centroamerica, Documentos, doc. 1512; Chapin, "Draft Memorandum of Conversation: Bilateral Between President Reagan and the President of Guatemala, Rios Montt," 6 Dec. 1982, RRPL, ESNSC, CF, box 52, folder "Guatemala, Vol. I, 1/20/81–7/31/84 [2 of 5]."

67. Per interviews with and reports from administration aides. Fred Francis and Chris Wallace, "Headline: Reagan/Guatemala Aid," NBC Evening News, 5 Dec. 1982.

68. Lauren Turek, "To Support a 'Brother in Christ': Evangelical Groups and US-Guatemalan Relations during the Ríos Montt Regime," *Diplomatic History* 39, no. 4 (2015): 707–716.

69. Chester A. Crocker, "South Africa: Strategy for Change," *Foreign Affairs* 59, no. 2 (1980): 323–351.

70. CIA, "South Africa: The Politics of Racial Reform," 4 Jan. 1981, http://www.foia.cia.gov/document/0000568199.

71. NSC, "Southern Africa Status Report," RRPL, African Affairs Directorate, box 6, folder "NSDD 187—South Africa (1 of 4)."

72. Marjorie Hyer, "Bishop Tutu Talks at Howard on Apartheid Struggle," *New York Times*, 10 Nov. 1984.

73. Allen Boesak, "An Open Letter to Desmond Tutu from Dr. Allan Boesak of the Nederduitse Gereformeerde Sendingkerk," *The Sowetan*, 24 Sept. 1981; Marjorie Hyer, "Bishop Tutu Rallies Anglicans for Justice," *Washington Post*, 29 Jan. 1984.

74. Pope John Paul II, "Address of Pope John Paul II to Members of the Special Committee of the United Nations Organization Against Apartheid," http://www.vatican.va/content/john-paul-ii/en/speeches/1984/july/documents/hf_jp-ii_spe_19840707_onu-apartheid.html. Emphases in original.

75. "Transcript of Talk by Reagan on South Africa and Apartheid," *New York Times*, 23 July 1986.

76. "Transcript of Talk by Reagan on South Africa and Apartheid."

77. It also reflected the ways in which Reagan and his conservative religious allies downplayed racism and racial violence. For recent work that examines the links between politically-conservative Christianity and white supremacy, see Anthea Butler, *White Evangelical Racism: The Politics of Morality in America* (Chapel Hill, NC: The University of North Carolina Press, 2021); Robert P. Jones, *White Too Long: The Legacy of White Supremacy in American Christianity* (New York: Simon & Schuster, 2020).

78. A brief sampling of the many speeches in which he referred to religious persecution in Nicaragua includes Reagan, "Radio Address to the Nation on Central America"; Reagan, "Remarks to Jewish Leaders during a White House Briefing on United States Assistance for the Nicaraguan Democratic Resistance," 5 Mar. 1986, https://www.reaganlibrary.gov/archives/speech/remarks-jewish-leaders-during-white-house-briefing-united-states-assistance; Reagan, "Remarks on Signing the Captive Nations Week Proclamation," 16 July 1984, https://www.reaganlibrary.gov/archives/speech/remarks-signing-captive-nations-week-proclamation-1.

79. Reagan, "Message on the Persecutions and Repression in Iran," 22 May 1983, https://www.reaganlibrary.gov/archives/speech/message-persecutions-and-repression-iran.

80. "Khomeini Criticizes Reagan for Backing the Bahais in Iran," *New York Times*, 29 May 1983.

81. Reagan, "Remarks on Signing the Bill of Rights Day and the Human Rights Day and Week Proclamation," 10 Dec. 1985, https://www.reaganlibrary.gov/archives/speech/remarks-signing-bill-rights-day-and-human-rights-day-and-week-proclamation-0; Reagan, "Remarks at a Conference on Religious Liberty."

82. Reagan, "Remarks on Signing the Bill of Rights Day and the Human Rights Day and Week Proclamation."

Part Four

Latin America

CHAPTER 11

Reframing Human Rights
Reagan's "Project Democracy" and the US Intervention in Nicaragua

WILLIAM MICHAEL SCHMIDLI

In the late 1960s, the bipartisan Cold War consensus among American policymakers collapsed. The foundation of American foreign policy since the late 1940s, the consensus reflected a shared commitment among centrist liberals and conservative internationalists to project American political, economic, and military power abroad to contain the spread of Soviet communism. Amid the failed US intervention in Vietnam, however, the Democratic Party fractured under the strain of widespread domestic opposition to the war and rising New Left political activism, leaving liberal cold warriors increasingly overshadowed by "new politics liberals"—liberal internationalists who rejected the Cold War logic of the previous two decades. Correspondingly, human rights emerged as a defining issue in the fierce struggle over the direction of American foreign policy in the aftermath of the Vietnam War. With the issue embraced by both liberal internationalists and Cold War hawks, congressional lawmakers inserted human rights conditionality piecemeal into the US foreign policymaking process over the opposition of the Nixon and Ford administrations. At the end of the decade, Jimmy Carter's effort to bring "competence and compassion" to the White House further advanced human rights as a US policy priority.

In an era defined by the breakdown of the Cold War consensus, Ronald Reagan's vision of an American victory over the Soviet Union harkened back to the bipartisan anticommunism of early Cold War US foreign policy. Yet as

Reagan was well aware, implementing a muscular US approach to the Cold War would require confronting the advances liberal internationalists had made into the very heart of the American foreign policy establishment. Reagan's Cold War victory, in other words, would require a strategy of dual containment: rolling back Soviet gains abroad while containing liberals at home. On both fronts, the politics of human rights played a central role. The Reagan administration effectively used human rights rhetoric as a vehicle to build domestic support for expanded US security assistance to anticommunist forces in the Third World. The White House placed special emphasis on democracy promotion—as the centerpiece of its human rights policy—to justify interventionist policies abroad.

Nicaragua was a defining test case for the Reagan administration's democracy promotion initiative. After taking power following the bloody 1979 revolution that ousted the dictator Anastasio Somoza Debayle, the leftist Frente Sandinista de Liberación Nacional (FSLN, the Sandinista National Liberation Front) assumed the role of a political vanguard. The FSLN's dramatic increase in state social spending, emphasis on international nonalignment, and mixed-economy model were rooted in a conception of rights that sought to extend social and economic justice to ordinary Nicaraguans. Correspondingly, through mass-based political organizations, the FSLN sought to create a participatory democracy that would provide nonelites with avenues to participate in the nation's political life. In foreign policy, inspired by socialist Cuba, the FSLN aimed to serve as a model for Third World nations seeking to break free from the legacies of colonialism and underdevelopment; covertly, the FSLN funneled Cuban-supplied weapons to leftist revolutionaries in neighboring El Salvador.

The Sandinista revolutionary project was incompatible with the Reagan administration's aggressive effort to reassert American power in the global Cold War. The White House viewed Nicaragua as a defining challenge; as the influential UN Ambassador Jeane J. Kirkpatrick asserted, Central America was "quite simply the most important place in the world."[1] The administration energetically utilized the lexicon of human rights to portray US-funded counterrevolutionary forces, known as the Contras, as anticommunist democrats, despite evidence of extensive human rights abuses. Correspondingly, the Reagan administration worked to delegitimize the social and economic human rights initiatives of the Nicaraguan revolutionary government.[2]

Competing conceptions of human rights and democracy were thus at the heart of Cold War hostility between the Reagan administration and the FSLN, resulting in immense human and material destruction in Nicaragua and the destabilization of the Sandinista political project. More broadly, over the course of the 1980s, the Reagan administration's democracy promotion initiative gained traction in Washington as a legitimate foreign policy goal, drawing support from the foreign policymaking community, members of Congress, and nonstate actors. By the end of the decade, a distinctive form of US democracy promotion—legitimated by a rigorous use of human rights rhetoric, pursued through civil society or "low-intensity" military interventions, and rooted in the neoliberal imperatives of US-led globalization—had emerged as a central feature of US foreign policy, with significant implications for post–Cold War international relations.[3]

Throughout the 1980 election campaign, Reagan portrayed the Carter administration as embodying defeatism, isolationism, and self-abasement—characteristics that the Reaganite alliance of conservatives and liberal Cold War hawks (the latter increasingly referred to as "neoconservatives") associated with the George McGovern wing of the Democratic Party. Following the November 1980 election, the Reagan administration took office determined to redirect US foreign policy; not surprisingly, the Carter administration's human rights policy was a primary target.[4] As the Reagan administration distanced itself from Carter's human rights agenda, the White House also moved quickly to deepen American involvement in Central America. In the administration's aggressive effort to roll back perceived communist gains in the developing world, ousting the FSLN took center stage. "It's difficult to remember that Nicaragua was an absolute foreign policy focus of the Reagan administration," recalled Harry W. Shlaudeman, a career foreign service officer who served as the president's special envoy to Central America. "Nothing was more important, except the Soviet Union itself."[5]

What made Nicaragua, a deeply impoverished nation with a mere 3.6 million inhabitants a US foreign policy priority? First, the White House viewed the 1979 Sandinista revolution and the blossoming leftist insurgency in neighboring El Salvador through the lens of the East-West confrontation. Emphasizing Nicaragua's proximity to both the continental United States and geo-strategically vital sea lanes, top administration officials repeatedly warned that a Soviet satellite in Central America would pose a distinct threat to US security interests. Second, in light of Cuban involvement in major military operations in the Horn of Africa and Angola and the strong ties between the Cuban dictator Fidel Castro and top Sandinista officials, the Reagan administration expressed genuine concern at the possibility that a joint Cuban-Nicaraguan operation, armed and supplied by the Soviets, could threaten the entire isthmus. "We must not let Central America become another Cuba on the mainland," Reagan warned the National Security Council in February 1981. "It cannot happen."[6]

Third, the administration viewed Central America as an opportunity to roll back perceived Soviet gains in the Third World. In what would become known as the "Reagan doctrine," administration hard-liners sought to turn the tables on the Soviet Union by supporting anticommunist wars of national liberation.[7] As CIA Director William J. Casey emphasized in June 1986, "With a relatively few skilled officers and a tiny fraction of our military budget we can introduce new elements of stability into the Third World and check Third World Marxist-Leninist regimes that are stamping out democratic liberties and human rights and posing a threat to our national security."[8] Finally, the administration understood Central America as test case for defeating the perceived inroads of post-1968 liberalism in American foreign policy, particularly the Carter administration's emphasis on multilateralism, noninterventionism, and a human rights policy that, in the Reaganites' view, targeted right-wing allies but gave communist adversaries a free pass.

Accordingly, the Reagan administration quickly moved against the Sandinistas. Even before assuming office, the administration gave quiet assurances of support to Argentine efforts to turn former members of Somoza's National Guard into counterrevolutionaries, and in March 1981, Reagan signed a secret presidential finding on Central America providing $19.5 million to train, equip, and assist Central American efforts to "counter foreign-sponsored subversion and terrorism."[9] By the end of 1981, the framework of the US destabilization policy toward Nicaragua was in place. Reagan approved covert financial support for domestic opponents of the Sandinistas on November 23, along with a CIA plan to train a force of 500 Latin American commandos. The president also signed National Security Decision Directive (NSDD) 17, an eleven-point plan for Central America emphasizing the imperative of defeating the insurgency in El Salvador and halting Cuban and Nicaraguan interventionism. Although congressional constraints forced the White House to articulate its goal as interdicting arms flowing from Nicaragua to revolutionaries in El Salvador, from the outset, top Reagan administration officials conceived the real mission as sponsoring the overthrow of the FSLN. Likewise, for Central American revolutionaries and counterrevolutionaries alike, as the United States quickly monopolized control of the operation following Argentina's spectacular defeat in the Falklands War, the Reagan administration's ultimate goal was never in doubt.[10]

By early 1983, the Contras had mushroomed to a force of 7,000 combatants and were regularly attacking targets in northern Nicaragua. Yet opposition among congressional lawmakers and a majority of the American people constrained the scale of the Reagan administration's intervention in Central America. The successful passage of the first Boland Amendment (Boland I) in December 1982 prohibited the Department of Defense or the CIA from attempting to overthrow the FSLN with US funds. In June 1984, following revelations that the CIA had mined Nicaraguan harbors without appropriately informing congressional oversight committees, restive legislators passed Boland II, prohibiting all lethal aid to the Contras.[11] Confronting determined efforts by congressional Democrats to bring the Contra program to a halt and widespread opposition among the US public to a US military intervention in Central America, the Reagan administration increasingly turned to the rhetoric of human rights. Democracy promotion, in particular, would emerge as the centerpiece in the administration's strategy to garner votes on Contra assistance bills from uncommitted congressional moderates and deepen public support for the administration's Central America policy.

As the White House policy toward Nicaragua was taking shape, the Reagan administration stumbled into stiff congressional opposition to its effort to downgrade human rights as a US foreign policy priority. In mid-May 1981, the Senate Foreign Relations Committee refused to confirm Ernest Lefever to lead the Human Rights Bureau. A conservative political theorist and founder of a right-wing think tank, Lefever had openly encouraged dismantling the bureau during the 1980 presidential campaign. His rejection was the culmination of an intense lobbying campaign by liberal human rights advocates, and a clear demonstration of the human rights community's ability to mobilize effectively as well as the abiding bipartisan interest in human rights on Capitol Hill, all of which raised concerns within the Reagan administration that the effort to downgrade human rights was becoming a costly liability.[12]

By late 1981 the White House had undertaken a reorientation of the human rights policy. Reagan signaled the shift by nominating Elliott Abrams to head the Human Rights Bureau on October 30; in an unusual statement accompanying the nomination, the president emphasized human rights as "important in all aspects of our foreign policy."[13] A hard-nosed neoconservative, Abrams was a former aide to Senator Henry M. Jackson (D-WA), a leading congressional human rights advocate concerned with the plight of captive peoples in the communist world.[14] During his confirmation hearings, Abrams deftly balanced anticommunist rhetoric—describing the Soviet Union as "an enemy of the United States"—with a pledge to honestly report on human rights conditions abroad and to choose tactics "with a practical goal in mind."[15] In stark contrast with the Lefever episode, the thirty-three-year-old Abrams easily won unanimous confirmation. As Senator Paul E. Tsongas (D-MA) put it, "Being a neoconservative does not disqualify you from the job."[16]

The Reaganites' political worldview, however, would make a distinctive imprint on the administration's human rights policy. From the outset, the administration took a narrow approach to human rights that emphasized civil and political rights. By contrast, social and economic rights, which had been championed throughout the Cold War by the communist world and, in the 1960s and 1970s by many Third World nationalists were not only excluded from the Reagan administration's human rights framework, but dismissed as a poor disguise for communist tyranny. In the communist world, "from the government's point of view, the reason its subjects receive free education and medical care is in no way different from the reason its tractors receive mechanical care: if the services weren't provided, the machine—either animate or inanimate—wouldn't work," wrote Joseph Shattan, a neoconservative who served as an influential speechwriter for both Kirkpatrick and Abrams. "In such circumstances, the economic 'rights' of citizens under communism makes about as much sense as to speak of the economic 'rights' of automobiles to gasoline."[17] Abrams held a similar view. "You could make the argument that there aren't many countries where there are gross and consistent human rights violations" the human rights bureau chief told a reporter, "except the communist countries because they have the system itself."[18]

Corresponding with the Reagan administration's dismissal of social and economic rights claims, the White House used human rights rhetoric to justify aggressive Cold War policies in the Third World. Soviet and Cuban adventurism, not socioeconomic factors, the Reagan administration consistently argued, fueled insurgencies in peripheral locales such as El Salvador; as Jeane Kirkpatrick controversially asserted, "Revolutions in our times are not caused by social injustice."[19] Underscoring the influence of domestic politics on foreign policy, the administration also deployed human rights rhetoric as part of its broader effort to reverse the perceived inroads in US foreign policy of post-1968 American liberalism, particularly liberals' emphasis on nonintervention-ism abroad. In a mid-1983 foreign policy address, for example, Abrams told listeners that "the lesson of Vietnam" was that "where democracy and human rights are threatened . . . American power provides the necessary deterrent to aggression." Sidestepping both consistent American support for repressive and unelected governments in Saigon as well as the horrific human and material costs of the American military intervention in Southeast Asia, Abrams maintained that "where that shield is in place—as in Western Europe—democracy and human rights can flourish. Where that shield is removed—as in Vietnam—the prospects for democracy are destroyed."[20]

Influenced by neoconservatives such as Abrams and right-wing organizations such as the Heritage Foundation and Freedom House, the Reagan administration had seized upon democracy promotion as the centerpiece of its human rights policy by mid-1982. In a major address to members of the

British Parliament at Westminster in June, Reagan emphasized the need "to foster the infrastructure of democracy, the system of a free press, unions, political parties, universities, which allows a people to choose their own way to develop their own culture, to reconcile their own differences through peaceful means."[21] More concretely, in January 1983, the president signed NSDD-77, which mandated increased "aid, training and organizational support for foreign governments and private groups to encourage the growth of democratic political institutions and practices."[22] The following month the administration submitted a $65 million "Project Democracy" funding request to Congress for forty-four democracy assistance projects funded through the United States Information Agency. Although the Congress rejected the White House proposal, the administration's efforts ultimately bore fruit; after prolonged and rancorous debate lawmakers on Capitol Hill legislated seed money for a National Endowment for Democracy (NED), a bipartisan, nonprofit, private organization that would be annually funded by US government appropriations.[23]

Why did the Reagan administration embrace democracy promotion? On one level, the initiative served as shorthand for the Reagan administration's select emphasis on political and civil rights. "Democracy, after all, is a form of government which is based on the freely given consent of the governed," noted the introduction to the State Department's *Country Reports on Human Rights Practices for 1983*. "But consent can only be freely given if the means for the free expression of consent, or of dissent, exist; such means include freedom of speech, freedom of press, freedom of assembly and association, an independent judiciary, and free elections." Accordingly, respect for human rights, the report concluded, "is built into the very foundations of the democratic form of government."[24] Significantly, such statements were not merely public relations boilerplate but a reflection of the administration's vision of human rights and international relations. As Abrams asserted in a letter to Freedom House Executive Director Leonard Sussman, "Democratic institutions ... are the only guarantee of human rights over the long run."[25]

On another level, the emphasis on democracy fit nicely with the Reagan administration's hardline approach to East-West relations. According to the *Country Reports* introduction, the United States' democratic constitution protected diversity, pluralism, and minority rights; in the Soviet Union, on the other hand, "minority rights have been systematically, even brutally, eroded." More controversially, the report echoed Kirkpatrick's 1979 essay "Dictators and Double Standards," emphasizing that "while non-Communist dictatorships are capable, to varying degrees, of evolving into democracies, Communist dictatorships are singularly resistant to democratization."[26] Promoting human rights thus required a robust commitment to the global containment of communism, even if it meant supporting right-wing dictators. "Preventing Communist dictatorships from establishing themselves" the report maintained, "ought to be an especially high priority of any realistic and serious human rights policy.[27] Democracy promotion, in other words, served to legitimate the Reagan doctrine's call to roll-back perceived communist gains in the developing world.

The Reagan administration's proxy war on Nicaragua was a defining test case for the democracy promotion initiative. In the immediate prerevolution era, decades of greed, corruption, and nepotism at the hands of the Somoza family dynasty—combined with the massive destruction caused by the 1972 earthquake—had left Nicaragua one of the most unequal and impoverished nations in Latin America.[28] The revolution itself had resulted in enormous destruction: in a nation of three million, the conflict had cost an estimated 50,000 lives and left one-fifth of the population homeless and another 40,000 orphaned.[29] Much of the nation's infrastructure lay in ruins, and in addition to confronting massive capital flight, the revolutionary government inherited a foreign debt of $1.6 billion.[30] Yet as tens of thousands of Nicaraguans celebrated the revolution's final victory in Managua's main square on July 19, 1979, it was clear that the FSLN enjoyed widespread popular support. Moreover, although the individual members of the FSLN Directorate advanced a diverse range of political beliefs—influenced by interpretations of Marxist-Leninism, the ideas of early twentieth-century Nicaraguan nationalist Augusto Sandino, the example of the 1959 Cuban revolution, liberation theology, and anti-imperialism—they shared a vision of transforming Nicaragua in the post-Somoza era by extending social and economic rights to ordinary Nicaraguans.

The results were indeed transformative. In the field of education, in early 1980 the FSLN launched a massive literacy campaign directed toward the more than half of Nicaraguans who were functionally illiterate—nearly twice the average across the continent. Some 60,000 volunteers fanned out across the country to teach basic reading skills to 400,000 people over a five-month period, reducing illiteracy to 12.9 percent.[31] Correspondingly, the number of children attending preschool programs jumped from 9,000 to 66,850 between 1978 and 1984; primary school enrollment over the same period increased from 369,640 to 635,637; and more than 15,000 new teachers entered classrooms between 1980 and 1984.[32] By 1981, continuation programs for adult learners enrolled nearly 144,000 people; three years later the program's enrollment neared 200,000; remarkably, by the end of the year, one-third of Nicaragua's population was enrolled in formal or technical higher education programs.[33]

With significant support from Cuba, the Sandinistas also revolutionized the national health system.[34] By the end of 1980 the Health Ministry accounted for 14 percent of the national budget, a higher percentage than in any other Latin American nation and more than double the regional average.[35] Between 1980 and 1984, 309 new primary care facilities were constructed, as well as Nicaragua's first children's hospital. As a result, the number of medical visits jumped from 2.4 million in 1977 to 6.4 million in 1983, dental visits more than doubled, and the number of pregnant women under medical supervision increased from 23 percent in 1977 to 93 percent in 1983. Correspondingly, 1.2 million Nicaraguans received vaccinations against polio, measles, and tetanus in 1980; four years later, polio had been eradicated, and only 110 cases of measles were reported. Government-sponsored health campaigns, involving some 78,000 volunteers, spared Nicaragua from a regional outbreak of dengue in 1981 and reduced the number of Nicaraguans who contracted malaria from an annual average of 20,000 to only 505.[36]

The FSLN's most ambitious initiative was an attempt to fundamentally restructure the Nicaraguan economy. Following Somoza's overthrow, the FSLN immediately expropriated the land holdings of the dictator and his associates, giving the revolutionary government ownership of roughly 25 percent of Nicaragua's 3.6 million hectares of arable land. Combined with nationalization of the domestic banks and insurance companies and of the mining and forestry sectors, the FSLN increased the public sector's share of the gross domestic product (GDP) from less than 10 percent in 1978 to 40 percent by 1981.[37] Although the FSLN retained a mixed economy model—the private sector retained control of 80 percent of agriculture and 75 percent of manufacturing—the revolutionary government aimed to aggressively employ the levers of the state to benefit the majority rather than the top tier of income earners.[38] The FSLN, had adopted the "logic of the poor," Xabier Gorostiaga, an official at the Ministry of Planning, asserted in 1981. "Our strategy differs from other models of economic development whose first priority is to establish a model of accumulation," Gorostiaga continued. "Our first objective is to satisfy the basic needs of the majority of the population."[39]

The FSLN's social and economic initiatives were part of a larger effort to establish a unique form of participatory democracy in revolutionary Nicaragua. The FSLN envisioned a balance between top-down vanguardism and a form of direct democracy in which nonelites could participate in the nation's political life through newly created mass-based organizations at the grassroots level. Sandinista Defense Committees, for example, enrolled a remarkable 16 percent of the nation's population by the end of 1982.[40] Combined with the increase in social sector spending, the Sandinista effort to instill a popular democracy was rooted in a specific conception of human rights that emphasized social and economic rights and grassroots political participation.

From the outset, however, the paternalism characteristic of the FSLN's vanguardism led to constraints on Nicaraguan civil liberties. Unlike in neighboring El Salvador and Guatemala, where political activists and perceived subversives were kidnapped, tortured, and murdered in the tens of thousands, in Nicaragua opposition political parties continued to operate, and criticism from the church, media, and non-Sandinista labor unions was publicly aired. But following Somoza's overthrow, the FSLN moved quickly to consolidate political power; as the Contra war intensified, the FSLN regularly censored the opposition newspaper *La Prensa*, and mobs of Sandinista youth occasionally threatened outspoken opponents of the regime. The limits on Nicaraguan civil society illuminated the FSLN's distrust of electoral institutions as a mechanism of political participation. Sandinista officials were quick to point out that during the US-backed Somoza dictatorship, Nicaragua maintained the pretense of formal democracy. The regime, asserted FSLN official (and later vice president) Sergio Ramírez, "imported the political model of elections every four years, and elections existed here, a bi-partisan system existed here, and there was a two-chamber legislative system, a supreme court, and a constitution with laws. And it was all a bloody hoax."[41] More broadly, the Sandinistas dismissed "democratism" as a "liberal bourgeois ideology" that championed abstract notions of liberty in order to hide structural inequalities. "Bourgeois freedom has nothing to do with popular freedom that reflects the people's own objective interests in terms of their right to organize and to arm themselves (politically, militarily, and ideologically) *as a class*, in order to imbue the historical project of society in a way that corresponds with their interests as the majority," the FSLN asserted in the government-run daily *Barricada* in March 1980.[42] For the FSLN, *authentic* democracy flowed from the promotion of social and economic rights and was maintained through daily participation in grassroots political organizations.

By the time Reagan entered the Oval Office, the fortieth president of the United States confronted a revolutionary regime in Nicaragua that remained in the foundational stages of post-conflict recovery, but that could boast significant achievements. With its close ties to Cuba, emphasis on social and economic rights, and active participation in forums such as the Non-Aligned Nations Movement, the Sandinista revolutionary project was incompatible with the Reagan administration's effort to reassert American power in the global Cold War. In its effort to oust the Sandinistas, the White House pursued a three-pronged approach. First, the administration repeatedly accused the Sandinistas of supporting leftist insurgencies that threatened regional democracies. Using evidence of Cuban small arms shipments passing through Nicaragua to Salvadoran revolutionaries, the White House hyperbolically warned that the Sandinistas harbored aspirations of regional dominance and, with Havana's logistical and military support, posed a serious conventional military threat to the rest of Central America. With a barrage of press releases, white papers, reports, books, booklets, pamphlets, presentations, and interviews over the course of the decade, the administration pounded home the message that revolutionary Nicaragua had created a military far in excess of its needs and was dedicated to what Secretary of State Shultz described as a "revolution without frontiers."[43] Second, whether describing skirmishes between Contras and Sandinista draftees on the Honduran border or the possibility of a Soviet delivery of MIG fighter jets, the administration utilized the tactic of inversion: Sandinista militarism was the problem—not the marauding army of counterrevolutionaries and the constant threat of a US invasion. This approach was taken to the (il)logical extreme by Jeane Kirkpatrick, who argued that even the CIA's mining of Nicaraguan harbors was an act of self-defense, since "Nicaragua is engaged in a continuing, determined, armed attack against its neighbors."[44]

Third, the Reagan administration used the language of human rights, especially relating to democracy promotion, to criticize the Sandinistas for denying political rights and civil liberties. Eliding the FLSN's social and economic achievements, the administration consistently focused on freedom of the press in Nicaragua, particularly Sandinista censorship of *La Prensa*. The Reagan team accused the Sandinistas of illegally detaining perceived subversives, compared Nicaraguan political prisoners to captives in Soviet gulags, and asserted that the FSLN was cracking down on democratic labor federations and the Catholic Church.[45] Moreover, far from encouraging participatory democracy, Nicaraguan mass organizations were mechanisms, in the words of Abrams, to "monitor the populace, seek out dissidents and coerce people into participating in Sandinista-inspired activities."[46] In sum, Sandinista Nicaragua, Reagan asserted, was a "totalitarian dungeon."[47]

Correspondingly, the administration repeatedly argued that the Sandinistas had failed to keep a 1979 promise to the Organization of American States to hold democratic elections. According to this logic, the US was not the aggressor, but a supporter of ordinary Nicaraguans, whose hope of a democratic future had been subverted. "We ask of the Sandinistas only that they do what they have publicly committed themselves to do—and what their increasingly fearful neighbors are asking of them," asserted Assistant Secretary of State for Inter-American Affairs Langhorne Motley in April 1983.[48] Three weeks later,

Reagan articulated his request for congressional funding for the Contras in the language of human rights. "The Sandinista revolution in Nicaragua turned out to be just an exchange of one set of autocratic rulers for another," Reagan asserted, "and the people still have no freedom, no democratic rights, and more poverty."[49]

When the FSLN announced national elections would be held in November 1984, the Reagan administration responded by denouncing the vote as a fraud. Four months before the ballots were cast, the president dismissed the election as a "Soviet-style sham."[50] After the US-backed opposition candidate withdrew from the race, the State Department released an unusual report that dismissed the elections out of hand. "For many Nicaraguans, the Sandinista elections on November 4 will offer no choice at all. The promise of free elections the Sandinistas made to the Nicaraguan people and to the world before they seized power will remain unfulfilled."[51] The election itself—heavily scrutinized by more than 600 journalists and 400 international electoral observers—was chaotic but generally considered as free and fair as neighboring El Salvador's election two years earlier, which the US had heartily endorsed.[52] The White House, however, was unmoved. "I have just one thing to say," Reagan told reporters. "It's a phony."[53]

Reagan's rejection of the 1984 Nicaraguan election revealed the Manichean approach to the Cold War that undergirded the administration's democracy promotion initiative. Eschewing the complexities of the Nicaragua political landscape in favor of a stark vision of Central America as a battleground in the East-West confrontation, top US policymakers portrayed the Sandinistas as brutal Soviet satraps, committed to establishing totalitarianism at home and supporting like-minded revolutionaries abroad. As such, the Sandinistas could not, by definition, be democratic; nor could the FSLN be trusted to fulfill its side of any negotiation with the United States or the international community. "The Sandinistas are communists, therefore, such agreements are lies," Abrams bluntly asserted. "It is preposterous" he added, "to think we can sign a deal with the Sandinistas to meet our foreign policy concerns and expect it to be kept."[54] Despite repeated assurances that the United States was committed to successive rounds of high-level talks with Nicaragua as well as support for regional diplomatic initiatives, in private the Reagan administration viewed such initiatives as purely instrumental—a necessary sop to Congress in the effort to convince congressional moderates to support Contra funding. "If we are just talking about negotiations with Nicaragua, that is so far-fetched to imagine that a communist government like that would make any reasonable deal with us," Reagan told the National Security Planning Group in June 1984, "but if it is to get Congress to support the anti-Sandinistas, then that can be helpful."⁵⁵

The Reagan administration's democracy promotion initiative reached its apogee in early 1986. Secretary of State Shultz played a particularly important role in fusing the Reagan doctrine's vision of rolling back communist gains in the developing world with the liberal internationalist appeal of the democracy promotion initiative, aligning the United States rhetorically behind democratization processes in Latin America.⁵⁶ More concretely, in February 1986 in response to widespread popular unrest in Haiti, the Reagan administration withdrew US support for the brutal president Jean-Claude Duvalier, who subsequently fled to France. A few weeks later, as unrest in the Philippines intensified following fraudulent elections, the White House prevailed on autocratic president Ferdinand E. Marcos to step down.⁵⁷ The following month, Reagan embraced the "democratic revolution" in a defining address to a joint session of Congress. Lauding the wave of democratization that was sweeping Latin America, Reagan asserted that "the American people believe in human rights and oppose tyranny in whatever form, whether of the left or the right."⁵⁸

The Reagan administration's actions in Haiti and the Philippines, combined with the president's lofty rhetoric, signaled a shift away from administration's rejection of human rights at the outset of the decade. Reagan had undertaken a "turnaround on human rights," an influential article in *Foreign Affairs* asserted, "a 150- if not a 180-degree change."⁵⁹ Even stalwart critics of the administration were impressed. "American policy in this instance expressed what we want to believe are the deepest American values," wrote *New York Times* columnist Anthony Lewis following Marcos's departure. "We used our influence on the side of democracy. We made no excuses for dictators. And our means were peaceful: not weapons or covert military intervention but the words of politics and diplomacy."⁶⁰

The administration's melding of the Reagan doctrine's call to roll back communism with a more general emphasis on supporting democracy also won bipartisan support on Capitol Hill. Underscoring bipartisan support for the president's democracy initiative, by early 1986 Congress had continued to allocate funding for the National Endowment for Democracy, augmented US support for anti-Soviet fighters in Afghanistan, repealed the Clark Amendment prohibiting covert operations in Angola, legislated military assistance to noncommunist resistance in Cambodia, and approved nonlethal aid to the Contras.⁶¹ By 1986, in other words, the administration's emphasis on democracy promotion, as the core of its human rights policy, had made significant steps toward recreating the bipartisan Cold War consensus between the executive and legislative branches that had foundered in the late 1960s on the shoals of the Vietnam War.

Yet even as the Reagan administration was fashioning a new Cold War consensus, the administration failed to convince a majority of the American people of the imperative of the US intervention in Central America. Throughout the 1980s, a slim majority of the public had opposed US aid to the Contras; by the spring of 1988 a *Washington Post*–ABC News poll found that a majority of Americans opposed Contra aid by a margin of 55 to 40 percent.[62] Public opposition was fueled by a robust movement opposed to the Reagan administration's intervention. With the painful memory of the American defeat in the Vietnam War still fresh, US activists feared that Reagan's repeated condemnations of the Sandinistas, support for the Contras, and the extensive US military maneuvers in the region would lead to US soldiers fighting and dying on Nicaraguan soil. Correspondingly, as the Contra war intensified, the widespread abuses of the Contras against civilian targets elicited a rising chorus of criticism from US-based human rights organizations, churches, and Latin America–focused solidarity groups. By mid-decade, grassroots organizations such as Witness for Peace, formed in October 1983 as a vehicle for faith-based peace activism focused on Central America, had established a powerful voice in debate over US policy toward the region.[63] Hundreds of Americans were living and working in Nicaragua in capacities that ranged from university teaching to reporting Contra atrocities, and as many as 100,000 US "brigadistas" visited Nicaragua on short-term trips over the course of the 1980s to witness the achievements of the revolution first hand and engage in solidarity activities such as harvesting coffee.[64]

More importantly, the interventionism at the heart of the democracy promotion initiative nearly destroyed the Reagan presidency. Beginning in late 1986, investigations of the Iran-Contra scandal revealed that the White House had solicited funding from wealthy American conservatives and friendly foreign governments to support the Contras.[65] The administration had also violated US law by secretly shipping arms to Iran in exchange for promises that hostages held by Iranian terrorists in Lebanon would be released. Worse, National Security Council (NSC) staffer Oliver North, charged by President Reagan to "do whatever you have to do" to keep the Contras "body and soul together," had illegally diverted profits from the arms-for-hostages scheme to the Contras—a "Contra-bution" as North jocularly put it.[66]

Although Reagan avoided impeachment, the scandal significantly weakened the president, consuming his attention throughout 1987 and hamstringing executive oversight of US foreign policy.[67] The scandal also created an opening for congressional activism in US policy toward Central America; despite opposition from administration hard-liners, Speaker of the House Jim Wright (D-TX) managed to convince the White House to sign onto a peace plan for Central America. In turn, the Wright-Reagan plan, as it came to be called, accelerated ongoing Central American diplomatic efforts, led by Costa Rican president Oscar Arias. With the successful signing of the Esquipulas accord on August 7, 1987, the five Central American nations pledged themselves to "democratic pluralism, free elections, and a concerted effort to end internal fighting by seeking a cease-fire with its armed opponents, instituting an amnesty for them, and initiating a process of political reconciliation and dialogue."[68] Despite the Reagan administration's continued efforts to drum up congressional support for Contra funding, Washington's war on Nicaragua was increasingly supplanted by a regional effort to reach a negotiated solution.

Amid the spectacle and speculation surrounding the congressional hearings on Iran-Contra, the relationship between the illegalities at the heart of the scandal and the Reagan administration's democracy promotion initiative were largely obscured. Yet from the outset, Reagan's intervention in Central America was undertaken in the spirit of a human rights policy that defined communism as the ultimate violation and justified US efforts to orchestrate a regime change—to force the FSLN, in other words, "to say 'Uncle,'" as Reagan brashly told reporters.[69] Indeed, it was no coincidence that Oliver North referred to his expansive web of black operations in Central America, including offshore bank accounts, dummy corporations, hired ships and airplanes, and communications infrastructure, as "Project Democracy."[70] Embedded in the Reagan administration's democracy promotion initiative, in other words, were deeply *undemocratic* practices that misled the American people, violated US law, and fueled the conflicts in Central America.

The Reagan administration's promise to oust the Sandinistas was ultimately fulfilled by the George H. W. Bush administration. In the dry, dusty heat of late-February 1990, the Nicaraguan people decisively rejected incumbent president Daniel Ortega and the FSLN in favor of US-supported opposition candidate Violeta Chamorro. The election results shocked Sandinistas and Chamorro supporters alike. In the immediate aftermath, wrote journalist Alma Guillermoprieto, the nation "came to a complete halt while the stunned people of Nicaragua contemplated the magnitude of what they had done, and tried to imagine the unimaginable consequences of their act."[71] To be sure, Nicaraguan voters bore the ultimate responsibility for Chamorro's victory. Yet the extent of American involvement in supporting the Contras, pressuring the

Nicaraguan economy, and shepherding the fragile opposition coalition underscored the power and potential of the democracy promotion initiative in advancing US political goals.

Indeed, despite the Iran-Contra scandal, the Reagan administration's "low-intensity" war dealt the Sandinista revolution a mortal blow, as it immiserated Nicaraguans in a conflict that claimed more than 30,000 lives and an economic cost as high as $2.5 billion.[72] The US-backed Contra war also played into the hands of Sandinista hard-liners. Both fearing a US invasion and using the crisis as an opportunity to expand their own political power, the Sandinistas alienated many erstwhile supporters by curtailing opportunities for expression, harassing the political opposition, and cracking down on the private sector. By 1986, the state held roughly 7,000 political prisoners accused of collaboration with the Contras.[73]

At the same time, the Contra war diverted scarce resources and placed enormous burden on the Nicaraguan people. In the face of US economic pressure, the FSLN quickly became dependent on the Soviet bloc for food aid, imports, and oil. By 1984, approximately half of the national budget was going to defense, making the Sandinistas' social reform promises impossible to maintain, and, combined with poor government economic planning, contributing to widespread shortages of basic staples such as beans and rice. The situation was "hellish," President Daniel Ortega lamented in 1985: "of every 100 trousers and shirts produced, 40 are military uniforms; of every 100 pounds of corn consumed, 30 go to the warfronts."[74] In an attempt to alleviate the financial pressure created by defense spending and facing decreased Soviet support in the latter half of the decade, Sandinista policymakers increased the amount of paper money in circulation. By 1988, inflation had topped 36,000 percent and the cost of basic commodities had risen 600 percent—leaving most wage earners increasingly unable to afford basic goods and services.[75] That, combined with widespread opposition to the nationwide military draft, had Nicaraguans yearning for peace, stability, and economic opportunity by the end of the decade.[76] As Sergio Ramírez recalled in a recent memoir, "The war itself would prove to be the great electoral adversary, and we could not defeat it with its absences, its separations, its misery, its death, and the inability to imagine its end for people who suffered under its fatal weight."[77]

Moreover, in the months leading up to the 1990 Nicaraguan election, the United States played a central role in convincing fourteen diverse opposition parties to join the Unión Nacional Opositora (UNO, the National Opposition Union) coalition led by Chamorro. The White House also convinced congressional lawmakers to pass a special allocation of more than $7 million to "level the playing field" of the Nicaraguan election, in the words of Secretary of State

James Baker.[78] Channeled through the National Endowment for Democracy, the funds included civic and voter education programs and "training and the provision of infrastructure (including office supplies, equipment and vehicles), as well as to support voter registration, verification, and election monitoring activities intended to instill confidence in the electoral process."[79] Combined with covert US spending, estimates of the total amount of US funds channeled to the opposition range as high as $30 million, or $20 per voter in Nicaragua—five times as much per voter as George Bush spent in the 1988 US presidential campaign.[80] Simultaneously, in April 1989 Congress approved an aid package of nearly $49.7 million for the Contras, who increased both military actions and propaganda in favor of the opposition in the months leading up to the election.[81]

Correspondingly, the Bush administration's maintenance of economic pressure on Nicaragua in the lead-up to the election served as an unmistakable reminder to Nicaraguan voters of American pressure on the incumbent regime. "If they want 30,000% inflation, they can do that," warned a senior Bush administration official shortly before election day. "If I were sitting down there in their shoes," the official continued, "I'd want those economic sanctions off; I wouldn't want them tightened. And there are some things that we can do to tighten them."[82] Secretary of State Baker was equally candid. "We have the Sandinistas in an economic chokehold," he told members of Congress in September 1989.[83] Indeed, following Chamorro's victory, the Bush administration quickly lifted the five-year-old trade embargo, announced that the US would send $21 million in food and humanitarian aid to Nicaragua, and submitted a request to the Congress for $300 million in emergency funds for the Central American nation.[84]

The FSLN's defeat in the February 1990 election was viewed by many in Washington as a fitting coda to the dramatic and largely peaceful end of the Cold War in late 1989. In the heady months following the fall of the Iron Curtain, Ronald Reagan's 1982 declaration at Westminster that "day by day democracy is proving itself to be a not-at-all-fragile flower" appeared prescient, even prophetic. Moreover by the late 1980s, it was evident that the Reagan administration's embrace of democracy promotion had led to a greater institutionalization of human rights—albeit narrowly defined—in US foreign policy.[85] As the executive director of Human Rights Watch Aryeh Neier admitted in 1987, "The administration today solidly accepts the principle that it is the responsibility of the United States to promote human rights worldwide. That was not the view in 1981."[86] This development was not limited to the White House; the evidentiary record indicates that by the end of the decade human rights promotion had become increasingly accepted as a legitimate US foreign policy goal among the many players shaping foreign policy in the Washington beltway and in US diplomatic posts overseas. Yet as US policy toward Nicaragua made clear, the emphasis on democracy promotion also served to legitimate a distinctive form of interventionism. Pursued through civil society or "low-intensity" military interventions and rooted in the neoliberal imperatives of US-led globalization, democracy promotion in the Reagan era would have major implications for post–Cold War US foreign policy.

Notes

1. Kirkpatrick, Speech before the Conservative Political Action Conference, 21 Mar. 1981, Washington, DC, Hoover Institution Archives (HIA), Richard V. Allen Papers (RVAP), box 27, folder "White House Files—Kirkpatrick, Amb. Jeane, 1981."

2. Although an enormous volume of scholarship on US-Central American relations was produced during the 1980s, relatively few archive-based studies were published thereafter. Early but still insightful studies include Cynthia J. Arnson, *Crossroads: Congress, the President, and Central America, 1976–1993* (University Park: Pennsylvania State University Press, 1993); Walter LaFeber, *Inevitable Revolutions: The United States in Central America* (New York: W. W. Norton, 1993); Robert Kagan, *A Twilight Struggle: American Power in Nicaragua, 1977–1990* (New York: Free Press, 1996); William M. LeoGrande, *Our Own Backyard: The United States in Central America, 1977–1992* (Chapel Hill: University of North Carolina Press, 1998); Robert A. Pastor, *Not Condemned to Repetition: The United States and Nicaragua* (Boulder, CO: Westview Press, 2002). Later studies include Greg Grandin, *Empire's Workshop: Latin America and the Roots of US Imperialism* (New York: Metropolitan Books, 2005); Stephen G. Rabe, *The Killing Zone: The United States Wages Cold War in Latin America* (New York: Oxford University Press, 2011); Malcolm Byrne, *Iran-Contra: Reagan's Scandal and the Unchecked Abuse of Presidential Power* (Lawrence: University Press of Kansas, 2014).

3. For scholarship on Reagan's approach to human rights, see Sarah B. Snyder's chapter in this volume. Reagan's democracy promotion initiative remains underexplored in the existing academic literature. For a pair of early but still insightful studies, see Thomas Carothers, *In the Name of Democracy: US Policy toward Latin America in the Reagan Years* (Berkeley: University of California Press, 1991); Tony Smith, *America's Mission: The United States and the Worldwide Struggle for Democracy in the Twentieth Century* (Princeton, NJ: Princeton University Press, 2012). Twenty-first-century studies include Hal Brands, *Making the Unipolar Moment: US Foreign Policy and the Rise of the Post–Cold War Order* (Ithaca: Cornell University Press, 2016); Gregory F. Domber, *Empowering Revolution: America, Poland, and the End of the Cold War* (Chapel Hill: University of North Carolina Press, 2014); Nicolas Guilhot, *The Democracy Makers: Human Rights and the Politics of Global Order* (New York: Columbia University Press, 2012); Robert Pee, *Democracy Promotion, National Security and Strategy: Foreign Policy under the Reagan Administration* (New York: Routledge, 2015); Robert Pee and William Michael Schmidli, eds., *The Reagan Administration, the Cold War, and the Transition to Democracy Promotion* (Cham: Palgrave Macmillan, 2019).

4. On this point see William Michael Schmidli, *The Fate of Freedom Elsewhere: Human Rights and US Cold War Policy toward Argentina* (Ithaca, NY: Cornell University Press, 2013), 182–183.

5. Harry W. Shlaudeman Interview, 24 May 1993, Association for Diplomatic Studies and Training (ADST), http://adst.org/oral-history/oral-history-interviews.

6. NSC meeting minutes, 11 Feb. 1981, Ronald Reagan Presidential Library (RRPL), Executive Secretariat–NSC (ESNSC), Meeting Files (MF), box 1, folder "NSC 00002."

7. The term "Reagan doctrine" was originally coined by neoconservative columnist Charles Krauthammer. See Krauthammer, "The Reagan Doctrine," *Time*, 1 Apr. 1985,. For a useful overview, see Dustin Walcher, "The Reagan Doctrine," in *A Companion to Ronald Reagan*, ed. Andrew L. Johns (Hoboken, NJ: John Wiley and Sons, 2015), 339–358.

8. William J. Casey, Address to the Society for Historians of American Foreign Relations, 25 June 1986, Hoover Institution Library & Archives (HIA), William J. Casey Papers (WJCP), box 312, folder "1986 June 25."

9. "Presidential Finding on Covert Operations in Central America," 9 Mar. 1981, Digital National Security Archive (DNSA), doc. NI01287. On Argentine support for the Contras, see Ariel C. Armony, *Argentina, the United States, and the Anti-Communist Crusade in Central America, 1977–1984* (Athens: Ohio University Center for International Studies, 1997).

10. LeoGrande, *Our Own Backyard*, 118. See also, Duane R. Clarridge with Digby Diehl, *A Spy for All Seasons: My Life in the CIA* (New York: Scribner, 1997), 197; Edgar Chamorro and Jefferson Morley, "Confessions of a 'Contra,'" *New Republic*, 5 Aug. 1985.

11. LaFeber, *Inevitable Revolutions*, 296, 302.

12. On this point, see Sarah B. Snyder's chapter in this volume.

13. "Nomination of Elliott Abrams to be an Assistant Secretary of State," October 30, 1981, *Public Papers of the Presidents of the United States: Ronald Reagan (PPP: RR), 1981* (Washington, DC: US Government Printing Office, 1982), 1004.

14. On Jackson and human rights, see Barbara J. Keys, *Reclaiming American Virtue: The Human Rights Revolution of the 1970s* (Cambridge, MA: Harvard University Press, 2014), 103–26.

15. Don Oberdorfer, "Panel Approves Abrams, Sees 'Commitment' to Human Rights," *Washington Post*, 18 Nov. 1981.

16. Judith Miller, "A Neoconservative for Human Rights Post," *New York Times*, 31 Oct. 1981.

17. Joseph Shattan, "Economic 'Rights' Under Communism," HIA, Joseph Shattan Papers (JSP), box 2.

18. See Vita Bite, "Human Rights in US Foreign Relations: Six Key Questions in the Continuing Policy Debate" 10 Dec. 1981, HIA, Latin American Strategic Studies Institute Records (LASSIR), box 11; quoted in Charles Maechling Jr., "Human Rights Dehumanized," *Foreign Policy* 52 (1983): 124.

19. Jeane J. Kirkpatrick, Speech before the Conservative Political Action Conference.

20. Elliott Abrams, Address to the Education and Research Institute, 2 Aug. 1983, HIA, JSP, box 14. On the legacy of the Vietnam War for the Reagan administration, see Mark Atwood Lawrence's chapter in this volume.

21. Reagan, Address to Members of the British Parliament, 8 June 1982, http://millercenter.org/president/reagan/speeches/speech-3408.

22. National Security Decision Directive 77, "Management of Public Diplomacy Relative to National Security," 14 Jan. 1983, DNSA, doc. IC00088.

23. Carothers, *In the Name of Democracy*, 203–205.

24. Department of State Bureau of Public Affairs, "1983 Human Rights Report," *Country Reports on Human Rights Practices for 1983* (Washington, DC: US Government Printing Office, February 1984).

25. Abrams to Sussman, 28 Apr. 1983, Princeton University Archives, Freedom House Records, box 37, folder 8.

26. DOS, "1983 Human Rights Report." See also Jeane J. Kirkpatrick, "Dictatorships and Double Standards," *Commentary* 68, no. 5 (1979): 38.

27. DOS, "1983 Human Rights Report."

28. Despite a rapidly rising GNP, in the 1970s Nicaragua was characterized by extreme income inequality and a growing number of landless peasants. A mere 5 percent of Nicaraguan income earners garnered 30 percent of national income and controlled 85 percent of the nation's farmland. Dennis Gilbert, *Sandinistas: The Party and the Revolution* (New York: Wiley-Blackwell, 1991), 3.

29. LaFeber, *Inevitable Revolutions*, 238.

30. Thomas W. Walker, *Nicaragua: The Land of Sandino* (Boulder, CO: Westview Press, 1981), 78.

31. Xabier Gorostiaga, "Some Aspects of Nicaragua's Economy," *Envío*, no. 5 (October 1981), https://www.envio.org.ni/articulo/3117.

32. FSLN Fact Sheet, "Five Years of Transformations in Education, Health and Housing" 1984, HIA, Nicaragua Subject Collection, box 2, folder "General Subject Area: 1984."

33. Gorostiaga, "Some Aspects of Nicaragua's Economy."

34. On Cuban medical assistance, see K. Cheasty Anderson, "Doctors within Borders: Cuban Medical Diplomacy to Sandinista Nicaragua, 1979–1990," in *Beyond the Eagle's Shadow: New Histories of Latin America's Cold War*, ed. Virginia Garrard-Burnett, Mark Atwood Lawrence, and Julio E. Moreno (Albuquerque: University of New Mexico Press, 2013), 200–225.

35. Harry Nelson, "Sandinistas Revolutionize Health Care in Nicaragua," *Los Angeles Times*, 25 Aug. 1983, C1.

36. "Nicaragua: Three Years of Achievements" *Envío*, no. 13 (July 1982), https://www.envio.org.ni/articulo/3368.

37. CIA, "Nicaragua: Slow Rebuilding of a Shattered Economy," Jan. 1981, DNSA, doc. NI01246.

38. Haig, "Assessment of Nicaraguan Situation," 30 July 1981, DNSA, doc. NI01364.

39. Gorostiaga, "Some Aspects of Nicaragua's Economy."

40. "Nicaragua: Three Years of Achievements." See also Dennis Gilbert, *Sandinistas: The Party and the Revolution* (New York: Wiley-Blackwell, 1991), 64–65; Luis Hector Serra, "The Grass-Roots Organizations," in *Revolution and Counterrevolution in Nicaragua*, ed. Thomas W. Walker (Boulder, CO: Westview Press, 1991), 49–75.

41. Sergio Ramírez, address to the Conference on Central America, sponsored by the Sandinista Association of Cultural Workers; reprinted as Ramírez, "The Unfinished Revolution and Nicaragua Today," *Contemporary Marxism* 8 (1984): 215.

42. Italics added. "Sandinismo no es democratismo," *Barricada*, 14 Mar. 1980, in *Sandinistas: Key Documents*, ed. Dennis Gilbert and David Block (Ithaca, NY: Cornell University Latin American Studies Program, 1990), 112–113.

43. Between October 1983 and November 1984, for example, the State Department's Office of Public Diplomacy for Latin America and the Caribbean (S/LPD), under the direction of the intensely anticommunist Otto J. Reich, booked 1,570 speaking engagements and radio, television, and editorial board interviews on Central America. Correspondingly, the Central America Outreach Program, run out of the White House by Assistant to the President for Public Liaison Faith Whittlesey, offered up to five briefings a day to special interest groups visiting Washington, ranging from the "Turkey Farmers of America, the National Florists . . . [to] the National Cattlemen's Association." Reich to Egan, "Organization of Office of Public Diplomacy for Latin America and the Caribbean," 8 Feb. 1985, DNSA, doc. IC00814; Faith Ryan Whittlesey Interview, 7 Dec. 1988, ADST; Shultz quoted in Joanne Omang, "Shultz Accused of Misquoting Sandinista Policy," *Washington Post*, 4 Oct. 1983.

44. Jeane J. Kirkpatrick, "What We're Doing in Nicaragua: A Matter of Self-Defense," *Washington Post*, 15 Apr. 1984.

45. On the gulag comparison, see Juan Williams, "White House Pitches Latin Policy to Public," *Washington Post*, 24 Sept. 1983.

46. Abrams, "Human Dimension: Human Rights in a Troubled Area," 4 Apr. 1984, HIA, JSP, box 7.

47. Philip Taubman, "New Effort to Aid Nicaragua Rebels," *New York Times*, 19 July 1984.

48. Langhorne Motley, "Diplomacy and Force Needed to Managua See Reason," *Los Angeles Times*, 8 Apr. 1983.

49. Reagan, Address before a Joint Session of Congress, 27 Apr. 1983.

50. Doyle McManus, "Reagan Sees Nicaraguan Vote as 'Soviet-Style Sham,' Urges Regional Leaders to Cooperate," *Los Angeles Times*, 20 July 1984.

51. DOS, "Resource Book: Sandinista Elections in Nicaragua," 1984, HIA, LASSIR, box 1, folder 15.

52. Dennis Volman, "Nicaragua Campaign Races to Chaotic Finish," *Christian Science Monitor*, 2 Nov. 1984.

53. Roy Guttman, "Nicaraguan Vote a Setback for US," *Newsday*, 5 Nov. 1984.

54. Wayne S. Smith, "Finding the Truth in US Policy on Nicaragua," *Los Angeles Times*, 25 Aug. 1985.

55. National Security Planning Group meeting minutes, 25 June 1984, DNSA, doc. IC00463.

56. On this point see George P. Shultz, *Turmoil and Triumph: Diplomacy, Power, and the Victory of the American Ideal* (New York: Scribner, 1995), 640. See also Shultz, "The Resurgence of Democracy in Latin America," 12 Nov. 1984, in DOS, *Current Policy*, 633; Shultz, "Nicaragua: Will Democracy Prevail?" 27 Feb. 1986, in DOS, *Current Policy*, 797.

57. Bernard Gwertzman, "Shultz Denounces Philippine Fraud: Statement Is Administration's Strongest on Election but also Opposes Aid Curb," *New York Times*, 20 Feb. 1986.

58. Reagan, "Freedom, Regional Security, and Global Peace," 14 Mar. 1986, *PPP:RR, 1986*, 386.

59. Tamar Jacoby, "The Reagan Turnaround on Human Rights," *Foreign Affairs* 64, no. 5 (1986): 1067.

60. Anthony Lewis, "Why We Celebrate," *New York Times*, 27 Feb. 1986.

61. Charles William Maynes, "Reagan and the American Resolve: A US Policy for Intervention Everywhere," *Los Angeles Times*, 9 Feb. 1986.

62. Lou Cannon and Tom Kenworthy, "Reagan Again Vows Support for Contras: Most in US Oppose New Aid, Poll Shows," *Washington Post*, 23 Mar. 1988.

63. Witness for Peace, "Annual Report 1987: Retrospective, 1983–1988," Swarthmore College Peace Collection, Witness for Peace Records, box 1, folder "Annual Report, 1987."

64. Roger Peace, *A Call to Conscience: The Anti-Contra War Campaign* (Amherst: University of Massachusetts Press, 2012), 3. On US solidarity activism and Nicaragua, see also Van Gosse, "'The North American Front': Central American Solidarity in the Reagan Era," in *Reshaping the US Left: Popular Struggles in the 1980s*, ed. Mike Davis and Michael Sprinkler (London: Verso, 1988), 11–50; Héctor Perla Jr, "Heirs of Sandino: The Nicaraguan Revolution and the US-Nicaragua Solidarity," *Latin American Perspectives* 36, no. 6 (2009): 80–100; Christian Smith, *Resisting Reagan: The US Central America Peace Movement* (Chicago: University of Chicago Press, 1996).

65. On the role of US right-wing activism in Central America see Byrne, *Iran-Contra*; Kyle Burke, *Revolutionaries for the Right: Anticommunist Internationalism and Paramilitary Warfare in the Cold War* (Chapel Hill: University of North Carolina Press, 2018), 118–196.

66. Quoted in Michael Schaller, "Reagan and Foreign Policy," in *Deconstructing Reagan: Conservative Mythology and America's Fortieth President* (New York: Routledge, 2007), 27, 29.

67. In particular, as former NSC staffer Jack Matlock writes, the Iran-Contra scandal arrested developments in US-Soviet Relations, "delay[ing] decisions that could have produced treaties on strategic and conventional arms in 1988" (Jack Matlock, *Reagan and Gorbachev: How the Cold War Ended* [New York: Random House, 2004], 321).

68. LeoGrande, *Our Own Backyard*, 515.

69. Reagan, News Conference, February 21, 1985, *PPP: RR, 1985*, 209.

70. Joel Brinkley, "Iran Sales Linked to Wide Program of Covert Policies," *New York Times*, 15 Feb. 1987.

71. Alma Guillermoprieto, *The Heart That Bleeds: Latin America Now* (New York: Vintage, 1995), 23.

72. Robert A. Pastor, *Not Condemned to Repetition: The United States and Nicaragua* (Boulder, CO: Westview Press, 2002), 214.

73. D'Amato to Byrd, "Report on Trip to Central American Countries, July 5–16, 1986," 5 Aug. 1986, DNSA, doc. NI02858.

74. Tony Jenkins, "Impoverished Nicaragua Blames Reagan," *Guardian*, 11 Feb. 1985; Larry Rohter, "Nicaragua Says Its Fiscal Shape Is 'Hellish,'" *New York Times*, 10 Feb. 1985.

75. Harry E. Vanden, "Democracy Derailed: The 1990 Elections and After," in *The Undermining of the Sandinista Revolution*, ed. Gary Prevost & Harry E. Vanden, (New York: St. Martin's Press), 53.

76. See Stephen Kinzer, "Military Draft in Nicaragua Is Meeting Wide Resistance" *New York Times*, 26 June 1984; Walker, *Nicaragua*, 84; Katherine Hoyt, *The Many Faces of Sandinista Democracy* (Athens: Ohio University Press, 1997), 111; Lynn Horton,

Peasants in Arms: War & Peace in the Mountains of Nicaragua, 1979–1994 (Athens: Ohio University Press, 1999), 201.

77. Sergio Ramírez, *Adiós Muchachos: A Memoir of the Sandinista Revolution* (Durham, NC: Duke University Press, 2011), 192.

78. Baker, quoted in "Updated Alert: Aid to the Nicaraguan Opposition," 17 Oct. 1989, DNSA, doc. NI03201.

79. NED, 1990 Annual Report, http://www.ned.org/wp-content/uploads/annualreports/1990-ned-annual-report.pdf.

80. William I. Robinson, *A Faustian Bargain: US Intervention in the Nicaraguan Elections and American Foreign Policy in the Post-Cold War Era* (Boulder, CO: Westview Press, 1992), 62. See also, LeoGrande, *Our Own Backyard*, 561.

81. Robert Pear, "Congress Votes $49.7 Million in Aid for Contras," *New York Times*, 14 Apr. 1989; Lee Hockstader, "In Rural Nicaragua, War Dominates Politics," *Washington Post*, 12 Nov. 1989.

82. Norman Kempster, "Way Is Open for Nicaragua to Normalize US Ties, Baker Says," *Los Angeles Times*, 2 Feb. 1990.

83. "Congressional Meetings on Central America: Draft Talking Points," 11 Sept. 1989, Princeton University Archives, Seeley G. Mudd Manuscript Library, James A. Baker III Papers, box 108, folder 9.

84. Congressional Research Service, "Nicaraguan Elections and Transition: Issues for US Policy," 26 Mar. 1990, DNSA, doc. NI03233.

85. The shift in US policy toward Chilean dictator Augusto Pinochet is an important case in point. See Evan McCormick's chapter in this volume.

86. Neil Lewis, "'Quiet Diplomacy' in a Loud Voice" *New York Times*, 12 May 1987.

CHAPTER 12

Reagan and Pinochet's Chile
The Diplomacy of Disillusion

Evan D. McCormick

Fernando Zegers had come to the US ambassador's residence in Santiago with what he described an "urgent matter." It was the evening of December 2, 1982, and Zegers—formerly the Chilean ambassador to Brazil, now director general of the Chilean foreign ministry—joined US ambassador James Theberge in the residence's lush garden. The atmosphere was ethereal—"the sweet sound of the waterfall behind us, the green grass, flowers, and twilight-hushed scene before us," Theberge wrote in his personal notes later that night—but Zegers's visit was due to a more intrusive reality. Chilean officials, including General Augusto Pinochet, who had ruled as a military dictator since a violent 1973 coup, were "deeply disturbed" by recent statements in which President Ronald Reagan and Secretary of State George Shultz had spoken of the US desire to spread democracy and defend human rights. Of course, Zegers insisted, Chile's military regime shared these values and applauded Reagan's commitment to them. But concerns were growing that Reagan's idealistic turn might lead the United States to "put pressure on countries where political democracy was absent." Zegers put the matter to Theberge point blank: "What we want to know is whether there has been a change in US policy," he stated. "Is the Reagan administration returning to the old Carter policy of human rights pressures and discriminatory treatment of Chile?"[1]

Theberge assured Zegers that this was not the case. The intensity of media coverage ahead of the president's trip through Latin America had mistakenly given the impression of a policy in flux, he suggested. The administration had made clear throughout its first two years that while it supported democracy, it remained "just as deeply committed to the principle of nonintervention." Committed to strengthening relations with anticommunist allies, Reagan would not single out Chile for criticism, Theberge promised. In his official cable to Washington, he wrote that the incident "graphically illustrates the extreme touchiness of President Pinochet and his closest advisors," as they faced mounting economic trouble and political pressure to relinquish power. In his private notes, Theberge's assessment of the Chilean *démarche* was more sympathetic: "skillful diplomacy," he wrote in shorthand, "flagging early potential problem, intimately engaged and alert to dangers." Pinochet's "brilliant diplomatic team," he assessed, was "trying to head off any incipient shift in US policy."[2]

The garden meeting—and the Chilean government's fears of a shift in Reagan's foreign policy—is notable not just for its tone and substance but for its timing, less than two years into Reagan's first term. Upon coming to office in 1981, Reagan officials stated clearly the administration's desire to resume normal bilateral relations with the Pinochet regime, ostracized in the 1970s by liberal Democrats in Congress and the Carter administration for its abysmal human rights record and policies of state terror. Reagan officials considered Pinochet's Chile to be a darling of free market capitalism and a vital ally in the fight against revolutionary Marxism in the hemisphere. And yet, by the end of Reagan's second term, the United States returned to policies that alienated the military government, publicly criticizing its disregard for human rights, actively encouraging the political opposition to Pinochet, and lending instrumental support to the plebiscite that ended the dictatorship in October of 1988.

This about-face has been acknowledged by scholars—namely, Morris H. Morley and Chris McGillion in their exhaustive *Reagan and Pinochet*—who have begun to treat the evolution of Reagan's policies as a significant development worth studying.[3] However, that scholarship continues to reflect a narrow and static focus on Reagan's ideology and US politics. Needing political support for its more controversial Central America policies, the typical narrative goes, the Reagan administration eventually acceded to a limited transition to democracy in Chile, where vital US interests were not at stake.[4] For the most part, scholars of US foreign relations have yet to incorporate the Chilean case during the Reagan years into a burgeoning historiography on the inter-American Cold War focused on the complex international and transnational dynamics of that conflict.[5]

This chapter asks what documents from official Chilean archives can tell us about that story. Chilean records demonstrate that US policy toward Chile did evolve, in ways that reflected a dynamic relationship between the Reagan administration's ideology, its national security goals, and political realities in Chile and, more broadly, Latin America. The documents suggest that US-Chilean relations were, after 1983, defined foremost by disillusion: on the Chilean side, a palpable frustration with the Reagan administration's failure to overcome domestic political opposition to normalizing relations and, on the US side, a disillusion with Pinochet's failure to curtail the regime's blatant repression of political opponents and to oversee a prompt transition to civilian democracy.

Cables and memos from the Chilean foreign ministry archive illuminate Reagan's policies as they were perceived in Santiago and highlight several conclusions related to the administration's evolving grand strategy and to politics in Latin America.[6] First, while the Reagan administration initially pursued a policy guided by ideological anticommunism—a belief that relations with Chile should be defined by a shared interest in counterrevolutionary national security policies—that ideology proved more malleable, and dissipated more quickly, than previously thought. Second, political changes in Chile, and in Latin America more broadly, prompted Reagan officials to revisit their core assumptions about the relationship between supporting the Pinochet regime and the administration's goal of undermining the revolutionary Left. Finally, notwithstanding its early ideological posturing vis-à-vis the Carter administration, from the Chilean government's vantage point the Reagan administration did not abandon human rights as a component of US foreign policy. Instead, the impression of its policies in Chile suggests that the Reagan administration sought to alter the focus of human rights policies to emphasize electoral democratization as the key condition for those rights, in ways that are echoed by Michael Schmidli's and James Cameron's analyses in this volume regarding Reagan's approaches to Nicaragua and Brazil, respectively. The administration undertook this reframing, Chilean officials perceptively realized, because democracy promotion gave US foreign policy elites a way to reconcile the national security objective of defeating the Left in Latin America with a deeper political and ideological inclination to see free markets and free elections as the keys to preserving regional stability and US hegemony amidst global change. By 1988, the illusion that engaging with Pinochet offered a better path to those goals than did engaging with the moderate opposition had been exposed as just that—an illusion.

In 1981, there was no mistaking the Reagan administration's intentions. As they prepared to take office, Reagan officials signaled a desire to repair diplomatic relations with anticommunist military governments throughout Latin

America. Taking their cues from Jeane Kirkpatrick's influential *Commentary* essay, "Dictatorships and Double Standards," Reagan officials vowed not to make pariahs out of those regimes whose brutal campaigns against revolutionary Marxists in the 1960s and 1970s had made them the *bêtes noires* of newly emergent human rights nongovernmental organizations (NGOs) and advocates in the US Congress. Chile in particular had been central to the growing salience of a human rights politics in the 1970s. US complicity in the overthrow of Salvador Allende in 1973, the Nixon and Ford administrations' support for Pinochet's regime, and the assassination of former ambassador Orlando Letelier and an assistant, Ronni Moffitt, in a bloody car bomb attack in Washington in 1976 were key episodes in the congressional-executive struggle over the importance of values in US foreign policy that preceded Reagan's election.[7]

The decisive legislative stroke in this battle had been a 1976 amendment to the foreign aid bill, originally introduced by Senator Ted Kennedy (D-MA), which—building on earlier legislation that linked human rights to US security assistance and foreign aid—terminated commercial weapons sales, military training, and credits to Chile due to its status as a gross violator of human rights.[8] After 1977, the Carter administration embraced congressional momentum on human rights, further slicing economic aid to Chile and publicly castigating the regime for human rights violations and its failure to cooperate in the Letelier-Moffitt investigation.[9] Though the Carter administration struggled to wield US influence in ways that promoted meaningful change in Chile, it remained committed to applying human rights pressure as leverage against the right-wing regime.[10] Now in office, Reagan sought to discard human rights pressure in favor of returning to comity on the issue of anticommunism. This was more than just an issue of rhetoric: Reagan believed that downplaying human rights would help the United States bolster strategic allies against the destabilization wrought by public criticism. Across the globe, the administration must "change the attitude of our diplomatic corps so that we don't bring down governments in the name of human rights," Reagan told his National Security Council (NSC) during a February 6, 1981, meeting. "None of them are as guilty of human rights violations as are Cuba and the USSR. We don't throw out our friends just because they can't pass the 'saliva test' on human rights."[11]

Anticommunist regimes welcomed the new approach that soon manifested toward Chile, Argentina, and Brazil.[12] In a report on the incoming administration, the Chilean foreign minister speculated that Reagan's election would bring a "fundamental change" in US diplomacy with Latin America, one that would "create propitious conditions to establish close political and economic relations with the countries that have traditionally been its friends and allies—including Chile."[13] He further speculated that unlike the "moralistic and discriminatory" human rights policy of the Carter administration, Reagan would apply a "conservative and pragmatic" approach to human rights. These perceptions were reinforced by interactions among key officials. Not even a week after the inauguration, a Chilean diplomat reported that he had spoken with Jeane Kirkpatrick, soon to be appointed as the US ambassador to the United Nations, at a social event. In his report, he stated that Kirkpatrick "made clear her conviction that in the future, Chile would be treated in a different manner" by the Reagan administration, particularly on the issue of human rights.[14]

This discourse played out primarily at the level of intentions and signals. Both Reagan policymakers and Chilean officials knew that in order to deliver on this newfound good faith, the administration would have to reverse the punitive policies enacted against Chile in the years after the 1973 coup, particularly the "Enmienda Kennedy" (Kennedy amendment) as the embargo was colloquially known to Chilean policymakers. Unlike in Central America, where US military aid and training directly supported brutal counterinsurgency campaigns, in countries such as Chile, Argentina, and Brazil, military sales served largely symbolic purposes, reinforcing legitimacy and bolstering professional ties among elites with similar worldviews.[15] Beginning in the spring of 1981, when Reagan announced his intention to lift an arms embargo enacted against Argentina in 1976, the foreign ministry in Santiago watched intently, expecting that the Reagan administration would deliver a similar outcome for Chile.

The administration began by dialing back rhetorical criticism, adopting a human rights policy of "quiet diplomacy." Quiet diplomacy, articulated most coherently by Elliott Abrams after his appointment as assistant secretary of state for human rights in late 1981, was premised on the idea that by avoiding public criticism of allies over human rights, the administration could increase its leverage with friendly regimes and more effectively encourage better behavior. Chilean officials noticed this policy change, and references to quiet diplomacy—or, in a telling translation to Spanish, "silent diplomacy"—are common in the cable traffic during this time. They welcomed Reagan's apparent commitment not to intervene in Chile's internal political affairs. In June 1981, after meeting with Secretary of State Alexander Haig, Chilean ambassador José Miguel Barros cabled the ministry to remark on the "new and favorable disposition" of the Reagan administration toward the Pinochet regime.[16]

The Chilean government believed that quiet diplomacy empowered those US officials who interacted directly with the Pinochet regime, away from the oversight of critical legislators. As a result of this assessment, there was initially very little perception among Chilean diplomats or foreign ministry officials of divisions that would emerge within the Reagan administration over policy toward the Southern Cone or of the scale and persistence of congressional opposition to any sort of rapprochement with Chile. Chileans tended to view officials such as Jeane Kirkpatrick and Vernon Walters, Reagan's special envoy for Latin America who carried a deep rapport with Latin American military elites, as Reagan's key decision-makers on Latin America.

Along with Walters, the most important figure in this early human rights approach to Chile was Reagan's man in Santiago: US ambassador James Theberge, a political appointee with unassailable anticommunist credentials. When he arrived in Santiago in March 1982, Theberge's tone gelled with the Pinochet regime's view of communism as a civilizational threat. In one early speech to the chamber of commerce he outlined his belief that governments in the Western Hemisphere had come to a crucial decision point "as to whether we shall continue as before, defending the status quo and business as usual, and watch the map of Western freedom shrink further under the relentless onslaught of the Soviet Union and international communism, or whether the Western ruling and intellectual elites are capable of recognizing the danger, overcoming internal divisions and exercising the will to reverse the process."[17] The Chilean embassy lauded Reagan's appointment of Theberge, noting that his selection was "positive for Chile . . . as much for his personal convictions as for the political support . . . he has in [the Reagan] administration."[18]

The Chilean records of early meetings with US officials reveal how "quiet diplomacy" created the sense that ideological allies were driving bilateral relations toward a new moment. US officials typically began by voicing their approval for the Chilean regime's economic, political, and security policies. Human rights topics, if they were addressed at all, were accompanied by US assurances that Reagan did not wish to intervene in Chile's internal affairs. When US officials did press—such as when State Department official Sam Eaton told a Chilean official in March 1981 that permitting the return of political exiles and assisting the United States in the ongoing investigation into the 1976 assassination of Orlando Letelier in Washington, DC, would be constructive steps toward normalizing relations—they were promptly reminded by their interlocutors that "Chile was a sovereign state," governed by its own laws.[19]

Pinochet felt so confident in this argument that he expressed it to Reagan personally. In September 1981, Pinochet passed a letter to Reagan via Bill Wilson, a diplomat and close personal friend of Reagan's, so that the correspondence might "differ from the rigid ceremonial norms and exceed the limitations imposed on us by regular information channels." In the letter, the general appealed to what he perceived to be Reagan's sense of Chile's strategic importance in the fight against communism. "We know that. . . . the stability of the present Chilean political regime would form part of a desirable Latin American political scheme for your country. This is particularly important for us, as a nation, considering the international problems we proudly and bravely face, the importance of which we cannot possibly disregard."[20]

The first eighteen months of US-Chilean relations saw little deviation from the Reagan administration's—or Pinochet's—ideological map. Although the administration proved extremely hesitant to certify Chile and thus to overcome the Kennedy Amendments, a deep sense of shared anticommunism pervaded bilateral meetings, informing a feeling of confidence that an *aproximación*—a "rapprochement," as Chilean officials would often refer to it—was underway.

Between 1982 and 1985, the solidity of this ideological foundation proved illusory, as Reagan policymakers learned that quiet diplomacy, based solely on shared anticommunist values, was both politically costly and counterproductive to their goal of solidifying alliances with stable governments in the region. These policy adaptations in the Reagan administration were part of a larger policy shift engineered by mid-level bureaucrats responding to political changes in Chile and throughout the hemisphere after 1982 under the leadership of Reagan's second secretary of state, George Shultz. As the Pinochet regime weathered its first major political upheavals in the wake of the global debt crisis, Washington increased its pressure on human rights issues, particularly the regime's timetable for carrying out a transition to civilian rule. Although the Pinochet regime continued to view the Reagan administration as an ally, the records from these years demonstrate a growing sense of disillusion, as Chilean officials perceived Reagan's policies evolving toward a universal—if at this stage largely rhetorical—support for liberal democracy that would return the Chilean military regime to its pariah status.

It was events in Chile's neighbor, Argentina, that most dramatically altered the regional politics and began to reshape diplomatic relations with the United States. Throughout 1981, Chilean officials had watched keenly as the Reagan administration courted the military government in Buenos Aires, vowing to lift the legal sanction on military sales by granting a presidential certification acknowledging Argentina's improved human rights record. Chile, in the midst of a territorial dispute with Argentina over islands in the Beagle Channel, was deeply suspicious of its neighbor and protested to Reagan counterparts regarding the wisdom of this policy. When one of Pinochet's chief officials in the finance ministry told Vernon Walters in 1981 that military officials' visits to Argentina created the appearance of a "flagrant disequilibrium" in the region,

Walters assured his interlocutors that the administration was seeking a way to end the arms embargo on both countries simultaneously.[21]

But by the spring of 1982, Chilean officials noted that key Reagan officials such as Elliott Abrams and Assistant Secretary of State for Inter-American Affairs Tom Enders remained reluctant to commit to a similar certification for Chile so long as outstanding human rights issues remained. The most glaring of those were the status of Chilean political exiles and the regime's noncooperation with the United States in the ongoing Letelier assassination investigation. In several meetings in the spring of 1982, State Department officials told their Chilean counterparts that certifying Chile, unlike Argentina, would be too politically costly for Reagan. Deputy Secretary of State Walter Stoessel told the Chilean defense minister during a visit in March 1982 that the media and Congress shared a perception that Argentina was making good faith efforts to improve human rights. Chile would have to "do something that would help the administration to better [present] our case," Stoessel told the minister, according to a Chilean summary of the meeting.[22]

Just days after this meeting, on April 2, Argentine military forces launched a surprise invasion of the British-held Falkland Islands. Counting on American support and hoping to present the British with a fait accompli that would alter the terms of negotiations over the islands' colonial status, the Argentine regime instead found itself locked in a military contest that lasted for two months and ended in defeat. Coinciding with mounting public pressures to account for human rights crimes and metastasizing economic debt, the Falklands crisis led to the downfall of the Argentine military regime. This in turn had far-reaching consequences for the Reagan administration in Latin America. Argentina's belligerent action had made certification of that country's government impossible in the US Congress, and—even though the Chilean regime had supported Great Britain in the conflict—had further soured the prospects for certifying the Pinochet military regime. Pinochet's officials in the foreign ministry were outraged by this political effect of Argentina's misadventure. When Haig notified the Chilean foreign minister and ambassador that the Falklands Crisis would likely postpone any votes on certification, the ambassador angrily confronted Haig: "If the United States does not wish to collaborate militarily with us," he warned in a meeting, "we will stay within our borders and look to other markets, but the United States would pay the cost for this." Failing to normalize relations with Chile created a "power vacuum" in South America, he warned, and invited "Soviet penetration."[23]

For the Reagan administration, siding with its transatlantic ally over Argentina meant scuttling its earlier effort to cultivate ideologically driven special relationships with anticommunist regimes in the Americas. The congenial attitude toward military regimes' appeals to sovereignty would be an inevitable casualty of such a shift. In late 1982, the administration produced National Security Decision Directive 71, which outlined a strategy to shore up relations with South America in the wake of the crisis. While the Reagan administration would continue to pursue "a region free of Soviet-dominated or hostile governments," it would likewise seek "the development of stable and democratic political systems and institutions which promote respect for basic human rights." In this regard, NSDD-71 marked the first step away from "quiet diplomacy"—an acknowledgment that the administration could no longer treat human rights issues as separate from its political and security goals. Managing relations with Chile and Argentina was an explicit impetus for this strategic shift: while attempting to "restore and reassert US influence in South America," the document read, the administration would need to carefully preserve the existing political and military balance by "seeking certification for Argentina and Chile, as eligible for US military sales, jointly if possible." In order to do so, "the State Department will intensify efforts to resolve those issues that currently proscribe arms transfers" to both countries.[24]

The strategy outlined in NSDD-71 nonetheless pointed to an ongoing policy dilemma: How could the administration satisfy legislators who opposed arms sales to human rights violators without further jeopardizing its influence with military governments in the region? The administration answered that question by embarking on a policy that encouraged transitions to civilian rule through electoral democratization. Argentina served as a primary test case for this policy shift. Immediately following the election of Raúl Alfonsín as president of Argentina in October 1983, the Reagan administration announced that it would certify Argentina, paving the way for resumed arms sales. Reagan wrote personally to Pinochet in December to assuage his concerns about this decision, notifying him that the administration would continue to monitor Chile's human rights record and progress toward elections. Fearing damage to the relationship, Reagan sent General Vernon Walters to deliver the letter. Pinochet responded "more in sorrow than in anger," telling Walters that because of his belief that Reagan was "the best possible president in terms of US-Chilean relations," he would not "cause the US any problems" over the rebuke.[25] In a private conversation with the Chilean ambassador in January 1984, Elliott Abrams admitted that it would be impossible to certify Chile until an election had taken place.[26]

Chilean officials saw the decision to certify Argentina and not Chile as an abandonment of quiet diplomacy, as well as confirmation of their fears that a policy shift that would favor promoting democratic change throughout the hemisphere was underway. This was the urgent matter that brought Zegers to Theberge's garden on the evening of December 2, 1982. Despite Theberge's sanguine reaction, Pinochet's officials were right to be anxious. Beginning in 1983, the Reagan administration seized on democratic elections in places such as El Salvador, Brazil, and Guatemala to argue that human rights in those countries were improving. In a lengthy report on US grand strategy in the middle of 1983, the Chilean embassy noted that in response to congressional opposition, "democracy is again a primary objective in American foreign policy and . . . relationships with democratic governments were [now] preferential." Reagan would continue to be guided by counterrevolutionary impulses, but, in the Third World, the administration would "insist on the values of democracy as the only valid and alternative government to Marxist totalitarianism."[27]

Chilean diplomats and foreign ministry officials astutely understood that this new focus on promoting elections reflected increased control over South America policy by the State Department and coincided with the replacement of Al Haig by George Shultz. Though Shultz was concerned primarily with Atlantic diplomacy and US-Soviet relations, he saw respect for human rights and free elections in Central and South America as compatible with his preference for encouraging economic liberalization.[28] In their first meetings with Shultz, Chilean policymakers found the new secretary enamored of the Chilean economic model, but more than willing to press them on the need to improve human rights. Shultz "personally admires Chile," one report written after a 1983 meeting stated, "but in the matter of certification, [Shultz emphasized] there needs to be progress on the matter of human rights and the evolution of the democratic process."[29]

The strategic shift to democracy promotion in Washington did not occur in a vacuum. Politics in Chile and effects of the global debt crisis ensnaring Latin America's biggest economies—including Brazil, as James Cameron describes elsewhere in this volume—affected US officials' perceptions of the relationship between the Pinochet regime and US objectives in the region. Skyrocketing unemployment and surging inflation led to widespread labor demonstrations against the Pinochet regime that began in May 1983 and continued monthly throughout the year. Pinochet's response to the first major popular challenge to the regime's legitimacy was mixed. The general harshly cracked down on protesters but, at the same time, replaced his cabinet with a group of pragmatic officials who urged him to undertake an *apertura* (opening). Pinochet allowed 1,500 exiles back into the country, loosened restrictions on the media and civil society groups, and began a limited dialogue with the opposition. The *apertura* was small but significant in a country where the elimination of democratic politics had been at the core of the military regime's ideological program and practical authority.

In relations with the United States, the opening that took place in 1983 and 1984 created a moment of opportunity and risk. To that point, the Pinochet regime insisted on carrying out the transition plan laid out in the 1980 Chilean constitution: after eight years of institutional transition, a nation-wide plebiscite would affirm or reject a single candidate put forth by the regime to oversee the final steps of democratization. Reagan officials disagreed over whether the United States should encourage the opening and risk interfering with the regime's complete management of the transition. On the one hand, ideological conservatives—most notably James Theberge in Santiago—wanted to remain firmly supportive of Pinochet's campaign against the threat of destabilization by the political Left. On the other, moderate officials in the State Department argued that Pinochet's refusal to undertake a democratic transition in earnest would undercut the moderate opposition and only increase the power and appeal of the armed Left. "The key to protecting long-term US interests," Assistant Secretary of State for Inter-American Affairs Tony Motley wrote in late 1984, was "strengthening the disorganized moderates, specifically weaning them away from the radical Left."[30]

The administration's concern with Chile's political deterioration—the Chilean ambassador was called in to the State Department four separate times between November and December 1984—emboldened US officials to directly engage with moderate opposition groups. This pivot was conditioned not simply by internal debates, but also by the administration's growing commitment to democracy promotion on a global scale. The founding of the National Endowment for Democracy in 1983 was particularly notable in this regard. Although the NED was ostensibly "quasi-nongovernmental" (it received congressionally appropriated funds that were independently channeled through the Republican and Democratic Parties, the Chamber of Commerce, and the AFL-CIO to pro-democracy civil society groups abroad), it gave the administration a crucial tool for supporting moderate unions, think tanks, and interest groups in Chile.[31] One of the NED's first beneficiaries was the Chilean National Accord, the first broad-based political coalition formed to oppose the regime. With NED funding, the National Democratic Institute had hosted the 1984 meeting at which the National Accord parties had agreed to cooperate.[32]

Chilean officials took note of this newly interventionist approach and, unsurprisingly, opposed it. Writing to Reagan in December 1983, Pinochet insisted that "constitutional consolidation"—the general's euphemism for a military-controlled transition—would "continue at the pace determined by the Chileans." The regime was committed, Pinochet wrote, to its "relentless fight against Soviet imperialism, which will continue with or without support of those that find themselves with the same objective, [and] despite the misunderstandings that may exist about my government."[33] In October 1984, Chilean ambassador to the United States, Hernán Felipe Errázuriz met with the Central Intelligence Agency (CIA) director, William Casey, and warned him that the moderate opposition had "aggravated the situation by not presenting viable alternatives" to the regime's transition plan, which he called "the only one capable of carrying forward an orderly and peaceful transition."[34]

Political and economic turmoil in Chile ruptured the connection, long cherished by Reagan conservatives, between military dictatorship and free-market economic development. At a breakfast with Latin American delegations to the United Nations in October 1984, Shultz called the "advance toward democracy" the "principal and positive development" in the region, according to the Chilean foreign ministry's report on the event. "At one time it was believed that harsh authoritarian governments were an adequate instrument to solve countries' problems, particularly economic," Shultz explained to attendees, many of them representing debt-ridden economies. Now, "experience has shown that is not the case, and that, to the contrary, it is the democratic regimes that have shown more effectiveness to those ends."[35] Even more glaring to Chilean diplomats was the way that Reagan officials were increasingly linking the issue of democratic political transition to human rights. In a meeting in December 1984, State Department officials told Ambassador Errázuriz that human rights votes in international organizations were putting the Reagan administration in an "awkward position" that "can only be resolved if the GOC carries through on the commitments we have heard from GOC officials by taking tangible steps toward the transition to democracy." Errázuriz complained that US policy was changing "with great speed, placing tremendous pressure on the GOC."[36] That change was on full display in a Human Rights Day speech by Ronald Reagan later that month, in which he characterized Chile's "lack of progress toward democratic government" an "affront to the human conscience."[37]

Together with the increasingly public human rights criticism, US abstentions from votes on loans to Chile in the Inter-American Development Bank (IADB) and the World Bank in early 1985 signaled outwardly that the tenor of US-Chilean relationship was undergoing an incipient shift.[38] But evidence of a more fundamental policy change can be found in records of Chilean officials' internal attempts to explain US behavior. Chilean Ambassador Errázuriz wrote to the foreign ministry in March 1985 that Chile had become the source of "the most disillusion for the administration in the area of human rights."[39] Even though the criticisms of the Reagan administration were more muted than those of Carter, Errázuriz noted, the fact that human rights language was being marshaled against Chile by Republicans meant that Chile had little hope of finding political allies in the United States to oppose such pressure. When Argentine president Alfonsín enjoyed a warm visit with Reagan in 1985, Chilean diplomats noted that it confirmed the administration's policy of "solidly linking itself with the democratic governments in Latin America."[40] Summarizing Argentina's burgeoning relations with the United States, the embassy wrote that "democratic expansion has come to constitute a fundamental part of the Reagan administration's diplomacy in Latin America."[41]

Nonetheless, by the end of 1986, the Reagan administration's policy remained carefully calibrated not to upset the status quo. There were internal disagreements between the State Department and the NSC over how best to maximize US leverage in urging along the democratic transition, but there was also broad agreement that the goal of engaging with the opposition was to keep Pinochet honest in carrying out the regime's plan for a managed transition. As Pinochet proved ever more intransigent, however, there were growing signs that Chile was becoming—as George Shultz put it early in 1986—one of the "odd men out" in a hemisphere that was rapidly democratizing.[42]

Between 1986 and 1988 Chilean perceptions of evolving Reagan administration policy crystalized into outright disillusion among regime elites. Although Reagan officials maintained support for Pinochet's commitment to crush the militant Left—particularly in the wake of a failed assassination attempt against Pinochet in September 1986—the general's intransigence on the issue of the transition to civilian rule sent bilateral relations into a period of dénouement.

The impetus for a policy shift came from two key personnel changes, a fact noted in the Chilean documents. The first was Elliott Abrams's transition from assistant secretary for human rights to assistant secretary for inter-American Affairs in April 1985. As his record on Nicaragua during the same period makes clear, Abrams had lost none of his virulent anticommunism, but he had above all advocated for consistency in US human rights policy, and Pinochet's brazen dictatorship had long been a source of frustration. Responding to a 1983 memo on the human rights situation there, Abrams scrawled a handwritten note that Chile would be a "terrific place when these guys throw Pinochet out."[43] Chileans bristled at Abrams's insistence that progress toward a democratic transition should be treated as a formal aspect of human rights, and they saw his appointment as ushering in "a variation in the style" of US diplomacy, which would "eventually manifest in a more direct rhetoric" toward Chile.[44] Abrams's policies also earned him the scorn of conservatives within the administration. James Theberge, for one, complained in personal notes that Abrams was part of "a ruthless group of careerists" running the State Department, whose "main aim is to forward the career, forget the national interest." By insisting on democratization, he wrote, Abrams had shifted US policy "towards the old tried and failed Carter policy of primacy of human rights."[45]

The second key personnel change was the replacement of James Theberge as ambassador to Chile by Harry Barnes in 1986. It would be hard to overstate the sea change in bilateral diplomacy that resulted from the appointment of Barnes, a career diplomat whose experience in India from 1981 to 1985 had immersed him in the language of human rights diplomacy in ways that were never true of James Theberge. The Barnes and Abrams appointments, Chile's ambassador wrote in September 1985, "would indicate that the State Department is searching for a new and more active approach to its relationship with Chile, with special emphasis on institutional development" (a euphemism for the transition). Chile should expect Barnes, the ambassador wrote, to approach government officials, opposition factions, and even the Catholic Church "with the purpose of actively serving as a catalyst in the Chilean institutional process."[46] Indeed, Barnes's diplomatic methods quickly ran afoul of Chilean officials, who saw his appointment as the official end of quiet diplomacy. One 1987 foreign ministry cable described the "discomfort of diverse government authorities," and Pinochet in particular, with Barnes's "numerous activities and declarations that have constituted intervention or, at least, imprudent acts." The tension surrounding Barnes grew so bad that US officials accused the foreign ministry of deliberately restricting Barnes's diplomatic access.[47]

In 1986 and 1987, while Pinochet's continuing lack of progress toward the plebiscite was the primary bone of contention with Reagan officials, two specific human rights issues intensified the discord. First was perhaps the most egregious case of the decade, the so-called *quemados* case, in which a teenage Chilean resident of the United States, Rodrigo Rojas, was burned alive by Chilean soldiers during a demonstration against the regime in July 1986. When Harry Barnes attended the funeral procession for Rojas, Pinochet was incensed, believing that the United States was making common cause with the regime's communist opponents. The Chilean embassy in Washington was bombarded with human rights correspondence from US citizens and legislators. The replies from the embassy were contentious and defensive, pointing out, for example, that "coverage of the press . . . can be very misleading."[48] When the ambassador met with Abrams in September, he shockingly defended Pinochet's action, pointing out to Abrams that Rojas had been "an activist" and his mother a communist. Abrams told him there was no escaping the effect that the death of an American citizen would have on bilateral relations.[49]

The second human rights issue was Chile's ongoing noncooperation on the Letelier assassination investigation. In 1987, the CIA informed Shultz that it had intelligence that Pinochet had personally ordered the killing in 1976. Upon receiving the report, Shultz wrote to Reagan that it was "a blatant example of a chief of state's direct involvement in an act of state terrorism, one that is particularly disturbing both because it occurred in our capital and since his government is generally considered to be friendly." Shultz told Reagan that knowledge of Pinochet's involvement "must affect both our overall policy towards Chile and the general conceptual framework of how we make decisions regarding that country."[50] While the Chilean foreign ministry documents do not contain revelations regarding Pinochet's involvement in the Letelier murder, they register dismay at the renewed interest in the United States in Pinochet's human rights record. The embassy cabled the foreign ministry to report that the pressure facing the embassy was as bad as it had been in 1979, during the height of Carter-era criticism. The ambassador suggested that the foreign ministry should do all it could to distance Pinochet from the ongoing Letelier controversy.[51]

Try as the Chileans might, relations had, by the end of 1987, begun to sour completely. The foreign ministry and embassy cable traffic during this time contains remarkably perceptive analysis of the forces shaping Reagan's second-term foreign policy. In October 1987, the Chilean embassy drafted a lengthy memorandum that sought to explain the energy with which US officials were now promoting the Chilean plebiscite. The second-term foreign policy team, the ambassador wrote, has "put an end to the attempt to incorporate foreign policy into [Reagan's] conservative agenda, essentially anti-communist and pro-freedom in economic and political terms." Instead it has returned to "the traditional post-war pragmatism of the Department of State, trying to find an understanding with Moscow, accommodating itself to congressional pressure, and looking for bipartisanship after the Republicans lost control of the congress in 1984."[52] The reasons for this about-face, the Chilean embassy reasoned, were many: Iran-Contra; a weakening of European support for Reagan's policies in the Global South; and a lack of foreign policy leadership from the White House, which empowered State department bureaucrats.

The Chilean analysis was astute, but diplomats underestimated the extent to which the Reagan administration's return to this deeper strain of US support for liberalization abroad had made getting Pinochet out of political power a basic objective. The announcement that the plebiscite would be held in 1988 completely refocused US diplomatic efforts. Indeed, the United States spent roughly $2.9 million through the aforementioned NED and the US Agency for International Development to ensure that Pinochet would not be able to manipulate the results of the plebiscite that eventually took place in October of that year.[53] In private meetings, Ambassador Barnes, Elliott Abrams, and others warned the regime not to interfere with the results; meanwhile the regime complained that Reagan was unwittingly supporting the radical Left.[54] Privately, US pressure had a strong effect. In October, the Chilean embassy cabled yet another lengthy report analyzing the US turn to democracy promotion. While it located the causes of the shift in entrenched opposition to the Chilean military government in Congress and the US "bureaucracy," it also acknowledged that Pinochet's stubborn handling of human rights had encouraged the United States to press more aggressively for political change. The ambassador recommended "major changes" in the way that human rights were handled in order to combat perceptions about the Chilean dictatorship.[55] "More than two years removed from the end of 'silent diplomacy,'" another cable noted, "and US interventionism has been growing with subtle hostility toward the government."[56]

The climax of the evolution of US policy was the plebiscite of October 5, 1988, in which the coalition of parties comprising the "No" campaign defeated the regime, paving the way for elections the following year. The regime was blindsided by the results. Pinochet had not expected to lose the vote, and he held US officials responsible for what he saw as a decisive role in his defeat. When the ambassador met with Abrams on October 7, he condemned Harry Barnes, calling him an "unacceptable interlocutor" in league with Chilean communists. Abrams listened patiently to the ambassador's criticism and emphasized that US policy in Chile was consistent with Reagan's foreign policy in the second term of "favoring competitive elections in all of Latin America without exception." Insisting to Abrams that Chile was "fed up with intervention," the ambassador cabled Santiago saying that he had put Abrams on the defensive, making him "conscious of the pain and risks" that the State Department had caused to bilateral relations. Errázuriz instructed the foreign ministry to keep "the most cold and distant relations possible" with the US embassy and not to meet with Ambassador Barnes before his expected departure from Chile. When Barnes's tour did end shortly after the plebiscite, Pinochet came to see him off but—rejecting diplomatic protocol—refused to shake the ambassador's hand.

In Chile, the Reagan administration faced a policy dilemma that was emblematic of diplomacy following the human rights "breakthrough" of the 1970s.[57] How could the United States best handle relations with countries that shared its goals but did not share its ideals? Should policymakers seek to pressure allies into changing their behavior and risk alienating friendly governments? Or should they first seek to bolster alliances, seeking improved behavior in conjunction with the benefits of geopolitical cooperation?

What is perhaps most interesting about the experience with Chile is that Reagan officials discovered that these were not binary options. Ideology and geopolitics were not exclusive policy considerations, but were completely intertwined in the way officials perceived their interests in the Southern Cone, and then in the policy options they formulated to deal with the Pinochet regime as it was weakened by the debt crisis and turned increasingly stubborn in the face of political opposition. Reagan officials learned that a public posture of unconditional support for anticommunism in Chile was politically costly and counterproductive to US leverage in the region; they learned as well that a policy of promoting democratic liberalization could be wielded to achieve specific objectives vis-à-vis allies, just as it could be against foes such as the Sandinista regime in Nicaragua.

There were no more astute observers of the Reagan administration's embrace of democratic liberalism than the Chilean officials who saw themselves unexpectedly end up on the short end of this policy, along with strange bedfellows Cuba and Nicaragua. In the ethereal garden scene in December of 1982, Ambassador Theberge had witnessed the earliest signs of Chilean disillusion—a recognition that the Reagan administration lacked the political power or will to deliver on the promise of normalizing relations with a brazenly authoritarian ally. By 1985, the Chilean foreign ministry sensed that a growing emphasis on promoting change through democratic elections would leave Chile once again as a pariah in the hemisphere. Overt US support for the "No" campaign in the 1988 plebiscite, while infuriating to Pinochet, was merely the culmination of a shift that institutions within the regime had seen developing for years.

That the evolution of the Reagan administration's policy toward Chile has failed to permeate analyses of Reagan's broader foreign policy, and his administration's policy in Latin America specifically, is due to the fact that the resulting policy, ironically, looked familiar in the longer context of the Cold War. By advancing elections, supporting moderate political parties and free market solutions, the Reagan administration hoped to undermine revolutionary movements in Latin America, much as its predecessors had done during previous decades. What was new, however, was the idea that the solutions at work in Chile—the overt support of free elections and free markets—could serve as the basis for US hegemony and regional order in Western Hemisphere, even when divorced from the Cold War threat of geopolitical competition with the Soviet Union that had made political revolution so intimidating. In that regard, the Chilean case, while hardly the only example of US democracy promotion efforts in Latin America, is one that best suggests the limits, costs, and contradictions of the liberalization policies that became entrenched in the neoliberal "Washington Consensus" of the 1990s. Finding those underlying frictions requires challenging unitary views of Reagan's legacy in Latin America, in large part by engaging with the evidence to be found in archival sources from the region itself.

Notes

1. On this meeting, see cable, Santiago to DOS, "Chilean Government Fears Prejudicial Shift in US Policy," 3 Dec.1982, DOS Electronic Reading Room, https://foia.state.gov; Theberge notes, 2 Dec. 1982, Hoover Institution Archives (HIA), James Daniel Theberge Papers (JDTP), box 13, folder "Chron File 1982." Theberge's papers contain voluminous rough notes and observations—some of which formed the basis for cables, but which often contained additional, revealing commentary left out of official records. The official cable is discussed in Morris H. Morley and Chris McGillion, *Reagan and Pinochet: The Struggle over US Policy toward Chile* (New York: Cambridge University Press), 47–48.

2. Theberge notes, 2 Dec. 1982.

3. Morley and McGillion, *Reagan and Pinochet*.

4. See, for example, Sarah Snyder's chapter in this volume. For an example of the most critical view, see Stephen Rabe, *The Killing Zone: The United States Wages Cold War in Latin America*, 2nd ed. (New York: Oxford University Press, 2016). For a view that takes democracy promotion seriously but still downplays Chile's importance relative to the administration's other priorities, see Thomas Carothers, *In the Name of Democracy: US Policy towards Latin America in the Reagan Years* (Berkeley: University of California Press, 1991).

5. The scholarship of the new inter-American Cold War has been typified by international research in Latin American archives and, to varying degrees, engagement with cultural and social approaches advanced by historians of Latin America. For representative approaches, see Virginia Garrard-Burnett, Mark Atwood Lawrence, and Julio E. Moreno, eds., *Beyond the Eagle's Shadow: New Histories of Latin America's Cold War* (Albuquerque: University of New Mexico Press, 2013); Gilbert M. Joseph and Daniela Spenser, eds., *In from the Cold: Latin America's New Encounter with the Cold War* (Durham, NC: Duke University Press, 2008); and Max Paul Friedman, "Retiring the Puppets, Bringing Latin America Back In: Recent Scholarship on United States-Latin American Relations," *Diplomatic History* 27 no. 5 (2003): 621–636. This chapter takes its cues from international works that have mined state archives to pierce (as opposed to simply acknowledge) the complexity of the Cold War in the region. See, for example, Renata Keller, *Mexico's Cold War: Cuba, the United States, and the Legacy of the Mexican Revolution* (New York: Cambridge University Press, 2015); Tanya Harmer, *Allende's Chile and the Inter-American Cold War* (Chapel Hill: University of North Carolina Press, 2011).

6. The Chilean Foreign Ministry was purged of nearly 40 percent of its career diplomats in the wake of the 1973 coup, greatly weakening its diplomatic service during

a time when diplomacy mattered greatly. It was dominated by naval officers until roughly 1978, when professional civil servants began to reestablish control. While it reflects the centralized ideological predilections of the Pinochet regime, the archival record also contains dispassionate analysis of the regime's foreign relations. See Mary Helen Spooner, *Soldiers in a Narrow Land: The Pinochet Regime in Chile* (Berkeley: University of California Press, 1994), 98, 112; Carlos Huneeus, *The Pinochet Regime* (Boulder, CO: Lynne Rienner Publishers, 2007).

7. Barbara Keys, "Congress, Kissinger, and the Origins of Human Rights Diplomacy," *Diplomatic History* 34, no. 5 (2010), 823–851; Alan McPherson, *Ghosts of Sheridan Circle: How a Washington Assassination Brought Pinochet's Terror State to Justice* (Chapel Hill: University of North Carolina Press, 2019), 216–220.

8. Amendment to *The International Security Assistance and Arms Export Control Act of 1977* (PL 94-329), which terminated cash sales of weapons, military training, and credits to Chile due to its status as a gross violator of human rights. For a summary of human rights legislation relating to Chile, see Peter Kornbluh, *The Pinochet File: A Declassified Dossier on Atrocity and Accountability* (New York: The New Press, 2003), 222–230; John R. Bawden, "Cutting off the Dictator: The United States Arms Embargo of the Pinochet Regime, 1974–1988," *Journal of Latin American Studies* 45, no. 3 (2013): 525–528.

9. Vanessa Walker, "At the End of Influence: The Letelier Assassination, Human Rights, and Rethinking Intervention in US-Latin American Affairs," *Journal of Contemporary History* 46, no. 1 (2011): 114–115.

10. Walker, "At the End of Influence," 114–115.

11. NSC, "Summary of Conclusions," 6 Feb. 1981, Ronald Reagan Presidential Library (RRPL), Executive Secretariat–NSC (ESNSC), Meeting Files (MF), box 91282.

12. See James Cameron's contribution to this volume.

13. Memorandum no. 3, Ministry of Foreign Relations (MRE) to Washington, 5 Feb. 1981, Archive of the Chilean Ministry of Foreign Relations (AGH).

14. Telex no. 39, Washington to MRE, 26 Jan. 1981, AGH.

15. Bawden, "Cutting off the Dictator," 45.

16. Telex no. 306–308, Washington to MRE, 10 June 1981, AGH.

17. Theberge speech to Chilean Chamber of Commerce, 30 Mar. 1982, HIA, JDTP, box 6.

18. Telex no. 462, Washington to MRE, 29 Sept. 1981, AGH.

19. Telex nos. 154–155, Washington to MRE, 23 Mar. 1981, AGH.

20. Letter (Free Translation), Pinochet to Reagan, September 3, 1981, HIA, JDTP, box 19.

21. Telex no. 229, Washington to MRE, 1 May 1981, AGH.

22. Telex no. 157, Washington to MRE, 31 Mar. 1982, AGH.

23. For the Chilean summary of this lengthy meeting, see Telex nos. 318–325, Washington to MRE, 16 June 1982, AGH. These themes were echoed in other meetings with US officials during the same round of talks. For meeting with Frank Carlucci of the Defense Department, see Telex nos. 329–334, Washington to MRE, 17 June 1982, AGH.

24. NSDD-71, "US Policy in the Wake of the Falklands Crisis," 30 Nov. 1982, https://fas.org/irp/offdocs/nsdd/nsdd-71.pdf.

25. DOS, "Meeting with Enrique Valenzuela" 17 Jan. 17, 1984, RRPL, ESNSC, Country Files (CF), box 20.

26. DOS to Santiago, "Chilean DCM Discusses Human Rights Issues with HA Assistant Secretary," Jan. 1984, RRPL, ESNSC, CF, box 20.

27. Memorandum no. 151, Washington to MRE, 31 Mar. 1983, AGH.

28. NSC, "NSC Meeting Minutes of November 23rd," RRPL, ESNSC, MF, box 91284.

29. Telex nos. 304–306, Washington to MRE, 28 Mar. 1983, AGH.

30. Motley to Deputy Secretary, "US Policy toward Chile," 20 Dec. 1984, Digital National Security Archive–Chile Collection.

31. See Evan D. McCormick, "Breaking with Statism? US Democracy Promotion in Latin America, 1984–1988," *Diplomatic History* 42, no. 5 (2018): 745–771.

32. National Endowment for Democracy, *Annual Report 1985* (Washington, DC: 1985), 16.

33. Telex no. 557, MRE to Washington, 13 Dec. 1983, AGH.

34. Telex nos. 893–896, Washington to MRE, 16 Oct. 1984, AGH.

35. Memorandum no. 11836, MRE to Washington, 18 Oct. 1984, AGH.

36. DOS to Santiago, "Undersecretary Armacost Meeting with Chilean Ambassador," 8 Dec. 1984, RRPL, Latin American Affairs Directorate–NSC, box 91172.

37. Reagan, "Proclamation 5287—Bill of Rights Day, Human Rights Day and Week, 1984," 10 Dec. 1984, https://reaganlibrary.archives.gov/archives/speeches/1984/121084c.htm.

38. See Morley and McGillion, *Reagan and Pinochet*, 111–120.

39. Memorandum no. 13, MRE to Washington, 7 Mar. 1985, AGH.

40. Memorandum no. 40, Washington to MRE, 31 Jan. 1985, AGH.

41. Memorandum no. 124, Washington to MRE, 18 Apr. 1985, AGH.

42. Joanne Omang, "Shultz Puts Chile on List of Latin Dictatorships," *Washington Post*, 30 Mar. 1986.

43. Abrams to Lister, 26 Nov. 1983, UT-Austin Benson Latin America Collection, George Lister Papers, https://law.utexas.edu/humanrights/lister/chile/chile.php.

44. Memorandum Washington to MRE, "Apreciación Marzo-Abril," 10 May 1985, AGH.

45. Theberge notes, "Policy Confusion," HIA, JDTP, box 25, folder "Chron File April–June 1985"; Morley and McGillion, *Reagan and Pinochet*, 74–75.

46. Memorandum, Washington to MRE, "Expectations for Reagan's Second Terms—New Factors," 9 Sept. 1985, AGH.

47. Telex no. 307, MRE to Washington, 2 June 1987, AGH.

48. Memorandum no. 171, Washington to MRE, 20 Aug. 1986, AGH.

49. Memorandum no. 52, Washington to MRE, 24 Sept. 1987, AGH.

50. Pascale Bonnefoy, "CIA Believed Pinochet Ordered 1976 Assassination in US, Memorandum Reveals," *New York Times*, 9 Oct. 2015.

51. Telex nos. 196–206, Washington to MRE, 14 Feb. 1987, AGH.

52. Memorandum no. 86, Washington to MRE, 28 Oct. 1987, AGH.

53. Amounts are taken from NED annual reports, as well as summaries in Morley and McGillion, *Reagan and Pinochet*, 255–256, and Carothers, *Name of Democracy*, 158–159.

54. Telex nos. 255–257, Washington to MRE, 26 Feb. 1987, AGH.
55. Memorandum no. 86, Washington to MRE, 28 Oct. 1987, AGH.
56. Telex nos. 550–551, Washington to MRE, 8 Dec. 1987, AGH.
57. See several essays, particularly those by Samuel Moyn and Patrick William Kelly, in Jan Eckel and Samuel Moyn, eds., *The Breakthrough: Human Rights in the 1970s* (Philadelphia: University of Pennsylvania Press, 2014).

CHAPTER 13

Anticommunism, Trade, and Debt
The Reagan Administration and Brazil, 1981–1989

JAMES CAMERON

Brazil underwent a profound transformation during the 1980s. A military dictatorship at the beginning of the decade, the country inaugurated its first civilian leader in over twenty years in 1985 and held the first fully democratic presidential election in its history in 1989. With a population of 146 million, Brazil thus became the largest democracy in Latin America—a region that experienced eight such transitions during Reagan's years in office, in what constituted a major part of the "Third Wave" of democratization.[1]

American officials were quick to ascribe Latin America's democratic turn during these years to US policy. The Reagan administration's "strong belief in individual freedom," Assistant Secretary of State Elliott Abrams argued in 1988, had made it "a more effective advocate and supporter of democracy in the region than any of its predecessors."[2] In private, Reagan himself claimed that he had made "a democratic Western Hemisphere ... a priority for this administration."[3] Samuel P. Huntington, originator of the Third Wave theory, agreed that "during the 1970s and 1980s the United States was a major promoter of democratization."[4]

While the Reagan administration took a more active role in other South American countries, such as Chile, its support for the democratic transition in Brazil amounted to "democracy by applause." Unlike in other Southern Cone countries such as Chile and Argentina, the gradual transition in Brazil was already underway by the time Reagan took office. Seeing their ability to affect Brazilian domestic politics as limited, US officials confined their support to praising the dictatorship's liberalizing steps after they had been taken. Instead of focusing on the challenges of democratization, the White House saw Brazil through the prism of its global preoccupations, principally the Cold War and its push to create a world economy that safeguarded US business interests and maximized their access to foreign markets.[5]

Reagan's strategy toward Brazil went through two phases. In the early 1980s, the White House attempted to enlist Brazilian help in prosecuting its renewed crusade against communism. Questions on which the two countries had clashed severely during the Jimmy Carter period, notably the US administration's confrontational approach to Brazil's nuclear program and its emphasis on human rights, were set to one side. With these points of contention removed, the two countries cooperated on preserving "hemispheric stability"—in short, maintaining a South America free from revolutionary disruption and communist influence.[6] Newly released documents show the extent to which the United States and Brazil worked together to contain the Falklands/Malvinas crisis. Ties reached their height with a secret joint initiative to entice the dictator of Suriname, Desi Bouterse, away from a closer relationship with Cuba and the Soviet Union.

The second phase saw an extended US-Brazilian clash over the shape of the emerging knowledge-based global economy. Even during the period of improved political relations in the early 1980s, major economic problems were never far below the surface. While the emergence of newly competitive Brazilian manufactured products worried US domestic interests, the United States' shift toward growth based on services and high technology led to an emphasis from Washington on the protection of intellectual property rights and free access for US software. Trade relations between the two countries had never been easy, but the 1980s saw a fundamental clash between the Brazilian model, which sought to foster national champions behind tariff barriers, and the renewed American enthusiasm for free trade—particularly when it came to new world-beating industries that would become one of the pillars of American power in the post–Cold War world.

Brazil's central role in the less developed country (LDC) debt crisis weakened its ability to press its views. By the middle of the decade, US diplomats told their Brazilian colleagues that "economic and financial issues" had assumed "overwhelming importance" in the US-Brazilian relationship.[7] Throughout its time in office, the Reagan team focused on protecting the interests of US lender banks at the expense of a more comprehensive approach to bringing the debt standoff to a conclusion. Officials resisted pressure for debt relief for the LDCs, and it was only after the inauguration of a new president, George H. W. Bush, that the United States unveiled a plan that married significant economic reforms by debtors with market-based reduction of those countries' obligations.

The Reagan administration therefore marks a transition away from the concerns that characterized Cold-War era US policy with regard to Brazil toward a new post–Cold War world. This shift had little to do with democratization, however; instead, it involved a fundamental tilt in the balance of economic power away from Brasilia toward Washington. As the 1980s progressed, Brazilian leaders had to cope with a newly assertive United States that was willing to use the levers at its disposal to press for a combination of open markets and structural reform that would become the keystone of the Washington consensus during the 1990s. While the United States emerged from the Reagan era re-empowered, a newly democratic Brazil found itself struggling to assert its interests in a unipolar world.[8]

There was much room for improvement in US-Brazilian relations when Reagan assumed the presidency on January 20, 1981. Whereas the administrations of Richard Nixon and Gerald R. Ford had attempted to prioritize the military dictatorship's role as a regional anticommunist gendarme, Reagan's immediate predecessor, Jimmy Carter, had precipitated a major rupture in ties by confronting Brasilia on two issues that went beyond the Cold War: the Brazilian nuclear program and the dictatorship's record on human rights. Brasilia had reacted angrily, canceling military cooperation and expelling American advisers. Despite limited attempts at a rapprochement, relations between the two countries remained cool. The US Congress had solidified the US-Brazilian standoff over the latter's nuclear program in 1978, banning exports of nuclear fuel to any state that did not accept nuclear safeguards on all of its facilities. Frustratingly for Brasilia, which had signed a contract with the United States for construction of its Angra I nuclear power plant before proliferation concerns had moved up the political agenda, this meant that the country was caught between either accepting inspections of its entire nuclear complex or paying a fine to the US Department of Energy for sourcing fuel from another supplier.[9]

With a renewed emphasis on combatting communism on a global scale, the Reagan administration sought to right US relations with South America's "major power," which, it judged, had "seriously deteriorated" and "been allowed to drift" under Carter.[10] Viewing its policy toward Brazil primarily through the prism of its predecessor's failed efforts, the new administration believed that this could be achieved by reversing US stances on nuclear and human rights issues. When Vice President George H. W. Bush visited Brasilia in October 1981, he agreed that Brazil could buy fuel for Angra I from another country on an interim basis, pending further work by the Reagan White House to reverse restrictions on US nuclear fuel exports. The administration also scaled back US criticisms of Brazil's human rights record, making the most of the country's gradual political liberalization (*abertura*) under President João Baptista Figueiredo.[11] "The human rights problems that did exist in the 70s have, in fact, disappeared," declared a senior administration official. "You mean the people, or the problem?" a waggish correspondent shot back.[12]

In justifying the prioritization of cooperation at the government-to-government level in retrospect, Reagan-era officials pointed to the relatively limited influence that the United States had over the course of Brazilian domestic politics. By his own account, US ambassador to Brazil Langhorne Motley "counseled . . . that *abertura* was made in Brazil, and from a public and private posture the United States was better off staying out of it. . . . All we did was applaud the process."[13] Indeed, Brazilian political reform had been moving apace regardless of the dictatorship's poor relations with the Carter administration. After assuming office in March 1979, Figueiredo had moved quickly to implement significant measures, including an amnesty law in August of that year that allowed political exiles to come home. In November 1979, Brazil's Congress lifted restrictions on the formation of political parties, ushering in the slow reestablishment of pluralistic democracy. Liberalization was halting, and the regime aspired to retain control of the process for as long as possible. However, taking into account entrenched suspicion of the United States' role in Brazil's domestic politics, Motley was probably right that "the dumbest thing [the Reagan administration] could have done was to have been in the middle of it."[14]

US interest in renewed ties with Brazil led to a period of heightened dialogue and cooperation during Reagan's first term, manifest in Figueiredo's visit to Washington, DC, in May 1982 and Reagan's return trip in December of the same year. In the course of these encounters Reagan and Figueiredo, a former cavalry officer, struck up a good personal rapport, based partly on their mutual American-Brazilian passion for horses, barbecue, and country music.[15] As Reagan remembered years after the event, Figueiredo gave him a "thoroughbred" named Giminich, "a German Hanaford" that could "jump six foot, nine inch hurdle."[16] Yet the two presidents also reached a mutual understanding that was uncommon between Brazilian and US leaders and one that the US president did not achieve with Figueiredo's successor and the first civilian president of Brazil, José Sarney. Figueiredo "understands us," Reagan wistfully remembered as he struggled with the complex of US-Brazilian disagreements during the Sarney period.[17]

It was in the political and military spheres that the two parties managed to make the most progress, centered on their joint interest in "hemispheric stability"—that is, the exclusion of communist influence from South America and the maintenance of control over the pace and extent of any political reform undertaken by the region's existing right-wing authoritarian governments. While claims that "Brazil had no interest in the global Cold War" are wide of the mark, this interest extended only as far as its immediate neighborhood and was balanced by a desire to maintain freedom of action beyond US influence. Brasilia strongly resisted US entreaties to lend support to Reagan's anticommunist campaign in Central America, publicly laying blame for the escalation of violence there at the door of both superpowers. It also pushed back against American attempts to formalize an anticommunist military alliance in the Southern Cone.[18] However, the military dictatorship was ready to act on a selective basis on issues where it saw the potential for conflicts to destabilize its own precarious situation during a period of economic difficulty and domestic political transition.

The first significant evidence of Brazil's usefulness to the Reagan administration in this regard came during British-Argentine Falklands-Malvinas conflict of 1982, which broke out in April and became a major topic of discussion during Figueiredo's visit to Washington between May 11 and 13. Despite officially taking opposite sides in the dispute, Washington and Brasilia shared an interest in its peaceful resolution in a way that would preserve the domestic political status quo in Argentina. Brasilia was most concerned by the possible consequences of Buenos Aires' "humiliation" at the hands of the British, which "would destabilize the Argentinian regime . . . opening the way for the Soviet Union." The Americans, who shared these concerns and agreed that the USSR "was fishing in troubled waters," asked if the Brazilians could use their contacts with the dictatorship in Buenos Aires to persuade it to take a more accommodating position in negotiations before any ground war started in earnest. While maintaining deep doubts regarding the likelihood of success for such an approach, the Brazilians agreed.[19]

Despite the failure of Brazilian mediation prior to the British landing to retake the islands, the United States continued to see Figueiredo's government as a useful tool of crisis diplomacy. As the course of the conflict swung increasingly against Argentina in late May, the United States sought to enlist Brazil in a final attempt to save the junta from absolute defeat. Under an American ceasefire proposal both Argentina and Britain would withdraw their forces, which would be replaced by Brazilian and American peacekeepers. Brasilia and Washington would also act as mediators between London and Buenos Aires as part of a four-nation contact group intended to find a permanent solution to the dispute. British Prime Minister Margaret Thatcher, seeing total victory within her grasp, rejected these overtures out of hand, and the Argentine regime subsequently collapsed—though without the ensuing rise of communism both Washington and Brasilia feared.[20]

While these US-Brazilian negotiation efforts over the Falklands/Malvinas failed, Brasilia's willingness to help strengthened the American perception of the country's "increased importance as a potential stabilizing factor in South America." Reagan paid a return visit to Brazil during a wider tour of Latin America in December 1982, seeking to capitalize on these beginnings.[21] Praising the Brazilian role in the South Atlantic crisis as one of "moderation and reason," Reagan sought to broaden the relationship.[22] The two sides agreed to the establishment of a series of working groups designed to form the basis for strengthened ties in the realms of trade, nuclear cooperation, science, military industry, and space.[23] The Brazilian democratic transition also received public American endorsement. Despite the administration's general wariness of commenting on Brazilian domestic politics, the president nevertheless praised the November 1982 legislative and mayoral elections as "a celebration of freedom."[24] The first free contests since the military coup of 1964, the elections had delivered a stunning victory to the democratic opposition.

US-Brazilian cooperation during the 1980s reached its height in the wake of Reagan's visit, again on issues related to hemispheric security. At about the time of Reagan's trip to Brazil, the United States became increasingly preoccupied with the deteriorating political situation in the small nation of Suriname, a country of 440,000 people on Brazil's northern border. In early December 1982 Suriname's de facto leader, Desi Bouterse, rounded up and executed a number of important figures in the country's democratic opposition movement, precipitating a crisis in relations between Suriname and the United States, as well as the Netherlands, the former colonial power. Both countries suspended aid, intensifying Bouterse's existing search for other sources of external support, most notably from Cuba and the Soviet Union. Fearing the possibility of a Cuban takeover, Washington began to prepare for various contingencies, including overthrowing Bouterse.[25]

While sharing some of Washington's worries about Cuban influence, the Brazilian government was also worried by the potential instability that could be injected into South American politics by a covert or overt US intervention in the region.[26] The Brazilian side initially attempted to quiet American fears regarding a possible Cuban outpost in South America. However, by March 1983 this strategy had run out of time, with Reagan writing to Figueiredo that, in the US view, "Bouterse [had] chosen a course which places him clearly and, in our view, unalterably in the Cuban/Soviet sphere."[27] In early April, Reagan dispatched his national security adviser, William P. Clark, to Venezuela and Brazil in order to ascertain their governments' views and pressure them into supporting some form of intervention.[28]

With Venezuela unwilling to assist the United States, the task of squaring American anxieties regarding communist influence with its own desire for tranquility in the hemisphere fell to Brazil. In doing so, Figueiredo's team came up with a scheme to mediate the brewing conflict, suggesting to Clark and his team that General Danilo Venturini, the secretary of the Brazilian National Security Council, should travel to the Surinamese capital, Paramaribo, to negotiate a pact with Bouterse. The Brazilian president kept the American role in "Operation Giminich"—named after the horse Figueiredo had given Reagan—secret, both from Bouterse and his own foreign ministry. During his two-day visit between April 15 and 17, Venturini managed to persuade Bouterse to limit his ties with Cuba in exchange for a new aid package from Brasilia. Although the evidence is not conclusive, it appears that at least some of the funding for the Brazilian aid program came from the United States.[29]

While Bouterse eased up on his growing relationship with Castro, US intervention in Grenada in October 1983 was likely decisive in precipitating a series of moves by the Surinamese leader that led to the final de facto cessation of relations between Paramaribo and Havana.[30] Nevertheless, the White House was happy with the outcome of the Venturini mission, seeing it as yet more evidence of the newly budding relationship with the hemisphere's southern giant. Brazilian openness impressed US diplomats. Motley observed that it had "been some twenty years since [the Brazilians] shared such sensitive information at the presidential/cabinet level with [the United States]."[31] While not agreeing on every point, by mid-1983 Washington and Brasilia had forged a renewed working relationship based on their common interest in minimizing potential threats to the Brazilian regime on the latter's immediate periphery.

With hindsight, however, the presidential visits of 1982 and the Suriname crisis of the following year marked the zenith of US-Brazilian relations during the Reagan administration. Cooperation on broader issues was patchy. The working groups established during Reagan's trip wrapped up in October 1983 with a visit from US Secretary of State George Shultz to Brasilia. As Shultz noted in his toast to his hosts, much progress had been made in some areas: a long-term route out of the impasse regarding fuel supply to Angra I was in prospect, while the two sides would enhance information sharing and cooperation the areas of nuclear power, space, science, and technology. "The biggest surprise," for Shultz, however, was the working group on industrial-military initiatives, which came to a memorandum of understanding on the exchange of classified military information and technical teams.[32]

While somewhat vague and requiring further elaboration, much of the language stemming from most of the US-Brazilian working groups was positive. This could not be said, however, for the most important working group on trade and bilateral economic relations. Shultz was frank that US-Brazilian cooperation in this field was "difficult" and could express only the wish that the exchange of views between the teams from the US Treasury and Brazilian Ministry of Finance would "lead eventually to pragmatic, equitable solutions to these issues."[33]

The fact was that US-Brazilian economic and trade relations—never particularly smooth—were deteriorating. Trade disputes had abounded in the early years of the administration, on everything from the United States' sugar quotas, to Brazilian export subsidies, to the US proposal to "graduate" Brazil from its Generalized System of Preferences of granting lower tariffs to developing-world importers. Reagan had provided limited respite from some of these policies during his December 1982 visit, granting temporary relief from the sugar quota program and postponing a confrontation on Brazilian subsidies. However, he had also put the country on notice that the United States would not give up its quest for trade liberalization.[34] Further difficulties came from the US Congress, many members of which were under pressure from local industries that were being undercut by cheaper Brazilian imports. Wary of Brazil's need for a positive balance of trade in order to service its debt obligations and reasoning that domestic manufacturing in certain goods, such as shoes, was perennially uncompetitive without significant technological reform, the Reagan administration successfully resisted a number of such protectionist calls.[35]

Yet these problems escalated from the mid-1980s onward. In 1984 the Brazilian Congress passed the Informatics Law, which limited the domestic micro- and minicomputer market to Brazilian companies for a period of eight years. The law also required foreign companies to disclose proprietary information to facilitate interoperability, which, given the lack of appropriate Brazilian copyright legislation, was likely to facilitate piracy. While the Brazilian side saw these protections as necessary in order to protect its domestic information-technology (IT) industry, US officials argued that the lack of competition hobbled the sector's development, describing Brazilian computers as "antiquated and derivative," far more expensive than comparable American products, and thereby entailing a consequent additional cost for the rest of the country's economy. In the fall of 1985, the Reagan administration initiated an investigation under Section 301 of the Trade Act of 1974, which authorized the US government to impose tariffs on imports from countries that imposed "unjustifiable, unreasonable, or discriminatory" measures on American goods.[36]

The US-Brazilian negotiations over informatics dragged out for several years, spanning the latter's transition from military to civilian rule. In January 1985 Tancredo Neves won election to Brazil's presidency through a one-off electoral-college vote in Congress. Neves fell ill before his inauguration, and his vice president, José Sarney, assumed the presidency after Neves's death in April of that year. After unsuccessful negotiations with President Sarney in Washington in October 1986, Reagan determined that the Informatics Law did fall under the definition of discrimination against US products. However, the Brazilian side headed off imminent retaliation by proposing a new law that would include the introduction of twenty-five-year copyright protection on software. The legislation passed the Brazilian Congress in June 1987.[37] Despite this, other problems abounded with Brazil's IT regulator rejecting an application to license Microsoft's MS-DOS operating system due to the fact that a Brazilian company had already produced a similar product. Claiming that the "decision establishes a precedent which effectively bans US companies from the Brazilian software market," the Reagan administration increased tariffs on $105 million of Brazilian goods in November 1987 in a course of action that the Brazilian minister of finance, Luiz Carlos Bresser-Pereira, branded "absurd."[38] Buckling under pressure, the Brazilian regulator licensed MS-DOS in January 1988, and the Reagan administration postponed the introduction of sanctions a few weeks later. The US government eventually shelved the 301 investigation in October 1989.[39]

It might appear strange that such a seemingly minor dispute over IT licensing could assume such a prominent place in the US-Brazilian relations. Part of the problem was the mishandling of certain procedural elements of the dispute by the American side, as well as an apparent underestimation of the impact that democratization was having on the domestic politics of Brazilian trade policy. The Reagan administration announced its Section 301 investigation on September 7, Brazilian Independence Day, touching a nationalist nerve in the country's increasingly liberalized press and solidifying the perception, as US Trade Representative Clayton Yeutter put it, that "the gringos" were "pushing [Brazil] around."[40] Despite some cognizance of the domestic political dynamics at play, Reagan subjected Sarney to a public dressing down during his September 1986 visit. "Prosperity should not be constructed at the expense of others," Reagan intoned to the acute frustration of the Brazilian delegation, "but rather based on the principle of mutual benefits." Such a public rebuke and the ensuing uproar in Brazil made the task of compromise even harder.[41]

Fundamentally, however, the informatics dispute and other similar standoffs over issues such as patent protection for pharmaceuticals were a clash over conflicting protectionist and neoliberal models of economic development.[42] Brazil saw its measures as essential for the evolution of its own indigenous high-tech industry; Sarney went so far as to describe the informatics regulations as "fundamental to [Brazil's] survival as a sovereign nation."[43] To concede, Brazilian officials feared, would be to leave the country completely dependent on US products. This was already a problem due to the American refusal to export advanced supercomputers on national security grounds.[44] From the American perspective, Brazil and other nations—particularly in Asia—were cynically taking advantage of protectionist measures, combined with lax intellectual property laws, in order to effectively steal products that were central to the Reagan administration's vision of the United States' economic future.[45] Given this, feelings ran high on the American side too. The actions taken by the Brazilian IT regulator were nothing short of "pathetic," Apple's head of government relations wrote to the Brazilian ambassador to Washington, Marcílio Marques Moreira. Yeutter privately described Brazilian policy as "shortsighted and cocky."[46] The Americans attempted to convince their Brazilian interlocutors that economic openness was really in the interest of all parties. "We are in a new age," Shultz told his Brazilian counterpart in more diplomatic tones. "Nobody looks at [the] steel mill and [the] assembly line as symbols of economic power." In the "information age," Shultz advised, "societies that are closed cannot take advantage of these changes."[47] Yet it was precisely the fear of technological dependence and consequent loss of autonomy in this new information age that drove Brazilian resistance.[48]

Conflicts over trade and development were sharpened by the LDC crisis.[49] A major energy importer, Brazil had borrowed heavily on international markets during the 1970s in an attempt to maintain the country's high growth rate after the price rises of 1973–1974 by the Organization of the Petroleum Exporting Countries (OPEC). Brazil's foreign debt rose to $49 billion by 1979. Financing from abroad and continued growth also facilitated the further industrialization of the Brazilian economy. Helped by large government subsidies, industrial goods grew from 32.4 percent to 56 percent of Brazilian exports in the period 1974–1979. Brazil had also diversified the destinations significantly by the end of the 1970s, with a shift away from North America, Western

Europe, and Japan toward Latin America, Africa, and the Middle East. While the developed world remained the largest customer, its share had shrunk from 78.5 percent of exports in 1969 to 57.1 percent in 1980.[50]

However, by the early 1980s high interest rates in the United States combined with the second oil shock, a global recession, and the increasing wariness of foreign lenders left Brazil acutely sensitive to any further disruption in its ability to borrow. This disruption duly arrived with Mexico's moratorium on payments to its international creditors in August 1982, sparking the LDC debt crisis. The loss of confidence in emerging-market government debt, combined with Brazil's high dependence on borrowing, forced the country into the arms of the International Monetary Fund (IMF) in November of that year. As in all crises of this type, the risk initially cut both ways. US banks such as Citicorp, Chase Manhattan, and Manufacturer's Hanover, heavily exposed to developing-world debt, were at the front of the queue for any losses resulting from default.[51]

Given the perilous situation of many of its major financial institutions, the US government played an active role in the early phases of the crisis. As Brazil's problems mounted in the months after the Mexico moratorium, the United States, in concert with the Federal Reserve, facilitated private talks between Brazil and its major creditor banks in order to prevent a total collapse in confidence in the country's ability to service its obligations. In the fall of 1982, the US Treasury extended emergency loans totaling almost $1.5 billion to Brazil through its Exchange Stabilization Fund, as well as organizing a further $1.2 billion credit via the Bank of International Settlements. On January 6, 1983, the Brazilian authorities signed a letter of intent with the IMF in exchange for necessary financing from official and private creditors, which agreed to a large rise in Brazil's trade surplus through domestic austerity and tax increases, as well as measures designed to get the country's 100 percent annual inflation under control. In May 1983, however, it became clear that Brazil would miss its economic targets, necessitating a revision of the IMF program.[52] Thus commenced a series of false starts between 1983 and 1985, during which Brazil would sign a letter of intent with the IMF, only for it to fail to meet the conditions under the agreement and thereby necessitate a new letter.[53]

While the pace and dynamics of Brazil's growth during the 1970s had fueled its aspirations to greater independence from the United States, the 1982 debt crisis shifted economic power back in favor of the latter. It also contributed to the deterioration of US-Brazilian relations during the second Reagan administration.[54] Frustration was palpable on both sides. While recognizing Brazil's difficulties, US officials asserted that the country was "in a crisis largely of its own making: many of its economic problems result from inappropriate policies followed for too long."[55] Shultz believed the primary problem for Brazil was its failure to implement pledged austerity measures. "It's not the debt," the secretary of state argued. "It's that they didn't do what they had to do."[56] For its part, the Brazilian side saw the international community as unwilling to do anything more than safeguard the viability of its major banks at the expense of all else. As one contemporary analyst noted, "The primary objective of many banks [was] not to find a long-term solution to the debt crisis but to protect their balance sheets and income statements in the short term."[57] This focus on regular debt servicing required the imposition of austerity measures that, Brazilian diplomats argued, facilitated a huge "transfer of resources from Latin America to its creditors" at the cost of living standards and economic output throughout the region. Consequently, Brazilian diplomats concluded, "the great majority of debtor countries today confront a dilemma: service the debt or grow." Numerous countries, including Bolivia and Peru, chose the latter and suspended debt payments in 1984.[58]

As with trade, the Reagan administration saw Brazil's democratization as adding a further layer of complexity. While US officials welcomed the return of civilian rule, they saw Sarney as rolling back IMF-sponsored austerity "in order to win popular support"—a policy that helped Brazil's gross domestic product grow by 8 percent in 1985.[59] "Brazil would honor its international commitments," Finance Minister Dilson Funaro told an IMF board meeting in early October of that year, "but the government must also fulfill its responsibilities to its people. In the present circumstances, growth was an imperative dictated by the legitimate demands of the Brazilian population. . . . Any debt restructuring exercise would have to comply with that growth requirement."[60]

Realizing its existing debt strategy was unsustainable, the Reagan administration responded with the Baker plan in October 1985, named after Treasury Secretary James A. Baker III, which sought to bring commercial creditors and international financial institutions together to provide a route out of the crisis. The Baker plan proposed additional lending from the World Bank and the Inter-American Development Bank, as well as commercial banks, in return for which recipient governments would agree to programs of labor market reform, privatization, and trade liberalization.[61] Brazilian officials, however, considered Baker's demands for reform "excessive," while faulting the plan for offering new lending well below that considered necessary to return the debtor countries to growth—approximately $13 billion per year compared with an estimated baseline of $20 billion. In the event, while multilateral lending institutions were forthcoming with new funds, commercial banks were not so enthusiastic, and total lending fell short of the lower figure. The Baker plan consequently failed to provide the necessary boost to growth required for countries to exit the debt trap.[62]

Domestic problems added to Brazil's woes. The failure of the Sarney government's Cruzado plan, designed to beat the country's ruinous triple-digit annual inflation, produced conditions in which the trade balance deteriorated rapidly in late 1986 for the first time in several years. In February 1987, citing the intolerable burden of existing arrangements, Sarney announced a suspension of interest payments on Brazil's obligations to commercial banks, necessitating a further round of crisis diplomacy between the US and the Brazilian governments. In early September 1987, the Brazilian finance minister, Luiz Carlos Bresser-Pereira, believed he had an agreement with Baker for a scheme that would have allowed Brasilia to securitize its debt obligations through new bonds. Judging that he had secured a dramatic breakthrough, he announced it to reporters waiting at the US Treasury. However Baker denied he had done any such thing, spelling "disaster," as the aggrieved Bresser later recalled, for the finance minister's political career and placing further strain on an already difficult US-Brazilian relationship.[63] While Brazil concluded a series of new agreements with the IMF and its commercial creditors in 1988, which facilitated a return to the debt markets, the country would continue to stumble forward for a number of years after both Reagan and Sarney had left office.[64]

The truth was that neither side could look back on the debt crisis with much satisfaction. By the end of the Reagan administration the perception that its strategy had been insufficient was widespread within the international financial community, from liberal economists such as Jeffrey Sachs and the government of Japan, both arguing explicitly for debt-reduction measures, to a high-level group of former policymakers and bankers, including Paul Volcker and Henry Kissinger, who called more elliptically for a greater emphasis on debtor countries' "ability to pay."[65] Brazil's 1988 agreement with its private creditors, involving a $7 billion reduction in long-term obligations, in fact suggested that a change in US policy might be in prospect. Solidifying this perception, in December President-Elect George H. W. Bush called for "a whole new look" at the debt problem.[66] The Brady plan of March 1989, devised by Bush's treasury secretary, Nicholas Brady, offered a way for debtor countries to significantly reduce their obligations in exchange for market reforms. Brazil would eventually finalize an agreement under the plan in 1994. For many in the international financial community such a scheme was long overdue. "In short," as one World Bank official wrote to another after Brady's announcement, "it is as if the US has finally added to the previous cliché 'Growth is essential but it will not be achieved without domestic reforms' the crucial sentence: 'Nor (for many countries) without a reduction of debt service.'"[67]

The year 1989 would prove pivotal for both Brazil and the United States: the unexpected end of communism in Eastern Europe coincided with the first popular elections for the Brazilian presidency in over twenty years. Yet, buffeted by the dual headwinds of political transition and economic upheaval, many Brazilians entered that year with a sense of anxiety. In the short term, the country's leaders openly worried that economic instability and the resulting "despondency and lack of confidence" could facilitate "an unprecedented deterioration of the social and political environment in Latin America." In the long term, observers wondered about the viability of democracy Brazil and the region more widely, given their pervasive and entrenched economic inequality, a situation that both the debt crisis and the orthodox solutions supported by the US government had only exacerbated. In this context the United States, newly empowered to push the doctrines of economic liberalization, was perceived as a potential source of domestic instability.[68]

Brazil's travails were beyond the power of the United States to fix. The intertwined economic and political challenges were too complex, while the country was too large and resistant to influence from its northern neighbor. However, the piecemeal manner in which Washington had approached the debt problem had not helped. US distance from Brazilian democratization during the early 1980s was probably well advised, but the lack of a comprehensive solution to the debt crisis during the latter half of the decade made the task of democracy building even harder than it might have been.[69]

US lobbying during Brazil's constitution-drafting process of 1987–1988 was indicative of how economic imperatives trumped concerns with Brazil's democratic transition. While careful to limit their public criticism of the nascent constitution for fear of an anti-American domestic backlash, in private the United States attempted to pressure the Brazilian government into ensuring the interests of US business would be met. The American side presented a list of demands to Moreira, Brazil's ambassador in Washington, in the form of a non-paper, including the removal of proposed barriers to US investment in healthcare, natural resources, and transportation.[70]

During the early years of the decade, Brazilian dictatorship's interest in a quiet neighborhood and the Reagan administration's focus on the global Cold War had converged temporarily on maintaining anticommunist continuity in Argentina and Suriname. By the time Reagan left office, however, relations between the two governments were at a low. Sarney made Brazilian dissatisfaction with this state of affairs explicit during his first meeting with President

Bush in February 1989. "The relationship with the US had not been successful in recent years," Sarney told Bush, partly because it had lacked "a positive agenda."[71] There was frustration on the American side as well. Brazil was "very much like a teenager," Deputy Secretary of State John Whitehead complained at a 1986 National Security Council meeting, "They want us to treat them like they are still a developing country and believe they deserve access to our markets. But they are not willing to give us access to their markets." Brazil was "unwilling to accept [its] place in the world," James Baker chimed in. According to Baker, Brazil "still" acted like developing country and needed to "grow up."[72]

The truth was that neither the Brazilian dictatorship nor civilian governments fully accepted the Reagan administration's conceptions of Brazil's "place in the world'"—a regional anticommunist policeman in the early 1980s or an open market for US goods, faithfully toiling to repay its insurmountable international debts, during the second half of the decade. Grappling with an economic crisis and democratic transition, Brazilian diplomats saw their mission as "focused primarily on securing conditions for [Brazil's] own national economic and political development." That vision of development, which placed a greater emphasis on economic autonomy and national sovereignty than the emerging Washington consensus would allow, never fully coincided with that of the United States. Such tensions were not unique to the Reagan period and would continue to shape Brazil's foreign policy during the 1990s, 2000s, and beyond, as it sought to use a mixture of regional and global forums such as the Mercosul trade bloc and the Brazil, Russia, India, China, and South Africa (BRICS) grouping to balance against an over-mighty United States.[73] As a result, the United States and Brazil have continued to pass like ships in the night, with brief attempts at a deeper partnership undone by the more profound gulf in expectations between the two sides.

Notes

1. Samuel P. Huntington, "Democracy's Third Wave," *Journal of Democracy* 2, no.1 (1991): 13.
2. Elliott Abrams, "Latin America in the Time of Reagan," *New York Times*, 27 July 1988.
3. NSC meeting, 13 Mar. 1987, http://www.thereaganfiles.com/870313.pdf
4. Huntington, "Democracy's Third Wave," 15.
5. Thomas Carothers, *In the Name of Democracy: US Policy toward Latin America in the Reagan Years* (Berkeley: University of California Press, 1991), 117–148; Andrew Hurrell, "The International Dimensions of Democratization: The Case of Brazil," in

International Dimensions of Democratization: Europe and the Americas, ed. Lawrence Whitehead (Oxford: Oxford University Press, 1996), 148–153.

6. Carothers, *In the Name of Democracy*, 120–127; Andrew Hurrell, *The Quest for Autonomy: The Evolution of Brazil's Role in the International System* (Brasilia: FUNAG, 2014), 315–320.

7. Hoar to Moriera, 22 Oct. 1986, Centro de Pesquisa e Documentação de História Contemporânea do Brasil (CPDOC), Marcílio Marques Moreira Papers (MMMP), MMM.ew.1986.10.22/2, folder 1.

8. Matias Spektor, "Brazilian Assessments of the End of the Cold War," in *The End of the Cold War and the Third World: New Perspectives on Regional Conflict*, ed. Artemy M. Kalinovsky and Sergey Radchenko (Abingdon: Routledge, 2011), 229–244.

9. Warren Hodge, "Bush Tells Brazil Atom Ban Is Eased," *New York Times*, 16 Oct. 1981; Matias Spektor, *Kissinger e o Brasil* (Rio de Janeiro: Zahar, 2009).

10. Shultz, "Your Visit to Latin America," 10 Nov. 1982, Ronald Reagan Presidential Library (RRPL) Roger Fontaine Files (RFF), box 20; Clark, "Your Meeting with João Baptista Figueiredo," 1 Dec. 1982, RRPL, RFF, box 50.

11. Hurrell, *Quest for Autonomy*, 315–316; Hodge, "Bush Tells Brazil Atom Ban Is Eased."

12. "Background Briefing by Senior Administration Official on President Figueiredo's Visit," 12 May 1982, RRPL, Office of Media Relations, box 7, folder "Brazil, Federal Republic of."

13. Carothers, *In the Name of Democracy*, 133.

14. Hurrell, "International Dimensions of Democratization," 150–151; Leslie Bethell and Celso Castro, "Politics in Brazil under Military Rule, 1964–1985," in *The Cambridge History of Latin America: Brazil Since 1930*, ed. Leslie Bethell (Cambridge: Cambridge University Press, 2008), 213–216.

15. Britta H. Crandall, *Hemispheric Giants: The Misunderstood History of US-Brazilian Relations* (Lanham, MD: Rowman and Littlefield, 2011), 139.

16. NSC meeting, 15 Aug. 1986, 1986, http://www.thereaganfiles.com/19860815-nsc-136-brazil.pdf.

17. NSC meeting, 15 Aug. 1986.

18. Crandall, *Hemispheric Giants*, 142; Hurrell, *Quest for Autonomy*, 317.

19. "Encontro do Secretário de Estado Alexander Haig com Sua Excelência o Senhor Presidente da República Federativa do Brasil, João Baptista de Oliveira Figueiredo: Síntese da posição brasileira," 11 May 1982, Brazilian National Archive (AN), BR DFANBSB N8.0.PSN.EST.47; "Encontro do Secretário de Estado Alexander Haig com Sua Excelência o Senhor Presidente da República Federativa do Brasil, João Baptista de Oliveira Figueiredo," 11 May 1982, AN, BR DFANBSB N8.0.PSN.EST.47; "Visita do Presidente João Baptista de Oliveira Figueiredo aos EUA. Encontros com o Secretário de Estado Haig, dia 11, e com o Presidente Reagan dias 12 e 13: A Questão das Malvinas," AN, BR DFANBSB N8.0.PSN.EST.47.

20. "Draft Proposal Prepared by the Department of State," 29 May 1982, in *Foreign Relations of the United States (FRUS), 1981–1988*, vol. 13, *Conflict in the South Atlantic, 1981–1984*, ed. Alexander R. Wieland (Washington, DC: US Government Printing Office, 2015), doc. 314; "Transcript of Telephone Conversation between President Reagan and British Prime Minister Thatcher," 31 May 1982, *FRUS*, vol. 13, doc. 315.

21. "National Security Directive 71," 30 Nov. 1982, *FRUS*, vol. 13, doc. 416.

22. Reagan, "Toast at a Dinner Hosted by Brazilian President João Baptista Oliveira de Figueiredo in Brasilia," 1 Dec. 1982, The American Presidency Project (APP), https://www.presidency.ucsb.edu.

23. Arthur Herman, "Reagan Shakes Hands with Brazil," 5 Dec. 1982, http://www.upi.com/Archives/1982/12/05/Reagan-shakes-hands-with-Brazil/7897407912400/.

24. Reagan, "Toast at a Dinner."

25. Paul Kengor and Patricia Clark Doerner, *The Judge: William P. Clark, Ronald Reagan's Top Hand* (San Francisco: Ignatius Press, 2007), 203–210.

26. Carlos Federico Domínguez Avila, "Guerra Fria na Região Amazônica: um estudo da Missão Venturini ao Suriname (1983)," *Revista Brasileira de Política Internacional* 54, no. 1 (2011): 11–15.

27. Reagan to Figueiredo, 24 Mar. 1983, RRPL, William P. Clark Files (WPCF), box 5, folder "Suriname Cables February-March 1983."

28. Kengor and Clark Doerner, *The Judge*, 211–218.

29. Hill to Clark, "US Assistance for the Brazilian Initiative in Suriname," 25 May 1983, RRPL, WPCF, box 5, folder "Suriname 05/20/1983-07/20/1983"; Kengor and Clark Doerner, *The Judge*, 211–218.

30. George P. Shultz, *Turmoil and Triumph: My Years as Secretary of State* (New York: C. Scribner's Sons, 1993), 344.

31. Motley to Clark, 15 Apr. 1983, RRPL, WPCF, box 5, folder "Suriname Cables 04/13/83-/04/19/83"; Motley to Clark, "Veturini [sic] Trip Report," 20 Apr. 1983, RRPL, WPCF, box 5, folder "Suriname Cables 04/20/1983."

32. Washington to Ministry of Foreign Relations (MRE), "Visita do Secretario de Estado ao Brasil. Texto de Discurso," 21 Oct. 1983, Brazilian Ministry of Foreign Relations Archive (AMRE), Séries A/Z, Rolo 1714—Secreto—Telegramas Recebidos ano 1983; Washington to MRE, "Brasil-EUA. Visita do Secretario de Estado. Relatórios dos Grupos de Trabalho," 15 Oct. 1983, AMRE, Séries A/Z, Rolo 1714—Secreto—Telegramas Recebidos ano 1983.

33. Washington to MRE, "Visita do Secretario de Estado ao Brasil. Texto de Discurso," 21 Oct. 1983, AMRE, Séries A/Z, Rolo 1714—Secreto—Telegramas Recebidos ano 1983.

34. Hurrell, *Quest for Autonomy*, 319; Steven R. Weisman, "Reagan, in Brazil, Warns on Trade," *New York Times*, 3 Dec. 1982.

35. Mitchell, Danforth, et al. to Reagan, 25 July 1985, RRPL, Thomas G. Moore Files (TGMF), box OA18897, folder "Trade—Footwear (Domestic) (3 of 4)"; Jones to Sprinkel, "Background for Meeting with the Footwear Industry," 16 July 1985, RRPL, TGMF, box OA18897, folder "Trade—Footwear (Domestic) (2 of 4)"; "Statement by the President," 28 Aug. 1985, RRPL, TGMF, box OA18857, folder "Trade—Footwear (Domestic) (4 of 4)."

36. John J. Gallagher, "The United States–Brazilian Informatics Dispute," *International Lawyer* 23 no. 2 (1989): 512–514; "Testimony of Ralph R. Johnson, Deputy Assistant Secretary of State for Trade and Commercial Affairs, before the Subcommittee on Commerce, Consumer Protection, and Competitiveness, Energy and Commerce Committee United States House of Representatives," 15 July 1987, CPDOC, MMMP, MMM.ew.1986.06.24, folder 1.

37. Gallagher, "The United States–Brazilian Informatics Dispute," 512–514.
38. Maria Inês Bastos, *Winning the Battle to Lose the War? Brazilian Electronics Policy under US Threat of Sanctions* (Ilford, UK: Frank Cass, 1994), 80; Ira R. Allen, "President Reagan Retaliated Friday against Brazilian Trade Restrictions," 13 Nov. 1987, http://www.upi.com/Archives/1987/11/13/President-Reagan-retaliated-Friday-against-Brazilian-trade-restrictions-on/8465563778000/.
39. Maria Inês Bastos, "The Interplay of Domestic and Foreign Political Constraints on the Informatics Policy of Brazil," United Nations University–Institute for New Technologies Working Paper, no. 6 (1992): 8.
40. Sara Schoonmaker, *High-Tech Trade Wars: US-Brazilian Conflicts in the Global Economy* (Pittsburgh, PA: University of Pittsburgh Press, 2002), 90; NSC meeting, 15 Aug. 1986, http://www.thereaganfiles.com/19860815-nsc-136-brazil.pdf; Octávio Henrique Dias Garcia Cortes, *A Política Externa do Governo Sarney: O início da reformulação de diretrizes para a inserção internacional do Brasil sob o signo da democracia* (Brasilia: FUNAG, 2010), 123–124.
41. Jeff Seward, *The Politics of Capitalist Transformation: Brazilian Informatics Policy, Regime Change, and State Autonomy* (New York: Routledge, 2017), 129.
42. Hal Brands, *Latin America's Cold War* (Cambridge, MA: Harvard University Press, 2010), 226–227; Schoonmaker, *High-Tech Trade Wars*, 15–18.
43. Alan Riding, "US-Brazil Computer Dispute Brews," *New York Times*, 5 May 1985.
44. Seward, *The Politics of Capitalist Transformation*, 129.
45. Norman Gall, "Does Anyone Really Believe in Free Trade?" *Forbes*, 15 Dec. 1985.
46. Johnson to Moreira, 7 June 1988, CPDOC, MMMP, MMM.ew.1986.06.24, folder 3; NSC meeting, 15 Aug. 1986, http://www.thereaganfiles.com/19860815-nsc-136-brazil.pdf.
47. Moreira, "Sec Shultz MRE 9:00h," 6 Aug.1988, CPDOC, MMMP, MMM.ew.1986.10.22/2, folder 1.
48. Schoonmaker, *High-Tech Trade Wars*, 90.
49. Brands, *Latin America's Cold War*, 225–236.
50. Marcelo de Paiva Abreu, "The Brazilian Economy, 1930–1980," in *The Cambridge History of Latin America: Brazil since 1930*, ed. Leslie R. Bethell (Cambridge: Cambridge University Press, 2008), 381–386; Hurrell, *Quest for Autonomy*, 352.
51. De Paiva Abreu, "The Brazilian Economy, 1980–1994," 397–398; James M. Boughton, *Silent Revolution: The International Monetary Fund, 1979–1989* (Washington: IMF, 2001), 336–337; Jeffrey Sachs and Harry Huizinga, "US Commercial Banks and the Developing-Country Debt Crisis," *Brookings Papers on Economic Activity*, no. 2 (1987): 555.
52. Boughton, *Silent Revolution*, 337–344.
53. De Paiva Abreu, "The Brazilian Economy, 1980–1994," 399–404.
54. Hurrell, *Quest for Autonomy*, 191–343.
55. "Testimony of Robert S. Gelbard, Deputy Assistant Secretary of State for Inter-American Affairs, before the Subcommittee on Commerce, Consumer Protection, and Competitiveness, Energy and Commerce Committee, United States House of Representatives," 15 July 1987, CPDOC, MMMP, MMM.ew.1986.06.24, folder 1.
56. NSC meeting, 13 Mar. 1987, http://www.thereaganfiles.com/870313.pdf.

57. Christine A. Bogdanowicz-Bindert, "The Debt Crisis: The Baker Plan Revisited," *Journal of Interamerican Studies and World Affairs* 28, no. 3 (1986): 39.

58. Washington to MRE, "Brasil/EUA. Visita do Presidente Sarney aos EUA. Subsídios. Divida Externa: 1. Quadro Atual e Perspectivas," 20 Aug. 1986, MREA, MBAS—Maço Básico do Pais ou de Assunto (G14), 1986.

59. NSC meeting, 15 Aug. 1986, http://www.thereaganfiles.com/19860815-nsc-136-brazil.pdf.

60. Boughton, *Silent Revolution*, 384.

61. Bogdanowicz-Bindert, "The Debt Crisis," 34.

62. Washington to MRE, "Brasil/EUA. Visita do Presidente Sarney aos EUA. Subsídios. Divida Externa: 1. Quadro Atual e Perspectivas," 20 Aug. 1986, MREA, MBAS—Maço Básico do Pais ou de Assunto (G14), 1986; Boughton, *Silent Revolution*, 427–428.

63. De Paiva Abreu, "The Brazilian Economy, 1980–1994," 407–410; Craig Webb, "Brazil Tuesday Claimed It Has US Support," 8 Sept. 1987, http://www.upi.com/Archives/1987/09/08/Brazil-Tuesday-claimed-it-has-US-support-for-a/7083558072000/; Luiz Carlos Bresser-Pereira, "A Turning Point in the Debt Crisis: Brazil, the US Treasury and the World Bank," *Revista de Economia Política* 19, no. 2 (1999): 114–118.

64. Boughton, *Silent Revolution*, 529–531.

65. Jeffrey D. Sachs, "New Approaches to the Latin American Debt Crisis," *Essays in International Finance*, no. 174 (Princeton, NJ: International Finance Section, Department of Economics, Princeton University, 1989); "A Route Map for the Seven Summiteers," *The Economist*, 18 June 1988; Hobart Rowen, "Volcker Group Calls for New Initiative on Third World Debt," *Washington Post*, 18 June 1986.

66. Peter T. Kilborn, "Bush Backs US Shift on World Debt," *New York Times*, 20 Dec. 1988.

67. Wiesner to Malan, "Secretary Brady's 'Remarks' on Debt," 13 Mar. 1989, CPDOC, MMMP, MMM.ew.1986.09.00/2, folder 30. Emphasis in original.

68. Brands, *Latin America's Cold War*, 234–236, 252–253; Spektor, "Brazilian Assessments of the End of the Cold War," 231–232; "Presentation by Mailson Ferreira da Nobrega, Finance Minister of Brazil, to the International Financial Community, Amsterdam," 19 Mar. 1989, CPDOC, MMMP, MMM.ew.1986.09.00/2, folder 30; Levinson, "Latin American Dilemmas: Some Speculative Thoughts," CPDOC, MMMP, MMM.ew.1987.01.00, Marcílio Marques Moreira Papers, folder 5.

69. Carothers, *In the Name of Democracy*, 138–147.

70. Note, CPDOC, MMMP, MMM.ew.1986.10.13, folder 2.

71. "President's Meeting with Jose Sarney of Brazil," 25 Feb. 1989, https://bush41library.tamu.edu/files/memcons-telcons/1989-02-25—Sarney.pdf.

72. NSC meeting, 15 Aug. 1986, http://www.thereaganfiles.com/19860815-nsc-136-brazil.pdf.

73. Washington to MRE, "Brasil-EUA. Visita de Estado do Presidente Sarney, Subsídios, Relações Bilaterais: Principais Aspectos, Historia Imediata, Perspectivas," 27 Aug. 1986, AMRE, MBAS—Maço Básico do Pais ou de Assunto (G14), 1986; Spektor, "Brazilian Assessments of the End of the Cold War," 239–242.

Part Five

The Middle East and Africa

CHAPTER 14

The Limits of Triumphalism in the Middle East

Israel, the Palestinian Question, and Lebanon in the Age of Reagan

SETH ANZISKA

It is increasingly clear that US foreign policy in the Reagan era had a far-reaching impact on the global South, particularly the Middle East and Africa.[1] While scandals such as Iran-Contra highlighted the domestic fallout of covert Cold War action in Washington, US diplomatic and military intervention in the Levant had tragic consequences on several interconnected fronts, fomenting local violence and entrenching conflict. In re-examining flashpoints such as the Israeli-Palestinian conflict and Lebanon against the backdrop of wider transformations, regional specialists can help explain how the Middle East was directly affected by Reagan's foreign policy in the closing years of the Cold War.[2]

Reagan's approach to Israel, the Palestinian question, and Lebanon was a stark departure from that of Jimmy Carter's administration. After the fitful pursuit of an equitable outcome to Israel's conflict with the Palestinians through the Camp David process and the signing of a bilateral Egyptian-Israeli peace treaty in March 1979, Reagan's choices further exacerbated conflict in the region.[3] As newly available evidence suggests, the administration's national security strategy intensified an alliance with Israel and marginalized Palestinian nationalists as agents of Soviet influence in the Middle East. The Reagan White House also inaugurated a shift in the US approach to international law with regard to settlement building in the West Bank and Gaza Strip, empowering the government of Israeli Prime Minister Menachem Begin to build further settlements in the occupied territories. Most damaging, however, was the green lighting of Israel's June 1982 invasion of Lebanon. The war abetted the military targeting of the Palestine Liberation Organization (PLO) and wreaked havoc on a civilian population already consumed by an internal civil war, and it drew US forces into their deadliest confrontation abroad since Vietnam.

In deferring the possibility of US engagement with the PLO leadership and explicitly supporting Israel's actions in the occupied territories and in Lebanon, Reagan signaled the reordering of American regional priorities in the 1980s. But the limits of this approach quickly became apparent, as open clashes with the Israelis over Lebanon and the introduction of a diplomatic plan aimed at resolving the Palestinian question underscored a tacit return to Carter-era principles. At a decisive juncture in the international history of the Middle East, following the Iranian revolution in 1979 and the outbreak of the Iran-Iraq War in 1980, Reagan's policies in the region aggravated Arab attitudes toward the United States and set the stage for protracted conflict well into the twenty-first century.

When it came to the Middle East, Reagan's abiding affinity was for Israel. His memoirs reflect this. "I've believed in many things in my life, but no conviction I've ever held has been stronger than my belief that the United States must ensure the survival of Israel."[4] During an early meeting about the Middle East, one participant remembers the candidate talking fondly about *Exodus*, the wildly popular Otto Preminger film based on the novel by Leon Uris that celebrated the miraculous victory of Israel over the Arabs in 1948. Reagan's approach during the campaign was an extension of this worldview.[5]

On September 3, 1980, Reagan addressed a Jewish American group at the B'nai Brith Forum in Washington, DC. "While we have since 1948 clung to the argument of a moral imperative to explain our commitment to Israel," Reagan argued, "no Administration has ever deluded itself that Israel was not of permanent strategic importance to America. Until, that is, the Carter administration, which has violated this covenant with the past."[6] Reagan's extensive repudiation of Carter encompassed his predecessor's attempt at a comprehensive settlement between Israel and the Arabs and the inclusion of the Soviet Union in these negotiations, as well as US arms sales to Saudi Arabia and Jordan. This criticism was reflected in the pages of the staunchly pro-Israel *Commentary* magazine, an intellectual home for many of Reagan's foreign policy advisors. The magazine characterized Carter's hands-on approach to resolving Israel's conflict with the Arab world as appeasement.[7]

In Reagan's view, Israel was clearly part of an anticommunist struggle that would keep Soviet influence in the Middle East at bay. "Without this bastion of liberal democracy in the heart of the area," Reagan wrote in the *Washington Post* in 1979, "our own position would be weaker."[8] Such an approach mirrored his actions in Latin America, as Michael Schmidli describes with regard to democracy promotion in Nicaragua.[9] After taking office, this anticommunist view was emphasized by leading neoconservative advisors. In the view of one scholar who has closely examined US perceptions of the region, officials within the Reagan administration promoted the idea "that Israel was a vital Cold War ally of the United States and that Palestinians were tools of the Soviet Union in its campaign of international terrorism."[10] Under the growing influence of these staunch anticommunists, Reagan's worldview reconstituted the Middle East as a site of contestation between the United States and the Soviet Union.

Secretary of State Alexander Haig, who had been chief of staff in the Nixon White House and Supreme Allied Commander of NATO in Europe, was a chief architect of this new approach. In his memoir, Haig described a radical rethinking of US priorities in the Middle East. To address concerns about the Soviet Union and the "fear of Islamic fundamentalism," Haig instituted a policy of "strategic consensus."[11] This policy had the dual aim of fighting communism and bolstering moderate Arab states, while upholding Israel's security.[12] Recoiling at Carter's perceived weakness toward the Soviet Union, especially after the Soviet invasion of Afghanistan, the emerging "Reagan doctrine" incited a late Cold War revival.[13] Through military interventions and the arming of anticommunist resistance movements in an effort to "roll back" Soviet-supported governments in Latin America, Africa, and Asia, the Reagan White House embarked on what the Cold War scholar Odd Arne Westad has called an "anti-revolutionary offensive in the Third World."[14]

In the Middle East, this doctrine collided with events on the ground. Nicholas Veliotes, Reagan's assistant secretary of state for Near Eastern and South Asian Affairs, said that there was "a determination to globalize everything in the Middle East" in a remark that underscored the incompatibility of this new approach.[15] "In part," Veliotes explained some years later, "if your analysis of the Middle East always started from the East-West focus, you could obscure the regional roots of the problem."[16] Both the internecine violence of the Lebanese civil war and the outbreak of the first Palestinian Intifada in 1987 undercut the Reagan doctrine and forced a return to Carter-era restraint in executing Middle East policy. This reversal occurred as the administration's sweeping anticommunist rhetoric gave way to growing accommodation with the Soviet Union during Reagan's second term in office.[17] But a globalist outlook—which oversimplified regional complexities and positioned Israel as a key asset—characterized the early months of Reagan's first term.

In his first trip to the Middle East as secretary of state in April 1981, Alexander Haig focused on strengthening US relations with Israel along these Cold War lines. His counterparts in Jerusalem were very encouraged by the new administration in Washington, having openly clashed with Carter's expansive aspirations for a settlement to the Palestinian question throughout the forging of the Camp David Accords.[18] Israeli Prime Minister Menachem Begin had entered office in 1977 after the surprise overthrow of the dominant Labor Party by the right-wing Likud. Begin was a staunch defender of his country's territorial acquisitions in 1967 and promoted a narrow vision of autonomy for the Arab inhabitants of the newly occupied territories. He did not see Palestinians as a national movement requiring self-determination in the West Bank and Gaza, but rather as a national minority in "Judea and Samaria" whom Israel could treat with greater benevolence under Jewish sovereignty.[19]

The Israeli prime minister drew on a Cold War framework to justify his views. During his opening meeting with Haig, Begin stressed Israel's deep opposition to a Palestinian state. "It would be a mortal danger to us," Begin implored. "It would be a Soviet base in the Middle East, after all the Soviets achieved: Mozambique, South Yemen, Ethiopia, invading Afghanistan, etc. . . . Unavoidably the Judea, Samaria and Gaza District and those settlements would be taken over by the PLO and the PLO is a real satellite of the Soviet Union."[20] The inclusion of the PLO into the Soviet orbit solidified the link between Palestinian state prevention and shared US-Israeli foreign policy goals in the Cold War. Secretary Haig's official toast that same evening underscored this interdependence. Turning to his Israeli hosts gathered in Jerusalem's King David Hotel, Haig praised the country for playing "an essential role in protecting our mutual strategic concerns against the threats of the Soviet Union and against the threats of its many surrogates."[21]

Growing mutual interest between the US and Israel was encapsulated by Haig's effort to initiate a strategic dialogue beyond military channels. Throughout the summer and fall of 1981 the US secretary of state convened meetings intended to formalize the first strategic alliance between the two countries.[22] As part of these talks, Israeli Defense Minister Ariel Sharon outlined an expansive vision of Israel's strategic value to Reagan during Begin's first official meeting with the Americans in Washington. "Israel can do things, Mr. President, that other countries cannot do. We have the stability of a real democracy. . . . We can both act in the Mediterranean theatre and in Africa. We are capable of embarking upon cooperation immediately. We have American equipment which we can put at your disposal in the shortest time."[23] One American participant recalls seeing Secretary of Defense Caspar Weinberger "blanch visibly" at Sharon's presentation, which outlined Israeli military assistance as far east as Iran and as far north as Turkey. Weinberger, who had pushed harder for engagement with moderate allies in the region, was wary of any sign that the US was turning away from key Arab states, particularly the Gulf countries.[24] "Everyone on the American side was shocked by the grandiose scope of the Sharon concept for strategic cooperation," observed US ambassador to Israel, Samuel Lewis.[25]

The gap between the expansive Israeli concept of strategic cooperation and the tempered enthusiasm of some US officials was linked to competing interests across the Middle East. One of the primary beneficiaries of US Cold War strategy in the region was now Saudi Arabia, a country that defense officials such as Weinberger hoped would move closer, like Egypt before it, toward the West. This duality bred a great deal of tension. Israeli leaders and American Jewish organizations vocally opposed the sale of F-15 fighter jets and airborne warning and control systems (AWACS) to Riyadh, threatening to undermine an emerging regional constellation of power.[26]

On November 30, 1981, Israel and the United States signed a memorandum of understanding promoting strategic cooperation to deal with the Soviet threat. Emphasizing the importance of a unified front against communism, it encompassed joint military exercises and preventative threat measures.[27] While leading supporters of Israel such as Secretary Haig were pleased to formalize a strategic relationship, conservative critics such as Weinberger worked to strip the memorandum of real content. As Lewis recalls, "Weinberger managed to have it signed in the basement of the Pentagon without any press present, so that it didn't get any attention. The Israeli press was fully briefed and made a big thing out of it, but there were no photographs of Weinberger signing this document with Sharon—they might have been used in the Arab world to undermine his position."[28]

In forging a strategic alliance with Israel, the Reagan administration turned a blind eye to the more troubling aspects of the Begin government's agenda, such as settlement expansion in the West Bank. It also put aside strident arguments that had erupted over Israel's highly provocative bombing of Iraq's Osirik nuclear reactor on June 7, 1981.[29] But not long after the signing of the memorandum in December 1981, a major crisis erupted when Begin moved to extend Israeli law to the Golan Heights through implicit annexation, and the agreement was suspended.[30] Critics of Israel in the administration were furious, with Weinberger exclaiming, "How long do we have to go on bribing

Israel? If there is no real cost to the Israelis, we'll never be able to stop any of their actions."[31] Reagan took decisive action by suspending millions in potential arms sales, infuriating the Israeli prime minister. Begin responded directly to Ambassador Lewis. "Are we a state or vassals of yours? Are we a banana republic?" he exclaimed. "You have no right to penalize Israel. . . . The people of Israel lived without the memorandum of understanding for 3,700 years, and will continue to live without it for another 3,700 years."[32] This angry reaction, like the sensitive discussions over the Osirik bombing, revealed hidden tension in the US-Israeli relationship in the early Reagan years.[33]

Despite these disagreements, Israel emerged in the early 1980s with a new rationale to entrench its global Cold War standing and solidify its regional position. The strategic alliance helped the Begin government counter Palestinian demands for self-rule by dismissing the PLO as a Soviet proxy and denying Palestinians substantive political standing. Furthermore, the alliance enabled intensified settlement building in the occupied territories, providing a justification for Israel's internal hold over the West Bank and Gaza Strip. Most dramatically, the relationship abetted Israel's invasion of Lebanon, drawing the US into a longstanding civil war and igniting a regional backlash.

Since 1975, the US government had vowed to marginalize the PLO until the organization accepted relevant UN Resolutions 242 and 338 and recognized Israel.[34] During the November 1980 US presidential campaign, when asked whether he thought the PLO was a terrorist organization, Reagan answered affirmatively, albeit with an important distinction. "I separate the PLO from the Palestinian refugees. None ever elected the PLO."[35] His views were connected to broader conservative antipathy toward the violence of anticolonial movements in the 1960s and 1970s. "We live in a world in which any band of thugs clever enough to get the word 'liberation' into its name can thereupon murder schoolchildren and have its deeds considered glamorous and glorious," Reagan said during the campaign. "Terrorists are not guerrillas, or commandos, or freedom-fighters or anything else. They are terrorists and should be identified as such."[36]

For all Reagan's symbolic warnings of "appeasement" when he was asked about whether the US should establish diplomatic relations with the organization, the PLO was undergoing a transformation from military resistance to a diplomatic track, one that had largely been achieved by the late 1970s.[37] There were important fissures within the constituent factions of the Palestinian national movement, and incidents of armed violence and terror attacks persisted into the 1980s. Although carried out by dissident splinter groups and rejectionist factions such as the virulently anti-PLO Abu Nidal Organization, officials in the Reagan White House often blurred the distinction.[38] Richard Allen, Reagan's national security advisor, dismissed countervailing influences within the PLO. During an interview on the ABC news program *20/20*, he labeled the group a "terrorist organization" until "it provides convincing evidence to the contrary."[39] According to Allen, moderate factions within the organization had little bearing on the administration's overall stance. "I've heard descriptions that identified [PLO chairman Yasser] Arafat as a moderate. . . . One man's moderate is another man's terrorist."[40]

Some Reagan White House officials understood that the PLO was a complex, dynamic organization. Raymond Tanter, a National Security Council (NSC) staffer who focused on the Middle East, cautioned Allen in November that "the President should not brand all of the PLO organizations as terrorists since the PLO includes a number of social and political institutions."[41] He cited the Central Intelligence Agency's (CIA's) *Palestinian Handbook*, which recognized nonterrorist entities such as the PLO Research Center and the Palestine Red Crescent Society. There was also ample evidence of direct low-level contact with moderate members of the PLO. A series of newspaper articles in the summer of 1981 revealed that contacts had been ongoing since Henry Kissinger's time in office, with Reagan's contacts facilitated primarily through the CIA and the American Embassy in Beirut.[42] The administration also had less formal discussions with PLO members through third-party interlocutors such as John Mroz, the director of Middle East Studies at the International Peace Academy in New York.[43]

Palestinian factions in Beirut took note of the dominant hostility toward the PLO in Washington, as did the active Arabic press at the time. One leading weekly, *Al-Hadaf* (The Target) was unrelenting in its critique of what it characterized as American neo-imperial aspirations in the Middle East. The newspaper, founded by the Palestinian writer Ghassan Kanafani, was the mouthpiece of the Marxist leaning Popular Front for the Liberation of Palestine (PFLP).[44] Reagan himself, in the eyes of *Al-Hadaf*, was restoring the use of force as the primary tool of US foreign policy in the region. Along with Haig, the president was portrayed as a radical departure from Carter and his US human rights agenda.[45] From the perspective of Palestinian activists in the global South, Reagan offered little hope for improving America's standing abroad.[46] The brunt of *Al-Hadaf*'s fury, however, was directed at Israel and Prime Minister Menachem Begin. Under a grotesque cartoon of Begin, face deformed, blood dripping from his hands, and a dagger at the ready, the paper attacked Israeli settlement policy in the West Bank and Begin's undermining of Palestinian national identity.[47]

The Reagan administration's support for Begin's settlement expansion was evident in the changing US position toward the legality of ongoing building projects in the West Bank. Throughout Carter's presidency, US policy on the settlements had been "clear and consistent."[48] They were considered illegal under international law and detrimental to the peace process, and the administration opposed both new settlements and expansion of those already built.[49] During the 1980 campaign, Reagan took a different stance. In an interview with *Time* magazine on June 30, 1980, he was asked whether he would "try to persuade Israel to stop settling on the West Bank?" His response underscored a clear difference with Carter. "Frankly, I don't know the answer to that. Under U.N. Resolution 242, the West Bank was supposed to be open to all, and then Jordan and Israel were to work out an agreement for the area." In light of these terms Reagan argued, "I do not see how it is illegal for Israel to move in settlements."[50]

In the week after his inauguration, Reagan expanded on this new position after lawmakers in Jerusalem approved three new West Bank settlements. When asked about the expansion during a press conference, he replied: "I believe the settlements there—I disagreed when the previous administration referred to them as illegal, they're not illegal."[51] In the NSC staff, Middle East adviser Raymond Tanter vigorously defended the administration's new approach. "The settlements *are legal*, but the issue is properly a *political* question, *not* a *legal* question. . . . There is no law that bars Jews from settling in the West Bank. No one should be excluded from an area simply on account of nationality or religion."[52] Eugene Rostow, the Sterling Professor of Law at Yale University, was an influential voice in facilitating this legal and semantic shift. Rostow's adamant defense of the settlements entrenched a viewpoint that the territories were never occupied, contradicting Israeli jurists as far back as 1967.[53]

The consequence of this policy reversal was borne out by the rapid pace of Israeli expansion through the 1980s. Five thousand Jewish settlers lived in the West Bank when Begin entered office in 1977. There were more than 80,000 by the late 1980s. In the interim, commuter towns and bypass roads for settlers bisected the actual ground upon which Palestinian sovereignty could be achieved, as Israel consolidated a durable matrix of control.[54] In February 1982, Reagan's ambassador to Israel, Sam Lewis, widely circulated an urgent memo detailing recent developments in the West Bank, writing that "settlement activity goes on at an accelerated pace, although in new and potentially more serious directions."[55]

Reagan was personally aware of the aftermath of settlement expansion. On Valentine's Day 1983, the president wrote in his diary: "Had a brief on the West Bank. There can be no question but that Israel has a well thought out plan to take over the W. B. [West Bank]"⁵⁶ In his memoirs, he would write that settlements were a "continued violation of UN Security Council Resolution 242."⁵⁷ This was at odds with his stance during the campaign, but did not signify a shift in policy. As late as 1988, upon hearing that Israel was planning new settlements, Reagan was subdued: "We are going to try and talk them out of that."⁵⁸

In actuality, the Reagan administration took a permissive attitude toward settlement expansion, as the Israelis were acutely aware. In a January 1982 meeting with US officials, Prime Minister Begin recalled the first time he met Carter in the Cabinet Room and the president told him "we consider your settlements to be illegal and an obstacle to peace." He had seen Carter more than ten times, and at each meeting, Carter repeated this message, and Begin disagreed. "I answered: legal and not an obstacle to peace. He didn't tire; I didn't tire." For Begin, who had long championed the expansion of the Jewish presence beyond the 1967 borders, settlements were not an obstacle to peace with the Palestinians. "On the contrary," he added, "they are a great contribution to peaceful relationships between the Jews and the Arabs in Judea and Samaria and the Gaza District." Without them, PLO fighters would come down from the mountains to the plains of Israel and carry out attacks on Jews. "If there are no settlements there, they can just come down."⁵⁹ "Mr. Ronald Reagan, put an end to that debate," Begin reminisced. "He said, the settlements are not illegal. A double negative gives a positive result. In other words, they are legal or legitimate."⁶⁰

Against the backdrop of Reagan's approach to Israel, the Palestinian national movement, and the occupied territories, Lebanon emerged as the region's Cold War battlefield.⁶¹ The PLO had relocated to Lebanon after the outbreak of the Jordanian civil war in 1970, shifting the center of nationalist politics to the Palestinian refugee camps inside the country.⁶² Israeli leaders were increasingly anxious about the power of Palestinian nationalism and the growing links between Palestinians inside the occupied territories and in the Arab diaspora. By targeting the PLO in Lebanon and forcing its withdrawal, strategic thinkers in Israel believed that Palestinian national aspirations for a homeland could be quashed and a pliant Maronite Christian ally established to the north.⁶³ An ideological alignment between Menachem Begin's Likud government and the Reagan administration helped foment the invasion, which sowed regional upheaval and drew the United States into the largest quagmire since the Vietnam War.

Israel's decision to militarily target the PLO grew alongside the launch of Palestinian autonomy talks in the spring of 1979. In Defense Minister Ariel Sharon's view, the failings of the Camp David Accords justified a display of force that would somehow defeat Palestinians in their Lebanese stronghold. There remains disagreement about both what precipitated the invasion and the American role in triggering the war. While there had been PLO attacks on Israel's northern border towns, they ceased after the July 1981 ceasefire brokered by Reagan's special envoy to Lebanon, Ambassador Philipp Habib. Israel would cite attacks outside of Lebanon, including the assassination of an Israeli diplomat in Paris and cross-border raids from Jordan, as further evidence of the need to strike the PLO.

Sharon revealed his military plans during a meeting with Ambassador Habib in December 1981 at the Israeli Foreign Ministry. Habib's assistant, Morris Draper, would recall the substance of this meeting ten years later. "In graphic detail he [Sharon] described to Haig and people like Larry Eagleburger that we were going to see American-made munitions being dropped from American-made aircraft over Lebanon, and civilians were going to be killed, there was going to be a hell of a big uproar, and the United States—which didn't look very good in the Middle East anyway at the time, for being so inactive—was going to take a full charge of blame."[64] US ambassador to Israel Samuel Lewis corroborated Draper's recollections, adding that "Habib and everybody else was thunder-struck by Sharon's plan, although I think our Embassy staff were not quite as surprised, except for the fact that Sharon was being so open about his views."[65] Habib reportedly asked Sharon what Israel would do with the thousands of Palestinians in the country, and Sharon allegedly replied, "We'll hand them over to the Lebanese. In any case, we expect to be in Lebanon only for a few days. The Lebanese Christians will take care of them."[66]

Sharon's presentation, as one US policymaker later explained, was intended "to prepare the Reagan administration for a large Israeli operation in Lebanon."[67] It did not take much convincing. A few days before the invasion, Sharon came to Washington and explained in detail to Haig what he was planning. The notebooks of Charles Hill, a top State Department aide, clearly indicate his boss issued a "green light" for Israel's actions. Haig told Sharon that an invasion required *"a recognizable provocation,"* akin to the Falklands intervention. "Hope you'll be sensitive to the need for provocation to be understood internationally," Haig said. Sharon replied that he was "aware of your concern about size. Our intent is *not a large operation. Try to be as small and efficient as possible.*" "Like a lobotomy," Haig replied approvingly.[68]

An assassination attempt several days later against Israel's ambassador to Great Britain, Shlomo Argov, provided the necessary spark. Even though the Abu Nidal Organization rather than the PLO had carried out the attack,

Israel launched "Operation Peace for Galilee" on June 6, 1982. The Begin government's stated war aim was to ensure the immediate cessation of cross-border violence.[69] But the invasion extended well beyond the forty-kilometer line Sharon had initially suggested would be the military theater of operation, and Israeli troops headed toward Beirut to link up with Maronite forces. Promising the Americans that they had no intention of staying in Lebanon and occupying the country, the Israelis simply asserted that they would not tolerate a return to the status quo of PLO shelling in the Galilee region.[70]

American officials debated the extent to which the administration should endorse Israel's "lobotomy" in Lebanon. Secretary Haig and US ambassador to the UN Jeane Kirkpatrick felt that Israel should be left to destroy the PLO, which they saw as a proxy of the Soviet Union. The more cautious trio of Secretary of Defense Caspar Weinberger, White House Chief of Staff James Baker, and National Security Advisor William Clark favored holding Israel to a more limited operation.[71] On June 8, Prime Minister Begin and Ambassador Habib met to discuss Israeli war aims. Habib was deeply concerned with Israel's mounting bombing campaign in Beirut. Along with Ambassador Sam Lewis, he argued that the PLO was not responsible for the assassination attempt against Argov and that the Israelis were exceeding the forty-kilometer threshold. Reagan's senior advisers were cognizant that their close alignment with Israel posed problems for US Middle East policy more broadly. There was a growing fear in Washington that the Arab world would view American silence as a sign of complicity or even a signal that the United States had helped to initiate the violence.[72]

The Israeli Prime Minister knew that US support was subject to internal debate, and the disagreements intensified on the eve of Begin's pre-planned visit to Washington in June 1982.[73] His first meeting with Reagan about Lebanon was a tense forty-five minutes with just the two leaders and their notetakers present. The meeting opened with Reagan's assertion that the invasion had exceeded its stated goals of responding to PLO attacks with the incursion toward the Lebanese seaside capital of Beirut. The United States, Reagan said, could not offer unconditional support to a "military operation which was not clearly justified in the eyes of the international community." Even in light of the terrible attack on the Israeli ambassador in London, he argued, "Israel has lost ground to a great extent among our people," who had recoiled at "the death and destruction that the IDF [Israel Defense Forces] brought to so many innocent people over the past two weeks."[74]

Given his overarching anti-Soviet agenda, Reagan believed that the United States could manage its long-standing friendship with Israel without alienating wealthy anticommunist Arab states. But Israeli overreach in Lebanon disabused him and his administration of this notion. As Reagan told Begin, "US influence in the Arab world, our ability to achieve our strategic objectives, has been seriously damaged by Israel's actions."[75] Begin, in turn, deployed the same Cold War logic that he had invoked to justify Israel's battle against the PLO. Detailing stockpiles of Soviet weaponry, he told Reagan that the south of Lebanon had become "the principal center of Soviet activities in the Middle East . . . a true international terrorist base." When Reagan pushed him to account for the civilian casualties, Begin denounced a media "biased against Israel." The meeting ended abruptly, sending a clear signal that the two countries' interests were diverging and that the Reagan administration would not remain silent in the face of Israeli aggression.[76]

US-Israeli tensions increased markedly throughout the summer months.[77] The Israelis lost a close ally after Alexander Haig was forced to resign for overextending his reach and was replaced by a more restrained secretary of state, George Shultz.[78] As Ambassador Lewis explained, "The sympathy of the administration, which up to early July, had been strongly pro-Israel, increasingly shifted towards the Palestinians."[79] Reagan himself was intensely disturbed by the barrage of TV images coming from Beirut as the Israeli army shelled the Lebanese capital. As he wrote in his diary one evening in late July, "Calls and cables back and forth with Lebanon. U.N. [Security Council] with us supporting voted 15 to 0 for a ceasefire and U.N. observers on the scene. Israel will scream about the latter but so be it. The slaughter must stop."[80]

On August 12, an intense day-long bombing of West Beirut by the Israelis inflicted over 500 casualties in what would be the last day of the summer siege on the Lebanese capital.[81] Reagan's diary reveals the depth of his anger and a growing rift between two stalwart Cold War allies. "I was angry—I told [Begin] it had to stop or our entire future relationship was endangered. I used the word holocaust deliberately & said the symbol of his war was becoming a picture of a 7 month old baby with its arms blown off. . . . Twenty mins. later he called to tell me he'd ordered an end to the barrage and pled for our continued friendship."[82] Ambassador Habib eventually negotiated a ceasefire, and PLO leader Yasser Arafat agreed to the withdrawal of his men from Lebanon.[83] On August 25, 800 US Marines began to arrive in Beirut, equipped for a noncombat role of assisting the Lebanese Armed Forces alongside French and Italian military personnel in the withdrawal. In side letters to Arafat during the arduous negotiations, Habib guaranteed the protection of Palestinian civilians remaining behind after the armed PLO guerilla fighters were evacuated.[84] But these promises were blatantly ignored—with calamitous results—in the weeks that followed.

Soon after the Marine deployment, Reagan announced a formal peace plan on September 1, 1982, from his "Western White House" in Santa Barbara, California. This was Reagan's first and only major speech on the Arab-Israeli conflict during his eight years in office. Building on Jimmy Carter's Camp David framework, he acknowledged that movement on implementing the Camp David Accords had been slow even as Israel had completed its withdrawal from the Sinai. Noting that the "opportunities for peace in the Middle East do not begin and end in Lebanon," Reagan recognized that "we must also move to resolve the root causes of conflict between Arabs and Israelis." In his view, the central question was "how to reconcile Israel's legitimate security concerns with the legitimate rights of the Palestinians."[85] Shultz had already underscored the importance of a "solution to the Palestinian problem" in a meeting with Defense Minister Ariel Sharon several days before the plan was announced.[86] Events in Lebanon had forced a reckoning with the very questions that Reagan had sidestepped when entering office.

The September 14 assassination of Lebanese President Bashir Gemayel, a Maronite ally of Israel and close confidant of Ariel Sharon, upended Reagan's initiative and shattered Begin's grand plans for the emergence of a Lebanese state remade under a strong Christian leader. The Israeli army broke the cease-fire and entered West Beirut, an act that Shultz deemed "provocative" and "counterproductive."[87] Israeli ambassador to the US Moshe Arens insisted that the Israelis did not want to deceive the Americans and that these were merely precautionary measures, as Israel "did not have ambitions in Beirut, not in the West, not in the east, and not in Lebanon at all." Shultz responded tersely: "Your activity in West Beirut will engender a situation where Israel is controlling an Arab capital." There would be "psychological" consequences.[88] Weinberger had already ordered the US Marines back to their ships, with the PLO evacuation now complete. As a result of the ensuing vacuum, Lebanese Christian militias who sought revenge for Gemayel's assassination were free to terrorize Palestinian civilians who had remained behind.

Between the evening of September 16 and the afternoon of September 18, Phalange militia fighters launched a cold-blooded attack on defenseless Palestinian civilians in the Israeli-controlled Sabra and Shatila refugee camps, killing at least 800 people, mostly women, children and elderly men.[89] Newly uncovered evidence in the Israel State Archives reveals that the US government was unwittingly complicit in this three-day massacre.[90] The Reagan administration's role was a moral stain and a strategic disaster, undercutting US influence in the region and precipitating further military involvement in the Lebanese civil war.[91] Weinberger's critics blamed him for enabling the violence by withdrawing the Marines, and even Ambassador Habib later admitted that the US had failed to keep its word to protect those Palestinians left behind.[92]

On October 23, 1983, an enormous explosion ripped through the US Marine barracks in Beirut, killing 241 American servicemen—the single deadliest attack against the US Marine Corps since World War II.[93] Minutes later, a second suicide bomber hit the French military barracks in the "Drakkar" building, killing fifty-eight paratroopers in France's single worst military loss since the Algerian War. These attacks led to open warfare with Syrian-backed forces and, soon after, the rapid withdrawal of the Marines and Multinational Forces to their ships, accelerating the end of US and European involvement in Lebanon. Despite Reagan's pledge to retaliate against the perpetrators and not to withdraw until the mission was complete, US troops departed within months.[94] In the words of US Ambassador Sam Lewis, the United States left the country "with our tail between our legs."[95] The Lebanese civil war would facilitate Syria's regional ascendency and incubate other important regional transformations, in particular the growing influence of Iran and Hezbollah, the emergent Shia paramilitary group.[96]

In the wake of the 1982 war, the Israeli government remained determined to preempt Palestinian self-determination. American officials did not force the issue, having shifted gears away from the Reagan plan toward secret peace talks with Jordan's King Hussein and local "quality-of-life" initiatives in the occupied territories in twin bids to circumvent the PLO. This line of approach would last until nearly the end of Reagan's second term in office. The outbreak of the first Intifada in December 1987 shattered illusions that Palestinian national movement could thus be sidestepped. After twenty years of Israeli military control, inhabitants of the occupied territories erupted in demonstrations and widespread civil disobedience that captured global attention.

The Intifada exposed the Reagan administration's policy vacuum in the Arab-Israeli conflict. After five years of inaction, Shultz formulated a new approach to the Palestinian issue, the first serious peace proposal since Reagan's September 1982 plan. Yet King Hussein, whose support was crucial for its success, relinquished Jordan's legal and administrative ties to the West Bank in July 1988, forcing the United States and Israel to deal solely with the PLO, a prospect which had been unthinkable years earlier. In the final days of the Reagan administration, the United States reluctantly agreed to begin an official dialogue with the PLO.[97] Like Reagan's reversal when it came to dealing with the Soviet Union, this shift was a striking turn for an administration so adamantly opposed to engagement since its first months in office.

The signing of a memorandum of understanding between Israel and the United States during Reagan's first year as president may have marked the formal onset of an alliance, but relations with the Palestinians and Lebanon complicate the dominant narrative of abiding friendship between stalwart allies in the 1980s. By enabling a new strategic rationale to bilateral ties, the Reagan administration empowered Israel to shut down political horizons in the occupied territories and intervene in the broader region. At the same time, open clashes with Israel, as well as the gradual recognition that Palestinian nationalism was not going to be defeated militarily, yielded a return to the comprehensive peace principles that Carter had sought on the road to Camp David.

When it came to Israel's conflict with the Palestinians, Reagan's marked shift from Carter's approach linked American foreign policy with the most reactionary elements of Israel's Likud party. The administration's revival of a global Cold War in the Middle East cast Palestinian nationalists as proxies of the Soviet Union, while a permissive legal turn emboldened advocates for settlement building in the occupied territories of the West Bank and Gaza Strip. The administration's early and unchecked impulse for military intervention by proxy across the global South fueled the green light offered by Alexander Haig to Ariel Sharon ahead of Israel's June 1982 invasion of Lebanon.

In reassessing Reagan's approach and legacy, historians must account for the actions of local actors in the region alongside developments in Washington. There was a host of dynamics at play in US relations with Israel, the Palestinians, and Lebanon, and the reinscription of a Cold War context was interwoven with domestic pressures, the ascent of the Likud, and the internal struggles of Palestinian nationalists and the Lebanese themselves. Although it is clear that Palestinian nationalists were seeking to move into the diplomatic arena, the bellicose rhetoric of the White House alienated moderate elements of the PLO, and the 1982 war fractured the Palestinian national movement while raining tragedy upon civilians in Lebanon. Rather than a triumphal story of the United States defeating communism in the periphery, events in the Levant highlight US agency in the intensification of regional violence in the 1980s. Against this backdrop, Reagan's time in office should be viewed as a period that contributed significantly to the erosion of a just and equitable outcome to Israel's conflict with the Palestinians, along with more corrosive developments—an "adders' nest of problems" in Reagan's revealing words—elsewhere in the wider Middle East.[98]

Notes

1. On US-Middle East relations in the late twentieth century, see Osamah Khalil, *America's Dream Palace: Middle East Expertise and the Rise of the National Security State* (Cambridge, MA: Harvard University Press, 2016); Mahmood Mamdani, *Good Muslim, Bad Muslim: America, the Cold War, and the Roots of Terror* (New York: Pantheon Books, 2004); Andrew Bacevich, *America's War for the Greater Middle East: A Military History* (New York: Random House, 2016); Rashid Khalidi, *Sowing Crisis: The Cold War and American Dominance in the Middle East* (Boston: Beacon Press, 2009); Salim Yaqub, *Imperfect Strangers: Americans, Arabs and US–Middle East Relations in the 1970s* (Ithaca, NY: Cornell University Press, 2016); James R. Stocker, *Spheres of Intervention: US Foreign Policy and the Collapse of Lebanon, 1967–1976* (Ithaca, NY: Cornell University Press, 2016); Patrick Tyler, *A World of Trouble: The White House and the Middle East—From the Cold War to the War on Terror* (New York: Farrar, Straus and Giroux, 2009); Mattia Toaldo, *The Origins of the US War on Terror: Lebanon, Libya and American Intervention in the Middle East* (New York: Routledge, 2013); Paul Thomas Chamberlin, *The Global Offensive: The United States, the Palestine Liberation Organization, and the Making of the Post–Cold War Order* (New York: Oxford University Press, 2012); Douglas Little, *American Orientalism: The United States and the Middle East Since 1945* (London: I. B. Tauris, 2003); Lloyd C. Gardner, *The Long Road to Baghdad: A History of US Foreign Policy from the 1970s to the Present* (New York: The New Press, 2008); Nicholas Laham, *Crossing the Rubicon: Ronald Reagan and US Policy in the Middle East* (Aldershot: Ashgate, 2004).

2. Although Odd Arne Westad has forced a necessary reckoning with Western military intervention in the global South, his work has avoided the Arab-Israeli arena. Odd Arne Westad, *The Global Cold War: Third World Interventions and the Making of Our Times* (Cambridge: Cambridge University Press, 2005), 4, 398. For an outline of how to approach the region in the post-1945 era, see Paul Thomas Chamberlin, "Rethinking the Middle East and North Africa in the Cold War," *International Journal of Middle East Studies* 43, no. 2 (2011): 317–319.

3. On the adverse consequences of the Camp David process, see Seth Anziska, *Preventing Palestine: A Political History from Camp David to Oslo* (Princeton, NJ: Princeton University Press, 2018). Material in this chapter is drawn from that work.

4. Ronald Reagan, *An American Life* (New York: Simon and Schuster, 1990), 410.

5. Rita Hauser, interview by author, 4 Apr. 2008. On the American embrace of Uris's novel, see M. M. Silver, *Our Exodus: Leon Uris and the Americanization of Israel's Founding Story* (Detroit, MI: Wayne State University Press, 2010).

6. Reagan, Address to the B'nai B'rith Forum, 3 Sept. 1980, Ronald Reagan Presidential Library (RRPL), Geoffrey Kemp Files (GKF), box 90494, folder "Israel Settlements 1981."

7. See, among others, Norman Podhoretz, "The Future Danger," *Commentary*, Apr. 1981; Menahem Milson, "How to Make Peace with the Palestinians," *Commentary*, May 1981: Robert C. Tucker, "The Middle East: Carterism without Carter?" *Commentary*, Sept. 1981.

8. Ronald Reagan, "Recognizing the Israeli Asset," *Washington Post*, 15 Aug. 1979.

9. See William Michael Schmidli's chapter in this volume.

10. Kathleen Christison, *Perceptions of Palestine: Their Influence on US Middle East Policy* (Berkeley: University of California Press, 2000), 198.

11. Alexander Haig, *Caveat: Realism, Reagan and Foreign Policy* (London: Weidenfeld and Nicolson, 1984), 170.

12. William B. Quandt, *Peace Process: American Diplomacy and the Arab-Israeli Conflict since 1967* (Washington, DC: Brookings Institution Press, 2005), 248–249. For detailed attention to Haig's views on strategic consensus, see Juliana S. Peck, *The Reagan Administration and the Palestinian Question: The First Thousand Days* (Washington, DC: Institute for Palestine Studies, 1984), chap. 2; Helena Cobban, "The US-Israeli Relationship in the Reagan Era," *Conflict Quarterly* 9, no. 2 (1989): 5–32. For the Israeli view of Haig, see "Alexander Haig v'Hamizrach Ha'Tichon," 27 Jan. 1981, Israel State Archives (ISA), MFA-8467/4.

13. On the Reagan doctrine, see Chester Pach, "The Reagan Doctrine: Principle, Pragmatism and Policy," *Presidential Studies Quarterly* 36, no. 1 (2006): 75–88.

14. See Odd Arne Westad, "Reagan's Anti-Revolutionary Offensive in the Third World" in Olav Njølstad, ed., *The Last Decade of the Cold War: From Conflict Escalation to Conflict Transformation* (London: Routledge, 2004), 241–262.

15. Nicolas Veliotes Interview, *Frontline Diplomacy*, Library of Congress Manuscript Division, (LOC).

16. Veliotes Interview.

17. See Beth A. Fischer, *The Reagan Reversal: Foreign Policy and the End of the Cold War* (Columbia: University of Missouri Press, 1997); James Mann, *The Rebellion of Ronald Reagan: A History of the End of the Cold War* (New York: Viking, 2009).

18. The Israeli Ministry of Foreign Affairs North America division conducted extensive analysis of Reagan's views and noted this favorable departure from Carter. See ISA, MFA/8467/1, 4, 5, 15 and MFA/8652/ 2, 3, 4.

19. Seth Anziska, "Autonomy as State Prevention: The Palestinian Question after Camp David, 1979–1982" *Humanity* 8, no. 2 (2017), 287–310.

20. Meeting between Begin, Haig, and delegations, 5 Apr. 1981, ISA, MFA-7083/12.

21. Toasts by Shamir and Haig after Dinner Hosted by Shamir, 5 Apr. 1981, SA, A-4341/1.

22. For full records of these top-secret meetings between Robert McFarlane and Israeli officials, see ISA, A-7384/6.

23. Meeting between Reagan and Begin, 9 Sept. 1981, ISA, A/7384/9.

24. Quandt, *Peace Process*, 247. Weinberger had been vice president of the Bechtel Corporation and was a strong advocate for rebuilding American military strength. On his approach to the use of force, see Gail E. S. Yoshitani, *Reagan on War: A Reappraisal of the Weinberger Doctrine, 1980–1984* (College Station: Texas A&M University Press, 2011).

25. Samuel Lewis Interview, *Frontline Diplomacy*, LOC. See also David Crist, *The Twilight War: The Secret History of America's Thirty-Year Conflict with Iran* (New York: Penguin, 2012), 57.

26. Reagan insisted to Begin that Saudi Arabia could be "brought around" to the US orbit. See Meeting between Reagan and Begin, 9 Sept. 1981, ISA, A-7384/9.

27. For the full text of the Memorandum, see Walter Laqueur and Barry M. Rubin, *The Israel-Arab Reader: A Documentary History of the Middle East Conflict* (New York: Penguin Books, 2001), 238–239.

28. Samuel Lewis Interview.

29. Israeli archives now reveal that the Osirik attack elicited furious American opposition, even from neoconservatives such as UN Ambassador Jeanne Kirkpatrick. See ISA, A/7384/4, 6.

30. For the administration's angry reaction, see RRPL, GKF, box 2, folder: "Golan Heights 1982."

31. Quoted in Haig, *Caveat*, 328.

32. Haig, *Caveat*, 329.

33. This strain is evident in a personal letter from Reagan to Begin after the suspension of the memorandum of understanding in the wake of the Golan Heights Law. See Reagan to Begin, 8 Jan. 1982, ISA, A-4342/1.

34. Despite the ban on direct diplomatic communication with the PLO put in place by the Ford administration in 1975, the CIA maintained regular contact with members of the organization. See Kai Bird, *The Good Spy: The Life and Death of Robert Ames* (New York: Crown, 2014); Osamah Khalil, "The Radical Crescent: The United States, the Palestine Liberation Organisation, and the Lebanese Civil War, 1973–1978," *Diplomacy and Statecraft* 27, no. 3 (2016): 496–522; James R. Stocker, "A Historical Inevitability? Kissinger and US Contacts with the Palestinians (1973–1976)," *International History Review* 39, no. 2 (2017), 316–337.

35. "Msibat Itonaim-Reagan," 6 Nov. 1980, ISA, MFA-8652/3.

36. Reagan, Address to the B'nai B'rith Forum, 3 Sept. 1980, RRPL, GKF, box 90494, folder "Israel Settlements 1981."

37. See Yezid Sayigh, *Armed Struggle and the Search for State: The Palestinian National Movement 1949–1993* (Oxford: Clarendon Press, 1997); Helga Baumgarten, "The Three Faces/Phases of Palestinian Nationalism, 1948–2005," *Journal of Palestine Studies* 34, no. 4 (2005): 25–48. On the consequences of nonengagement with the PLO, see Chamberlin, *The Global Offensive*, 256.

38. The Abu Nidal Organization was formed after a 1974 split in the PLO and was supported by Baathist Iraq in a highly visible and destructive terror campaign against Israel and Western targets, as well as PLO members who pursued negotiations. See Patrick Seale, *Abu Nidal: The Secret Life of the World's Most Notorious Arab Terrorist* (New York: Random House, 1992).

39. Allen Interview, *20/20: The ABC News Magazine*, 2 Apr. 1981, RRPL, GKF, box 90220, folder "PLO 1981."

40. Allen Interview.

41. Tanter to Allen, "The PLO and the President's Press Conference," 9 Nov. 1981, RRPL, GKF, box 90220, folder "PLO 1981."

42. "US, PLO: 7 Years of Secret Contacts," *Los Angeles Times*, 5 July 1981; "US, PLO Reportedly Have Custom of Secret Dealings," *Philadelphia Inquirer*, 6 July 1981.

43. This is clear from letters provided directly to Geoffrey Kemp, senior director for Near East and South Asian Affairs at the National Security Council in the White House. See Sartawi to Mroz, 27 May 1981, RRPL, GKF, box 90220, folder "PLO 1981." For more on this secret channel, see Christison, *Perceptions of Palestine*, 205.

44. Kanafani was born in Acre and forced into exile in 1948. He was later recruited by Dr. George Habash into the Arab Nationalist Movement (ANM), a left-wing pan-Arab organization whose membership evolved into the PFLP and served as a strong counterweight to the dominant Fatah party. Kanafani was assassinated in 1972 along with his niece in a Beirut car bombing by the Israeli Mossad. See Ronen Bergman,

Rise and Kill First: The Secret History of Israel's Targeted Assassinations (New York: Random House, 2018), 656n144; and Rashid Khalidi, *The Hundred Years' War on Palestine: A History of Settler Colonialism and Resistance, 1917–2017* (New York: Metropolitan Books, 2020).

45. "Il-Rais Reagan yusalam risala muhima fi beit il-abyad," *Al-Hadaf* 12, no. 522 (24 Jan. 1981), Beirut Institute for Palestine Studies (IPS).

46. "Idarat Reagan tu'hadad," *Al-Hadaf* 12, no. 525 (14 Feb. 1981), IPS.

47. "Hukumat Begin tas'ad min il-nisha't il-istitani," *Al-Hadaf* 12, no. 524 (7 Feb. 1981), IPS.

48. Peck, *The Reagan Administration and the Palestinian Question*, 11.

49. This position was based on Article 49 of the Fourth Convention Relative to the Protection of Civilian Persons in Time of War, which states clearly that "the Occupying Power shall not deport or transfer parts of its own civilian population into the territories it occupies"; see International Committee of the Red Cross, *The Geneva Conventions of August 12, 1949* (Geneva: International Committee of the Red Cross, 1949), 172.

50. "An Interview with Reagan," *Time*, 30 June 1980.

51. "Excerpts from President Reagan's Answers in Interview with Five Reporters," *New York Times*, 3 Feb. 1981.

52. Tanter to Allen and Feith, "Thoughts on Legality of Israel's West Bank Settlements," 3 Aug. 1981, RRPL, White House Office of Records Management (WHORM) case file 037386, folder CO074. Emphasis in original.

53. Eugene V. Rostow, "'Palestinian Self-Determination': Possible Futures for the Unallocated Territories of the Palestine Mandate," *International Journal of Yale Law School* 5, no. 2 (1979), 147–172. An abbreviated version of this argument appeared as "Israel's Settlement Right Is 'Unassailable,'" *New York Times*, 19 Sept. 1982. For the origins of Israeli legal thinking that justified expansion, see "Hitnachluyot: P'sak Hadin Hamaleh," ISA, MFA-9336/10.

54. A contemporaneous study of the expansion can be found in Peter Demant, "Israeli Settlement Policy Today," *Middle East Report* 116 (1983): 3–29.

55. Lewis to Shultz et al., 2 Feb. 1982, RRPL, GKF, box 90494, folder "Israel Settlements, 1982."

56. Douglas Brinkley, ed., *The Reagan Diaries* (New York: HarperCollins, 2007), 130.

57. Reagan, *An American Life*, 441.

58. Brinkley, *The Reagan Diaries*, 577.

59. Meeting between Burg and Haig, 28 Jan. 1982, ISA, MFA-6898/8.

60. Meeting between Burg and Haig, 28 Jan. 1982, ISA, MFA-6898/8.

61. On the history of violent battlefields during the Cold War, see Paul Thomas Chamberlin, *The Cold War's Killing Fields: Rethinking the Long Peace* (New York: HarperCollins, 2018).

62. Palestinians refer to the events of 1970 as "Black September." For Israel's role, see Ziv Rubinovitz, "Blue and White 'Black September': Israel's Role in the Jordan Crisis of 1970," *International History Review* 32, no. 4 (2010): 687–706. On the history of the PLO inside Lebanon and the lead up to 1982, see David Hirst, *Beware of Small States: Lebanon, Battleground of the Middle East* (New York: Nation Books, 2010); Rosemary Sayigh, *Too Many Enemies* (London: Zed, 1994); Helena Cobban, *The Palestinian*

Liberation Organisation: People, Power, and Politics (Cambridge: Cambridge University Press, 1984); Yezid Sayigh, "The Palestinians," in *The Cold War and the Middle East*, ed. Yezid Sayigh and Avi Shlaim (Oxford: Clarendon Press, 1997).

63. On Israel's motivations in Lebanon, see Kirsten E. Schulze, "Perceptions and Misperceptions: Influences on Israeli Intelligence Estimates during the 1982 Lebanon War," *Journal of Conflict Studies* 16, no. 1, (1996), 134–152; Avner Yaniv and Robert J. Liber, "Personal Whim or Strategic Imperative?: The Israeli Invasion of Lebanon," *International Security* 8, no. 2 (1983), 117–142.

64. Morris Draper, "Marines in Lebanon—A Ten Year Retrospective: Lessons Learned," Quantico, VA, 1992 (courtesy of Jon Randal).

65. Samuel Lewis Interview.

66. Samuel Lewis Interview.

67. Samuel Lewis Interview.

68. Below this, Hill wrote: "A GREEN LIGHT FROM HAIG ON LIMITED OPERATION" (Hill notes, 25 May 1982, Hoover Institution Archives, Charles Hill Papers, box 76, folder 17). Emphasis in original. While recent scholarship still upholds Haig's denial of having given Sharon permission, the minutes of the meeting prove otherwise; see Crist, *The Twilight War*, 109. For an earlier study on the green light, without access to Hill's notebooks, see Ze'ev Schiff, "The Green Light," *Foreign Policy* 50 (Spring 1983), 73–85.

69. See Eyal Zisser, "The 1982 'Peace for Galilee' War: Looking Back in Anger—Between an Option of a War and a War of No Option," in *A Never-Ending Conflict: A Guide to Israeli Military History*, ed. Mordechai Bar-On (Westport: Praeger, 2004). Begin admitted that 1982 was a war of "option" and it would cure "trauma of 1973" (cited in Zisser, 194–195).

70. Meeting between Begin and Habib, 7 June 1982, ISA, MFA-7080/3.

71. Detailed accounts of the administration's policy debate over Lebanon can be found in Quandt, "Reagan's Lebanon Policy."

72. George J. Church, "The Shakeup at State," *Time*, 5 July 1982.

73. See Ministerial Committee meeting, 13 June 1982, ISA, MFA-7080/4.

74. Meeting between Reagan and Begin, 21 June 1982, RRPL, Near East and South Asian Affairs Directorate–National Security Council, box 91987/3.

75. Meeting between Reagan and Begin, 21 June 1982.

76. For a detailed account see "Summary of the President's Plenary Meeting" and "Summary of the Working Luncheon," 21 June 1982, both in RRPL, Near East and South Asian Affairs Directorate–National Security Council, box 91987/3.

77. See, for example, the letter exchange between Reagan and Begin on July 8, 1982, in ISA, A-4178/4.

78. On Haig's resignation and conduct in Lebanon, see Stanley Hoffmann, "The Vicar's Revenge," *New York Review of Books*, 31 May 1984.

79. Samuel Lewis Interview.

80. Brinkley, *The Reagan Diaries*, 95.

81. For details on the siege and a periodization of the fighting, see Rashid Khalidi, *Under Siege: P.L.O. Decisionmaking during the 1982 War*, 2nd ed. (New York: Columbia University Press, 2014).

82. Brinkley, *The Reagan Diaries*, 98.

83. For a study of Arafat and his decision-making during the war, see Rashid Khalidi, "The PLO's Yasser Arafat," in *Leadership and Negotiation in the Middle East*, ed. Barbara Kellerman and Jeffrey Z. Rubin (New York: Praeger, 1988).

84. See "Preface to the 2014 Reissue" in Khalidi, *Under Siege*.

85. "Address to the Nation on United States Policy for Peace in the Middle East," 1 Sept. 1982, https://www.reaganfoundation.org/media/128673/nation.pdf.

86. Meeting between Sharon and Shultz, 27 Aug. 1982, ISA, A-4342/10.

87. Washington to Jerusalem, 15 Sept. 1982, ISA, A/4317/3.

88. Washington to Jerusalem, 15 Sept. 1982, ISA, A/4317/3.

89. See Seth Anziska, "Sabra and Shatila: New Revelations," *NYR Daily*, 17 Sept. 2018, https://www.nybooks.com/daily/2018/09/17/sabra-and-shatila-new-revelations/.

90. On the new evidence, see Seth Anziska, "A Preventable Massacre," *New York Times*, 17 Sept. 2012; Meeting between Shamir, Sharon, and Draper, 17 Sept. 1982, ISA, A-4317/3. For the authoritative account on the massacre and victims, see Bayan Nuwayhid al-Hout, *Sabra and Shatila: September 1982* (London: Pluto Press, 2004).

91. On the US reaction to the revelations of the massacre, see Meeting between Arens and Shultz, 18 Sept. 1982, ISA, MFA-6875/11; Conversation between Shultz and Arens, 20 Sept. 1982, ISA, A-4317/3.

92. See John Boykin, *Cursed Is the Peacemaker: The American Diplomat versus the Israeli General, Beirut 1982* (Belmont: Applegate Press, 2002), 266–273.

93. Quandt, *Peace Process*, 258. For an insider's perspective on the end of American involvement in Lebanon, see George P. Shultz, *Turmoil and Triumph: My Years as Secretary of State* (New York: Scribner, 1993), 220–234. For an account of the Marine mission in Lebanon and the barracks bombing, see Eric M. Hammel, *The Root: The Marines in Beirut, August 1982–February 1984* (San Diego: Harcourt Brace Jovanovich, 1985).

94. On Reagan's pledge to retaliate and remain, see "Transcript of President Reagan's News Conference on the Attack in Beirut," *New York Times*, 25 Oct. 1983. On Reagan's about-face, see Micah Zenko, "Reagan's Cut and Run," *Foreign Policy*, 7 Feb. 2014, http://foreignpolicy.com/2014/02/07/when-reagan-cut-and-run); Crist, *The Twilight War*.

95. Telephone interview with Ambassador Samuel Lewis, 6 Sept. 2012.

96. See Crist, *The Twilight War*; Augustus R. Norton, *Hezbollah: A Short History*, updated ed. (Princeton, NJ: Princeton University Press, 2014).

97. Quandt, *Peace Process*, 277–285, recounts the evolution of the dialogue in some detail. See also Mohamed Rabie, *US-PLO Dialogue: Secret Diplomacy and Conflict Resolution* (Gainesville: University Press of Florida, 1995).

98. Reagan, *An American Life*, 407.

CHAPTER 15

The Central Front of Reagan's Cold War
The United States and Afghanistan

ROBERT B. RAKOVE

No Cold War–era battleground has endured greater devastation, political upheaval, or human suffering over the past quarter century than Afghanistan. The civil war of the 1990s, the encroachment of al Qaeda, the US-backed campaign to oust the Taliban, and two ensuing decades of warfare and troubled state-building have each tarnished what seemed earlier to be the Ronald Reagan administration's greatest victory in the Third World. The choices made in Moscow, Washington, Kabul, and Islamabad during the 1980s have consequently received much critical scrutiny.

Scholarship on the end of the Cold War has argued, generally critically, that the Reagan administration drove a hard bargain in securing a Soviet withdrawal from Afghanistan, particularly in its refusal to respond in kind, by ceasing aid to the Afghan rebels (mujahideen).[1] This chapter does not question this verdict, but the absence of an archival-researched account of the Reagan administration's decision-making on Afghanistan hinders our understanding of why it acted as it did. Afghanistan is something rare in the historiography of Cold War battlegrounds: a case where the scholarship on the Soviet side has significantly outpaced studies of US policy. In surveying the administration's internal debates and policy statements, efforts at public diplomacy, and the comparatively unexamined role of US domestic politics, this chapter examines the broader significance of Afghanistan in Reagan's Cold War.

Among the battles Reagan waged around the world, Afghanistan should be understood as the central front. It cannot claim this distinction because it received the most detailed attention from Reagan's national security team—sustained deliberation about it occurred only during the second term. The resources expended on the CIA's aid pipeline to the mujahideen, a covert enterprise of unprecedented scale, argue in favor of its centrality, but only and especially if one considers, in addition, the broader politics of the war. The Afghan war's centrality should be understood in terms of the expectations and hopes that Reagan, George Shultz, and other policymakers affixed to victory there. No other battlefield held the broad, globally symbolic ramifications attached to Afghanistan. Nor was any other anticommunist cause in the world nearly as popular within the US political spectrum. Challenged by the opposition on his policies in Central America, Southeast Asia, and southern Africa, Reagan enjoyed (if that is the word) a surfeit of enthusiasm for his Afghan endeavor. Yet consensus and belief carried their own costs, and the pursuit of victory limited what diplomacy could achieve—to the detriment of Soviets, Americans, and Afghans alike. This was true, even in the early months of the Reagan administration, when the Soviet Union first broached the possibility of serious negotiations.

To the shock of observers around the world, in December 1979 the Soviet Union invaded Afghanistan, ousting and murdering its Marxist strongman, Hafizullah Amin, and replacing him with a more pliable rival, Babrak Karmal. Within months, Leonid Brezhnev's Politburo began to realize that it had made a grave mistake. Fed up with the outgoing President Jimmy Carter and hopeful that the new administration would prove a better negotiating partner, the Soviet government repeatedly inquired in 1981 and 1982 about holding substantive talks on Afghanistan. Although Soviet officials insisted upon the cessation of foreign aid to the mujahideen and sought international recognition of the Karmal government, hints of flexibility in their position were visible. Soviet Ambassador Anatoly Dobrynin suggested the possibility of a withdrawal in spring 1981 meetings with Secretary of State Alexander Haig.[2] In a major address in Tbilisi, Brezhnev introduced the possibility of a phased withdrawal.[3] "We miscalculated," lamented a well-placed Soviet official to Jack Matlock, the senior US diplomat in Moscow in 1981.[4] In a conversation with French Foreign Minister Claude Cheysson, Foreign Minister Andrei Gromyko even broached the possibility of removing Karmal from office.[5]

By no means were these admissions of error or hints of potential concessions the party line. Soviet officials, in other venues, adamantly rejected US criticism of their Afghan venture and fought to establish the legitimacy of the embattled Karmal regime. The Soviet government rejected a summer 1981 proposal for negotiations by the European Economic Community (EEC), faulting it for excluding the Afghan government and infringing on Afghan sovereignty. In a July 24, 1981, meeting with Matlock, First Deputy Foreign Minister Georgii Korniyenko delivered a "disjointed shotgun polemic," accusing the United States of using Afghanistan as an excuse to wreck the détente system.[6] US-Soviet conversations on the issue—which occurred far more regularly in 1981 than they would in subsequent years—usually fell into an awkward pattern of repetition and mutual recrimination. US representatives insisted upon an immediate and unconditional Soviet withdrawal; their adversaries countered by demanding a halt to external interference in internal Afghan affairs.

Yet, for reasons that remain open to speculation, Moscow directed one serious entreaty to the Reagan administration. On September 28, Haig spent four hours in dialogue with the visiting Gromyko. In an often-strained conversation, Haig—for reasons unknown—strayed from the existing US position on Afghanistan, which called for an immediate Soviet withdrawal. He suggested, instead, that a withdrawal could coincide with efforts to broaden the base of the Afghan government and to limit cross-border activities. Gromyko gave little indication of having noticed the change.[7] Nevertheless, at the end of the following month, Dobrynin presented Haig with a demarche professing interest in discussions to be held "in a business-like manner, in the spirit of realism, and without unnecessary polemics."[8]

Haig found the communiqué unusual. He was struck by the "non-polemical tone" and the absence of language referring to prior, "unacceptable" Soviet-Afghan proposals. Although he allowed that the demarche could very well be a ploy intended to alter US policy toward the Soviet occupation or perhaps to drive a wedge between Washington and Islamabad, Haig urged Reagan to take it seriously and to consider its "important positive implications" for the broader relationship between the superpowers.[9]

Haig's hopes for serious dialogue were dashed by his numerous rivals in the White House, by the worsening Cold War climate, and by his own peculiar machinations. Hard-liners Richard Pipes and James "Bud" Nance of the National Security Council (NSC) staff, supported by their boss, National Security Advisor Richard Allen, worked to undercut Haig. For his part, Haig refused to share transcripts of his conversations with Dobrynin and Gromyko. "The White House is denied by the State Department information that the Kremlin has!" observed Pipes. "Is this Alice in Wonderland?"[10] Nor was Haig well served by his peculiar decision to wait nearly three weeks after the Dobrynin meeting before notifying Reagan.[11] The NSC staff independently secured a Haig-Gromyko transcript while withholding Haig's memo from Reagan. Having discovered Haig's departure from policy in his September 28 meeting, Nance finally released Haig's memo, attaching his own rebuttal. Claiming that the Kremlin "almost certainly interpreted this statement as an about face," he dismissed the possibility that Moscow held "a more conciliatory attitude on Afghanistan."[12] Perhaps so, but Nance and his allies made, at most, a circumstantial case.

Ten days after Reagan finally learned of the demarche, a new crisis surfaced. The Polish government commenced a comprehensive crackdown on the anticommunist Solidarity trade union. Solidarity had first emerged in summer 1980, amid worker strikes that initially protested rising food prices but that soon posed a fundamental challenge to the wavering government in Warsaw. Under considerable Soviet pressure, Poland's beleaguered communists finally acted, unleashing elite police units on the evening of December 12, 1981. The outraged Reagan—who had derived inspiration from the striking Poles—pondered "a total quarantine on the Soviet Union," but settled for the adoption of a broad new round of sanctions against Moscow and its allies in Warsaw.[13] Substantive superpower dialogue on Afghanistan could scarcely occur in such circumstances. In unwitting collaboration, Haig and his adversaries had run out the clock.

It was unsurprising that Afghanistan represented one point of conflict between the brash secretary of state and the White House staff. Even so, this was more than a clash of personalities; fundamentally different interpretations of the Soviet war and its broader importance animated the respective combatants. The tendency, noted elsewhere in this volume by Elisabeth Leake, to regard the Soviet invasion as a drive toward the Persian Gulf was strongest in the early years of the Reagan White House. Some within the White House further embroidered the thesis by rendering Brezhnev the long-awaited executor of centuries-old tsarist schemes to acquire a warm-water port. Chief among them was Pipes, who claimed that Moscow had effectively "annexed" Afghanistan as a "military springboard" for subsequent invasions of Iran and Saudi Arabia.[14] Secretary of Defense Caspar Weinberger accepted the imperial thesis as well.[15] Haig, on the other hand, understood the invasion much as his predecessor, Cyrus Vance, had: as a consequence of Soviet insecurity and anxiety about its own growing Muslim population.[16]

Even as interpretations of the intervention differed, a belligerent spirit held sway across the administration's divide. Haig could see beyond historical clichés, but was as eager as anyone else to approach the war as a Soviet Vietnam, succumbing in the process to the temptation to seek retribution. The events of December 1981 and reports of the Soviet use of chemical weapons in Afghanistan pushed him toward a more hawkish stance. Meeting with his aides on January 21, 1982, he asked for memoranda of Henry Kissinger's conversations with Gromyko on Soviet support for North Vietnam, "so that we might throw some of the Soviets' own language back at them" and thereby show them "that we think historically and keep a long memory." He concluded, "They stuck it right in our eye back then and we should not miss an opportunity to return the favor."[17]

Yet Haig continued to argue for dialogue during the remainder of his short, stormy secretaryship. Soviet diplomats, referring to previous exchanges, repeatedly inquired about the possibility of expert-level talks on Afghanistan, only to be told that the question was still under consideration.[18] Haig urged that Reagan pursue the talks.[19] Once again, his foes within the NSC staff rose to counter him. Prompted in part by Pipes, National Security Advisor William Clark wrote, "The current economic and imperial crisis of the Soviet regime, acute though it is, does not offer good opportunities for negotiations."[20] Haig forged ahead, nevertheless. Meeting Gromyko in June, he was finally able to agree to an exchange on Afghanistan, to be held in Moscow the following month.[21] When they finally occurred, talks between US Ambassador Arthur Hartman and Korniyenko were unproductive (and Haig was out of office). Hartman's instructions had been merely to reiterate the prior US stance.[22] Brezhnev died in November, and no significant US-Soviet exchanges on Afghanistan occurred during the remainder of Reagan's first term.[23] In any event, stated positions left little room for progress; Anglo-Soviet exchanges on the subject in the same period deadlocked on fundamental questions of the Kabul government's legitimacy.[24]

The faltering of diplomacy encouraged both sides to seek their desired ends on the battlefield. Hawks within the Reagan administration, initially limited by budgetary exigencies, sought to expand military aid to the rebels.[25] The Soviets increased their troop strength in Afghanistan in 1981 and sought strategic victories the following year, particularly against the elusive Tajik rebel leader, Ahmed Shah Massoud. Intensified counterinsurgency operations led to a number of mass killings, particularly in the province of Logar, southeast of Kabul. In one infamous episode, which received widespread publicity in the West, an estimated 105 Afghan civilians, hiding in an underground irrigation tunnel, were burned to death by Soviet forces. Such atrocities bolstered the confrontational course emerging from the Reagan White House.

The failure of US-Soviet diplomacy on Afghanistan during the Haig period was unsurprising. This chapter does not posit the existence of a lost opportunity for peace. Yet the factors apparent in this phase of the Afghanistan conflict shed broader light on the Reagan administration's approach to the struggle. More persistent than the thesis of Soviet imperialism, which cast Brezhnev as an improbable reincarnation of Peter the Great, was a deep-seated skepticism toward negotiations with the Soviet Union. Broadly speaking, the hawks distrusted diplomacy, viewing Soviet entreaties as efforts to legitimate the Kabul government or delay a Soviet withdrawal. "The record of US-Soviet summit meetings would indicate that they should be avoided altogether," William Stearman of the NSC staff wrote in March 1981.[26]

They were especially skeptical that diplomacy could secure a Soviet withdrawal from Afghanistan. Stearman decried the "common fallacy [that] the Soviets can be negotiated out of Afghanistan."[27] Moscow appeared to them immune to the domestic costs of counterinsurgency warfare. The fusion of tsarist and totalitarian traits common to Reagan-era assessments of the Soviet Union created a hybrid foe with the combined strengths of both, and none of the weaknesses. Stearman doubted in January 1982 that "the world's strongest land power" could be defeated "by a ragtag collection of very courageous, but poorly armed and poorly organized, Afghan irregulars." "Historically," he reasoned, "the Russians . . . are used to long 'pacification' campaigns in this area."[28] Comparing the Soviet casualty rate in Afghanistan to that experienced by the United States in Vietnam furthered his disquiet. An estimated 106 dead Soviet soldiers each month were "not likely to have a significant impact on the Soviet population." Nor would the Kremlin need to "worry about an organized peace movement."[29]

Such grim assessments baldly contravened repeated signals from Moscow that it was reconsidering its intervention, as well as intelligence analyses that noted waning morale within the Red Army, factionalism within the Afghan government, and the unreliability of the Afghan military.[30] "Afghanistan is a mistake, and we are paying for it," lamented Gosbank Chairman V. S. Alkhimov to a US diplomat in March 1982.[31] Yet these estimates dovetailed broadly with the outlook of the early administration, which perceived a global crisis of confidence in American leadership and the expansion of Soviet power into the Third World. As Haig foundered, the NSC staff succeeded in making the reversal of this trend a core objective of the administration. National Security Decision Directive (NSDD) 32, signed on May 20, 1982, affirmed that US national security strategy should "contain and reverse the expansion of Soviet control and military presence throughout the world."[32] This, in turn, was consolidated by the pivotal NSDD-75, drafted by Pipes and signed by Reagan on January 17, 1983.

James Graham Wilson and Elizabeth Charles write judiciously about NSDD-75 in their chapter in this volume, where they note that both Reagan and Secretary of State George Shultz were not constrained by it in their subsequent pursuit of superpower diplomacy and nuclear abolition. Yet the directive appears to have been more influential within the realm of Afghanistan policy. It specified "external resistance to Soviet imperialism" as a core national objective. The Afghan conflict, now entering its fourth year, was identified as one of several "important weaknesses and vulnerabilities within the Soviet empire." The directive called for keeping "maximum pressure on Moscow" to withdraw, while ensuring that Soviet "political, military, and other costs remain high while the occupation continues." NSDD-75 also invoked the imperial thesis, calling for "blocking the expansion of Soviet influence" in the Middle East and Southwest Asia.[33]

Battles over the implications of NSDD-75 for US-Soviet diplomacy raged through the first half of 1983, pitting Shultz against National Security Advisor William Clark.[34] They pertained not to the substance of the US stance on Afghanistan, but rather to the nature of dialogue with the Soviet Union. Shultz argued for renewed diplomacy, yet focused more on human rights and arms control, relegating Afghanistan to the category of a regional issue and maintaining the existing US position.[35] In conversation with the UN mediator Diego Cordovez, he stressed that the United States could not be a party to an agreement leading to "either the perpetuation of a Marxist-Leninist regime or an explosion into renewed widespread civil war."[36] Two months later, Shultz reported to Reagan that "positive results have been meager" in bilateral dialogue on Afghanistan, among other issues. "Our task," he wrote, "remains to drive home to the Soviets the importance of progress on these issues if there is to be a meaningful and lasting improvement in relations."[37]

The Shultz-Clark argument, insofar as it touched on Afghanistan, pertained to means, not ends. Shultz did not embrace the imperial explanation for the Soviet invasion, but he regarded an unconditional Soviet withdrawal as essential. He recalled, in a December 2016 interview, "We didn't spend a lot of time trying to figure out why they did what they did. They did it." In 1985, Shultz explained the Soviet intervention as an expression of the Brezhnev doctrine, colloquially describing it as: "What's mine is mine, what's yours is up for grabs."[38] The intervention was thus not the result of a grand (tsarist) design, but still constituted a de facto form of expansionism. Shultz's diplomatic project toward Moscow envisioned compelling the Soviet Union toward responsible behavior in the world. Yet by this point, US-Soviet dialogue on the matter had withered, and the UN mediation effort assumed greater centrality, as it would until the conclusion of the Geneva Accords. "If it works, fine," Shultz said to Dobrynin, about the UN effort. "We do not need to be involved in everything."[39] In part, this shift occurred because the Reagan administration had already managed to raise the cost of Soviet withdrawal through public and private diplomatic campaigns.

Even as the Reagan administration bickered about the prospects of dialogue with the Soviet Union, it moved ahead in an energetic and ambitious campaign to condemn the Soviet invasion and marshal world opinion in favor of an unconditional withdrawal. Annual resolutions in the United Nations General Assembly castigating Moscow passed by overwhelming margins, opposed only by the Soviet Union and its closest Warsaw Pact and Third World allies. Pakistani appeals to Islamic countries were particularly effective, while friends of Moscow, such as India, Nicaragua, Algeria, and Iraq, consistently abstained. Within the body, and in international media, the US government repeatedly accused the Red Army of committing atrocities and employing chemical weapons against Afghan civilians. An energetic publicity campaign directed by Charles Z. Wick of the United States Information Agency, which included broadcasts into Afghanistan, further added to Moscow's distress.[40]

Much of this effort dated back to the Carter administration's response to the invasion. Yet the Reagan White House sought, from its inception, to exploit the Soviet war in the battle for global opinion. In a July 1981 cable sent to all US diplomatic posts, Haig announced "a major public and diplomatic effort to challenge the Soviets to come to the negotiating table on Afghanistan" but explained it not as a response to events in that country, but as a reaction to Soviet propaganda against the administration. Insofar as it constituted Moscow's "most pressing problem," Afghanistan represented the opportune pressure point.[41] Early results disappointed the administration. By the summer of 1981, the Soviet intervention was no longer a new development. The eruption or escalation of crises and conflicts elsewhere—in the Persian Gulf, Central America, and Poland—had done much to divert attention. A sympathetic senior Brazilian diplomat observed that Afghanistan "is not on people's minds."[42]

The apparent indifference of the world galled the White House. "When the United States was involved in Vietnam," wrote Nance, "the moral indignation of the rest of the world knew no bounds." Moscow's invasion of its southern neighbor, on the other hand "evokes little excitement."[43] Writing in July 1984, NSC staff members Donald Fortier and Shirin Tahir-Kheli dubbed it the "forgotten war."[44] If it expected a new generation of Tom Haydens or Rudi Dutschkes—student radicals famous for their anti–Vietnam War activism—to stride forth in righteous opposition to the Soviet war, the Reagan administration was setting itself up for disappointment. Even so, international sympathy for Afghanistan afforded the US government a unique opportunity to wage political warfare against the Soviet Union.

In this arena, Congress—responsive to networks of human rights activists and the small but vocal Afghan-American community—undertook the first significant step. Following the lead of the European Parliament, the US Congress designated March 21, 1982—the start of the new year according to the Persian calendar—as "Afghanistan Day." Official preparations began late, barely two months before the given day.[45]

Presidential efforts to commemorate the Afghan struggle reached their crescendo as Afghanistan Day drew near. In his spoken remarks upon signing the bill, on March 10, Reagan praised "a nation of unsung heroes whose courageous struggle is one of the epics of our times." "Nowhere," Reagan argued, "are human rights more brutally violated than in Afghanistan today." He dedicated the March 22 launch of the space shuttle *Columbia*, representing "man's finest aspirations in the field of science and technology," to the Afghan people, whose struggle represented "man's highest aspirations for freedom."[46] The following evening, Ronald and Nancy Reagan attended a performance of the Joffrey Ballet dedicated—with the cooperation of company co-founder Robert Joffrey, himself an Afghan American—to the Afghan people. Tying geopolitics to a dance performance proved a fraught enterprise, as a small group of patrons booed the president and first lady upon their arrival and again during the intermission.[47]

During the brief span of its observance within the United States, Afghanistan Day drew the interest of US citizens—and not only those with family connections to Afghanistan. Communal associations for Americans with Eastern European ancestry took to the cause with particular enthusiasm. Two hundred Chicagoans met at Carl Schurz High School in northwest Chicago in a spirited rally jointly supported by the Afghan Relief Committee, the Captive Nations Committee, and the Polish American Congress. Polish American attendees enthusiastically linked the struggles of their ancestral homeland with that of Afghanistan. The famed Cambodian journalist Dith Pran accompanied a group of protesters outside the New York offices of Aeroflot. In Boston, a small but lively demonstration on a rainy afternoon brought together one hundred marchers from the local Free Afghanistan Alliance, Support of Solidarity, Latvians for Latvia, the AFL-CIO, and the Massachusetts Libertarian Party. The varied protesters marched from the Boston Common to Faneuil Hall, burning two Soviet flags along the way. Its first observance, in March 1982, attracted the most media attention, but Reagan, Congress, and a disparate group of activists continued to declare and commemorate Afghanistan Day for the remainder of his tenure.[48]

Elsewhere, its observance varied by country to country. The Egyptian government, a supplier of weapons for the rebels, staged *two* Afghanistan Days in three months.[49] Betamax tapes of the documentary film *Afghanistan 1981* received some airing in Europe and Latin America. D. J. Gowan of the British Foreign Office's South Asian Department, wrote, "It is difficult to judge how useful Afghanistan Day has been."[50] The anger it had evoked in Kabul and Moscow appeared to be perhaps the most useful gauge; in Kabul a counterprotest put the US embassy on a state of high alert.[51] Over time, the weight of international condemnation seemed to take a toll on the Soviets. "The world around them seems too much for the Russians," wrote J. N. Dixit, India's ambassador in Kabul. "There is an acknowledgement of a feeling of isolation."[52]

Repeated US accusations of chemical warfare in Afghanistan further incensed the Soviets. Dobrynin and Gromyko each demanded an end to the accusations—to no avail.[53] In November 1982, Shultz presented Congress with a report charging the Soviet Union and Vietnam with employing chemical weapons in their respective Afghan and Cambodian wars.[54] The rhetorical escalation of the White House's Afghan war helped to place the Soviet Union on the defensive on the world stage. Simultaneously, it raised the cost of conceding ground to Reagan, as Cold War tensions elsewhere continued to deepen. Reagan's public diplomacy campaign constitutes the earliest evidence that his White House perceived the intervention more as a Soviet vulnerability than as a geostrategic threat.

Repeated presidential efforts to draw public attention to the Soviet war engaged Reagan's own interest and sympathies. He repeatedly welcomed Afghan refugees and rebels to the White House. As in the cases of persecuted Russian Pentecostals and the families of Middle East hostages, these interpersonal contacts moved him deeply, attaching faces to a humanitarian calamity. He wrote in his diary, in February 1983, after the first visit by Afghans to the White House, including survivors of the tunnel massacre in Logar:

> Finally had a visit with 6 Afghan Freedom Fighters here in this country to tell of inhumanity of the Soviets. One's wife had been executed while her 2 children watched. One was a young, pretty and tiny lady—held in custody for four months—tortured daily. She had been a medical student. Her crime? Caught looking at a "freedom" leaflet. The others were from a village where the Russians had burned 105 people alive with gasoline & chemicals in an irrigation tunnel.[55]

"They were mere babys [sic]," an outraged Reagan wrote after meeting a group of grievously wounded Afghan children in January 1986. "I'd like to send the photos to Gen. Sec. Gorbachev."[56] He pointedly recounted Soviet atrocities to visiting foreign leaders.[57]

When he did so, he generally found a sympathetic audience. Within the North Atlantic Treaty Organization (NATO) and the EEC, the Reagan administration enjoyed strong support on Afghan issues, bolstered by conservative British and Canadian governments. The July 1981 EEC initiative incorporated the US position of nonrecognition of the Kabul regime, and failed for that reason. NATO affirmed the need to press the Soviet Union on Afghanistan, and North Atlantic Council declarations included, from December 1982 until July 1984, language on chemical warfare in Afghanistan, despite the fact that only the US government believed the accusation.[58] Nevertheless, the issue mustered less urgency in transatlantic dialogue than questions of nuclear armaments. The only ally, outside of the Islamic world, with equal if not greater ardor for the Afghan struggle was the People's Republic of China. Beijing sent considerable aid to the rebels and placed even greater stress on the need for a Soviet withdrawal in its own bilateral dialogue with Moscow than did Washington.[59] It also warned against Haig's project of expert-level talks in 1982.[60]

Nonaligned countries were a particular target of Reagan's Afghanistan diplomacy, and none more so than India. Although Indira Gandhi's government declined to condemn the Soviet invasion and abstained on UN resolutions, its discomfort with the Soviet war was apparent to the United States and its NATO allies. Visiting Washington in July 1982, Gandhi attempted to assuage Reagan by reiterating India's traditional opposition to "the use of foreign troops"—a placebo of sorts for outright condemnation of the Soviet invasion. In approaching India, Reagan chose persuasion over condemnation, asking both Indira Gandhi and her son and successor, Rajiv, to raise the question of serious negotiations in Moscow.[61] The Reagan administration ventured a double bet in encouraging Indian mediation of the Afghanistan conflict: repeated entreaties from New Delhi might either drive the Soviets to moderate their position, or they might drive a wedge between the two. Shultz attached particular significance to India's potential role and took New Delhi's reports seriously.[62] Although National Security Adviser Robert McFarlane cautioned against trying to "get a new friend (India) at the expense of our old one (Pakistan)," the administration nevertheless hoped—not unlike some of its predecessors—that the two South Asian giants could be induced to set aside their rivalry, lean toward the West, and jointly confront the threat of communist expansion.[63]

In the end, South Asian realities proved inescapable, chief among them Pakistan's control over the aid pipeline and its undiminished nuclear ambitions. Maintaining the Afghan war effort required continual entreaties and aid to Pakistan, which allowed President Mohammed Zia ul-Haq's government discretion over the disbursement of aid, even as Islamabad concealed the extent of its nuclear program from Washington.[64] Pakistan faced continual incursions by Afghan and Soviet forces. Moscow and Kabul offered carrots as well, hinting at times that they might affirm the previously disputed border between the two countries.[65] The complexities of Pakistani domestic politics, as well as bureaucratic infighting between the diplomatic corps, intelligence agency, civilian leadership, and military, added to the uncertainty. Also present—as Elisabeth Leake's chapter reveals—were fundamental concerns about the potential disintegration of the Pakistani state. Consequently, Islamabad's leverage never diminished, even in the final months of the Soviet presence, bolstering an already prevailing tendency in Washington to seek victory on the battlefield.[66]

So, too, did repeated unsolicited efforts by Congress to shape Afghan policy. Democratic Representative Charles Wilson of Texas famously fought to increase aid allotments to the mujahideen.[67] Less convenient for the executive branch was the entirely superfluous autumn 1982 resolution submitted by the liberal Senator Paul Tsongas (D-MA) calling for material support for the mujahideen. His hometown newspaper, the *Boston Globe*, wondered what purpose such a bill served when US aid to the rebels was already an open secret.[68] As James M. Scott observes, even opponents of the Reagan doctrine accepted aid to the mujahideen.[69] Conservatives needed little convincing that the rebels were fighting the good fight, and liberals otherwise opposed to Reagan's foreign policy embraced Afghanistan as their best opportunity to demonstrate their own anti-communist bona fides. Ultimately, it proved to be too much of a good thing.

For all the internal acrimony over Afghanistan that marred Reagan's first term, the objectives of aiding the rebels received little explicit discussion. Grand directives such as NSDD-32 and NSDD-75 addressed Afghanistan either implicitly or concisely, but serious, consequential dialogue within the administration did not occur before 1984. Thus, Donald Fortier of the NSC staff wrote to his boss, McFarlane, on February 21, 1984: "The fundamental issue of course is where we are headed with our basic strategy in Afghanistan. Are we merely trying to be of nuisance value to the Soviets?" Or was there the potential to "dramatically stress Soviet capabilities in Afghanistan?" If the latter, was the United States to do so "on behalf" of the mujahideen or "in accord with our displeasure" over Soviet activity elsewhere in the world?[70] These were questions that might profitably have been posed *much* earlier. As Fortier wrote in a later memo, "Our present policy appears to be one in which means are seldom reexamined and basic ends remain only loosely defined."[71]

Having diagnosed the deficiencies with the existing program, Fortier appears to have been one the earliest NSC staffers to address Afghan policy lucidly and systematically.[72] Writing to McFarlane in March, he outlined what would be the contours of the Reagan doctrine as applied to Afghanistan, solidifying the notion of treating it as a Soviet pressure point:

> *In short, any improvement in relations that the two sides are able to achieve will endure only if the US retains the ability to compete in those areas where agreement is not reached. This is particularly true for Afghanistan. If—given Soviet actions in Vietnam, Central America and Syria—we fail to seriously stress the Soviets where they are vulnerable, how can we expect them to take seriously our willingness to compete on vital Third World issues at all?*

"Indeed," Fortier concluded, "precisely because the Soviets can be made to hurt more there, Afghanistan ought to be a mirror reflecting our own displeasure for Soviet subversion elsewhere."[73] Under McFarlane's direction, the NSC staff increasingly invested itself in broadening US support for the Afghan cause by addressing questions of media outreach, collaboration with NGOs, psychological warfare, and humanitarian assistance.[74]

The expansion of the US aid program in 1983–1984, and the later announcement of the Reagan doctrine heightened the salience of an Afghan settlement to US-Soviet relations. In a February 22, 1985, speech before the Commonwealth Club in San Francisco, Shultz declared US support for "those struggling against the imposition of communist tyranny."[75] In March, responding to signs of a Soviet offensive in Afghanistan, Shultz and Casey convinced Reagan to expand assistance to the rebels. NSDD-166, drafted afterward, recommitted the administration to forcing a Soviet withdrawal from the country, denying Moscow a base in Afghanistan, and fostering Soviet isolation in the world on the issue. The directive linked US support of the rebels to US credibility throughout the Third World. It also posited that with "the resumption of arms control talks in Geneva, it is important to signal to the Soviets that we will continue to oppose unacceptable Soviet behavior in other fields."[76]

Even as he championed dialogue with the new Soviet regime, Shultz remained a firm proponent of aiding the mujahideen. He wholeheartedly supported, for example, the pivotal decision to supply Stinger missiles to the rebels.[77] Shultz perceived Afghanistan as a pressure point and a Soviet withdrawal as an event of profound global significance. His deputy, Michael Armacost, flatly told the Soviets during a March 1987 trip to Moscow that "if they chose to prolong their involvement, we will obviously not abandon our friends."[78] NSDD-270, signed on May 1, 1987, reaffirmed the objective of maintaining "strong pressure" on the Soviets in pursuit of a "prompt, complete, and irrevocable" withdrawal.[79] Nonetheless, suspicion of the State Department lingered in the White House, Defense Department, and Congress, amplified by the tumult of the administration's final years.[80]

Until the end of 1987, Shultz and Armacost maintained that the United States would insist upon a right to aid the mujahideen, so long as Soviet aid flowed to the Kabul government. Yet at the end of the year, Shultz and his department seemed to concede ground on this point. Pressed by Gorbachev in a December 10 luncheon, Shultz affirmed that US support would cease sixty days after the commencement of a Soviet withdrawal.[81] This set the stage for the final US-Soviet argument about Afghanistan, the following year, after Reagan reiterated that aid to the rebels would continue.[82]

It is unclear why Shultz departed from prior policy. He later told journalist Selig Harrison that he had made the remark with the assumption that Moscow would also cease aiding the Kabul regime.[83] The tenor of US-Soviet dialogue on Afghanistan in the autumn of 1987 suggests a related possibility: that he hoped for sustained efforts by the two to establish an independent, neutral Afghan state through a long process of national reconciliation. In September, he had accepted a suggestion by the visiting Foreign Minister Eduard Shevardnadze that postwar Afghanistan might pledge permanent neutrality, in exchange for guarantees of its independence and territorial integrity. Concurrent arms cutoffs by Washington and Moscow, in the wake of a Soviet withdrawal, were a necessary and logical step toward longer-term superpower collaboration in reconstructing the country.[84] Gorbachev, for his part, hoped to make Afghanistan an example of superpower cooperation, applicable to other conflicts in the Third World.[85] For more than eight years, the two adversaries had proclaimed to each other their respective interest in the restoration of a peaceful, independent, nonaligned Afghanistan, and Soviet officials had pointedly noted that neither country had any interest in seeing a fundamentalist regime emerge in Kabul.[86]

Yet in the end, the two superpowers signed an agreement in which neither believed and which neither would attempt to enforce. Each side continued aiding its favored Afghans, and the country remained wracked by warfare. In part this occurred because the Soviet Union remained unwilling to abandon its client, perceiving its broader global credibility to be at stake. Fifteen years earlier, Richard Nixon and Henry Kissinger had confronted much the same predicament in Vietnam. But the limited scope of the Geneva Accords also attested to divisions within the Reagan White House and its relative weakness during its final years. Distrust of the State Department pervaded the NSC, which ultimately held the same views as the president. Reagan had remained silent at the December 10 luncheon and spoke only of securing a Soviet withdrawal from Afghanistan. Above all—and like many Americans—he idealized the Afghan resistance. "They have fought valiantly and against heavy odds to free themselves from the yoke of oppression," he proclaimed, while signing the final Afghanistan Day declaration, "from assaults on their liberty, their sovereignty, their dignity, their lives, and their very way of life."[87]

Even as he did so, Reagan's Afghanistan policy had come under attack from both parties. The Democrats, returned to the majority in the Senate by the 1986 midterm elections, joined conservative Republicans who were increasingly uneasy with Reagan's Soviet policy. Predicting that the White House would "sell the Afghan resistance down the river," Senate Majority Leader Robert Byrd (D-WV) suggested that he would watch the ongoing negotiations closely before he scheduled consideration of the INF Treaty.[88] On February 29, 1988, the Senate voted unanimously on a measure rejecting any early cutoff of aid to the Afghan resistance.[89] Republican Senator Gordon Humphrey of New Hampshire assailed the administration's policy from the Right, charging that the Geneva Accords were "dangerously defective."[90] "He is wrong as H—l," Reagan wrote, after a meeting with Humphrey.[91] Yet conservative scrutiny of the White House—heightened after the much-decried signing of the Intermediate-Range Nuclear Force (INF) Treaty—applied as well to its Afghan diplomacy. Reagan observed, of these critics, "It's amazing how certain they can be when they know so d—n little of what we're really doing."[92]

Were these attacks consequential? They did drive the administration to elevate the visibility of its support to the mujahideen. "We must avoid giving grist to those who accuse us of 'selling out' the Afghans," wrote Edward Djerejian, of the State Department's Near East and South Asia bureau.[93] The White House staged the seventh and final proclamation of Afghanistan Day with added pomp and circumstance and several mujahideen guests, despite the awkward fact that Shevardnadze was due to arrive the following day. When pressing the Soviets during Shevardnadze's March visit, both Shultz and Armacost argued that they would need to sell any deal to Congress.[94] The White House may have feared, as well, that acrimony over the accords might impede ratification of the INF Treaty. Separately, and perhaps most significantly, challenges to the Geneva Accords precluded other forms of legislative oversight. In farcically questioning Reagan's pro-rebel sympathies, amid the clamor of an election year, Congress neglected to pose critical questions about the future of Afghanistan after a Soviet withdrawal.

Undoubtedly, Reagan never envisaged withdrawing support from the mujahideen. He never had to confront the problem, as the Soviet presence in Afghanistan outlasted his administration by nearly a month. He commemorated the ninth anniversary of the invasion on December 27, 1988—a few weeks after his final meeting with Gorbachev—with a presidential statement condemning the Red Army's closing offensive and questioning whether the Soviet Union was truly committed to a peaceful solution.[95] Although evidence of their political fractiousness was abundant, the military limitations of the rebels remained to be discovered. In the Red Army's absence, the cause of Afghan liberation lost its urgency to Americans, in and out of government.

This outcome was telling: Reagan's war in Afghanistan, although sometimes rationalized by the hyperbolic thesis of a Russian drive to the gulf, was never primarily about securing a Soviet withdrawal. Had the Soviet intervention represented the dire threat posited by so many to the world's oil supplies, the early Reagan team might have responded more seriously to early Soviet entreaties and attached less importance to the question of who governed in Kabul. Although the imperial thesis had its adherents, its importance has likely been overstated. NSDD-166 did not postulate a Soviet drive toward the gulf. It also defined US policy toward the conflict instrumentally: as a means to demonstrate to the Soviet Union the costs of "unacceptable behavior" in the world. Shultz and Reagan believed, furthermore, as the former recalled in 2016, that "a [Soviet] withdrawal from Afghanistan would be noticed in Poland and in [Eastern Europe]. . . . And I think it was." Helpless in the face of the Polish crackdown, the Reagan administration chose instead to challenge the Brezhnev doctrine in the mountains of Afghanistan.[96]

That is not to say that Americans adopted the Afghan struggle dispassionately, concerned only with its global implications. Indeed, while Afghan relief attracted support throughout the Western world, Americans felt a special sympathy for the Afghan resistance. Perhaps this feeling came in part because of the lingering wounds of Vietnam, but more of it stemmed from Reagan's success in defining the Afghans in ways congruent with the American self-image: as a courageous, pious, self-reliant people. Fractious, disorganized, ruthless, and sometimes deeply hostile to the West, the mujahideen nevertheless enjoyed a level of American esteem never remotely equaled by the Nicaraguan Contras or the National Union for the Total Independence of Angola (UNITA) in Angola. Outrage over Soviet atrocities in Afghanistan—verifiable or otherwise—affirmed the morality and righteousness of their cause and their pursuit of outright victory. As a result, the domestic politics of Afghan aid took on an exceptional (if not bizarre) dynamic, with Congress striving to outdo the administration in displays of support for the rebels.

A similar consensus of sorts reigned within the otherwise fractious, chaotic Reagan White House after Haig's departure. The fundamental divisions described in Melvyn Leffler's chapter in this volume—between advocates of confrontation and those of realistic, prudent negotiations—had little effect on

Afghanistan policy. If Shultz did not share the belief of Pipes and others that the invasion constituted the first act in a broader drive toward the gulf, he nevertheless agreed that it could not stand. To some, Afghanistan constituted the frontlines in the modern struggle against Soviet expansionism; to others, it represented an opportune location to compel Moscow toward reasonable behavior. Either diagnosis yielded the same fundamental prescription.

Enthusiasm was no substitute for prudence, however. While the State Department came to question the imminence of mujahideen victory by 1988, there existed little political room to maneuver in the administration's final year and to pursue some of the more extensive negotiated solutions discussed during the previous year. Heartened by their achievements to date, the Reagan team and their immediate successors were—as the historian David Anderson writes in another context—trapped by success.[97] Meanwhile, interest in Afghanistan proved historically fleeting. After the Reagan-era pursuit of victory came abandonment and indifference. Reagan's former acting CIA director, Robert Gates, later wrote, of the post-Geneva period: "Now the Afghans could resume fighting among themselves—and hardly anyone cared."[98] For a while, anyway.

Notes

I would like to thank Will King for his assistance in researching at the British National Archives, George Shultz and Howard and Teresita Schaffer for consenting to interviews, and Michael Armacost and Thomas W. Simons Jr. for corresponding with me. James Graham Wilson and Elisabeth Leake offered helpful suggestions over email. Thanks also go to James, Elizabeth Charles, and their colleagues in the Historian's Office for compiling, editing, and publishing several superb volumes of the *Foreign Relations of the United States* series, cited often in this chapter.

1. See Artemy M. Kalinovsky, *A Long Goodbye: The Soviet Withdrawal from Afghanistan* (Cambridge, MA: Harvard University Press, 2011); Melvyn P. Leffler, *For the Soul of Mankind: The United States, the Soviet Union, and the Cold War*, 1st ed. (New York: Hill and Wang, 2007), 403–14; Odd Arne Westad, *The Global Cold War: Third World Interventions and the Making of Our Times* (New York: Cambridge University Press, 2005), 376–77; Diego Cordovez and Selig S. Harrison, *Out of Afghanistan: The Inside Story of the Soviet Withdrawal* (New York: Oxford University Press, 1995); Hal Brands, *Making the Unipolar Moment: US Foreign Policy and the Rise of the Post–Cold War Order* (Ithaca, NY: Cornell University Press, 2016), 114–16; Paul Thomas Chamberlin, *The Cold War's Killing Fields: Rethinking the Long Peace* (New York: Harper, 2018), 418–51, 454–63, 494–501, 529–48.

2. Department of State (DOS) to Moscow, 1 May 1981, Ronald Reagan Presidential Library (RRPL), Jack Matlock Files (JMF), box 40, folder "US-USSR Relations (May 1981)."

3. DOS to NATO, 23 May 1981, RRPL, JMF, box 40, folder "US-USSR Relations (May 1981)."

4. Moscow to DOS, 6 July 1981, Digital National Security Archive (DNSA).

5. Notes on the Meeting with the Permanent Representative of Pakistan, Javier Perez de Cuellar and N. Naik, September 30, 1981, Secretaries General Area, AG-006 Waldheim, S-0904, box 72, "4—Afghanistan 6/79-12/81," UN Archive, New York, NY.

6. Moscow to DOS, 24 July 1981, *Foreign Relations of the United States (FRUS), 1981–1988*, vol. 3, *Soviet Union, January 1981–January 1983* (Washington, DC: US Government Printing Office, 2015), 225–231.

7. Haig and Gromyko meeting, 28 Sept. 1981, *FRUS*, 3:292; see also Simon Miles, *Engaging the Evil Empire: Washington, Moscow, and the Beginning of the End of the Cold War* (Ithaca, NY: Cornell University Press, 2020), 40–42.

8. Soviet Demarche, *FRUS*, 3:372–373.

9. Haig to Reagan, 17 Nov. 1981, *FRUS*, 3:371–372

10. Pipes to Allen, 18 Nov. 1981, RRPL, Executive Secretariat–NSC (ESNSC), Country File (CF), box 34, folder: "Afghanistan, 7/14/81–12/28/81."

11. Most likely, he was attempting to secure further evidence of Soviet intentions, through conversations in Moscow.

12. Nance to Reagan, 2 Dec. 1981, *FRUS*, 3:370.

13. Gregory F. Domber, *Empowering Revolution: America, Poland, and the End of the Cold War* (Chapel Hill: University Of North Carolina Press, 2016), 24–35; James Graham Wilson, *The Triumph of Improvisation: Gorbachev's Adaptability, Reagan's Engagement, and the End of the Cold War* (Ithaca, NY: Cornell University Press, 2014), 27–30.

14. Pipes to Clark, 29 July 1982, RRPL, ESNSC, CF, box 34, folder "Afghanistan, 7/29/82–5/2/83."

15. Caspar Weinberger Interview, 19 Nov. 2002, Miller Center, http://millercenter.org/oralhistory/interview/caspar-weinberger.

16. Haig and Chatham House Group meeting, 17 Oct. 1981, *FRUS*, 3:336–340.

17. Haig meeting with aides, 21 Jan. 1982, *FRUS*, 3:426.

18. See, for example, DOS to Moscow, 25 Feb. 1982, *FRUS*, 3:486–487; DOS to Moscow, 11 May 1982, *FRUS*, 542–542; DOS to Moscow, 25 May 1982, *FRUS*, 565–571.

19. Haig to Reagan, 2 Apr. 1982, *FRUS*, 3:512–520, esp. 3:517.

20. Clark to Reagan, "When to Negotiate with the Soviet Union," 5 Apr. 1982, *FRUS*, 3:523–524.

21. Haig and Gromyko meeting, 15 June 1982, *FRUS*, 3:610–614.

22. At this writing, there is no available record of the Hartman-Korniyenko talks. Shultz briefly mentioned their outcome in a subsequent conversation with Gromyko. See Memcon, Shultz and Gromyko, September 28, 1982, *FRUS*, 3:723. On Hartman's instructions, see Washington to Foreign and Commonwealth Office (FCO), 18 June 1982, UK National Archives (TNA), FCO 37/2630.

23. Telegram 136834, State to Islamabad, May 4, 1985, RRPL, Shirin Tahir-Kheli Files, box 91880, folder "US-Pakistan Military 1985."

24. See, for example, "Record of Anglo/Soviet Planning Talks," 20–21 Jan. 1983, TNA, FCO 37/3052.

25. Robert M. Gates, *From the Shadows: The Ultimate Insider's Story of Five Presidents and How They Won the Cold War* (New York: Simon and Schuster, 1996), 250–252.

26. Allen to Reagan, 2 Mar. 1981, *FRUS*, 3:55–58.

27. Stearman to Clark, 22 Jan. 1982, *FRUS*, 3:435–436.

28. Stearman to Clark, 22 Jan. 1982.

29. Stearman to Allen, 7 Oct. 1981, RRPL, ESNSC, CF, box 34, folder "Afghanistan, 7/14/81–12/28/81."

30. Eliza Van Hollen, "Afghanistan: 18 Months of Occupation," Aug. 1981, DNSA.

31. Moscow to DOS, 4 Mar. 1982, *FRUS*, 3:496.

32. NSDD-32, "US National Security Strategy," 20 May 1982, https://fas.org/irp/offdocs/nsdd/nsdd-32.pdf.

33. NSDD-75, "US Relations with the USSR," 17 Jan. 1983, *FRUS*, 3:861–869. See as well Brands, *Making the Unipolar Moment*, 85–88.

34. Wilson, *The Triumph of Improvisation*, 68–75.

35. Shultz to Reagan, "Next Steps in US-Soviet Relations," 16 Mar. 1983, RRPL, *Foreign Relations of the United States (FRUS), 1981–1988*, vol. 4, *Soviet Union, January 1983–March 1985* (Washington, DC: US Government Printing Office, 2021), 68–70.

36. Shultz to Reagan, 2 Mar. 1983, RRPL, ESNSC, CF, box 34, folder "Afghanistan, 7/29/82–5/2/83."

37. Shultz to Reagan, "Next Steps in US-Soviet Relations," 21 May 1983, *FRUS*, 4:177–179.

38. Shultz, "America and the Struggle for Freedom," 22 Feb. 1985, *Department of State Bulletin* 85, no. 2097 (1985), 16–23; George Shultz interview with author, 12 Dec. 2016.

39. Meeting, 15 February 1983, *FRUS*, 4:33-41. The essential work on this remains Cordovez and Harrison, *Out of Afghanistan*.

40. Nicholas J. Cull, *The Cold War and the United States Information Agency: American Propaganda and Public Diplomacy, 1945–1989* (New York: Cambridge University Press, 2008), 417–418, 428, 448.

41. DOS to all posts, 25 July 1981, RRPL, ESNSC, CF, box 34, folder "Afghanistan, 7/14/81–12/28/81."

42. The Hague to DOS, 20 Aug. 1981, RRPL, Sven Kraemer Files (SKF), box 90103, folder "NATO-Shaping European Attitudes—Afghanistan"; Rome to DOS, 9 Sept. 1981, RRPL, SKF, box 90103, folder "NATO-Shaping European Attitudes—Afghanistan"; Brasilia to DOS, 27 July 1981, RRPL, SKF, box 90103, folder "NATO-Shaping European Attitudes—Afghanistan."

43. Nance to Meese, Baker, and Deaver, RRPL, SKF, box 90103, folder "NATO-Shaping European Attitudes—Afghanistan."

44. Fortier and Tahir-Kheli to McFarlane, 16 July 1984, RRPL, ESNSC, CF, box 34, folder "Afghanistan 6/28/84–7/23/84."

45. Clark to Dole, 15 Jan. 1982, RRPL, Elizabeth Dole Files, box 2, folder "Afghanistan Day (1/2)."

46. Reagan, "Remarks on Signing the Afghanistan Day Proclamation," 10 Mar. 1982, https://www.reaganlibrary.gov/research/speeches/31082b.

47. Lois Romano, "Reagan Booed at Joffrey Gala," *Washington Post*, 11 Mar. 1982.

48. Eileen Ogintz, "200 Rally Here for Afghanistan Day," *Chicago Tribune*, 22 Mar. 1982; Maryellen Kennedy, "Boston Rally Protests USSR in Afghanistan," *Boston Globe*, 22 Mar. 1982; Caption, *New York Times*, 22 Mar. 1982.

49. Cairo to DOS, 25 Mar. 1982, DNSA.

50. Gowan to Somersall, 26 Mar. 1982, TNA, FCO 26/2348.

51. Kabul to DOS, 20 Mar. 1982, RRPL, ESNSC, CF, box 34, folder "Afghanistan 1/21/82–4/1/82."

52. J. N. Dixit, *An Afghan Diary: Zahir Shah to Taliban* (New Delhi: Konark Publishers, 2000), 92.

53. Haig and Gromyko meeting, 26 Jan. 1982, *FRUS*, 3:467; Shultz to Reagan, 7 Dec. 1982, RRPL, JMP, box 40, folder "US-USSR Relations (December 1982)."

54. DOS, "Chemical Warfare in Southeast Asia and Afghanistan: An Update," Nov. 1982, DNSA.

55. Douglas Brinkley, ed., *The Reagan Diaries* (New York: HarperCollins, 2007), 128–129.

56. Brinkley, *The Reagan Diaries*, 385–386.

57. See, for example, Reagan and Gandhi meeting, 12 June 1985, RRPL, ESNSC, CF, box 91981, folder "Visit of Prime Minister Rajiv Gandhi (June 14, 1985) (1/7)"; Reagan and Eanes meeting, 15 Sept. 1983, RRPL, ESNSC, Subject File, box 51, folder "Memorandums of Conversation—President Reagan (08/15/1983–09/25/1983)."

58. Loten to James, 17 Nov. 1983, TNA, FCO 37/3057; FCO to NATO, 23 Nov. 1983, TNA, FCO 37/3057. The British embassy in Islamabad cast doubt on early US claims of the use of lethal agents. See Masefield to Archer, 13 Apr. 1980, TNA, FCO 37/2278.

59. Sergey Radchenko, *Unwanted Visionaries: The Soviet Failure in Asia at the End of the Cold War* (New York: Oxford University Press, 2014), 10–50.

60. Beijing to DOS, 21 June 1982, RRPL, JMP, box 40, folder "US-USSR Relations (May–June 1982)."

61. Kimmitt to Hill, RRPL, ESNSC, CD, box 34, folder "Afghanistan, 6/8/84–6/21/84."

62. George P. Shultz, *Turmoil and Triumph: My Years as Secretary of State* (New York: Scribner, 1993), 570.

63. McFarlane to Reagan, "Setting Priorities for the Next Four Years," 19 Nov. 1984, RRPL, Donald Fortier Papers, box 13.

64. Dennis Kux, *The United States and Pakistan, 1947–2000: Disenchanted Allies* (Washington, DC: Woodrow Wilson Center Press, 2001), 266–291.

65. On this see Elisabeth Leake, *The Defiant Border: The Afghan-Pakistan Borderlands in the Era of Decolonization, 1936–65* (New York: Cambridge University Press, 2017).

66. Brands, *Making the Unipolar Moment*, 115–116.

67. Steve Coll, *Ghost Wars: The Secret History of the CIA, Afghanistan, and Bin Laden, from the Soviet Invasion to September 10, 2001* (New York: Penguin Press, 2004), 91–93.

68. Benjamin Taylor, "Tsongas Urges US to Aid Afghans against Soviets," *Boston Globe*, 1 Oct. 1982; "A Too-Easy Resolution," *Boston Globe*, 9 Oct. 1982.

69. James M. Scott, *Deciding to Intervene: The Reagan Doctrine and American Foreign Policy* (Durham, NC: Duke University Press, 1996), 26.

70. Fortier to McFarlane, 21 Feb. 1984, RRPL, ESNSC, CF, box 34, folder "Afghanistan, 11/14/83–3/13/84."

71. Fortier to McFarlane, 5 Mar. 1984, RRPL, ESNSC, CF, box 34, folder "Afghanistan, 11/14/83–3/13/84."

72. The Afghanistan-related folders of Geoffrey Kemp of the NSC staff remain, at this writing, closed to researchers.

73. Fortier to McFarlane, 5 Mar. 1984, RRPL, ESNSC, CF, box 34, folder "Afghanistan, 11/14/83–3/13/84." Emphasis in original document.

74. Raymond to Afghan Political Group, 20 March 30, 1984, RRPL, ESNSC, CF, box 34, folder "Afghanistan, 3/30/84–5/18/84"; Raymond and Kemp, 21 June 1984, RRPL, ESNSC, CF, box 34, folder "Afghanistan, 6/6/84–6/21/84."

75. Shultz, "America and the Struggle for Freedom"

76. NSDD-166, "US Policy, Programs, and Strategy in Afghanistan," 27 Mar. 1985, https://reaganlibrary.archives.gov/archives/reference/Scanned%20NSDDS/NSDD166.pdf. See, as well, Scott, *Deciding to Intervene*, 58–59; Gates, *From the Shadows*, 319–321.

77. Shultz, *Turmoil and Triumph*, 691–692.

78. Armacost to Shultz, 20 Mar. 1987, *FRUS, 1981–1988*, vol. 6, *Soviet Union, October 1986–January 1989* (Washington, DC: US Government Printing Office, 2015):94–96.

79. NSDD-270, "Afghanistan," 1 May 1987, https://reaganlibrary.archives.gov/archives/reference/Scanned%20NSDDS/NSDD270.pdf

80. Ermath to Carlucci, 26 Mar. 1987, *FRUS*, 6:108–109; Peter W. Rodman, *More Precious than Peace: The Cold War and the Struggle for the Third World* (New York: Scribner, 1994), 341–349.

81. Meeting, 10 Dec. 1987, *FRUS*, 6:673.

82. Kalinovsky, *A Long Goodbye*, 138–139.

83. Cordovez and Harrison, *Out of Afghanistan*, 262–263. This is also discussed in Kalinovsky, *A Long Goodbye*, 129–130.

84. Meeting, 16 Sept. 1987, *FRUS*, 6:350–355.

85. Westad, *The Global Cold War*, 376.

86. Meeting, 4 Dec. 1987, *FRUS*, 6:595–600.

87. Reagan, "Afghanistan Day, 1988," 21 Mar. 1988, https://www.reaganlibrary.gov/research/speeches/032188c.

88. Helen Dewar, "Senate Sets Hard Line on Afghanistan," *Washington Post*, 1 Mar. 1988.

89. Byrd to Reagan, 22 Mar. 1988, RRPL, White House Office of Records Management (WHORM), box 36, folder "CO002 (651000-562235)."

90. Humphrey to Reagan, 12 Apr. 1988, RRPL, WHORM, box 36, folder "CO002 (651000-562235)."

91. Brinkley, *The Reagan Diaries*, 594.

92. Brinkley, *The Reagan Diaries*, 595.

93. Djerejian to Armacost, 15 Mar. 1988, RRPL, Nelson Ledsky Files (NLF), box 1, folder "Afghanistan 1988 Memos-Letters 1/3."

94. Meeting, 23 Mar. 1988, *FRUS*, 6:872; Meeting, 22 Mar. 1988, RRPL, NLF, box 1, folder "Afghanistan 1988 Memos-Letters 2/3."

95. Reagan, "Statement on the Ninth Anniversary of the Soviet Invasion of Afghanistan," 27 Dec. 1988, https://www.reaganlibrary.gov/research/speeches/122788a.

96. George Shultz interview with the author, 12 Dec. 2016.

97. David L. Anderson, *Trapped by Success: The Eisenhower Administration and Vietnam, 1953–1961* (New York: Columbia University Press, 1991).

98. Gates, *From the Shadows*, 433.

CHAPTER 16

The Reagan Administration and the Cold War Endgame in the Periphery
The Case of Southern Africa

FLAVIA GASBARRI

In 1965, the future general secretary of the Communist Party of the Soviet Union, Yuri Andropov, stated that the "future competition with the United States will take place not in Europe, and not in the Atlantic Ocean directly. It will take place in Africa, and in Latin America. We will compete for every piece of land, for every country."[1] When US President Ronald Reagan and Soviet General Secretary Mikhail Gorbachev met in Geneva for the first time twenty years later, it was clear that Cold War competition had unfolded along many fronts, but the Third World "periphery," as Andropov predicted, had played a surprisingly central role. Since the 1960s, with the division of Europe completed and dozens of new independent states emerging from decolonization, the geo-ideological struggle between the two blocs had rapidly expanded to Asia, Africa, the Middle East, and Latin America.[2] It was not surprising, therefore, that when the 1985 Geneva summit opened the doors to an unprecedented relationship between the leaders of the two superpowers, the regional conflicts and proxy wars in the Third World became a fixture of this and all subsequent US-Soviet summits. These conflicts had shaped the development of the bipolar rivalry during the 1960s and the 1970s, and they would likewise significantly affect the way in which that rivalry concluded in the 1980s.

Among the Third World battlefields, the Reagan administration invested considerable political capital in southern Africa through the policy of "constructive engagement," with Assistant Secretary for African Affairs Chester Crocker taking a lead role for eight years. Under this policy, and also through dialogue with its Soviet counterparts, the US government brokered a complex negotiation that eventually led to the 1988 Tripartite Accord, which settled a chain of conflicts and proxy wars throughout southern Africa. This agreement was a watershed for military and political developments in the region, with direct bearings on the broader US dialogue with the Soviets to end of the Cold War.

The case of southern Africa reveals how the Reagan administration's management of the Cold War endgame in the Third World was strongly influenced by the lessons it had drawn from the failure of détente in the 1970s. As a result, the "regional aspect" of bilateral relations with the Soviet Union, which was animated by fears of "burying" the talks on arms control anew, was the central framework for US efforts at conflict resolution in southern Africa. On a broader level, the complex way in which the bipolar confrontation ended in this region raises questions about the significance of the Cold War finale for the Third World. The events leading up to the Tripartite Accord, in fact, had their own peculiar logic and unique timing, which show how the end of the Cold War in the Third World does not always fit in the narrative centered on Europe, which lowers the curtain on the decades-long conflict in 1989 or 1991.

Since 1945 Washington's main interests in the southern Africa region had revolved around its relationship with the apartheid state of South Africa. The economic and strategic relevance of this country, rich in uranium deposits and other valuable minerals, as well as its government's strident anticommunism, made South Africa an important ally for the Western bloc in the first postwar decade.[3] The growing racial discrimination of the apartheid system and Pretoria's intransigence over the colonial issue in Namibia was, by contrast, a source of embarrassment in Washington.[4] Through different policies and alternative outcomes, all US presidential administrations from Harry Truman to Ronald Reagan tried to resolve a dilemma between two opposing needs: encouraging Pretoria to move away from the apartheid system and protecting US interests in the area.[5]

The end of Portuguese colonial rule in Angola and Mozambique in 1974 upended the balance of power that Washington had painstakingly cultivated in southern Africa. The turmoil that the collapse of the Portuguese empire left in its wake prompted, directly and indirectly, the white minority-dominated countries on South Africa's borders—Angola, Mozambique, and, later, Rhodesia (future Zimbabwe)—to move toward black majority rule. These new governments were hostile to Pretoria's white supremacy and provided wide support to anti-apartheid organizations in South Africa, as well as to the groups fighting for independence in Namibia.[6] The political orientation of the parties that took power in Angola, Mozambique, and Zimbabwe also disrupted US policy toward the region. The Movimento Popular de Libertação de Angola (MPLA), the Frente de Libertaçao de Moçambique (FRELIMO), and the Zimbabwe African National Union (ZANU) were all Marxist-inspired and received wide support from the Eastern bloc and the People's Republic of China.[7] The Soviet Union also backed the African National Congress and the South African Communist Party, which led domestic opposition to the apartheid system.[8] Furthermore, the civil war between the three principal liberation movements in Angola—the MPLA, the Frente Nacional de Libertação de Angola (FNLA), and the União Nacional para a Independência Total de Angola (UNITA)—which followed independence rapidly assumed the features of a proxy war, with the two blocs backing opposing sides. In 1975, Washington supported the FNLA and UNITA against the MPLA with a covert CIA operation, while the South African Defence Force (SADF) began a military invasion of Angola to assist these parties as well.[9] The South African invasion, however, triggered an increase in the Soviet military aid and a massive deployment of Cuban troops to Angola in support of the MPLA's military efforts against its enemies.[10] These developments complicated Washington's handling of the region. The collusion between the United States and the South African apartheid government poisoned relations with other African countries and gave rise to public opposition in the United States and Western Europe.[11] In this climate, the White House's public acknowledgement at the end of 1975 of US covert intervention in Angola prompted Congress to pass, a few months later, the Clark Amendment, which cut off all aid to any faction fighting in the Angolan civil war.[12]

From the mid-1970s, therefore, southern Africa became the theater of a complex convergence between a dramatic exacerbation of the "old" racial issue and the development of a "new" Cold War paradigm.[13] This convergence became the most evident symbol of how the Cold War extended to the region through an overlap of the global bipolar logics with the military and political dynamics of the local and regional crises. Two phenomena arose as a result. On the one hand, this overlap generated a strict interdependence among several distinct local conflicts in the region, such the civil war in Angola, the anticolonial struggle in Namibia, and the apartheid question in South Africa. On the other hand, it connected these local African crises to global Cold War dynamics in a mutually reinforcing "core-periphery" linkage. Superpower and

Cuban intervention intensified the local conflicts, while these local conflicts disrupted US-Soviet détente under the presidencies of Gerald Ford and Jimmy Carter. In fact, the persistent disagreement between Washington and Moscow on their respective policies and interventions in the Third World hampered dialogue on the core issue of nuclear arms control. In this way, the Angolan civil war became one of those regional conflicts that—together with the Shaba crises, the Ogaden War, and the Soviet invasion of Afghanistan in 1979—contributed to the failure of the Strategic Arms Limitation Talks (SALT II) and to the collapse of the détente process between Moscow and Washington as the 1970s came to a close.[14]

When Ronald Reagan became president in 1981, the US government developed a wider policy of "constructive engagement" in southern Africa, devised and enunciated by a new assistant secretary for African Affairs, Chester Crocker.[15] The strategy was based on two "pillars," which aimed at addressing the two main problems for US policy in the region: relations with apartheid South Africa and the regional proxy war. As for the first point, recognizing that the nature of the South African system prevented Washington from pursuing its interests without political costs, Crocker proposed a policy that combined diplomatic pressure with calls for reform. Rather than focusing on the long-term, ideal goal—a nonracist, democratic South Africa—constructive engagement focused on the process that would precede this outcome: "If this means that the United States becomes engaged in what some observers label as only 'amelioration,' so be it, provided that the process is open-ended and consistent with a non-racial order."[16] This policy was also proposed as a positive response to some modest, and controversial, reforms of the apartheid system that South African Prime Minister Pieter W. Botha concurrently introduced in the early 1980s.[17]

The second pillar of the constructive engagement policy was the strategy adopted to address the chain of conflicts in the region. This strategy established the so-called linkage: diplomatic negotiations on the independence of Namibia would be made conditional on a total withdrawal of Cuban troops from Angola.[18] The "linkage" formula was rooted in the assumption that there was a strict interdependence among all the conflicts that afflicted southern Africa. This assumption was a direct consequence of the overlap between the local conflicts and the Cold War logic that had affected southern Africa since the disintegration of the Portuguese empire in the 1970s. Indeed, Crocker's view of the regional picture was heavily influenced by this interaction, and he saw the independence of Namibia and the civil war in Angola as two sides of the same coin. As he summarized in a memorandum to Under Secretary of State for Political Affairs Michael Armacost in July 1988:

The continuing Angolan civil war had invited and sustained foreign intervention. The massive Cuban presence in Angola has been seen by South Africa as ultimately directed against it. South Africa has intervened in Angola with its own forces. Thus the civil war in Angola has become linked to the South African occupation of Namibia.... South Africa has made it clear that it will agree to Namibia's independence only when the withdrawal of Cuban forces from Angola is assured. Angola has insisted with equal force that the Cubans will depart only when Angola's security is assured by a process leading clearly to Namibian independence and the removal of South African military forces from Angola's borders.[19]

Therefore, the true connecting point between the two conflicts in Angola and Namibia was that "massive Cuban presence" on Angolan territory, which was in turn also a crucial piece of the broader Cold War competition in Africa as well as one of the main threats that Washington saw on the continent. In other words, the Cuban troops were the "knot" that tied together the regional situation and broader Cold War imperatives, as well as the local conflicts among themselves, creating strict connections and interdependence between domestic, regional, and international dynamics in southern Africa. Therefore, the cornerstone of the negotiations had to be the withdrawal of the Cuban troops from Angola, and Namibian independence became a tool for creating leverage in pursuit of that goal.[20] The United States thus expanded the agenda settled with United Nations General Assembly (UNGA) Resolution 435, which required the end of South Africa's illegal occupation of Namibia by linking its implementation to a timetable for Cuban troop withdrawals from Angola. This holistic regional strategy would put Washington in a position to liberate "two African countries for the price of one."[21] At the same time, it would serve the broader and more pressing goal of undermining the communist presence on the continent.[22] Crocker accordingly reached out to both Pretoria and the MPLA government led by José Eduardo dos Santos in 1981 in a bid to launch a round of talks that would untie the regional knot.

The constructive engagement policy, however, faced harsh criticism from the transnational anti-apartheid movement, and by the mid-1980s both "pillars" of the strategy had reached a deadlock. Increasing unrest, political violence, boycotts, and strikes that were spreading in the black townships in South Africa were the first signs that the "constructive" approach had failed. In 1985, Botha decided to declare a state of emergency, which further exacerbated domestic conflict and triggered a huge wave of state-sanctioned repression. These events received wide media coverage, particularly in the United States and Western Europe, and a broad anti-apartheid campaign rapidly mounted across influential sections of civil society on both continents.[23] In the United States, the situation in South Africa became a domestic political issue that eventually reached the halls of the Capitol. One of the most contentious points was the prospect of economic sanctions against South Africa, a measure that Crocker and President Reagan strongly opposed. However, the persisting violence in the South African townships and the increasing pressure from the US public led Congress to approve, in the face of Reagan's presidential veto, the 1986 Comprehensive Anti-Apartheid Act (CAAA), which established a broad range of US economic sanctions against South Africa for the first time. In 1986, this act seemed to represent the definitive failure of the constructive engagement with Pretoria.

At the same time, a fresh upsurge of the Cold War confrontation in the first half of the 1980s hindered Crocker's diplomatic efforts to address the regional turmoil. In the spirit of the Reagan doctrine—which aimed to "roll back" self-proclaimed Marxist regimes in the Third World by arming rival guerrillas and insurgents—conservative hawks within the administration requested and obtained the repeal of the Clark Amendment in 1985.[24] The Reagan doctrine had profound effects on US foreign policy across all the regional battlefields of the Cold War.[25] However, as White House Communications Director Pat Buchanan stressed in a memo to the President, "The single place where America can best send back a message that the one-sided rules of détente do not apply in the Reagan Era is the same place where, in 1975, it was made evident that détente was a Western delusion: Angola." From the mid-1980s, the United States resumed its covert action program in support of UNITA and its leader Jonas Savimbi. The US decision to resume funding to UNITA led the MPLA to abandon the bilateral negotiations started with Washington in 1981. By the mid-1980s, therefore, the regional peace process had reached an impasse, and Crocker's linkage strategy seemed fatally undermined.[26]

It was auspicious that 1985 was also the year Mikhail Gorbachev took power in the Kremlin.

Gorbachev's rise to power in 1985 and the launch of dialogue with Reagan opened a new relaxation of tensions between the superpowers and lent fresh momentum to critical arms control talks. The relationship that developed between the two leaders resulted most concretely in the signing of the Intermediate-Range Nuclear Forces (INF) Treaty in December 1987. This improvement in US-Soviet relations and in the international balance also affected the regional scenarios of bipolar competition and thus the development of events in southern Africa. From the first Reagan-Gorbachev meeting in

Geneva in 1985 to the final one in Moscow in 1988, regional conflicts in the Third World were a constant topic of discussion. Although the problem of nuclear arms control and disarmament dominated discussions between the principals, there was a simultaneous effort to find a solution for the ongoing proxy wars in Latin America, the Middle East, and Africa and thus diminish Cold War tensions on the so-called periphery.

Secretary of State George Shultz pointed out the nub of the problem during a meeting with Soviet Foreign Minister Eduard Shevardnadze in October 1985: "We need in the first instance to work on those conflicts—Afghanistan, Cambodia, Nicaragua, Angola and Ethiopia—which directly contributed to the deterioration of our relations. These issues are at the core of international tensions and were largely responsible for shattering efforts to improve US-Soviet relations in the 1970s.... With all due respect to arms control agreements, they can be readily derailed by an atmosphere created by regional conflicts."[27] Indeed, learning from the lessons of the collapse of the détente in the 1970s, the American perception was that a failure to move forward on the solution of regional issues could once again hamper the overall relaxation of tensions and lessen the likelihood of arms reductions, as well as the ratification process of the INF Treaty.[28]

This "core-periphery" dynamic was repeatedly acknowledged in meetings between US and Soviet leaders from 1985 to the collapse of the Soviet Union. Before the Geneva summit in November 1985, a memorandum dictated by the US president summarized his thoughts: "To those who believe arms control must be the goal as an end in itself with no connection to regional issues, let us ask ... did SALT II fail ratification on it's [sic] own or did the invasion of Afghanistan have something to do with it? They should be told in the coming meeting that Congressional approval on trade or arms control or whatever else they want will be difficult if not impossible to get if they continue to support their clients in Southeast Asia, the Middle East and Latin America."[29]

The preparatory documents for the Reykjavik meeting in 1986 included a "President's initiative on regional conflicts," which entailed a program of negotiations among the warring parties of each of those conflicts in parallel with joint US-Soviet talks to support them. As Reagan pointed out, this plan was considered a framework for the Soviet Union to cooperate with the United States in forging peace, as well as "an extraordinary opportunity for the Soviet side to make a contribution to regional peace which in turn can promote future dialogue and negotiations on other critical issues."[30]

In September 1987, when Reagan met Shevardnadze two months before the Washington summit with Gorbachev, he stressed anew the importance of the regional conflicts:

> These conflicts have blocked cooperation in the past and could continue to do so. . . . Our concern with Soviet policy is that it causes or inflames such conflicts by seeking to impose a political system unwanted by the people and by its lavish supply of arms to aggressive and irresponsible regimes. There can be no general improvement in our relations while such Soviet policies continue. But if those policies change for the better, then great improvements are possible.[31]

The connection between the resolution of regional conflicts and the improvement of superpower relations offered a powerful incentive to Moscow as well. The reformist impulse of Gorbachev's "new thinking," together with mounting economic difficulties and domestic criticism of past Soviet Third World policy, led the new Soviet leader and his lieutenants to seek a withdrawal from global commitments on the periphery, though this process was neither linear nor free from obstacles and setbacks.[32] According to Soviet Deputy Minister of Foreign Affairs Anatoly Adamishin, from the mid-1980s the decision about Soviet policy in regional conflicts was absolutely clear: "We had to go away. . . . Disengagement from regional conflicts also meant for us more possibilities to work with the Americans on more substantial issues, such as disarmament."[33]

Despite some persistent disagreements between Washington and Moscow, the core-periphery dynamic that marked the overall approach to Third World conflict resolution gave rise to two different yet interconnected processes. On the one hand, it progressively dampened a source of tension in the global chess match; on the other, it removed the external interferences from many conflicts across the Third World. This held true on the African continent. By the late 1980s, efforts to resolve the nesting civil and proxy conflicts that had wracked southern Africa for more than a decade became part of the more general dialogue between Washington and Moscow. Talks among the warring parties of those conflicts thus intersected with US-Soviet discussions at the global level, as well as among the parties and their superpower patrons. Autonomous military developments on the ground, as well as local and regional politics, also contributed to the development of those two processes.

In the mid-1980s the whole constructive engagement policy was in trouble. The problems of apartheid and political change in South Africa emerged as critical issues in US public opinion and Congress, creating a rift in the domestic political debate. The repeal of Clark Amendment had meanwhile caused the regional peace process to break down.

The passage of the 1986 CAAA, however, while restricting the Reagan administration's freedom of action, had the additional effect of dampening the domestic struggle on the issue of apartheid, leaving the initiative in southern Africa in the hands of the executive branch.[34] As stated by Shultz in a cable to the US embassy in Pretoria in January 1987: "Despite continuing interest in South Africa we can expect respite from Congressional action on South Africa. . . . Last year the momentum was against administration policies. For the first half of this year, barring a major atrocity in South Africa, the momentum is with us. Our conclusion is thus that a defensive approach to Congress is no longer appropriate."[35] Furthermore, since the spring of 1987 a chain of events had afforded an opportunity to overcome the stalemate in regional talks. As a consequence, in the last two years of its term, the administration tried to regain the initiative in southern Africa with the effect that, in Crocker's words, "the final eighteen months of the Reagan era proved to be the most eventful in the modern history of the region."[36]

After a hiatus of almost one year in US-Angolan relations, in April 1987 the MPLA government moved to resume contacts with Crocker and his shuttle diplomacy between the regional capitals.[37] This was due mostly to the increasing economic difficulties that a collapse in world oil prices and a consequent fall in oil revenues had caused and, relatedly, an unsustainable defense budget which absorbed almost half of total government expenditure.[38] The diplomatic push proceeded alongside dramatic military developments. In August 1987, the war in Angola reached its peak with a major clash between UNITA/SADF combined forces and the MPLA with Cuban reinforcements around Cuito Cuanavale in the southeast of the country. Cuba deployed 15,000 additional troops in Angola and in March 1988 launched a major counteroffensive by advancing toward the Namibian border with the declared intent of expelling the South Africans from Angolan territory.[39] The massive Cuban military buildup in southern Angola in close proximity to the Namibian border raised the possibility of Havana bringing the offensive inside Namibia, resulting in a full-scale war between the Cubans and the South Africans.[40]

This was probably the apex of tensions during the Angolan civil war, as it happened just before the launch of the first quadripartite talks between Angola, Cuba, South Africa, and United States, which Crocker had organized in London for May 1988. This coincidence created a back-and-forth tug of war and diplomacy between mid-1987 and spring 1988. Both the South Africans and the Cubans worked to exploit military advances in "blackmail" strategies during the peace conference. For their part, the Cubans used the threat of crossing the Namibian border as a bargaining chip at the negotiating table.[41] Meanwhile, the South Africans implicitly threatened the use of nuclear weapons with the twofold aim of warning the Cubans and sending a message to the superpowers in order to influence the future negotiations.[42]

This complex situation reached a breakthrough during a meeting held at Sal Island, Cape Verde, on July 22–23, 1988. South African, Angolan, and Cuban senior military representatives eventually agreed to take "practical measures" of restraint to maintain a de facto cessation of hostilities. These measures included no further southward movement of Cuban troops and the beginning of the withdrawal of the South African troops from Angola, which would be completed by September 1, 1988.[43] Following the end of the hostilities, both parties would claim victory on the basis of having forced the enemy to the negotiating table.

Regardless of who won the war, military developments on the ground between 1987 and 1988 showed two important realities. The first one was the danger of military escalation, in particular of a major direct clash between the Cuban and the South African forces at the Namibian border.[44] The second was the military stalemate, in which neither side was able to achieve victory. As summarized by a précis of the US Bureau of Intelligence and Research: "The South African intervention . . . made it clear to Luanda and its allies that the military approach would fail as long as South Africa held Namibia. . . . However Cuba, by sending more troops and increasing its role has counterbalanced SADF military pressure. Pretoria appears to be taken aback by the Cuban reaction to its own involvement and may now realize that it cannot unilaterally force concessions from Luanda, renewing its interest in negotiations."[45] There was a shared recognition among the belligerents in early 1988 that their positions could hardly be improved through military action. The chain of conflicts in southern Africa required a negotiated settlement.[46]

The diplomatic and military situation developing in southern Africa, particularly the tension in Cuito Cuanavale, was inextricably linked to the improvement of US-Soviet relations at the highest levels, which had the further effect of bolstering regional diplomacy in southern Africa. Both the risk of a military escalation and the benefits of a negotiated solution were acknowledged and stressed on several occasions during the meetings between US and Soviet officials. In a meeting with Adamishin on April 29, 1988, Crocker stressed the perils of a military escalation that the movement of Cuban forces toward the Namibian border had created.[47] Considering that in June 1988 South Africa called up Citizen Force personnel to ensure necessary forces to maintain border security at an acceptable level in Namibia, Adamishin was on firm ground when he later stated that "we could have a war for real. Neither the Cubans, nor the South African, nor us wanted this."[48] Chris Saunders argues that the events in Angola-Namibia at the end of the 1980s were, at least potentially, one of the last serious crises of the Cold War. A military escalation could have halted the dialogue between Gorbachev and Reagan and replicated the impact of Cuban and Soviet intervention in Angola in the mid-1970s on US-Soviet relations at that time.[49]

The Angola-Namibia conflict was thus considered "ripe" for negotiation and suitable for removal as a bone of contention between Washington and Moscow.[50] In 1987 and 1988, in particular, Crocker made a strong case for getting southern Africa to the top of the agenda; he believed that the United States faced the best opportunity in six years for a real breakthrough and that there was an opening for genuine US-Soviet cooperation to resolve a conflict that "had burdened our relations for more than a decade."[51] Another event boosted that hope in April 1988: the signature of the Geneva Accords to settle what Robert Rakove, in his contribution to this volume, has called "the central front" among the battles Reagan waged around the world, namely the war in Afghanistan.[52] Given the resolution of such an important conflict of the Cold War in the Third World, Crocker considered the negotiations over southern Africa a test of the superpowers' ability to move beyond Afghanistan to resolve all their Third World disputes.[53] "We had developed a framework with the Soviets to talk about all the regional conflicts," Crocker said "They were not all of the same importance: the high-ranking was Afghanistan. In terms of US domestic politics I think the second most important probably was Central America, but in terms of the broader geopolitical framework I would argue that it was Southern Africa."[54] Adamishin shared this view: "We were involved in many regional conflicts. First of all Afghanistan. We were fighting in Afghanistan and we were able to withdraw only in 1989. After Afghanistan, Angola was number two, for our political involvement and for the economic resources we were investing there."[55] Consequently, even though the Kremlin continued to transfer arms to Luanda in 1987, by 1988 Soviet policymakers were persuaded that Moscow should work to withdraw from Angola, though this process had to be gradual in order not compromise its international prestige.[56] The southern African issue was thus on the agenda in the last two meetings between Reagan and Gorbachev in Washington in 1987 and in Moscow in 1988. It was also the topic of several rounds of discussion at the ministerial level, which went on between Crocker and Adamishin, among others, throughout 1988[57]

Those final eighteen months of the Reagan era were perceived in the US Bureau for African Affairs as a window of opportunity that would shut after the US presidential elections in November 1988. This feeling of "time running out" added a further incentive for the US diplomatic effort. As Crocker stated in April 1988 during a meeting with an Organization of African Unity delegation, the upcoming election campaign would monopolize attention in the United States.[58] Furthermore, since 1981 the Reagan administration had invested considerable political capital in southern Africa under the umbrella of Crocker's constructive engagement. It was unlikely that another administration would be more committed.

It was Washington's perception that this idea was shared by all parties as well, in particular by the Angolans and the South Africans. The MPLA told the Americans that they were aware of the desirability of reaching an agreement while Reagan remained in office.[59] The same applied to the South Africans, who, in Washington's view, saw in Reagan their best interlocutor, all the more because the Democratic Party platform for the 1988 elections called for declaring South Africa a terrorist state.[60] As South African Foreign Minister R. F. "Pik" Botha told US Ambassador Edward Perkins in May 1987, "Even with a Republican President there was no guarantee, given the American system of government, that a new incumbent in the White House would continue to insist on Cuban withdrawal."[61]

Between 1987 and 1988, therefore, all these elements came together in support of the final phase of constructive engagement. The resumption of Crocker's shuttle diplomacy in 1987 led to the first official meeting between South Africa, Angola, and Cuba, in London on May 3 and 4, 1988, with the mediation of the United States. On that occasion, all the parties acknowledged the linkage, which would become the basis for a settlement.[62] The Soviet Union, while registering "pro-forma" objections to the legality of linkage, found the US approach "broadly acceptable."[63] The London summit inaugurated a cycle of twelve quadripartite meetings to discuss the complex chain of conflicts in southern Africa, which, as noted above, involved a close interaction of three different levels of political dynamics: domestic affairs, regional situation, and global scenario. The negotiations eventually reached a turning point on December 22, 1988, when Angola, Cuba, and South Africa signed the Tripartite Agreement in New York. With this document the parties agreed to the implementation of UN Resolution 453, which established the independence of Namibia and the withdrawal of all the South African military forces from its territory. Havana and Luanda committed to a calendar for the withdrawal of all Cuban troops from Angola by July 1991. In addition, all parties agreed to refrain from the threat or use of force and to ensure that their respective territories were not used for acts of war or aggression against any State of south-western Africa.[64]

The 1988 agreement was a watershed for southern Africa and US policy toward the region. The implementation of the linkage concept untied the knot among domestic, regional, and international politics. The removal of all foreign forces from Angola meant that the civil war, which was still ongoing, could finally be addressed as a purely internal matter.[65] The same applied to

South Africa, which, with the end of the struggle over Namibia and the disappearance of the "communist threat" on its border, lost two strong justifications for its domestic regime and was forced to turn its attention to the internal battle against apartheid. More generally, the end of the massive Cuban presence in the region helped to remove this conflict "from the list of issues which poison east-west relations."[66] As a consequence, it ended the paradigm of the Cold War competition in southern African regional and internal dynamics and brought about change in the rationale and logics that underpinned US policy and intervention in the wider region.

After the agreement, US policy in southern Africa had to deal with Washington's longstanding support for UNITA and the ongoing civil war in Angola against a backdrop of warming US-Soviet relations, the fall of the Berlin Wall, and the revolutions in Eastern Europe. The end of the second Reagan presidential mandate in January 1989 meant that a new administration would have to manage the implementation of the Tripartite Agreement and the legacy of almost one decade of constructive engagement.

George H. W. Bush continued to move on the pattern inaugurated by his predecessor through regular meetings and consultations with Gorbachev. As far as policy in the Third World was concerned, the new administration maintained the same core-periphery connection that had emerged in the dialogue with the Soviets during the Reagan years. Like Reagan, Bush still saw the cooperation with the Soviet Union in the Third World as a way to support the broader relationship with Moscow, particularly as the Soviet empire started to crumble in Eastern Europe and the Baltics.[67] Once again, this approach was evident in southern Africa, as the Bush administration continued to engage in the conflict resolution process in Angola, where, following the withdrawal of the Cuban troops, the civil war between UNITA and MPLA still raged.

In December 1990, after two years of unsuccessful negotiations led first by Zaire and then by Portugal, Washington and Moscow decided to involve themselves directly in the peace process. The two superpowers developed a joint sponsorship for the negotiations in Angola, which led in 1991 to the signature of the Bicesse Agreement between dos Santos and Savimbi and to the first democratic election in Angola in September 1992. Unfortunately, the refusal of Jonas Savimbi to accept the result of the election, won by the MPLA, led to a resumption of the civil war between UNITA and MPLA and to an ensuing struggle to keep the peace process on track. A new phase of negotiations was carried on between 1993 and 1994, this time under the auspices of the United Nations, ending with the signing of the Lusaka Accord in 1994. This agreement gave Angola four years of "neither war nor peace": at the end of 1998 the parties went back to a full-scale war.[68] The Bicesse Agreement thus failed to solve the riddle of the Angolan civil war, but it was a triumph for the broader goal of US involvement in the Angola peace process—namely, cooperation with Moscow. As Secretary of State James Baker explained to his Soviet counterpart Aleksander Bessmertnykh after the signing of the agreement: "Our coordination on Angola is another indication of the positive spirit of cooperation that marks US-Soviet relations. I am also gratified that we were able to work together constructively to resolve a conflict that once divided us."[69] Many years later, talking about the outcome of the Angolan elections, Baker stated in his memoirs: "The pain and suffering unfortunately was not over. However, at least the Angolan conflict was no longer a proxy war."[70]

When the Reagan administration entered the White House, its approach to the many conflicts in southern Africa reflected the interplay between the global Cold War and local military and political dynamics, through which the Cold War was extended into the region. The "linkage strategy" devised by Crocker was a clear example of how, in Washington's view, this overlap was inextricable and the local roots of the various conflicts could not be untangled from the campaign against Soviet and Cuban influence in the region. The beginning of Reagan's and Gorbachev's dialogue in 1985 marked a major turning point, as it inserted US policy in southern Africa within the broader policy framework of cooperation with the Soviet Union in solving the conundrum of the regional conflicts in the Third World. This framework built on the same core-periphery logic that had characterized détente during the 1970s and had shown that there was a clear mutual influence between the negotiation on arms control and the superpowers' policies in the Third World.

The lesson learned from détente's failure—that regional conflicts had contributed to SALT II's collapse—strongly influenced Reagan's effort to pursue negotiated solutions toward Third World proxy wars amid a new relaxation of tensions with Moscow. This time dialogue between Moscow and Washington featured mutual reinforcement between negotiations on arms control and those to solve regional disputes and end superpower involvement in Africa and kindred hotspots in Latin America, Asia, and the Middle East. Whereas the two tracks of the core-periphery dynamic had diverged during the 1970s, during the 1980s they finally converged.

This change in the global-local interplay was an important boost for Crocker's diplomacy in southern Africa. The desire to remove this nest of conflicts from the list of issues that bedeviled US-Soviet relations was one of those factors that ultimately yielded the tripartite New York Agreement in 1988. This agreement operationalized the "linkage" and cut the "knot" that tied the Cold War paradigm to the regional conflict in Southern Africa. In this sense, the year 1988 and the New York Agreement became for southern Africa what the year 1989 and the fall of the Berlin Wall would be for Europe—the milestone that marked the end of the Cold War. In fact, given that the Cold War's extension to the region in the 1970s resulted in an overlap of global, regional, and local political and military dynamics, the true meaning of the end of the Cold War for this specific battlefield was the reversal of that process. In 1988 this "de-linkage" was complete.

Even after that date, however, the core-periphery interplay survived and adapted to the ongoing transformations. The Bush administration's involvement in the peace process in Angola between 1988 and 1991 fully responded to this core-periphery framework again. Washington devoted a lot of effort to that peace process mostly because it was critical to the broader foreign policy goal of cooperating with Moscow. After 1991, when the Bicesse Agreement failed, the task of restarting the negotiations and the peace process was taken up by the United Nations. By then, the Soviet Union was no longer extant, so Washington had lost an important point of reference for its policy in Southern Africa—namely, that global-local interplay that had guided the US involvement in the region for almost fifteen years, first in terms of confrontation with the Soviet Union during the 1970s and then in terms of cooperation at the end of the 1980s.

Notes

1. Svetlana Savranskaya and David Welch, "Global Competition and the Deterioration of US-Soviet Relations 1977–1980," 23–25 Mar. 1995. http://www2.gwu.edu/~nsarchiv/carterbrezhnev/docs_global_competition/part7.PDF.

2. As Artemy Kalinovsky and Sergey Radchenko argue, "The Cold War was fought, to some extent, for and in the name of the Third World"(Artemy Kalinovsky and Sergey Radchenko, *The End of the Cold War in the Third World* [London: Routledge, 2011], 7).

3. On the close economic and trade relationships between the United States and South Africa in the 1940s, see Thomas Borstelmann, *Apartheid's Reluctant Uncle* (New York: Oxford University Press, 1993), 38–55.

4. After 1945, South Africa refused to renounce to the League of Nations' mandate for the administration of Namibia. In 1971, the International Court of Justice declared the South African occupation of Namibia illegal. See International Court of Justice, "Legal Consequences for States of the Continued Presence of South Africa in Namibia (South West Africa) notwithstanding Security Council Resolution 276 (1970)," 21 June 1971, http://www.icj-cij.org/files/case-related/53/5597.pdf.

5. Alex Thomson, *US Foreign Policy towards Apartheid South Africa, 1948–1994: Conflict of Interests* (New York: Palgrave Macmillan, 2008).

6. For South Africa's response to the turmoil of the 1970s, see Jamie Miller, *An African Volk: The Apartheid Regime and Its Search for Survival* (New York: Oxford University Press, 2016).

7. Vladimir Shubin, *The Hot "Cold War": The USSR in Southern Africa* (London: Pluto Press, 2008).

8. Shubin, *The Hot "Cold War,"* 239–263.

9. Piero Gleijeses, *Conflicting Missions: Havana, Washington, and Africa, 1959–1976* (Chapel Hill: University of North Carolina Press, 2002), 273–300; John Stockwell, *In Search of Enemies: A CIA Story* (London: Futura Publications, 1979), 40–57, Chester Crocker, *High Noon in Southern Africa: Making Peace in a Rough Neighborhood* (New York: Norton, 1992), 48–50; Edward George, *The Cuban Intervention in Angola, 1965–1991: From Che Guevara to Cuito Cuanavale* (London: Frank Cass, 2005), 68–81.

10. Odd Arne Westad, *The Global Cold War: Third World Interventions and the Making of Our Times* (Cambridge: Cambridge University Press, 2007), 234; Gleijeses, *Conflicting Missions*, 300–328.

11. Thomson, *US Foreign Policy*, 84.

12. Peter Schraeder, *United States Foreign Policy toward Africa: Incrementalism, Crisis and Change* (Cambridge: Cambridge University Press, 1994), 47.

13. John Daniel, "Racism, the Cold War and South Africa's Regional Security Strategies, 1948–1990," in *Cold War in Southern Africa: White Power, Black Liberation*, ed. Sue Onslow (London: Routledge, 2009), 35.

14. "SALT lies buried in the sands of Ogaden," in the words of Zbigniew Brzezinski, *Power and Principle: Memoirs of the National Security Adviser 1977–1981* (London: Weidenfeld and Nicolson, 1983), 188.

15. Chester Crocker, "South Africa: Strategy for Change," *Foreign Affairs* 59, no. 2 (1980): 323–351.

16. Crocker, "South Africa," 327.

17. Thomson, *US Foreign Policy*, 12–14; Nigel Worden, *The Making of Modern South Africa: Conquest, Apartheid, Democracy* (Oxford: Wiley-Blackwell, 2012), 131–140.

18. Crocker to Shultz, 22 Sept.1982, in *South Africa and the United States: The Declassified History*, ed. Mokoena Kenneth (New York: New Press, 1993), 261; Crocker, *High Noon*, 63–67.

19. Crocker to Armacost, July 25, 1988, National Security Archive (NSA), Incoming FOIA, box 2, folder "Angola—8180 2 of 2."

20. Zachary Kagan-Guthrie, "Chester Crocker and the South African Border War, 1981–1989: A Reappraisal of Linkage," *Journal of Southern African Studies* 35, no 1 (2009): 11.

21. Crocker, *High Noon*, 64–67.

22. To some extent, it is possible to see some similarities with the policy of "strategic consensus" that the Reagan administration was implementing in the Middle East. As argued by Seth Anziska in his chapter in this volume, that policy had the dual aim of fighting communism and bolstering moderate Arab states in the Middle East, while upholding Israel's security.

23. Crocker, *High Noon*, 257–258; Schraeder, *United States Foreign Policy*, 217–218.

24. Buchanan to Reagan, Nov. 7, 1985, Ronald Reagan Presidential Library (RRPL), White House Office of Records Management (WHORM), CO006.

THE REAGAN ADMINISTRATION AND THE COLD WAR ENDGAME   361

25. See for instance, Robert Rakove's chapter on the war in Afghanistan and Seth Anziska's chapter on Israel, the Palestinian question, and Lebanon, both in this volume.

26. "Memorandum on the talks between the People's Republic of Angola and the United States of America," 22 Mar. 1988, South African Foreign Affairs Archives (SAFAA), 1/22/1/5/2, vol. 1; Crocker, *High Noon*, 302; Kagan-Guthrie, "Chester Crocker and the South African Border War," 71–73.

27. Meeting record, 25 Oct. 1985, RRPL, Jack Matlock Files (JMF), box 47, folder "Memcons-Shultz/Shevardnadze Meetings Helsinki and New York." See also Blakey, 8 Dec. 1987, RRPL, WHORM, FO006-11; George Shultz, *Turmoil and Triumph: My Years As Secretary of State* (New York: Macmillan, 1993), 266, 278.

28. Stevens to Risque, 24 Nov. 1987, RRPL, WHORM, 528155–528851, FO006-11. See also Shultz to Reagan, RRPL, JMF, box 46, folder "Briefing Book Material (1/3) [Talking Points]."

29. Reagan, "Gorbachev," Nov. 1985, in *The Last Superpower Summits*, ed. Thomas Blanton and Svetlana Savranskaya (Chicago: University of Chicago Press, 2016), 44.

30. "Speaker's Package for Reykjavik Meeting," Oct. 1986, RRPL, WHORM, 440053, FO006-11.

31. Ermarth to Carlucci, 21 Sept. 1987, RRPL, Executive Secretariat–NSC (ESNSC), box 11, folder "#8790982."

32. Raymond Garthoff, *The Great Transition: American-Soviet Relations and the End of the Cold War* (Washington, DC: Brookings Institution Press, 1994), 733–748; Svetlana Savranskaya, "Gorbachev and the Third World" and Chris Saunders, "The Ending of the Cold War in Southern Africa," in *The End of the Cold War in the Third World*, ed. Artemy Kalinovsky and Sergey Radchenko (London: Routledge, 2011), 21–45 and 265–266; Westad, *The Global Cold War*, 364–387.

33. Anatoly Adamishin Interview with the author, 2 May 2014. See also: "Conversacion del Comandante en Jefe Fidel Castro con Anatoli Adamishin," 28 Mar. 1988, http://digitalarchive.wilsoncenter.org/document/118132.

34. In 1988 the Congress eventually voted not to further assert its authority in this area; Thomson, *US Foreign Policy*, 150.

35. Shultz to Pretoria, 30 Jan. 1987, RRPL, African Affairs Directorate–NSC (AADNSC), box 16, folder "[South Africa—General] (9 of 14)."

36. Crocker, *High Noon*, 353.

37. The contacts resumed in Brazzaville in April 1987. Three months later the Angolan government invited Crocker in Luanda. In the interim between the two meetings, Crocker also met with Adamishin to discuss the Angolan situation. See "US/Soviet Talks and the Upcoming US/MPLA Talks: Embassy Report" and "US Report: Comparison of Contents," July 1987, SAFAA, 1/22/1/6/1, vol. 2; Crocker, *High Noon*, 342–352.

38. Crocker, *High Noon*, 341; Kagan-Guthrie, "Chester Crocker and the South African Border War," 74; Gerald Bender, "Peacemaking in Southern Africa: The Luanda-Pretoria Tug-of-War," *Third World Quarterly* 11, no. 2 (1989): 21–22. See also David Painter's chapter in this volume for an overview of how the developments in the world oil economy at the end of the 1980s contributed to the crisis of the Soviet Union.

39. Abramowitz to Shultz, 13 May 1988, NSA, FOIA, box 2, folder "Angola—8670 1987-88 Military Action in Angola"; Piero Gleijeses, "From Cassinga to New York:

The Struggle for the Independence of Namibia," in *Cold War in Southern Africa: White Power, Black Liberation*, ed. Sue Onslow (London: Routledge, 2009), 210.

40. Gleijeses, "From Cassinga to New York," 214; Chris Saunders, "The Angola/Namibia Crisis of 1988 and Its Resolution," in *Cold War in Southern Africa: White Power, Black Liberation*, ed. Sue Onslow (London: Routledge, 2009), 232.

41. "Entrevista de Risquet con Chester Crocker," 26 June 1988, http://digitalarchive.wilsoncenter.org/document/118144. See also Piero Gleijeses, *Visions of Freedom: Havana, Washington, Pretoria and the Struggle for Southern Africa, 1976–1991* (Chapel Hill: University of North Carolina Press, 2013), 454–455; Crocker, *High Noon*, 399.

42. Frank Pabian, "South Africa's Nuclear Weapon Program: Lessons for US Nonproliferation Policy," *Nonproliferation Review* 3, no. 1 (1995): 8.

43. "Summary of points of agreement and others discussed at the South African and Angolan/Cuban military meetings," 22–23 July 1988, http://www.aluka.org/action/showMetadata?doi=10.5555/AL.SFF.DOCUMENT.rep19880722.035.017.d1.18.

44. DOS to Pretoria, 29 June 1988, NSA, FOIA, box 2, folder "Angola—8180 2 of 2"; DIA, 31 Mar. 1988, NSA, FOIA, box 2A, folder "Angola—24769—Military Action in Southern Angola"; DIA, 5 Apr. 1988, NSA, FOIA, box 2A, folder "Angola—24769—Military Action in Southern Angola"; DIA, 22 Apr. 1988, NSA, FOIA, box 2A, folder "Angola—24769—Military Action in Southern Angola."

45. Kamman to Bentley, 28 Apr. 1988, NSA, FOIA, box 2, folder "Angola—8670 1987–88 Military Action in Angola."

46. DOS to Kingston, 16 Feb. 1988, NSA, FOIA, box 2, folder "Angola—8180 2 o f2"; Abramowitz to Armacost, 15 June 1988, NSA, FOIA, box 2, folder "Angola—8180 2 o f2"; Shultz to Moscow, 8 Apr. 1988, NSA, FOIA, box 2, folder "Angola—8180 2 o f2"; Shultz to OAU, 11 May 1988, NSA, FOIA, box 2, folder "Angola—8180 2 o f2"; Van Heerden to Stroebel, 9 July 1987, SAFAA, 1/22/1/6/1, vol. 1.

47. London to Shultz, 4 May 1988, NSA, FOIA, box 2, folder: "Angola—8180 2 of 2."

48. The Citizen Force was a reserve component of the South African armed forces. Cable to DIA, NSA, FOIA, box 2A, folder: "Angola—24769—Military Action in Southern Angola"; Adamishin interview.

49. Saunders, "The Angola/Namibia Crisis of 1988 and Its Resolution," 225.

50. Briefing book, RRPL, Kenneth Duberstein Files, box 4, folder "Washington Summit Briefing Book: The Meetings of President Reagan and General Secretary Gorbachev, Washington, DC, 12/08/1987–12/10/1987 (3)"; Crocker to Armacost, 25 July 1988, NSA, FOIA, box 2A, folder "Angola—8180 2 of 2"; Shultz to Kinshasa, 28 May 1988, NSA, FOIA, box 1, folder "Angola—8180 US pressure on MPLA to negotiate with UNITA 1 of 2."

51. Crocker, *High Noon*, 361; Crocker to Shultz, 10 June 1988, NSA, FOIA, box 2, folder "Angola—8180 2 of 2."

52. See Robert Rakove's chapter in this volume.

53. Shultz to OAU Collective, 11 May 1988, NSA, FOIA, box 2, folder "Angola—8180 2 of 2"; Crocker to Armacost, 25 July 1988, NSA, FOIA, box 2, folder "Angola—8180 2 of 2."

54. Chester Crocker Interview with the author, 8 Aug. 2012.

55. Adamishin Interview.

56. Crocker, *High Noon*, 360; Shubin Vladimir, "Were the Soviets 'Selling Out'?" in *The End of the Cold War in the Third World*, ed. Artemy Kalinovsky and Sergey

Radchenko (London: Routledge, 2011), 246–247; Saunders, "The Angola/Namibia Crisis of 1988 and its Resolution," 225.

57. "Reagan-Gorbachev Working Luncheon," 10 Dec. 1987 and "Reagan-Gorbachev Second Plenary Meeting," 1 June 1988, in *The Last Superpower Summits*, ed. Thomas Blanton and Svetlana Savranskaya (Chicago: University of Chicago Press, 2016), 347–355 and 428–442.

58. Shultz to OAU, 11 May 1988, NSA, FOIA, box 2, folder "Angola—8180 2 o f2".

59. Shultz to Lisbon, 1 Jan. 1988, NSA, FOIA, box 1, folder "Angola—8180 US pressure on MPLA to negotiate with UNITA 1of2".

60. Moscow to Shultz, 10 July 1988, NSA, FOIA, box 2, folder "Angola—8180 2 of 2"; Democratic Party platform, 18 July 1988, http://www.presidency.ucsb.edu/ws/index.php?pid=29609; "Michael Dukakis: A Platform for Africa," *Africa Report* 33, no. 3 (1993): 13–15.

61. "Meeting of Minister R. F Botha with American Ambassador: 12 May 1987," 18 May 1987, SAFAA, 1/33/3, vol. 110. In this regard, however, Piero Gleijeses states that there is "no evidence in the available South African, Cuban, or US documents that the November 1988 US Presidential elections influenced Pretoria's stance in the negotiations" (Gleijeses, *Visions of Freedom*, 507).

62. London to Shultz, 4 May 1988, NSA, FOIA, box 2, folder "Angola—8180 2 of 2"; "Summary Minutes of Exploratory Discussions held in London on 3 May and 4 May 1988 between a South African Delegation and an Angolan Delegation, facilitated by a Delegation from the United States," 5 May 1988, SAFAA, 1/22/1/5/4, vol. AJ.

63. Shultz to OECD capitals, 7 Apr. 1988, NSA, FOIA, box 2, folder "Angola—8180 2 of 2"; "Non-Paper on US-Soviet Talks on Southern Africa and Upcoming US-MPLA Talks," July 1987, SAFAA, 1/22/1/6/1, vol. 2; Adamishin interview.

64. United Nations Security Council, 22 Dec. 1988, S/20346, A/43/989.

65. "The December 1988 accords in effect reduced the Angolan conflict from a 'regional conflict' with outside parties to a civil war, although warfare resumed . . . , with continuing supply of arms by the external powers, for two and a half years more" (Garthoff, *The Great Transition*, 740).

66. Shultz, 22 Dec. 1988, NSA, FOIA, box 2, folder "Angola—8180 2 of 2."

67. "Theme Paper: US–Soviet Priorities in 1990," Dec. 1989, George Bush Presidential Library (GBPL), National Security Council (CF), Subject Files (SF), Condoleeza Rice Files, box OA/ID CF00717, folder "Malta Summit Papers (Preparation) December 1989 [2]"; "The President's Meeting with President Gorbachev, Dec. 2–3, 1989," GBPL, NSC, SF, Susan Koch Files, box OA/ID CF01337, folder "Malta [2]"; Scowcroft to Bush, 29 May 1990, GBPL, NSC, SF, Nicholas Burns Files, box OA/ID CF01309, folder "Chron File: May 1990–June 1990 (3)."

68. Ian Spears, "Angola's Elusive Peace: The Collapse of the Lusaka Accord," *International Journal* 54, no 4 (1999): 566.

69. Shultz to Moscow, 10 May 1991, NSA, FOIA, box 2, folder "Angola—10572—Angolan Peace Accords."

70. James Baker, *The Politics of Diplomacy: Revolution, War and Peace, 1989–1992* (New York: Putnam, 1995), 600–601.

Part Six

South and East Asia

CHAPTER 17

Reagan and the Crisis of Southwest Asia

ELISABETH LEAKE

On April 25, 1981, some one hundred days after Ronald Reagan became the fortieth president of the United States, his secretary of state, Alexander Haig, spoke to the American Society of Newspaper Editors. He outlined Reagan's foreign policy objectives, pledging that "America will act in a manner befitting our responsibilities as a trustee of freedom and peace." He made special mention of "the Middle East and Southwest Asia" as sites of "a new, intensive effort . . . to protect our vital interests and to help assure peace."[1] That Haig returned to this regional imaginary throughout his speech was unsurprising—there were many obstacles to declared US interests in the region. The overthrow of the Shah in Iran in February 1979 and the Soviet invasion of Afghanistan in December 1979 had thrown regional planning into disarray, renewing the threat of Soviet expansionism and introducing a new ideological challenger—political Islam.

How would US officials comprehend and address these new threats to their relationships in the region? Events across Southwest Asia—also called the greater Middle East or the "Near East and South Asia," depending on the observer—posed formidable problems for the Reagan administration. The host of crises across that part of the world threatened US Cold War policy, access to energy reserves, and increasingly, national security interests. Moreover, they endangered regional balances of power and ultimately the body of nation-states with which US policymakers had become used to engaging.

This chapter considers how the Reagan administration wrestled with a broader sense of crisis across Southwest Asia. Rather than a specific predicament—the Soviet invasion of Afghanistan or the Iranian revolution—the overarching crisis in Southwest Asia involved the future of the sovereign, modern, and, to an extent, secular nation-state in this region. Local secessionist movements and religious reformers threatened this system, as, of course, did Soviet encroachment. Indeed, the 1979 Soviet invasion of Afghanistan seemed to indicate the potential fusion of regional and international crises, whereby Soviet intervention could have a domino effect, leaving a trail of crumbling states in its wake. Even if Reagan was not intent on a Soviet withdrawal from Afghanistan, as Robert Rakove argues in this volume, the foundational political order upon which US policymakers relied for allies and influence was in jeopardy.

Records from the State Department, the Central Intelligence Agency (CIA), and the National Security Council (NSC) reveal that US policymakers were above all concerned with the survival of those nation-states that preexisted Reagan's presidency. Even while Reagan made passionate campaign promises to rethink US foreign policy, his policies were fundamentally premised on an international system of states. This worldview, inherited from multiple generations of earlier policymakers, meant that officials working under Reagan had certain expectations as they crafted policy. States' political boundaries needed to remain largely unchanged, even if different factions vied for power within them. Neither the Cold War nor regional nor domestic dynamics could be allowed to reshape, multiply, or reduce the basic units of international politics. In other words, the political map of Southwest Asia circa 1979 had to endure.

This focus on state sovereignty and survival had two key consequences. First, officials agonized about the potential for ethnonationalist autonomy movements to disrupt state-centered politics. Second, analysts wrestled with the prospects of political Islam in the region. While Washington clearly identified and understood how secessionists could undermine state sovereignty, its understanding of the role that Islam in its politicized and orthodox manifestations might play was more ambivalent. They could agree that autonomy movements presented a clear threat but were divided as to whether Islamism was largely reactionary, and therefore "backward," or instead merited serious consideration as a competing political system. Washington's reliance on state-led politics fundamentally shaped how the Reagan administration approached this regional crisis but also left officials unable to understand fully how and why opponents to the extant system had emerged or the potential consequences of this resistance. The administration never reached a clear consensus on the Southwest Asian system of states, to the detriment of US relations with local actors and governments in the 1980s and on into the twenty-first century.

The United States' relationship with Southwest Asia experienced a crisis in the late 1970s. Long before this, US policymakers had encountered the greater Middle East, in the words of Osamah Khalil, as "an ideational construct produced and maintained by geographical, ideological, and intellectual representations."[2] Since the beginning of British and French decolonization processes in the early to mid-twentieth century, US officials had taken an increasingly active interest in this region. Not only was access to oil increasingly critical for fueling a superpower intent on extending its influence and economic prosperity, but the Middle East was a crucial link in the United States' strategy of containing Soviet expansion. This could be clearly seen by the mid-1950s with the establishment of a "northern tier" of US allies (Iraq, Iran, Turkey, and Pakistan, united in the Baghdad Pact/Central Treaty Organization), as well as the 1957 Eisenhower doctrine of military and economic aid to any Middle Eastern state, which avowed to "secure and protect the territorial integrity and political independence of nations" in the region.[3]

While definitions of Southwest Asia or the greater Middle East remained fluid in geographical terms—at some points it narrowly referred to the Arabian peninsula, Iraq, and Iran, and at others included the expanse from Sudan and northern Africa east to India and Sri Lanka—US policy toward the various states in the region was often unified and defined by a focus on economic development initiatives, preservation of oil access, and the Israel-Palestine conflict.[4] Countries such as Afghanistan and Egypt became key sites for testing the tenets of modernization theory, with American technocrats advising on industrialization, dam-building, mass agriculture, or urban policies intended to overturn "traditional" society.[5] Reliance on Middle Eastern oil meant that successive presidential administrations strengthened ties with authoritarian regimes in prerevolution Iran and Saudi Arabia or authorized covert actions to support sympathetic political leaders in the name of resource access.[6] Meanwhile, US support for Israel complicated relations with Muslim-majority states across the region, especially in times of conflict such as the 1956 Suez crisis and the 1967 and 1973 Arab-Israeli wars.

United States policy toward the countries comprising Southwest Asia consequently relied on state authority. This aligned with the primacy of the state as the key apparatus of sovereignty in international politics after the Second World War, the establishment of the United Nations, and decolonization. Thus, throughout the twentieth century, US officials dealt almost exclusively with state representatives in Southwest Asia and avoided talks with nonstate actors such as the Palestinian Liberation Organization or the Awami League in East Pakistan (modern-day Bangladesh).[7]

The official mind in Washington therefore operated amid a set of established postcolonial nation-states that shared internationally recognized borders. Notably, and often controversially, these borders were largely colonial inheritances rather than reflections of local ethnic, social, or political divisions. This meant that the states system across the region relied on international recognition and top-down efforts by states to assert and affirm their right to govern all the territory up to their borders. Thus, on one hand, Southwest Asia's political geography frequently divided ethnic populations with historical ties that cut across new borders, giving rise to resistance movements against state-based governance.[8] On the other, presidential administrations did not allow these local dimensions to shape policy, instead deferring to state leaders to contain local dissatisfaction.

Developments beginning in 1978 forced the Jimmy Carter and Ronald Reagan administrations to revisit their strategic priorities in Southwest Asia. The revolution in Iran from December 1978 to February 1979 and the Soviet invasion of Afghanistan in December 1979 left the United States without one key ally (Mohammad Reza Shah) while also facing the prospect of expanding Soviet influence in the strategically vital Persian Gulf. In his State of the Union address on January 23, 1980, President Carter called Soviet interventionism a threat to "all those who rely on oil from the Middle East and who are concerned with global peace and stability." He went on not only to reemphasize the importance of the region's natural resources to the global economy but also to re-pledge to all "countries in the region" the United States' support for their "independence, security, and prosperity."[9] The Carter doctrine, as it became known, placed Southwest Asia, broadly defined, at the heart of US national security policy. It emphasized the need for cooperation with local states, as well as preventing Soviet expansion. However, Carter was able to do little to pursue his announced doctrine before losing the presidential election to Reagan. While authorizing covert aid to a growing anti-Soviet Afghan resistance, he failed to retrieve American hostages from a hostile Iran. Instead, Reagan was left to wrestle with an ongoing Southwest Asia crisis—one that increasingly extended from India to north Africa. The Reagan administration thus took on the task of both identifying and resolving the key elements of the crisis in order to preserve US interests, and perhaps win the Cold War.

The Soviet invasion of Afghanistan and the Iranian revolution occurred within a broader crisis of statehood in Southwest Asia in the late 1970s and 1980s. While Afghanistan and Iran underwent the most extreme political transformations, other countries also faced threats that often transcended national borders. Alongside the Soviet-Afghan war, the 1980s saw war erupt between Iran and Iraq, an ongoing civil war in Lebanon, worldwide anti-Western terrorist activities, and the assassination of at least one prominent world leader in South Asia, India's Indira Gandhi. (Speculation persists whether Pakistan's Mohammad Zia-ul-Haq's death in a plane crash was accidental.)

While many different causes fueled these conflicts, US-based observers sought to discern patterns in disaster. For the US government, political stability was paramount to preserving its regional interests, and national security officers soon focused on the ethnic fragmentation of the region and the multitude of autonomy movements that challenged its political geography. As one CIA analyst explained, "The ethnic geography of Southwest Asia is such that crisis and confrontation in the region are particularly prone to stir up separatist activity and the self-determination issue, both of which can then spread to other regions."[10] Local calls for self-determination had the potential to spark additional autonomy movements, engulfing the entirety of Southwest Asia.

Separatism was a particularly fraught topic because of its potential to disrupt the local states system on which US strategy relied. Upholding the states that comprised Southwest Asia provided a systemic means for preserving US regional interests. Carter's National Security Council (NSC) affirmed in August 1980 the "great significance [of] the sovereignty and independence of the states of the region." Reagan made clear he agreed when in July 1983 he issued National Security Decision Directive (NSDD) 99, which highlighted the necessity of "supporting the sovereignty of all countries in the region."[11] Even following the establishment of a hostile regime in Iran, US officials relied on the continued existence of an Iranian state. A complete breakdown of law and order was even more problematic than Ayatollah Khomeini's fiery anti-US rhetoric, as it could invite Soviet intrigue and influence. As a draft NSDD in June 1985 argued, one of the United States' most pressing concerns was "preventing the disintegration of Iran and preserving it as an independent strategic buffer which separates the Soviet Union from the Persian Gulf."[12]

Autonomy movements threatened to disrupt this system. Throughout the 1980s, ethnonationalists across the region came into conflict with state leaders or pursued demands for their own nation-states. This brought existing state borders into question, introducing conflict between states and also insecurity and instability within them. This was not symptomatic of an ostensibly "Muslim world." Secessionist demands cut across religious divides. This was most clearly demonstrated by the explosive rise of violent Sikh nationalism in India, which threw the state into disarray much as demands for ethnic Pashtun, Baluch, and Kurd autonomy threatened to undermine neighboring Pakistan and nearby Iran. While there were numerous examples of autonomy movements across Southwest Asia during this decade, three merit extended discussion: Pashtun ethnonationalism across Afghanistan and Pakistan; Sikh demands for an independent state between Pakistan and India; and Kurd secessionist movements in Iran. Together, these three case studies highlight how Washington saw autonomy movements as ripe for Soviet manipulation amid concerns that local political dynamics would explode into crises of state stability and regional security.

Pashtun ethnonationalism in the Afghan-Pakistan borderlands had been a major stumbling block in US relations with both Afghanistan and Pakistan throughout the twentieth century.[13] Afghan demands for the creation of an autonomous, ethnically defined "Pashtunistan" was a sore point in Afghan-Pakistan relations and one that US officials had never felt capable of resolving. The border between the states had remained extremely fluid, and in this context, the specter of Pashtunistan exacerbated US fears about Soviet expansion across Southwest Asia following the invasion of Afghanistan.

The Soviet intervention in Afghanistan posed a direct threat to the established states system in Southwest Asia. Reagan's White House and State Department largely agreed that the Soviet presence in Afghanistan meant the country no longer existed. As a memorandum from Richard Pipes to William P. Clark, deputy secretary of state, noted, "From the Soviet point of view, the situation in Afghanistan has become 'irreversible,' i.e. for all practical purposes *Afghanistan has been annexed to the Soviet Union.*"[14] In their eyes, the Soviet invasion amounted to the effective re-colonization of Southwest Asia, the creation of a Soviet empire in which the states that had previously populated the region were dismembered, and the potential resulting loss of US allies and oil access. Officials across the CIA, State Department, and NSC uneasily highlighted the longstanding belief that the Soviets desired a warm-water port with access to the Indian Ocean and the Persian Gulf.[15] By this logic, the invasion of Afghanistan was a mere steppingstone to further expansion.

This fear of Soviet expansionism played out in two specific ways. First, it renewed attention to the security and stability of the Pakistani state. Second, it led to reflection about the potential for Soviet encouragement of secessionist movements across the Persian Gulf and beyond. In the fight to prevent further Soviet expansion and undermine the Soviet presence in Afghanistan, Pakistan was a frontline state. Covert aid from the US government to Afghan resistance fighters, first authorized by Carter and then continued and expanded under Reagan, was distributed via Pakistan's Inter-Services Intelligence.[16] These funds cemented Pakistan as a key regional partner in limiting the spread of Soviet influence. As Reagan's NSC acknowledged, thanks to "its geographic location and its large well-trained armed forces, a strong, independent, anti-Soviet Pakistan that is willing to cooperate with the US can play a key role in our overall regional strategy."[17]

But the US-Pakistan relationship rested on a shaky foundation. Pakistan was weak. During the 1970s, the state had absorbed a string of setbacks. It had undergone a bloody bifurcation, with the emergence of independent Bangladesh in 1971. It had faced an additional, violent autonomy struggle from Baluch nationalists along the border with Afghanistan and Iran. And it had weathered the overthrow, execution, and replacement of its leader, Zulfikar Ali Bhutto, by a military dictatorship under Mohammad Zia-ul-Haq. In the 1980s, Pakistan's disintegration remained a real possibility: despite extensive counterinsurgency activities, Baluch nationalism persisted, and the transborder Pashtun community remained a source of tension between Afghanistan and Pakistan. These interethnic dynamics were exacerbated by the millions of Pashtuns fleeing the Afghan communists and settling in Pakistan, putting unprecedented pressure on Pakistan's local infrastructures and politics. US Secretary of State Alexander Haig could only conclude that Pakistan was "woefully unprepared to counter [Soviet] increased pressure or to deter aggression."[18]

The inference of such analysis was clear: US aid would be of little use if Pakistan succumbed to intranational conflict or external pressure from the Soviets. Intelligence services in the United States focused on the potential for the Soviets to exacerbate local secessionist movements, leading to Pakistan's total disintegration. An early memorandum sent to President Carter by Stansfield Turner, director of the CIA, noted that the Soviet invasion of Afghanistan "has created possibilities for direct large-scale Soviet aid to Baluchi [in Pakistan and Iran] as well as to Azari and Kurdish separatist movements [in Iran]." He went on to predict that Soviet leadership, if faced with resistance, was likely to encourage these autonomy movements as well as long-standing border disputes between neighboring countries such as Afghanistan, Pakistan, and India.[19] CIA intelligence analyses throughout the 1980s highlighted Pakistani fears about Soviet and Afghan subversion operations among Pakistan's Pashtun population.[20] The infringement of Pakistani airspace by Afghan planes and bombings on Pakistan's side of the border authenticated these anxieties.[21] Such activities threatened to blur the border between Afghanistan and Pakistan and turn fears of subversion into reality.

Thus, the stability and continued existence of Pakistan had ramifications far beyond US support for the Afghan resistance against the Soviets. As members of the NSC pointed out, "Pakistan's geographic location adjacent to Iran, Afghanistan, the PRC and India, and close to the mouth of the Persian Gulf underlines its importance to the power balance in Southwest Asia. Of prime importance is the denial of Pakistan's strategic location and political alignment to the USSR."[22] A November 1982 Department of State briefing paper similarly argued that the "fundamental aim of US policy toward Pakistan today is to help this front-line nation provide for its own security and independence in the face of the threat from 100,000 Soviet troops across the border in Afghanistan."[23] In effect, Pakistan could not be allowed to succumb to Soviet pressure or internal dissent. Local autonomy movements thus gained significance for the broader security of Southwest Asia.

Fears of disintegration fed Washington's resolve that the Pakistani state deserved support and preservation. Linking anxieties about the potential for local autonomy movements to undermine Pakistani sovereignty, subversion of the Soviets in Afghanistan, and US regional strategy more broadly, James A. Phillips, a senior policy analyst at the Heritage Foundation, recommended that US economic aid be used specifically in the Pakistani provinces bordering Afghanistan and Iran. This would not only lighten the burden of the Afghan refugees on the Pakistani state, he argued, but equally "could blunt [the] appeal of pro-Soviet Pushtun and Baluchi separatists by giving these ethnic minorities more of a stake in Pakistan's future."[24] NSDD-99 explicitly mentioned the potential Soviet threat to Baluchistan and the need to discuss strategy with Pakistan with this in mind.[25] For Pakistan, as for much of Southwest Asia, local hotspots acquired far greater importance within a broader US worldview and global strategy that relied on the survival and stability of extant states.

Even in states that appeared ostensibly stable, autonomy movements had the potential for huge disruption. This became obvious with India, frequently seen as an exceptionally resilient (and secular) state in comparison with others in Southwest Asia. The shocking assassination of Prime Minister Indira Gandhi on October 31, 1984, by two of her Sikh bodyguards brought international attention to communal tensions within India and the Akali Dal party's demand for an independent Sikh state, "Khalistan."

Since the creation of independent India and Pakistan in 1947, Sikhs in the Indian state of Punjab, which bordered Pakistan, had agitated for increased rights and autonomy. The movement for Khalistan began in earnest in 1978. Under the Akali Dal party and its charismatic leader, Jarnail Singh Bhindranwale, the demand for a Sikh state became increasingly militant. By the end of 1983, the state of Punjab was under President's Rule, or direct executive authority, in response to Sikh terror attacks. Gandhi's government resorted to "Operation Blue Star" in June 1984, during which the Indian Army, in an attempt to root out Bhindranwale, laid siege to the Golden Temple in Amritsar, the holiest Sikh shrine, and killed a number of Akali Dal leaders.[26] The assassination of Gandhi was in retaliation for Operation Blue Star.

The demand for Khalistan and Gandhi's assassination sparked a moment of crisis in South Asia. Domestically, it unleashed a wave of violence across India. In Delhi, more than 1,000 Sikhs were killed within two days of Gandhi's death. In Ramachandra Guha's words, "The police's indifference was shocking, the role played by Congress politicians positively immoral."[27] Abroad, it provoked questions about India's future as a unified state. The *New York Times*, whose front page on November 1 was devoted almost entirely to coverage of Gandhi's death, predicted a "period of prolonged uncertainty, with the potential for greater domestic instability and new tensions with its neighbors, particularly Pakistan." Policymakers in Washington reportedly worried the country would fragment and "explode in general violence."[28] A report from the CIA's Directorate of Intelligence six days after Gandhi's assassination predicted, "Sikh discontent is the most serious domestic problem facing new Prime Minister Rajiv Gandhi," Indira's son. It went on to conclude that in "our judgment, Sikh alienation from the government in the wake of the crackdown in Punjab—and now, the Hindu attacks on Sikhs outside Punjab—will result in long-term resistance to New Delhi's policies."[29] Indira Gandhi's death looked like the start of a greater crisis for Indian statehood.

The assassination of Indira Gandhi provided an important lesson at a critical point in time. Even the most stable state in Southwest Asia was susceptible to autonomy movements. The threat of fragmentation was not distant. For US officials intent on preserving states in the region, Sikh demands for Khalistan created additional concerns. It posed questions about the future of India and its regional relations. The Directorate of Intelligence predicted that "the Soviets will be well placed to manipulate India's heightened security concerns," and feared "overt and covert Soviet efforts to implicate the US and Pakistan" in Gandhi's assassination.[30] The CIA's Office of Near Eastern and South Asian Analysis in 1986 also mooted the potential for the increased militarization of the Indian state in response to autonomy movements and noted that Rajiv Gandhi could be targeted by secessionist assassins from among Khalistan supporters or Kashmiri nationalists.[31] In such a scenario, analysts, citing the "volatility of communal, ethnic, and caste tensions," predicted that Gandhi's death "would spark further demands for concessions from militant minority groups."[32] The Indian state's experience with militant Sikh nationalism had created opportunities for further (violent) anti-state movements that could disrupt India's stability and provide further opportunities for Soviet interference.

The crisis also had regional implications. Even before Gandhi's assassination, Reagan's NSC identified Sikh unrest along the Indo-Pakistan border as a potential threat to Pakistan's ability to withstand Soviet and Afghan pressure.[33] Indian leaders accused Pakistan of encouraging unrest in Indian Punjab. When US Congressman Stephen Solarz met with Arun Singh, Indian minister of state for defense, Singh claimed that "slippery" Zia-ul-Haq was training Sikh fundamentalists in the Faisalabad jail in Pakistani Punjab.[34] By 1986, Shirin Tahir-Kheli, the NSC's director of Near East and South Asian Affairs, noted in a memorandum titled "A Legacy of Peace in South Asia" that "a worsening internal situation in the Panjab has fed Indian suspicions that Pakistan is bound to exploit the Sikhs against New Delhi." She concluded that whether Pakistan "is actually doing so has become secondary to the fear of *potential* involvement," before pointing out that "Panjab is currently Rajiv Gandhi's most vulnerable point."[35] For US officials, the fear became that the local demand for Khalistan could spiral into a regional crisis that would ultimately undermine US regional strategy and allow the Soviets to reinforce their influence in India while extending their position elsewhere in Southwest Asia.

The potential for local autonomy movements to undermine Southwest Asian interstate and intrastate relations—and thereby provide a space for new Soviet influence and manipulation—was a common theme of many strategy discussions in Washington. This was clear in the case of Sikhs and Indo-Pakistan relations, as well as Baluch and Pashtuns in Afghan-Pakistan relations. It also was evident in US governmental debates on nearby Iran. In this case, the Iranian revolution, the Soviet presence in Afghanistan, and finally the 1980–1988 Iran-Iraq war exacerbated concerns about local autonomy movements. As previously mentioned, the Soviet invasion had sparked fears about Baluch nationalists residing in Pakistan and Iran and Soviet willingness to encourage renewed resistance from this community. However, concerns about Iran's Baluch population paled in comparison with those about its Kurds.

Ethnic Kurds were a truly transborder community, spread across Iran, Iraq, Turkey, and the western Soviet Union. Demands for an independent Kurd state, or "Kurdistan," were made during the dissolution of the Ottoman Empire after the First World War and again during the formation of the United Nations. In both instances, the movement was quashed by great-power politics and local state interests. A Kurdish Republic was briefly established in 1945–1946 before being violently suppressed. Nevertheless, Kurdish ethnonationalism continued, and was (and is) a major issue in regional relations. It was a source of tension within Iran, where Kurdish nationalists were heavily policed by the Shah's regime. It also had an impact on Iran-Iraq relations. Kurdish nationalists moved across the border, seeking safe haven in Iraq or Iran, depending on each state's policies of the time. The practices of one state toward the Kurds had ramifications for the neighboring state's relations with the same community.[36]

At the time of the Iranian revolution, a CIA intelligence memorandum had noted renewed Kurdish dissident activity. While it acknowledged that these Kurds shared the same frustrations as other Iranians disillusioned with the shah's regime, it warned of renewed Kurdish nationalism taking advantage of the state's political disarray.[37] These concerns were justified. On March 2, 1979, the Kurdish Democratic Party issued a statement promoting a Kurd state encompassing the Iranian provinces of Kurdistan, Kermanshah, Ilam, and Western Azerbaijan—a territory of 140,000 square kilometers.[38] It seemed to indicate that local Kurds intended to use Iran's political upheaval to again pursue an independent state.

CIA analysts identified Iranian Kurds as one of the key opposition forces within Iran. While analysts argued that "their political concerns will remain limited by parochial goals" and highlighted the fragmentation of the transborder Kurdish community, they also pointed out existing transnational ties between some Kurdish leaders and the Soviets, as well as cooperation between the Kurdish Democratic Party and the Iraqi state.[39] Despite concluding that a Kurdish autonomy movement was unlikely to unseat Khomeini's regime, this population became critically important as a source of potential instability during the Iran-Iraq war. In this instance, the Iraqi and Iranian governments attempted to use their Kurdish minority populations to sway Kurdish resistance in the opposing country.[40] For both neighbors, Kurdish ethnonationalism served as a political tool in the two countries' disputes, much as Sikh nationalism affected Indo-Pakistan relations.

For the United States, the potential for Iran to exploit Iraq's Kurd population—or vice versa—was particularly disconcerting. Stuart D. Goldman, a specialist in Soviet affairs advising Congress members, pointed out in 1986 that "Moscow continues to provide enough low-level support to Azeri and Kurdish nationalists to retain good contacts and some influence in Iran's northern borderlands." Autonomy movements still provided the easiest outlet for increased Soviet influence and further disintegration of political relations across Southwest Asia.[41] In the eyes of the US government, the Iran-Iraq war opened this region up to Soviet infiltration, and the Kurdish community provided ready local allies.

The CIA's Office of Near Eastern and South Asian Analysis worried about not only the spread of Soviet influence but also Khomeini's anti-Westernism. One report called Iraq "one of the most fragmented societies in the Middle East." In a parallel to concerns about the potential domino effect of the

Soviet invasion of Afghanistan, CIA watchers considered the possible ramifications of the spread of Iranian influence by exploiting Iraq's Kurds. In light of the Iran-Iraq war, intelligence analysts concluded, a "long war of attrition, the most likely scenario, will primarily benefit the Kurds, who will gradually take over large areas of the north [thereby weakening the Iraqi position].... A total Iraqi defeat would be the outcome most damaging to US interests. Without Iraq to act as a break on its activity, Tehran would export its revolution throughout the region. Iraq, under an Islamic regime, would work in tandem with Iran to subvert moderate Gulf states."[42] The war's implications thus were twofold: the expansion of Soviet and Iranian influence and potentially a new Kurdish state. Both of these factors endangered the region's stability, as well as its political geography, threatening to redraw the political map of Southwest Asia through both violence and state collapse.

Demands for Kurdistan had a potentially huge impact on regional relations and US strategy, much as did other autonomy movements in Southwest Asia. In this case, the concerns of national security and intelligence elites in Washington were less about the internal stability of Iran or Iraq than about the regional balance of power. Analysts remained confident that without an interstate war, the regimes of either country could easily, if brutally, quash local autonomy movements. Much as Sikh nationalism threatened to disrupt Indo-Pakistan relations, Kurdish nationalism complicated Iran-Iraq relations, and thus US interests. The threat of such ethnonationalist movements lay partly in their ability to destabilize local states and partly in their potential to disrupt established balances of power and create new opportunities for Soviet influence. Washington's focus on Kurdish autonomy movements, much like those of Sikhs, Baluch, and Pashtuns, related to a web of local, regional, and international political concerns.

But the Kurdish nationalist movement also brought an additional question to the table. The Iran-Iraq war, and the Kurdish role within this conflict, forced relevant US officials to consider the ramifications of extended Iranian influence—specifically, the spread of Khomeini's strident anti-US pronouncements and his brand of political Shi'ism. The ethnonationalist threat and that of political Islam comingled. Those whose portfolios touched on Southwest Asia also had to come to terms with the ways in which spreading interest in political Islam could potentially destabilize US strategy there.

Elite US fears about the spread of Iranian influence reflected not only concerns about the potential disruptive force of minority ethnonationalism, but also a broader sense of insecurity about the future role of religion across the larger region. Islam was not the only cause for concern. By mid-1986, CIA analysts had identified Hindu revivalism in India and religious extremism in Israel as critical issues in Southwest Asia, alongside the rise of Islamism.[43] Focusing specifically on Islam, officials throughout the Reagan administration recognized that Islam was a potentially potent political force across Southwest Asia. Nonetheless, US government approaches to the question of religion were largely ambivalent. Whether Islam would prove transformational was an object of debate rather than consensus.

There was a paradox in official Washington's conception of political Islam. US observers recognized that leaders could position Islam as the antidote to Western influence and expansionism, but many officials continued to explain and understand the appeal of Islam dismissively as a rejection of modernity and a return to "traditional" society. Although this led many in Washington to see political Islam, especially its more radical strains, as a potential threat to US interests, they simultaneously dismissed it due to its supposedly backward-looking orientation. Such a view left policymakers bereft of the analytical tools necessary to enact policies that adequately addressed this region-wide issue.

The Reagan administration's approach to Islam was not framed purely as "us" versus "them." Certainly, some intelligence analysts focused their explanations of the rise of political Islam, especially in Iran, on how the United States was perceived by devout Muslim leaders. They described the United States as epitomizing the "cultural seduction of the West's materialism, secularism, and sexual liberalism," or cited the US alliance with Israel as making the country "antipathetic to Islamic culture and aspirations."[44] This couched tensions in a total cultural rupture between Southwest Asia and the United States.

But analysts more frequently spoke in terms of local political dynamics and a Third World reaction against modernization. According to one CIA Near Eastern and South Asian Analysis paper, the Islamic revival was "born out of the anxieties and frustrations of the disproportionately youthful Third World countries striving to demonstrate their autonomy."[45] The CIA's Office of Political Analysis concluded: "The root cause for the intense expressions of anti-US feelings is the dissatisfaction and humiliation the Muslim peoples are experiencing in their collective lives. As the traditional social order breaks down, the answers drawn from the past are insufficient for coping with the complexity of the modern world; the structure provided by Islam cannot contain the anger and frustration of the Muslim people uprooted from their traditional milieu."[46] These statements were more inward-looking than focused on a binary division between the Western and Islamic worlds. But they nonetheless revealed the limited scope of many CIA analysts' understanding of

Islam. Time and again, officials pointed to Islam as belonging to the "traditional social order." As such, they believed locals turned to Islam as a comforting relic from the past. The Iranian revolution, according to one report, "sought to return Iranian society to more traditional ways with all aspects of life governed by Islamic teaching, tradition, and law."[47]

But such analysis was inherently self-limiting. It did not recognize that a singular Islamic "traditional way" did not exist, much as a singular "Muslim world" was largely a figment of twentieth-century state politics, as Cemil Aydin has shown.[48] Moreover, it left little room for reflection about the changing nature of political Islam and the ways that some Islamic thought was in direct dialogue with contemporary developments, not just "tradition."[49] Analysts acknowledged a schism between Sunni and Shi'ite Muslims, but they did not delve into what Ayesha Jalal has called the "fissured nature of globalized Islam in the contemporary world."[50]

As a consequence, US observers did not recognize Islam as a potentially destabilizing factor in the same vein as ethnonationalism. CIA analysts tended to downplay the durability and likely impact of Islam as a political factor across Southwest Asia. More than seven years after the Iranian revolution, a major analysis of Islamism in the region concluded, "We believe radical fundamentalist groups will gradually weaken politically, with some members adopting a more moderate outlook."[51] Similarly, while a 1987 report predicted that the "Islamic resurgence is likely to be the most powerful, widespread political force in the Arab world for the remainder of this century," it went on to argue that Islamic revivalism would more probably result in a "shift toward an authentic Islamic culture," with some social and political impacts, not radical regime changes. It identified two competing institutional perspectives. One upheld Islam as a "stabilizing agent holding society together in the face of enormous social and economic challenges." The more pessimistic perspective focused on "reactionary impulses that distort Islamic tradition, the rigidity that often prevails over reasonable application of Islamic thinking, and the zealotry that makes compromise, flexibility, and adaptability dangerous offenses."[52] In either definition, Islam was described as a social phenomenon with potential political ramifications, rather than as a potent governing force.

One great irony of the Reagan administration's approaches to Islam was that while analysts mused on the role of political Islam for the future of Iran, Iraq, and the "Arab world," they largely dismissed the role of Islam in wartorn Afghanistan. This was critical. With the benefit of hindsight, scholars frequently emphasize Reagan's administration public embrace of an Islamic "jihad" in Afghanistan. Andrew Preston describes the situation more accurately: "Both [the United States and the Afghan resistance] hated the Soviet

Union for its aggression, its communism—and its atheism."[53] In essence, religion was not the main motivating factor for cooperation, even if US support ultimately went to supporting some militant Islamists.[54] As Rakove shows in his chapter in this volume, Reagan emphasized the United States' and Afghanistan's shared love of freedom and sense of self-reliance. US analysts, particularly in the CIA, largely dismissed Islam as an important factor in Afghan politics. Notably the same report that predicted that fundamentalist groups were likely to decline did not even include Afghanistan in its analysis. Another CIA situation report observed that "insurgents in the field have usually said they are fighting to defend Islam, but their definition of Islam appears to include all traditional ways including the Pashtun code of revenge and other customs that are not Islamic."[55] Even as talks for a Soviet withdrawal progressed, analysts concluded that insurgents were not motivated by religion, or even a nationalist agenda. The "majority" wanted "considerable autonomy for their region or ethnic group and favor[ed] a minimum of interference in local affairs from Kabul."[56] They concluded that local tribal and social dynamics were more likely to determine the actions of the Afghan resistance and the future of the Afghan state. Little in these reports could have predicted the post-withdrawal rise of the Taliban.[57]

The official mind in Washington thus took an ambiguous approach to political Islam across Southwest Asia. To an extent, it recognized Islam as a potential source of social mobilization, especially in Iran, Iraq, and the Arab world. However, at the same time, it dismissed Islam as a political force in war-torn Afghanistan, even while describing the resistance movement as a jihad. Analysts recognized the potential danger of the relationship between Islamic fundamentalism and spreading anti-US sentiment, but clearly they did not perceive religion as a potential source for regional instability in the same vein as autonomy movements. Instead, the Islamic threat became increasingly conflated with the threat of transnational terrorist activities targeting the United States and its allies, specifically as orchestrated by Hezbollah in Lebanon, Libya's Muammar Gaddafi, and later by al Qaeda and Osama bin Laden.[58] Yet, as Chris Fuller argues in this volume, Reagan's counterterrorism policy remained as uncoordinated and ambiguous as his administration's approach to Islam. Islam's significance lay not in the stability of Southwest Asia but in its potential to motivate attacks elsewhere in the world.

Events in Southwest Asia posed a threat to the Reagan administration's worldview, as well as its foreign policies. His government undoubtedly recognized that political and ethnonationalist instability, coupled with the potential for Soviet expansion, threatened Southwest Asia. Political Islam was recognized as an additional potential hazard, but it was largely dismissed as a relic of traditional societies. What remained paramount for Reagan and those who worked in his administration was to preserve the existing states system across the "greater Middle East." Afghanistan may have fallen to Soviet influence, but other countries could not be allowed to follow. Washington accordingly provided extensive aid to Pakistan to prevent the disintegration of this frontline state; maintained an uneasy neutrality in the Iran-Iraq war, providing limited aid to Saddam Hussein while supplying Iran with weapons in return for help returning US hostages (the infamous failed Iran-Contra affair); and kept tabs on India's Rajiv Gandhi, his relationship with the Soviet Union, and his approach to domestic unrest.[59] These activities were intended to preserve the status quo—the balance of power between neighboring states within the region.

But maintaining the status quo did not solve many of the issues confronting the diverse peoples of Southwest Asia. Ethnonationalism has continued to be a critical source of weakness for many of the states there. It has been compounded by the powerful influence of political Islam, which, despite US analysts' predictions otherwise, has shaped the region in numerous political, social, and cultural ways—and not merely as a return to "tradition." The fate of Afghanistan perhaps best exemplifies the weakness of the US policy of maintaining the political geography of Southwest Asia without adequate consideration of local dynamics. Reagan's focus on a Soviet withdrawal, and thus the restoration of an independent Afghan nation-state on the political map of Southwest Asia, was single-minded. It did not extend to planning, or supporting, a stable, functioning post-withdrawal Afghanistan. The country was allowed to succumb to civil war, and later the Taliban, in the name, according to President George H. W. Bush, of "self-determination."[60]

Southwest Asia thus came to represent an enduring paradox in US foreign policy. The Reagan administration's policies toward the states in this region demonstrated the postcolonial importance of the international states system and also states (and their leaders) as the main protagonists in international politics. By the time Reagan came to office, this international status quo fundamentally shaped US approaches to foreign policy. This, in turn, limited his administration's capacity to address events in Southwest Asia, where, during the 1980s, this post-1945 system entered a period of sustained crisis, as it could accommodate neither local political aspirations nor swelling transnational support for political Islam. Many Washington elites recognized the perils of ethnonationalism—less so Islam. But both issues were largely referred to in the ways in which they potentially threatened the region's extant states, rather than their potential for engendering alternative political systems. To this day their inability to come to grips with local threats to the states system in Southwest Asia persists in complicating US relations with state and nonstate actors across this vital region.

Notes

1. "Text of Haig's Speech on American Foreign Policy," *New York Times*, 25 Apr. 1981.

2. Osamah F. Khalil, "The Crossroads of the World: US and British Foreign Policy Doctrines and the Construct of the Middle East, 1902–2007," *Diplomatic History* 38, no. 2 (2014): 302.

3. Cited in Khalil, "Crossroads of the World," 323.

4. See Seth Anziska, *Preventing Palestine: A Political History from Camp David to Oslo* (Princeton, NJ: Princeton University Press, 2020); Peter Hahn, *Crisis and Crossfire: The United States and the Middle East since 1945* (Lincoln: University of Nebraska Press, 2005); Douglas Little, *American Orientalism: The United States and the Middle East since 1945* (Chapel Hill: University of North Carolina Press, 2002); Michael Oren, *Power, Faith and Fantasy: America in the Middle East 1776 to the Present* (New York: Norton, 2007).

5. See Khalil, "Crossroads of the World," 328; Nathan J. Citino, "The 'Crush' of Ideologies: The United States, the Arab World, and Cold War Modernisation," *Cold War History* 12, no. 1 (2012): 89–110; Nick Cullather, "Damming Afghanistan: Modernization in a Buffer State," *Journal of American History* 89, no. 2 (2002): 512–537; Timothy Mitchell, *Rule of Experts: Egypt, Techno-Politics, Modernity* (Berkeley: University of California Press, 2002).

6. See Christopher R. W. Dietrich, *Oil Revolution: Anticolonial Elites, Sovereign Rights, and the Economic Culture of Decolonization* (New York: Cambridge University Press, 2017); Daniel Yergin, *The Price: The Epic Quest for Oil, Money, and Power* (New York: Simon and Schuster, 1990).

7. See Paul Thomas Chamberlin, *The Global Offensive: The United States, the Palestine Liberation Organization, and the Making of the Post–Cold War Order* (New York: Oxford University Press, 2012); Gary J. Bass, *The Blood Telegram: Nixon, Kissinger, and a Forgotten Genocide* (New York: Knopf, 2013). This would gradually change from 1978–1979, with US support for the Afghan antistate resistance and later under President Bill Clinton and the 2000 Camp David Summit.

8. South Asia provides a number of clear examples of this. See Willem Van Schendel, *The Bengal Borderland: Beyond State and Nation in South Asia* (London: Anthem Press, 2004).

9. Carter, State of the Union Address, 23 Jan. 1980, http://www.presidency.ucsb.edu/ws/?pid=33079.

10. CIA, "Effects of the Southwest Asian Crises on Key Global Issues (An Intelligence Assessment)," May 1980, CIA Electronic Reading Room (CIAERR), https://www.cia.gov/library/readingroom/home.

11. NSC, "Discussion paper for SCC-Security Framework," 26 Aug. 1980, Digital National Security Archive (DNSA); NSDD-99, "United States Security Strategy for

the Near East and South Asia," 12 July 1983, Ronald Reagan Presidential Library (RRPL), National Security Decision Directives, 1981–1989.

12. Draft NSDD, "US Policy toward Iran," 11 June 1985, DNSA.

13. See Elisabeth Leake, *The Defiant Border: The Afghan-Pakistan Borderlands in the Era of Decolonization, 1936–65* (New York: Cambridge University Press, 2017).

14. Pipes to Clark, "Afghanistan," 29 July 1982, RRPL, Executive Secretariat–NSC (ESNSC), Country Files (CF), box 34, folder "Afghanistan 7/29/82–5/2/83." Emphasis in original.

15. Goldman, "Soviet Policy toward Iran and the Strategic Balance in Southwest Asia," 7 Oct. 1986, DNSA.

16. See Steve Coll, *Ghost Wars: The Secret History of the CIA, Afghanistan and Bin Laden* (New York: Penguin Books, 2004).

17. "Study Memorandum: Pakistan," 6 Mar. 1981, RRPL, Near East and South Asian Affairs Directorate–NSC (NESAAD), box 91134, folder "IG on Pakistan, March 6, 1981."

18. Haig to Reagan, "Soviet Pressure on Pakistan," 1 July 1981, RRPL, ESNSC, CF, box 46, folder "Pakistan 1/20/81–12/31/81 [6 of 7]."

19. CIA, "Soviet Union and Southwest Asia," 15 Jan. 1980, DNSA.

20. See, for example, CIA, "Pakistan: Prospects for the Zia Government," Feb. 1981, CIAERR; CIA, "Near East and South Asia Review," 11 Oct. 1985, CIAERR; CIA, "The Afghan Regime: Prospects for Political Consideration," Dec. 1986, CIAERR.

21. See, for example, Nawaz to Perez de Cuellar, 1 Apr. 1986, United Nations Archives and Records Management Section (UNARMS), S-1024-2-2; S. Nawaz to Perez de Cuellar, 8 May 1986, UNARMS, S-1024-2-2.

22. "Strategic and Contingency Dialogue," March 2, 1981, RRPL, NESAAD, box 91134, folder "IG on Pakistan, March 2, 1981 (2 of 2)."

23. DOS, "US-Pakistan Relations," 29 Nov. 1982, DNSA.

24. Phillips, "Updating US Strategy for Helping Afghan Freedom Fighters," 22 Dec. 1986, DNSA.

25. NSDD 99, "United States Security Strategy."

26. See Rajshree Jetly, "The Khalistan Movement in India: The Interplay of Politics and State Power," *International Review of Modern Sociology* 34, no. 1 (2008): 61–75; Ramachandra Guha, *India after Gandhi: The History of the World's Largest Democracy* (London: Pan, 2008), ch. 24.

27. Guha, *India after Gandhi*, 572.

28. Cited in Guha, *India after Gandhi*, 574.

29. CIA, "India: The Sikh Challenge," 6 Nov. 1984, CIAERR.

30. CIA, "Prospects and Implications for USSR of Gandhi Assassination," 1 Nov. 1984, CIAERR.

31. In the end, the CIA was not far off: Gandhi was assassinated in 1991, though by suspected Tamil nationalists from Sri Lanka, affiliated with the Liberation Tigers of Tamil Eelam.

32. CIA, "India after Rajiv [Redacted]," Mar. 1986, CIAERR.

33. National Security Planning Group meeting, "Pakistan and NSDD-99 Work Program," 31 Aug. 1984, DNSA.

34. "CODEL Solarz's Meeting with Arun Singh," 24 Dec. 1986, DNSA. See also Michael Hamlyn, "Peace Pact on Ice until after Elections," *The Times*, 11 Oct. 1984.

35. Tahir-Kheli, "A Legacy of Peace in South Asia: A Strategy," September 30, 1986, RRPL, ESNSC, Meeting Files, box 12, folder: "NSC 00138 3 October 1986 (2/2)." Emphasis in original.

36. See Hashem Ahmadzadeh and Gareth Sansfield, "The Political, Cultural, and Military Re-Awakening of the Kurdish Nationalist Movement in Iran," *Middle East Journal* 64, no. 2 (2010): 11–27.

37. CIA, "Iran's Minorities: The Kurds," 2 Feb. 1979, DNSA.

38. US Embassy Iran, "Kurdish Particularist Activities," 6 Mar. 1979, DNSA.

39. CIA, "Iran: A Handbook," May 1982, CIAERR.

40. Nader Entessar, "The Kurdish Factor in Iran-Iraq Relations," 29 Jan. 2009, Middle East Institute, http://www.mei.edu/content/kurdish-factor-iran-iraq-relations. See also Bryan Gibson, *Sold Out? US Foreign Policy, Iraq, the Kurds and the Cold War* (London: Palgrave Macmillan, 2015).

41. Goldman, "Soviet Policy toward Iran and the Strategic Balance in Southwest Asia," 7 Oct. 1986, DNSA.

42. CIA, "Iraqi Opposition: Status and Prospects," Dec. 1983, CIAERR.

43. CIA, "Emerging Issues in the Near East and South Asia," 13 May 1986, CIAERR.

44. CIA, "Iranian Factionalism in Perspective," 25 Nov. 1987, CIAERR; Fuller, "Iran/Iraq War: The Worst Prospects," 24 Feb. 1984, CIAERR.

45. CIA, "Islam and Politics: A Compendium," Apr. 1984, CIAERR.

46. CIA, "Resurgent Islamic Nationalism in the Middle East: An Intelligence Assessment," Mar. 1981, CIAERR.

47. CIA, "Iran: A Handbook."

48. Cemil Aydin, *The Idea of the Muslim World* (Cambridge, MA: Harvard University Press, 2017).

49. On links between radical Islam and globalization, see Faisal Devji, *Landscapes of the Jihad: Militancy, Morality, Modernity* (London: Hurst, 2005); Faisal Devji, *The Terrorist in Search of Humanity: Militant Islam and Global Politics* (London: Hurst, 2008). Specifically on Iran, see Said Amir Arjomand, *The Turban for the Crown: The Islamic Revolution in Iran* (Oxford: Oxford University Press, 1988).

50. Ayesha Jalal, "An Uncertain Trajectory: Islam's Contemporary Globalization, 1971–1979," in *The Shock of the Global: The 1970s in Perspective*, ed. Niall Ferguson, Charles S. Maier, Erez Manela, and Daniel J. Sargent (Cambridge, MA: Belknap Press of Harvard University Press, 2010), 319–336, 334.

51. CIA, "Islamic Fundamentalism in the Middle East and South Asia: Looking Ahead," Dec. 1986, CIAERR.

52. NIE, "Islamic Fundamentalism: Implications for the Arab World and the United States," Dec. 1987, CIAERR.

53. Andrew Preston, *Sword of the Spirit, Shield of Faith: Religion in American War and Diplomacy* (New York: Alfred A. Knopf, 2012), 586.

54. See Zahid Shahab Ahmed, "Political Islam, the Jamaat-e-Islami, and Pakistan's Role in the Afghan-Soviet War, 1979–1988," in *Religion and the Cold War: A Global Perspective*, ed. Philip E. Muehlenbeck (Nashville, TN: Vanderbilt University Press, 2012), 275–295.

55. CIA, "Afghanistan: Goals and Prospects for the Insurgents," May 1983, CIAERR.

56. CIA, "Insurgency: 1985 in Review (An Intelligence Assessment)," Apr. 1986, CIAERR.

57. See Elisabeth Leake, "Spooks, Tribes, and Holy Men: The Central Intelligence Agency and the Soviet Invasion of Afghanistan," *Journal of Contemporary History* 53, no. 1 (2018): 240–262.

58. See Kiron K. Skinner, "The Beginning of a New US Grand Strategy: Policy on Terror during the Reagan Era," in *Reagan's Legacy in a World Transformed*, ed. Jeffrey L. Chidester and Paul Kengor (Cambridge, MA: Harvard University Press, 2015), 101–123.

59. See Hal Brands and David Palkki, "'Conspiring Bastards': Saddam Hussein's Strategic View of the United States," *Diplomatic History* 36, no. 2 (2012): 625–659.

60. Coll, *Ghost Wars*, 191, 195.

CHAPTER 18

Adam Smith's Arthritis
Japan and Fears of American Decline

JENNIFER M. MILLER

On March 4, 1981, the editorial page of the *New York Times* published an unusual plea: "Please, Japan, Return the Favor: Occupy Us." Author John Curtis Perry, an associate at Harvard University's Japan Institute, argued that the United States' economy, corporate practices, and democracy could all benefit from intensive Japanese oversight. "The United States needs renewal, 'a new beginning' in the words of President Reagan. Japanese leadership, supported by American hard work, could accomplish this noble purpose.... We should ask the Japanese to come here, occupy us, and do exactly the things we did for them from 1945 to 1952."[1] On the one hand, Perry's piece was an exercise in self-congratulation for the generosity and forward-thinking nature of the American occupation: Perry argued that wise American policies had placed Japan on its path to miraculous economic growth and democratic stability. It also expressed sentiments common to the 1980s, especially the belief that Japan was leading the way to a prosperous, technologically advanced, and globalized future.[2] As Harvard University sociologist Ezra Vogel wrote in his unexpected 1979 best seller *Japan as Number One*, Japan had "dealt more successfully with the problems of postindustrial society than any other country."[3] Americans, Perry and Vogel claimed, could and should learn from Japan.

On the other hand, Perry's editorial also revealed a widespread anxiety that dominated the 1980s, specifically the fear that the United States was facing a

387

new and audacious challenge from Japan, its former enemy turned close, if decidedly junior, ally. While the United States struggled with unemployment, inflation, high interest rates, trade deficits, and industrial transition, Japan had become the second largest economy in the world. According to historian Paul Kennedy's bestselling *The Rise and Fall of the Great Powers* (1987), Japan could economically overtake the United States, becoming "*much* more powerful" in the "early twenty-first century."[4] The prospect of such a transformation sparked deep fears of Japanese global economic dominance as a broader manifestation of American decline. Some observers, such as New York real estate developer Donald J. Trump, proclaimed that Japan's rise was the product of American weakness; after all, it was American leaders who opened US markets to Japanese products, accepted Japanese protectionism, and secured Japan though military bases and a nuclear umbrella. As Trump ranted in a 1987 open letter in the *New York Times*, the *Boston Globe*, and the *Washington Post*, "For decades, Japan and other nations have taken advantage of the United States. . . . The Japanese, unimpeded by the huge costs of defending themselves (as long as the United States will do it for free), have built a strong and vibrant economy with unprecedented surpluses." Articulating narratives that he would ride to the presidency three decades later, Trump called on American leaders to take a stand to "end *our* vast deficits by making Japan, and others who can afford it, pay. . . . Let's not let our great country be laughed at any more."[5]

Trump was not alone in sounding this alarm. For many Americans, the specter of Japanese success hung heavily over the 1980s. In particular, American policymakers, economic leaders, and industrial lobbyists expressed intense anxiety about the trade deficit between the United States and Japan. In 1981, Japan exported $16 million more goods to the United States than the United States did to Japan; by the end of the decade, this gap had reached $60 billion.[6] Japanese cars, Walkmans, and semiconductors became potent symbols not just of Japanese success but also of American failure. Business leaders, lobbyists, labor unions, and policymakers became frantic about access to the Japanese market, with products such as beef, oranges, Little League bats, and tobacco assuming a symbolic importance far beyond their actual financial value. They excoriated Japan for excluding American products and claimed that Japanese industrial policy was unfair, anticapitalist, and undemocratic. While the United States, the argument went, doggedly maintained its commitment to the proper ethics of free trade, Japan was violating the rules of the game, utilizing protectionism, industrial collusion, government subsidies, and unsavory practices such as dumping to prey on the United States. Such claims often expressed racist panic that an inhuman and decidedly foreign Japan was actively and nefariously targeting the United States in a conspiracy akin to Pearl Harbor. Some went so far as to assert that Japan's economic success was the final end to World War II, with Japan as the ultimate victor.[7]

Why did Japan play such a prominent role in the American political, economic, and public consciousness throughout this decade? Hard economic realities were certainly a key to this story, as was protectionist political pressure at home, racism, and the still-powerful memories of World War II. The ubiquity of Japanese consumer products raised fears that the consumption of foreign goods was undermining not only American industry but also an authentic American community.[8] Indeed, as this chapter argues, these intense fears were not fully about Japan. Rather, political and public discussions about Japan became an important site to articulate potent criticism of the United States, to question American values, and to challenge the supposed benefits of American global leadership and the larger project of postwar liberal internationalism. What did it say about the United States—and American power, values, and purpose—that a smaller, Asian country was able to amass such economic and cultural power? Japan offered an imposing mirror for Americans in 1980s, and many did not like what it reflected back to them.[9]

In utilizing Japan as a site to develop these critiques of the United States, Americans also tapped into longer Cold War narratives about the potential weaknesses of democracy and capitalism, especially vis-à-vis an untrustworthy and anticapitalist adversary. In the early Cold War, policymakers such as State Department director of policy planning Paul Nitze warned that communism would triumph not through brute strength, but by exploiting the freedoms and openness of the democratic system; communism would utilize free speech, propaganda, and demagoguery to turn American democracy against itself. If the United States and its allies could lose the Cold War, this way of thinking suggested, it was because a ruthless enemy bent on global domination exploited the ideological, political, and structural weaknesses of democracy.[10] This argument also had a more crudely anti-elite manifestation, best exemplified by Wisconsin Senator Joseph McCarthy. McCarthy claimed that the communist enemy had help from within, at the highest reaches of the American government, where "bright young men who are born with a silver spoon in their mouths" and soft, unmasculine "pompous diplomat[s] in striped pants" "sold out" the American people to communism. Their weakness, disloyalty, lack of masculinity, and immorality made them susceptible and willing agents in the triumph of a foreign adversary.[11]

In the 1980s, it was Japan's economic might that offered a new test to American capabilities and upended American conceptions of global power. To be sure, Japan did not pose the specter of communist domination. Instead, it was a potent combination of threats—the loss of American power and independence, the decline in American industry, the seeming challenge to American individualism, and the specter of an alternative form of capitalism—that confronted Americans across the political spectrum. Despite placing increased pressure on Japanese policymakers through repeated negotiations, the Reagan administration struggled to address Japan's newfound economic power, especially as it became increasingly dependent on foreign—particularly Japanese—capital to fund its domestic agenda.[12] Similar to the Reagan administration's approach to China, as discussed by Jonathan Hunt in this volume, its approach to Japan also demonstrated the tensions between its "reputation as free-market fundamentalists" and its actual support for "regulatory regimes."[13] Unwilling to fully shift away from free trade policies, the Reagan administration instead sought out voluntary export restraints and targeted Japanese industrial policy, seeking to force Japan not only to buy American products but to change the way that it funded and promoted exports.

Such policies did little to change the trade deficit or Japan's corporate, financial, and real estate presence within the United States. Policymakers and observers continued to declare that Japan was single-mindedly pursuing global economic domination. It was taking advantage of the United States' commitment to free enterprise and open trade to undo the United States itself. Japan's rise, these critics declared, demonstrated the wishful thinking that had undergirded postwar liberal internationalism, especially the decision to allow former enemies full access to the American market in the service of creating a strong, integrated global economy. Such criticisms reveal the extent to which postwar dreams of "capitalist convergence" were, at their core, dreams of unlimited American hegemony.[14] Some further posited that the Japanese were aided by weak and foolish Americans: from the naiveté of a postwar occupation that rebuilt Japan to the present-day lobbyists who advised Japanese companies in their alleged quest to dominate the United States, Japan's success could not come from Japanese strengths, but only from American weaknesses. Perhaps most alarming, Japan's economic model—one that some observers described as "totalitarian"—seemed more successful than that of the United States. A wave of literature argued that Japan was "winning" precisely because of active government planning and industrial policy, a group-centered culture, and a clear sense of national purpose and motivation. These interpretations directly challenged American celebrations of individualism, the free market, and free trade, key ideological claims behind Reagan's administration and, more broadly, American global leadership since 1945. Japan's rise, premised on ideas and practices that many Americans characterized as dirty, dangerous, illegal, and abhorrent, was so troubling because its seemed to stem from flaws and weaknesses embedded in the United States itself.

In the aftermath of World War II, Japan lay in ruins, its largest cities bombed to ash. Yet even before the beginning of the postwar occupation, American policymakers had decided that a destroyed and ruined Japan was in nobody's interest, least of all the United States'.[15] Throughout the 1950s and 1960s, American policymakers encouraged Japanese trade with the United States, even as US politicians and industrial leaders complained about the deleterious impact of low-priced Japanese goods such as textiles and silverware.[16] Americans also developed an extensive technical assistance program in Japan, sharing management and production techniques and licensing technology and bringing Japanese executives and labor leaders on tours of American businesses and factories.[17] Coming in the aftermath of depression and global war, this policy was part of a larger project that sought to foster international economic recovery and growth to prevent the rise of extremist ideas and secure American hegemony through the stability of international capitalism. US policymakers therefore emphasized the necessity of an integrated global economy, especially through trade, with the United States serving as a vital market for a variety of international goods. The postwar US-Japanese relationship also had a significant security component. During the occupation, Japan's new US-authored constitution prevented Japan from acquiring offensive military forces or "war potential." At the end of the occupation, the United States signed a security treaty with Japan that stationed US military forces throughout Japan and Okinawa and, in a 1960 revision, committed the United States to defending Japan in times of attack.[18]

Japan's economic recovery was swifter than expected. By the late 1950s, Japan had entered a period of unprecedented economic growth, bolstered in part by American military spending in Korea (and later Vietnam) and American trade and technical assistance policies.[19] Between 1955 and 1960, Japan's gross national product (GNP) grew at an average annual rate of 9 percent, spurring widespread talk of an "economic miracle."[20] Japanese exports were central to this growth. So concerned were American policymakers that President Richard Nixon actively forced the Japanese to voluntarily limit their textile exports in the early 1970s. Both Nixon and his national security adviser, Henry Kissinger, were heavily critical of Japanese political and industrial policy. Dubbing it "Japan Inc.," they decried that all of Japan—government, industry, and people—collaborated to economically assault the American market.[21] Yet the trade deficit between the United States and Japan continued to grow throughout the 1970s despite American efforts to increase American imports to Japan.[22] By the time that Ronald Reagan entered office in 1981, it had reached $10 billion, boosting US-Asian trade past US-European trade for the first time in history.[23] While Americans had once derided Japanese products as "Gimcracks" and "Jap Crap," they now came to admire Japan's technological prowess while watching Japanese televisions, listening to Japanese Walkmans, and driving Japanese cars.[24]

Equally alarming for Americans, Japan's surging growth also facilitated an unprecedented Japanese financial presence in the United States. As Michael De Groot notes, the high interest rate regime of the early 1980s drew in large amounts of foreign capital, including Japanese capital newly available for foreign investment because of Japan's economic success.[25] Japanese investors purchased 35 percent of the debt sold by the US Treasury between 1980 and 1985, with the 1984 yen-dollar agreement further facilitating these trans-Pacific capital flows.[26] By the mid-1980s, the Reagan administration was actively seeking foreign capital, and members of the Treasury Department even visited Tokyo to market American bonds to Japanese investors.[27] This influx of Japanese money helped the Reagan administration operate with large deficits, which fostered a "debt-financed consumption boom in the US economy."[28] The financial transformations of the early 1980s thus fundamentally shaped the American economy in ways that continue until today. As Greta R. Krippner asserts, the inflow of Japanese capital was central to the financialization of the American economy and dramatically accelerated the shift from the state-based controls and policies that had marked the Bretton Woods era to a new world shaped by a "sea of capital flows."[29] In the second half of the 1980s, Japanese investors shifted focus to American properties and companies, buying resorts and hotels in Hawai'i and on the West Coast, major entertainment companies, including Columbia Pictures and Universal Studios, and signature landmarks such as Rockefeller Center. Throughout the 1980s, then, Japanese money—in the form of products, investments, and property—became a major feature of American economic, political, cultural, and material life.

Japan's economic rise seemed especially ominous because it coincided with—and perhaps exacerbated—the United States' own economic difficulties.[30] Throughout the 1970s and early 1980s, the United States suffered from "sustained economic turmoil," marked by inflation, stagflation, recessions, and rising unemployment, which climbed past 10 percent in September 1982.[31] The large-scale international investment in the dollar had also increased the value of the dollar against other currencies, making imports cheaper for Americans but raising the price of US exports.[32] At the dawn of 1980s, no product better symbolized these changing economic fortunes than the automobile. As successive oil crises dramatically raised prices, Japanese cars—smaller and more fuel efficient than their American counterparts—made dramatic inroads into the American market. Japanese imports made up 11 percent of US auto sales in January 1979 and rose to a peak of 25 percent in July of 1980.[33] This success reflected changes in global trade; as tariffs plunged, US imports had first exceeded exports in 1971, the beginning of a growing trade deficit that Japan would come to symbolize. It also coincided with an accelerating transformation from an industrial to a service economy. The United States lost more than 30 million jobs in the 1970s, the majority in manufacturing; even American companies such as Ford were producing more cars overseas than at home and the unemployment rate in some midwestern cities reached 20 percent.[34] Between 1978 and 1981, US auto industry production declined 30 percent, and unemployment in the auto industry reached a peak of 300,000; to many Americans, every Honda, Subaru, or Toyota seemed to represent the loss of a job in Detroit or Kansas City.[35]

Not surprisingly, many members of the auto industry blamed Japan for their fate. In 1981, Ford and the United Auto Workers (UAW) filed a complaint with the International Trade Commission arguing that Japanese auto imports had severely harmed the domestic industry. Chrysler chairman Lee Iacocca became notorious for his anti-Japan rhetoric; in a 1985 speech to the American Chamber of Commerce in Japan, for example, he declared that "it's not fair that Japan has open season on our markets, and we have to crawl through a maze of bureaucratic regulations in order to sell over there."[36] Lobbyists, company heads, and union leaders regularly appealed to Congress, requesting legislation that would require cars to be manufactured with American parts and pushing for tariffs or import restraints on Japanese cars.[37] As *Time* magazine wrote in March 1981, "Detroit's problems have come to symbolize the ills of US business in general." American industry used to dominate the manufacturing of textiles, steel, and ships, the author bemoaned, "but then US executives watched almost helplessly as their customers were snatched away by industrious Japanese competitors selling better products at lower prices."[38]

In 1981, under intense pressure, the Japanese government agreed to voluntarily restrict auto exports to the United States to 1.7 million vehicles per year.[39] Companies such as Honda and Nissan also built plants inside the United States, which were often welcomed by local communities as vital sources of employment.[40] Yet such measures could not diminish American enmity. Some Americans engaged in violent protests; a group of autoworkers in Detroit staged a "mock execution" and burial of a Toyota.[41] Most tragic was a June 1982 murder, when the combination of economic anxiety and racism proved toxic and deadly. After leaving a bar in a Detroit suburb, Vincent Chin, a twenty-seven-year old

Chinese American, was heavily beaten by a Chrysler plant supervisor and his stepson. His assailants blamed him for Japan's success, allegedly shouting, "It's because of you we're out of work." Chin died four days later, while his assailants were convicted of manslaughter and received three years of probation.[42] Throughout the 1980s, car advertisements played on such sentiments by stoking the fires of history, urging consumers to buy American and halt the advance of the Japanese, all while remembering Pearl Harbor. A Pontiac ad created by the Deutsch agency for New York auto dealers ominously warned consumers that if they "keep buying Japanese cars," they might someday visit "the big Christmas tree at Hirohito Center," a reference to the recent Japanese purchase of Rockefeller Center.[43] Such racialized discourses depicted Japan as a potent and extraordinarily foreign other that sought not only to decimate the United States' economy, but also to destroy American sovereignty, culture, and traditions.

Fears about Japanese domination thus loomed large when Reagan came into office in 1981, riding his campaign pledge to restore American power, purpose, and prosperity. In his speeches, Reagan promised to rescue the United States' economy from recession, stagflation, and decline by removing regulations, lowering taxes, and unleashing market forces. He celebrated free enterprise as the core not only to rebuilding the American economy, but also to American individualism and the American character.[44] As he proclaimed in a 1982 speech, "We're not afraid of free enterprise or free trade unions or freedom of thought. We depend on them, because only when individuals are free to worship, create, and build, only when they're given a personal stake in deciding their destiny and benefiting from their own risks—only then do societies become dynamic, prosperous, progressive, and free."[45] In the eyes of Reagan and his administration, American vibrancy and greatness stemmed from capitalist markets and individual enterprise. It was the free market, he repeatedly claimed, that was the pillar of political and personal freedom and the primary source of efficiency, prosperity, and growth.[46]

Reagan's promise to rebuild US economic prosperity only increased the focus placed on Japan. Though he rarely publicly engaged in "Japan-bashing," Reagan's speeches often mentioned Japan as a rationale for his policies. In an April 1981 statement on the American auto industry, Reagan announced his plan to restore US competitiveness by removing "excessive regulation and interference," including provisions from the Environmental Protection Agency and the National Highway Traffic Safety Administration. Japan was the only foreign country mentioned in the speech as part of Reagan's promise to "monitor the effect of international trade on our domestic automobile industry."

"In observing the principles of free trade," Reagan asserted, "we expect our trading partners to do so, as well," and he noted that a briefing delegation would soon go to Japan.[47] In a 1982 speech at the AFL-CIO, he declared that "America's working men and women are every bit as dedicated, skilled, and productive as their German and Japanese counterparts," but that they could succeed only if the government lowered taxes and reduced regulations.[48] Japan therefore served as a potent and threatening symbol that Reagan utilized to viscerally illustrate the necessity of his domestic economic agenda. In his telling, the United States was losing out to foreign competitors like Japan because "we have become over-governed, over-regulated, and overtaxed."[49]

With the trade deficit growing and the United States mired in recession, opening the Japanese market to American products quickly became a central focus in the Reagan administration's diplomacy. As National Security Council (NSC) staffer Douglas McMinn wrote in 1983, "There is the perception widely held in America that the US-Japanese trading relationship is inequitable. While our market is wide open to Japanese exports, the Japanese restrict access to their own market for our own products. . . . In this context, Japanese autos have become a highly visible symbol of this inequity."[50] National Security Directive 62, signed on October 25, 1982, placed access at the center of the US-Japanese economic relationship. The United States, it stated, should "persist in continuing to have Japanese economy opened on a broad front" and "object to any policy or practice that discriminates against imports, especially in the realm of high-technology."[51] In his meetings with Japanese leaders and bureaucrats, Reagan regularly pressed them on alleged Japanese protectionism and access for American companies and products.[52] Throughout the 1980s, the United States and Japan routinely engaged in prolonged negotiations over tariffs and quotas on products such as beef, citrus, and tobacco, a process that fostered constant tension in their relationship.

Reagan and his advisors sought more than just a market for American products. They were also deeply concerned that Japan's meteoric success would provoke protectionism at home. As a briefing paper for the president's 1983 meeting with Japanese prime minister Nakasone Yasuhiro noted, "Protectionist reactions threaten to close US markets to Japanese goods and begin the unraveling of the multilateral trading system. . . . Japan has become the most prominent symbol for American and Congressional frustrations over domestic economic problems and perceived inequities in the international trading system."[53] These fears about domestic protectionism only grew as Reagan began to campaign for reelection in 1983 and 1984. Indeed, Reagan's advisers recommended that the United States communicate a desire for Japan to continue the voluntary export restraints on cars for one more year, lest Reagan be "perceived as 'selling-out' to the Japanese. The president would be accused of taking away jobs from Americans without getting anything tangible and balanced in return," they warned. "Congress would use this emotional issue to revive protectionist legislation."[54]

This fear of protectionism was both political and economic. Reagan and his advisors certainly worried that an economically nationalist narrative would be a powerful tool in a Democratic campaign. But Reagan also believed that economic nationalism and protectionism could have significant economic consequences. He therefore regularly spoke in favor of free trade, even as he sought Japanese restrictions. As he proclaimed in a 1984 speech at a Ford assembly plant in Kansas City Missouri, "Some advocate far harsher methods. They believe we should run up the flag in defense of our markets, embrace protectionism, and insulate ourselves from world competition." In response, Reagan offered a cautionary tale: the Great Depression, he argued, was caused by the "Smoot-Hawley tariff bill, which literally destroyed free trade worldwide and . . . which, incidentally, was only cured then by World War II." He even heralded Japan's commitment to voluntary import restraints—even through these were not an example of free trade—declaring that they gave the American industry "breathing room" to recover, modernize, and build new plants.[55] In a bevy of similar speeches and radio addresses, Reagan repeatedly warned that a trade war would hurt everyone, especially American workers.[56] Yet to American industries and workers, it often seemed as though free trade, not a trade war, was the primary problem. In the late 1970s and early 1980s, the US trade commission ruled against petitions for trade relief from industries such as the auto industry and the footwear industry, declaring that their problems were due to the recession and that American companies had to play by the rules.[57] The Reagan administration therefore never reconciled its claim about free trade's ability to usher in American prosperity with the reality that such policies seemed to undermine key sectors of the American economy. This contradiction left ample rhetorical and ideological space for Japan to shoulder the blame.

While Reagan may have been restrained in his use of Japan as an ominous threat, others described Japan in far cruder terms. Bob Dole, Republican senator from Kansas, condemned Japanese "selfishness and myopia" for their refusal to open markets.[58] John Danforth, Republican senator from Missouri, harkened back to World War II propaganda that depicted the Japanese as inhuman, calling them "leeches."[59] In 1983 hearings in the House of Representatives' Ways and Means Committee about Japanese trade practices, trade subcommittee chair, Florida Democrat Sam M. Gibbons, declared his desire to "specifically" look "at Japanese targeting because it smacks to me of being pernicious and predatory upon on markets." California Democrat Pete Stark agreed: "To speak bluntly," he declared, it was time for the Japanese "to grow up and become a member of the world community."[60] Michigan's Democratic Congressman John Dingell was perhaps the most openly racist, blaming the auto industry's woes on "those little yellow people."[61] According to members of the US Congress, the Japanese were sneaky, inhuman, childlike, immature, and decidedly foreign. These traits, many claimed, had a malevolent and noxious impact on the world community. Drawing heavily from the racist language and images of World War II propaganda, politicians in both parties called for a more bellicose and nationalist response, especially new rules and tariffs to curb the Japanese "assault."

Indeed, American observers repeatedly invoked the historical framework of World War II to convey the seriousness of the threat posed by Japan, from car commercials to congressional discussions to the pages of leading newspapers. In July 1985, for example, the *New York Times Magazine* ran a lengthy article by Theodore H. White, Pulitzer Prize winner and longtime reporter on Asian affairs, entitled "The Danger from Japan." White opened by describing Japan's surrender on the USS *Missouri* in September 1945, revealing his—and perhaps the United States'—longing for certitude. "We had won out over them. We lost more than 100,000 men to prove we could not be lacerated without warning, without seeking revenge." Yet Japan's economic success, White claimed, threatened to overturn the United States' greatest triumph. "What we are faced with now is the idea that events contradict history's logic. Perhaps we did not win the war, perhaps the Japanese, unknown even to themselves, were the winners." At stake in the US-Japanese trade relationship was far more than access to Japanese markets or even the prospect of a trade war; at stake was the outcome of World War II itself, and by extension, the United States' past, present, and future. "Today, 40 years after the end of World War II, the Japanese are on the move again in one of history's most brilliant commercial offensives, as they go about dismantling American industry. Whether they are still only smart, or have finally learned to be wiser than we, will be tested in the next 10 years. Only then," he mused, "will we know who finally won the war 50 years before."[62]

White's article was significant not only for its use of World War II to convey the stakes of contemporary economic and trade policy. Equally important was his explanation of Japan's success. White argued that the United States had made a fundamental "blunder" in 1945 by underestimating the Japanese; in choosing to rebuild Japan, politically and economically, it created the conditions that would facilitate its rise mere decades later. As US policymakers sought to construct a global order premised on free trade, "for the Japanese it must have seemed too good to be true.... The Americans had rewarded them with a world market far larger than the Great East Asia Co-Prosperity Sphere." Japan, White claimed, was succeeding beyond belief in the world that the United States had created. It had taken the United States' own plans and goals and improved on them. "What the Japanese have done since in remodeling the American model is no less than spectacular. They have devised a system of government-industry partnership that is a paradigm for directing a modern industrial state for national purposes—and one designed for action in the new world of global commerce that the United States blueprinted."[63] In making this claim, White offered a larger critique of US foreign policy since World War II, which stemmed in part from the liberal internationalist belief that global economic recovery and international alliances were necessary to US security and prosperity. In White's telling, such a policy was not the product of concrete historical experience or wise global leadership, but instead demonstrated US leaders' naïveté, shortsightedness, and a fundamental unwillingness—or inability—to take the necessary steps to protect and assist Americans.

This claim that Japan's success came not in spite but *because* of American economic, trade, and political policy was not limited to White. Trump similarly used Japan to lambast "soft" and unmasculine American leaders, scoffing that they needed to show "a little backbone.... Make Japan, Saudi Arabia and others pay for the protection we provide as Allies. Let's help our farmers, our sick, our homeless," he wrote in his 1987 letter, "by taking from some of the greatest profit machines ever created—machines created and nurtured by us."[64] Trump made a similar complaint when speaking with Oprah Winfrey in 1988. "We let Japan come in and dump everything right into our markets and everything—it's not free trade. If you ever go to Japan right now, and try and sell something, forget about it, Oprah. Just forget about it. It's almost impossible."[65] Speaking to the Ways and Committee in 1983, Congressman Gibbons offered his own criticisms of American policy. He bemoaned how the Japanese took advantage of American openness and access to business and industrial data provided by the Department of Commerce. "You can just wander in and get the information" he exclaimed in disbelief. Gibbons in fact had sent a staffer to see how this information was being used, and the result was jarring. Americans largely ignored the data made available by the US government, he warned, "but that office was always full of Japanese. They were in there ferreting out the information that we were making public and apparently doing something with it."[66]

Gibbons's racialized language—"ferreting," implying Japanese deviousness—certainly harkened back to World War II. But his claim that the Japanese were turning the American system against itself tapped deeply into the anxieties and narratives of the early Cold War, when American policymakers feared that the Soviet Union would utilize free speech and the openness of American civil society to undermine American democracy. This idea was best expressed in a National Security Council policy paper known as NSC-68, issued under Paul Nitze in the spring of 1950. NSC-68 is largely remembered for its recommendation for a massive military buildup to defeat communism. Yet Nitze and other national security bureaucrats also reflected extensively on the inherent difficulties of combatting totalitarian enemies in a democratic society. "The democratic way," NSC-68 declared, "is harder than the authoritarian way" because it could not rely on total government power to mobilize or control the people; the United States was disadvantaged by the very free speech, individualism, and open thought that it waged the Cold War to protect.[67] According to Nitze and his staff, communism was dangerous not just because of its quest for dominance, violence, atheism, or opposition to private property. It was also alarming because of its nefarious ability to take advantage of democratic institutions, freedoms, and principles in order to destroy them from within.

Updated for the 1980s, the conflict was not between democracy and communism, but between the United States' proclaimed commitment to free enterprise, a free market, and free trade and Japan's alleged quest for global market dominance, based on government planning and widespread collusion between business, bureaucracy, and the state. Steel industrialist and political scientist William S. Dietrich described the threat in language akin to the 1947 Truman Doctrine: "Today we face a new challenge [that] threatens our way of life and ultimately our freedoms as much as past challenges from Nazi Germany and the Soviet Union. This new challenge," he wrote in his *In the Shadow of the Rising Sun: The Political Roots of American Economic Decline* (1991), "comes from Japan."[68] In the same spirit, government officials lamented that Japan was overtaking the United States by its brazen willingness to subvert and undermine the structures and values of the American economy and the broader free world. Commerce Secretary Malcolm Baldrige, for example, reached back to the World War II and early Cold War dichotomy of free and unfree worlds, musing in a 1984 meeting that he "could not accept the argument that Japan is part of the same world. . . . Japan is in fact getting stronger, seeing its goals in high tech and satellites, and is keeping the United States out. They clearly intend to dominate by 1990/2000. Can we afford to be 'Adam

Smith' if they do not want to play?"[69] Baldrige bemoaned that the United States' commitment to Smith's "invisible hand" of the market had done little to slow Japanese intrusion; Japan, he claimed, did not "play by the rules" and was "the rotten apple that spoils the entire world trade barrel."[70]

For some observers, it was in fact Japan, not the Soviet Union, that was the true threat to world freedom. Writing in *Parade* in 1983, historian David Halberstam declared that Japan was the United States' "most difficult challenge ... a much harder and more intense competition than.... the political-military competition with the Soviet Union."[71] Writer Marvin J. Wolf took this claim even further in *The Japanese Conspiracy* (1983): "Behind [Japan's] major penetration of foreign markets is a system of business activity which can best be describe as economic totalitarianism, a government-directed enterprise in which all the energies of Japan have been mobilized to overwhelm the world competition." The Japanese, he thundered, were as dangerous as the political and military threat of the Soviet Union, but "the Japanese have brilliantly disguised their conspiracy in the convincing cloak of free enterprise. They thus confound and confuse those in the West who have become unwitting partners in Japan's economic aggression."[72]

Not all saw Japan's key American partners as "unwitting." Other observers placed a Joseph McCarthy-esque spin on this narrative, asserting that Japan was succeeding with the assistance of craven Americans. Economist Pat Choate's book *Agents of Influence* (1990), opened by declaring that Japan was spending "at least $100 million each year to hire hundreds of Washington, D.C. lobbyists, super-lawyers, former high-ranking public officials, public relations specialists, political advisors,—even former presidents."[73] By taking advantage of US lobbying practices, its open political system and constant political campaigns, and its dependence on foreign capital, Japan's "trade negotiations and companies succeed, while America's fail." This outcome "reflects the cumulative personal and profession decisions made by hundreds of Americans who constitute an important segment of this nation's governing class." The consequences could be dire, Choate warned. "No American industry—regardless of how competitive—is safe."[74]

The film adaption of Michael Crichton's novel *Rising Sun* (1992) showed the resonance of Choate's message. Set in Los Angeles, *Rising Sun* told the story of two American detectives investigating the murder of a young American white woman who had worked as an escort for Japanese businessmen; the murder took place at a fictional Japanese corporation.[75] The book attributed Japanese behavior to a fundamentally distinct, irrational, and racist Japanese "culture."[76] Crichton sought to warn Americans about the cultural and economic threat posed by Japan by depicting, in the words of historian Andrew C.

McKevitt, a future of American "subservience to Japan as a new colonial master—the United States' vast natural resources, including its people, and particularly its women, were open to plunder by Japan's economic and cultural imperialists."[77] While in the novel the killer is a Japanese executive assistant, the film changed the killer to be an American, a lawyer and lobbyist who works on behalf of the Japanese corporation. The message was clear; Japan's rise was enabled by immoral and traitorous American elites, willing to sell out the United States' future to a nefarious, foreign enemy.

While Choate and Crichton wrote at the height of the "Japan panic" in the early 1990s, they drew from the well-developed narrative that the United States was facing an economic takeover enabled by a misguided commitment to free trade. This argument conveniently ignored the numerous tariffs that the United States government had placed on imports, especially in agriculture.[78] It also grossly exaggerated Japanese tariff barriers. Still, Reagan's appointees often complained about Japan's abuse of the free trade system. Japan's entire industrial policy, they declared, was a perverse betrayal of American principles. As Assistant Secretary of the Treaty Marc E. Leland asserted, "Japan is still xenophobic, its industrial structure is cartel-like, anti-competitive practices are tolerated, dealing with government officials is time-consuming and difficult, the distribution system is impossible." Racial and cultural differences only exacerbated the problem: "the Japanese language is hard," Leland complained, "and the Japanese are truly foreign. It is much like France, only much more so."[79]

Reporting on a November 1982 trip to Japan to study industrial policy, Lionel Olmer, the Commerce Department's undersecretary for international trade, similarly described a system of careful coordination between private industry and government that fostered a "strong base from which the chosen firms can launch aggressive export drives." The role of the Japanese government, Olmer asserted, was to "select target industries, to reduce risks, and to facilitate large scale economies in research, development, and production. The process for achieving these goals is for MITI [the Ministry of Trade and Industry] to work closely with industries to identify promising technologies, to establish cooperative research programs, to select a leading foreign company as a model, and then to foster protection of the domestic market." In particular, MITI, the large government agency that directed Japanese industry policy, had taken an active role in building Japan's semiconductor industry; it brought together Japan's largest technology firms, including Hitachi, Toshiba, and Fujitsu, and gave them substantial financial assistance, tax relief, and de facto exemption from anti-monopoly laws.[80] In the 1983 Ways and Means hearing, Congressman Gibbons professed astonishment at similar descriptions of Japanese industrial practices by a representative from Motorola. Motorola's pursuing such cooperation "under our laws would have been a violation of our antitrust laws. You would have all been in jail had you done that in our country."[81]

In light of these growing fears, the US government adopted a more aggressive approach toward Japan, which explicitly targeted Japanese industrial policy. When Prime Minister Nakasone arrived for a visit in January 1985, American officials pursued a policy known as market-oriented, sector-selective (MOSS), the goal of which was "reorienting the Japanese economy through intense talks to make manufactured imports on beachhead sectors fully responsive to market forces."[82] The chosen "beachhead sectors"—a term directly taken from military terminology—were telecommunications, electronics, forest products, and medical equipment and pharmaceuticals, and the US officials planned to press Nakasone on all four during his visit.[83] MOSS was essentially an attempt to change Japanese industrial policy; rather than emphasizing lower tariffs, it sought to "free" the market by pressuring the Japanese government to stop the targeting and support of key industries, reduce its funding for private research and development, and change sales and distribution techniques. As such, it reflected the deep belief of some members of the Reagan administration that the "the power of market forces, given sufficient time" could transform "even the most illiberal of societies."[84] Yet not all of Reagan's advisers supported such an ambitious and aggressive policy. William Niskanen of the Council on Economic Advisors, for example, warned that "if that goal [changing the American system] had been outlined in a Japanese paper, we would be infuriated." But other officials, such as US trade representative Bill Brock, were far more enthusiastic. Even though the United States had trade deficits with other counties, such as Canada and Taiwan, "some things [in Japan] are different, requiring a different approach.... We must deal with Japan before it is seen as a successful model for others."[85] Commerce Secretary Baldrige agreed, tapping into existing emphases on Japan's "foreignness" to proclaim that the arrogant Japanese were uninterested in truly liberalizing or opening trade. It was time, he implied, for a far more aggressive approach.[86]

At its heart, MOSS relied on the logic that American products would naturally dominate the market, if only Japan stopped its nefarious meddling. This belief was best seen in the emphasis on market share for products such as semiconductors. While American-made semiconductors topped the market in other countries, they struggled to surpass 10 percent of the market share in Japan, a fact that American officials and manufacturers repeatedly attributed to Japanese trade policy and industrial policy. As Alexander Lidow, vice president of research and development in the semiconductor division of the

International Rectifier Corporation declared in 1983, "We submit that given Japan's recent history of protectionism in this industry, and the low sales performance of United States firms in Japan as compared to their performance in the rest of the world, the Japanese market cannot be regarded as 'open' until US firms' sales as a percent of total sales in Japan show a very substantial increase."[87] The office of the US Trade Representative therefore sought to place a series of far-reaching requirements on the Japanese to facilitate American access, including a guaranteed market share by the end of the decade. The United States should require "leading Japanese end users to buy specific additional amounts of US goods . . . [and] to price [them] according to an imposed formula."[88] Such a policy was far from Reagan's proclamations about the importance of free trade.

This pressure bore some fruit in 1986, when the United States and Japan signed a trade agreement that was specifically about semiconductors and was designed to increase American access to the Japanese market. This agreement, however, was signed under the shadow of a formal American investigation into alleged Japanese semiconductor dumping that could have resulted in severe import quotas or even the suspension of Japanese semiconductor imports.[89] Indeed, the United States placed new duties in Japanese semiconductors in 1987, citing continued dumping and other unsavory trade practices by Japan.[90] In speeches and statements, Reagan announced that all these agreements were evidence that "we will not stand idly by as American workers are threatened by unfair trading practices. We have and we will take the tough actions that are necessary to ensure that all nations play by the same rules."[91] Where Reagan had once described the United States as being committed to free trade, he now regularly talked about "free and *fair* trade" to make clear that the United States would seek to punish upstarts such as Japan that succeeded despite the United States' dominance of the global economy.[92]

Behind the scenes, however, the United States' changing approach to the semiconductor industry reflected fears that Japan, with its government-corporate coordination, had developed a more successful economic model. In 1987, with $100 million in yearly funding from the Department of Defense, fourteen American semiconductor manufacturers created a research and development consortium called SEMATECH, short for Semiconductor Manufacturing Technology. SEMATECH followed in MITI's footsteps and explicitly hoped to expand market share by increasing cooperation in an acrimonious and competitive industry, yet it sought this goal through perhaps the most American of ways: military spending. It was not through the free market, but through a government agency and public funds that these American corporations hoped to increase their competitiveness. SEMATECH also proved to be successful, at least within the United States, as the companies' domestic market share doubled over the next five years.[93] As such, SEMATECH symbolized the contradictions of the Reagan administration's approach to Japan: a constant rhetorical and ideological emphasis on power of the free trade and free enterprise, undergirded by a willingness to use state regulatory and funding power in a quest to secure the United States' triumph in this allegedly "free" market.

Even with Reagan's attempts to rein in Japan and establish "free and fair trade," Japan's global economic triumph continued to spark deep anxieties. Perhaps Japan's ascent augured a permanent weakening of American capabilities and American resolve; no matter what US policymakers did, after all, the trade deficit only continued to rise throughout the decade. Some writers and commentators offered a deeply troubling explanation: the structures and values that Americans had lionized as central to their superior political, economic, and ideological system—free enterprise, low government regulation, and American individualism—were the source of the United States' weakness. Some of these observers reflected positively on Japanese industrial policy, singling out its consensus-based management style, its emphasis on group life, and its ability to foster loyalty and commitment from its employees. Others contended that Japan's ascent showed that the United States lacked resolve and purpose. As the 1980s progressed, a growing number of Americans across the political spectrum wondered if the entire model of American economic leadership was in profound decline. Japan's rise seemed to show a defeat not just of American production, but of American economic practices and foundational ideologies.

This was a dramatic reversal. In the 1950s, US technical assistance programming in Japan had celebrated American production practices, managerial techniques, and attitudes as a guaranteed route to success. As an industrial consultant wrote in a 1956 report, "The Japanese way of life is pleasant in many respects, but will have to depart from some of their time honored traditions, and Japanese businessmen must adopt more of the Western psychology, if we are to have the right foundation for further gains in productivity."[94] Yet in the 1980s, US bookstores were flooded with literature extolling the success of Japanese management, celebrating Japanese corporate philosophy, and calling for the import of Japanese communalism to revitalize a moribund United States. American businessmen suddenly extolled Japanese practices such as quality control circles and consensual decision-making, which urged employees to take responsibility for the success of the products they produced.[95]

Perhaps the most visible book in this vein was Vogel's *Japan as Number One*. In his chapter on Japanese corporate life, Vogel asserted that the Japanese valued agreement and consensus rather than individual brilliance or charismatic and authoritative leadership. "Good decisions emerge not from brilliant presentations of alternatives but from section people discussing all aspects of the question over and over with the most knowledgeable people."[96] Productive management practices such as these had allowed the "large modern Japanese corporation" to become a "highly successful institution. It is successful," Vogel proclaimed, "not because of any mystical group loyalty embedded in the character of the Japanese race but because it provides a sense of belonging and a sense of pride to workers, who believe their future is best being served by the company."[97] Others parroted this notion that Japan's communal capitalism was the source of its success. In his *Miracle by Design: The Real Reasons Behind Japan's Economic Success* (1982), Frank Gibney favorably contrasted Japan's "Confucian capitalism," founded on economic planning, government-business cooperation, and "respect for relationship and harmony" with the United States' "market rational" system, based on an adversarial and counterproductive "cops and robbers" relationship between government and business.[98] Japan's "people-centered business thinking" had developed not only "a new kind of capitalism," but also "the kind best suited to take the capitalist system into the strains and conflicts of the twenty-first century."[99]

These celebrations of Japanese planning challenged values that politicians such as Reagan extolled as the center of American political and economic life: individualism, the free market, and free enterprise. Indeed, these authors claimed that these values had not only harmed American economic and political life, but were the cause of the United States' decline. As Vogel proclaimed, "In the guise of pursuing freedoms, we have supported egoism and self-interest and have damaged group or common interests. . . . [The] Japanese have been at the forefront of making large organizations something people enjoy. Americans tend to think of the organization as an imposition, an outside force restraining the free individual. Japanese from an early age are taught the values of group life."[100] Nor was this assessment limited to scholars. A 1981 article in *Time* magazine offered similar view, proclaiming that Japan offered a useful corrective to American values run amok. "Americans are reared with a commitment to individual liberty and freedom. . . . It has taken a successful country on the rim of Asia to remind the US that teamwork, however it is organized, is still the prerequisite for a prosperous society."[101]

Such assessments crossed the political spectrum. Even members of the Reagan administration contended that Japan demonstrated the United States' flaws. Clyde V. Prestowitz had worked in the Reagan administration's Commerce Department and accompanied Olmer on his 1982 trip to study Japanese industrial policy. In his *Trading Places: How We are Giving Our Future to Japan and How to Reclaim It* (1988), Prestowitz decried how "the easy assumptions and tranquilizing bromides" that underpin "American economic and strategic thinking are faulty and have contributed immeasurably to the US decline." Particularly damaging, he claimed, was the "issue of fundamental American values. Deeply rooted in the American spirit is the concept of individualism—a concept most completely embodied in the myth of the lone cowboy standing tall, who succeeds without help against long odds by dint of ingenuity, zeal, and determination. It has long been a seductive picture for Americans, but can all too easily develop into an ethic of every man for himself, as in the 'me generation' of the 1980s."[102] In *Miracle by Design*, Gibney concurred, though he placed responsibility squarely on the Reagan administration's emphasis on lower taxes, individual enterprise, and market competition as the keys to economic growth. "The peculiar Reagan version of supply-side economics, supported by so many businessmen, premises a world where Horatio Alger's maxims all come true, with prosperity as unlimited as opportunity if we just give entrepreneurial free enterprise its head. Planning is anathema.... The true capitalist," Gibney bemoaned, "professes that Adam Smith's invisible hand will do the job. Unfortunately, judging from the current bad state of the American economy, Adam's hand seems to have a bad case of arthritis."[103] Commentators such as Prestowitz and Gibney pursued this line of argument with zeal; the United States' flawed lionization of the individual was the very weakness that allowed Japan to succeed.

Ultimately, the increasing fear over Japan's economic success during the Reagan years did not stem just from the direct economic impact, political pressure, racism, or the use of historical analogies, though all of these concerns were central to the American response. Equally important was what Japan's rise said about the United States itself: that the American people were being taken advantage of, that the United States had lost control over a global system it had created, that it had the wrong values, that the free market, the individual, and even capitalism itself were on trial. Indeed, the United States' inability to effectively reverse the seemingly inexorable flood of Japanese goods raised questions about a disturbing lack of power, purpose, and resolve in the nation. Prestowitz hammered this theme home.

> Ultimately, I have come to the strong belief that the issue is neither Japan nor the US-Japan relationship. Rather, it is the United States. In the words of Pogo, we have met the enemy and he is us. Our problems with Japan are only symptomatic of a larger flight from reality. In the final analysis, our trade deficit and our inability to compete with Japan spring

from the same willful disregard of reality and self-delusion as the decay of our central cities, the permeation of our society with drugs, and the decline of our educational system.[104]

Japan's successes revealed that the United States was "a stumbling, declining society," undermined by the very policies, practices, and values of the vaunted "American way of life."

This belief that Japan was profiting not simply because of its illiberal practices but also because of the United States' own institutional, ideological, and moral weaknesses was not new. Rather, it reiterated language, ideas, and anxieties that deeply shaped the United States' conceptualization of the communist enemy throughout the Cold War. This line of argumentation also perpetuated a long-standing, populist critique of postwar liberal internationalism, claiming that naïve, immoral, and myopic Americans had "sold out" the American people to the Japanese. Former Massachusetts Senator Paul Tsongas made these connections explicit in his 1992 campaign for the Democratic presidential nomination. Campaigning on a theme of economic nationalism, Tsongas called on the United States to "counter the 'attack' from 'foreign ownership of industry.'"[105] He turned the United States' seeming Cold War triumph into an ominous warning: "The Cold War is over," Tsongas declared, "and Japan won."[106] William S. Dietrich, for his part, used a metaphor that would be familiar to fans of horror movies: while the United States sought to directly confront the communist enemy, "the Japanese quietly and unobtrusively moved in through the back door and occupied much of the house."[107] The economic success of the United States' most important ally in Cold War Asia no longer seemed to serve as a potent symbol of the power of democracy and capitalism; instead it came to represent American weakness.

By the mid-1990s, such declarations looked silly. With the collapse of Japan's so-called bubble economy and the United States' economic boom, it seemed as though the global economy had returned to what Americans saw as its "natural" order. But fears of decline remained lurking beneath the surface. As the new trade pacts such as the North American Free Trade Agreement and the World Trade Organization proceeded alongside continued declines in American manufacturing and production, some commentators again warned of a nefarious plot to destroy American prosperity. No one articulated this message more powerfully than Trump, whose 2016 presidential campaign resurrected his decades-old fixation with tariffs and the "unfair" nature of global trade. Drawing directly from his anti-Japan language of the 1980s, Trump excoriated "stupid" American leadership that allowed countries such as China and Mexico to cheat the global trading order and thrive in the global economy.[108] It was not the shortcomings of American products, skills, or ingenuity, he declared, but American leaders' naïve, weak, and treasonous surrender to international trade laws, and thus foreign states and peoples, that had left the United States in "carnage." The electoral resonance of such narratives, fraught with nativist and racist anti-immigration rhetoric, showed the long emotional and political legacies of the 1980s. First articulated with Japan in mind, anxieties about the United States' "rightful" position in the global economy—and US leaders' ability and willingness to safeguard American hegemony—remained potent for decades, with far-reaching consequences.

Notes

1. John Curtis Perry, "Please, Japan, Return the Favor: Occupy Us," *New York Times*, 4 Mar. 1981.

2. Andrew C. McKevitt, *Consuming Japan: Popular Culture and the Globalizing of 1980s America* (Chapel Hill: University of North Carolina Press, 2017), 7.

3. Ezra Vogel, *Japan as Number One: Lessons for America* (Cambridge, MA: Harvard University Press, 1979), viii.

4. Paul Kennedy, *The Rise and Fall of the Great Powers* (New York: Random House, 1987), 467. Emphasis in the original.

5. Ilan Ben-Meir, "That Time Trump Spent Nearly $100,000 on an Ad Criticizing US Foreign Policy in 1987," 10 July 2015, https://www.buzzfeed.com/ilanbenmeir/that-time-trump-spent-nearly-100000-on-an-ad-criticizing-us?utm_term=.ggnGPaxMl#.rqxX26Wq7. Emphasis in the original. See also Jennifer M. Miller, "Let's Not Be Laughed at Anymore: Donald Trump and Japan from the 1980s to the Present" *Journal of American-East Asian Relations* 25, no. 2 (2018): 138–168.

6. Michael Schaller, "Reagan and Asia," in *A Companion to Ronald Reagan*, ed. Andrew Johns (Malden, MA: John Wiley and Sons, 2015), 422.

7. See, for example, Theodore H. White, "The Danger from Japan," *New York Times Magazine*, 28 July 1985.

8. McKevitt, *Consuming Japan*, 3.

9. For the concept of Japan as mirror, see Helen Mears, *Mirror for Americans, Japan* (Boston: Houghton Mifflin, 1948).

10. This fear is best expressed in NSC-68, written under Nitze's supervision in the fall of 1949 and the spring of 1950. See A "Report to the National Security Council–NSC 68," 12 Apr. 1950, https://www.trumanlibrary.org/whistlestop/study_collections/coldwar/documents/pdf/10-1.pdf (esp. 20–24); Jennifer M. Miller, *Cold War Democracy: The United States and Japan* (Cambridge, MA: Harvard University Press, 2019), 53–57.

11. McCarthy, "Speech at Wheeling, West Virginia," 9 Feb. 1950, in *The Age of McCarthyism: A Brief History with Documents*, ed. Ellen Schrecker (Boston: Bedford Books of St. Martin's Press, 1994), 211–214. See also Robert Dean, *Imperial Brotherhood: Gender and the Making of Cold War Foreign Policy* (Amherst: University of Massachusetts Press, 2003), 63–87.

12. On the Reagan administration's embrace of foreign capital, see Michael De Groot's chapter in this volume.

13. See Jonathan Hunt's chapter in this volume, 427.

14. See Hunt's chapter, 414.

15. See Dayna L. Barnes, *Architects of Occupation: American Experts and the Planning for Postwar Japan* (Ithaca, NY: Cornell University Press, 2017); Miller, *Cold War Democracy*, 26–39.

16. See Sayuri Shimizu, *Creating People of Plenty: The United States and Japan's Economic Alternatives, 1950–1960* (Kent, OH: Kent State University Press, 2001).

17. Miller, *Cold War Democracy*, 227–250.

18. These commitments to international alliances was not limited to Japan; the United States signed a wide array of alliance treaties after World War II, including with the Philippines, Australia, and New Zealand, and a multilateral security alliance with many Western European countries known as the North Atlantic Treaty Organization (NATO).

19. See Aaron Forsburg, *America and the Japanese Miracle: The Cold War Context of Japan's Economic Revival* (Chapel Hill: University of North Carolina Press, 2000); Richard Samuels, *Rich Nation, Strong Army: National Security and the Technological Transfer of Japan* (Ithaca, NY: Cornell University Press, 1996), 130–269.

20. Scott O'Bryan, *The Growth Idea: Purpose and Prosperity in Postwar Japan* (Honolulu: University of Hawaii Press, 2009), 4.

21. Michael Schaller, *Altered States: The United States and Japan since the Occupation* (New York: Oxford University Press, 1997), 221–222. The Nixon administration also regularly derided the Japanese as free riders, arguing that they had gotten rich on US defense spending, especially the war in Vietnam, while refusing to spend on their own defense. See Schaller, "Reagan and Asia," 421.

22. For example, Jimmy Carter's vice president, Walter Mondale, visited the Japan to urge an increase in American imports but left with no firm commitments. Judith Stein, *Pivotal Decade: How the United States Traded Factories for Finance in the 1970s* (New Haven, CT: Yale University Press, 2010), 161.

23. Walter LaFeber, *The Clash: A History of US-Japanese Relations* (New York: Norton, 1997), 371.

24. See Meghan Warner Mettler, "Gimcracks, Dollar Blouses, and Transistors: American Reactions to Imported Japanese Products, 1945–1964," *Pacific Historical Review* 79, no. 2 (2010): 202–230.

25. De Groot's chapter in this volume.

26. Schaller, *Altered States*, 255; Schaller, "Reagan and Asia," 423; De Groot, in this volume.

27. Greta R. Krippner, *Capitalizing on Crisis: The Political Origins of the Rise of Finance* (Cambridge, MA: Harvard University Press, 2012), 100–101. See also Schaller, *Altered States*, 255; Schaller, "Reagan and Asia," 423.

28. Krippner, *Capitalizing on Crisis*, 104; De Groot, in this volume, ch. 4.

29. Krippner, *Capitalizing on Crisis*, 25, 102; De Groot, in this volume, ch. 4.

30. Judith Stein argues that "economic competition from Japan and Germany battered the economy in the 1970s" and that growing of trade deficits "are at the root of contemporary global crises" (Stein, *Pivotal Decade*, xi).

31. Daniel T. Rodgers, *Age of Fracture* (Cambridge, MA: Belknap Press of Harvard University Press, 2012), 43–44.

32. De Groot, in this volume, ch. 4. The 1985 Plaza Accord aimed to depreciate the dollar against foreign currencies such as the yen, with the hope that this would lower the prices of American exports and prevent protectionist legislation.

33. Department of State, "Japanese Automobile Sales to the US," 21 Nov. 1980, Digital National Security Archive (DNSA), *Japan and the United States: Diplomatic, Security and Economic Relations, 1977–1992*.

34. Thomas Borstelmann, *The 1970s: A New Global History from Civil Rights to Economic Inequality* (Princeton, NJ: Princeton University Press, 2012), 62; McKevitt, *Consuming Japan*, 80.

35. Christopher Byron, "How Japan Does It," *Time*, 30 Mar. 1981; Department of State, "Japanese Automobile Sales to the US."

36. Quoted in Matthew W. Seeger, ed., *"I Gotta Tell You": Speeches of Lee Iacocca* (Detroit, MI: Wayne State University Press, 1994), 184. Iacocca continued in this vein in the early 1990s, referring to Japanese cars "massing on our borders" in a 1991 speech to forty-two members of the House of Representatives; Seeger, *"I Gotta Tell You,"* 192.

37. Department of State, "Japanese Automobile Sales to the US."

38. Byron, "How Japan Does It."

39. Schaller, *Altered States*, 254–255.

40. See McKevitt, *Consuming Japan*, 79–130, for a detailed exploration of the first American Honda plant, which opened in Marysville, Ohio, in 1982.

41. Schaller, *Altered States*, 253–255.

42. Frank H. Wu, "Why Vincent Chin Matters," *New York Times*, 22 June 2012.

43. Stuart Elliot, "The Media Business: Advertising; Anti-Japan Auto Ads May Backfire," *New York Times*, 30 Jan. 1992. See also Schaller, *Altered States*, 256.

44. Lawrence B. Glickman, *Free Enterprise: An American History* (New Haven, CT: Yale University Press, 2019), 3, 9.

45. Ronald Reagan, "Remarks at the National Legislative Conference of the Building and Construction Trades Department, AFL-CIO," 5 Apr. 1982, American Presidency Project (APP), http://www.presidency.ucsb.edu/.

46. Rodgers, *Age of Fracture*, 70–76.

47. Ronald Reagan, "Statement on Assistance for the Domestic Automobile Industry," 6 Apr. 1981, APP.

48. Ronald Reagan, "Remarks at the National Legislative Conference of the Building and Construction Trades Department, AFL-CIO."

49. Quoted in Alfred E. Eckes Jr. and Thomas Zeiler, *Globalization and the American Century* (New York: Cambridge University Press, 2003) 208.

50. Douglas McMinn to William P. Clark, "Japanese Automobile Restraints," 13 Oct. 1983, DNSA, *Japan and the United States: Diplomatic, Security, and Economic Relations, Part III, 1961–2000*.

51. National Security Decision Directive 62, "United States–Japan Relations," 25 Oct. 1982, https://fas.org/irp/offdocs/nsdd/nsdd-62.pdf.

52. As Reagan officials repeatedly acknowledged in meetings, Japanese tariffs were generally lower than those in the United States, though other business practices made it difficult for American products to enter the Japanese market.

53. William P. Clark, "Meeting with Japanese Prime Minister Nakasone, January 18, 1983," DNSA, *Japan and the United States: Diplomatic, Security, and Economic Relations, Part III, 1961–2000*.

54. McMinn to Clark, "Japanese Automobile Restraints."

55. Ronald Reagan, "Remarks at the Ford Claycomo Assembly Plant in Kansas City, Missouri," 11 Apr. 1984, APP.

56. See Ronald Reagan, "Radio Address to the Nation on Free and Fair Trade," 31 Aug. 1985, APP.

57. Stein, *Pivotal Decade*, 257; Eckes and Zeiler, *Globalization and the American Century*, 209.

58. LaFeber, *The Clash*, 376.

59. LaFeber, *The Clash*, 376. For a detailed exploration of US propaganda about Japan during World War II, see John W. Dower, *War without Mercy: Race and Power in the Pacific War* (New York: Pantheon Books, 1986).

60. Hearings before the Subcommittee on Trade of the Ways and Means, House of Representatives, 98th Congress, 1st Session, 10 Mar. and 17, 26 Apr. 1983, 6, 44.

61. McKevitt, *Consuming Japan*, 81.

62. White, "The Danger from Japan."

63. White, "The Danger from Japan."

64. Ben-Meir, "That Time Trump Spent Nearly $100,000 on an Ad."

65. Quoted in Charles Laderman and Brendan Simms, *Donald Trump: The Making of a World View* (New York: I. B. Tauris, 2017), 41.

66. Hearings before the Subcommittee on Trade of the Ways and Means, 65.

67. "A Report to the National Security Council—NSC 68," 23.

68. William S. Dietrich, *In the Shadow of the Rising Sun: The Political Roots of American Economic Decline* (University Park: Penn State University Press, 1991), xii.

69. Senior Interdepartmental Group on International Economic Policy, 5 Dec. 1984 Meeting, DNSA, *Japan and the United States: Diplomatic, Security, and Economic Relations, Part III, 1961–2000*. On the free world/slave world dichotomy, see *Why We Fight: Path to War* (Dir. Frank Capra, 1942) and NSC-68.

70. Senior Interdepartmental Group on International Economic Policy, 5 Dec. 1984 Meeting.

71. Quoted in Kennedy, *The Rise and Fall of the Great Powers*, 465.

72. Marvin J. Wolf, *The Japanese Conspiracy: The Plot to Dominate Industry Worldwide—and How to Deal with It* (New York: Empire Books, 1983), 15.

73. Choate ran as Ross Perot's vice-presidential candidate on the 1996 Reform Party ticket.

74. Pat Choate, *Agents of Influence* (New York: Alfred A. Knopf, 1990), xi–xii.

75. Such a setting was not new. The 1988 film *Die Hard* took place at Nakatomi tower, and John McClane's wife worked for a fictional Japanese corporation. The film depicts her Japanese boss as noble; he is murdered after refusing to give terrorists the code to the building's vault. However, the film also asserts that this nobility was misguided; only John McClane's quick thinking and cowboy individualism, under the catchphrase "Yippie-ki-yay, motherfucker!," is able to defeat a nefarious and greedy German enemy.

76. For an excellent discussion of conceptions of race in *Rising Sun*, see McKevitt, *Consuming Japan*, 68–75.

77. McKevitt, *Consuming Japan*, 68.

78. In 1989, the US government formally labeled Japan an unfair trading partner under the 1988 Omnibus Trade and Competitiveness Act.

79. Mark E. Leland to Donald Regan, "Japanese Protectionism," 18 Mar. 1981, DNSA, *Japan and the United States: Diplomatic, Security and Economic Relations, 1977–1992*.

80. Lionel H. Olmer, "Japan Trip Report, November 26–December 4, 1982," DNSA, *Japan and the United States: Diplomatic, Security, and Economic Relations, Part III, 1961–2000*.

81. Hearings before the Subcommittee on Trade of the Ways and Means, 53.

82. Senior Interdepartmental Group on International Economic Policy, 5 Dec. 1984 Meeting.

83. National Security Division Directive 154, "US-Japan Trade Policy Relations," 31 Dec. 1984, https://fas.org/irp/offdocs/nsdd/nsdd-154.pdf. See also Senior Interdepartmental Group on International Economic Policy, 14 Dec. 1984 Meeting, DNSA, *Japan and the United States: Diplomatic, Security, and Economic Relations, Part III, 1961–2000*.

84. Hunt, in this volume, 426.

85. This concern that Japan would become a model for other nations grew over the latter half of the 1980s. In 1993, the World Bank published *The East Asian Miracle: Economic Growth and Public Policy* (New York: Oxford University Press), which examined the role of industrial policy in the rapid economic growth of eight Asian countries. The report concluded that while government intervention was common, it was difficult to demonstrate its concrete benefits or causal consequences. Reflecting the zeitgeist of the early 1990s, especially the embrace of the market as the main engine of growth, the report instead argued that the market-oriented aspects of the Asian experience were the most significant: "The fact that interventions were an element of some East Asian economies' success does not mean that they should be attempted everywhere, nor should it be taken as an excuse to postpone needed market-oriented reform" (World Bank, *The East Asian Miracle*, 26).

86. Senior Interdepartmental Group on International Economic Policy, 5 Dec. 1984 Meeting.

87. Hearings before the Subcommittee on Trade of the Ways and Means, 95.

88. Ann L. Hollick to Douglas McMinn, "Views of State and Other Agencies on USTR Non-Paper," 25 Feb. 1986, DNSA, *Japan and the United States: Diplomatic, Security, and Economic Relations, Part III, 1961–2000*.

89. Both Japanese and American authors further asserted that Japanese dominance of semiconductor manufacturing could threaten American military capabilities; modern military technology was so dependent on them that access to Japanese products was becoming a security imperative. See Akio Morita and Shintaro Ishihara, *The Japan That Can Say "No": The New US-Japan Relations Card*, quoted in "Extension of Remarks," *Congressional Record*, 14 Nov. 1989, and Clyde V. Prestowitz, *Trading Places: How We Are Giving Our Future to Japan and How To Reclaim It* (New York: Basic Books, 1989).

90. Eckes and Zeiler, *Globalization and the American Century*, 228.

91. Ronald Reagan, "Statement on the Japan-United States Semiconductor Trade Agreement," 31 July 1986, APP.

92. Emphasis added. See, for example, Ronald Reagan, "Radio Address to the Nation on Free and Fair Trade," 31 Aug. 1985, APP; Ronald Reagan: "Radio Address to the Nation on Free and Fair Trade," 2 Aug. 1986, APP.

93. Eckes and Zeiler, *Globalization and the American Century*, 228.

94. W.S. Landes, "Survey of Japanese Industrial Productivity," 1 Jan. 1956, US National Archives and Records Administration, Record Group 286, Office of Indonesia Affairs, Entry #P 368, Closed Project Files, 1955–1964, box 6, folder "Landes Report." National Archives, College Park, MD.

95. Stephen P. Waring, *Taylorism Transformed: Scientific Management Theory Since 1945* (Chapel Hill: University of North Carolina Press, 1991), 160, 166.

96. Vogel, *Japan as Number One*, 144.

97. Vogel, *Japan as Number One*, 157.

98. Frank Gibney, *Miracle by Design: The Real Reasons behind Japan's Economic Success* (New York: Times Books, 1982), 8, 15.

99. Gibney, *Miracle by Design*, 9.

100. Vogel, *Japan as Number One*, 235.

101. Byron, "How Japan Does It."

102. Presowitz's book went through multiple printings; this quotation comes from the 1989 edition of the book; Prestowitz, *Trading Places*, 103.

103. Gibney, *Miracle by Design*, 10.

104. Prestowitz, *Trading Places*, 81–82.

105. McKevitt, *Consuming Japan*, 21.

106. McKevitt, *Consuming Japan*, 21.

107. Dietrich, *In the Shadow of the Rising Sun*, 7.

108. Laderman and Simms, *Donald Trump*, 3.

CHAPTER 19

One World, Two Chinas
Dreams of Capitalist Convergence in East Asia
JONATHAN R. HUNT

When the People's Republic of China (PRC) became the first communist country Ronald and Nancy Reagan had travelled to, what impressed them most was an open-air street market. To ease the septuagenarian couple's westward journey across eleven time zones and the international date line, the presidential retinue had made daylong stops in California, Hawaii, and Guam, before landing in Beijing on Thursday, April 26, 1984. What followed were five nights and six days of dinners, meetings, ceremonies, speeches, and sightseeing, with a soupçon of cluelessness for added measure. After a formal greeting in the East Court of the Great Hall by PRC President Li Xiannian and his wife, the Reagans settled into the Diaoyutai State Guesthouse before heading to dinner. The next day Reagan jotted down in his official diary how he and Nancy had "heeded Dick Nixons [sic] advice & didn't ask what things were—we just swallowed them. There were a few items I managed to stir around on my plate & leave."[1] He enjoyed the give-and-take with Premier Zhao Ziyang, Lieutenant General Secretary Hu Yaobang, and Vice Premier Deng Xiaoping more than the cuisine, as he seized the occasion to warn the three members of the Standing Committee of the Chinese Communist Party's (CCP) Politburo that although Taiwan's future was for Beijing and Taipei to work out themselves, it nevertheless "must be worked out peacefully."[2]

Later in his visit, Reagan waxed poetic about the alpine vistas he surveyed from atop the Great Wall and the 800 life-sized terracotta warriors that had been unearthed from the first Qin emperor's tomb in Xian, China's ancient capital. What really piqued his interest, however, were signs of burgeoning private industry six years after Deng Xiaoping unveiled "reform and opening up" at the Third Plenum of the Eleventh Party Congress and four years after the Fifth Plenum of the Central Committee had devolved responsibility for agriculture to rural households, clearing the way for city markets in the villages and townships of China's heartlands.[3] Cultural differences were nonetheless sources of the occasional faux pas. After touring the mausoleum on Sunday, the Reagans stopped at a pop-up bazaar that the CCP had specially arranged for them:

> We wanted to see the real thing because it's part of their departure from communism—individuals selling their wares in the open market for profit.... Nancy bought some decorative items for our Xmas tree. There was an incident—her bill came to 5 Yuan ($2.50). The poor gal selling didn't have any change. I'm aware there is no tipping in China but she was so embarrassed and looking to others for help. I said "keep it," & we moved on. She caught up with us & gave me the change she'd gotten from someone for the 10 Yuan note I'd given her. Our T.V. press made a big thing of it—that I had committed a blunder & tried to tip her.[4]

However minor, the misunderstanding evoked the contradictions at play in Reagan's greater China policy: a Potemkin village where a new thread in China's social fabric had been placed on display; a deep cultural chasm illustrated by a open-hearted gaffe; a reform campaign that aimed to foster personal initiative in what remained an authoritarian, one-party state.

Reagan returned from the trip trumpeting "the injection of a free market spirit" and the promise of trade, investment, and friendship "with this so-called Communist China."[5] In his memoirs, George Shultz, the former Stanford economist who became Reagan's second secretary of state on July 16, 1982, registered greater ambivalence. "We knew that China wanted to have it both ways," he noted, "to gain the benefits of a booming economy while maintaining state control over key aspects of economic and political behavior. They would have to face the reality that a society cannot be Communist and capitalist at the same time," he predicted; "this they were not ready to do."[6]

Shultz's crystal ball was imperfect. China's authoritarian globalizing would work better than he had foreseen, in part because diplomatic entrepreneurs in the White House, the Republican Party, and corporate America saw in the

Chinese mainland a market whose vast potential could line their pockets while bridging the gulf between the PRC, the Republic of China (ROC) on the island of Taiwan, and Hong Kong. While Reagan and Shultz worked to ensure that China's reentry into the US-led international economic order did not come at the expense of America's global military preponderance, they struggled to tame the animal spirits that dreams of the mainland market had unleashed. As a result of their neoliberal idealism, they planted the seeds of a rising power in the Asia-Pacific, whose liberalization would stop far short of the values of human rights and democracy in which Reagan would elsewhere profess his faith.

The typical story of US–East Asian relations in the 1980s features four subplots: Beijing and Washington's anti-Soviet partnership; Tokyo's rising clout; pouncing Asian Tigers in Singapore, South Korea, Hong Kong, and Taiwan; and the ascent of democracy in Seoul, Hong Kong, Taipei, and the Philippines. The common denominator is East Asia's maturation into, first, a workshop of global capitalism and, then, a conveyor belt of goods and investment, as capital and culture flowed in from North America and Western Europe as well as within the region between the Asian Tigers and developing markets in Malaysia, Indonesia, Thailand, and the PRC. Relatively cheap commodities and manufactures went out in return, as a fusion of ideas, people, and technology drove shifting patterns of industrialization, urbanization, consumption, and expectations in the long arc from Singapore to Sapporo. From 1985 to 2005, Japan's share of global merchandise declined from 12 to 6 percent, while that produced by emerging Asian economies doubled from 10 to 20 percent. The PRC became a magnet for intermediate goods used to make consumer exports as intraregional trade exploded, replacing, for instance, the United States as Hong Kong's and Taiwan's largest export markets in these years. From 1986 to 1991, the value of PRC exports grew by 18.2 percent and, from 1991 to 1996, by another 19.2 percent. During the first five-year period, Beijing's exports to the United States tracked the mean at 18.0 percent; during the second, they jumped up by a whopping 38.9 percent, for an annual growth rate of 6.9 percent.[7]

For all the ways East Asian societies moved toward convergence with North America and Western Europe after 1978, the Taiwan issue still dominates accounts of US-PRC relations during the Reagan years, with early reactions accusing him of dumping Taipei in exchange for Beijing's help with Moscow.[8] Historians have developed a keener appreciation for how he pursued a marriage of convenience with the PRC without altogether abandoning Taiwan, most consequentially by linking future military sales to the strategic balance in the Taiwan Straits.[9] Today, the bargain whereby Washington lowered barriers for technology and knowledge transfers into the PRC in return for an open door into Beijing's "planned commodity economy" is garnering ever more attention.[10] Reagan and his allies were dedicated to the universal triumph of US-style electoral capitalism and, to that end, to China's reintegration into the world economy as a prerequisite for Deng's four modernizations: of agriculture, of industry, of national defense, and of science and technology.[11]

The commercial dimensions of "reform and opening up" softened US attitudes toward the PRC in ways that went well beyond Richard Nixon's trip to Beijing in 1972 or Carter's normalization of diplomatic relations with communist China in 1979. International economics in fact competed with and at times trumped Cold War strategy in how the Reagan administration handled the PRC. Congressional requirements for continued military sales under the 1979 Taiwan Relations Act had always barred a Sino-American entente, while the Taiwan dispute and the geostrategic imperatives of the "Second Cold War" had largely fallen by the wayside by late 1982. By the end of 1984, the Sino-British Joint Declaration had eased concerns that Hong Kong would remain a financial powerhouse after London's ninety-nine-year lease lapsed in 1997. Zhao's and Reagan's reciprocal visits that same year sealed China's new license to purchase military and nuclear equipment from the United States and its rich allies. It was an unmarked milestone as US-PRC relations were superseded by a framework that encompassed Hong Kong and Taiwan, as well as communist China. In the 1970s, the dial had turned three times: from animus to recognition to normalization. In the 1980s, it ventured one step further—to economic harmonization across what many in these four polities hoped would be a "greater China."[12]

Private actors and government officials took the stage together in trans-Pacific relations during the 1980s. Reagan's reputation as Taiwan's best friend and some campaign indiscretions had caused heart palpitations in 1980, leading both Beijing and the Republican Party to worry that as president he would re-recognize diplomatic officials from Taipei. When Reagan floated the idea on the campaign trail, running mate George H. W. Bush, former US ambassador to Beijing under President Gerald Ford, was dispatched to assure Deng that Reagan would not "set back the clock."[13] After the Reagan-Bush ticket won in November, congressional Republicans moved to reassure Deng once more after Ray Cline, a former CIA analyst on the transition team, attacked Carter's normalization while touring Taiwan and Southeast Asia that December. No less a grandee than Senate Majority Leader Howard Baker of Tennessee was to bear words of reassurance to Beijing—that is, until his wife, Joy, took ill. The Republican Party was sensitive enough to Deng's potential displeasure that the Senate majority whip from Alaska, Ted Stevens, made the trip in Baker's stead, on a three-day "honeymoon" with his new wife, Catherine.[14]

The newlyweds were accompanied by Anna Chennault, whose acquaintance with Stevens went back thirty-five years to his wartime service under her dead husband, Lieutenant General Claire Chennault. Chairwoman of the Republican National Heritage Foundation—the party's central organization for ethnic voters—she was "to many Americans," the writers at the *Christian Science Monitor* among them, "the very embodiment of the so-called Taiwan lobby." A businesswoman, writer, and fundraiser whose rolodex overflowed with top powerbrokers across the Pacific, she resented her twin reputation as a Georgetown hostess and a "Dragon Lady."[15] Her three-part journey from an implacable critic of communist China, to a go-between for it, the United States, and Taiwan, and, finally, to an investor in its globalizing economy was a testament to how dreams of a Pacific gold rush in the 1980s were turning former foes into business partners.

Born Chen Xiangmei to a family of diplomats in Beijing in 1925, Chennault attended Hong Kong's Lingnan University before she became a war correspondent for its Central News Agency after Japan's invasion of Manchuria. During her travels, she met Claire Chennault, who led the First American Volunteer Group, known more widely as the vaunted Flying Tigers, in the Republic of China. They married in 1947 after he divorced his first wife.[16] The Chennaults quickly became prominent members of the pro-Kuomintang (KMT) China lobby in the United States after the Chinese Revolution in 1949. Following his death in 1958, Anna became vice president of Flying Tigers Line (FTL), an air freight and military charter service founded and crewed by former Flying Tiger pilots, where she excelled at cultivating connections with Asian governments willing to approve landing rights for what became the aviation company's lucrative trans-Pacific and intra-Asian network.

Her association with FTL gained her access, clout, and over time a large fortune. A celebrated Mandarin-language writer, she befriended politicians and businessmen throughout Asia, and especially on Taiwan, where she often called on Chiang Ching-kuo, who had acceded to the presidency after the death of his father, Chiang Kai-shek, in 1972. She also counted friends and contacts in the turnstile between the Pentagon and major defense contractors. In 1976 she founded TAC International, an aerospace and transportation consulting firm, whose client list grew to include FTL, General Electric, Northrop, Grumman International, and various Asian and European enterprises. When Fred Smith of FedEx purchased FTL for $880 million in December 1988, the shares Claire had bequeathed to her and their children may have been worth millions.

Anna had pressed for a diplomatic mission in the weeks before Cline's comments, citing the need to foster dialogue between Beijing and Taipei. After conversations with PRC Ambassador Chai Zemin she described as undertaken "with the approval of my Taiwan friends," she wrote to Vice President-elect Bush to volunteer herself for the assignment:

> You probably also realize that I have been in contact with the highest levels of both the Peoples [sic] Republic of China and Taiwan. Officials of both of these governments have quietly expressed to me their wish and desire to have me serve as a bridge for future negotiations. They feel I, as an American citizen, with my understanding of Chinese background, would be able to talk and carry messages for the three sides—United States, Peoples [sic] Republic of China and Taiwan.[17]

She sent copies of her letter to Reagan and his presumptive national security adviser, Richard Allen. Chennault's celebrity, even stronger in Taiwan and communist China than in the United States, may have prompted the Chinese Communist Party to reach out initially. Considering her closeness to congressional Republicans, notably Baker and Stevens, it was unlikely that they were not also privy. While disclaiming her "own glory"—she merely wanted to "be of much service to my adopted country and my mother country, China"—she had ulterior motives. A second letter addressed to Bush that same day requested positions in the administration for her ranging from "Ambassador without Portfolio" to "Special Assistant to the President on Ethnic Affairs."[18]

That such a vocal and prominent Chinese-American defender of Taiwan would sit down for tea with Deng Xiaoping was sure to draw attention. For all Stevens's denials that it was the president-elect who had sent him, his description of Reagan as "very realistic," when combined with Chennault's presence, signaled that business should return to normal.[19] The headlines (some peddling rank orientalism) wrote themselves: "New Views Hinted by Mrs. Chennault," "A Native Critic Returns," "No Longer Breathing Fire, 'Dragon Lady' Anna Chennault Adopts a Two-China Policy."[20] The *Washington Post* asked what it likened to a "fortune cookie riddle. . . . Do Flying Tigers change their stripes?" After all, just fifteen months earlier, Chennault had castigated the Carter administration for normalizing relations with communist Beijing.[21]

The meeting lasted two hours in the Fujian room of the Great Hall. The symbolism was clear: Fujian was the mainland region neighboring Taiwan. Deng dwelt on China's need for Western technology and techniques while lamenting the damage wrought by the Soviet model and the Cultural Revolution, but he also insisted that the Taiwan issue could cancel out all recent progress in US-PRC relations. "While it is improper to dwell too much upon this matter," the paramount leader warned, "China will not simply set aside the Taiwan question out of consideration of its strategy against the Soviet Union."[22] Chennault translated for the two men, though she and Deng lapsed into Mandarin for stretches. Some details of their dialogue remain unknown. Baker later joked that he knew "everything that was talked about in English. Only Anna knows what was talked about in Chinese."[23]

At the press conference afterward, Stevens stated he would not "rule out" the sale of lethal arms to the PRC, framing mutual beneficial relations between the two countries in terms of their common antagonist—the Soviet Union. His words carried weight: Stevens would chair the Senate's Defense Appropriations Subcommittee in the next session. Chennault's comments were more personal, circumspect, and philosophical.[24] Having taxed Deng for lagging so far behind Taiwan, she promised an "open mind," extolling the need to "look at the world in reality," and maintaining how, in its treatment of communist China, the United States could not "afford to be isolated."[25] She cast her visit back to her birthplace as a "sentimental journey."[26]

Chennault's Chinese identity was an important credential for her entrepreneurial diplomacy. While in Beijing, she reconnected with her second cousin, Liao Chengzhi, vice chairman of the Standing Committee of the National People's Congress and honorary president of the Office of Overseas Chinese Affairs. His position showed how Chinese nationalism could transcend Cold War feuds. Years later, Chennault would claim that she had counseled Deng against mimicking the West, encouraging him to forge a Chinese model of development and globalizing instead: "[He] talked about westernisation, and I said to him: 'China should not talk about westernization. After all, our culture, the Chinese culture, the background certainly could not adapt the western way of doing things.' I said, 'you should talk about modernisation.' And, I am so glad that he, although . . . an elderly statesman, was pretty smart to take advice from a woman."[27]

While her claim to have coined "the four modernizations" was boastful fiction—the phrase dated from 1978—there was truth in her recollection beyond her constant struggle to be taken seriously as an Asian woman. After three days in Beijing, she and Stevens jetted to Taipei to brief Chiang. What messages she ferried remain unknown. Back in Washington, Baker, Allen, Senator Jesse Helms, White House Counsellor Edwin Meese, and Secretary of State Alexander Haig, Jr., all received copies of Stevens and Chennault's confidential report.[28] A letter to Reagan from Thomas Corcoran, the New Deal fixer and K-Street lawyer whom Chennault was then romantically involved with, suggested that Chennault had made it "feasible that any representative of the United States may from now on visit *both* Peking and Taiwan."[29] If she had secured such a tacit concession from Deng, its limitation to US congressional visitors would soon be made clear.

Once back in Washington, Chennault envisioned new business opportunities. She shared the report with at least two of her clients, Northrop Corporation and Grumman Corporation, the latter with reference to an "ongoing business opportunity . . . on the mainland."[30] Her informal diplomacy on behalf of three nation-states gave rise to conflicts where her business interests intersected. In a one-party, communist state where self-dealing was the norm, Chinese Civil Aviation Administration (CAA) officials had had no compunctions about scheduling a meeting with her to discuss landing rights for FTL, whose leadership was eyeing landing rights on the mainland, where Chennault had negotiated charter arrangements two years prior, to add to its lucrative trans-Pacific portfolio.[31] When the Associated Press caught wind of the meeting, Chennault dubbed even the appearance of wrongdoing "completely absurd," assuring FTL Vice President Paul Stokes that she had not spoken for the company before acknowledging that Beijing had bent "backward to accommodate me."[32] She assured FTL's head of public relations that although it had not been "a business trip . . . it is the general opinion that Tiger has been benefitted by my visit to both Peking and Taipei. Since Washington, the People's Republic and Taiwan are happy with my trip," she attested. "I presume we can say we have another breakthrough."[33]

The Republican Party had averted an early crisis between the wealthiest and the most populous nations on Earth. Even as Chennault's new role as liaison between Beijing and American aerospace and defense firms took flight, however, her mission to have Deng acquiesce to official Taiwanese calls on the United States self-destructed. When pro-Taiwan representatives of the Republican Party asked her as a member of Reagan's inauguration committee "to make arrangements to get official invitations for Taiwan officials to attend," the aspiring bridge builder sparked the first international crisis of the new presidential administration.[34] Her invitation to Secretary-General Tsiang Yien-si drew a high-level rebuke from Beijing, which threatened to shun the event entirely. Tsiang had to make a show of battling the flu in order to avert a major incident.[35]

US-PRC relations were highly personalized in the 1980s, with members of the US national-security establishment eyeing Deng's political fortunes in hopes of expanding Beijing's ties to the capitalist world rather than solely, or even principally, of maintaining an anti-Soviet common front. "Chinese connections with the West—especially the United States," a CIA report noted, "not only serve the PRC's strategic needs but also further Deng's design for China's rapid modernization."[36] The CIA's China watchers continued to distinguish between "demaoification" and "liberalization," however, and their belief that "to a great degree, the CCP is condemned if it does reform and condemned if it does not" betrayed deep-seated assumptions about the lethality of social and economic liberties to authoritarian rule. Accustomed to viewing PRC politics through a Maoist lens after decades during which Mao Zedong and his cult of personality had dominated mainland politics and international radical politics, the CIA assigned utmost importance to septuagenarian Deng's survival.[37]

To the CIA the Taiwan issue looked like Deng's greatest challenge. An early review concluded with a dark premonition: to restore harmony with Taipei might not itself "lead to Deng's fall. Repair of Sino-US relations and of Deng's political standing, however, would take time, and at age 76 he may not have enough."[38] While he had proved capable of outmaneuvering his political rivals after sidelining Hua Guofeng, who had lost the premiership of the PRC in September 1980, the CIA's National Foreign Assessment Center remarked in March 1981 that the Taiwan issue was the "one in which he has the least room to maneuver by sharing responsibility with other leaders." His personal investment in US-PRC normalization ruled out buck-passing, indicating that Reagan should tread carefully there, lest he hand conservative forces within the CCP a wild card to play.[39] Deng was a survivor, having been purged by Mao twice during the Cultural Revolution on account of his reformist economic views. Given that the "climate favoring increased foreign economic dealings with China, rests finally on the overall stability and longevity of Deng's overall reform program," Langley warned that the reintegration of one-fifth of humanity into the global capitalist economy would hinge on his political fate.[40]

With intelligence analysts confident that steady US-PRC relations were a necessary precondition for Deng's reforms, they harbored aspirations that Taiwan could chart a more independent course. Taiwanese society would struggle throughout the decade with the grievances stoked by the minority rule of *Waishengren* (mainland Chinese transplants), who accounted for approximately three in twenty residents. The claims put forward by the dictatorial KMT to represent greater China sounded ever more foolish in the early 1980s. President Chiang had long ago accepted that his father's dream of retaking the mainland was dead. Deng's concession that Beijing would only reunify the two territories by force of arms under extreme circumstances, most notably a Taiwanese declaration of independence, had been a welcome change. The question for pro-unification Chinese across the Taiwan straits had therefore become whether their two social systems could coexist or even converge successfully enough for Taipei to accept Beijing's preeminence.

Communist Chinese and Taiwanese propaganda reflected this ambivalence. When Reagan took office, Chiang cast his country as "a model province whose example [would] someday inspire the people of mainland China to overthrow Communist rule."[41] By the same token, Deng characterized the Taiwanese economic miracle as a model for his reforms and the Chinese diaspora as a vital source of financial and human capital with which to rebuild the Middle Kingdom.[42] While cross-strait talks were a non-starter, Taipei's acquiescence to indirect trade via Hong Kong amounted to a lucrative firewall around commerce, with flows of capital and goods growing from $320 million in 1980 to around $9 billion by mid-1992, by which point Taiwan manufacturers would bankroll 5,517 enterprises in south China to the tune of $4.75 billion.[43]

The initial tensions in Reagan's East Asia trade policy centered on arms sales.[44] From early on, the US Congress and the executive branch wrestled with how to react to a rapidly changing East Asia without abandoning the Taiwan Relations Act. In the early summer of 1981, the House Subcommittee on Asian and Pacific Affairs met eight times to discuss numerous topics: political and human rights in China and Taiwan, Deng's reform campaign, the military balance, arms sales, and the strategic implications of more harmonious US-PRC relations.[45] The issues covered included the nascent Taiwanese independence movement, martial law under the KMT, democracy movements, textile dumping, and Soviet power in the Far East. The likelihood of peaceful reunification loomed over proceedings. The last US ambassador to the Republic of China, Leonard Unger, spoke for many when he asserted that mainland reforms would have to "continue in the same direction, that is, an opening up of both the political and the economic processes. I can imagine that over time there would be a mutually acceptable arrangement. But I certainly would not see it today, or anytime soon." What he meant by "anytime soon" was left unsaid.[46]

Deng had made four points to Stevens and Chennault in Beijing. First, however much China remained "a weak and poor country," the size of its territory and population made "self-reliance" a strategic option. Second, openness to foreign influences would not proceed at the expense of the historic claims of the Chinese nation. Third, and relatedly, Taiwan was part of historic China. Lastly, the CCP forswore communist expansion beyond the borders claimed by the Qing dynasty. This last point was not a major concession—the CCP had distanced itself from wars of national liberation since Saigon's fall in 1975. By the same token, the *People's Daily*'s attacks on Dutch submarine sales to Taiwan represented shots across the bow of the United States in a context of conservative attacks on Deng's reform and opening up.[47] Hardline Politburo members were mounting a rearguard defense of Marxist-Leninist liturgy in universities and attacking Special Economic Zones in Shenzhen, Zhuhai, Shantou, and Xiamen. In this context, Deng risked an elite revolt if US arms sales to Taiwan went forward.[48]

The Soviet menace therefore clarified rather than drove US-PRC rapprochement. For all the Kremlin's meddling in Afghanistan or Cambodia or the Red Fleet's expansion in the Pacific Ocean, Reagan's foremost ambition was the global spread of electoral capitalism. When his administration finalized its strategic blueprint, National Security Decision Directive (NSDD) 32, on May 20, 1982, it listed eleven objectives. The first six involved deterring, containing, neutralizing, restraining, or reversing Soviet influence. Communism went unmentioned. Instead, NSDD-32's last five objectives painted a positive vision for US global strategy: to preserve access to foreign markets, in particular "energy and mineral resources;" to keep open "space and the oceans;" to regulate nuclear technology under the 1968 Nuclear Non-Proliferation Treaty (NPT); to seed capitalism, human rights, and the rule of law throughout the "Third World" with the tools provided by "aid, trade, and investment;" and to support a rule-based international trade and investment regime.[49]

The arms sales question set these two sets of strategic ends at odds. White House plans to arm Taiwan with advanced F-5G fighters that Northrop and McDonnell-Douglas had developed in line with Carter's embargo of more advanced fighter jets competed with US State Department efforts to sell the PRC hitherto-restricted military equipment. Secretary Haig, who had been present when Kissinger "opened" communist China, claimed that Beijing was key to a favorable balance of power versus the Soviet bloc. He therefore made the People's Republic his first trip abroad, bypassing allied Tokyo en route to Beijing. Then Haig buried the F-5G sale in red tape. His efforts yielded dividends on September 22, 1981, when the National Security Council (NSC) approved "case-by-case" munition and arms transfers to the PRC, only for Haig's unilateral expansion to all "defensive" weapons a few weeks later to induce the White House to publicly contradict the secretary of state.[50]

The Taiwan Relations Act directed the executive branch to treat "any attempt to resolve the Taiwan issue by other than peaceful means" as a direct threat to peace. It would continue to furnish the island in consultation with Congress and the Pentagon the weapons sufficient for its defense.[51] In a bid to overturn this state of affairs, Zhao unveiled a nine-point plan to Reagan in October 1981 in which Taipei would retain local autonomy under Beijing's rule. According to the PRC's new premier, this early presentation of "one country, two systems" would render the Taiwan Relations Act null and void.[52] In the absence of the KMT's acceptance of the CCP's terms, however, the legal and political cases for ending the arms sales were not compelling, and ensuing mid-level talks languished as a result. In May, President Reagan sent Vice President Bush to Beijing to inform Deng that he rejected a hard cut-off date. Reagan then softened the blow by publicizing letters to Deng, Zhao, and Hu that promised to peg the quality and quantity of arms transfers to the intensity of cross-strait tensions.

Congressional friends of Taiwan had now trained their sights on Haig, however. Arizona Senator Barry Goldwater, Reagan's earliest political mentor, was in high dungeon on June 18, 1982, after an administration official leaked to the Washington Post that Haig had informed Beijing in December that Taiwan would receive obsolescing F-5Es rather than modernized F-5Gs. Goldwater handed his list of one dozen grievances to a sympathetic audience; Reagan had already castigated the "China Lobby" in the US State Department in his diary twice that year.[53] Haig's ensuing push to decouple US-Taiwan arms sales from the state of play in the Taiwan Straits was the final straw. The secretary of state had a habit of submitting a resignation letter whenever he felt outflanked. When he did so on July 5, 1982, Reagan chose to accept. In his memoirs Haig named "the China question" as the leading cause of his break with the president.[54]

Haig's resignation did not resolve the arms sales bind; it would take considerable finesse to avert a major setback to US-PRC relations. The 1972 Shanghai Communiqué and the 1979 Joint Communiqué on the Establishment of Diplomatic Relations had been silent on the matter, which necessitated some form of reciprocal public action that recognized common principles without crossing any redlines. Pro-Taiwan voices in the US Congress ruled out a formal treaty. The United States–China Joint Communiqué on United States Arms Sales accordingly reaffirmed the principles of sovereignty, territorial integrity, and noninterference on August 17, along with US recognition of "one China." It went on to limit the level of arms sales to Taiwan, qualitatively and quantitatively, to that which had obtained since normalization in 1979.[55] Reagan caught flack for reversing a key feature of his anti-détente crusade in the 1970s and felt insulted by charges that the joint communiqué amounted to "a betrayal of Taiwan." While his insistence that Beijing had in fact "made all the concessions" was at best wishful, six corollary statements that he issued on the occasion made clear that any alteration of arms sales would be contingent on a peaceful resolution to the relationship between the two states. For the rest of his presidency, Reagan strictly observed the Taiwan Relations Act, refusing any end date on arms sales, eschewing consultations with Beijing about them, refraining from mediation, respecting Taipei's attitude, and guaranteeing its self-determination.⁵⁶ President Chiang may have had some foreknowledge of the six assurances when James R. Lilley, the director of the American Institute in Taiwan, briefed him on the so-called Third Communiqué on July 14. Regardless of whether they were purely an American initiative or the product of the Taiwan lobby in Washington, DC, the timing suggested they had been a proximate cause of Haig's resignation nine days earlier.⁵⁷

Just as the Third Communiqué smoothed over the largest cracks in their relationship, Beijing and Washington's strategic outlooks began to diverge. In a conciliatory speech on March 23, 1982, Soviet Premier Leonid Brezhnev spoke favorably of negotiating Sino-Soviet border issues while building the trust necessary to end their mutual military buildup. Although the Chinese response sounded dismissive, Brezhnev's outreach induced a rethinking of Soviet policy in the CCP Politburo, culminating in a speech by Hu Yaobang to the Twelfth Party Congress in September, when the foreign minister asserted that "international circumstances" would henceforth dictate how Beijing dealt with Moscow and Washington's "hegemonism," effectively opening the door for Sino-Soviet rapprochement.⁵⁸ With the Taiwan issue shelved for now and PRC foreign policy exhibiting newfound flexibility, Deng's thirst for Western technology and rich-world hunger for China's continent-sized market (and boundless cheap labor) remained the Sino-American relationship's central pillars.

Shultz brought a different temperament, outlook, and skillset to the US State Department. While he did not share Haig's conviction that Beijing was key to checking Moscow strategically, the former student of the libertarian economist Milton Friedman, president of California-based Bechtel Corporation, and US treasury secretary appreciated the economic transformation then unfolding in East Asia. When Shultz made his first visit to the PRC and the Far East in February 1982, the *Economist* noted how, in contrast to Kissinger and Haig, it was international finance rather than geopolitics that he knew "inside and out." The financial weekly concluded that US foreign policy was likely to grow "more sensitive towards third-world bankruptcies and the accompanying threats to the international banking system." In truth, Shultz's deepest commitment was to the power of market forces, given sufficient time, to liberate individual genius in even the most illiberal of societies.⁵⁹

Technology and knowledge transfers thus became the new hallmarks of US-PRC affairs. On January 18, 1983, Reagan signed NSDD-76, which authorized peaceful nuclear cooperation with the PRC on three conditions: high-level nonproliferation pledges, controls on nuclear exports (mainly International Atomic Energy Agency safeguards on those to nonnuclear-weapon states), and bilateral safeguards for US-supplied technology.⁶⁰ Notwithstanding their reputation as free-market fundamentalists, Reagan and Shultz endorsed regulatory regimes that established a level playing field in global markets, particularly when they bolstered US military prerogatives, as in the case of the global nuclear nonproliferation regime.[61] While they had concerns about Chinese nuclear assistance to Pakistan and Iran, the Pentagon's interest in reclassifying the PRC as a friendly, nonaligned country rather than as a potential adversary—a matter in which military contractors had a considerable stake—bore fruit when Commerce Secretary Malcolm Baldrige traveled to Beijing in May with word that Reagan had authorized the reclassification of US export controls on the country. Communist China's upgrading expanded the types of advanced electronics and telecommunications equipment that Beijing could purchase, even if, over the next five years, the exceptions would prove so frequent that the PRC would be treated more like Romania or Poland than like France or West Germany.[62]

Nuclear exports were a tougher nut to crack. There was considerable interest among US-based industrial firms with large nuclear operations, namely Westinghouse and General Electric, to compete with Japanese and West European rivals to build reactors in a massive, developing market, all the more in light of the domestic fallout from the Third Mile Island accident in March 1979.[63] Shultz encountered this entrepreneurial exuberance on his first trip to Beijing in February 1983, when he met with US corporate salesmen, including those of Westinghouse, who were eager to obtain a license to sell nuclear power plants there despite Beijing's missing signature on the NPT. Their lack of fidelity to US national policy exasperated Shultz: "The question carries the implication, as most of your questions do, that there is something wrong with the United States. Our regulations are based on a deep concern about the problems of proliferation of nuclear weapons technology. That is a legitimate problem. The question suggests in a rather cavalier fashion that you brush it off. I don't brush it off." Their common knowledge that Chinese microphones were recording their conversation led the secretary of state to conclude that "some of the businessmen were trying to make points that would ingratiate themselves with the Chinese authorities." The experience left him "with a sour taste" in his mouth because it summed up the dilemma at the heart of the bilateral relationship: Could Washington harness the Promethean forces of global capitalism without losing control over an global order that sought, among other matters, to restrict the atomic franchise to responsible stakeholders?[64]

Ultimately, Washington moved to harmonize China's status in the liberal international order. The two sides continued an itinerary of reciprocated high-level visits through the end of Reagan's presidency. Shultz's first visit had been preceded by PRC Foreign Minister Huang Hua in October, as bilateral relations attained a one-step-backward-two-steps-forward rhythm. Two weeks after Huang's visit to the United States, the People's Liberation Army announced it had successfully fired a sub-launched ballistic missile. Two weeks before Shultz landed in Beijing, the PRC declared it would ban cotton, soybeans, and chemical fibers purchases from the United States in protest against US restrictions on low-cost Chinese textiles. Then, on March 1, Beijing and Moscow resumed bilateral contacts after a three-year hiatus. Shultz would later credit Secretary Baldrige's visit as the moment when momentum shifted, with Beijing inviting Secretary of Defense Caspar Weinberger to visit China in late September, with PRC Foreign Minister Wu Xueqian to reciprocate one month later. At an NSC meeting on September 20, 1983, Shultz observed that they had "made quite a bit of headway in . . . relations with China in the last year," noting that the state of their relations was "in reasonably good shape." He ended with plaudits for Deng's reform campaign: "The Chinese have taken a number of steps in the economic area which we would like to encourage. They are experimenting with the rudiments of a market system. They have also introduced private incentives into the communes and into industry."[65]

Weinberger's and Wu's visits set the stage of the presidential visit to communist China in April. Zhao Ziyang called on Reagan in Washington in January 1984 to iron out nuclear exports beforehand. Much had changed since the two heads of state had met in Cancun two years earlier, when Zhao's proposal of "one country, two systems" failed to resolve the arms sales dispute over Taiwan. His words of "friendship" between the two countries at a formal White House dinner on January 10 marked Reagan's evolution from heaping scorn on Carter's normalization of US-PRC relations to its torchbearer. The remainder of his remarks made clear that the reform campaign and US investments in its promised returns were the root cause. Zhao's introduction of market-oriented reforms in Sichuan after 1975 had turned the poor, populous province into China's breadbasket. Upon his return to Beijing in 1979, the "Sichuan experience" had served as a model for reforms elsewhere, a record that Reagan applauded in his toast to the premier's "efforts to modernize by offering incentives to your people in stimulating economic competition." After noting that the Taiwan issue remained "the principal obstacle" to further headway, Zhao's return toast signaled that China's longstanding opposition to the NPT as an unequal treaty had softened: "We do not engage in nuclear proliferation ourselves, nor do we help other countries develop nuclear weapons."[66]

While a Chinese representative would not sign the NPT for another thirteen years, Reagan and Zhao would go on to sign a nuclear power agreement in the Great Hall on April 30, clearing the way for representatives of the US nuclear-power industry to bid on as many as twelve new nuclear power plants there. Afterward, Reagan took a tour of the Shanghai-Foxboro Company facility, the first high-technology joint venture between a US company and the Chinese government, before returning to his accommodations in the massive new Great Wall Hotel, for whose mirrorlike exterior the Hyatt Regency in Dallas had been the model. Back in Washington, DC, a few months later, Reagan sat down with the representatives of Allied/Bendix, Boeing, General Electric, Lockheed, Loral, McDonnell Douglas, Martin Marietta, RCA, Rockwell International, and Textron traveling with the China trade commission to explore the market for civilian aviation purchases on the Chinese mainland.[67] Leading the trans-Pacific mission were White House Assistant for Cabinet Affairs Craig L. Fuller, Deputy Under Secretary of Commerce for International Trade Olin Wethington, Assistant Secretary of Commerce for Trade Development H. P. Goldfield, and the vice president of Reagan's Export Council, Anna Chennault.[68]

Shultz would profess in his memoirs that neither he nor Reagan had held any "illusions about China," yet both assumed free enterprise would in time sweep all before it. He ended his chapter on US-China relations on a breathless note: "As the Chinese are increasingly set free, their accomplishments could be spectacular."[69] For all his complaints about profit-loyal American businessmen in Beijing, Shultz would benefit financially from the gold rush set off by visions of greater China. He joined Bechtel Corporation's board of directors after leaving government at the end of Reagan's second administration in 1989. Three years later, the company won a $16 billion contract to build the world's longest suspension bridge, a harbor tunnel, a rail network, and Hong Kong International Airport—the world's "gateway" to mainland China, the main hub for Cathay Pacific, and the world's busiest entrepôt for logistic firms such as FedEx.[70]

For his part, Reagan grew ever more optimistic about the PRC over the course of his presidency. Taiwan and arms sales dominated the relevant diary entries in 1981. After Foreign Minister Huang tried to dictate terms on Taiwan on October 29, the president tersely noted, "I don't like ultimatums."[71] Five years later, a meeting with Chinese Vice Premier Yao Yilin yielded no such fireworks: "Our relationship with China seems to be on solid ground & they continue to swing more & more to a free mkt e[t]c."[72] While ballistic-missile sales in the Middle East and the China National Space Administration's low-cost, commercial-satellite launches would cause trouble toward the end of his presidency, the White House increasingly let the private sector set the agenda in East Asia as the climate in US-Soviet affairs warmed. Reagan's native

California was uniquely situated to reap the windfalls of the new Pacific economy. Under Mayor Tom Bradley, who served five sequential terms from 1973 to 1993, Los Angeles, America's second-largest city, built new ports and Los Angeles International Airport (LAX) with a view to becoming "the new command center of the California and Pacific Rim economies, the 'headquarters of the 21st century,'" regardless of how hard the end of the Cold War hit the region's world-leading aerospace firms.[73]

The 1984 peaceful nuclear cooperative agreement paved the way for the United States to become the leading foreign investor in the PRC. And for however much US, Japanese, Taiwanese, and West European businesses coveted the mythical China market, the Chinese were just as aware of what a large share of the enormous US consumer market their bargain-basement manufactures could capture.[74] South of San Francisco, Apple Computers would close its Fremont-based assembly lines by 1992. While Silicon Valley had long ago started offshoring its semiconductor packaging, first to Japan, then to South Korea and Taiwan, today boxes of Apple's iconic iPhone all feature the label "Designed by Apple in California. Assembled in China."[75]

Taiwan did not trail far behind the United States or Japan in mainland investments—a development that led one scholar to figure that "on a per capita basis, Taiwan has sent more capital to China than has any other country." Taipei's rise as an exporter of value-added goods and capital eased misgivings about its post-1979 isolation. By the end of the 1980s, Taipei had removed capital controls on investments bound for the PRC. Labor-intensive businesses in Taiwan—notably, textiles, clothing, footwear, and cheap consumer electronics—moved en masse to south China, while at the same time massive flows of capital transited from Taiwan via Hong Kong and other British territories to the mainland. According to some estimates, between 1991 and 2000 nearly two-thirds of Taiwanese foreign investment found its way to communist China.[76]

The Joint Sino-British Declaration on December 19, 1984, preserved Hong Kong as a regional financial hub under "one country, two systems," turning the British colony into a laboratory for relations across the Taiwan Straits. Its early success also calmed the nerves of entrepreneurs and capitalists. As Jennifer Miller explains in her chapter in this volume, Tokyo's growing economic sway discomfited American elites who remained skeptical of corporatist planning yet keen to compete in the world's fastest-developing markets. In the 1980s, the promise of an open door to "greater China" enchanted Washington politicians, New York bankers, and Silicon Valley technologists, who collectively believed that the corporatization of the PRC's state-owned enterprises had validated their free-market views of the world.[77]

Chennault proved more loyal to herself and her Chinese self-identity than to either Taiwan or the United States. Her greatest source of frustration with the Republican Party was not its failure to welcome Chinese-Americans, "the minority of the minorities," as political equals.[78] Her service on Reagan's Export Council, the Republican National Heritage Council, and Chinese Americans for the Reagan-Bush Campaign, not to mention her tireless organizing and fundraising, never netted her the presidential appointment that she considered her due. Beijing's reform and opening up generated exuberance, at times irrational, in the fabled riches of the China market. When Northrop's board despaired as to whether it would ever find a buyer for the F-5G (rechristened the F-20 Tigershark), Chennault suggested that if stymied in Taipei, they might approach Beijing: "Northrop has been a friend to Taiwan, R.O.C. for over three decades.... However, the time has come that we as a company can no more ignore the PRC['s] existence and her relationship with the United States."[79] American aerospace firms envisioned big profits in greater China, with Boeing, the country's largest exporter by dollar value, seizing a head start when it inked a deal for ten Boeing 707s three weeks after Kissinger and Nixon drank tea with Mao. From 1980 to 1989, the Civil Aviation Administration of China ordered an additional thirty-five Boeing 737s, thirty-three Boeing 757s, and ten Boeing 767s, and, in 1990, it placed an order with Seattle-based firm for another thirty-six airplanes with a reported total value of $9 billion. In Shaanxi Province, where the Reagans overpaid for knick-knacks back in 1984, Xian Aircraft was poised to receive some of that windfall, thanks to the PRC's insistence in contracts with Boeing and its European rival, Airbus, on offset agreements requiring direct or indirect technology transfers to Chinese startups.[80]

The region's ideological momentum reversed polarity in the 1980s. Where the Chinese revolution had inspired fears of toppling dominoes from 1949 to 1975, the rise of the Asian Tigers implied that history was back on capitalism's side. While Deng's reform agenda was neither universally loved within the ranks of the CCP nor without its setbacks, its survival heightened Western investment in its success. The working assumption was that China, Hong Kong, and Taiwan would prioritize economic growth by means of trade, industrialization, and technology transfers, climbing up the value chain from agriculture to light industry and eventually information-age electronics. The Taiwan Straits began to look less like a Cold War flashpoint and more like a conduit for ideas, trade, and capital. Until the Tiananmen massacre, some even expressed hope that Beijing would match Hong Kong and Taipei's moves toward democracy. Afterward, major exporters like Boeing continued to lobby to extend and even make permanent China's most-favored-nation status in the face of protests over human rights and democracy. On December 11, 2001, such efforts to welcome the communist state into the World Trade Organization bore fruit, inaugurating an era in which "Made in China" consumer goods would fill bargain bins even as US-based exporters signed offset agreements with Chinese firms that would contribute to the siphoning of jobs and technology off US shores.

The removal of barriers to foreign entry in China, however gradual or limited, fitted the dispensation then ascendant in the United States that sought to transfer government functions to private interests even as it encased vital markets from democratic interference.[81] Throughout the 1980s, it looked as if China would pour out wealth without jeopardizing Washington's status as the chief guarantor of global order. If all went as planned, Beijing, Hong Kong, and Taipei would each be too busy making money together to rock the boat. What did it matter, then, if there were one or many Chinas, as long as everyone grew ever more richly embedded within the global free market?

Notes

1. Reagan diary, 26 Apr. 1984, https://www.reaganfoundation.org/ronald-reagan/white-house-diaries/diary-entry-04261984/.
2. Reagan diary, 28 Apr. 1984, https://www.reaganfoundation.org/ronald-reagan/white-house-diaries/diary-entry-04281984/.
3. Ezra F. Vogel, *Deng Xiaoping and the Transformation of China* (Cambridge, MA: Belknap Press of Harvard University Press, 2011), 217–373; David L. Shambaugh, *The Making of a Premier: Zhao Ziyang's Provincial Career* (New York: Routledge, 2019).
4. Reagan diary, 29 Apr. 1984, https://www.reaganfoundation.org/ronald-reagan/white-house-diaries/diary-entry-04291984/.
5. Hedrick Smith, "Reagan, in US, Says China Trip Advanced Ties," *New York Times*, 2 May 1984.
6. George P. Shultz, *Turmoil and Triumph: My Years as Secretary of State* (New York: Scribner, 1993), 396.
7. Joanne Cutler, Kevin Chow, Carrie Chan, and Unias I, "Intra-Regional Trade and the Role of Mainland China," *Hong Kong Monetary Authority Quarterly Bulletin*, no. 41 (Dec. 2004): 5–24.
8. Kishore Mahbubani, *The Great Convergence: Asia, the West, and the Logic of One World* (New York: PublicAffairs, 2013); For an account of how Reagan broke ranks with the many neoconservatives among his backers, see James Mann, *The Rebellion of Ronald Reagan: A History of the End of the Cold War* (New York: Viking, 2009); Michael P. Riccards, *The Presidency and the Middle Kingdom: China, the United States, and Executive Leadership* (Lanham, MD: Lexington Books, 2000), 202–208.
9. Michael J. Green, *By More than Providence: Grand Strategy and American Power in the Asia Pacific since 1783* (New York: Columbia University Press, 2017); James Mann,

About Face: A History of America's Curious Relationship with China, from Nixon to Clinton (New York: Vintage, 2000).

10. Julian Gewirtz, *Unlikely Partners: Chinese Reformers, Western Economists, and the Making of Global China* (Cambridge, MA: Harvard University Press, 2017).

11. Michael Schaller, "Ronald Reagan and the Puzzles of 'So-Called Communist China' and Vietnam," in *Reagan and the World: Leadership and National Security, 1981–1989*, ed. Bradley Lynn Coleman and Kyle Longley (Lexington: University Press of Kentucky, 2017).

12. David L. Shambaugh, ed., *Greater China: The Next Superpower?* (New York: Oxford University Press, 1995).

13. Harry Harding, *A Fragile Relationship: The United States and China since 1972* (Washington, DC: Brookings Institution Press, 1992), 100.

14. Donnie Radcliffe, "Return Engagement," *Washington Post*, 14 Jan. 1981.

15. Clare Crawford-Mason, "No Longer Breathing Fire, 'Dragon Lady' Anna Chennault Adopts a Two China Policy," *People Magazine*, 26 Jan. 1981, https://people.com/archive/no-longer-breathing-fire-dragon-lady-anna-chennault-adopts-a-two-china-policy-vol-15-no-3/.

16. Takashi Oka, "Deng Plan to Woo Taipei Gets a Boost from Key Member of Taiwan Lobby," *Christian Science Monitor*, 5 Jan. 1981; Catherine Forslund, *Anna Chennault: Informal Diplomacy and Asian Relations* (Wilmington, DE: SR Books, 2002).

17. Chennault to Bush, "China Mission," 21 Nov. 1980, Arthur and Elizabeth Schlesinger Library on the History of Women in America (AESL), Anna Chennault Papers (ACP), box 43.

18. Chennault to Bush, "Appointment," 21 Nov. 1980, AESL, ACP, box 43.

19. Cass Peterson, "Kissinger, Chennault Trips Are Cockleburs for Reagan Advisers," *Washington Post*, 7 Jan. 1981; Michael Weisskopf, "Senator Will Not Rule Out Sale of US Weapons to China," *Washington Post*, 4 Jan. 1981.

20. Fox Butterfield, "New Views Hinted by Anna Chennault," *New York Times*, 5 Jan. 1981; Crawford-Mason, "No Longer Breathing Fire"; "A Native Critic Returns," *Washington Post*, 5 Jan. 1981.

21. Forslund, *Anna Chennault*, 133.

22. Vogel, *Deng Xiaoping*, 654–655; Xiaoping Deng, *Selected Works of Deng Xiaoping, 1975–1982* (Beijing: Foreign Languages Press, 1984), 371–372.

23. Donnie Radcliffe, "The Transformation of Anna Chennault," *Washington Post*, 15 Feb. 1981.

24. Weisskopf, "Senator Will Not Rule Out Sale of US Weapons to China."

25. Oka, "Deng Plan to Woo Taipei Gets a Boost."

26. Raymond Wilkinson, "A Sentimental Journey," United Press International, 4 Jan. 1981.

27. "Deng Xiaoping and the Four Modernisation Slogan: The Untold Story," *The Correspondent* 2, no. 3 (1989): 13.

28. Meese to Chennault, "PRC and Taiwan Reports," 4 Feb. 1981, AESL, ACP, box 43; Helms to Chennault, "PRC/ROC Report," 22 Jan. 1981, AESL, ACP, box 45.

29. Corcoran to Reagan, "Anna Chennault," 11 Feb. 1981, AESL, ACP, box 43. Emphasis in the original.

30. Chennault to Hannan, "March Consultant Report," Mar. 1981, AESL, ACP, box 61; Chennault, "Report of January 1981, to Northrop Corp.," AESL, ACP, box 64.

31. Chennault to Jordan, "The Asian Market," April 15, 1986, AESL, ACP, box 57.
32. "Mrs. Chennault Meets a Second Time with Taiwan President," Associated Press, 7 Jan. 1981; "Denies Discussing Airline Operation with Peking," Associated Press, 8 Jan. 1981; Chennault to Stokes, "Trip to Beijing," 29 Jan. 1981, AESL, ACP, box 43.
33. Forslund, *Anna Chennault*, 137.
34. Chennault, "Report of December 1980," AESL, ACP, box 64.
35. Lung-chu Chen, *The US-Taiwan-China Relationship in International Law and Policy* (New York: Oxford University Press, 2016), 135.
36. CIA, "Political Constraints on China's Economic Reforms," Feb. 1981, CIA Electronic Reading Room (CIAERR).
37. Julia Lovell, *Maoism: A Global History* (New York: Alfred A. Knopf, 2019).
38. CIA, "Political Constraints."
39. CIA, "Deng Xiaoping and the Taiwan Question," 27 Mar. 1981, CIAERR.
40. CIA, "Political Constraints."
41. CIA, "Taiwan: Midterm Prospects," Feb. 1981, CIAERR.
42. Nancy Bernkopf Tucker, "Dangerous Strait: Introduction," in *Dangerous Strait: The US-Taiwan-China Crisis*, ed. Nancy Bernkopf Tucker (New York: Columbia University Press, 2008), 1–15.
43. CIA, "Taiwan: Midterm Prospects"; Nancy Bernkopf Tucker, *Taiwan, Hong Kong, and the United States, 1945–1992: Uncertain Friendships* (New York: Maxwell Macmillan International, 1994), 161.
44. "Dinner in Honor of Mr. and Mrs. Wang Guang Ying—Guest List," 28 June 1985, AESL, ACP, box 50.
45. "The New Era in East Asia," 19 May–16 July 1981, Hearings before the Subcommittee on Asian and Pacific Affairs of the Committee on Foreign Affairs, United States House of Representatives, 97th Congress, 1st Session (Washington, DC: US Government Printing Office, 1981).
46. "The New Era in East Asia," 9.
47. Deng Xiapiong, "Our Principled Position on the Development of Sino-US Relations," *Selected Works of Deng Xiaopoing*, https://archive.org/stream/SelectedWorksOfDengXiaopingVol.1/Deng02_djvu.txt.
48. CIA, "Warning Assessment: East Asia," 28 Jan. 1981, CIAERR.
49. National Security Decision Directive 32, "US National Security Strategy," 20 May 1982, https://fas.org/irp/offdocs/nsdd/nsdd-32.pdf.
50. Green, *By More than Providence*, 395–396.
51. Quoted in Dennis Van Vranken Hickey, "The Taiwan Relations Act: A Mid-Life Crisis at 35?," Woodrow Wilson International Center for Scholars, Policy Brief, Mar. 2014, https://www.wilsoncenter.org/publication/the-taiwan-relations-act-mid-life-crisis-35.
52. Harding, *A Fragile Relationship*, 113.
53. Reagan diary, 11 Jan. 1982, https://www.reaganfoundation.org/ronald-reagan/white-house-diaries/diary-entry-01111982/.
54. Alexander Haig, *Caveat: Realism, Reagan, and Foreign Policy* (New York: Macmillan, 1984), 195.
55. "United States–China Joint Communiqué on United States Arms Sales to Taiwan," 17 Aug. 1982, in Harding, *A Fragile Relationship*, 383–384.

56. "Statement of President Reagan on United States Arms Sales to Taiwan," in Harding, *A Fragile Relationship*, 385–386.

57. Harvey Feldman, "Taiwan, Arms Sales and the Reagan Assurances," *American Asian Review* 19, no. 3 (2001): 75–101.

58. Sergey Radchenko, *Unwanted Visionaries: The Soviet Failure in Asia at the End of the Cold War* (New York: Oxford University Press, 2014), 10.

59. "A Manager for All Seasons." *Economist*, 12 Feb. 1983.

60. National Security Decision Directive 76, "Peaceful Nuclear Cooperation with China," 18 Jan. 1983, https://fas.org/irp/offdocs/nsdd/nsdd-76.pdf.

61. Francis J. Gavin, "Strategies of Inhibition: US Grand Strategy, the Nuclear Revolution, and Nonproliferation," *International Security* 40, no. 1 (2015): 9–46.

62. Shultz, *Turmoil and Triumph*, 142; Benjamin H. Flowe Jr., "Export Licensing of Computer Equipment and Technology—A Practitioner's Perspective," *North Carolina Journal of International Law and Commercial Regulation* 10, no. 3 (1985): 645n62.

63. Natasha Zaretsky, *Radiation Nation: Three Mile Island and the Political Transformation of the 1970s* (New York: Columbia University Press, 2018); J. Samuel Walker, *Three Mile Island: A Nuclear Crisis in Historical Perspective* (Berkeley: University of California Press, 2004).

64. Shultz, *Turmoil and Triumph*, 390–391.

65. NSC meeting, "Review of US-China Relations," 30 Sept. 1983, Ronald Reagan Presidential Library, David Laux Papers, box 14.

66. "Toasts of the President and Premier Zhao Ziyang of China at the State Dinner," 10 Jan. 1984, https://www.reaganlibrary.gov/research/speeches/11084d.

67. Reagan diary, 18 July 1984, https://www.reaganfoundation.org/ronald-reagan/white-house-diaries/diary-entry-07181984/.

68. "Statement by the Principal Deputy Press Secretary," 18 July 1984, AESL, ACP, box 78.

69. Shultz, *Turmoil and Triumph*, 399.

70. Tucker, *Taiwan, Hong Kong, and the United States*, 224.

71. Reagan diary, 29 Oct. 1981, https://www.reaganfoundation.org/ronald-reagan/white-house-diaries/diary-entry-10291981/.

72. Reagan diary, 15 Mar. 1986, https://www.reaganfoundation.org/ronald-reagan/white-house-diaries/diary-entry-05151986/.

73. Mike Davis, *City of Quartz: Excavating the Future in Los Angeles* (New York: Verso, 2006), 11.

74. Warren I. Cohen, *America's Response to China: An Interpretative History of Sino-American Relations* (New York: Wiley, 1971), 229–230.

75. Margaret Pugh O'Mara, *The Code: Silicon Valley and the Remaking of America* (New York: Penguin, 2019), 264; John Markoff, "Past Tense: Apple Computers Used to Be Built in the US: It Was a Mess," *New York Times*, 15 Dec. 2018.

76. T. J. Cheng, "China-Taiwan Economic Linkage: Between Insulation and Superconductivity," in in *Dangerous Strait: The US-Taiwan-China Crisis*, ed. Nancy Bernkopf Tucker (New York: Columbia University Press, 2008).

77. For the distinction between "privatization" and "corporatization" in China's new stock markets, see Carl E. Walter and Fraser J. T. Howie, *"To Get Rich Is Glorious!": China's Stock Markets in the '80s and '90s* (Basingstoke, UK: Palgrave, 2001), xiv.

78. Anna Chennault, "Chinese American Heritage," *Asian Week*, 24 Aug. 1984.

79. Chennault to Ebner, "The F-20," 19 May 1986, AESL, ACP, box 64.

80. Stanley Holmes, "How Boeing Woos Beijing," *Seattle Times*, 26 May 1996; Neil Thomas, "For Company and for Country: Boeing and US-China Relations," Macro Polo: Decoding China's Economic Arrival, 26 Feb. 2019, https://macropolo.org/analysis/boeing-us-china-relations-history/.

81. Quinn Slobodian, *Globalists: The End of Empire and the Birth of Neoliberalism* (Cambridge, MA: Harvard University Press, 2018).

Conclusion

Reagan Reconsidered

SIMON MILES

On December 6, 1986, without knowing it, the weekly televised sketch show *Saturday Night Live* broke new historiographical ground. In a skit entitled "President Reagan, Mastermind," the Canadian-born actor Phil Hartman showed a different side to the fortieth president than most in the United States saw—or believed they saw. Hartman's Reagan knew the details of covert flight times and arms shipment manifestos, did mental math on exchange and interest rates in third countries laundering secret US government funds, brokered deals in fluent Arabic and German, quoted Montesquieu, introduced Chief of Staff Don Regan to the word processor, and even had his picture taken with the top seller of Girl Scout cookies—"the part of the job I hate."[1] This was a very different Reagan from that perceived by Hartman's fellow countryman, Canadian Prime Minister Pierre Elliott Trudeau, who considered the US president a simpleton, intellectually unequal to the office he occupied. His "profound ignorance ... was a depressant."[2] Unbeknownst to the *SNL* writers' room, live from New York, "Reagan revisionism" was born—before its subject was even out of office.

The preceding chapters illustrate the value and importance of taking a fresh look at the Reagan administration, with both the benefit of distance and increasing access to archival materials. The assumptions of Trudeau—and many others—who considered the president to be out of his depth in the Oval Office have been displaced by more balanced appraisals. In fact, the pendulum has swung so far back from the initial disdain that even one of his most sympathetic biographers worries about the coopting of his legacy by "the media-academic complex."[3]

Regardless of whether he has been portrayed as a dunce who brought the world to the brink of Armageddon or as the Cold War's conquering hero, the chapters in this book show that Reagan's role in the world, and that of the nation he led, defies caricature. The tensions and discrepancies—between good and ill, between success and failure, and indeed between right and wrong—are not unique to the Reagan administration, to be sure. But scholars of US foreign relations in the 1980s, as the authors of these chapters demonstrate, must grapple with these complexities and seeming inconsistencies.

The Cold War looms large in these accounts, but it varies widely across time and space. The early 1980s were a time of tension, most dramatically in transatlantic relations over the stationing of new US nuclear weapons in Europe and the fears of many thousands that this would lead to a nuclear war on the continent. At decade's end, by contrast, the perception of a Soviet threat had practically disappeared in the White House (even if not throughout official Washington) as Reagan and Mikhail Gorbachev looked beyond ideological differences and great-power rivalries to sign the agreement that removed those very same missiles. In Europe, that war never came, as strategic stability held, and the superpowers and their allies successfully and—for the most part—responsibly managed their complex relationships and kept the peace.

Elsewhere, however, war was a daily fact of life. In Africa, Asia, and Latin America, as the chapters in this volume illustrate, the human toll of that ideological and systemic conflict mounted apace, reaching almost unimaginable proportions. In "the Cold War's killing fields" the superpowers' policies often created the circumstances for violence, and it was all too often local populations who paid the price for the competition between Washington and Moscow.[4]

Reagan figures in all of these stories, for better and for worse. Of course, there is much that transformed international politics for which the fortieth president was not directly responsible. He did not, for example, invent the personal computer, which changed how business is done and how people around the world communicate; nor did he liberalize the economy of the People's Republic of China, which reshaped the global balance of power, both economically and, increasingly, militarily. But he did make some critical choices. It was Reagan who recast the US wars in Indochina in the public discourse and reframed how Americans saw their country's military capabilities and the use of force in a bid to put an end to the "Vietnam syndrome." But the specter of the Vietnam War still haunted the president, his advisors, and Americans, as it reared its head in Beirut, compelling policymakers to precipitously curtail the US military presence there after a suicide bomber attacked Marines on peacekeeping operations in Lebanon and to confine themselves to the use of force in the small Caribbean island of Grenada. The Reagan administration recognized that the power of the United States came not only from the might of its military or the nation's willingness to use force, but also from the strength of liberal ideas; for this administration, human rights were not just a soft-power consideration, but an integral part of the US arsenal. Similarly, the anticommunist tenor of US policies in Latin America and Afghanistan bore the hallmarks of Reagan's drive to quash that ideology. The near-miss with eliminating nuclear weapons between the United States and the Soviet Union at Reykjavík in late 1986 also illustrated the power of Reagan's conviction—even as it outpaced his advisers—to drive policy, albeit not quite as far as he might have hoped. Reagan and his ideas shaped many important aspects of international politics in the 1980s, to be sure, but sheer force of presidential will (and bureaucracy) alone could not overcome every obstacle.

Reagan's famous description of his Cold War grand strategy as "we win, they lose" is, as the authors in this volume demonstrate, not the whole story of US foreign policy under his administration.[5] Reagan wanted to end the Cold War, to be sure, but any observer comparing the situation in the United States to that in the Soviet Union after the Cold War had at last ended, after Reagan had left office, would likely agree that something akin to a US victory had in fact come to fruition, whether Reagan sought it or not. The means of organizing economies and societies that Reagan had espoused (even if he did not always practice what he preached) seemed on the march. Around the world, markets and political systems were becoming less regulated and more integrated. A quasi-autarkic, single-party state such as the Soviet Union found its room for maneuver shrinking over the course of the 1980s and, by the dawn of the 1990s, gone entirely.[6]

In the ten years following the disintegration of the Soviet Union in 1991, Russia faced near-constant turbulence. Beginning in 1992, Boris Yeltsin, the country's first post-Soviet president, implemented an economic program of "shock therapy" that caused the value of Russians' savings to plummet overnight. While the roots of this crisis lay in the Soviet era, Russian citizens blamed the leaders of the present, not the past. Disputes over economic policy escalated such that Yeltsin took the drastic step of ordering the Russian military to shell the country's own parliament in late 1993. Again, in 1998, yet another economic crisis rocked the country—and its citizens' savings.[7] No one was immune: the final general secretary of the Communist Party of the Soviet

Union was reduced to starring in Pizza Hut commercials just to make ends meet as the successive crashes of the 1990s left the Gorbachev family with savings equivalent to $2.00.[8]

Russia's current president does not want to revive the Soviet Union; but Vladimir Putin does want to restore Russia to the position of international influence the Soviet Union once enjoyed. Putin has made no secret of his dissatisfaction with—and disdain for—the so-called unipolar moment of unquestioned and unchallenged US supremacy that Reagan helped to usher in.[9] Before the Munich Security Conference in 2007, Putin famously denounced Washington's "unrestrained hyper-use of force," which, instead of solving problems, only created new ones and caused further suffering. "No one feels safe!" he declared.[10]

Others around the world have reason to look back on the foreign policy of the Reagan administration with regret, at least for its apparent consequences. Washington's activities in places such as Brazil, Chile, and Nicaragua, detailed in the previous chapters, along with other cases, all contributed to upheavals that have led thousands to seek safety and a better life to the north—as, of course, did Soviet and Cuban involvement. Today's stories unfolding on the southern border of the United States are in many ways the legacy of foreign interventions in Latin America over the course of the 1980s and the strife they provoked and perpetuated.[11] In Afghanistan, US policies designed to inflict maximum pain on the Soviet Union after Moscow's December 1979 intervention may not have created Vietnam War–like circumstances for the Kremlin, but it did contribute to the collapse of a functioning state in southwest Asia, which proved fertile ground for terrorist organizations such as al Qaeda after the Soviet Union finally withdrew in early 1989 and the Taliban took over half a decade later. The vision of the Stinger missile–armed mujahideen fighting the Soviet Army, which the Reagan administration invoked to build support for Operation Cyclone—the Central Intelligence Agency's program of support for the Afghan resistance fighters—may have been more fantasy than fact, but the image of what al Qaeda, thanks to its Afghan sanctuary, wrought some two decades later became a nightmare for Americans watching the collapsing World Trade Center. Since September 11, 2001, over 2.77 million US military personnel have served more than 5.4 million deployments around the world in the name of the Global War on Terror.[12]

If the threat of terrorism was not central to how the Reagan administration saw the world during the 1980s (the bombing of Pan Am flight 103 over Lockerbie, Scotland, on the orders of Libyan dictator Muammar Gaddafi notwithstanding), it is now at the forefront of policymakers' minds the world over. How the United States manages this threat, and particularly its reliance on intelligence services to conduct paramilitary—if not outright military—operations, is a legacy of policy choices made under Reagan. So, too, are the circumstances in which terror groups have flourished, and not just in Afghanistan. Reagan's staunch support for Israel, for example, created a permissive context for some of that country's politicians, especially in the then–newly formed Likud party, to use force in their neighborhood, be it in the south of Lebanon or against the Osirak nuclear reactor in Iraq. The fire of resentments stoked, or at least fanned, by US policy during the 1980s remains a feature of the Middle East today and a present and future challenge for the region's leaders and peoples.

Discontinuities also abound between the world as the Reagan administration left it and as it is today—and in some of Washington's most critical relationships. Beijing was Reagan's first communist destination as president when he visited in April 1984, and over the course of the decade, its economy began to look more and more like the economic system Reagan espoused as leaders like Deng Xiaoping concluded that measured market reforms offered the greatest promise, not only for national prosperity in an increasingly globalized world economy, but also for the endurance of communist rule in the People's Republic of China.[13] The United States was a key player in that process, which was made possible by liberal international trade regimes: US capital flowed into the country, and in exchange inexpensive manufactured goods flowed back. But these goods replaced many of those manufactured in the United States beforehand, and it was working-class Americans who lost their jobs to competitors overseas as a result. Because of that, the global architecture of free trade in which Reagan believed is no longer assumed to benefit the United States, with leaders on both sides of the aisle promising to "bring back our wealth" and put "America first" or to "buy American" and "work with allies to reduce their dependence on competitors like China."[14] The work of the Reagan administration to bring Beijing into the international market and put Sino-American relations on a new, improved footing is largely a thing of the past. Now, the White House's vision is more in line with how Americans saw Japan during the Reagan years, with proclamations that "the days of accepting unfair trade practices are over." Many of those practices now perceived as unfair nevertheless began under an earlier Republican president.[15]

The same can be said of US relations with its Western European allies, chiefly in the context of NATO, where tensions at the beginning of the administration over the implementation of the dual-track decision and the new Reagan administration's skepticism of the policy of détente gave way to an even more united alliance eight years later and the Western cooperation necessary to end the Cold War and reunify Germany. Throughout the many trials and tribulations over the Euromissiles, the White House made choices that reflected an appreciation that allies were a critical component of Western strength.[16] Even if he did not always make the best choices when it came to picking them (particularly in the Third World), Reagan nevertheless appreciated the value of allies for US foreign policy. Twenty-first century accusations that other NATO members, or Japan and South Korea, "owe massive amounts of money" and warnings of a "dwindling appetite and patience . . . in the American body politic . . . to expend increasingly precious funds on behalf of nations that are apparently unwilling to devote the necessary resources or make the necessary changes to be serious and capable partners in their own defense" do not only undercut the cohesion of US alliances.[17] They ignore the fact that, while prior leaders—including Reagan—called on partners to do more, they also did not want them to do too much more, and preserve the critical US role in Europe and East Asia—in furtherance, not to the detriment, of Washington's interests.[18]

Assessments of the successes and failures of US foreign policy during the 1980s are not of interest to scholars alone. We live in a world shaped to an extraordinary degree by the events of that decade, when many of the leaders of today's great powers—such as Vladimir Putin in Russia and Xi Jinping in the People's Republic of China—formed their basic ideas about the international system.[19]

During the 1980s, Reagan's White House confronted a vast array of issues; the chapters in this volume evaluate some of the most important. Through these studies we are reminded not only of the sheer scope and scale of US power in the world, but also its important limitations. For all his talk of the need for Washington to engage globally, much happened around the world not merely without Reagan's involvement, but in spite of it. Taken together, the chapters in this collection situate the Reagan administration and the United States in broader context, blending domestic histories with international ones. What they illustrate are the president's successes and failures, the debates that shaped his administration and the world in which they created policy, along with the limitations to and often unintended consequences of Washington's actions around the globe. Much, of course, still remains to be written about Ronald Reagan, his presidency, and his policies. But the chapters here highlight the possibilities ahead as historians continue to make sense of the contradictions and nuances of Reagan and his world.

The path to the Cold War's end was far from straightforward, nor was Reagan always the one who steered the ship of state in that direction. It was not a journey without casualties: Reagan's successes in US-Soviet relations must be weighed against the human costs of his failings in Latin America and the

Middle East, for example. This tension is at the core of the debate over Reagan's legacy, especially in foreign policy—and the debate playing out in these pages. With the passage of time, as all the authors here illustrate, historians will have even more resources at their disposal to weigh in as archival access continues to expand in the United States and around the world. As our perspective broadens and our knowledge of the past deepens, historians will have much more to say about whether Reagan left the world better off than he found it.

Notes

1. James Downey and Al Franken, "President Reagan, Mastermind," *Saturday Night Live*, season 12, episode 6, 6 Dec. 1986, National Broadcasting Corporation.
2. Ivan L. Head and Pierre Elliott Trudeau, *The Canadian Way: Shaping Canada's Foreign Policy, 1964–1984* (Toronto: McLelland and Stewart, 1995), 159.
3. Steven F. Hayward, "Reagan Reclaimed," *The National Review* 63, no. 2 (2011): 34.
4. Paul Thomas Chamberlin, *The Cold War's Killing Fields: Rethinking the Long Peace* (New York: Harper Collins, 2018).
5. Richard V. Allen, "Ronald Reagan: An Extraordinary Man in Extraordinary Times," in *The Fall of the Berlin Wall: Reasserting the Causes and Consequences of the End of the Cold War*, ed. Peter Schweizer (Stanford, CA: Hoover Institution Press, 2000), 52.
6. Hal Brands, *Making the Unipolar Moment: US Foreign Policy and the Rise of the Post–Cold War Order* (Ithaca, NY: Cornell University Press, 2016), 7–8.
7. Chris Miller, *Putinomics: Power and Money in Resurgent Russia* (Chapel Hill: University of North Carolina Press, 2018), 3–7.
8. Paul Musgrave, "Mikhail Gorbachev's Pizza Hut Thanksgiving Miracle," 28 Nov. 2019, https://foreignpolicy.com/2019/11/28/mikhail-gorbachev-pizza-hut-ad-thanksgiving-miracle/.
9. Charles Krauthammer, "The Unipolar Moment," *Foreign Affairs* 70, no. 1 (1990): 23.
10. Vladimir V. Putin, remarks at the Munich Conference on Security Policy, 10 Feb. 2007, http://kremlin.ru/events/president/transcripts/24034.
11. Eric L. Olson, testimony before the US Senate Committee on Homeland Security and Governmental Affairs, 16 July 2014, https://www.wilsoncenter.org/article/challenges-the-border-examining-and-addressing-the-root-causes-behind-the-rise-apprehensions.
12. Jennie W. Wenger, Caolionn O'Connell, and Linda Cottrell, *Examination of Recent Deployment Experience across the Services and Components* (Santa Monica: RAND Corporation, 2018), 1.
13. Odd Arne Westad, *Restless Empire: China and the World Since 1750* (New York: Basic Books, 2012), 383–384.
14. Donald J. Trump, inaugural address, 20 Jan. 2017, https://www.whitehouse.gov/briefings-statements/the-inaugural-address/; "The Biden Plan to Ensure the Future is 'Made in All of America' by All of America's Workers," https://joebiden.com/made-in-america/.

15. Peter Navarro, "The Era of American Complacency on Trade Is Over," *New York Times*, 8 June 2018.

16. Susan Colbourn, "President Trump's Rejection of a Key Pillar of Reagan Conservatism," 28 Oct. 2018, *Washington Post*.

17. Donald J. Trump, remarks at NATO Headquarters, 25 May 2017, https://www.whitehouse.gov/briefings-statements/remarks-president-trump-nato-unveiling-article-5-berlin-wall-memorials-brussels-belgium/; Robert M. Gates, remarks at the Security and Defense Agenda, 10 June 2011, https://www.atlanticcouncil.org/blogs/natosource/text-of-speech-by-robert-gates-on-the-future-of-nato/.

18. Joshua R. Itzkowitz Shifrinson, "Trump and NATO: Old Wine in Gold Bottles?," 29 Sept. 2017, http://issforum.org/roundtables/policy/1-5BA-NATO.

19. Odd Arne Westad, "Has a New Cold War Really Begun? Why the Term Shouldn't Apply to Today's Great-Power Tensions," 27 Mar. 2018, https://www.foreignaffairs.com/articles/china/2018-03-27/has-new-cold-war-really-begun.

Contributors

Seth Anziska is the Mohamed S. Farsi-Polonsky Associate Professor of Jewish-Muslim Relations at University College London. He is the author of *Preventing Palestine: A Political History from Camp David to Oslo*.

James Cameron is a postdoctoral fellow with the Oslo Nuclear Project in the Department of Political Science, University of Oslo. He is the author of *The Double Game: The Demise of America's First Missile Defense System and the Rise of Strategic Arms Limitation*.

Elizabeth C. Charles is a Historian in the Office of the Historian at the US Department of State. She researches and compiles the *Foreign Relations of the United States* series, and has completed volumes on the Soviet Union 1983–1985, Soviet Union 1985–1986, and the Intermediate Range Nuclear Forces Treaty 1984–1989.

Susan Colbourn is the Associate Director of the Triangle Institute for Security Studies at Duke University. She is the author of *Euromissiles: A Transatlantic History* and editor, with Timothy Andrews Sayle, of *The Nuclear North: Histories of Canada in the Atomic Age*.

Michael De Groot is Assistant Professor of International Studies in the Hamilton Lugar School of Global and International Studies at Indiana University Bloomington. His research focuses on the political economy of the Cold War.

Stephanie Freeman is Assistant Professor of History at Mississippi State University. She is completing a book manuscript on nuclear abolitionism and the end of the Cold War.

Christopher J. Fuller is Associate Professor in Modern US History in the History Department at the University of Southampton. He is the author of *See It/Shoot It: The Secret History of the CIA's Lethal Drone Program*.

Flavia Gasbarri is Lecturer in the War Studies Department at King's College London. She is the author of *US Foreign Policy and the End of the Cold War in Africa*.

Mathias Haeussler is Assistant Professor of Modern European History at the University of Regensburg (Germany). He is author of *Helmut Schmidt and British-German Relations: A European Misunderstanding* and *Inventing Elvis: An American Icon in a Cold War World*.

Jonathan R. Hunt is Assistant Professor of Strategy at the US Air War College. He is the author of various articles and chapters on international nuclear history and global affairs as well as the forthcoming book, *The Nuclear Club: How America and the World Governed the Atom from Hiroshima to Baghdad*.

William Inboden is the William Powers Jr. Executive Director of the Clements Center for National Security and Associate Professor at the LBJ School of Public Affairs, both at the University of Texas at Austin. He is completing a book on Reagan administration foreign policy titled *The Peacemaker: Reagan in the White House from War to Peace*.

Mark Atwood Lawrence is Associate Professor of History at the University of Texas at Austin. He is author of *Assuming the Burden: Europe and the American Commitment to Vietnam*, *The Vietnam War: A Concise International History* and *The End of Ambition: The United States and the Third World in the Vietnam Era*.

Elisabeth Leake is Associate Professor of International History at the University of Leeds. She is the author of *The Defiant Border: The Afghan-Pakistan Borderlands in the Era of Decolonization, 1936–65* and a global history of the Soviet-Afghan war, *Afghan Crucible: The Soviet Invasion and the Making of Modern Afghanistan*.

Melvyn P. Leffler is Professor Emeritus at the University of Virginia. Most recently, he is the author of *Safeguarding Democratic Capitalism: US Foreign Policy and National Security, 1920–2015*. His book *A Preponderance of Power: National Security, the Truman Administration, and the Cold War* won the Bancroft, Ferrell, and Hoover Prizes, and his volume *For the Soul of Mankind: The United States, the Soviet Union, and the Cold War* won the Beer Prize.

Evan D. McCormick is Associate Research Scholar at Columbia University's Interdisciplinary Center for Innovative Theory and Empirics (INCITE), where he works on the Obama Presidency Oral History project. His first book, on US-Latin American relations during the Reagan years, is under contract with Cornell University Press. His writing has appeared in *Diplomatic History*, *Journal of Cold War Studies*, and *Foreign Affairs Latinoamérica*.

Simon Miles is Assistant Professor in the Sanford School of Public Policy at Duke University. He is the author of *Engaging the Evil Empire: Washington, Moscow, and the Beginning of the End of the Cold War*.

Jennifer M. Miller is Associate Professor in the History Department at Dartmouth College. She is the author of *Cold War Democracy: The United States and Japan* and "Neoconservatives and Neo-Confucians: East Asian Growth and the Celebration of Tradition" in *Modern Intellectual History*.

David S. Painter is Associate Professor of History Emeritus at Georgetown University. His research focuses on oil, the Cold War, and US relations with the Third World. He is the author of *Oil and the American Century: The Political Economy of U.S. Foreign Oil Policy, 1941–1945*; *The Cold War: An International History*; and articles and chapters on international oil, the Cold War, and US relations with the Third World.

Robert B. Rakove is Lecturer in International Relations at Stanford University. He is the author of *Kennedy, Johnson and the Nonaligned World* and is currently writing a history of the US-Afghan relationship in the years preceding the Soviet invasion of 1979.

William Michael Schmidli is Associate Professor in the Institute for History at Leiden University. He is the author of *The Fate of Freedom Elsewhere: Human Rights and US Cold War Policy toward Argentina*.

Sarah B. Snyder is Professor in American University's School of International Service. She is the author of two award-winning books, *From Selma to Moscow: How Human Rights Activists Transformed US Foreign Policy* and *Human Rights Activism and the End of the Cold War: A Transnational History of the Helsinki Network*.

Lauren F. Turek is Associate Professor of History and Director of the Mellon Initiative for Undergraduate Research in the Arts and Humanities at Trinity University in San Antonio. She is the author of *To Bring the Good News to All Nations: Evangelical Influence on Human Rights and US Foreign Relations*.

James Graham Wilson is a Historian at the Department of State, where he compiles volumes for the Foreign Relations of the United States series. He is the author of *The Triumph of Improvisation: Gorbachev's Adaptability, Reagan's Engagement, and the End of the Cold War*.

Index

Able Archer 83 exercise, 5, 131
Abrams, Elliott, 191–192, 201, 217, 219, 241, 242, 243, 247, 248, 264, 267, 268, 272, 275, 281
Abu Nidal Organization, 308–309, 312–313, 320n38
Adamishin, Anatoly, 352, 354, 355, 361n37
Adelman, Ken, 26, 29–30, 31–34
Afghanistan: Geneva Accords (1988), 337–338, 340, 355; history (post-occupation), 324, 381, 382; jihadism history, 75–78, 80, 380–381; Pakistan and, 75–77, 78, 331, 334–335, 372–374, 376; policy studies, 324, 340; Reagan, and Cold War, 8–9, 10, 75–76, 77–78, 107, 324–340, 368, 380–381, 382, 440; Soviet invasion/occupation, 1, 8–9, 10, 45, 75–78, 107, 125–126, 324–340, 351, 355, 368, 370, 372, 373–374, 380–381, 382, 440; US foreign policy history, 369, 372; US support of rebels, 56, 75, 76–78, 80, 324, 325, 328, 333, 335–340, 372–373, 380–381, 440; US war, 11, 64, 324
"Afghanistan Day," 332–333, 338
Africa. *See* Southern Africa; specific nations
African National Congress, 223, 347
Akali Dal party, 374–375
Akhromeyev, Sergei, 107
Alfonsín, Raúl, 268, 272
Alkhimov, Vladimir, 329
Allen, Richard, 28, 29, 105–106, 128, 309, 326, 419, 420
Allende, Salvador, 263, 264
Amin, Hafizullah, 325
Amnesty International, 188–189, 194
Anderson, David, 340
Anderson, Martin, 26, 147
Andropov, Yuri: arms negotiations, 155; Cold War geopolitics, 345; communication paths, 112
Angola: civil war, 8, 347–349, 350, 353–355, 356, 357–358; colonial history, and liberation movement, 346–347; elections, 357; US relations and policy, 223, 239, 347, 348, 350, 353–356
Anti-Ballistic (ABM) Treaty (1972), 117
anticommunism. *See under* communism
antitrust policy, 401–402
apartheid, South African: anti-apartheid organizations, 346–347; international anti-apartheid movement, 223–224, 349–350, 356; US policy legislation, 199–200, 350, 352–353; US/Reagan relations and policy, 8, 189, 198–200, 223–224, 346–350, 352–353, 356
approval/disapproval ratings, 180–181
Aquino, Corazon, 200
Aquino, Ninoy, 200
Arab-Israeli conflicts, 10, 177, 303–304, 306–317, 369, 441
Arab-Israeli peace process, 303, 306, 310, 311, 315
Arab Nationalist Movement, 320n44
Arafat, Yasser, 309, 314–315
Argentina: economic crises, 97, 267; elections, 268; human rights issues, 190, 192–193, 204–205n15, 266, 267; leaders, 190, 204–205n15; military activity and conflicts, 240, 267, 285–286; US relations and policy, 190, 192–193, 240, 263, 264, 266–268, 272
Argov, Shlomo, 312, 313
Armacost, Michael, 336–337, 338, 348–349
Armitage, Richard L., 169
arms control policy and negotiations: Cold War "periphery" distractions, 345, 347–348, 350–352, 354–355, 358; disarmament policy/treaties, 2, 5, 8, 29, 33–35, 105, 115, 116–117, 120, 133–134, 138, 145–146, 156–157, 350, 439; DoD attitudes, 112, 113, 133; local resolutions, 148, 152; planning and methodology, 8, 34–36, 111, 112, 113, 117, 128, 132–133, 144–145, 147–148; summit meetings, 7, 16, 29, 34–35, 107,

449

INDEX

arms control policy and negotiations (*continued*) 115, 132–133, 156, 345, 350–351. *See also* arms race; diplomacy; specific agreements

arms race: nuclear freeze movement, 8, 144–157; Reagan interest and focus, 111, 144, 152; SDI and avoidance, 30–31; spending comparisons, 87–88; works about, 146, 149

arms trade: arms-for-hostages deals, 10, 74–75, 79, 182, 250–251; nuclear materials and classification, 426–427, 428; Soviet sales, 53; US sales and provisions, 10, 56, 75–77, 263, 264, 266–267, 268, 304, 307–308, 312, 336, 347, 350, 352, 417, 420, 423, 424–425

atheism, 218, 221

Attali, Jacques, 93

austerity measures, 95–96, 291, 292

automobile manufacturing, and economic parallels, 91, 392–396

Azeri nationalists, 377

Bahá'í faith, 225

Bailey, Norman, 48, 88

Baker, Howard, 417–418, 419, 420

Baker, James: in Bush administration, 17, 202, 252–253, 295, 358; on Reagan, 29, 30, 32, 34; in Reagan administration, 27, 29, 135, 149, 173, 292–293, 313

balance of power: détente effects, 124, 126–127; nature of, and shifts, 137, 350; superpowers, and European security, 124, 125, 127, 133–134

Baldrige, Malcolm, 399–400, 402, 427, 428

ballistic missiles: arms control, 8, 16, 132–134, 151, 152–154; China, 428; Soviet arsenal and European locations, 109, 125; US arsenal and European locations, 1, 8, 109, 125, 127, 148, 441–442

Baluch people and autonomy, 371–372, 373, 374, 376

Bangladesh, 370, 373

Barnes, Harry, 273, 275

Begin, Menachem, 10, 303–304, 306–311, 313–315

Beirut, Lebanon: Israeli bombing and fire, 313, 314, 315; US Embassy bombing (1983), 65, 66; US Marine barracks bombing (1983), 10–11, 65, 66, 67, 130, 176–178, 181, 316, 323n94; US Marine Corps deployment, 315–316, 439

Berlin Wall, 14, 31, 118–119, 138, 359

Bessmertnykh, Alexander, 30, 358

Bhindranwale, Jarnail Singh, 374–375

Bhutto, Zulfikar Ali, 373

Bicesse Agreement (1991), 357–358, 359

Bingham, Jonathan, 149

bin Laden, Osama, 73, 79

Bitburg affair (1984), 136–137

Boeing Company, 429, 431

Boesak, Allan, 223

Bolivia, 292

bond markets, and US foreign investment, 15–16, 89, 90, 91, 392

Botha, Pieter W., 348, 350–351

Botha, R.F. "Pik," 356

Bouterse, Desi, 282, 286–287

Bradley, Tom, 430

Brady, Nicholas, 293–294

Brazil: economic crises, 97, 269, 282–283, 290–294; elections, 269, 281, 286, 289, 294; foreign investment, 15–16; history, 281, 284–285, 286, 289, 294; human rights, 283–284; trade, 282, 283–284, 286, 287–293, 294–295; US relations and policy, 263, 264, 281–295

Bresser-Pereira, Luiz Carlos, 289, 293

Bretton Woods system, and changes, 12, 392

Brezhnev, Leonid, 108–109, 195, 325, 327, 328, 329, 330, 339, 426

Brezhnev doctrine, 5, 7, 330

BRICS nations, and trade, 295

Brock, William, 46, 402

Brzezinski, Zbigniew, 75, 126

Buchanan, Pat, 171, 350

budget deficits and balancing, 3–4, 84–99, 136

Bulgaria, 95

Bush, George H.W., 16–17; Afghanistan policy, 382; arms reduction agreements, 5, 8, 156; China policy, 15, 417, 419, 425; Cold War and, 17, 19n15, 31, 156, 253, 357, 359; economy under, 3; election, 9, 355–356, 357; era, and historic events, 4, 5, 8, 16–17, 31; foreign policy, 17, 293, 294–295, 357–359; Latin America policy and spending, 9, 16, 251–252, 252–253; military policy, 11; in Reagan administration, 27, 32–33, 71, 74–75, 182, 194, 284, 417, 419, 425

Bush, George W.: counterterrorism policy, 64, 440; economic policy, 3–4; military policy, 11, 64, 65

Byrd, Robert, 338

Caldicott, Helen, 144–145
Callaghan, James, 125
Cambodia, 171, 249, 333
Camp David Accords (1978), 303, 306, 311–312, 315
Canada: Afghanistan policy, 334; trade, 134–135, 407
Cannistraro, Vincent, 75
capital flows: Asian change and growth, 96, 416, 430, 441; deregulation and, 90; global shifts, 13, 17, 89–90, 92–94, 96, 98, 391–392, 430; "international Reaganomics," 84–99, 136
capital markets, 85, 94–98
Card, Andrew, 64
Caribbean region, 174–176, 179–180, 182. *See also* Grenada invasion (1983)
Carlucci, Frank, 26, 29, 35
Carrington, Peter, 129
Carter, Jimmy: arms control talks, 125, 348; economy under, and economic policy, 17, 85, 86, 93; election campaigns, 11, 65–66, 78, 107, 166, 213, 239, 370; foreign policy, 12, 15, 16, 45, 56, 65–66, 68, 70, 75, 76, 109, 124–126, 213, 216, 239, 240, 260–264, 282, 283–284, 303, 304, 305, 306, 310, 311, 315, 317, 348, 370, 371, 372, 373, 417, 419; human rights policy, 15, 124–125, 188–190, 192, 203, 213, 216, 237, 239, 240, 260–261, 263–264, 273; military policy, 8, 70, 75, 87, 109, 125, 146; presidency and events, 1, 66, 68, 70, 370; trade policy, 409n22; veterans affairs, 168
Carter doctrine, 56, 370
Casey, William: as CIA director, 11, 47, 48, 56, 67–68, 111–112, 240, 271, 336; CIA/DoD relations, 11, 45–46, 70–71, 108; counterterrorism, 11, 67–68, 70–71, 72–75, 76–78; energy intelligence and policy, 45–46, 47, 48, 49, 56
Castro, Fidel, 239
Catholic organizations and values, 214, 215, 223–224, 227n13
Central America. *See* Latin America; specific nations
Central Intelligence Agency (CIA): China information, 422; counterterrorism and CTC, 11, 64, 67–68, 72–80; DoD and, 11, 45–46, 64, 70–71, 73–74, 79, 87–88, 108; economic and trade information and policy, 47, 48, 50, 53, 56, 422; fiction and entertainment, 69; military spending reports, 87–88, 116; operations, 10, 11, 55, 56, 75, 79, 240, 247, 271, 274, 309, 325, 336, 347, 381, 422, 440; Palestine information, 320n34; South/Southwest Asia policy, 75, 368, 371, 372, 373, 375, 377–380, 381, 440; staff, 26, 36
Chai Zemin, 419
Chamooro, Violeta, 2, 251–252, 252–253
chemical weapons: Afghanistan use, 327–328, 331, 333, 334; arms control, 133, 134
Cheney, Richard "Dick," 3–4, 30
Chennault, Anna, 15, 418–421, 423, 429, 431
Chennault, Claire, 418
Chen Xiangmei. *See* Chennault, Anna
Chernenko, Konstantin, 32–33, 115, 132
Chernobyl disaster (1986), 208n86
Chernyaev, Anatoly, 30, 34–35, 96
Cheysson, Claude, 137, 325
Chiang Ching-kuo, 418, 420–421, 422–423, 426
Chiang Kai-shek, 418
Childress, Richard T., 171–172
Chile: economy, 201–202, 261, 269, 271; foreign investment, 15–16; history, 260, 263, 264, 277–278n6; human rights issues, 16, 189, 192–193, 200–201, 209n98, 260–276; national archives, 261–262, 265, 266, 269, 271–272, 277; US relations and diplomacy, 260–277, 277–278n6
Chin, Vincent, 393–394
China, People's Republic of: Afghanistan policy, 334; economic conditions and power, 3, 4, 14–15, 416, 430, 441; economic reform and change, 415–417, 420, 421–422, 423–424, 428, 430, 431, 441; human rights, 2, 14–15, 423, 431–432; modernization, 417, 420, 422, 428; Reagan visits, 414–415, 417, 428–429, 441; Soviet policy and relations, 416, 419–420, 421–422, 423–424, 426, 428; US relations, 14–15, 414–432, 441
Choate, Pat, 400, 401
Christian nationalism, and rhetoric, 214, 227n13
Chrysler Corporation, 91, 393, 410n36
Chun Doo-hwan, 190, 204–205n15
Church, Frank, 74
Civil Aviation Administration (China), 421, 431
Clark, William: appointment and activity, 27, 28, 48–49, 112–113, 174–175, 287, 313, 328, 330, 372; arms reduction and negotiation policy, 149–150, 155; on Reagan, 29; resignation, 50
Clark Amendment repeal (1985), 347, 350, 352

Clarridge, Duane, 73, 75
Cline, Ray, 417
Clinton, Bill, and administration, 9, 79, 383n7
Cohen, William, 154
Cold War, 6; aftermath, 17, 19n15, 239, 253–254; Bush era and, 17, 19n15, 31, 253; economic systems and, 1, 6, 7, 85, 95–96, 389, 399, 407; end, 3, 5–6, 7, 25, 28–31, 35–37, 44, 56, 85, 106–107, 119, 156–157, 253, 294, 346, 358–359, 407, 439, 442–443; focus, vs. terrorism, 11, 65, 68, 71, 74, 77–78, 79–80, 440–441; Gorbachev's work to end, 33, 106–107, 119, 156; historical events and elements, 75–76, 107, 121n7, 237–238, 369; Reagan and, 5–8, 16, 17, 25–42, 65, 68–69, 71, 74, 85, 105–120, 156–157, 173, 179, 183–184, 237–240, 246–252, 285–287, 304–308, 313–314, 317, 324–340, 346, 417, 438, 439, 441–444; regional variation and proxy conflicts, 8–9, 10–11, 74, 75–76, 108–109, 173, 174–175, 179, 193–194, 212, 222, 223, 224–225, 238–240, 246–250, 261, 265–266, 267, 277n5, 282, 285–287, 304–308, 311–314, 317, 325, 335–336, 345–359, 376, 438–439, 440; "Second," 93, 109, 417. *See also* arms control policy and negotiations; diplomacy; Europe
communism: anticommunism military supports, 8, 15–16, 74, 171, 222–223, 238–254, 304–305, 347; anticommunist ideology and figures, 4, 8, 12, 15–16, 74, 108, 137, 171, 179, 242, 243–244, 265–266, 389, 399, 423; capitalism pairings, 414–432; nations and change, 3, 5, 7, 108, 415; Reagan policy, 4, 8, 12, 15–16, 74, 108, 112, 118–119, 175–176, 179, 194, 195, 202, 221–223, 224–225, 237–238, 248–249, 262–264, 265–266, 282, 285–287, 295, 305, 325, 439. *See also* Cold War
Comprehensive Anti-Apartheid Act (1986), 199–200, 350, 352–353
Conference on Security and Cooperation in Europe (CSCE), 189, 195–196, 217, 219. *See also* Helsinki Accords (1975)
Congress. *See* United States Congress
conservatism: Cold War policy, US, 237–238, 242–243; issues and values, 15, 213–214, 220–221, 225–226, 227n13; modern movement history, 15, 214, 220, 227n13; political engagement and deployment, 214, 220–221, 223, 224, 226, 227n13; Reagan policy and values, 108, 213–214, 218, 222–223, 224, 225–226, 227n13, 237–239, 242–243
Conte, Silvio, 149
copyright law, 288–290
Corcoran, Thomas, 420–421
corporate diplomacy interests and involvement, 421
corporate life and leadership, 404–405
Council of Economic Advisers, and staff, 89, 98
counterterrorism policy: entities and operations, 11, 67–68, 70, 71–72, 73–75, 78, 181, 324; public opinion, 71, 72; Reagan era, and evolution, 11, 64–80, 189–190, 381, 440–441; reports, 75, 77–78, 79
coups: Chile, 260, 264, 277–278n6; Guatemala, 222; Pakistan, 76
Cranston, Alan, 180, 205n23
credit crunch conditions, 85, 94–97
Crichton, Michael, 400–401
Crocker, Chester, 8, 199, 345–346, 348, 349–350, 353–356, 358, 361n37
Cuba: Angolan intervention, 347–349, 353–354, 356, 357; human rights issues and policy, 263; regional influence, 173, 238, 239, 240, 245, 246–247, 282, 286–287
currency and exchange systems, 12, 17, 52, 85, 90–91, 92–93, 392

Daalder, Ivo, 133
Danforth, John, 396
Davis, Patti, 144
Deaver, Michael, 27, 147, 149, 173
debt crises: Eastern Europe, 85, 94–96, 98; least-developed countries, 96–98, 282–283, 290–294; South America, 97, 267, 269, 271, 276, 282–283, 290–294
defense industry manufacturers, 421, 424, 429, 431
de Gaulle, Charles, 124
Delta Force, 68, 70
democracy: exploitation of, 389, 399; global rates and states of, 1, 2, 4, 222, 245–246, 247–248, 251, 281, 416; organizations, 201–202, 243, 249, 252–253, 270; theory, 9, 243; US ideals, 106, 238, 243, 389; US promotion and interventionism, 9, 15, 16, 201–202, 221, 222, 224–226, 237–254, 260–264, 266, 268–273, 274–277, 281–282, 284, 286, 289, 292, 294–295, 331. *See also* elections

INDEX 453

Deng Xiaoping, 15, 414, 415, 417–418, 419–420, 421–422, 423–425, 426, 428, 431, 441
Deppe, Martin, 215
Derian, Patricia M., 190
détente: European policy, 7–8, 47, 123–126; ineffectiveness, 107–108, 125–126, 350, 358; Reagan views, 7–8, 12, 87, 109, 112, 123, 124, 126, 127, 138, 425; shifts from, 7–8, 109, 110, 123, 124–125, 146, 346, 348, 441
diary writings (Reagan), 33, 48, 88, 108, 112, 113–114, 131, 132, 136, 144, 197, 310–311, 314, 333, 414–415, 425, 429
"Dictatorships and Double Standards" (essay; Kirkpatrick), 228n18, 231n65, 263
Dietrich, William S., 399, 407
Dingell, John, 397
diplomacy: informal and "volunteer," 418–421, 423; POW/MIA efforts, 169; "quiet," 7, 27, 112–115, 118, 216, 264–266, 268, 273; summit meetings, 7, 33–35, 107, 132–133, 156, 196, 197, 345, 350–351; trust within, 32–33, 34–35, 114–115, 131–132; US/Africa, 199, 349, 353–358; US/Asia, 394–395, 401, 402, 414–416, 417–432; US/Europe, 123–138; US/Latin America, 248–249, 251, 257n43, 260–277, 281–282, 284–288, 291–293, 294–295; US/Middle East, 303–311, 315, 316–317; US principles and paradigms, 110–115, 127–128, 131–132, 137, 178–179, 216, 249, 263–264, 268, 273, 275–276, 328–329, 330, 351–352; US/Soviet Union, 7, 27, 32–37, 85, 105–107, 110–114, 116–120, 124, 127, 128, 131–134, 150–151, 194–198, 325–331, 337, 345, 350–352, 358, 439–440. *See also* arms control policy and negotiations
disarmament. *See* arms control policy and negotiations
Djerejian, Edward, 338
Dobrynin, Anatoly, 30, 112, 113, 114, 195, 218, 325, 326–327, 330, 333
DoD. *See* US Department of Defense
Dodd, Christopher, 178, 205n23
Dole, Bob, 396
domestic spending, US, 87, 90, 98–99
dos Santos, José Eduardo, 349, 357
Draper, Morris, 312
drones, development and use, 73–74, 79
dual-track decision (1979), 125, 127–128, 130, 134, 137, 148, 441

Dujmovic, Nicholas, 55
Duvalier, Jean-Claude, 249
Dyess, William J., 174

Eagleburger, Lawrence, 217, 312
East Asia. *See* China, People's Republic of; Hong Kong; Japan; Taiwan
economic conditions: Asia, 2–3, 14–15, 85, 91, 96, 387–408, 412n85, 414–432, 441; Europe, 2, 13, 14, 47, 48, 49, 85, 92–96, 98, 125–126, 129; global and market shifts, 12–13, 14, 17–18, 32, 84–85, 89–90, 92–94, 387–388, 391–392, 416; Latin America, 13, 91, 96–97, 98, 244–245, 282–283; least-developed countries, 96–98, 282–283, 290–294; Russia, 439–440; Soviet Union, 32, 33, 35, 43–44, 45–46, 48–49, 52–55, 56–57, 85, 96, 109, 116, 129; US, 1970s-90s, 1, 2–4, 13, 14, 32, 85–94, 387–388, 391–392, 394–395, 399–400, 401, 404, 406–407
economic inequality, 12, 84, 256n28, 294
Economic Recovery and Tax Act (1981), 86
economic sanctions: on Chile, 263, 264; on Nicaragua, 253; on Poland, 128, 198; on South Africa, 199, 223, 224, 350; on Soviet Union (Carter), 12, 45, 125–126; on Soviet Union (Reagan), 12, 47, 48–50, 110, 128–130, 198, 327
economic theory, and US, 3, 399–400, 405
"economic warfare": US-Europe, 14, 49–50; US-Soviet, 27, 49, 56–57
Egypt, 303, 332–333, 369
Eisenhower, Dwight D., 75, 150, 369
elections: Europe, 31, 36; global democratic, 4, 268–269, 357; Latin America, 2, 4, 9, 222, 246, 247–248, 251–253, 268–269, 275, 281, 286, 289, 294; US midterm, 87, 89, 152, 274, 338; US presidential, 2, 9, 11, 68–69, 78, 126, 147, 155–156, 166, 168, 182, 188–189, 213, 239, 355–356, 370; US presidential primaries, 3, 126, 166; US rejections, 248, 249
El Salvador: civil war and human rights, 174, 194, 222, 238, 246; in Cold War, 108, 173, 193; elections, 222, 248, 269; US relations and intervention, 171, 172, 173–174, 193, 194, 222, 239, 240
emigration policy, Soviet, 114, 189, 195–198, 207n63
empathy, 33–34, 37, 132

energy industries: alternative energy sources, 51, 52; efficiency and conservation, 51; and energy consumption, 51, 54; organizations, 51, 52; and Saudi-US relations, 13–14, 55–56; shocks and embargoes, 44, 46–47, 51, 291; Soviet infrastructure and production, 14, 44–51, 55–56, 109–110, 129; Soviet performance and economy, 43–57; and US economic power, 13–14, 43–44, 45–46, 47–51, 55–56, 369. *See also* natural gas; oil reserves and prices

entertainment media and storytelling, 69, 167, 168

Errázuriz, Hernán Felipe, 271–272, 275

ethnonationalist movements: political Islam mixtures, 10, 378, 380, 382; South and Southwest Asia, 368, 371–372, 373, 374–379, 381, 382

Europe: Cold War positions and perspectives, 123–126, 126–131, 133–134, 135–138, 346; East/West relations, 7–8, 31, 47–48, 94–97, 109, 118–119, 123, 125, 128–131, 195; economic conditions, 2, 13, 14, 47, 48, 49, 85, 92–96, 98, 125–126, 129; energy needs and trade, 14, 43–44, 45, 46–57, 109–110, 129–130; energy reserves and production, 46–47, 51; NATO missiles and placement, 1, 7–8, 109, 115, 125, 127, 130, 134, 137–138, 148, 438, 441–442; 1970s-1980s events, 1, 5–6; US and transatlantic relations, 123–138, 441–442; US economic investment, 14, 89. *See also* specific nations

European Economic Community, 326, 334

European Union (EU), formation, 2

evangelical organizations, 214, 215, 223, 226–227n11, 227n13

exchange systems. *See* currency and exchange systems

Fahd, King of Saudi Arabia, 13–14, 56
Fairbanks, Charles, Jr., 191
Falklands War (1982), 240, 267–268, 285–286
Farabundo Martí National Liberation Front (FMLN), 194
Federal Bureau of Investigation (FBI), 78
Federal Reserve, 86, 88–89, 90, 92, 291
Feith, Douglas, 121n23
Feldstein, Martin, 89
Figueiredo, João Baptista, 284–287
financialization and globalization. *See* globalization and financialization
First Intifada (1987–93), 316–317

first-strike capability: arms negotiations and discussion, 33–34, 117, 156; simulations and exercises, 131
Flying Tigers, 418, 419, 421
Ford, Gerald: economic policy, 17; foreign policy, 124, 126, 263, 283, 320n34, 348
Ford Motor Company, 393, 396
foreign investment: into Africa, 98; into Asia, 14–15, 430; into Europe, 93; into South America, 15–16; into Soviet Union, 45; by US, 15–16, 84, 282, 387, 390, 397–398, 430; into US, 14, 84, 89, 91–92, 98, 387–388, 392, 394
foreign policy and relations. *See under* human rights; Reagan, Ronald, and administration; US Department of State; specific nations and regions
Forsberg, Randall, 146
Fortier, Donald, 331, 335–336
France: Lebanon war and peacekeeping, 314, 316; US relations in Cold War, 93, 130, 136, 137
free market values, 16, 276, 394, 399–400, 404, 405, 406, 430
Frente de Libertação de Moçambique (FRELIMO), 347
Frente Sandinista de Liberacion Nacional (FSLN). *See* Sandinistas and Sandinista government (Nicaragua)
Friedman, Milton, 12, 426
Friends Committee on National Legislation, 151
Fukuyama, Francis, 9
Fuller, Craig L., 429
Fuller, Graham, 69

Gaddafi, Muammar, 65, 71–72, 381
Gaffney, Frank, 121n23
Gandhi, Indira, 334, 371, 374–375
Gandhi, Rajiv, 334, 375, 376
Gates, Robert, 36, 340, 442
Gaza Strip, 303–304, 306, 308, 311, 317
Gemayel, Bashir, 315
Geneva Accords (1988), 337–338, 340, 355
Geneva meeting and walkout (1983), 115, 130
Geneva summit (1985), 33–34, 156, 196, 345, 350–351
genocide, 193, 213, 222
Germany: border and peoples, 1, 14, 118–119; economic conditions, 14, 92–97; reunification, 2, 4, 14, 31, 36, 441; terrorism, 71; US relations in Cold War,

92–93, 124–125, 127–129, 130, 134, 136–137; US weapons placement, 1, 8, 109, 119–120, 127, 130, 134
Gibbons, Sam M., 396–397, 398–399, 401–402
Gibney, Frank, 405, 406
Giscard d'Estaing, Valéry, 124
glasnost', 7
globalization and financialization: changing economic conditions, 12–13, 32, 392, 416; Chinese economic changes, 415–432, 441
Golan Heights, 307–308
Goldfield, H.P., 429
Goldman, Stuart D., 377
Goldwater, Barry, 12, 425
"good vs. evil" narrative, in entertainment, 69
Gorbachev, Mikhail: biography and historiography, 31; economy of Russia and, 439–440; economy under, 32, 33, 35, 53–55, 56; military policy and changes, 5, 7, 29, 116; Reagan/US relations and diplomacy, 5, 7, 10, 29–37, 55–56, 85, 106–107, 115, 116–118, 119, 132–134, 156–157, 195–197, 202, 337, 350–352, 438; and SDI, 30–31, 34–35, 107, 117–118, 132–133, 156; START Treaty/Bush relations, 5, 31, 156; tenure, 30, 32–33, 37, 53–55, 56, 106, 111, 115, 120, 155, 350, 352
Gordievskii, Oleg, 131
Gotlieb, Allan, 135
government size, 86, 87
Greenspan, Alan, 3
Grenada invasion (1983), 11, 130, 136, 179–181, 182, 439
Gromyko, Andrei, 111, 115, 207n66, 325, 326–327, 328, 333
ground-launched cruise missiles. *See* INF weapons
Ground Zero, 149
Guatemala: civil war and human rights, 8, 193, 222–223, 246; elections, 269; US relations, and intervention, 8, 15, 193, 222–223
guerrilla warfare, and classification vs. terrorism, 74, 76, 308–309

Habib, Philipp, 312, 313, 314–315, 316
Haig, Alexander: on arms control negotiation, 150–151; on global economy, 93; Middle East policy, 305–307, 309, 312–314, 317, 322n68, 367; resignation and replacement, 27, 28, 49, 50, 110, 129, 192, 202, 217, 269, 314, 425–426; as secretary, and foreign policy, 46, 108, 110, 127–128, 150–151, 173, 174–175, 189–190, 191, 192, 202, 204n14, 206n39, 215–216, 216, 264, 267, 305, 306, 312, 313, 322n68, 325, 326–328, 331, 367, 373, 420–421, 424, 425
Haiti, 249
Halberstam, David, 400
Hart, Gary, 180
Hartman, Arthur, 328
hate crimes, 393–394
Hatfield, Mark, 149
health care systems, 245
Helms, Jesse, 420
Helsinki Accords (1975), 126, 129, 196, 197–198, 219–220, 230n45
Hezb-i-Islami, 76
Hezbollah, 65, 68, 74, 79, 178, 316, 381
Hill, Charles, 312, 322n68
Hong Kong, 416, 417, 423, 430, 431, 432
Howe, Geoffrey, 92
Hua Guofeng, 422
Huang Hua, 428, 429
human rights: Afghanistan, 328, 331, 332–333, 339; Carter administration policy, 15, 124–125, 188–190, 192, 203, 213, 216, 237, 239, 240, 260–261, 263–264, 273; China, 2, 14–15, 423, 431–432; international movement and tenets, 198, 199, 225–226, 230n45, 263; organizations, 188–189, 202, 208n82, 214–215, 217, 253; policy critiques and commentary, 188–189, 190–191, 192–194, 198–199, 201, 204n7, 204n13, 213–226, 237–254, 260–267; Reagan administration framing and foci, 9, 189–190, 192, 195, 202, 213–215, 216–226, 237–254; Reagan administration policy, 15, 111, 114–115, 188–203, 208n82, 212–226, 237–239, 241–244, 249–251, 253–254, 260–276, 332, 349–350; religious values and tenets, 213–215, 218, 220, 221, 223–224, 226–227n11; Soviet Union, 114, 189, 192, 194–198, 213, 215–220, 263
Humphrey, Gordon, 338
Hussein, King of Jordan, 316
Hussein, Saddam, 11, 382
Hutchings, Robert, 17
Hu Yaobang, 414, 425, 426

Iacocca, Lee, 393, 410n36
India, 75; Afghanistan policy, 333, 334; Pakistan and, 334–335, 371–372, 373, 374, 375–376

industrial sabotage, 55
inflation: Brazil, 293; Nicaragua, 252, 253; Reagan era and Reaganomics, 84–85, 86–87, 88–89, 89, 95; US conditions, 1, 2, 85, 86, 88, 392
informatics law, 288–290
INF Treaty (1987): background/planning, 112, 115, 117–118, 128, 132–133, 149; congressional opinions, 338; details and signing, 5, 35, 105, 107, 133–134, 156, 350; new challenges from, 119–120
INF weapons: arms control negotiations, 115, 128, 132–134, 138, 156; development and arsenal, 109, 116, 148; NATO and, 109, 115, 130, 133–134; nuclear freeze movement and, 130, 148; zero option, 116–117, 128, 133–134, 150. *See also* arms control policy and negotiations; arms race; ballistic missiles; INF Treaty (1987); nuclear weapons
innovations. *See* technology and innovations
Institute on Religion and Democracy, 220–221
intellectual property law, 288–290
intercontinental ballistic missiles (ICBMs). *See* ballistic missiles
interest rates: debt payment, 95; investment vehicles, 89; US global influences, 89, 92–93, 95, 96, 97, 136, 291; US policy and conditions, 13, 88–90, 93, 392
intermediate-range nuclear forces (INF). *See* INF weapons
Intermediate-Range Nuclear Forces Treaty (1987). *See* INF Treaty (1987)
international economy. *See* economic conditions; "Reaganomics"; trade relations
International Energy Agency (IEA), 50–51
International Monetary Fund (IMF), 13, 97–98, 201, 291, 292
Inter-Services Intelligence (Pakistan), 75–76, 372–373
investment banks, 3
Iran: history, and Islamic Republic, 1, 10, 15, 367, 370, 371, 376, 379–380; human and religious rights, 225; Kurdish nationalism, 376–379; regional influence, 377–379; state-sponsored violence, 65, 74, 316
Iran-Contra scandal, 10, 11, 74–75, 79, 250, 382; background and lead-up, 175, 182, 193, 212, 224–225, 238–241; and Reagan presidency, 250–251, 258n67, 274
Iran hostage crisis (1979–1981), 1, 66, 68, 70, 370

Iran-Iraq War (1980–1988), 52, 304, 371, 376, 377–378, 382
Iraq: Kurdish nationalism, 376–378; Osirak nuclear reactor, 10, 307, 308, 320n29, 441
Iraq War (2003–2011), 11
Islamism, and Islamist regimes: Afghan jihad, 75–78, 80, 380–381; assumptions vs. reality, 379–381; Iran, 1, 10, 370, 371, 377–378, 379–380; Iraq, 378; Pakistan, 76–78; Southwest Asia, 10, 367, 368, 378–382; US takes, and policy, 10, 305, 367, 368–369, 378–382, 378–383, 441
Israel: Lebanon invasion, 304, 308, 311–316; regional and military conflicts, 10, 177, 303–304, 306–317, 369, 441; settlement building, 10, 303–304, 306, 307–308, 309–311, 317, 321n49; US relations and treatment, 10, 303–308, 310–317, 369, 379

Japan: auto industry and exports, 91, 393–394; books about, 387, 388, 399, 400–401, 404–407; culture, and economy, 390, 398, 400–401, 404–405; economic investment by US, 387, 391; economic investment into US, 12, 14, 89, 90, 390; economic power, 3, 14, 387–389, 389–408, 412n85, 416; history, 391, 397–398; technology industry and exports, 2–3, 91, 96, 388, 391–392, 395, 401–402, 402–404, 412n89
Jaruzelski, Wojciech, 47, 198, 209n98
John Paul II, Pope, 215, 219, 223–224
Johnson, Lyndon, 108
Jordan, 304, 310, 311, 312, 316

Kampelman, Max M., 195
Kanafani, Ghassan, 309, 320n44
Karmal, Babrak, 325–326
Kennedy, Richard, 191
Kennedy, Ted, 149, 263, 264
Khalistan, 374–376
Khamenei, Ayatollah Ali, 2
Khomeini, Ayatollah Ruhollah, 1, 2, 225, 371, 377–378
Kirkpatrick, Jeane, 9, 15, 174, 189, 193, 204n13, 228n18, 238, 242, 243–244, 247, 263, 264, 265, 313
Kissinger, Henry, 124, 183, 206n39, 293, 328, 337, 391, 424
Kohl, Helmut, 130, 132, 133, 136–137
Korean Air Lines flight 007 (1983), 5, 111, 115, 130
Korniyenko, Georgii, 326, 328

INDEX

Krauthammer, Charles, 175
Kurdistan, 376–378
Kurd people and movements, 371–372, 373, 376–379
Kuwait, 11

labor: Eastern European movements, 14, 47–48, 198, 327; US unions and relations, 393, 395
Latin America: civil wars, and military supports, 8, 74, 171, 173–175, 182, 193–194, 202, 238–241, 244–254, 440; economic conditions/crises, 13, 91, 96–97, 98, 244–245, 282–283; human rights issues, 189, 193–194, 202, 212–214, 215, 222–223, 224–225, 246, 260–276, 440; 1970s-1980s events, 1, 2, 440; Vietnam comparisons, 171–172, 173–175, 176, 250. *See also* specific nations
least-developed countries (LDCs), and economies, 96–98, 282–283, 290–294
Lebanon: Israel invasion and civil war, 304, 305, 308, 311–316, 371; regional conflict, and US policy, and presence, 10–11, 65, 68, 176–178, 179–181, 182, 303, 304, 305, 308, 311–314, 315–316, 317, 322n68, 439
Lefever, Ernest W., 190–191, 205n17, 205n23, 215–216, 228n18, 241
Leland, Marc E., 401
Letelier, Orlando, 201, 263, 265, 267, 274
Lewis, Samuel, 307, 308, 310, 312, 313, 314, 316
Liao Chengzhi, 420
Libya, 65, 71–72, 371
Likud Party, 10, 306, 311, 317, 441
Lilley, James, 15, 426
Lin, Maya, 11, 169–171
linkage (policy), 147, 348, 350, 356, 358–359
Li Xiannian, 414
lobbying industry, 400, 418
López Portillo, José, 97
Los Angeles, California, 430
Lusaka Accord (1994), 357

Maastricht Treaty (1992), 2
MacEachen, Allan, 135
madrassas, 77
Madrid, Miguel de la, 97
management systems, industrial, 404–405
manufacturing industries: automobile, and economic parallels, 91, 392–396; China growth and trade, 430, 431–432, 441; defense, 421, 424, 429, 431; management and quality theory, 404–405; outsourcing and offshoring, 393, 430, 432, 441; semiconductors, 401, 402–404, 412n89, 430
Mao Zedong, 422
Marcos, Ferdinand, 200, 249
Markey, Edward, 149
Martin, Preston, 89
Matlock, Jack, 27, 28, 111, 195, 197, 258n67, 325, 326
McCarthy, Joseph, 389
McFarlane, Robert "Bud," 10, 27, 71, 151, 153, 171, 175, 220, 334, 335–336
McMinn, Douglas, 395
McNamara, Robert, 107
Meese, Edwin, 27, 149, 173, 420
Mexico: economy, 97, 291; trade agreements, 135, 407
Middle East: oil producers and industry, 13–14, 46–47, 51–52, 53, 56, 369; peace process, 303, 306, 310, 311, 315; US foreign policy history, 369; US/Reagan foreign policy, 10–11, 13–14, 56, 176–178, 179–181, 182, 303–317, 360n22, 367, 382, 441; weapons imports, 53, 304, 307, 312. *See also* Southwest Asia
military and defense spending: Soviet Union, 30, 87–88, 109, 116, 124–125; US, 16, 68–69, 87–88
military-entertainment complex, 69, 71
missile defense. *See* Strategic Defense Initiative (SDI)
missiles. *See* ballistic missiles; INF weapons
missing in action (M.I.A.) military personnel, 168–169, 171–172
Mitterrand, François, 93, 130, 136, 137
Mondale, Walter, 409n22
monetary policy, 13, 85, 88–90; Europe, 93, 95, 136; least-developed countries, 97–98, 252, 291, 292–293; US, 95, 98, 291
Moscow summit (1988), 197, 355
Motley, Langhorne, 247, 270, 284, 287
Movimento Popular de Libertação de Angola (MPLA), 347, 349, 350, 353, 356, 357
Mozambique: colonial history, and liberation movement, 346–347; US relations and policy, 223, 347
Mulroney, Brian, 134, 135
Mundell, Robert, 12, 13
Mutual and Balanced Force Reduction (MBFR) talks, 125
mutually-assured destruction: Reagan opinions, 26, 88, 147; vs. survivability, 107, 116

Nakasone, Yasuhiro, 402
Namibia: independence movement, and South Africa, 346, 347, 348–349, 353, 354–355, 356–357, 359n4; US relations and policy, 223, 346, 348
Nance, James "Bud," 326–327, 331
national debt: 1980s, 3–4, 84, 86, 88, 98; 2000s, 3–4; US history and growth, 84, 88
National Endowment for Democracy, 201–202, 243, 249, 252–253, 270
National Intelligence Estimates, 47, 116, 120
National Park Service, 170–171
national security: Bush (G.H.W.) administration, 17; Bush (G.W.) administration, 64; Carter administration, 75, 126, 370; economic and trade policy, 395, 399; Reagan administration staff and relations, 7, 26, 27, 28, 29, 34, 48–49, 50, 67–68, 70–71, 72–73, 75, 79, 108, 110, 111–114, 128, 147–148, 313, 326–327, 328; Reagan administration strategy, 27, 28–29, 33–34, 67–80, 108–120, 145–146, 154, 174–175, 195, 213, 239–240, 268, 309, 325, 328, 329–330, 335–340, 421–422, 424. *See also* National Security Decision Directives (NSDDs)
National Security Council (NSC): Cold War policy, 7, 17, 27, 34, 48–49, 55, 67–68, 110–117, 147–148, 239, 263, 326–327, 329–330, 335–336, 339–340, 368, 371, 372–374; economic policy, 48, 88, 90; workings, and administration relations, 26, 27, 34, 48–49, 55, 68, 111–114, 171–172, 250, 326–327, 328, 337–338, 424
National Security Decision Directives (NSDDs): #17, 240; #32, 26–27, 49, 329, 335, 424; #62, 395; #71, 268; #75, 7, 26–27, 28, 50, 76, 111, 113, 115, 118, 131, 195, 218, 243, 329–330, 335; #76, 426–427; #99, 371, 374; #138, 67–68, 73; #165, 115–116; #166, 76–77, 336, 339; #207, 73; #270, 336
natural gas: production and prices, 43–44, 45, 46, 53; reserves and infrastructure, 44, 45, 46, 51, 129
Neier, Aryeh, 202, 204n7, 253
neutron bomb, 148
Neves, Tancredo, 289
Nicaragua: civil war and human rights, 193, 212–214, 224–225, 246, 250, 252; economy, 244–245, 252, 253, 256n28; elections, 2, 9, 246, 247–248, 251–253; insurgents funding, and Iran-Contra affair, 74, 174, 175, 182, 193, 212, 238–251; leadership, US relations, and intervention, 1, 10, 15, 74, 171, 172, 193, 212–213, 238–241, 244–254; social programs, 244–246, 252
1970s (decade), 1, 2
1980s (decade), 1–3, 4–5, 442
1990s (decade), 2, 277, 283, 407, 412n85
Nippon Life Insurance Company, 14
Niskanen, William, 402
Nitze, Paul, 107, 117, 389, 399
Nixon, Richard: China visit, 414, 417; domestic policy, 108; economic policy, 12, 17; foreign policy, 12, 263, 283, 337; trade policy, 391, 409n21
North, Oliver, 10, 67–68, 71–72, 74–75, 250–251
North American Free Trade Agreement (NAFTA), 135, 407
North Atlantic Treaty Organization (NATO): Able Archer exercise, 5, 131; history, 123, 124, 442; missile capabilities and military placement, 1, 5, 8, 115, 125, 127, 130, 134, 137–138, 148, 438, 441–442; US Cold War diplomacy, 7–8, 110, 123–125, 129–131, 133, 441–442; US Cold War policy planning, 48, 109–110, 334. *See also* Dual-Track Decision (1979)
Nuclear and Space Talks (NST) (1985), 115, 132, 155, 334
Nuclear Non-Proliferation Treaty (NPT) (1968), 424, 427, 428–429
nuclear programs: Brazil, 283–284, 287–288; China, 417, 426–429; trade and materials, 426–427, 428
nuclear weapons: assumptions of Soviet arsenal, 116, 144–145, 147; disarmament, 2, 5, 8, 29, 105, 115, 116–117, 128; freeze and peace movements, 8, 127, 130, 138, 144–154, 155–157; nonproliferation policy, 424, 427, 428–429; parity and balance of power, 124, 125; pre-Reagan strategies, 8, 146, 150; Reagan attitudes and policy, 5, 26, 29, 33–37, 111, 116–118, 128, 131, 138, 144–157, 424; South Africa, threats, 353; Soviet policy/capabilities, 5, 107, 109, 116–117, 120, 125, 150–151; and war dangers, 5, 26, 33, 34, 131, 144, 146, 148, 149–150, 438. *See also* ballistic missiles
Nunn, Sam, 154

occupied territories, 10, 303–304, 306, 307–308, 309–311, 316, 317, 321n49
Office of Management and Budget (OMB), 85, 86–87
offshoring, manufacturing, 393, 430, 432, 441
oil reserves and prices: global, 13–14, 44, 51–56, 53t, 94, 290, 353; Saudi Arabia, 13–14, 52, 55–56; Soviet Union, 43–45, 51, 52–53, 53t, 54
Olmer, Lionel, 401, 405
O'Neill, Paul, 3–4
Operation Desert Shield (1990), 11
Operation Eagle Claw (1980), 70
Operation El Dorado Canyon (1986), 71–73
Organization for Economic Cooperation and Development (OECD), 51
Organization of the Petroleum Exporting Countries (OPEC), 51, 52
Orlov, Yuri, 196–197, 207n63
Ortega, Daniel, 2, 251, 252
Osirak nuclear reactor (Iraq), 10, 307, 308, 320n29, 441

Pakistan: Afghanistan and, 75–77, 78, 331, 334–335, 372–374, 376; domestic politics and strife, 76, 335, 373; India and, 334–335, 371–372, 373, 374, 375–376; non-state actors, and regional conflict, 370, 371–372; US policy and relations, 75–77, 334, 372–374, 376
Palestine: Cold War position and framing, 10, 305–308, 317; Israel conflicts, 10, 177, 303–304, 305–317; refugees, 177, 308, 312, 315–316; US policy, 308–310, 313, 315–317, 320n34
Palestinian Liberation Organization (PLO): Arab-Israeli conflicts and negotiation, 10, 176–177, 304, 306, 308–309, 311–313, 314–315, 316–317, 320n34; Cold War framing, 306, 308, 309; as non-state actor, US relations, 369–370
Pan Am flight 103 bombing (1988), 72
paranoia, 131
Pashtun people and ethnonationalism, 371–372, 373, 374, 381
peace initiatives: antinuclear movements, 8, 127, 130, 138, 144–154, 155–157; Central America, 250, 251; leaders and peace "credit," 5, 25, 33, 34–37, 150, 303; leaders' peace "missions," 130; Middle East, 303, 306, 310, 311, 315; Southern Africa talks and agreements, 346, 353–354, 356, 357–359
"peace through strength": explanations and illustrations, 36, 114, 144–145, 147; as Reagan strategy/touchstone, 29, 88, 109, 146–147
Pentecostalists, in US Embassy Moscow, 7, 110–111, 113–115, 118, 195, 207n63, 218–219
People's Republic of China. See China, People's Republic of
Pepper, Claude, 87
Percy, Charles, 154, 190–191, 205n23
perestroika, 7
Perkins, Edward, 356
Perle, Richard, 116
Perot, H. Ross, 170
Perry, John Curtis, 387
Peru, 292
Peterson, Pete, 110
petroleum industry. See energy industries
Philippines: economy, 416; human rights issues, 15, 189, 192–193, 200, 249; US relations and policy, 15, 189, 192–193, 200, 249
Phillips, James A., 374
Pinochet, Augusto, 16, 200–201, 260–277
Pipes, Richard, 7, 26, 27, 34, 48, 326, 327, 328, 329, 340, 372
Poland: economic instability, 95–96; human rights issues, 128–129, 198, 220; labor movements, 14, 47, 198, 327; Soviet influence/intervention, 47–48, 108–109, 128–129, 189, 198, 327, 339
political Islam. See Islamism, and Islamist regimes
Popular Front for the Liberation of Palestine, 309, 320n44
Portuguese colonialism, 346–347, 348
Powell, Colin, 26, 183
Prestowitz, Clyde V., 405–407
prisoners of war, 168–169, 171–172
production management and philosophy, 404–405
propaganda: Afghanistan occupation, 331; American anti-Japanese, 396–397, 398–399; military entertainment, 69, 71; religious schools, 77; Soviet foreign influence, 108; Taiwanese, 423
Punjab (Indian state), 374–376
Putin, Vladimir, 440, 442

Qaeda, al-: in Afghanistan, 64, 78, 324, 440; background and growth, 9, 64–65, 78, 381; terrorist actions, 64, 79
"quiet diplomacy," 7, 27, 112–115, 118, 216, 264–266, 268, 273

racism and racial violence: South Africa, 199–200, 224, 232n77; United States, 393–394, 396–397. *See also* apartheid, South African
Reagan, Nancy, 25, 26, 27, 414
Reagan, Ronald, and administration: anticommunism, 4, 8, 12, 15, 112, 118–119, 175, 195, 202, 237–239, 248–249, 262–264, 265–266, 282, 285–287, 295, 305, 325, 439; biography, 3, 9–10, 12, 179; Cold War and, 5–8, 16, 17, 25–42, 65, 68–69, 71, 74, 85, 105–120, 156–157, 173, 179, 183–184, 237–240, 246–252, 285–287, 304–308, 313–314, 317, 324–340, 346, 417, 438, 439, 441–444; counterterrorism policy and shortcomings, 11, 64–80, 181; death and funeral, 4, 36, 134; diary, 33, 48, 88, 108, 112, 113–114, 131, 132, 136, 144, 197, 310–311, 314, 333, 414–415, 425, 429; domestic policy, 108; economic and trade policy, 3–4, 12–14, 16, 17–18, 45–46, 84–99, 128–129, 135–136, 388, 389–390, 392, 394–396, 401, 402–404, 406, 423, 426–427, 431, 441; elections, 2, 11, 126, 147, 166, 168, 188–189, 239, 370, 395–396; energy economy strategy, 13–14, 43–44, 45–46, 47; era, and historical context, 1–18; foreign policy, 5, 6–9, 10–16, 18, 31–32, 35, 56, 72, 74–80, 85, 111–112, 123–138, 166–169, 171–184, 188–203, 212–226, 237–254, 260–277, 281–295, 303–317, 345–359, 360n22, 367–383, 402, 414–416, 417–432, 438–444; historiography and reconsideration, 4–7, 25, 437–443; human rights policy, 15, 111, 114–115, 188–203, 208n82, 212–226, 237–239, 241–244, 249–251, 253–254, 260–276, 332, 349–350; humorous portrayals, 437; legacies, 3–4, 18, 25, 30, 317, 438, 440–444; military/defense policy and spending, 5, 7–8, 10–11, 16, 17, 25, 33–34, 64, 68–69, 71–72, 74, 87–88, 111, 116–118, 144–145, 156, 166–167, 173–184, 439; nominations, 190–192, 205n17, 205n23, 215–216, 228n18, 241; peace policy and "credit," 5, 25, 29, 33, 34–37, 147, 150; personality, 3, 9–10, 12, 25–26, 29–30, 33–35, 37, 66, 105, 106, 110–111, 112, 114, 184, 437–438; revisionism, 4, 437; Soviet opinions on, 105, 107; Soviet relations and diplomacy, 5, 6–8, 10, 27–31, 32–37, 47–48, 55–57, 74, 85, 105–120, 124, 127, 128, 131–134, 147, 150–151, 194–198, 218–220, 325–331, 337, 345, 350–352, 358, 438, 439–440; speeches and quotations, 28, 65–67, 106, 118–119, 127, 128, 132, 147, 149, 165–166, 172, 176, 179–181, 183, 304, 394; staff and personalities, 7, 10, 11, 17, 26–29, 50, 70–71, 108, 110–114, 326–328; transatlantic relations, 123–138
Reagan doctrine: term, applications, and illustrations, 68–69, 74–80, 175, 240, 249, 305, 335–336, 350; unforeseen consequences: terrorism, 77, 78, 79–80
"Reaganomics," 84–99, 136
real estate investment, 14, 392, 394
Reed, Thomas, 28–29, 49, 55
refugees: Afghan, 77, 333–334; Palestinian, 177, 308, 312, 315–316
Regan, Donald, 46, 85, 437
regulations, US, and economy, 13, 393, 394–395, 403–404
Reich, Otto J., 257n43
religious interests and groups: global human rights, 15, 213–215, 223–224; language and rhetoric, 213–214, 215, 216–217, 221, 223–224, 229n24; political uses, 212–213, 220–223, 224–225, 227n13; religious freedom issues, 114–115, 197, 209n91, 216–217, 218–223, 224–225, 227n13
religious right, 214, 220–221, 227n13. *See also* conservatism
religious schools, 77, 227n13
Renouard, Joseph, 204n14, 209n91, 213
Republic of China. *See* Taiwan
Reykjavik summit (1986), 16, 29, 34–35, 107, 132–133, 138, 156, 197, 351, 439
Rhodesia, 346–347
Rice, Condoleezza, 64
Ríos Montt, Efraín, 193, 222–223
Robinson, Roger W., Jr., 55
Rogers, Bernard, 134
Rojas, Rodrigo, 273
Romania, human rights issues, 209n98
Rostow, Eugene, 121n7, 147–148, 150, 310
Rumsfeld, Donald, 64, 110
Russian Federation and Russia, 2, 439–440, 442

sabotage, 55
Sabra and Shatila massacre (1982), 177, 315

Sachs, Jeffrey, 293
Sakharov, Andrei, 118, 119, 189, 196
Sandinistas and Sandinista government (Nicaragua), 1, 2, 74, 193, 212–213, 224–225, 238–241, 244–253
Sarney, José, 284–285, 289–290, 292–293, 294–295
Saturday Night Live (television program), 437
Saudi Arabia: mujahideen support, 76–77; oil production and revenues, 13–14, 52, 56, 369; US relations, 13–14, 55–56, 76, 307, 369
Savimbi, Jonas, 350, 357
Schifter, Richard, 204n14
Schmidt, Helmut, 13, 92–93, 124, 125, 126, 127–128, 129, 130, 136
Scowcroft, Brent, 17, 154–155
"Second" Cold War, 93, 109, 417
self-dealing, 421
semiconductor industry, 401, 402–404, 412n89, 430
September 11, 2001 terrorist attacks, 64–65, 73, 75, 79, 440
settlement building, Israel, 10, 303–304, 306, 307–308, 309–311, 317, 321n49
Shah of Iran (Mohammad Reza Pahlavi): Kurdish relations, 376–377; overthrow, 1979, 15, 367, 370; US foreign policy, 15, 56, 370
Sharia, 77
Sharon, Ariel, 306–307, 311–313, 315, 317, 322n68
Shcharansky, Anatoly, 118, 119, 195, 196–197
Shevardnadze, Eduard, 115, 118, 197, 337, 338, 351–352
Shultz, George: counterterrorism, 67–68, 69–70, 70–71, 77–78, 181; economic policy and expertise, 16, 415, 426–427, 429; interagency relations, 11, 27, 28, 70–71, 107, 113–114; on Reagan, 29, 31, 32, 34, 35, 111–112, 113–114; as secretary, and foreign policy, 7, 11, 27, 28, 33, 50, 67–68, 69–70, 70–71, 106, 107, 110–112, 113–115, 117, 118, 119, 120, 129–130, 131–132, 134–135, 171–172, 177, 178, 181–183, 192, 194–195, 197, 201–202, 217–218, 247, 249, 253, 260, 266, 269, 272–273, 274, 287–288, 290, 291–292, 314, 315, 316, 325, 330–331, 334, 336–337, 339–340, 351, 415–416, 426–429
Sichuan province (China), 428
Sikh nationalism, 371–372, 374–376
"silent diplomacy," 264–266, 275

Silva-Herzog, Jesús, 97
Singh, Arun, 376
Single Integrated Operational Plan (SIOP), 33
Snowe, Olympia, 87
social programs: Nicaragua, 244–246, 252; US, and tax policy, 87, 90, 98–99
Social Security, 87
Somoza, Anastasio, 1, 15, 238, 240, 244, 245, 246
South Africa: apartheid and human rights, 8, 15, 189, 199–200, 222, 223–224, 346, 347, 349–350, 356, 357; Namibia occupation, 346, 347, 348–349, 353, 354, 356–357, 359n4; regional military conflicts, 347–349, 353–355, 356–357; US foreign policy, 8, 15, 31–32, 189, 198–200, 202, 222, 224, 346, 347, 348–350, 352–357
South African Defence Force, 347, 353, 354
South America. *See* Latin America; specific nations
South Asia: Afghanistan wars, 1, 8–9, 10, 75, 76–77, 78, 324–340; jihadism history, 75–78, 80; Pakistan conflict and relations, 75–77, 334–335
Southeast Asia: American POW/MIA issues, 168–169; US and "Vietnam syndrome," 11, 165–166; Vietnam War, 107, 165–168, 171–172, 173, 176, 183
Southern Africa: Cold War proxies and communism, 8, 223, 345–350, 352–359; national liberation movements, 346–347, 348–349; sub-Saharan national debts, 97–98; US foreign policy, 8, 199, 345–346, 348–350, 352–359. *See also* specific nations
South Korea: economy, 416; human rights issues, 190, 193, 204–205n15; leaders, 190, 204–205n15
Southwest Asia: instability and crisis, 10, 335, 367–383; US/Carter policy, 370, 371; US/Reagan policy, 10, 330, 335, 367–383, 440–441. *See also* Middle East; South Asia
sovereign debt crises. *See* debt crises
Soviet Union: Afghanistan invasion/occupation, 1, 8–9, 10, 45, 75–77, 107, 125–126, 324–340, 351, 355, 368, 370, 372, 373–374, 380–381, 382, 440; China relations and policy, 416, 419–420, 421–422, 423–424, 426, 428; Cold War grand strategy and policy, 6, 27–28, 245, 327, 329, 339, 352, 355, 372; Eastern Bloc relations and influence, 47–48, 94, 96, 108–109, 120, 128–129, 189, 198, 220, 327, 339; economic

Soviet Union (*continued*)
  conditions, 32, 33, 35, 43–44, 45–46, 48–49, 52–55, 56–57, 85, 96, 109, 116, 129; economic warfare on, 27, 49, 56–57; end, 2, 4, 5, 31, 32, 36, 43, 54–55, 120, 439; energy industry and economy, 13–14, 43–57, 109–110, 129; human rights issues and policy, 114, 189, 192, 194–198, 213, 215–220, 263; nuclear buildup and capabilities, 5, 107, 109, 116–117, 120, 125, 150–151; Reagan administration diplomacy and policy, 5, 6–8, 10, 27–31, 32–37, 55–57, 85, 105–120, 124, 127, 128, 131–134, 147, 150–151, 194–198, 218–220, 325–331, 337, 345, 350–352, 358, 439–440; Saudi relations, 13–14
Spencer, Stuart, 28
Stark, Pete, 397
State Department. *See* US Department of State
state-led politics, and state sovereignty focus: vs. ethnonationalist conflicts, 368, 371–372, 374, 376–377, 381–382; US policy and preference, 368, 369–370, 371, 376–377, 382–383
Stearman, William, 329
Stein, Herbert, 98
Stevens, Ted, 418, 419, 420, 423
Stiglitz, Joseph, 18
Stockman, David, 26, 34, 46, 85, 86–87, 88
Stoessel, Walter J., Jr., 216–217, 219, 267
Stokes, Paul, 421
Strategic Arms Limitation Talks (SALT I): Carter policy, 125, 348; vs. START, 149
Strategic Arms Limitation Talks/Treaty (SALT II) (1979): failure, 348, 351, 358; opposition, 117, 146
Strategic Arms Reduction Talks/Treaties (START): background and formulation, 107, 115, 145–146, 149–152, 154–155, 156; content and goals, 150–151; signing, 5, 120, 156
Strategic Defense Initiative (SDI): first-strike capability, 34, 117, 156; importance, 30, 132–133; impracticality, 30–31; Reagan policy, 10, 29–30, 34–35, 88, 107, 117–118, 132, 156; sharing, 29–30, 34–35, 118
strength: national power and relations, 28–29, 107–108; "peace through" strategy, 29, 88, 109, 114, 144–145, 146–147
supply-side economics, 12–13, 85–86, 90, 406

Suriname, 282, 286–287
Syria: Cold War policy speculation, 180, 336; Lebanon civil war, 316

TAC International, 418–419
Tahir-Kheli, Shirin, 331, 376
Taiwan, 14–15, 414, 416–426, 428, 430–431, 432
Taiwan Relations Act (1979), 417, 423, 424–426
Taliban: in Afghanistan, 64, 324, 381, 382, 440; background and formation, 64, 78; counterterrorism efforts, 64, 73
Tanter, Raymond, 309, 310
tax policy: bracket creep and tax cuts, 86–87; budget decisions, 84, 87, 89, 90, 98–99; supply-side economics, 85–86
technology and innovations: counterterrorism and military, 73–74, 79; and economic systems and conditions, 12–13, 32, 401–402; for energy production, 45–47, 49–50; intellectual property, 288–290; missiles and bombers, 109, 148; sabotage stories, 55; trade issues, 2–3, 96, 388, 392, 395, 403–404; US industry and culture, 2–3, 288–290, 391, 430
Teltschik, Horst, 133
Tenet, George, 64
terrorism, 66–67; attacks, 10–11, 64–66, 67, 68, 71, 72, 73, 75, 78, 316, 371, 440; Cold War focus vs., 11, 65, 68, 71, 74, 77–78, 79–80, 440–441; guerrilla warfare vs., 74, 76, 308–309; state-sponsored, 65, 74, 274, 381; training and networks, 77, 78; US counterterrorism policy, 11, 64–80, 181, 189–190, 324, 381, 440–441
Thatcher, Margaret: arms diplomacy opinions, 127–128, 133, 135–136; economics and trade opinions, 48, 49, 89, 92, 110, 136; friendship and bond, 17, 49, 134; military policy, 136, 286
Theberge, James, 260–261, 265, 269, 270, 272–273, 276, 277n1
Thorn, Gaston, 93
Tiananmen Square massacre (1989), 15
Toyota, 393
trade agreements, 135, 403, 407
trade relations: balance of trade, 90–91, 94, 288, 390, 391–392, 393, 395; bloc power, 295; deficits, 91, 94, 388, 390, 391–392, 395, 404, 406–407; energy production equipment, 45–47, 49–50, 283; free trade, 12, 135, 282, 388, 390, 394–396, 397–398,

401, 403, 441; tariffs, 282, 288–289, 393, 395, 396, 397, 401, 407; US-Asia, 2–3, 85, 92, 290, 388–389, 389–408, 416–417, 419–420, 426–432, 441; US-Brazil, 282, 283–284, 286, 287–293, 294–295; US-Canada, 135, 407; US-China, 416–417, 419–420, 426–432, 441; US-Europe, 14, 48–51, 55, 85, 89, 92–94, 128–129, 392; US history and change, 13, 89–99, 391–392; US-Japan, 2–3, 92, 388–408; US-Soviet, 12, 45–46, 47, 48–51, 128–130, 140n24; US staff, 46, 402, 403, 429. *See also* arms trade

Treaty on the Non-Proliferation of Nuclear Weapons (NPT) (1968), 424, 427, 428–429

Tripartite Accord (1988), 346, 356, 357

Trudeau, Pierre, 130, 135, 437–438

Truman, Harry, and administration, 117, 389, 399

Trump, Donald, 14, 388, 398, 407–408, 442

trust, in negotiations and relationships, 32–33, 34–35, 114–115, 131–132

Tsiang Yien-si, 421

Tsongas, Paul, 3, 205n23, 241, 335, 407

Turkey, human rights, 193

Turner, Stansfield, 373

Tutu, Bishop Desmond, 223

unemployment: Europe, 47, 92, 93; US, 1, 85, 88, 91, 393

Unger, Leonard, 423

União Nacional para a Independência Total de Angola (UNITA), 347, 350, 353, 357

Union of Concerned Scientists, 148

United Auto Workers (UAW), 393

United Kingdom: Afghanistan policy, 333, 334; China and Hong Kong policy, 417, 430; Falklands War, 240, 267, 285–286; US relations in Cold War, 127–129, 133, 135–136

United Nations: ambassadors, 189, 264, 265; disarmament sessions, 151; General Assembly, 72, 201, 331, 334, 349; human rights entities and statutes, 196, 198, 201–202, 217; Palestine and, 308, 310, 311; Security Council, 314; Southern Africa policy, 349, 356, 359; US-Soviet mediation, 330–331

United States Agency for International Development (USAID), 77, 202, 274–275

United States Congress: democracy promotion, 239, 243, 252–253; diplomacy by, 417–418, 419, 423; economic and trade policy, 135, 393, 396–397, 398–399, 400, 401–402; economic policy and legislation, 86, 87, 92, 98–99; executive relations, 150, 154–155, 173, 180, 181, 182, 190–191, 191–192, 248–249, 250–251, 263, 338, 353; human rights policy, 190–191, 191–192, 193, 198–200, 215–217, 223–226, 241, 248, 249–251, 261, 263, 267, 269, 332, 350, 352–353, 423; lobbying, 400, 418; midterm elections, 87, 89, 152, 274, 338; military/defense powers and policy, 10, 16, 17, 67, 69, 70, 145, 146, 149, 150, 172, 174, 178, 181, 182, 212, 240–241, 248–249, 249–251, 253, 263, 335, 338, 339, 347, 417, 420, 423; military/nuclear policy, 152–154, 180; and Vietnam Veterans Memorial, 169–170

United States Information Agency, 243, 331

United States Marine Corps, 10–11

US Arms Control and Disarmament Agency (ACDA), 147–148, 150–151

US Arms Export Control Act (1976), 347, 350, 352

US Department of Commerce, 46, 48, 398, 399–400, 401, 402

US Department of Defense: budgets and spending, 16, 17, 68–69; Bush (G.H.W.) administration, 30; Bush (G.W.) administration, 64; CIA and, 11, 45–46, 64, 70–71, 73–74, 79, 87–88, 108; counterterrorism policy, 11, 64, 68–80; policy and actions, 10, 11, 27, 45–46, 56, 70–72, 111, 116, 150–151, 173, 174–175, 177–178, 181–183, 240–241, 307; POW/MIA efforts, 169; staff and Reagan relations, 26–27, 71, 177, 182–183, 307–308

US Department of Energy, 283–284

US Department of State: arms control negotiations, 150–151; arms sales policy, 424, 425; China and Taiwan policy, 424, 425–429; counterterrorism policy, 67, 70–71, 77–78, 181, 189–190; diplomacy policy and methods, 110–115, 126, 128, 178–179, 268, 326–328, 330–331; energy and trade policy, 46, 48, 49–50; Europe policy, 124, 127–128; Human Rights Bureau and policy, 189–192, 194–195, 197, 202, 204n14, 205n17, 205n23, 206n39, 215–226, 228n18, 241–243, 247, 248, 264, 265, 267, 268, 269–270, 272–275, 353; interagency relations, 27, 71, 107, 108, 110, 111–112, 113–114, 118, 121n23, 171, 182–183, 327–328, 330, 337, 339–340;

US Department of State (*continued*)
  Middle East policy, 305–307, 309, 310, 312–313, 314, 315–316; staff and figures, 7, 8, 9, 27, 31, 49, 50, 121n23, 129–130, 326–328
US Department of the Treasury, 3–4, 13, 86, 90, 91, 135, 291, 292–293, 392

Vance, Cyrus, 327
Vasilyev, Gennadiy, 105, 107
Veliotes, Nicholas, 305
Venezuela, 287
Vessey, John W., Jr., 177
video games, 2–3
"Vietnam syndrome": described, 69, 165; Reagan and, 11, 165–184, 239, 438–439
Vietnam Veterans Memorial, 11, 169–171
Vietnam War (1955–1975): Afghanistan involvement compared, 9, 327–328, 329, 331, 337, 339, 440; Latin America involvement compared, 171–172, 173–175, 176, 250; Reagan admin. takeaways, 107, 165–168, 171–172, 173, 176, 183, 242; skepticism of interventionism following, 166, 172, 173, 176, 250; veterans, 11, 165–166, 167–172
Viola, Roberto, 190, 204–205n15
Vogel, Ezra, 387, 404–405
Volcker, Paul, 13, 88–89, 90, 92, 98–99, 293

Walters, Vernon, 265, 266–267, 268
war gaming and exercises, 5, 131
war memorials, 11, 169–171
"War on Terror": Bush (G.W.) administration, 64–65, 73–74, 440; Reagan administration seeds, 67–80. *See also* counterterrorism policy
Warsaw Pact: dissolution, 138; NATO neighbors and relations, 7–8, 47–48, 109. *See also* dual-track decision (1979)
Washington summit (1987), 133, 197, 351–352, 355
Watt, James, 170–171
Webb, James H., 169
Webster, William, 26

Weinberger, Caspar: foreign economic policy, 45–46, 48, 49, 56, 109; military buildup under, 68–69, 70, 88, 111, 116–117; on military power, and doctrine, 11, 70–71, 182–183, 307, 319n24; as secretary, 11, 27, 29, 108, 109, 111, 115, 116–117, 128, 173, 174–175, 177, 178, 181, 182–183, 307–308, 313, 315–316, 327, 428
West Bank, 10, 303–304, 306, 307, 308, 310–311, 316, 317
Wethington, Olin, 429
White, Theodore H., 397–398
Wick, Charles, 25–26, 30, 331
Wiesel, Elie, 136
Wilson, Bill, 265–266
Wilson, Charles, 190, 335
Winthrop, John, 217
Wolf, Marvin J., 400
Wolfowitz, Paul, 30, 121n23, 191, 217
World Bank, 201, 271, 292–293
World Trade Center Bombing (1993), 78
World Trade Organization, 432
World War II: American anti-Japanese propaganda, 396–397, 398–399; Japan, postwar conditions, 391, 397–398
Wright, Jim, 251
Wright, Oliver, 130, 131
Wu Xueqian, 428

Xi Jinping, 442

Yao Yilin, 429
Yeltsin, Boris, 439
Yousef, Ramzi, 78

Zakhmatov, Vladimir, 55
Zawahiri, Ayman al-, 78
Zegers, Fernando, 260–261, 268–269
zero option, 116–117, 128, 133–134, 149–150
Zhao Ziyang, 14–15, 414, 417, 424–425, 428
Zia-ul-Haq, Muhammad, 76, 334–335, 371, 373, 376
Zimbabwe, 346–347
Zimbabwe African National Union (ZANU), 347

CPSIA information can be obtained
at www.ICGtesting.com
Printed in the USA
LVHW091905240921
698690LV00001B/1

9 781501 760686